# The Sources of Value

# THE SOURCES OF

# VALUE

Stephen C. Pepper

UNIVERSITY OF CALIFORNIA PRESS

Berkeley, Los Angeles, London

1970

UNIVERSITY OF CALIFORNIA PRESS
Berkeley and Los Angeles, California

UNIVERSITY OF CALIFORNIA PRESS, LTD.
London, England

© 1958 by The Regents of the University of California

Second printing, 1970

ISBN 0-520-01798-6

Library of Congress Catalog Card Number: 58-8657

Printed in the United States of America
Designed by Adrian Wilson

# To
the chief source of
my personal values
my wife
Ellen

# Contents

# 10

# 11

# 12

# Introduction

THIS BOOK, for all its length, is only a sketch. Its virtue lies in its being a comprehensive hypothesis of the main lines of relationship among the facts bearing on human decisions. The scope of the relevant facts is overwhelming. They extend all the way from fugitive impulse and the grammatical form of the imperative sentence to the effects of natural selection in organic evolution, and possibly even into the inorganic realm. Most treatments of the problem of values pinpoint some one relevant area of subject matter and set this up as value proper, or at least as an area that can be studied in isolation without distortion of the subject. A deceptive security is then engendered in the student by the neatness of his analyses within the arbitrary limits he himself has set up. So we have a variety of isolated approaches to the problem: a motor-affective approach, a linguistic approach, a culture-determined approach, a biological approach—each with a separate center minimizing its effective relationships with the other centers.

The value problem is one problem that cannot be profitably handled as a collection of unrelated special studies. Concentration on a limited topic offers constructive material only if it is seen as a contribution to an understanding of a much wider set of relationships. The act of concentration on a specific topic is itself an establishment of a value criterion, the legitimacy of which can be assessed only by considering its relationships to the topics excluded. Value is a subject in which a comprehensive hypothesis of the character of the total field is essential.

1

Such a hypothesis is here attempted. It is an empirical hypothesis, tentative and groping. It takes as its point of departure R. B. Perry's *General Theory of Value,* which, to my mind, is the most comprehensive empirical treatment of the subject to date. To this may be added its recently published sequel *The Realms of Value.* Broad as Perry's approach is, it seemed to me still too narrowly psychological at its base, and not as clear as it might be in the analysis of its key concept, 'interest.' So I entered the subject by what amounts to a critical commentary on Perry's analysis of interest. A great deal of psychological material has come in since Perry wrote, and I have sought to bring as much of this as I could assimilate to bear on the analysis of interest. In the course of this critical reconstruction, the term 'interest' lost its utility as a central value concept. A constellation of interrelated concepts took its place. Purposive value became identified with 'conation,' 'achievement,' and 'affection' interconnected within the articulations of purposive structures. And two types of purposive structure emerged for describing these value relationships: the appetitive and the aversive.

The steps by which this treatment of the structure of purposive values developed were gradual, as well as the steps that led to the successive levels of value above these. I have thought it wise to let the traces of this development be seen. Since this study makes no pretense at being a definitive theory, the process of thinking which led to each successive stage may turn out to be more helpful to other students of the subject than the actual conclusions reached. The chapters ahead may be truly considered as a report of one man's exploration and survey of this field as he penetrated deeper and deeper into its factual relationships. Following the evidence where it led, I found myself examining the subject matter in a range extending all the way from simple likings and purposes to personality structure, cultural pattern, religion, and natural selection.

There is a kind of empirical discovery that comes from philosophic reflection on empirical materials. Many of the concepts and relationships exhibited in these pages emerged in the writing as descriptive hypotheses for the handling of the data available. And the total comprehensive hypothesis of the interrelated levels of values and the polarity of value dynamics seemed forced upon me by the appearance of the facts.

Chief among these empirical discoveries of philosophic reflection is the concept of *selective system,* which has turned out to be the guiding concept linking the successive levels of values. It may even be regarded as the defining concept for the term 'value' as this is traced out in the present study. A selective system is a peculiar dynamic structure which allows one to describe errors as occurring within the system by virtue of the fact that these errors are corrected by the dynamics of the system itself. A selective system operates to eliminate errors and accumulate correct results in terms of criteria embodied in the system.

This concept did not register in my mind until the study was half completed. The first mention of it will be found in chapter 13, on "The Principles of Evaluation." Logically, such a chapter should come at the beginning of a study of value. But I purposely delayed taking up this topic until there was a good deal of empirical material to refer to. This delay was rewarded in that it brought to light a guiding principle for an empirical theory of value. Actually, I had been guided by this concept of selective system all along, but had not identified it. And I believe this has been the guiding concept intuitively used by empirical moralists seeking out the dynamics and sanctions for ethical judgments throughout the history of the subject. For if the sanctions for values are not to be sought in the supernatural or the a priori—and this I would take for granted—then where else would we expect to find these sanctions than in some natural dynamic system so constructed as to eliminate errors on its own plan? This is just what we find in a purposive structure—in a typical appetitive or aversive act—and once having insight into the nature of one selective system, we can then identify other selective systems operating upon human dispositions and conduct and instituting values generally.

On the basis of this insight it is possible to offer a salutary maxim for the guidance of any empirical study of value: Follow the *dynamics* of selective action. In traditional terms this means: Watch for the *sanctions.*

I began gathering material for this study about 1940. I had

drafted the first half of the project by 1948, when I was induced to break off the work for an aesthetics book which became *The Principles of Art Appreciation*. Knowing this interruption might be a long one, I summarized the conclusions I had reached up to that time in *A Digest of Purposive Values*. This little book was partly for class purposes over the intervening period and partly to invite criticism. When I came back to the uncompleted manuscript, I found it, as might be expected, so unsatisfactory that I laid it aside and began afresh. Nevertheless, there are not so many discrepancies between the *Digest* and this finished study as I would have anticipated. The latter takes up details and extends over areas that the *Digest* did not go into.

My indebtedness to R. B. Perry and Edward Tolman is spread over all the earlier pages of this book. Just what is owing to Perry comes out clearly. But what is owing to Tolman is so interwoven with my own ideas that there can be no unraveling of it. During the formative stages of the study of learning and the discovery of the details of purposive structures, we had many talks together, and many discussions of the implications of these discoveries in respect to value theory. Probably most of the empirical concepts given in my descriptions of purposive structures I owe to him. It was he, I am quite sure, who, for instance, suggested the concept of 'riddance pattern,' so important for distinguishing aversions from appetitions. But his analyses and mine often differ and he is not responsible for mine.

I am indebted also to the writings of C. I. Lewis much more than references to him would indicate—particularly in his handling of what he calls 'inherent values' and I call either 'objects of potential value' or 'conditional objects of value.' This important area of value theory I did not intensively go into, beyond showing rather precisely just where it came in. I was the more content to leave this gap because I knew I could refer the reader, with few reservations, to Lewis' careful treatment of the topic in his chapters on valuation in the *Analysis of Knowledge and Valuation*.

There are many other men to whom I am greatly indebted. David Krech, of our Psychology Department, went over the manuscript at a late stage and made constructive suggestions and a number of corrections. David Mandelbaum very carefully went over the anthropological sections, and these were discussed in seminar with students and staff of the Anthropology Department. Clyde Kluckhohn, while in this vicinity, also read these sections, which permitted me to benefit from his suggestions.

I wish particularly to thank Bernard Diggs, of the University of Illinois Philosophy Department. He became interested in my mode of empirical treatment of values through a seminar I gave at the University of Illinois in 1950, and has followed my manuscript ever since, chapter by chapter, giving me the benefit of his own intensive studies in the psychology of motivation and his rich historical background in ethics and other value fields. Much detailed revision has been done on his sympathetic advice. I am inexpressibly grateful to him.

There is, moreover, an unmeasurable contribution from my own departmental colleagues in Berkeley, and from many clear-headed graduate students who have participated in classes and seminars where material on the theory of value was under discussion.

Finally I wish to thank the University of California Press and all those connected with it who have made the publication of this book possible. And I wish to express a special appreciation to Miss Genevieve Rogers for her careful and thoughtful editing of the manuscript and for the hours of meticulous proofreading.

S. C. P.

# 1

# The Setting of the Problem

## 1. The Problem of Value and the Field of Study

'Theory of value' is the name for a set of problems common to a group of studies known as the value sciences. These include ethics, aesthetics, some phases of logic and theory of knowledge, economics, political science, anthropology, and sociology. Specialization has more and more separated and insulated these studies from one another. Theory of value is a movement in the opposite direction, drawing out a core of problems in which they all share. The movement is relatively recent, but the problems it deals with are very old. They are the problems of the good and the bad.

In the broadest sense anything good or bad is a value. Among such things have been considered: pleasures and pains; desires, wants, and purposes; satisfactions and frustrations; preferences; utility, means, conditions, and instruments; correctness and incorrectness; integration and disintegration; character, vitality, self-realization; health; survival, evolutionary fitness; adjustability; individual freedom, social solidarity; law, duty, conscience; virtues, ideals, norms; progress; righteousness and sin; beauty and ugliness; truth and error; reality and unreality.

Such a list or a portion of it is just what we get when we ask any ordinary group of people today for examples of good and bad. It is a fair sampling of the field of value in the common sense view, and constitutes a convenient point of departure for a study of the subject. It amounts to a common sense ostensive

7

definition of the field of value. Its utility consists precisely in its looseness, unreflectiveness, and freedom from theoretical bias. Moreover, a list of conceptions of value culled from the traditional literature of the value sciences would hardly differ, except in refinements of the concepts, from this list.

The first question that presents itself is how to bring order and clarity into this apparently heterogeneous mass of subject matter. Three principal ways have been employed singly or in combination by most writers on the subject. The first is to seek for a common trait or set of traits that runs through some or all of the suggested examples of value. This is the *method of generalization*. The second is to identify value proper with some conspicuous example of value and to attempt to reduce some or all other items to this one. This is the *method of reduction*. The third is to select some item or items as 'real values' or as value according to the writer's stipulated definition, and find reasons for excluding other items as unreal or mistaken or simply outside the writer's interest as indicated in his stipulated definition. This is the *method of exclusion*.

Each of these methods can be used in arbitrary ways that actually produce distortive descriptions of the field. Some of the commonest of these fallacious procedures will be pointed out presently. But if these methods are held to the empirical evidence, and the aim of investigating the whole common sense field is steadily kept in mind, they can bring order and clarity into the field without descriptive distortion. For they include the regular inductive procedures of classification, correlation, definition, and hypothesis.

By these means the rough common sense definition of the field offered by the items listed can be cognitively refined. For our knowledge develops in such matters by successive refinements. The steps in these refinements can be marked by successively more discriminating definitions of the field based on more and more detailed and verifiable hypotheses of the nature of the subject matter investigated. This procedure in the refinement of knowledge is sometimes called that of *successive definition*. It might also be called that of successive hypotheses. For the possibility of more refined and accurate definitions depends on the verification of more detailed and precise hypotheses.

Starting, then, from a vague common sense definition of the field of value, we shall expect the usual empirical methods to bring successively greater clarity and order into the material as our inquiry proceeds. From time to time the results may be gathered up in successively more refined definitions of the material studied.

In following this procedure, however, we should beware of certain pitfalls. Very few writers in the past have avoided them completely. Let us list the pitfalls now so that we may not fall into them ourselves. Moreover, in becoming aware of what to avoid we shall perhaps get some good positive ideas about how to work into our problem.

## 2. Some Common Fallacies in the Study of Value

We should not *assume that the common sense definition is final* or, what amounts to the same thing, that we have to be *bound by common usage* or even to the traditional usage of the body of experts. By the very nature of the case, a refined definition would never, or almost never, correspond exactly with a common sense definition or with traditional usage. Refinement of knowledge implies new or more precise observations and more careful analysis. Inevitably, the more developed field will be different from the common sense and traditional conceptions of it. It may well introduce some strange new items into the field, or show that some traditional items do not belong there, or that it would be profitable to divide the field into a number of radically different parts. Just as closer observation showed that whales and porpoises are more nearly related to bears and rabbits than to salmon and mackerel, so it might turn out among some items in the field of value.

Consequently, it is not necessarily a serious criticism of a theory of value that it excludes as an instance of value something commonly regarded as such. The question rests solely on the grounds for the exclusion. Are there good evidential reasons for it? Some writers, for instance, do not consider pleasure as a value for the very good reason (if it should be correct) that they believe they have sufficient evidence to deny the existence of a quality of pleasure. Common sense, however, would select pleasure as one of the most conspicuous examples of a value, an example of something indisputably good. Nevertheless, a theory of value which diverged from common sense in this respect would not necessarily be deficient. It might possibly be correct.

We must not assume, then, that a theory of value is necessarily inadequate because it diverges from common sense or common usage in some respect.

Second, and for very much the same reason, we must not *assume that there is a common character* of value running through all the instances in the field indicated by the term. That is to say, we cannot assume that the method of generalization will yield an adequate theory of value. This is no disparagement of an important inductive method, but only a warning against a way in which it can be misused.

The misuse usually consists in the method purporting to do something it does not do. If an impressive group of value items is presented, and then it is shown that these items possess a common character, it is almost impossible to resist the inference that this is the character that properly defines value. We presume that it is the character unreflectively meant by common sense or by the consensus of experts. There may, of course, be such a character, but the common sense list of items given earlier does not look entirely promising. Writers who appear to be using this method actually have prepared beforehand the field from which the inductive generalization is to be made, with the result that the generalization inevitably emerges. The negative instances that might spoil the induction are plausibly set aside by some phase of the method of reduction. The procedure is like that of carefully preparing to take a rabbit out of a hat by seeing that the rabbit is definitely placed in the hat beforehand.

It is principally because of this procedure that we find so many inductively plausible theories of value maintaining basic concepts which are incompatible or irrelevant to one another.

The generalizations from the facts presented are often true and illuminating so far as they go. The difficulty comes when these limited generalizations are put forward as *the* theory of value to the exclusion of all others.

Thus some writers say that all value is based on pleasure and displeasure; others, that it is based on desire; or on adjustment to the environment; or on what is required to bring harmony and fulfillment into a situation. All of these seem plausible as we read the books which explain these theories and marshal the evidence for them. Unfortunately, they cannot all be exclusively true. For the most part, the generalizations are confirmable, and the writers have merely deceived themselves about the adequacy of their views to displace many of the competing views. The results might be regarded as so many separate studies of separate fields. But this easy solution is probably too easy, as we shall see very soon. In the present context, it is enough if it has become clear that we cannot safely assume that simple inductive generalization from a number of proffered instances will give an adequate theory of value. The instances may have been carefully (even though unintentionally) biased in a certain direction.

One of the strangest misuses of an appeal to simple inductive generalization is that which led to G. E. Moore's theory of the 'indefinable good.' For the origin of Moore's argument is an appeal to all the various things that in common usage we call 'good.' Moore points out that an identification of 'good' with any one item such as pleasure or desire distorts the common sense meaning of the word, which applies indiscriminately to both pleasure and desire and to many other things as well. He then argues that the only common property that all things called 'good' seem to have is the attribute of their 'goodness' indicated by their being called so. He infers that there is a unique quality of 'good' analogous to the quality 'yellow,' for instance, which leads us to call all these things good just as the presence of the quality yellow leads us to call yellow things yellow. He then tries to make us believe that we have a sort of immediate cognition of this quality 'good' much as we sense yellow in immediate awareness. The burden of his argument, however, rests on the apparently simple induction to a quality of goodness to be found in all things called 'good.' The whole argument is now generally recognized as a verbalistic tour de force. The surprising thing is that it could ever have gained the rather large coterie of supporters that it did. The principal importance of the view now in the history of value theory is as an object lesson to warn us against a number of fallacious ways of approaching the subject. Actually, Moore's theory of the 'indefinable good' accepted uncritically both of the assumptions we have been warning against. He assumed the common sense definition of good as final, and he assumed that a common quality would be found in the field so indicated. He assumed the latter so intensely that he actually reified a quality of goodness out of the usage of a word.

Third, we must not *assume that all instances in the common sense field of value can be reduced to one sort of instance.* The method of reduction no more than the method of generalization can be safely relied upon to yield an adequate theory of value. That some reduction of certain items to others may be legitimate seems fairly clear from a cursory survey of the list. For instance, the dependency of means and instruments on the ends they serve suggests a sort of reduction of the values of instruments to the values of their ends. And preference may not be an independent value, but may be reduced to a stronger desire in comparison with a weaker one. A writer cannot assume, however, that items over the whole field can be thus reduced to one. We cannot assume, for example, that all the items will turn out to be various ways in which pleasantness and unpleasantness are manifested. Such may be the true theory, but we cannot assume it.

It is sometimes suggested that all forms of reduction are fallacious. Of course, some are and some are not. A reduction of a gallon to four quarts for liquid measurement is clearly legitimate. And most persons today would agree that a ghost can be reduced to a set of hallucinatory experiences. But it is not entirely certain that a musical chord can be reduced to the tones that make it up, or that a molecule of water can be reduced to its atomic elements.

The four commonest modes of reduction are (1) by *explaining away,* showing that a concept may be resolved without residue into something else (as with a ghost); (2) by *element analysis,* reducing a whole to a sum or configuration of its parts (as a gallon to four quarts); (3) by *analysis of origins,* reducing the character of a subsequent event to its antecedent causes; (4) by *correlation,* reducing one set of elements to another with which it is correlated (as, allegedly on some theories, sound to air vibrations). All of these have to be watched carefully, but each may be perfectly legitimate and may aid enormously in the simplification and clarification of a complex field of subject matter. Even the last one, correlation, may conceivably lead quite legitimately to the elimination of one set of correlates. For reasons may appear for explaining away one set. This is presumably the procedure of radical behaviorism of the J. B. Watson type. The question is whether the reasons for rejecting the introspective correlates are sufficient. In the present inquiry we shall hold that they are not, but the opposite point of view once had an impressive following.

When in laboratory contexts men speak of reducing qualitative differences to quantitative terms, and sound and color and heat and pressure are correlated with physical properties and units on scales, the reduction is only methodological and temporary. The physical properties give precise information much of which can be read back into the correlated introspective data, but the introspective data are not reduced away. For example, the precise analysis of musical timbre could never have been developed by introspective means alone. But having correlated musical tone with air vibrations, scientists could make quantitative studies of complex air vibrations and analyze timbres in physical terms. These analyses could then be correlated back into the experienced musical tones and could often be introspectively recognized. Behavioristic analyses of animal activities can similarly be highly informative of phases of human motivation. Methodological reduction of this sort is not a reducing away, and must be distinguished from the latter. What we need to watch out for is the procedure of reducing something away entirely into something else. The latter may sometimes be quite legitimate and a great simplifier of knowledge.

Fourth, we must not leap to the opposite extreme and *assume that there is no field of values.* It is, of course, possible that this would be the final conclusion. But we should not assume it, and on the cursory view it appears unlikely. The usual reason for denying a field of values is that we cannot assume a common trait among the common sense items or find a way of reducing them all to one. But even if this were true (and at the outset we cannot justifiably assert either that it is or is not), it does not follow that there is not a unified field of study. Even if it should be true that there is no common value trait covering, let us say, both aesthetic and ethical 'values,' it would not follow that the two subjects (and a number of others besides) were not so closely connected, and involved such similar problems, as to constitute a convenient unified field of study.

This is, in fact, the presumption which I propose to make in the present study. It may well be that there is no quality of value that is common to all or even to a large number of the things that men call good and bad, but there seems to be a common problem that runs through the field. This is *the problem of how to make well-grounded decisions in human affairs.* An inquiry into this problem is an important one, and constitutes a unified intent. It would be strange if, in man's long reflective history, this intent had not marked out a more or less unified field of study. My belief is that it has, that it was Plato's field of the good, the true, and the beautiful, and that it is the present-day field of value. It may well be that this field includes a variety of goods or values but so interconnected that a decision about one involves decisions about the others. And the ways of reaching well-grounded decisions may also be much the same in all instances. It is possible that this problem is precisely what has marked out the common sense field of value.

We might have set this problem for ourselves at the start and not have concerned ourselves with the intermediate discussion about the common sense definition of the field. But if it is true that the problem of making well-grounded decisions has tacitly marked out the field from the beginning, much is to be gained by keeping the traditional field in mind. There is a sort of wisdom in common sense that it is not well to dispense with, and there is much learning in the tradition of a subject. If we are mistaken about the decision problem defining the field, common sense will bring us back into line. We do not want to be too tightly bound by the common sense field, but constant reference to it may lead us into relevant material that will preserve us from unconscious dogmatism.

For in value theory conceived as an inquiry into the problem of how to make well-grounded decisions, there may enter a subtle dogmatism that comes simply from confining the inquiry to too narrow a field. It is a very subtle dogmatism because there is nothing unempirical about it except a too narrow restriction upon the facts taken to be relevant. In this subject more than in any other, a definition may be a principal source that distorts the empirical results. Here a definition is never wholly innocent. A writer may define value as pleasure, or as any interest in any object, or as preference, or as social solidarity. These are all presumably areas of fact and open to direct empirical study. They will yield grounds of judgment for decisions within their fields. But if (as is practically always done) it is assumed or asserted that the judgments reached within these special defined fields are final for all human decisions in which these subjects are involved, this may be entirely erroneous and highly dogmatic.

For if the facts in these restricted fields happen to be only a part of the material relevant to a decision in the total texture of a human situation, the writers in question are demanding that a decision be made on the basis of only a part of the relevant evidence. Satisfaction of desire may be always relevant to a considered judgment in human affairs. But so, also, may social solidarity. A well-grounded decision cannot safely neglect either. It would be dogmatic to assume that one of these was value proper and the other only a condition or symptom of value.

It would be just as dogmatic to stipulate that one of these should arbitrarily be defined as value (let other men define value as they please!) and proceed to evaluate human decisions in terms of this arbitrary stipulation, ignoring other equally justifiable ways of defining value. What is relevant to well-grounded human decisions remains, of course, factually just the same, whatever a writer's stipulated definition may be.

So we shall not assume that there is no field of values, for we suspect that a common problem sets the field. However, if the evidence should later indicate that this is not a single but a multiple problem, or (hard to conceive) that there is no such problem, we shall naturally follow the evidence.

Fifth, before moving directly into our investigation, we should consider two more matters of method, both of which have to do with the avoidance of dogmatism. We have just stated a promising guiding problem for our enterprise: that of how to make well-grounded decisions. We propose to seek the solution of this problem in purely empirical terms—purely by hypothesis and assemblage of evidence. No limitations will be set on the nature of the acceptable evidence relevant to the problem except that any evidence used will be regarded as open to criticism and corroboration.

This may appear so obvious a requirement for evidence in a factual inquiry as scarcely to need mentioning. But experience shows otherwise. A number of *traditional devices of dogmatism* have been and still are frequently resorted to. We need to be on our guard against them.

Dogmatism may be defined as insistence upon a belief in excess of the degree to which the evidence supports it. The devices referred to are means that have traditionally encouraged such excess of insistence. They are extremely plausible and appealing and it is only with experience that we learn to distrust them.

These devices are: (1) appeal to divine revelation, infallible authority, or any authority in excess of the 'experience' or evidence which the authority can present to support it; (2) appeal to self-evidence, certainty, the a priori, inconceivability of the opposite, or mere inconceivability as a test for certifying statements, principles, concepts, or ideas; (3) appeal to indubitability or certainty of immediacy to place data of sense and other intuitions outside the range of corroboration or criticism.

These are the typical devices for setting pet theories beyond the reach of criticism. Their purpose is to make it appear presumptuous to ask for confirming evidence. Norms of evaluation and data of value have over and over again been put forward with these plausible appeals. Unsupported authority is fortunately becoming a thing of the past, but some reputable writers still appeal to self-evidence, and many of them appeal to indubitable immediacy.

I shall not take the time here to justify in detail the rejection of these devices. The argument can be found elsewhere.[1] These devices add nothing to the credibility of the evidence. If, for instance, a proposed 'indubitable datum' is questioned, a conscientious writer is always willing to present confirming evidence to support his description. If a writer refuses to do this, and in effect calls the critic stupid or confused or unscientific or perhaps even wicked or unpatriotic who persists in asking for evidence, there is good reason to believe that the suggested 'indubitable' is doubtful.

In the discussions which follow, no appeals will wittingly be made to implicit authority, self-evidence, or indubitables. We shall make our appeal only to evidence that is open to critical examination and corroboration. There would be no need to mention these devices of dogmatism except that some readers might wonder why we make no use of them when an item seems patently indubitable or self-evident. We learn through the history of thought how often the appeal to certainty proves to have been unwarranted. Nothing is gained by the appeal, and reliance on it inhibits a scrutiny and search for corroboration.

Sixth and last, another mode of usually unintentional dogmatism may be called *the fallacy of clearing the field*. This consists in the examination and elimination of the principal alternative theories on any given subject with the apparent result of clearing the field for any new theory such as one's own. It is an appealing procedure and highly convincing when first encountered. The trouble is, one's own theory may be no better than some that have been rejected. There can be no harm in running over a number of other views to show their difficulties or to show what the relevant problems are. The fallacy arises only when it is implied that because earlier theories are not fully adequate, and so not absolutely true, they can thenceforth be ignored. In a complex subject like the one we are entering, alternative theories often stress areas of relevant evidence that the subject cannot afford to ignore. We shall not, therefore, follow the common procedure of first examining the theories that have gone before so as to clear the field for our own. We shall plunge immediately into our subject at some promising point and proceed from there. The only exceptions will be certain theories employing unempirical methods; we need to make a critical examination of these theories early in our study, because so many persons have accepted them uncritically, and might think we had not taken them into account. We turn to these in §3.

## 3. The Empirical versus the Linguistic Approach to Values

The program suggested in the preceding sections is clearly that of an empirical approach to the study of values. Many writers on the subject, however, recommend a quite different approach. These as a group constitute a special school of value theorists. They may be called the linguistic school.

The characteristic of the linguistic school is to seek the solution of value problems by an appeal to language. This appeal, as well as the empirical appeal to the facts of value, is as old as the interest in the study. Until lately, however, the two appeals have not been sharply separated. Plato's *Republic*, for instance, can with equal fairness be regarded as a study of the meaning of the word 'justice' or as an empirical study of the political constitution of society and the psychological dispositions of man in order to discriminate the better from the worse. Similarly with Aristotle's works on ethics and politics, and with most of the writings on value topics in Western culture till about thirty years ago.

It is doubtful whether writers on ethics or aesthetics previous to the twentieth century had more than an inkling of a possible issue in their fields between analyzing their pivotal value terms and analyzing the facts indicated by their terms. The meaning of a term passed for them so naturally through to the facts meant, and from an examination of the facts back to an enrichment and refinement of the meaning of the term, that no problem seemed to be involved.

But within the last few decades a great division has sprung up between those who conceive value theory as the study of value *terms* and those who conceive it as the study of value *facts*—between the linguists and the empiricists.

There are two schools of linguists. There are those who believe they can obtain insight into the character of values by analyzing selected value terms like 'good' and 'right.' These may be called the linguistic intuitionists. Then there are those who believe that the status of values is determined by an analysis of sentences containing value terms. The latter have come to be known as the value judgment (or emotive judgment) school.

The linguistic intuitionists need not delay us long. G. E. Moore, who hypostatized the word 'good' in a desperate effort to find a common quality among all the common sense items of value, is the arch exponent of this school. In fact, he can be regarded as the father of all modern linguists, of both the intuitional and the value judgment varieties. As the transitional man between his empirically minded predecessors and the out-and-out linguists whom he fathered, Moore retains a strong empirical element in his procedure. He purported to be looking for an empirical or at least a discriminable character, 'good.' What makes him a linguist is his method of looking for it. His method, as we saw, was that of examining instances of usage of the term. By this method he could easily show that the identification of 'good' with any empirical character like pleasure or desire did not exhaust the common sense uses of the term. In common sense, the language of the ordinary man (as the phrase now goes), we can appropriately speak of pleasure as sometimes bad. But no one would regard it as appropriate to say that good is sometimes bad. Consequently, Moore argued that the meaning of pleasure cannot be identified with the meaning of good. Then, setting aside the possibility that the word 'good' might be ambiguous, he proceeded to dub all such identifications of the good with commonly observable characters as 'the naturalistic fallacy.' By this device he cleared the field (cf. §2, sixth point) of all preceding empiricists in value theory. And then he argued to the existence of a simple and (in this sense) indefinable quality, 'good,' not to be identified or analyzed into any other empirically or intuitively found qualities. Having thus hypostatized a quality, 'good,' he had to hypostatize a faculty of intellectual intuition to cognize it.

To an empiricist it is obvious that Moore avoided his 'naturalistic fallacy' only to fall doubly deep into the fallacy of hypostatization. He also commits himself to the dogmatic device of indubitable immediacy with a view to forbidding criticism of his hypostatized quality. This should be condemnation enough of his mode of procedure. But, ironically, his own followers in his mode of linguistic analysis do not find their indubitable intuitions in agreement with his. It appears that by his own linguistic method some of his successors discover another quality, 'right,' which is intuitively distinct from the quality 'good.' Moore had written of 'right' as analyzable in terms of 'good.' Others of his students (those who developed the value judgment school) failed to experience any intellectual intuition of his indubitable nonnatural good at all. So, all in all, the intuitive linguistic method of generating indubitable values seems rather dubious. And we shall leave the method in this impasse.

In passing, it may be remarked that an ordinary empiricist would not regard Moore's 'naturalistic fallacy' as a fallacy at all, except as a question-begging epithet illicitly tossed by Moore at critics who are not impressed by his linguistic performances. In our own empirical approach we shall, of course, seek out definite areas of empirical fact referred to by various meanings of common sense 'good,' and shall try to refine and improve those meanings. If there is any fallacy in this procedure of correcting the meanings of empirical terms by reference to the facts that the terms refer to, then most empirical inquiries are fallacious. And, moreover, there is no reason why common sense meanings should be taken as infallible, or why 'facts' should be manufactured to comport with such meanings rather than meanings altered to conform with the facts.

So much, then, for the intuitive school of linguists. Strangely enough, the value judgment school seems to have grown out of a criticism of the intuitive school—a criticism that goes along halfway with the regular empiricist's criticism of that school. The value judgment men are not impressed any more than the empiricists with the intuitionists' dogma of one or more incorrigible value qualities. They question the empirical verifiability of such qualities. But they are still somehow impressed with the doctrine of the 'naturalistic fallacy,' and they are still ready to believe that there may be something incorrigible about values. Their solution is to discover in the linguistic analysis of *sentences* a way of lifting values entirely outside the empirical field. It is an extraordinary linguistic sleight-of-hand. This is the way of it:

They describe ethics (or any other value subject) as the study of sentences containing ethical (or other value) terms, such as 'good,' 'right,' 'ought.' Then they observe that these sentences often express commands, wishes, and the like. Now commands, wishes, and the like, they observe, are emotive expressions, and statements expressing them may be called 'emotive judgments.' Then these writers generalize value theory as the study of emotive judgments. This appears innocent enough till the next step is taken, which is that such judgments are not either true or false. Only declarative sentences are true or false. Imperatives and optatives are not declarative statements. Therefore they are neither true nor false. Then it turns out that the subject of ethics, and value theory generally, being occupied with emotive judgments, now called 'value judgments,' are likewise neither true nor false. Basic value judgments, then, turn out to be incorrigible, as, to be sure, Moore said they were, but not for the reason he said. They are incorrigible not because they refer to supposed objects of a special intellectual intuition, but because they are not declarative statements referring to objects at all.

Statements such as 'Spinach is good,' 'Lying is evil,' are interpreted as equivalent to 'Would that you liked spinach,' 'Don't lie.' They are expressions of someone's emotions. They do not, it is declared, predicate anything of the objects referred to or purport to be true or false.

It is not denied that declarative statements may be made about emotions. But these would be defined as part of psychology, not of ethics or value theory. And declarative statements may be made about people's judgments of approval and disapproval. But these would be defined as anthropological and sociological statements, not ethical or value judgments. Declarative statements may also be made about the means of getting spinach or inducing people not to lie. But these are judgments about means, not about intrinsic values or ends. Value judgments refer to ends, not to means. It is an empirical question whether anything is a means to something else. But the ultimate or end value is always an emotive expression, and a judgment expressing it is neither true nor false.

The value judgment theory is very plausible. But it does not, as superficially appears, escape from cognitive responsibility. It is, in a much subtler way, just as dogmatic as Moore's intuitionism. The dogmatism is one of definitional exclusion. The device is that of definitional stipulation. Certain entities are plausibly defined as comprising the field of value, and thereby the critic is estopped from ascribing value to any other entities—on pain of not talking about value, as this has been plausibly defined. The device is rather easily exposed when the entities stipulated are natural ones like pleasure or adaptation. It catches the critic off guard when they are linguistic ones. The device institutes a sort of linguistic a priori certainty on an apparently empirical base.

The form of the procedure is as follows. The first step is to make an empirical examination of the sentences appearing in writings on value and in common speech. Generally the examination is made of ethical statements. So we shall on the whole follow the procedure in this area of value. The inquirer notices in ethical writings and discussions a number of sentences in the imperative form, such as 'Don't lie,' 'Don't break a promise,' 'Don't cheat.' He observes that these sentences often take the declarative form without a change of intent or meaning: 'Lying is bad,' 'Telling the truth is good,' and so on. These, he declares, are concealed imperatives. Wherever he comes across terms like 'good,' 'bad,' 'right,' 'wrong,' 'ought,' 'ought not' which have a value or a normative reference, he interprets the sentences in which they occur as imperatives. On the basis of this empirical linguistic analysis, he defines ethical value in terms of imperatives. Then he generalizes and defines the field of ethics as that of imperatives.

There are three steps in the procedure: (1) an empirical examination of the sentences in traditional ethical works and common usage; (2) a definitional stipulation as a result of this investigation that an ethical statement is an imperative; (3) a more extended definitional stipulation that the field of ethics is that of imperatives.

The definitional stipulations 2 and 3 are then exhibited as being immune to cognitive criticism in terms of evidence that can be brought against them, partly on the ground that they are nominal definitions and a man may stipulate what meaning he pleases for a term, but mainly on the ground that an imperative is neither true nor false, whence questions of evidence regarding its truth are irrelevant. The novel feature in the position of the value judgment school is the tying in of an imperative immune to empirical criticism with a definitional stipulation also regarded as immune to empirical criticism.

Let us then look more closely at just what is contained in steps 2 and 3 and the transition from 1 to 2. What is an imperative statement and how does it differ from a declarative? One of the difficulties we shall encounter is the variety of interpretations that can be given to both the imperative and the declarative. However, the generic differences are sufficiently wide to permit us to find the source of the dogmatism in the value judgment theory without getting deeply involved in the diversity of theories about meaning and truth.

Roughly, a declarative sentence such as 'This table is black' or 'Tables are colored' is in the form '$x$ is $q$,' where $x$ is some object or event or class of objects that can be indicated and $q$ some quality or relation that can be predicated of $x$. The sentence '$x$ is $q$' has a reference to an existent object or event. The sentence is true if it meets certain requirements such as correspondence or operational verification. These requirements constitute the truth reference. The precise nature of this reference is still controversial and is the subject of inquiry in the various theories of truth. The sentence '$x$ is $q$' as it appears on a printed page is a set of symbols. These symbols acquire meaning only as they are interpreted by somebody reading or writing the sentence. There is sure to be some motivation for the person to perform the act of interpretation, but this motive is generally (though not always) considered irrelevant to the meaning of the sentence. The declarative meaning of the sentence is thus generally conceived as derived from its truth reference. So in a declarative sentence there is the symbol complex 'x is q,' a motive instituting the dynamics for interpreting its meaning, and a truth reference of the sentence to some existent object or event that can verify the sentence. Suppose we symbolize it thus:

$$M \dashrightarrow \text{'}x \text{ is } q\text{'} \rightarrow X \overset{?}{(Q)} \tag{1}$$

where $M$ is the motive giving the dynamics for interpretation, 'x is q' the printed sentence, $\rightarrow$ the truth reference to $X$, which is the existent object or event referred to, and $(Q)$ the quality or relation referred to which will be a character of $X$ if the sentence is true, but will not be a character of $X$ if the sentence is false. The relation of $M$ to 'x is q' is given in a dotted line to signify that this is not generally regarded as a part of the meaning of the sentence. The sentence, however, would never acquire meaning without it.

Now what is involved in an imperative sentence? A typical imperative is 'Tell the truth' or 'Don't lie,' or better, 'Thou shalt speak truthfully' or 'Thou shalt not lie.' The second form is better because it emphasizes the reference to the person at whom the imperative is directed. Here, as well as in the declarative sentence, is a symbol complex that can be uttered or written or read on a printed page. This we may call the printed sentence to stress its possible independence from an interpreter. An imperative, however, requires two interpreters: the person who commands and the person commanded. And the two must understand each other if the command is to be obeyed. In the value judgment theory, however, the focus of attention is on the person who makes the command. For on this view the ethical entity is the imperative itself, and that would be the command emanating from the person commanding.

Taking the command as a point of departure, we can make out a certain degree of parallelism between a declarative sentence and an imperative sentence. Both have a symbol complex, both require an interpreter with a dynamic motivation to give meaning to the symbols, and both have an objective reference to something beyond the symbol complex.

The form of the symbol complex, the printed imperative sentence, is roughly '$p$ do $a$,' where $p$ is some person or class of persons who can be indicated, and $a$ some act which $p$ is commanded to perform. There is a motive for the command on the part of the person giving it. This motive is the dynamic source for the meaning of the imperative. It is generally (and particularly by the value judgment school) regarded as intimately connected with the imperative. There is also the reference of the imperative sentence to the person commanded, and the act he is commanded to perform. This reference is likely to be relatively unemphasized by the value judgment school. But without it an imperative would at best be only an optative or just an exclamation. The reference of an imperative to the person commanded and the act commanded to be done is as essential to an imperative as the motive generating the command.

Suppose, then, we symbolize the imperative thus:

$$M \overset{(1)}{\to} \text{'$p$ do $a$'} \overset{(2)}{\to} P \text{ (does } A) \qquad (2)$$

where $M$ is the commander's motive for the imperative, '$p$ do $a$' the printed or spoken imperative sentence (the symbol complex), $P$ the person (or persons) commanded, and $A$ the act commanded, which may or may not be performed. If $P$ performs $A$, we say the imperative was obeyed; if not, it was disobeyed (provided $P$ understood the command) or unobeyed (provided $P$ did not understand, or perhaps there was no $P$). The first arrow $\overset{(1)}{\to}$ we may call the motivating reference, and the second arrow $\overset{(2)}{\to}$ the obedience reference.

Now we are in a position to examine the view of the value judgment school that ethical sentences are imperatives and are neither true nor false, and that accordingly ethics is not a scientific study for which empirical evidence is relevant to establish the truth of an ethical theory.

What specifically does a value judgment theorist refer to as an imperative? The first thing to observe is that the empirical examination of sentences constituting step 1 refers only to printed or uttered sentences (symbolic complexes). If, then, the critic holds the value judgment theorist to a strict accounting for what he declares he finds in books on ethics, the subject matter of ethics on this view is printed sentences in the imperative form—'*p* do *a*.' These are observably different from printed sentences in the form '*x* is *q*.' Moreover, it is also empirically discoverable that sentences of the form '*p* do *a*' have obedience references to events beyond themselves, which are distinguishable from the truth references characteristic of declarative sentences in the form '*x* is *q*.' Imperative sentences are not then literally true or false. They are obeyed or disobeyed.

But what have these distinctions to do with ethics or with values generally? These are interesting linguistic distinctions. Where does any value come in? Up to this point, it would appear, none—*unless,* by definitional stipulation, value is identified with printed imperative sentences and their objective obedience references. Printed sentences are traditional linguistic subject matter, but not the traditional subject matter of ethics. Ethics traditionally deals with human conduct and the motives for decisions of conduct. And if many moralists have been concerned with the meaning of 'good' and 'ought' and of sentences containing these terms, their concern was not to discover distinctions among forms of sentences but data on human conduct.

At this point the value judgment exponent is faced with a dilemma. He may insist by definitional stipulation that by value statements (regarding the 'good' and the 'ought') he means imperative printed sentences. By doing this he retains his distinctive paradox that these statements have no truth reference. But by this stipulation he removes himself from a long ethical tradition according to which the subject matter of ethics is human conduct, which can presumably be described in declarative sentences with truth references. He can retain imperatives as the subject matter of ethics if he is willing to conceive ethics as a branch of linguistics having no central concern with human conduct. But if he allows that human conduct is the subject matter of ethics, he must drop his idea that the subject matter of ethics is imperative sentences. For then it is not the sentences he is concerned with as a student of ethics, but the conduct leading up to and consequent upon such sentences. And his statements coming out of this study of conduct will be declarative sentences with a truth reference.

To repeat, the dilemma of the value judgment exponent at this point is: either he may hold that the subject matter of ethics is imperatives with no truth reference, in which case ethics becomes a branch of linguistics and is divorced from the tradition which, he maintains in step 1, is the source of his idea that ethical judgments are imperatives; or he may stand by his concern for the tradition expressed in step 1, in which case he will have to give up his imperatives and allow that ethics is composed of declarative sentences, true or false, about conduct.

But if he does take the first alternative, notice that he can maintain it only by his own arbitrary definitional stipulation. The tradition would appear to be against him.

An exponent of the value judgment school, however, would not want to admit that an imperative was a mere linguistic form or a mere symbol complex. His escape is by way of the motivating reference. An imperative, he declares, is an *emotive* judgment. It expresses the emotion of the agent.

This leads us into a second phase of the argument. In this phase the imperative is not a linguistic form or symbol complex primarily, but an act expressing an emotion. The central element about an imperative in this phase of the value judgment view is the emotion from which the imperative expression emanates, and the words are in the nature of active gestures directed at the object of the emotion, the person being ordered to do something.[2]

Now here we have an act of conduct, a purposive act, which would be acknowledged in the traditional ethical theories or by common sense and the man in the street as a typical act of ethical value, something to which we can properly attribute the character 'right' or 'wrong.'

Such an act, however, is an event that can be described in declarative sentences. It is, to be sure, an act of command, but being an act it is open to description, and the sentences describing it would be true or false like any other descriptive sentences.

Moreover, an observer can easily describe the conditions which lead us to ascribe the terms 'right' or 'wrong' to elements in the total action complex. If the person who is ordered to perform an act does so, it is customary to say he did the right act in obedience to the command; if not, he did wrong. The relation of obedience or disobedience is a verifiable character of the total action complex. And a right act is often called a good performance, and a man who has a disposition to perform right acts is customarily called a good man. These are all observable relations between an act of a person motivated to express a command and the act of a person to whom the command is given. The constituent acts and the relations between them are all describable and have for many generations been described in declarative sentences.

Not that all ethical writers agree in their descriptions of such acts. For such acts are full of complexities when followed through into their details. Commands may supervene over other commands, may overlap, may conflict. A variety of ethical theories arise from these circumstances and await ultimate confirmation. But nearly all ethical writers in discussing commands have assumed until lately (for they saw no reason to do otherwise) that they were making declarative sentences open to verification or confirmation.

Where, then, in this phase of the argument does the value judgment school find any purchase for its characteristic idea that ethical statements are neither true nor false? It finds it in the *act* of command. The emotive expression, being an act and not a description, is neither true nor false.

It is true that an act as an occurrence is never true or false. It just occurs. It is the object that verifies a declarative sentence describing the object, and so, of course, is not the sentence it verifies.

An imperative sentence, however, is neither true nor false for a quite different reason. It is neither true nor false not because it is an event which verifies sentences that are true or false, but because it is a sentence whose objective reference is not a truth reference but an obedience reference.

There is accordingly an equivocation at this point. An imperative sentence as a linguistic form is one thing; an imperative act as an emotive expression is quite another thing. The first is not a value act in any ordinary sense, but is a linguistic sentence. The second is a value act in the usual sense of the term, but not as such a purely linguistic sentence.

So here the value judgment exponent is confronted with another dilemma on top of the first one. If he takes the first meaning, he gives up talking about ethical values in any ordinary sense of the term; but if he takes the second meaning, he gives up the characteristic paradox of his view, that ethics is a set of sentences that are neither true nor false.

The plausibility of his view comes from his ability to slip from one meaning of imperative to the other without the reader noticing the equivocation. That an ethical theory is a system of sentences seems obvious enough. Then the suggestion that these sentences are all imperative sentences seems acceptable. The next observation, that imperatives are neither true nor false, comes as something of a shock. But if the critic begins to escape from this consequence by the idea that perhaps such imperatives are mere linguistic forms and empty of ethical values, he is blocked off by the assertion that these imperatives are emotionally expressive acts. The unwary critic is then reassured, since emotional expression is quite acceptable as a value act. The absurdity of the result will quickly come to light, however, if the critic will just complete the circle and contemplate an ethical theory as a set of emotionally expressive acts. Then it will dawn on him that a set of imperatives as linguistic forms is not identical with a set of imperatives as emotionally expressive acts.

And it is only by stipulating that imperatives be defined as linguistic sentences which are neither true nor false that the value judgment men can maintain their paradoxical dogma. I trust that it is now evident how unjustifiable this stipulation is. It probably would have been exposed very quickly but for the fact that imperative sentences actually have no truth references. This gave them a specious immunity from vigorous empirical criticism.

Nevertheless, even after this analysis of the value judgment school's procedure, there are sure to be readers who will be still unsatisfied, thinking something is omitted, and asking, "After all, can prescriptions ever be made into descriptions?" "Can the 'ought' ever be found in the 'is'?" "Isn't there something about normative judgments that can never be reduced to descriptive judgments?" [3]

Possibly there is, and of course an emotive fact can never be reduced to a description of it. But the value judgment school, in its disposition of ethics, is implying more than that. Our coming investigation will inform us of these things. All that need concern us at this preliminary stage is that a decision be not thrust upon us by dogmatic a priori devices or by a manipulation of definitional stipulations. Let us follow the evidence where it leads. If values are to be found among empirical facts, the facts should show them forth. If not, perhaps we shall find evidence for some other status for them, or perhaps there are no values in spite of the appearances. Of just one thing we may be reasonably sure, unless the preceding analysis is quite in error: the linguistic procedures of both the intuitive and the value judgment schools are such that they are not likely to yield ultimately acceptable results—because these procedures rest on devices calculated to isolate definitional stipulations from rational or empirical criticism.

At the same time, it should not be thought that the writings of these men have not made helpful contributions to the value field. They have swept out a good deal of irrelevant clutter. They have stimulated their opponents to greater analytical rigor than was customary earlier. G. E. Moore, particularly, pointed out the ambiguities in the term 'good' by the device of his 'naturalistic fallacy.' This did produce the value judgment school, but it could also have stimulated an opposite movement, that of accepting 'good' as indeed ambiguous, as a term referring to a collection of natural entities more or less closely connected and requiring only to have their connections discriminated and described. As for the value judgment school, much acute linguistic discrimination of subtle meanings in sentences employing value terms has come out by their analyses. And particularly through the work of Charles Stevenson we have inherited a sensitive and detailed analysis of the art of moral persuasion.

## 4. A Summary of Preliminary Conclusions

In our study thus far we have indicated the common sense and traditional field of our subject matter. This we are calling the common sense definition of the field. We have warned against a number of common assumptions and deceptive procedures that might distort our findings. We will be careful not to assume that the common sense field is final and incapable of revision; nor, will we assume, second, that there is necessarily a common trait or set of traits to be found among the items in the field; nor, third, that they can all be reduced to one; nor, fourth, that there is no field of subject matter for a theory of value if generalization or reduction is not fully applicable; nor, fifth, shall we resort to devices of dogmatism which seek to substitute an appeal to certainty for the empirical methods of corroboration of evidence and hypothesis and probability; nor, sixth, shall we yield to the allurement of the fallacy of clearing the field.

Meanwhile, we have come upon a problem which may turn out to be the unifying element in this area of subject matter: the problem of how to get well-grounded judgments for human decisions. Though there may be no common trait running through the items of the common sense field of value, the items may be connected with one another by way of the search for the solution of this common problem.

The hypothesis of a common problem of value offers a unifying guide for a study of the field of value—a guide flexible enough to avoid dogmatism and yet determinate enough to stimulate research for the discovery of whatever the evidence may yield. On this hypothesis we are free to discover anything in regard to the nature of the field. We may find it is, as it superficially appears, a collection of interconnected heterogeneous items; or we may find it a field which by a legitimate use of the reductive method and generalization may be unified in a single compact system; or we may discover that no fruitful field of study exists there at all, that on analysis the various items prove more and more discrete, and that the enveloping term 'value' and its synonyms 'good' and 'bad' had better be discarded.

Obviously, if we thought there was much chance of this third possibility, we should not be setting out on the present undertaking. At the very least, we do think it quite probable that the first alternative may prove true. Yet most theories of value assume the second alternative, and if the evidence shapes up in that direction, our method would reveal that outcome. The advantage of our method is that it does not assume any particular outcome. We rather anticipate that either the first or the second alternative will prove true. There seems to be a good deal of evidence to indicate that a field of value does exist for refined cognition approximating the field of the rough common sense definition. But whether the unifying element is a common problem or a single common quality or relation that may emerge when the field is suitably analyzed is a question that can be answered only after extensive study. The more conservative and undogmatic preliminary assumption seems rather obviously to be the former. That will be the tentative assumption on which we shall start. We shall begin with the hypothesis that the common sense field of value constitutes a sufficiently unified field for systematic study because of a common problem, but that we have no assurance yet that the items in the field are ultimately homogeneous.

## 5. A PROGRAM OF PROCEDURE

On the basis of these conclusions, how should we best proceed? Let us assume tentatively that we are dealing with a number of distinct but interconnected values rather than with a single quality of value. The common sense list can undoubtedly be simplified a good deal by legitimate uses of reduction and generalization, but we do not know how much. It would not, theoretically, make much difference where we began our study, but practically it would be most fruitful to pitch upon some item on the list that would rather quickly lead to the systematic organization of a large amount of our subject matter. Presumably such an item would be one already developed by some persistent and well-known type of value theory.

For our Western culture at the present juncture, the two most promising candidates for our choice would probably be affection (pleasure and pain) and conation (desire and purpose). Of the two, affection would probably, for most people, seem the more obvious. Hedonism, the pleasure theory of value, is one of the oldest and most persistent in all the value sciences—in ethics, in aesthetics, and indirectly in economics as the basis for utility, and in anthropology and sociology as the basis for social approval. In fact, the clear distinction between pleasure and desire is rather recent. Even so late a moralist as Mill failed to make it, naming desire indiscriminately with pleasure as if they were phases of the same thing, namely, pleasure. The distinction between them, however, made the first big schism in general theory of value, that between the Meinong school and the Ehrenfels school. Since then value theorists have often tried to cover up the opposition by enclosing it in the hyphenated word 'motor-affective.' Clearly, pleasure and desire are the areas of value that the history of the subject would indicate as early choices for study. And pleasure would appear to be the obvious first choice.

But I shall instead suggest desire in the form of purpose as our first choice. The reasons are these. There is no question that value is as widely and appropriately ascribed to purpose as to pleasure. The present advantage of selecting purpose over pleasure is that a great deal of objective behavioristic study has been done on the structure of purpose. There is available to us a thoroughly objective description of purposive behavior which does not require any dependence on introspective observation. This cannot be said of pleasure. Pleasure is much more distinctively an introspective term—so much so that some recent theorists have spoken of it as private and incommunicable. Although it can, beyond much question, be correlated with certain behavior patterns, nevertheless, if we started our study of value with pleasure as the point of departure, we would hardly begin with behavioristic descriptions of the experience. Yet this would be the most profitable procedure today in dealing with purpose. Pleasure is still predominantly an introspective item, whereas purpose can be treated either introspectively or objectively, and the latter has been highly developed. In selecting purpose instead of pleasure as our first subject of study we avoid the issue over the introspective[4] versus the objective method. We can actually begin with an objective study of value. The subject matter of purposive value then finds its place naturally in relation to biological and physical facts, and the relevant introspective data can be fitted in whenever desired to the objective descriptions of purposive behavior. These advantages cannot be expected yet of the subject matter of hedonic value or pleasure.

Closely allied with the introspective difficulties with pleasure is the fact that some highly competent writers have cast doubt on the very existence of pleasure as a specific quality of immediacy. Pleasure is explained away as a name for a collection of other identifiable qualities. This is because the identification of pleasure depends so heavily on introspective reports. No sense organ has been found for it, nor is there firm agreement as to what its physiological correlate may be; it is a bare possibility that there is none and that pleasure is a psychological fiction. This can never be said of purpose. We have too much objective information about purpose. So, on this ground, too, it is more secure to begin the study of value with purposive behavior than with pleasure and pain.

After we have made a careful study of the value elements to be found in purpose, we can take up pleasure and any other items in the common sense field that have not found an adequate treatment within purposive structures—unless by good fortune it should turn out that pleasure and pain are also elements of purposive activity.

Our program, then, is to enter the study of the common sense field of value by way of purposive behavior, and thence work, area by area, over the whole field. In carrying out this program I think we shall be on the way to finding the best available answers to man's most engrossing problem—how to obtain well-grounded decisions for action.

# 2

# The Main Features of
# Purposive Value

## 1. Sources of Data for Purposive Structures

Highly developed expositions of a purposive theory of value are
to be found in R. B. Perry's *General Theory of Value* and E. C.
Tolman's *Purposive Behavior in Animals and Men*. These two
books supplement each other and have nearly identical presuppositions. The differences that appear are generally very illuminating of the relevant facts and hidden issues. It should be remembered that Tolman's book was written as a contribution to
psychology and not to theory of value, but, if anything, this
renders his descriptions involving purposive value the more significant. The analysis of purpose in this and succeeding chapters
will lean heavily on the materials to be found in these two books.
But, for reasons that will appear, our treatment will not exactly
follow that of either writer.

One divergency consists in not following their rather thoroughgoing behaviorism. It appears to me unnecessary to limit a purposive theory of value to a behavioristic account and voluntarily
to reject the contributions of introspective reports where these
are helpful and often indispensable for reaching full descriptions
of purposive activity. This is not the place to revive the old
controversy between behaviorism and introspection. The fruitfulness of a behavioristic treatment of psychological facts has

35

become well established, and likewise the method of introspection has survived the behavioristic attack and, though somewhat chastened, is respectable again.

Introspection seems to be very secure wherever there is an objective framework into which the data of introspection may be fitted. One of the periods of most rapid advancement in psychology occurred in the late nineteenth century under men like Wundt and Helmholtz working out the details of sensory discrimination. This work was largely introspective, but the data were fitted into the detailed knowledge which had been acquired of the physiology of the nervous system and the sense organs. These objective physiological structures afforded a rigid framework within which introspective data could be placed with great precision. Visual sensations can be clearly ordered and separated from other sense qualities by their relation to the eye, auditory sensations by their relation to the ear, and so on. We can even now appreciate how difficult it would be to separate the taste sensations of sweet, salt, sour, and bitter from the sensations of odor if these were not clearly separated by their dependency on the sense organs of the tongue. But with these objectively described physiological structures established, we can rely safely upon introspective reports correlated with them. The introspective data then often give sense discriminations that would be very difficult to obtain without their help.

Now, we can expect somewhat the same situation as a result of the behavioristic descriptions of purposive structures. Once these structures have been objectively described and their articulation laid out in detail, it is safe to call in the introspective reports that can be correlated with the articulations of the purposive structures. These reports can often produce relevant data that would be very difficult to obtain otherwise. Sometimes there may be no other means of getting at a nest of relevant data. Introspective terms like 'sensuous satisfaction,' 'apprehension,' and 'anticipation' thrown out at large are vague and hard to verify, but when correlated and located in the articulations of an objectively described purposive structure they acquire precision and are easily open to confirmation.

Moreover, most actual decisions are made in the theater of

the mind in terms of felt satisfactions and pains, desires, apprehensions, and anticipations; and to think that these have to be interpreted behavioristically before they can be used practically is contrary to the momentum of actual human conduct. We ultimately act upon our decisions as they are qualitatively felt, and the values involved are qualitatively experienced. There would be a profound distortion of fact if it were implied that the quality of experience is superfluous. These qualities are the data which introspection reports. So, ultimately, the data of introspection are never dispensed with. They might as well be used to augment a behavioristic report wherever they can be helpful.

We shall begin our descriptions in behavioristic terms, in the manner of Tolman and Perry, but later we shall find it helpful to interpolate introspective data into our objective findings. The two types of reports can be used coöperatively.

## 2. The Definition of Purposive Behavior

What, then, is purposive activity? Where do we draw the line between purposive and other forms of activity? Here, as with the subject of value in general, we shall have to proceed by successive definition. We shall know with some precision how best to describe a purposive act only after we have made our analysis. In this instance, however, we do not have to start at the vaguest common sense level. We can take advantage of an excellent preliminary analysis by R. B. Perry.

Though purpose is sometimes attributed to inorganic nature, this is usually done on the assumption that mental activities are somehow involved in that sphere. Perry takes the more usual contemporary attitude that mind does not appear in nature outside of living things. Purpose is at the very least a form of biological activity. Consequently, any definition of purposiveness which would extend it into the inorganic realm would appear to him too wide to serve for a study of value. He then considers three characters that have frequently been used to differentiate purpose: organization, tendency, and adaptation.

*Organization* he finds at once to be too broad a character.

Many inorganic systems, such as the solar system, exhibit organization. Undoubtedly purpose involves organization, but it seems advisable and closest in conformity with usage to limit purpose to activities associated with living organisms.

*Tendency* has a similar defect. In the broadest sense, any determinate causal relation extending through time exhibits a tendency. By the law of inertia, any unimpeded body tends to move in a straight line. Such a tendency is hardly purposive. We come nearer what we are seeking if a tendency is conceived as heading for a terminus. As Perry says, "A determined temporal process is spoken of as a tendency whenever there is anything remarkable which distinguishes the later from the earlier stages, and may be regarded as that *toward* which the process moves, or that *in* which it culminates." [1] Thus two bodies tend to gravitate toward their center of mass. A purpose is clearly an instance of such a culminating tendency, but it is also clearly a more specific kind of tendency.

This brings Perry to *adaptation*. Can a purpose be identified with an adaptive tendency? Unqualified adaptation also proves too broad. Perry describes a number of forms of adaptation. He first considers what he calls 'compensatory adjustment,' which is the principle of *equilibrium* in simplest form. We conceive a normal state of a system. Then we observe a disturbance which upsets the normal state of the system. If, within the system, there is some mechanism which restores it to its normal state, this is a compensatory adjustment. A thermostat on a furnace would be such a mechanism, or the governor of an engine. A biological organism is provided with a great variety of such mechanisms for maintaining its life equilibrium in a changing environment. Purposive activity is clearly one of the mechanisms for maintaining a biological equilibrium, but, as generally conceived, purposive adjustment is more specific than the mere compensatory adjustment we find in purely mechanical things.

Perry next considers a process he calls 'preparatory adjustment.' Hibernation is an instance of this. It is an adjustment of the organism to a certain condition performed before the condition occurs. The various protective reflexes stimulated by distance sensations, like the winking of the eyes at an approaching cinder, are examples. All instinctive behavior is of this kind. Here we are getting very close to Perry's field of unquestionable purposive action. For purposive action conspicuously exhibits the character of preparatory adjustment. In purposive behavior we anticipate harm before it occurs. We avoid a thistle before it stings. We buy food before we begin feeling the pangs of hunger. More remarkable still, we anticipate satisfactions before they occur. We cook a dinner in the pleasant expectation of the delight of eating it.

All these examples illustrate preparatory adjustment. But there is obviously an important difference between the latter examples, which are unquestionably purposive, and the earlier, which would require some stretching of the term. The earlier acts are automatic, whereas the latter are *modifiable* or *docile*—acts which prepare against a future contingency, not automatically but in a *novel* manner specifically suited to the contingency. The organism *invents* the means of meeting the situation. He learns how to handle it. He exhibits *intelligent* behavior. Here we seem to have found the concept we were looking for. It is in terms of this sort of behavior that Perry defines purposiveness. Another name for it commonly used today, and the term Perry employs whenever he desires a technical term, is 'interest.'[2]

We shall accept this definition of Perry's as our first approximation to the field of purposive values. *Purposive activity is docile adaptive behavior.* Its nearest relative is automatic adaptive behavior. Perry identifies value (all value whatever) with the former and denies it to the latter. As our introductory approach to the problem showed, we should not wish to commit ourselves to this identification, at least not yet. We wish to leave the way open to regard anything as falling within the field of value which is relevant to the making of well-grounded decisions. There is no question that all docile adaptive behavior is relevant to this problem, and thus falls within our general field of values. But it is not clear to us yet that no other sort of behavior is relevant. So, provisionally, we shall call this field marked out by Perry that of purposive values—qualifying the values as purposive, thus leaving it open that there may be areas of values that are not strictly purposive.

One merit of Perry's approach, if the evidence will bear him out, is that it embeds values within the natural world in the life process. Among the forms of equilibrium which maintain themselves in the physical environment is that of living organisms having a capacity for modifiable adaptive behavior. Purposive values thus appear immersed in life, a stage in the biological evolutionary process. If the evidence will support this disposition of purposive values, they would appear to be biological facts of a kind, and many important consequences follow from this observation.

## 3. Isolation of a Purposive Act:
### Appetition versus Aversion

Having obtained a definition of our field of purposive values as that of docile adaptive behavior, we are ready to describe the nature of this behavior and see how values emerge from it. We shall begin with relatively simple instances and work up to complex manifestations. As human beings, we ourselves are, of course, too familiar with purposive behavior. We are immersed in it all the time. We practice it in the most complicated forms and the most intricate cultural patterns. Human life is a web of interacting purposes. How can we simplify this material and get hold of something that is open to observational control?

One answer has been to experiment with animals capable of docile behavior and then make inferences to comparable behavior in man. Rarely does a man act on a single purpose. There are times when he comes close to it, and we shall make the most of these instances. But usually he is acting under a variety of convergent or overlapping purposes. An animal's economy is generally much simpler than a man's, and under laboratory conditions this economy can often be still further simplified. Most animal behavior experiments have controlled the conditions so that only one or two purposive processes shall operate at a time. A precise description of the articulated structure of an isolated purposive act then becomes possible. More has been discovered in the last few years through controlled animal experiment about the detailed structure of a purposive act than for a long time previously. We shall want to take full advantage of this material.

Many persistent and troublesome issues in theory of value dissolve simply in the detailed description of typical forms of purposive activity. We shall, therefore, do well to begin our study with the examination and description of single purposes. Later we shall see how they combine in situations where a number of purposes are operating together, and how they integrate into personality structures, and finally how they become institutionalized as cultural patterns in societies. But it is highly advantageous to find out what the structures of single purposes are before trying to describe complexes of purposes.

This is, to be sure, the method of element analysis, which involves some risk of the reductive fallacy. But if we are aware of the ways in which the reduction of the complex to the simple may be misused, we shall be less likely to misuse it. When our analysis is completed, we can look back and see if we have fallen into any of the errors mentioned in chapter 1. And then we can make the necessary corrections. There is nothing intrinsically fallacious in selecting the simplest examples of a subject matter to examine in detail first. This is what we are proposing to do in seeking out examples of isolated or relatively isolated purposive acts. At this stage of our inquiry, then, we shall lean heavily on the material from animal psychology, and we shall refer also to a few human examples which resemble controlled animal experiments.

The typical conditions for animal experimentation consist in arousing a drive and then, by reward and punishment, inducing the animal to learn a set of actions. The drive is ordinarily directed from a basic need like hunger or thirst. The reward is food or liquid which satisfies the drive. The tasks to be learned are such performances as a cat getting out of a cage by pulling a cord which releases a catch on the door, or a rat learning a maze, or a chick or a dog getting around a wire barrier, or an ape obtaining with a stick a banana that is otherwise out of his reach. The inducement is some reward like food when the task is correctly performed. The performance may be further reinforced by punishment, such as a slight shock from an electric grill if a wrong choice is made, or simply the discomfort of being confined.

These experiments were designed by psychologists mainly to obtain detailed information about the learning process. But since it is docility, or adaptation through the capacity to learn, that defines our field of purposive behavior, these experiments inevitably dealt also with our subject matter of purposive values. This fact is plainly evidenced in the rewards and punishments that supplied the dynamics of the experiments. These terms in themselves indicate the presence of positive and negative purposes—purposes to attain something good, a reward; and purposes to escape from something bad, a punishment. Here obviously is the focus of our subject in this sort of behavior. A reward gives a positive value and a punishment a negative value. We find that there are two fundamental sorts of purposes: positive purposes, which seek a reward; and negative purposes, which avoid a harm. The structures of the two sorts of purposes are quite different. We shall call the positive type of purpose an *appetition*, and the negative type an *aversion*. Since the appetition is the form of behavior most fully associated with purposive activity, we shall turn to it first.

## 4. EXAMPLES OF APPETITIVE BEHAVIOR

We should, however, also have before us some examples of human behavior that are comparable to the controlled animal behavior of the psychological laboratory. Men, of course, can be induced to solve mazes and other puzzles, and be rewarded in a variety of ways. Men, too, are used as laboratory subjects. But the kind of inducement employed in the typical animal experiment is rather more important to us at this initial stage of our inquiry than the nature of the task learned. Human subjects, usually members of a psychology class, can be induced to learn a maze and other tasks simply at the request of the instructor. The inducement is strong enough, but just what is its source and what is the nature of the satisfactions that the students get in the solution? The motivation is obviously highly derivative and socialized. Animals in the laboratory, however, are motivated by basic needs such as hunger and thirst. If, therefore, we assumed that a psychology student solving a maze on the complex motivation of interest in the course, membership in a college class, desire for a degree, or fear of or affection for his instructor was acting in a manner comparable to that of a hungry rat solving a maze, we might be neglecting some crucial value facts. Nevertheless, we require examples of human purposive actions that come as close as possible to the isolated purposes of hungry animals learning a maze.

Men's actions may be brought close to the level of their basic needs in conditions of unusual emergency. Thus a single-minded purposive act on the intense urge of a basic need may occur in human behavior. Even though they are rare, such acts are extremely illuminating. For one thing, they keep us reminded of a connection between human and animal behavior. But just here they serve particularly to justify our carrying over into human behavior information about the structure of isolated purposive acts discovered in animal behavior.

Imagine a young geologist on a field trip who has been exploring arid mountain country. He is far from camp, and has become so absorbed in his work that he has lost all track of time. Late in the day he feels very thirsty, but discovers that his canteen is empty. There is no water in sight. He realizes, however, that if there were any sign of green he could probably find water by digging a hole to the underground seepage. If he could get up on an elevation with an outlook he might see such a spot. He selects a promising shoulder of a neighboring mountain, climbs it, sees a line of willows and a patch of grass in a fold of hills, makes his way to it, digs a hole, finds enough water for his purposes, drinks to his satisfaction, and fills his canteen.

Now let me quote from a report of a somewhat similar instance. An anthropologist is describing the actions of an Eskimo fishing:

> Half a mile from shore Utak began by clearing the snow off the surface of the lake with his native shovel in a circle about twelve feet in diameter. Then he knelt down, a hand shading his eyes, his nose to the ice, and tried to judge whether or not the depth of the

lake here was what it should be. I did as he did, and could see the bottom of the lake perfectly, the grasses waving and the fish moving past in their tranquil world. As soon as he spied the fish, Utak became feverish. He ran to the sled, which with the dogs had been left a hundred feet off, came back with an ice chisel, and now the ice was flying in an upward rain of chips. He was cutting out a hole, and it was incredible with what speed and precision he worked. I have seen Eskimos go through five feet of ice with one of these chisels in ten minutes. He would stop at every four or five inches, send down a sort of ladle made of bone, and slowly and cautiously bring up the chips.

When the hole had been pierced through, the water flowed in and brought to the surface the odd chips that still remained, which were carefully ladled off. Then, on the far side of the hole, Utak built a wind-screen of three snow blocks, one set straight ahead of him and each of the others serving as wings. This done, he spread a caribou skin, and knelt on it. With his left hand he unrolled a long cord at the end of which hung a small fish made of bone, with two fins. He let the decoy down into the water, and when he jigged, or pulled on the cord, which he did with the regularity of a clock, the fins beat. The little bone fish was like a water-bug swimming. In his right hand, held very near the hole, was the *kakivok*, the great three-pronged harpoon. When the fish, lured by the decoy, came swimming beneath Utak, he would lower his harpoon gently into the hole, and at the proper moment he would strike, and the fish would be speared.

. . . At first I knelt beside him. Then, my hands freezing and my muscles stiff, I stood up to stretch. He became furious, for a man walking round the hole frightens away the fish. But one could hum as much as one pleased without disturbing them, and as Utak peered into the hole he kept up a monotonous humming. I came back to where he crouched, for I was fascinated by what he was doing. . . .

With what patience that left hand, as regular as a metronome, rose and fell while the hours went by! And what passion the Eskimo put into this form of the chase! What intensity was in his gaze! The tiniest fish that passed drew from him muttered words, and it was clear that the game absorbed him, that time and space had fled leaving him only this hole in the ice over which he would peer for days if necessary. As far as the eye could see in every direction the scene was void of life; and in the midst of this immensity a single man, who might have been alone in the world, was absorbed with a scientist's concentration upon . . . upon what? Upon the art of filling his belly.[3]

There can be no question that these are typical purposive acts of the positive or appetitive type. The geologist wants water and performs a series of acts to get it. Utak wants fish and performs a series of intermediate acts till he gets them. Both are relatively isolated purposes. From the time the geologist discovers he is thirsty and his canteen empty, he bends all his efforts to the one end of obtaining the necessary water. When his thirst is satisfied and his canteen filled, his acts to that end are terminated, and he starts off on another set of aims. Similarly Utak is utterly absorbed in his fishing till he has made his catch and set off for home at the end of the day.

## 5. The Main Structure of an Appetitive Purpose

From these two examples and the earlier references to typical animal experiments the main features of an appetitive purpose can easily be discerned. They consist in an initiatory impulse, a terminating goal, and a set of intermediate acts connecting the impulse with the goal. The intermediate acts are furthermore determined in some manner by the impulse in reference to the goal. Following essentially Perry's terminology, which is conveniently expressive of the functions of the three main features, we may take as our first approximation toward a description of an appetition:

Governing propensity | Subordinate acts | Goal

The governing propensity institutes the demand which automatically endows the goal with value. Previous to the appearance of the demand, no purposive value exists. It was the geologist's thirst that made the water valuable, and Utak's need of food that made the fish valuable. And all the subordinate acts by which the geologist got his water and Utak his fish acquired their value only as they led to the attainment of the goal.

For a number of chapters now we shall be concerned with the detailed description of each of these main divisions of an appetition and of the ways in which they are connected. In terms of traditional value theory, we shall be analyzing a single interest. In an interest theory of value, the unit of valuation is an interest. It is then held that the way to increase value is to maximize the satisfaction of interests. The heart of such a theory of value is the individual interest. This is generally taken for granted as something that anybody should know. But an interest is a very complex thing with a determinate structure. Until the structure of an interest is known, the admonition to maximize the satisfactions of interests remains a rather formal maxim. It is like saying to a cook that he can increase the amount of bread he provides by increasing the number of loaves he bakes. This is perfectly true, but the crucial question is: What are the materials that go into a loaf of bread? So the crucial question for us is: What are the constituents of an interest? This is precisely what we shall be seeking to answer in our analysis of the structure of a purposive act.

# 3

# The Appetitive Drive

## 1. Functions of the Governing Propensity: Drive and Anticipatory Set

The governing propensity[1] has two parts, which I shall call the *drive* and the *anticipatory set*. The functions of the two parts overlap and cannot always be kept distinct. They sometimes appear to merge, and one of them, the anticipatory set, may temporarily be absent. But for a complete description of the governing propensity both parts are needed, and their particular functions must be kept in mind.

At this point an experiment of C. P. Richter's with hungry rats reported by Tolman is pertinent. It brings out in the simplest way the change of behavior in an appetition which marks the difference in the operation of a drive before and after the emergence of an anticipatory set.

Richter has shown that general exploratory activity of the rat occurs in cycles corresponding to the cycles in the contractive activity of the stomach. And, further, if there be attached to the rat's main living cage a small cage in which there is food, he found that it is at the height of each activity cycle that the rat passes into the food-cage and eats, after which the animal returns to the living cage, cleans himself and then subsides. . . . To quote [from Richter]: "Thus we see that the small contractions give rise to the diffuse activity in the large cage. The animal seems at first simply to be annoyed and becomes more and more restless as the contractions grow larger, until the 'main' contractions set in and the general discomfort becomes centralized in the hunger sensation. This stimulus dominates the behavior of the organism and it enters the food-box to eat. When its appetite has been satisfied, it passes into a period of quiescence which lasts until the stomach has become empty and the contractions have started up again." . . . It appears, in short, that it is the hungry, or satiation-demanding, rat who is the explorative-demanding rat. And further it also appears that at the height of hunger, the exploratoriness is specifically directed towards food.[2]

It is obvious from this experiment that the stomach contractions have a basic and continuous control over all the other activities of the rats. When these contractions begin, the rats start moving around and continue to be active as long as the contractions go on; when the contractions cease the other activities of the rats also cease. Furthermore, it is clear that through the agency of these contractions the energy of the organism is gradually being mobilized with the aim of eventually bringing these contractions to quiescence. The mobilization of energy to a final aim and the pattern of activities directly connected with this mobilization of energy is what we mean by a drive.

Now at a certain point in the rats' activities a definite change took place. At first, while the stomach contractions were mild, the rats exhibited exploratory actions, but later, when the main contractions occurred, the rats stopped their exploratory actions and went through a sequence of acts that brought them to food. The mobilization of energy became concentrated upon a definite aim and the pattern of actions changed to one that led immediately to food. "The exploratoriness is specifically directed towards food." This is the point at which an anticipatory set entered in. Previous to this point the rats were restless and their activity diffuse. We would say that the rats did not know what they wanted. But at this point they knew, in some sense or other, what they wanted and acted directly to get it.

The presence of this cognitive element is the essential difference between a drive and an anticipatory set. A drive is a mobilization of energy into a pattern of tensions, which continues until certain organic conditions are satisfied. An anticipatory set is a specific pattern of references directing action toward an object or situation which is expected to satisfy the organic conditions. This is a general statement of the difference. Now it is our task to describe each of these parts of the governing propensity in detail to see just how they function.

## 2. THE DRIVE: ITS IMPULSE PATTERN AND CONDITIONS OF QUIESCENCE

Roughly speaking, the drive supplies the energy for purposive activity; the anticipatory set, the goal. The one is the engine, the other the directing eye. The one is dynamic, the other cognitive. Essentially this is the great difference. But on closer examination we see that the ultimate specification of the goal is determined by the drive, and not, as we should expect, by the anticipatory set. The ultimate terminus of a purposive activity is the quiescence of the drive. Recall the terminus of the activity of Richter's rats. This quiescence is achieved only under specific conditions, and the ultimate goal is only that which will answer to those conditions. The satisfaction of those conditions is the consummatory act of an appetition, and we shall call it the *quiescence pattern*.

As the example of Richter's rats shows, once a drive like hunger starts to operate, it continues, generally increasing in intensity, until an object is found which produces the specific sort of quiescence peculiar to that drive. For hunger the quiescence pattern is the eating and digesting of food; for thirst, the drinking and bodily absorption of liquid. Every appetitive drive has its own specific quiescence pattern.

The quiescence pattern or consummatory act is the terminal goal of an appetitive drive. As such it cannot be considered as a feature of the drive, but the *conditions of quiescence* are definitely a property of the drive. For what gives the drive its particular purposive character is the persistence of the drive until the conditions for quiescence are achieved. The conditions of quiescence are the reciprocal, so to speak, of the pattern of tensions which constitute the dynamic core of the drive. They are the conditions which will release the tensions and return the organism to a state of quiescence.

The pattern of tensions which constitute the core of a drive we may call the *impulse pattern*. Literally, the impulse pattern consists of the total group of tensions which maintains the activity of the organism up to quiescence. These are rarely open to definite physiological description as are the stomach contractions of hunger. And there is evidence that even these do not exhaust the tension system involved. But the stomach contractions of hunger do exemplify the nature of an impulse pattern as it would be described in physiological terms. Theoretically, every impulse pattern is susceptible of a physiological description of this sort, and this would be the fundamental objective description of the core of a drive. But ordinarily we have to infer the presence of the physiological tension pattern and deal with its larger behavioral manifestations as the evidence for its pattern of activity.

Ordinarily, in fact, we are likely to describe an impulse pattern in terms of the sort of objects that produce its quiescence. This often proves to be the most accurate way of delimiting the operation of an impulse. So the hunger drive can be described as the tensions instituted by stomach contractions, or as the tensions that can be reduced only by eating certain things. The latter mode of description can be fairly precise, and is our only way of getting at quantitative systems of preference (for one food rather than another, for instance) at different degrees of intensity of a drive. The latter is also our only means of description when we are dealing with the complex derived drives that make up most of our human social activity. Nevertheless, to describe an impulse in terms of what satisfies it is a backhanded and indirect way of describing it. Such a description should never be mistaken for a direct description of the impulse pattern. For the impulse pattern is not the array of objects which will satisfy it, but the system of tensions which demands such objects for its satisfaction.

Similarly, the description of a drive in terms of the consummatory act or quiescence pattern to which it leads should not be mistaken for a description of the impulse pattern itself. So hunger described as the drive to eat, or thirst as the drive to drink, though true enough, is not a direct description of the impulse pattern itself. The latter is the system of tensions that requires eating or drinking as part of its quiescence pattern. This sort of indirect description, incidentally, is not usually so informative as that in terms of the objects which produce satisfaction. For the pattern of tension reductions which constitutes the quiescence pattern is often physiologically as difficult to describe adequately as is the tension system of the impulse pattern. But the array of objects that will satisfy a drive is something that can be experimentally discovered in ordinary large-scale observation.

Another way of indicating impulse patterns is by their characteristic sensory or emotional quality—that is to say, by the introspective report. Actually, the introspective report, when it is available for a basic appetitive drive, is the quickest and one of the most reliable ways of identifying an impulse pattern. The feeling of hunger and the feeling of thirst are very reliable indices of their respective physiological tension patterns. There is nothing indirect about these feelings either. They constitute the very quality of these drives in their vivid human immediacy. The reports of these feelings can be relied upon with great confidence because, like color for the eye and sound for the ear, we have so much information about their physiological correlates. We can place them with considerable precision in objectively described physiological and behavioristic structures. It is generally enough for somebody to say he feels hungry for us to credit him with the characteristic pattern of tensions, to expect his actions to show a bias toward food, and to anticipate that when he gets into contact with food he will eat it. Our expectations are usually confirmed, and these give us reason to believe that the stomach contractions were there too, as the physiologist assures us. In short, reports of feelings like hunger and thirst can be taken as very reliable indices of the impulse patterns with which they are ordinarily correlated.

We probably should not quarrel with a person who wished to identify the impulse with its qualitative feeling—to identify the hunger drive with the quality of feeling hungry. But this would raise the whole problem of introspection. In order to avoid the issue at this point, as well as to gain all the other advantages of an objective method, it will be wiser for us to describe the impulse pattern objectively. Let us therefore define it as a system of physiological tensions, and suggest that the introspective feeling of the quality of a drive is very closely correlated with the respective tension system.

## 3. Drive Distinguished from Need

We have already oversimplified the situation. Underlying many instinctive drives is a bodily *need*. For hunger it is food deprivation showing up in describable metabolic conditions; for thirst it is dehydration. Ordinarily a need sets off a drive specific to the need. Thus the hunger drive determines the organism specifically with conditions of quiescence for reducing food depletion, and the thirst drive for reducing dehydration. But there are needs that have no drives generated by them. Such are needs of the organism developed from many diseases such as anemia and diabetes. Diabetes generates a need for insulin, but the need does not generate a drive for insulin. There is no drive innately attached to the diabetic organism's need for insulin in the way that the thirst drive is attached to a dehydrated organism's need for liquid. The biological reason for this difference is clear enough. A bodily need for insulin is a relatively rare occurrence. The human species can survive without a special provision in the form of a drive to replenish such a bodily need. But dehydration is a daily occurrence in many animal species, and requires a special mechanism always ready to replenish this need for the survival of the species. Thus all biologically essential needs have specific drives, but unusual bodily needs ordinarily do not.

When a drive is attached to a bodily need, part of the character of its impulse pattern will come from the need. But part also comes from a specific set of neuromuscular tensions which puts the organism into action. The conditions of quiescence for the drive lie mostly in the requirements for reducing the bodily need, but the dynamics comes mostly out of the neuromuscular tensions. An impulse pattern, then, ordinarily has two contributing factors:

Impulse pattern

Bodily need | Neuromuscular tensions

The recognition of the contributory characters of bodily need in the impulse pattern of a drive helps solve otherwise puzzling occurrences connected with drives. It explains, for instance, how there can be many specific phases in a general hunger drive. The bodily need may change greatly while being served by practically the same neuromuscular tensions. Thus a pregnant woman may feel a calcium deficiency and exhibit a specific hunger for foods providing calcium. Laboratory experiments have shown specific hungers for protein, fat, carbohydrate, sodium, phosphorus, riboflavin, and other chemical constituents of foods. It is not that the organism knows, to begin with, what foods satisfy his bodily needs, but he learns the foods that reduce his cravings and then knows what foods to select. The character of the craving, however, clearly comes from the bodily need, not, except indirectly, from the neuromuscular tensions. Yet it is the latter that constitute the main dynamics of the drive.

Are there impulse patterns based solely on neuromuscular tensions without underlying bodily needs? Apparently there are. What we shall call 'gratuitous satisfactions' seem to be of this sort. They seem to consist of patterns of neuromuscular tensions, not strong enough to demand trial-and-error activity to reduce them, but ready to yield satisfaction whenever the appropriate stimulus is applied. Gratuitous satisfaction is derived from skillful massage, for example. The tensions are there to be relaxed, but usually not strong enough to start up a restlessness or trial-and-error activity to reduce them. Men are endowed with a large quantity of available gratuitous satisfactions from all the senses—touch, smell, taste, sight, hearing—and they make up most of the materials for our elementary aesthetic values. There are, besides, many gratuitous satisfactions attached to the consummatory acts or quiescence patterns of the principal appetitive drives, such as hunger, thirst, and sex.[3]

Besides gratuitous satisfactions, there are derived drives which are built up independently of bodily needs. These appear to be acquired sets of neuromuscular tensions operating on their own. There will be much to say about these in due time.

How do we distinguish a need from a neuromuscular tension? At the extremes there is no question. For then they plainly vary independently of each other. During starvation, bodily need increases steadily, whereas after two to four days the strength of the hunger drive decreases noticeably.

Metabolic *need* is an objective concept, important in the field of nutrition. To describe needs there must be some criterion such as survival, maintaining homeostasis, growth, reproduction, response to stimulation, etc. *Need* is always relative to a criterion; there is need of something for something. To illustrate, if maintaining homeostasis is the criterion, then the organism *needs* water, oxygen, protein, sodium, vitamin A, and other dietary elements. If reproduction is the criterion, then the laboratory animal needs vitamin E.[4]

The determination of needs would seem to be biological in terms of the normal requirements of a species for the maintenance of life or survival—*except* the requirements bearing on docility. The chemical and physical requirements for homeostasis, growth, and reproduction normal for the survival of a species constitute the needs of an organism, but the response requirements necessary for the survival of a docile animal in initiating its purposive behavior come under the head of neuromuscular tensions. Seeing that both factors are biologically determined for the survival of a docile species, we should not be surprised if sometimes they are difficult to tell apart. Where they cannot be precisely distinguished, there is obviously no reason to distinguish them, for we are induced to distinguish them only when it becomes clear that they are contributing unequally to the impulse pattern.

Where the two are distinguishable, the principal dynamics of the impulse pattern comes from the neuromuscular tensions, whereas the principal characteristics of the conditions of quiescence for reducing the drive come from the need. Thus in the hunger drive the principal dynamics comes from the neuromuscular stomach contractions and other tensions motivating the organism to action; but the principal characteristics of the conditions of quiescence for reducing the drive come from the metabolic needs, some of which may be very specific, such as a calcium deficiency. The reason for the close linkage of neuromuscular tensions to the need in such instances is that the biological function of the former is to serve the latter. But there are bodily needs which have no neuromuscular tensions to provide a drive for their reduction. We may, if we will, say that the conditions of quiescence are there in the need, but without any drive to activate them. And then there are neuromuscular tensions not based on bodily needs. These, however, have conditions of quiescence of their own which they can activate to bring their own activity to quiescence.

But ordinarily the impulse pattern of a drive is composed of two factors: a need and a set of neuromuscular tensions to activate the need.

## 4. Innate Readinesses of the Drive

The dynamic core of a drive, then, is its impulse pattern, but the ultimate function of a drive is to attain its conditions of quiescence. We have so far isolated two essential features of a drive, its impulse pattern and its conditions of quiescence, and seen how the first itself divides in two. There is yet a third, possibly not essential but probably always present: readinesses to act in specific ways on the impulse of the drive. These readinesses are customarily attributed to the drive if they are innate.

To understand the nature of such innate readinesses and their relation to the drive, it is useful at this point to compare an appetitive drive with the kind of instinctive behavior known as the chain reflex. This is the sort of behavior that governs most of the activity of insects. In the evolutionary tree, it is roughly true to say that the insect branch culminating in ants and bees has exploited the chain reflex mode of instinctive behavior, whereas the vertebrate branch has exploited the intelligent mode of behavior. Both are highly complex modes of adaptive behavior, the one unmodifiable and the other modifiable within the life of the organism.

A typical chain reflex of a species of digger wasp is the following succession of acts. Owing to some internal change at a certain time in her life, this wasp is stimulated to dig a hole, after which she flies about till she finds a grasshopper. She stings the grasshopper in a manner to paralyze it, drags it by the antennae to the edge of the hole, and, having reached the opening, drops the grasshopper, investigates the hole, and returns if it is clear. Then she drags the grasshopper into the hole by the antennae, lays an egg on it (which eventually hatches a wasp grub that eats the grasshopper), and ends the chain by closing up the hole. This is all automatic behavior very highly specialized for this particular mode of propagating the species.

Why is this called chain reflex behavior? Because one articulation of the sequence sets off the next and the next. The acts are linked in a definite sequence. The first act is internally stimulated, probably by some chemical hormone. On this stimulus the wasp digs the hole. The completion of the hole acts as a stimulus to seek a grasshopper. Finding a grasshopper, the wasp is stimulated to sting it. The paralyzed grasshopper then stimulates the wasp to seize the grasshopper's antennae and drag it to the edge of the hole. The sight of the opening stimulates the wasp to drop the grasshopper and investigate the hole. The emptiness of the hole then stimulates the wasp to drag the grasshopper in and lay the egg, which done the wasp is finally stimulated to close up the hole.

Each act stimulates the next in a succession of articulated links. The whole chain is inherited, automatic, unlearned. It is an innate behavior structure that goes into operation in the mature wasp at a certain time on some internal stimulus presumably of a chemical nature. If any link is disturbed, the wasp has to go back to a previous stimulus, or may have to repeat the whole chain from the beginning. No modifiability of any kind enters into this chain reflex. If, for instance, the grasshopper is taken a short distance away while the wasp is investigating whether the hole is clear, the wasp, on drawing the grasshopper once more to the edge of the hole, is stimulated to leave the grasshopper and investigate the hole again. The wasp will do this over and over again. She cannot skip a link of the chain. There is no provision in her behavior for even that little bit of learning. And if the antennae of the grasshopper are removed, the chain reflex action abruptly ends, even though the legs of the grasshopper would serve as well. This link of the chain reflex is so specialized that the chain is broken if the wasp cannot seize the grasshopper's antennae. The wasp has to go off and find another grasshopper.

Now the point of this description of a typical chain reflex is that there are certain striking similarities between chain reflex behavior and intelligent behavior along with the even more striking differences. These similarities go far to explain certain otherwise mysterious traits of intelligent appetitive behavior.

Both sorts of behavior involve a linkage of acts with an initiating and a terminal act. Just as the wasp is stimulated by certain internal chemical changes to start digging a hole, so a man is stimulated by certain internal changes producing stomach contractions to seek food. The initial articulation in both modes of behavior is a drive. Furthermore, the drive continues to operate in both kinds of behavior until a certain terminal act is performed. The striking difference between the two modes of activity is that a bridge of intermediate acts between the drive and the terminal act is innately provided in great detail for the wasp, whereas for man there is an open gap. But for most (possibly for all) human drives it is not a completely empty gap. Some fragments of the connecting links still survive. It is to explain these that I have made this long excursion into the detailed description of a typical automatic chain reflex. The innate readinesses attached to basic human drives are the remains, in all probability, of an original chain reflex structure that has broken up.

In the hunger drive in man, for instance, there is salivation, a tendency to carry edible things to the mouth, and, once food is in the mouth, a succession of acts—biting, chewing, and the muscular sequence of swallowing—which are linked so closely as to be literally a chain reflex in the consummatory area of this drive. Similarly with thirst. And in the human sex drive there are many such innate readinesses from the tendency to embrace to the final reflexes of the orgasm. It is to be expected that there would be more of these innate readinesses more closely linked in the consummatory area than in the earlier stages of an appetitive drive. Biologically, the advantages of modifiable behavior are negligible in the consummatory field of preparatory intermediate acts designed to provide the stimuli for consummatory acts.

A basic appetitive drive may therefore be conceived as a broken-down chain reflex system, where a gap has opened up between the initial act and the terminal act. Fragments of what would have been a chain reflex remain scattered along the way, particularly in the consummatory field, which may still consist of a fairly extensive and closely linked system.

It may at first seem strange to think of our highly developed intelligent behavior as based upon a gap opening up within an instinctive chain reflex system. But once such gaps begin to appear in the evolutionary process, their biological advantages to organisms would become apparent on one condition: the provision of a technique of behavior, such as trial and error, which could be thrown into gear when a gap appeared, so that an organism could acquire by learning, and then maintain, a successful bridge over a gap whenever such a bridge had been found. Once this condition was met, intelligent modifiable behavior became possible.

The biological advantage of such behavior is that it vastly enlarges the area of adjustment open to an organism. Chain reflex behavior limits an organism to the environmental conditions which support all the specific links of the chain of acts in the sequence required. If any change in the environment breaks off one of these links, the organism is helpless, and may not be able to survive in that environment. But with modifiable behavior an organism is capable of adjusting to extremely variable environments, through bridging the gap between the drive and the consummatory act by a variety of intermediate acts.

An organism limited to chain reflex behavior can never perform an incorrect act because it is incapable of learning and has no choice. That is why we do not ascribe purposive value to such acts. The organism cannot make any decision. It cannot make a wrong decision, because a chain reflex system, once initiated, has to go through according to the automatic inherited linkage of the acts. If the series is blocked at one point, the organism must start over again at some previous point where a stimulus is picked up, or possibly has to start all over again from the beginning. Only when such linkages are broken can choice enter in, and with it the capacity to make decisions, to act correctly or incorrectly, to do right or wrong, in short, to acquire purposive values. Purposive values emerge in the evolutionary process in the gap between the links of chain reflex behavior.

There are, however, many degrees of transition between tightly linked chain reflex behavior like that of the digger wasp and the widely open modifiable behavior of the higher vertebrates and man. Nest building among birds is a chain reflex system, but there is much acquisition of skill and precision between the links of the chain. A chick is endowed with a pecking instinct, but observation shows that at first the chick pecks at everything and has to learn to distinguish kernels of grain from pebbles. Even in the intricate instinctive systems of bees and ants, a good deal of learning seems to be interspersed. Varying amounts of modifiable behavior can thus be found running far out in the biological realm. But man has developed this mode of behavior to the maximum and, justifiably proud of his attainment, has given the name of *homo sapiens* to his species.

## 5. DEFINITION OF INSTINCTIVE BEHAVIOR

Intelligent behavior, as we see, is founded upon instinctive behavior. This is a good time, therefore, to come to a decision on the definition of instinctive behavior. It is convenient to have a term to refer to the relatively complicated forms of innate or inherited activity that lie between simple reflexes, which carry on most of the mechanics of the organism, and acquired or uninherited modes of behavior, which are the contributions of intelligence.

Such complex innate behavior is of two types, both of which may be called instinctive: chain reflexes and innate drives of modifiable purposive behavior. These two modes of instinctive activity are theoretically distinct, but they merge into one another in action. There are tight chain reflexes like that of the digger wasp. But there are also chain reflexes which permit of acquired improvements between some of the links. At the other extreme is the theoretically pure innate drive which is simply an initial tension, the first link of a dissolved chain reflex without any innate subsequent links. But actually, all appetitive drives probably have some innate links scattered along the way, particularly in the consummatory area. If there is a specific quiescence pattern, that is, a specifically fixed succession of acts innately required for the quiescence of the drive, these acts are functionally just like the terminal links of a chain reflex. There is a continuous spectrum of innate forms of complex adaptive activity from the tight chain reflex at one end to the innate drive with its conditions of quiescence at the other. If there are innate links scattered along the path of a purposive act, these are the innate readinesses which constitute the third of the three major characteristics of a drive. In an appetitive drive like hunger, thirst, or sex, innate readinesses are always present in the form of the determinate quiescence pattern or consummatory act which is the terminal goal of such positive purposes.

## 6. Innate Readinesses in Relation to the Goal

It is sometimes assumed that innate readinesses are essential at the beginning of a purposive act for directing a drive to its goal. This is not true, and it is important for value theory that the point be established early. For, if it is allowed to pass, it breaks down the very important distinction between the drive and the anticipatory set. The drive of an appetition can be cognitively blind and still attain its goal. A rat learns the successive linkage of acts of a maze without the help of innate readinesses until the goal is reached in the food chamber. The connections are made by trial and error on the pressure of the drive. The attainment of the goal is determined by the conditions of quiescence of the drive, because, as long as these conditions are not attained, the pressure of the drive continues, and the moment they are fully attained the pressure ceases. The drive may thus cognitively be utterly blind.

The cognitive blindness of a drive in contrast to the cognitive foresight of an anticipatory set is the distinction to be stressed. The relation of an anticipatory set to its goal object is entirely cognitive. It involves foresight and verification, and is altogether different from the relation of a drive to its consummatory goal, which depends only on its conditions of quiescence. The conditions of quiescence are not cognitive references. Essentially this means that they cannot be in error. They are literally the conditions which disperse the energy of a drive so that activity ceases.

It is true that the drives of instinctive appetitions include innate readinesses to perform a specific consummatory act when a suitable stimulus object is attained. But in aversions, as we shall see, the conditions of quiescence are simply absence of a disturbing stimulus, and do not involve any innate consummatory readinesses.

However, once the distinction is firmly made between the cognitive references of an anticipatory set and the conditions of quiescence of a drive, it can be admitted that the readinesses inherent in a drive do make it possible for an organism to have a sort of premonition of its quiescence pattern. This can happen if the innate readiness can be tentatively activated previous to normal stimulation. On the other hand, the fact that a drive possesses innate readinesses does not entail their being set off until the organism reaches a certain stage in the sequence of acts composing the appetition. There is no reason to believe that the digger wasp has any premonition of the later links in the chain reflex while acting on the earlier ones, even though every link is innately ready for its successor. Each act seems able to prepare only for its successor. That is why the wasp is so badly disturbed when the least break occurs in the chain. It is safe to assume that an instinctive drive in vertebrate behavior is cognitively blind in just the same way. To be sure, after one experience with the quiescence pattern of a drive, an intelligent organism can always thereafter anticipate it, and a cognitive reference may then be added to that of the conditions of quiescence intrinsic to a drive. But the essential point is that these two sorts of references shall not be confused. And the fact that a drive possesses innate readinesses does not mean that the drive has a cognitive anticipation of its goal. A drive is intrinsically blind in terms of cognitive reference.

## 7. Summary of Characteristics of the Drive

A drive, then, has three characteristics:

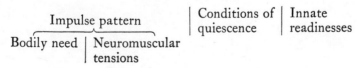

| Impulse pattern | | Conditions of quiescence | Innate readinesses |
| Bodily need | Neuromuscular tensions | | |

The dynamics comes from the impulse pattern. The goal of the impulse is referred to, and is determined by, the conditions of quiescence. There may also be some innate readinesses. These help to direct the impulse to its goal but are not essential to this function; if they can be prematurely activated, they may even give premonitions of a consummatory act previous to experience. These innate readinesses also show how closely related an instinctive appetitive drive is to a chain reflex instinct. The dynamic impulse appears to be identical in the two. This last point is important to remember, for it will keep us from falling into certain overintellectualistic theories of motivation. We should hesitate to say now, for instance, on the evidence before us, that the thirsty geologist was motivated in any literal sense by the end he was heading for. We may well hesitate to say that he was motivated primarily by the anticipation of the pleasure of drinking, though this might have entered in. We might also hesitate to say that he was motivated primarily by the discomfort or pain of his thirst. This may well have been a strong element, but it may not be essential to the impulsion of a drive. For there is plenty of evidence that the anticipation of pleasure in the terminus of the chain reflex did not enter into the digger wasp's motivation. And there is no evidence that pain or discomfort motivated her to start the impulse going. But we have plenty of evidence of the urgency of her drive and her persistence in carrying it through. We have reason to think that a man's instinctive appetitive drives have much the same sort of impulsion. This is the point we must keep in mind.[5] A drive seems to be primarily a pattern of tensions requiring release.

# 4

## The Anticipatory Set

### 1. The Cognitive Function of the Anticipatory Set

We now turn to the cognitive factor in the governing propensity —the anticipatory set. The function of this set is to specify a goal for the selective guidance of the organism toward the quiescence of the drive. It is to show the organism an object that will satisfy the drive or serve as a means to its attainment. The drive fails to do this. For the impulse pattern of a drive is cognitively blind, just a pattern of tensions; the conditions of quiescence are passive, just the set of conditions that will actually bring a drive to quiescence; the innate readinesses are incomplete and might be lacking. There is no cognitive guiding reference in a drive. It is the function of the anticipatory set to supply this cognitive guidance.

In highly developed conscious behavior, the name of this element is 'idea.' The geologist felt thirsty and the idea came to him that he needed water. Thirst was his drive, but the idea of water was his governing anticipatory set. In the consciousness of men, an idea is often represented by an image. But an image may be a very poor representative of the idea or anticipatory set that guides the purpose. There is no image that corresponds exactly with the geologist's guiding idea. He would have accepted water in many forms: clear or roiled, in a glass or a cup, from a running stream or a spring or a well. But any image would have to be a selection of one of these forms projected before his

63

mind's eye, and no image could be a clear composite of them all. An idea is a set of cognitive references, and almost always differs in the range of its references from any image attached to it. The term 'concept' comes closer, but this has certain limited logical connotations. It would be strained, for instance, to speak of the concept of a proper name. A concept ordinarily refers to a logical class. A new term is needed, and 'anticipatory set' is a good descriptive term that has gained some acceptance.

We shall presently discuss an apprehensive set, which functions in aversions in a manner comparable to that of anticipatory sets in appetitions. The general term 'cognitive set' could be used to cover the two. *A cognitive set may be defined as a set of references entertained or acted upon by an organism in a manner which shows that it is open to error.* Any element in the behavior of an organism which may be corrected as a false try is a cognitive set. It is the modifiable element in behavior. An instinctive drive is not modifiable and so cannot be in error. The geologist could not change his thirst. It would be senseless to assert that his thirst drive was in error. But his idea that water would quench it, or the idea that climbing a hill would give him a clue to the location of water, might have been in error, and would have been open to modification, for these are cognitive sets.

*An anticipatory set is a cognitive set conducive to the attainment of a purposive goal.* It is a characteristic element in appetitions and is essential to their successful achievement. Any extensive appetitive act includes a whole series of anticipatory sets referring to a sequence of objects or situations which, when acted upon, are expected to lead the organism to the quiescence pattern of the drive. They fill the gap between the initiation of the drive and the goal of the drive. The sequence of ideas from the moment the geologist realizes his thirst and his predicament to the final attainment of water is a series of anticipatory sets. The series is a hierarchy in which each set depends upon the one above. Granted the idea that water would quench his thirst, some sign of green must be found to indicate water, and to find a sign of green he must climb to a height, and so on. After the first idea, the other ideas are all subordinate to that. They develop, in fact, the subordinate acts which constitute the big intermediate division between the governing propensity and the goal in the structure of an appetition.

It is only the top set in the hierarchy that is, strictly speaking, considered as part of the governing propensity. For this is not strictly speaking a subordinate act. Given the cognitively blind drive, it is the highest superordinate set of the drive which gives a cognitive direction to the purpose. If the thirsty geologist had been unable to think of water as the goal, his actions would have been quite aimless—as indeed sometimes happens in a panic. The idea of what to aim for on the inception of a drive is thus an essential part of the directing of a purpose, an essential part of its governing propensity. And, strictly speaking, only the highest set of the series belongs in the governing propensity division of an appetition. All the other sets dependent upon it belong in the subordinate act division.

However, especially after a set of subordinate acts has been well learned, it is hard to draw a sharp line between the uppermost act of a hierarchy and neighboring subordinate acts. One act often slips into the next almost indistinguishably. So, in driving a car, we tend to throw the whole series of acts into a single act. Similarly, the geologist's act of digging would hardly be broken up, even in his anticipatory thinking, into the sequence of separate acts which make it up. A whole series of sets is thus often legitimately amalgamated into a single extended set, and this can apply even to the whole bridge of acts which connects a drive with its goal. The whole sequence may be referred to *the* anticipatory set for the drive. In practice there is a degree of arbitrariness in drawing the lines between successive subordinate acts. But this produces no serious difficulty, and a line springs up clearly enough whenever a subordinate act proves to be in error. That act cuts itself off definitely from its superordinate act.

The last act in the hierarchy that would be left if all other subordinate acts were in error is the superordinate act, whose anticipatory set should ultimately be ascribed to the governing propensity. But in practice the anticipatory sets can be much more loosely designated. It is often psychologically correct that they should be. Whenever a sequence of acts like driving a car, hammering a nail, cutting a loaf of bread, calling central on the phone, has become so mechanized as to go off as a whole, it is one act of behavior, and to describe it otherwise would falsify the description. In short, an anticipatory set may often properly designate a highly complex act, and this would apply to the superordinate set of the governing propensity as well as to any other.

Just how are the references of an anticipatory set conducted? Evidence indicates that they are in the nature of acquired readinesses to act in specific ways in commerce with the goal object referred to. The anticipatory reference to tying my shoe is a readiness to pull the shoestrings and shape them into a knot. The references to the shoe as a whole are similar readinesses for handling, touching, and seeing it. Previous to action, these readinesses are tensions. One of the best evidences for their existence is that they occasionally go off ahead of time.

Perry describes this very well in the succession of acts involved in the runback of a football player.

> A football player about to catch and run back a punt has the whole action outlined in advance. At the same time that he is watching the ball in its course through the air, he is ready with neuromuscular coördinations of the arms and legs to grasp the ball, ward off tacklers and run down the field. At any given instant in the course of this action some part of it is being carried out, while other parts are carried as far as possible without interference. So far are these anticipations carried that the organism is at the time incapable of doing anything else, and will if 'overanxious' carry the anticipation too far, as when the running-response crowds the catching-response and causes the player to fumble the ball. Or the anticipatory set may have so much momentum that it is impossible to readjust quickly to a change of situation.[1]

Here the readinesses are all muscle-joint readinesses. These are the most open to observation. But presumably there are pure neural readinesses also, and these may be the basic material of all cognitive anticipations. A pattern of neural tensions presumably lies behind any pattern of muscle-joint readinesses.

How do these acquired cognitive references of anticipatory sets differ from the innate readinesses of a drive, when the latter are present? Possibly not at all, except that the latter are innate and unmodifiable and operate like reflexes. It is probably the modifiability of a readiness, and consequently a degree of tentativeness that accompanies it, that constitutes its cognitive character. In short, it is the possibility of being in error that marks an anticipatory set and makes its pattern of readinesses cognitive. As further evidence of the correctness of this conclusion, consider what happens to a set of acquired readinesses when they are hardened into a mechanical habit. They lose much of their cognitive character and take on the feel of a chain reflex. At one time every movement in the tying of a bowknot was a tentative cognitive reference, because it might have been in error and in need of correction. Now I tie it automatically, and each movement stimulates the next as in a chain reflex and the cognitive character of the references has all but disappeared.

This brings out the fact that an anticipatory set is in the nature of a hypothesis. It is subject to verification. When the hypothetical character goes out of it, and it is no longer subject to change, it loses its cognitive character and becomes part of the automatic functioning of the organism.

Being a hypothesis, an anticipatory set is likewise a judgment. It is, in fact, the mediating judgment for the value of the object it refers to as a means to the attainment of the terminal value of the drive. This function of an anticipatory set as a mediating judgment of value is so pertinent to our subject that we shall wish to devote a section to it. But first we must speak of the object to which an anticipatory set refers.

## 2. The Goal Object of an Anticipatory Set

An anticipatory set is thus a disposition of the organism, a set of tensions or readinesses. It is instigated by the drive in the pressure toward quiescence. Anticipatory sets are not spontaneously generated: they are generated by drives. There is a good deal of evidence that this is always true. We were once taught that thought could arise by mere association of ideas. But it now appears that our associations are guided by our desires. It is remarkable how a hungry man finds his thoughts drifting toward food. In the complexity of our civilized interests, we often find it impossible to determine the impulse behind a thought. But the trend of evidence suggests that there is no such thing as a thought without a drive behind it. That will be our hypothesis in the field of purposive behavior. And we shall speak of the thought, the anticipatory set, as being charged by the drive.

The anticipatory set is both generated[2] and propelled into action by the drive that charges it. The ultimate function of an anticipatory set is to channel the energy of the drive toward the release of its tensions in quiescence. This function the anticipatory set performs by directing the actions of the organism upon some situation or object which is expected to produce the quiescence pattern. The object expected to produce this result is the object of cognitive reference for the set. It may be called the *goal object*. This is the goal of the anticipatory set.

It follows that a governing propensity refers to two goals. There is the terminal goal of the drive, which is the quiescence pattern. Then there is the goal object of the superordinate anticipatory set, which is expected to produce the quiescence pattern. These are quite distinct and very easily discriminated in basic appetitions like hunger and thirst. The quiescence pattern of the geologist's thirst drive was the act of drinking, but the goal object he sought was water. The quiescence pattern for Richter's hungry rats was the swallowing and digesting of food and the cessation of the stomach contractions. The goal object was the food.

The distinction between the two goals is easy to see in basic instinctive drives. But it often becomes hidden in modified derived drives which operate in a large part of civilized living. If, therefore, a writer chooses his illustrations from the derived drives and fails to notice the action of the instinctive basic drives, he may easily identify the ultimate goal of an appetition with the goal object of the anticipatory set, and never notice the terminal quiescence pattern of a basic instinctive drive. Perry does this. It gives an intellectualistic bent to his theory which distorts some of his conclusions. His error is a common one, and we shall point out its consequences in detail in chapter 9. The symptoms of such a view is that value comes to be attributed to objects, and little or no value is given to acts. Food and water are held up as ultimate values, but not much is said about the satisfactions they yield.

Tolman does not fall into this error. Since he is an animal psychologist, his principal illustrations all have to do with instinctive drives in which the difference between a goal object and the consummatory pattern of an act of quiescence is too striking to be missed. This fact is the more significant in that his views and those of Perry are otherwise very similar—so similar that in the early years each borrowed freely from the other, apparently without noticing the enormous difference in their conceptions of the terminal goal.

It is very important that the difference be stressed early, and that the evidence for Tolman's view and against Perry's be brought out. It might be argued—and this might be Perry's defense—that the difference is merely a matter of definition. Perry might hold that he defines the area of purposive value in a more limited way than Tolman does. Perry would not deny the evidence of blind satisfactions of animal instincts. But he would not call these values unless they resulted from the attainment of purposefully anticipated goal objects. And then not he but some less tough-minded writer might add that in the higher purposes characteristic of human as distinct from animal behavior, the satisfaction appears actually to consist in the attainment of the goal object. If you want a house or a job or a political office or a scholarly degree or the solution of a research problem, the attainment of these goal objects seems to constitute the satisfaction of the purpose. No bodily quiescence pattern like eating and digesting is needed, apparently. In the higher purposes the activity seems to have attained a level above the need of a quiescence pattern, which, it might be argued, indicates that the essential element in the definition of a purpose is the attainment of an anticipated goal object. It is immaterial whether or not a separate act of quiescence follows. I do not say that this would be Perry's defense. But many who share Perry's way of defining value in terms of the goal object, to the neglect of the quiescence pattern, would argue in this manner.

The answer would depend in part on the detailed analysis of derived drives, which we shall consider presently. But it cannot be taken for granted that the demands of instinctive drives for the satisfactions of their quiescence patterns disappear or become wholly transcended or transmuted in man's higher integrated purposes. Yet enough of an answer can be given at once to offer assurance that Perry's limitation is not advisable. Two points can be brought out.

First, a definition that excludes quiescence patterns as terminal values conflicts with our central aim of regarding anything as relevant to our study which bears on the making of well-grounded decisions. Certainly there is nothing more decisive in determining whether a goal object is well or ill grounded in a basic appetition than its quiescence pattern. All the decisions of the geologist were controlled by the conditions of quiescence of his thirst, and all of Utak's by the conditions of quiescence of the desire to provide against hunger. The quiescence pattern could not be excluded by definition without thereby excluding one of the most relevant facts bearing on our central problem.

Second, the quiescence pattern cannot be excluded from Perry's consideration as a terminal value element without distorting his description of facts included in the definition accepted by him of the value field as the field of docile behavior. In other words, Perry's concentration upon the goal object to the neglect of the quiescence pattern as the terminal goal of a purpose leads to descriptions at variance with the evidence. And no one engaged in empirical inquiry can, *by definition alone,* legitimately lop off the terminal segment of a structure which requires that segment for its functional integrity. This point has such extensive consequences that I shall expand upon it in chapter 9, where I analyze Perry's treatment of the subject, and show what difficulties he gets into by failing to notice the quiescence goal and trying to fit the facts into a definition of a purposive goal which the structure of the facts will not permit.

## 3. Do Animals Have Anticipations?

Most men are good visualizers, and since men depend greatly on their eyes, the early conceptions of ideas as the instruments of thinking were in terms of visual images. It was believed that men thought in terms of images, by which was uncritically meant visual images. To have the thought of a fish was to have the visual image of a fish. Even as late as the beginning of the twentieth century the hypothesis of imageless thought was regarded as paradoxical and almost inconceivable. Yet there are men who cannot visualize at all or very poorly. Images, in general, are very inadequate representations of thoughts.

Anticipatory sets were said to correspond with what in common sense are called ideas. Can animals be said to have anticipations like the geologist's anticipation of water and Utak's of fish? Whether animals have conscious images is difficult to determine. But since images are only incidental to anticipatory sets, the question whether animals have images is irrelevant to the question whether they have anticipations.

There is plenty of evidence that animals do have anticipations in the sense of readinesses to act upon objects in the future and out of sight. That is the significance of Richter's experiment. His rats began to move around as soon as the stomach contractions started. But while these contractions were weak, the movements of the rats were aimless and inconstant. When the contractions became strong, however, the nature of their activities changed completely. The rats, from wherever they were in the living cage, directed their movements to the food cage and began eating. What would account for this change to a directed activity? The inception of a strong hunger drive produced by the increased stomach contractions would account for a greater intensity of activity, but not for its definite direction and organization. A system of readiness to act in a specific directional manner has to be inferred. Such a system of readinesses is precisely what we mean by an anticipatory set. When the strong stomach contractions began, this system of readinesses was activated and organized so as to lead the rats to the food. The activation of this system was the arousal of a set of references to the food. They were cognitive references because they were learned, and if any of them proved erroneous they would be modified and corrected.

In terms of all the characteristics of an anticipatory set so far described, the rats were cognitively anticipating the food in the food cage. They were exhibiting references to the food which were open to verification and would be changed to fit the situation if they proved in error. These are all that are required to establish the existence of anticipatory behavior. Rats may lack human imagery, though there is evidence that some animals have it, and they may lack the qualitative character of human consciousness, though this may also be untrue. But that animals have cognitive anticipations in the sense of anticipatory sets is evidenced in every animal learning experiment.

## 4. The Mediating Judgment

We are now in a position to describe the most important cognitive element in the valuing process. Vagueness about its nature and operation has been one of the principal sources of confusion in value theory. The least ambiguous name for it in common use is 'the mediating judgment.'

A *mediating judgment is a set of cognitive references which mediate between something valued and something else that would not be valued except for the mediation of these references.* Obviously, an anticipatory set operates in an appetition as a mediating judgment between the drive and the goal object. It is the judgment that the goal object will produce the quiescence pattern of the drive. The organism acts to attain the goal object only on the belief that it will lead to the consummation of the drive. The geologist sought water on the belief that it would quench his thirst. The judgment implicit in that belief was the mediating judgment.

The action of the mediating judgment has long been noted in value theory, and some theories make it an essential element in a valuing activity. On the basis of our analysis, the mediating judgment of an appetition consists in the references, the acquired readinesses, of an anticipatory set. If these references do not lead to an object which produces the quiescence of the drive, that object and its anticipatory set drop out of the structure of the appetitive act. If the thirsty geologist thought of climbing a nearby hill to look for a green spot and then decided that the hill was not high enough, his interest in climbing that hill would cease at once. His interest in the hill was mediated by the belief in the implicit judgment that the view from the top of the hill would guide him to water. Utak dug his hole in the ice tentatively in the belief that he would see fish beneath. If he had not seen them swimming there, he would have abandoned that hole and tried another. That he would see fish swimming was the implicit mediating judgment which supported all his acts in making the hole till it was deep enough to give a view of the lake bottom. And Richter's rats likewise on the hunger stimulus went into the food cage in the anticipation that they would find food. Their action was mediated by the implicit judgment that food would be there to satisfy their hunger.

Now there are actually two implicit mediating judgments in such acts. This appears from the fact that there are two ways in which an anticipatory set may prove to be in error. The goal object may not, when attained, produce the quiescence of the drive. Or no such anticipated goal object may exist at all. If the hole Utak made in the ice had failed to reveal fish, it would have been an error in the first sort of mediating judgment. But if the thirsty geologist had seen a lake in the distance and, on a nearer view, it proved to be a mirage, this would have been the second sort of mediating judgment. An anticipatory set implicitly declares, in the fact that an organism acts upon it: first, that the goal object of the set will lead to the quiescence of the drive charging the set; and second, that such a goal object exists or can be brought into existence. These two mediating judgments are implicitly believed by the organism; otherwise he would not act on the anticipation.

Does this mean that Utak and the geologist had to make these judgments somehow by words? Obviously not. Though men do much of their thinking in words, it often goes too fast for that; and of course animals do not use words in their anticipations at all. What is meant by these implicit mediating judgments is simply that when we sophisticated observers of appetitive behavior try to analyze and make clear the elements in an anticipatory set which keep it in action and keep it from being abandoned, our only recourse is to describe the elements in the grossly expanded form of the verbal propositions implied in the organism's cognitive references. An animal would never be led to analyze the reason for abandoning an unsuccessful anticipatory set. Most men would not either. They would simply give up an unsatisfactory set and try another. But some men do try to find out what was wrong, and as students of the subject we ourselves have to do this. When we do analyze the problem, we see that it lies in the relation of the cognitive references to the factual conditions anticipated. The clearest expression of this relation is a verbal judgment. All we can do in the interest of explanation and clarity is to say that these judgments were implicit in the organism's behavior. But of course this does not entail the absurdity that verbal judgments necessarily accompanied the anticipatory sets.

A mediating judgment is simply the expectation of an organism that the references of his anticipatory set will prove successful. We observers can see that this expectation is dependent on two separate factual conditions: the capacity of the goal object to satisfy the drive, and the possibility of the existence of the goal object. We shall call the first the *instrumental mediating judgment,* and the second the *existential mediating judgment.*

## 5. THE ANTICIPATORY SET AND VERBAL EXPRESSION OF IT

Having been drawn into noticing the difference between an anticipatory set and a verbal statement of it, we might as well take advantage of this opportunity to go more fully into the matter, and point out some of the consequences of the distinction in human behavior, where verbal communication is so pervasive.

We have just seen that the anticipatory set is the actual mediating judgment which endows the goal object with value on the belief that this object will lead to the quiescence pattern of the drive. For purposes of communication among men the mediating judgment is ordinarily expressed in words. There is a tendency, then, among men (and that means also writers on value) to identify the mediating judgment with the verbal expression. The identification is the more insidious because sometimes, especially in highly intellectual procedures, the anticipatory set actually is a verbal pattern. In the solution of a mathematical problem, for instance, the anticipatory set is almost necessarily a verbal pattern, because the precision of the thought depends upon the symbols, and the thinking is often nothing but a manipulation of the symbols. But ordinarily, and in all our basic biological acts of loving and hating and raising a family and making a living, the anticipatory set is a pattern of readinesses to act and is not verbal at all. When men, however, are asked to communicate their purposive aims, they naturally do so in words. The words then express their anticipatory sets. The words are one thing and the sets another. And people speak quite correctly when they say they are trying to find words to express their thoughts, and often that they cannot find words adequate to express their meanings.

In all such reports they are calling attention to the gap they sense between their anticipatory sets and such verbal statements as they can find to communicate them. They are demonstrating what most people take for granted, but some writers have denied, that thoughts and judgments are different from the verbal statements of them. Of course, sometimes thoughts and judgments become clearer and better organized by the effort to express them in words. Then the anticipatory sets are adjusted to conform to the verbal expressions, in which the symbols in their interrelations and their references to the traits of goal objects can often be made more precise than by nonverbal references. The anticipatory sets may even merge with the verbal expressions of them and the two become identical. But generally there is a distinction between the two. Even when we are thinking consciously in verbal terms, the words usually follow a succession of potential acts or anticipatory nonverbal references. Otherwise, quite possibly we are merely verbalizing.

An important consequence is that a verbal expression or a sentence ordinarily has two sets of references: one to the anticipatory set which it expresses; the other to the acts or objects in the environment denoted by the words. In its intention to express the set, it means the set. In its intention to refer to acts and objects, it means these. Since the set as well as the sentence refers to acts and objects, and the sentence is supposed to express the latter references precisely, it is very easy to confuse the two meaning references of a sentence and to forget the first entirely. This can lead to a serious difficulty, which has greatly troubled Perry among others.

What does a sentence refer to if the object it refers to does not exist and possibly never can exist? Suppose Utak had asserted his intention to catch fish in the lake over the hill, and suppose there were no fish in that lake. Or, to make the illustration still more dramatic, suppose he said he was going out to catch a mermaid. We cannot say that such sentences are meaningless, for definite references are stated. These sentences express something that Utak wants, and we cannot say that there is no object of his desire, for he clearly refers to it. But the object does not or cannot exist. What, then, is the object he wants?

Perry, with Meinong and others, regards this situation as evidence that the object of a want (specifically, in terms of our preceding analysis, the object of a mediating judgment) must be not the goal object, such as a physical fish on the line, but an 'objective.' By 'objective' these writers mean a sort of Platonic entity having a special ontological status which may be designated 'subsistence.' A judgment expressing a desire for a mermaid is said to refer to a subsistent mermaid, which is the object of the cognitive references and gives them a meaning. Thus any judgment, whether verifiable or not, has a meaningful reference to a subsistent 'objective.' The 'objective' is always there to receive the references of a judgment. The only question then is to see if there are existent objects corresponding to the subsistent 'objectives.' If Utak expressed the desire for a mermaid, his mediating judgment would be referring to the subsistent mermaid. His judgment would have its objective reference in the 'objective,' but he would sooner or later find out that this 'objective' had no existent counterpart. Utak's mediating judgment to catch fish through the hole in the ice he actually made, did, however, have existing fish as counterparts to the subsistent 'objective' of fish referred to as the object of that judgment.

This seems to be an unnecessarily complicated and doubtful way of describing the situation. (We shall have to come back to it again in chapter 9.) Much of the difficulty arises from failing to distinguish between the two sets of references of a verbal sentence. A man's sentence about a mermaid already has two sets of references: one set to the thought of the mermaid, the anticipatory set; and one set to the physical world, if he believed he could find a mermaid there. The latter would turn out to have no terminus, but the former gives a firm objective reference to a judgment about a mermaid in the system of readinesses which is always there.

In short, the anticipatory set is the 'objective' of a sentence referring to an object that does not exist. There is no need of a subsistent entity to describe the situation. The anticipatory set exists as a disposition of the organism which has the readinesses involved. What Utak was ready to accept as a mermaid would be the object of his mediating judgment, and the character of that object existed in the pattern of readinesses which constituted his anticipatory set. A sentence about the mermaid would find its 'objective' *existing* in this actual pattern of the anticipatory set. Whether this existent pattern of references will lead to an existent goal object to satisfy them or will be doomed to frustration is a further matter for an interested organism to find out. And there is no need for a subsistent 'objective.'

The anticipatory set is the actual mediating judgment: it specifies the goal of an appetition and controls the choice of subordinate acts. This is not done by the verbal judgment. Or rather, the verbal judgment functions so only when it merges into the anticipatory set. The mediating value judgment is the anticipatory set.

## 6. The Anticipatory Set and Belief

When an anticipatory set goes into action it seems to imply belief on the part of the organism. We say that Utak chiseled out the hole in the ice in the belief that he would find fish. The organism must believe in the mediating judgment if he is going to act on its references. What is this belief? How is it related to the charge of a drive?

Clearly, in highly intellectualized behavior the two are not the same at all. The intensity of a drive varies in relation to the tensions involved, such as the strength of stomach contractions in hunger. But the intensity of belief has something to do with the balance of evidence. A very hungry man may act on a very weak belief as to the probable success of his act. The thirsty geologist as an intelligent man presumably felt no great certainty of belief that he would see a green spot by climbing the neighboring ridge. And as long as he retained his intellectual balance, we should expect the probability of his belief to remain the same whatever changes in intensity occurred in his thirst drive.

However, the charge of the drive is a necessary ingredient in the conception of belief in a judgment. A mere summary statement of the balance of evidence pro and con a particular judgment would not constitute belief in the judgment. Even if the evidence was heavily weighted pro, a statement of this fact would not necessarily entail a belief in the statement. Any fanatic who is immune to argument exemplifies this condition. In order that there should be belief in a judgment, this judgment must be charged with some drive. The act by which a judgment becomes charged with a drive is a *commitment*. Belief involves commitment. We may then tentatively define a belief as *a mediating judgment to which an organism is committed in the expectation that it will perform its function in a purposive structure*. The act of believing is the act of having such an expectation. The anticipatory set of an appetition thus involves belief, in that it is charged (committed) by the drive in the expectation that it will lead to the quiescence of the drive.

Now the distinction between intensity of drive and degree of belief arises when there is a probability judgment that the expectation of success in the action is less than certainty. This would be an additional judgment which underlies and itself mediates the mediating judgment. In intelligent human behavior this distinction is always latent, and often explicit. It is the distinction between having a hypothesis and estimating its chance of success. Whenever stress is put on the evidence of belief, the distinction is functioning in the behavior.

It is obvious that the success of an anticipatory set depends on the probability of its achieving its mediating function of guiding the organism to an object which produces the quiescence pattern of a drive. In short, the success of the set depends on the truth of the judgment implicit in the set. Consequently, if there is any means of gauging the probable truth of the judgment ahead of time, this will have a lot to do with the selection of this set for action. It will have a lot to do with the commitment of the organism to this set. Well, the process of reaching a judgment on the weight of evidence in favor of a proposed action is precisely the means of gauging the probable truth of a mediating judgment. This process is highly systematized in logic and scientific method. But the rudiments of it operate in much of the simplest behavior. Utak obviously started his hole in the ice without the certainty of its being the right place for a fishing hole. He would not have stopped halfway to look for signs of fish through the ice if he had not felt uncertain about the advisability of that hole. His belief in the suitability of this particular hole was affected by some insufficiency of evidence in its favor when he started chiseling. The report narrates that he worked with redoubled energy when he had the conclusive evidence of seeing fish through the ice.

The intensity of action clearly depends partly on the drive and partly on these other factors. The value of the hole apparently increased greatly as soon as Utak saw there would be fish under it. Now, how are these other factors to be described and distributed in a purposive act? For they are the factors which have to do with the influence of belief in values.

The answer is plainly not a single one. In this instance we shall begin with the most intelligent human action, in which the relations among the factors of belief are clearest, and then see what rudiments of these relations appear in animal behavior.

## 7. INERTIAL COMMITMENT AND THE PROBABILITY JUDGMENT

We have distinguished between the degree of evidence for a mediating judgment and the degree of commitment to it. Though it is too early in this study to mention standards of evaluation, there is not likely to be any question that the more evidence in favor of a mediating judgment, the better the judgment for attaining the goal of a purpose. With this standard in mind, we should expect it to follow that an intelligent organism would seek to correlate the degree of commitment to a judgment with the degree of evidence in its favor.

This is apparently about what Utak did. He worked fairly energetically in the beginning of his fishing hole on the basis of fairly good evidence in its favor, but worked most energetically when the evidence made the utility of the hole practically certain. Behavioristically, this probably meant that the absence of complete evidence and possibly the presence of some negative evidence inhibited or at least failed to facilitate the full discharge of the drive into the mediating judgment.

There is no question of a strong human and animal tendency to act in this rather peculiar way. If the evidence is weak, let the commitment be weak. The process is so widespread as to deserve a name. Let us call it the process of *inertial commitment*. By this process an organism would give full commitment only to an evidential certainty. The principle can frequently be justified on various grounds, such as the need of conserving energy when an act is so uncertain that the organism may have to try a long succession of acts before finding a right one.

## 8. INTELLIGENT COMMITMENT AND THE FEASIBILITY JUDGMENT

But in many situations this principle does not give the best results. It would have been unintelligent for the thirsty geologist to have dragged his legs slowly up the neighboring ridge, making his actions weak so as to correspond with the weakness of his evidence for success on reaching the top. Generally, it is wise to give full commitment to the best of a number of alternative actions, even though the evidence is far from conclusive. In short, the principle of inertial commitment is not really the most intelligent behavior. The intelligent thing is to give full commitment to the action for which the evidence is best, however weak the probability, unless there is good reason to do otherwise. And in an emergency, where perhaps only one trial will be possible—as when two cars are about to collide—complete commitment to whatever seems the best action, however slight the chance, is the intelligent decision. For indecision is itself a decision when the event occurs, and is almost always the worst one.

*Intelligent commitment* attempts to make the energy of action conform to the situation in the light of the evidence, whereas inertial commitment simply equates the energy of action to the chance of success. The former opens the situation to the full strength of the drive unless there is reason to conserve the drive for a possible long pull or some equally good reason. The latter tends to inhibit the drive.

## 9. INVERTED INERTIAL COMMITMENT

This last fact accounts for a strange compensating process very common in human social situations. It may be called *inverted inertial commitment*. On the assumption that men can be moved to full commitment only if they feel certain of the complete truth of their mediating judgments, means are found to give judgments the appearance of certainty without recourse to a weighing of the evidence. The devices of dogmatism are highly sophisticated instruments of this sort: appeals to self-evidence, indubitable immediacy, and infallible authority. But all the devices of propaganda and the instruments of fear and force employed to channel and maintain special beliefs are of this sort. The relation is inverted, for the original function of a belief in an appetition is to guide a drive to the attainment of its quiescence. But here drives are employed as a means of maintaining a belief. In common sense terms, there is a reversal of means and ends.

The danger of the procedure is obvious. If a belief is taken as certain, it is not easily susceptible to change when it is found not to conform to the facts. The organism tries to hold the belief in the face of the facts. It leads to rigidity and frustration, and failure to satisfy the drive that the belief was supposed to serve.

Inverted inertial commitment is characteristic of dictatorial societies and of many religions. It is ordinarily justified on grounds of a 'higher truth' (some authority claiming access to truths beyond the sphere of ordinary human observation, or some intuitive certainty open only to an initiated few), or realistically on grounds of social expediency. The plea for a higher truth can be discounted for reasons given in chapter 1. The plea of social expediency is harder to meet.

It is argued that the masses are not intelligent enough to act on the evidence of what is socially best for them. The guidance of society should be left to experts and the people told what to believe; and the more firmly they believe it, the greater the security of society. High morale in a society means confidence in it, and this means faith and full commitment to its basic ideals. Especially in the emergency of war must faith be instilled in the people.

There is enough evidence in support of some of these claims to require us to hold the hypothesis in abeyance. At present we have our hands full in an analysis of single appetitions and aversions. We shall be in a better position to consider the consequences of social policies after we have described the working of individual purposes. The social bearing of the issue is mentioned at this point merely to show its wide significance.

But this much on the issue can be said here: full commitment to a mediating judgment does not psychologically require belief in the certainty of a judgment. Belief in the fact that a particular hypothesis is the best in view of the available evidence plus a belief that the situation is urgent and requires energetic action is sufficient inducement for an intelligent man to commit himself fully to a doubtful mediating judgment. And men can be educated to the advisability of acting on this principle.

There are two means of getting full commitment on a mediating judgment for which the evidence is insufficient to yield a sense of practical certainty. One is that of intelligent commitment just described. The other is that of inverted inertial commitment. A choice between the two means is theoretically (and to any intelligent man also practically) open. For the achievement of a man's purposive aims the first is clearly the better. If the second is to be justified, it must be on grounds other than that of attaining the goals of purposive drives.

## 10. COMMITMENT IN ANIMAL BEHAVIOR

We have been analyzing commitment and belief solely in terms of human behavior, and especially of reflective behavior. What is the nature of belief and commitment in simpler human activities and among animals?

The problem of commitment affects behavior only when there is conflict of evidence bearing on a mediating judgment. In most of the areas of animal behavior there is no question of a balance of evidence. At a point of choice the animal knows just what to do in terms of what he has learned; or has no idea what to do if he is faced with a novel situation. In the first instance he acts with full commitment; in the second he throws into gear the trial-and-error mechanism. Strict trial-and-error action is random behavior within the capacities of the organism, and presumably receives the full energy of the drive. It is as if the organism said to itself, "I don't know what to do at all. So I might as well try everything." A sophisticated man could do this deliberately as a matter of last resort, where it would amount to full commitment to a *method* of search for an idea in the absence of an idea of what to do. In animal behavior, and in unreflective human behavior, resort to trial-and-error activity is automatic and instinctive.

An animal typically gives less than his full commitment to an act when there is a conflicting alternative. In a dangerous situation an animal may move gingerly toward its goal. A dog with a bone moves past another dog with great circumspection. The dog is acting on the evidences of the total situation, and commits himself to the drive for depositing his bone only so far as he believes safe. There is an implicit judgment here with inertial commitment (which I think, we should agree in this instance, happens to be also intelligent). This instance shows clearly that animals can express doubt in their behavior. The doubt arises from conflicting impulses which inhibit the full discharge into the dominant drive. Probably the most reflective human behavior expressing doubt is no different in principle. There is no question that animals often exhibit inertial commitment.

Whether animals exhibit intelligent commitment in the sense described above is more difficult to determine. When a bird with a morsel in its beak lands on a twig near its nest and looks all around before darting to its young, this looks like intelligent commitment. It looks as if the bird were examining the evidences of risk in the situation, and then discharging its drive into the conclusive act with full commitment. But this may be an instinctive mechanism in the form of intelligent commitment. The act of the digger wasp in exploring its hole before dragging the grasshopper in looks like an intelligent act, but the evidence shows it is entirely a chain reflex activity.

In order for intelligent commitment to take place, there must be a mechanism which inhibits the drag of the inhibiting impulses constituting doubt and permits the conclusive act to receive whatever degree of charge is appropriate to the situation, even to the full uninhibited charge of the drive. Men possess these mechanisms, which become highly refined in logic and scientific method. Whether animals have them in some rudimentary form is a question. In simple situations like that of the dog with a bone, inertial commitment yields a result which would conform to intelligent judgment of the appropriate action. Whether an animal can go farther than this is not certain. But it is quite certain that animals have nothing corresponding to inverted inertial commitment. For this seems to require language and communication, and grows out of institutionalized human society. It is produced by devices which give the appearance of intelligent commitment without the intelligent examination of a situation and the evidence available. It gives dubious action the appearance of reflective certainty. That is to say, inverted inertial commitment is an inhibition upon the normal action of intelligent commitment, which in turn is a control over the normal action of inertial commitment. We know that animals exhibit the last of these. They may exhibit the second in rudimentary ways. But quite surely not the first.

## 11. Final Conclusions Regarding Commitment to a Belief

In what follows, until we discuss the interaction of a number of purposes within a total situation, we shall ordinarily assume full commitment to an anticipatory set. For doubt arises only when there is a conflict of impulses—and such seems to be the nature of doubt even in the intellectually rarefied atmosphere of a conflict of evidence. The resolution of such a conflict goes on in terms of subsidiary judgments mediating the particular mediating judgment concerned. There is a judgment of probability, and possibly also a feasibility judgment (or possibly a judgment of certainty). Every anticipatory set that fills the gap between the drive and the quiescence goal may be supported by these subsidiary mediating judgments. They add intricacy to the structure of an appetition, but the skeletal structure of a purposive act remains the same whether they are needed in the act or not. It is extremely important to be aware of these judgments, for, when a situation requires them for successful achievement, they perform an essential function. Intelligent action in a doubtful situation would be very limited without them. A very large proportion of purposive human actions involves implicit if not explicit probability and feasibility judgments.

To clarify further the way in which these various judgments operate in mediating the flow of the drive toward its goal, I offer a schematic representation in table 1.

The value attributed to the goal object is in every instance proportional to the charge given the anticipatory set. That charge tells how much the organism wants that object. A person may very much want an object which he thinks he is unlikely to get. It is not the probability judgment that endows an object with value but the degree of commitment. Yet the probability judgment is extremely relevant to the attribution of value. For if there were thought to be no chance of attaining the goal, no hope at all, there would be no commitment. This is where belief is so important in the attribution of value. Unless there is some belief in the power of a goal object to produce the quiescence

TABLE 1

TYPES OF COMMITMENT

INERTIAL COMMITMENT

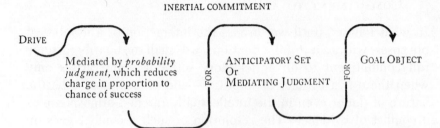

INTELLIGENT COMMITMENT

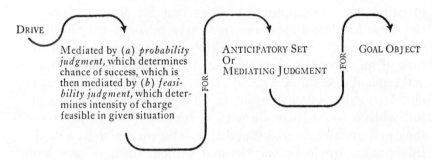

INVERTED INERTIAL COMMITMENT

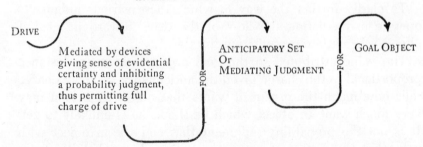

of a drive, the object would have no value for the organism. In this respect, belief contributes to the value of an object.

Belief, however, applies only to anticipatory sets and their goal objects—to the cognitive elements in purposive acts. It does not apply to instinctive drives and their quiescence patterns. A drive simply emerges as a flat fact and through its conditions of quiescence demands its quiescence pattern. It is not open to error and so is not susceptible to belief or disbelief. This is obvious enough from our analysis, but it needs to be stressed because some writers incorporate a cognitive element into all value, and make belief in the existence and efficacy of an object a requirement in the value of anything. The value of all goal objects of anticipatory sets does require belief in these objects. But the value of the quiescence pattern of an instinctive drive comes from the drive alone, and belief is irrelevant to it.

# 5

## The Conditioning Mutations
## and the Development
## of Anticipatory Sets

### 1. How Are Anticipatory Sets Developed?

Anticipatory sets come into being by a process of learning. Moreover, the process develops a mode of value mutation, and for
that reason alone would be a most important topic in value
theory. *A value mutation is a change in the values of an object
or act.* We shall discover that there are a number of distinct
modes of value mutation which either alter the nature of the
value for an act or endow objects with value which formerly
were valueless. The production of an anticipatory set is a value
mutation of the latter sort. It endows objects with value, which
formerly were neutral, by connecting them with the drive or its
goal. We need a name for this mode of mutation, and since the
name commonly employed today for the process is 'conditioning,'
let us call this the *conditioning mutation.*

Now, in spite of all the work that has been done on the learning process, the subject is still controversial. The factors involved
seem to be numerous. The tendency has been to oversimplify the
theory. We need not go into all the details, for not all of them are
relevant to the value problem. But some of the main issues
should be considered so as to avoid errors of an oversimplified
theory of the conditioning mutation. We can probably do no

88

better at this point than follow the main outlines of Tolman's analysis of the controversy in his *Purposive Behavior in Animals and Men*. He concludes that there are three modes of learning, involving a large number of generalizable factors, or laws. But each mode consists in the addition of certain laws lacking in the mode underlying it. The three modes in their order of complexity are *conditioned reflex learning*, *trial-and-error learning*, and *inventive learning*. Since the laws of conditioning underlie all three, it is appropriate to retain for the total value mutation the term 'conditioning.' The conditioning mutation will accordingly refer to value changes derived from any of these three modes of learning.

Certain classical experiments associated with each of these modes are so important both historically and empirically that descriptions of them will be quoted in detail. We shall wish to refer to them often. The oversimplified theories of learning come from a too hasty and undiscriminating generalization from the striking features of the original conditioned reflex and trial-and-error experiments.

We proceed now to present the classical experiments and a statement of the oversimplified theories derived from them, followed by Tolman's amplification of the laws necessary to make the theory of learning square with the full range of evidence available.

## 2. CONDITIONED REFLEX LEARNING

Pavlov's classical experiments for conditioned reflex learning, summarized by Woodworth, are quoted by Tolman as follows:

About the year 1900, Pavlov, while actively at work on the physiology of digestion, using dogs as subjects, introduced a minor operation, by which the saliva from one of the glands in the dog's mouth was carried out through the cheek by a little tube, so that it could be easily observed and measured. He then noticed that the saliva flowed rapidly, not only when food was actually in the mouth, but when the dog saw the food before him, or when he saw the dish in which the food was usually given him, or when he saw the person approach who usually brought him his food, or even when he heard the footsteps of that person in the next room. Now when the stimulus of food is actually in the mouth, the salivary response is a natural and permanent reflex, but the same response aroused by accessory stimuli, such as the sight of the food or of the dish or the sound of the feeder approaching, depended on the animal's past experience, and was thus artificial or subject to certain conditions. Pavlov therefore called it a conditioned reflex. . . .

Pavlov wished to discover how these artificial reflexes got started, and so attempted to establish a conditioned salivary response to the ringing of a bell, the flashing of a light, or the brushing of the animal's skin. He soon found the way to establish any such conditioned response. His procedure was as follows.

A hungry dog—a well-treated animal, quite at home in the laboratory—was placed standing on a table, and loosely secured by slings about the shoulders and hips, suspended from above, so that he could move only a step or two. When the animal was quiet, an electric bell began to ring, and after it had rung for a certain time (often for a minute, but a few seconds were sufficient), some food was placed in the dog's mouth and his saliva began to flow. After a pause of a few minutes, the bell started up again, and, as before, food was given after the bell had been ringing for a certain time. When this sequence of bell . . . food, bell . . . food had been repeated a number of times, the dog, however, still remaining hungry, the saliva was observed to flow before the food was supplied. The bell now caused the dog to look and turn toward the source of food, and at the same time his salivary glands became active. There was a complex motor and glandular feeding activity, initiated by the sound of the bell. Pavlov's attention was directed mostly to the glandular part of this total response, because it could be measured by measuring the flow of saliva. At the outset of the experiment, the bell did not excite any flow of saliva, but as the bell-food combination was repeated time after time, the bell began to give a small flow and then a progressively larger amount. Thus the conditioned reflex was established, at least for the moment.

Next day the same procedure was repeated. No saliva at the first sounding of the bell, but the bell-food combination needed only to be repeated a few times before the conditioned reflex was established . . . After a few days of this same procedure, the conditioned response (both motor and salivary) held over from one day to the next, without needing reëstablishment each day.[1]

On the basis of these experiments, an oversimplified conditioned reflex theory was developed, according to which the only factors necessary to explain conditioning were *frequency* and *recency* of presentation of the associated stimuli. Let $S_1$ represent the original unconditioned stimulus, such as the sight of the food, which starts the salivation. Let $S_2$ represent the conditioned stimulus, such as the sound of the bell. Let $R$ represent the response, such as salivation. Then, on the simplified conditioned reflex doctrine, the more frequent and recent the simultaneous or closely successive stimulation of $S_2$ with $S_1$, the firmer the attachment of the original response $R$ of $S_1$ to $S_2$. This was all there was to it. And for some writers like J. B. Watson, all learning was reducible to combinations of these simple conditional responses. What was observed was the mutation for $S_1 \rightarrow R$ to $S_2 \rightarrow R$. The cause of this mutation was ascribed simply to the frequency and recency of contiguous stimulation of $S_2$ with $S_1$ in an organism having capacities for learning. The process can be diagrammatically represented thus:

From:

$$S_1 \rightarrow R$$
$$S_2$$

(as a result of frequency and recency of $S_2$ with $S_1$)

To:

$$S_2 \rightarrow R \tag{1}$$

The great difficulty with this simple theory of conditioning is that it fails to describe a connection which holds between $S_2$ and $S_1$. A conditioned reflex is one that goes off literally only *on condition* that the stimulus of the conditioned reflex $S_2$ leads to the original unconditioned stimulus $S_1$. What is left out in the oversimplified theory is an anticipatory element (the anticipatory set). $S_2$ goes off only on the expectation of $S_1$. The organism must implicitly believe that $S_2$ is a sign of $S_1$. When this belief breaks down, or the connection is disproved (i.e., the implicit prediction is not confirmed), the conditioned response disappears. This is a fact of major importance.

The experiments of Pavlov established this fact of an implicit belief also for the conditioned salivary reflexes of his dogs. But the significance of the fact was not noticed by early behaviorists. Here is Woodworth's description, quoted from Tolman, of the process of extinction of a conditioned reflex due to lack of reinforcement:

Though the conditioned response can be well established by the procedure just described, we are not to suppose that it has anything like the fixity of the natural reflex. It can be trained out in much the same way as it was trained in. Simply apply the conditioned stimulus (i.e., the artificial stimulus which has come to give the salivary response) time after time *without following it by the natural stimulus.* Here, for example, is the record of one of Pavlov's experiments, in which the conditioned stimulus was the beating of the metronome. The salivary response to this stimulus had been well established. Now on a certain day the metronome was sounded for 30 seconds, without any food, and there was a large flow of saliva. Three minutes later, the same procedure was repeated, with a smaller resulting flow of saliva; and so on, till the flow of saliva was no longer excited by the metronome alone. The gradual decrease and final extinction of the salivary response can be seen in the following table of results:

| Time when each thirty-second stimulation by the metronome began | Quantity of saliva produced, in drops |
|---|---|
| 12.07 p.m. | 13 |
| 12.10 " | 7 |
| 12.13 " | 5 |
| 12.16 " | 6 |
| 12.19 " | 3 |
| 12.22 " | 2.5 |
| 12.25 " | 0 |
| 12.28 " | 0 |

This extinction, however, is only temporary, for if the dog is now taken away, and brought back the next day, the metronome again gives the salivary response. But if the food is omitted this day also, the extinction is more rapid than on the first day; and repetition of the extinguishing procedure, day after day, finally causes the conditioned response to disappear permanently. After one day's extinction of the conditioned response, it can be readily reëstablished by applying the food along with the metronome, but when the extinction has been very thorough, by repetition on several days, the conditioned response is very difficult to reëstablish.[2]

These experiments show that a conditioned reflex, even after it is established (learned), has to be reinforced from time to time; otherwise it will become extinguished. (Certain important exceptions will be pointed out later.) The significance of this fact is that it indicates the need for a set of anticipatory references (the anticipatory set) in order to maintain the conditioning. The diagram for conditioned reflex learning should provide for this added factor, and then it would come out something like this:

From:

$$A^N_1 \leftarrow S_1 \rightarrow R$$
$$S_2$$

To:

$$\left.\begin{array}{l} A^N_1 \\ \uparrow \\ A^N_2 \leftarrow S_2 \end{array}\right\} \rightarrow R \qquad (2)$$

Let $S_1$ be the sight of the meat for Pavlov's dog, and $A^N_1$ the anticipatory set references to eating meat. These together produce the salivary response $R$. From this more complex form of the unconditioned reflex it can be seen how, as a result of the frequent contiguity of the sound of the bell $S_2$ with $S_1$ and $R$, the conditioned reflex develops. It develops through the emergence of a new anticipatory set, $A^N_2$, which links $S_2$ with $A^N_1$, whence the response $R$ follows.

This diagram means that the mutation from an unconditioned to a conditioned response depends primarily on the development of an anticipatory set, $A^N_2$, which is quite literally the organism's prediction that $S_2$ can be reliably accepted like $S_1$ as a means of reaching the goal. The law of extinction signifies that the conditioned response will cease as soon as the predictive references $A^N_2$ cease to be supported: the heart of the conditioned response process lies in the anticipatory set linkage $A^N_2$.

The oversimplified doctrine of conditioning treated the process as a purely mechanical stimulus-response operation. That doctrine could give no adequate explanation of the experimental extinction of a conditioned reflex—not to mention other difficulties. In Tolman's theory, the process depends on the development of a new anticipatory set which links the conditioned stimulus with the expectancies of the unconditioned stimulus. In short, *the conditioned reflex process is purposive in nature.*

In the oversimplified doctrine, the only factors needed for conditioning in the stimulus situation were those of frequency and recency. Tolman names six other groups of factors. Let me list them and explain them. They will help us to understand the ways in which values change through conditioning.

1. Interrelations in the material
    m) 'Togetherness' of sign, significate, and means-end relation
    n) Fusibility of sign, significate, and means-end relation
    o) Other Gestalt-like laws
2. Presentation conditions
    u) Frequency and recency
    v) Revival after extinction, primacy, distributed repetitions, etc.
    w) Motivation [drive]
    x) Not 'effect' but 'emphasis'

By *togetherness* ($m$) Tolman is referring to a selective action. In any ordinary situation an organism is being bombarded by a huge number of stimuli—all sorts of visual, tactile, olfactory stimuli. What selects the particular set of stimuli to which the organism will respond? A person looks out the window and is stimulated by all sorts of visual forms. What leads him to see particularly the passing automobile? In part, interest or drive (the $w$ in Tolman's list). The person has an interest in automobiles, but not in birds, rocks, and so on. But in part what he sees is a group of stimulus characters that stick together, and also the relation of these characters to the goal of interest in the drive. The visual characters that belong to the car stick together as the car moves along. The bell sound for Pavlov's dog was coming up consistently together with the sight of meat in which he was interested. This fact of the togetherness of ($m$) of these characters in relation to the drive in operation led to the separation of these characters from all other environmental stimuli in the development of the complex:

$$\left.\begin{array}{c} A_1 \\ \uparrow \\ A_2 \leftarrow S_2 \end{array}\right\} \rightarrow R \tag{3}$$

By *fusibility* ($n$) is meant the important fact that a succession of acts which consistently lead to a goal tend to fuse into a single continuous act. In learning to run a car, each successive act of gear shifting, accelerating, steering, and so on is separately considered in relation to the next in sequence. In introspective terms, we feel conscious of each act as we perform it. But with practice these acts drop into a single thought and fuse into one continuous act. What was a succession of concatenated anticipatory sets turns into a single extended set. We merely think of starting the car, and all the rest follows. So to a beginner a scale passage is a succession of separate finger movements, but to the trained pianist it is fused into one articulated sweep of the hand.

Another aspect of fusibility is the mechanization of habit. Introspectively, this means that when conditioning has been carried far, a person becomes unconscious of the succession of acts involved. We are particularly aware of this process in muscular activity. In most skills the acts required in a sequence are not only fused but mechanized and largely unconscious. But mechanization also occurs in the visual field and elsewhere in our experience. A familiar face is hardly seen at all in its details. The room we live in, unless it is deliberately changed from time to time, becomes an unconscious habit. Mechanization of response is aesthetically a very important mutation, for it removes objects, both pleasant and unpleasant, from the field of conscious appreciation. Here objects of a certain kind of value lose their value as a result of the action of conditioning.[3]

By *other Gestalt-like laws* (*o*) Tolman refers to a tendency, whenever a degree of forgetting sets in, for the characters of the stimulus object to become simplified and formalized in certain ways. This amounts to a mutation in the character of the conditioned object valued. There is some evidence that these simplifications proceed in the direction of references to forms which arise at the time of learning. So a squarish form (but not quite square) after an interval of time tends to be remembered as square, or a nondescript treelike form (but not a tree) tends with time to be remembered as the form of a tree. These facts indicate meaningful references from the beginning of learning, which become more prominent as there is less reinforcement. The mechanical conditioning doctrine could hardly explain these. Such changes are of interest in value theory because they represent changes in the character of objects valued even apart from actual conditioning. In our terms, what has happened is a change in an anticipatory set and its goal object as a result of mere partial forgetting.

About *frequency and recency* (*u*) nothing needs to be added. These are the factors referred to in the doctrine of mechanical conditioning. They are essential to conditioning, but not sufficient.

*Revival after extinction* (*v*) refers to the experimental fact that a conditioned reflex which has been extinguished on one day from lack of confirmation will nevertheless for a time revive on another day or in another situation. Even after these revivals cease, it retains a *primacy*. For if in a new situation the old correlation begins to hold once more, the organism becomes reconditioned much more quickly than on the first occasion. Apparently an organism never completely forgets what was once well learned. This means that potential interests or values are stored away as dispositions ready for re-arousal in docile organisms far beyond what used to be imagined.

By *distributed repetitions* is meant the fact that the most efficient learning is not obtained by means of the greatest frequency. Certain distributions of repetitions give the most effective learning with the least expenditure of time. This law yields a standard for efficiency of learning which is relevant to all acts of achievement where new processes of behavior have to be learned.

*Motivation* [*drive*] (*w*) is almost surely another essential factor in conditioning. An organism notices only what it is interested in. Nearly all the learning experiments on animals get their dynamics from the easily controllable instinctive drives of hunger and thirst and the instinctive pain reactions of electric shock and the like.

The only controlled experiments that cast any serious doubt on the need for a drive in learning are the so-called latent learning experiments. If two groups of hungry rats are placed in a maze, and the first group is fed at the end of the maze during a series of trials and the second is not fed, the rats that are fed learn the maze fairly quickly, as would be expected, and those that are not fed maintain a high level of errors. What is unexpected is that as soon as the second group is rewarded at the end of the maze, its learning curve drops abruptly. It would appear that a rat learns the maze even when nothing is to be gained by learning it and when no sign of learning has appeared in its behavior. This is known as *latent learning*.

This looks like evidence of a rather mechanical process of learning without any anticipatory sets referring to goal objects or the terminal goal of a drive. But we must remember that there was a strong drive in action. The rats were hungry and consequently alert and ready to learn any means that would produce food if the means should turn up. Since there was nothing else to learn, what they evidently did learn was the geography of the maze; their drive to get food somehow was sufficient inducement for them to keep trying on the chance that a way of getting food might turn up—as it finally did. Then it was evident in the speed of their solution of the problem that they had learned the maze on the drive that kept them restlessly exploring—presumably the same hunger drive that motivated the first group of rats.

But what kind of references are developed in latent learning when no satisfying goals are obtainable? In ordinary appetitive learning the organism learns the anticipatory set that leads to the goal, and drops and forgets the sets that have been tried and proved unsuccessful. In the latent learning experiment the early runs of the experimental group of rats were so arranged that there was no goal for their hunger drive, and consequently no correct or satisfying anticipatory sets leading to such a goal. All acts were of necessity unsuccessful. We would expect that none would register, that no anticipatory references would develop, and that nothing would be learned. Nevertheless, the experimental rats had pretty well learned the maze without reward.

Tolman suggests that the rats were acting on a curiosity drive. This may be. But other drives will also work. It has been discovered that latent learning is much reduced if there is a strong drive operating in a solvable setup or if the drive is very weak. Introspectively, we can confirm these facts in human terms. If you have very important practical business on hand, you go as straight as you can from one place to another without paying much attention to your surroundings. And similarly, you are inattentive if you are not particularly interested in anything. But if you are on important business and find yourself blocked halfway at a washed-out bridge, you are likely to be alert and observant, especially if something might turn up to shorten your delay. The restlessness due to the blockage of your dominant interest and the chance that something relevant might turn up, institute a secondary goal of familiarizing yourself with the landmarks and mapping them in your mind. Toward this secondary goal, anticipatory references develop in regard to the relations of the various features of the landscape. If the delay is fairly long you will have learned these relationships very thoroughly, even though they serve no dominant goal. And if suddenly a knowledge of these relationships does prove instrumental to your main goal, you discover that you have the knowledge and do not have to acquire it. So, possibly, with the experimental group of rats in the latent learning experiment. By being delayed while hungry and restless in the maze, they were alert to the relationships of its alleys and learned the references of one alley to another. But the learning was done, according to this hypothesis, on the motivation of the hunger drive.

On our hypothesis, a drive is necessary to learning. But the latent learning experiment shows that it is not necessary that what is learned should be immediately conducive to the goal of the drive.

Tolman's phrase *not 'effect' but 'emphasis'* (x) states that anything which places emphasis on certain features of a set of references to be learned will facilitate learning. Many writers have held that learning is determined in part by the satisfactoriness of the effect of what is learned in respect to the drive. The latent learning experiments show that this is not true. Learning may occur without reward. But an intense reward tends to hasten learning, and, strangely enough, under certain circumstances *so does punishment*. Two groups of subjects were given the task of punching holes for a problem solution. In one group an electric shock was administered when the incorrect hole was punched, but the other group was given a shock when the correct hole was punched. The *latter* group learned quicker! So it seems to be emphasis rather than correctness that facilitates learning.

However, it should not be thought that the factor of correctness is not important, for, of course, it is primarily the anticipatory references of the correct responses that are being learned in purposive behavior. The drive sees to it that the correct response comes through. What is principally learned is the way to get the correct response for the quiescence of the drive. Only under the special situations for latent learning are other sets of references learned through conditioning.

## 3. TRIAL-AND-ERROR LEARNING

Trial-and-error learning differs from conditioned reflex learning in that the organism makes a choice among alternatives. In simple conditioning, as with Pavlov's dog, the organism is relatively passive, and a significant connection in his environment is forced upon him or borne in upon him. But in trial-and-error learning the organism actively makes choices among alternatives; the errors get eliminated while the correct choices are learned by the regular laws of conditioning.

The classic example of trial-and-error learning is that of Thorndike's cat. With a number of cats Thorndike made a study of the kind of behavior employed in escaping from a box with a latched door.

> The behavior of all but 11 and 13 was practically the same. When put into the box the cat would show evident signs of discomfort and of an impulse to escape from confinement. It tries to squeeze through any opening; it claws and bites at the bars or wire; it thrusts its paws out through any opening and claws at everything it reaches; it continues its efforts when it strikes anything loose and shaky; it may claw at things within the box. It does not pay very much attention to the food outside, but seems simply to strive instinctively to escape from confinement. The vigor with which it struggles is extraordinary. For eight or ten minutes it will claw and bite and squeeze incessantly. With 13, an old cat, and 11, an uncommonly sluggish cat, the behavior was different. They did not struggle vigorously or continually. On some occasions they did not even struggle at all. It was therefore necessary to let them out of the box a few times, feeding them

each time. After they thus associate climbing out of the box with getting food, they will try to get out whenever put in. They do not, even then, struggle so vigorously or get so excited as the rest. In either case, whether the impulse to struggle be due to an instinctive reaction to confinement or to an association, it is likely to succeed in letting the cat out of the box. The cat that is clawing all over the box in her impulsive struggle will probably claw the string or loop or button so as to open the door. And gradually all the other nonsuccessful impulses will be stamped out and the particular impulse leading to the successful act will be stamped in . . . until, after many trials, the cat will, when put in the box, immediately claw the button or loop in a definite way.[4]

As the Pavlov experiments precipitated an oversimplified theory of learning in terms of only one of a number of factors required for the conditioned reflex, so the Thorndike experiments precipitated an oversimplified generalized theory from trial-and-error learning. This theory pounced upon the effect of the successful choice in learning, and stated that learning resulted from frequency and recency plus the 'good' effect of the successful choice and the 'bad' effect of the unsuccessful choices. For Thorndike the 'good' effect was the satisfactoriness of the correct choice and the 'bad' effect the annoyingness of the incorrect choices. For others the effect was described as confirmation versus inhibition, or congruity with some total instinctive activity versus incongruity. These suggestions are particularly interesting to us because they make *some value* the decisive factor which stamps in the correct alternative.

But a 'good' effect does not seem to be necessary for learning. The two sets of experiments described in the previous section bring this out. The latent learning experiments show that learning of associated connections among objects occurs even when no 'good' result for any drive in action is evident. And the experiment in which subjects were punished for the correct choice and yet learned sooner than those who were not punished indicates that it is *emphasis* rather than a 'good' effect that improves learning. However, a 'good' effect is one way of obtaining strong emphasis.

At this point Tolman propounds a very important thesis for value theory, namely, that what is uniquely determined by the 'good' effect is not the learning of cognitive sets but the *per-formance*. Many cognitive sets are learned by latent learning and otherwise, but in appetitive action only those sets which are believed to be anticipatory sets for the achievement of a goal of a drive in action are charged by the drive and acted on. Learning and speed of learning are one thing. Performance on the basis of connections learned is another. Drives are necessary for both learning and performance. Many cognitive sets are learned that are never acted upon, never become anticipatory sets for an appetition (nor, as we shall see later, apprehensive sets for an aversion). And the speed of learning depends on other things besides the success of an act in furtherance of a drive. But the performance, the selection of one alternative rather than another when learning has occurred, does depend on the 'good' anticipated effect of the act. An anticipatory set, and the action performed through it, is dropped out the moment an organism ceases to believe it may lead to the goal of the drive charging the act. The performance ceases. And yet the connection that was learned is not thereby forgotten, and still maintains a primacy if ever again it receives encouragement.

In short, the laws of learning and the laws of performance are not identical, though they are interconnected. The over-simplified trial-and-error theory of learning, which sought to make out that a 'good' effect stamped an act in and a 'bad' effect stamped an act out, was an attempt to identify the laws of learning with those of performance. Anticipatory sets are acquired by the laws of learning, but their attachment to appetitive drives and the purposive action passing through them follow other laws.

Tolman suggests two added factors bearing on trial-and-error learning not involved in conditioned reflex learning. In addition to the $m$, $n$, and $o$ factors having to do with the interrelations in the materials, Tolman suggests a $p$ factor consisting of 'interrelations among the spatial, temporal, and other characters of the alternatives' favorable to learning. For instance, if alternatives are spatially close together, the learning of the correct alternative seems to be quicker than if they are far apart.

And in addition to the $u$, $v$, $w$, and $x$ factors for conditioned reflex learning, Tolman suggests a $y$ factor of 'temporal orders and sequences in the presentations of the alternatives' favorable to learning.

Trial-and-error learning is consequently for Tolman simply a complication upon conditioned reflex learning due to the need of the organism actively to select a correct act from among a number of incorrect ones. The crux of the learning process is not a mechanical result of recency, frequency, and satisfactory effect, but the establishment of an anticipatory set linkage. Thorndike's cat, having learned that the correct act is to claw the loop or button, now performs that act because it anticipates that this will open the door, which mediates the superordinate anticipation of getting food. It is because the subordinate antici- pation is linked with the superordinate anticipation that the response is performed.

This mutation is, however, more remarkable than the condi- tioned reflex mutation, because there is a complete blockage on the superordinate response, such that the latter cannot occur. The cat cannot reach its food. Only the drive for the response is present, and perhaps the stimulus in terms of sight or smell of the food (not always that). Pavlov's dogs were getting their food, and the stimulus of the bell was simply an added source of anticipation for the food. But Thorndike's cats were not get- ting their food. They had to discover not only a new stimulus but *a new response to a new object* (the latch) which would release their response to the food. Hence diagram 2 for the conditioned reflex mutation will no longer do. The trial-and- error learning mutation must be represented in some such way as this:

From:

$$A^{N_1} \longrightarrow O^{G_1}$$
$$\underbrace{SR}$$
$$\uparrow SR$$
$$O^{G_2}$$

To:

$$\left. \begin{array}{c} A^{N_1} \\ \nwarrow \\ A^{N_2} \end{array} \right\} \longrightarrow O^{G_2} \quad SR \tag{4}$$

$A^N_1$ = anticipatory set for food    $O^G_2$ = latch open, goal object of
$O^G_1$ = food, goal object of $A^N_1$          $A^N_2$
$A^N_2$ = anticipatory set for opening    $SR$ = stimulus-response activity
   latch                          on object

The mutation is from a situation in which, as a result of trial-and-error activity, the cat by chance opens the latch $O^G_2$, and thereby finds that it can act on an anticipation, $A^N_1$, to get food, $O^G_1$; and leads to the situation in which the cat, as a result of frequent successes and the other factors of learning, comes to anticipate that, through the opening of the latch $A^N_2$ it can reliably anticipate the getting of food, $A^N_1$. When these two anticipations are linked ($A^N_2 \rightarrow A^N_1$), the cat will act to open the latch immediately at any time it is in the cage and wants food. We say the cat has learned how to get at its food when it is in the cage. And the latch, which formerly had no value for the cat, now acquires value through the anticipation that action upon it will lead to food, which the cat already values. The cat has acquired a new instrumental value.

Of course, just as with conditioned reflex learning, this connection has to be constantly reinforced; otherwise it will be extinguished. All the laws of the conditioned reflex apply to trial-and-error learning, but there is an added complexity due to the trial-and-error activity by which an organism acquires a new correct response to a new object among a number of possible incorrect choices.

## 4. Trial-and-Error Activity
### an Instinctive Technique

An important point about trial-and-error activity is that it is an instinctive technique of action which normally comes into play whenever a docile organism is blocked in the attainment of a goal or the quiescence of a drive. It is an essential technique for bridging the gap between the drive and its quiescence pattern. A docile organism with a strong drive in action, like hunger or thirst, when faced with a novel environment would be at a loss what to do, if it were not for the instinctive technique of trial-and-error activity that automatically goes into gear at such a

time. If such an organism had to rely solely on conditioned reflex learning, it would be at the mercy of the immediate environment. It is the impulse for trial and error that actively sends
the organism out into the environment to find the correct act
for the quiescence of a drive. An organism with an impulse for
the trial-and-error technique would obviously have a much better chance of survival than one that had to rely entirely on
passive conditioning. Trial-and-error activity is therefore a sure
sign of docility in an organism. It is also a sign that the organism is contending with a gap between a drive and a goal, and
that at this point the drive is cognitively blind and lacks an
anticipatory set with cognitive references by which the organism would know what to do.

Just what is trial-and-error activity? It is not doing the same
act over and over again, like William James's pickerel in a tank
that ran into the glass partition between it and a minnow hundreds of times. This is the way of the chain reflex instincts. They
have no flexibility, because there is no gap between one reflex
link and the next, and no trial-and-error technique to develop a
novel link. Trial-and-error activity is guided by an impulse
constantly to change the act if it does not lead to the desired
goal or quiescence. In its most primitive form it seems to be
random action within the stimulus-response capacities of the
organism. No anticipation of what may follow seems to be necessary. At the other extreme the trials may be based on carefully
thought-out predictions, as in scientific experimentation. And
there may be any degree of anticipatory preparation in trial-and-
error activity between these extremes.

The trial-and-error acts of Thorndike's cats indicate both random action and action with a degree of anticipation based on
somewhat similar experiences in the past. Clawing and biting
at the bars suggest anticipations, based on previous success, of
breaking down such obstructions. But 'clawing all over the box,'
which finally produced the correct response by accident, looks
like random action devoid of anticipatory references. In general,
it would seem that the more unfamiliar an obstruction, and the
longer it resists solution, and the more urgent the impulse, the

greater the tendency for trial-and-error activity to deteriorate to the primitive form of purely random action devoid of specific anticipatory references. Human introspection would certainly bear out such a generalization. In situations similar to that of Thorndike's cats, when a man is trying to open a window that is stuck, or to mend a break in a water pipe, or to find his way back to camp in a snowstorm, he begins with well-planned hypotheses, but, as he becomes more and more desperate, gives way to random, irrational actions devoid of any cognitive expectations that could be called anticipatory sets. This blind sort of trial-and-error activity occurs in its most primitive form when men are panic-stricken.

This point is an important one to make, since Tolman, and Perry even more, always include an anticipatory (that is to say a cognitive) element in every articulation of a purposive act. My view is that the peculiarity of docile behavior is precisely the lack of a cognitive element in the crucial gap between a drive and its goal, and *what is learned is the cognitive anticipatory reference* that was previously lacking. On my view, *blind* trial-and-error behavior is the basic technique for discovering a connection between a *blind* drive and its quiescence goal.

True, in an animal that has had much experience in many kinds of situations, the form that trial-and-error activity first takes is cognitively anticipatory rather than cognitively blind. He tries out anticipatory sets that have worked in the past in similar situations. But if the blockage continues, the behavior deteriorates cognitively until it comes close to the primitive instinctive cognitively blind form. Biologically, cognitively blind trial-and-error behavior is a docile animal's ultimate resource for adjustment to a totally new environment. It is paradoxically the sign of the animal's docility, of its capacity for intelligence, of its freedom from the rigidity of chain reflex activity which can act only on the anticipation of the next link in the chain and go on doing the same inappropriate act over and over when faced with an inauspicious environment. The cognitive *blindness* of the instinctive trial-and-error technique together with the cognitive *blindness* of the instinctive appetitive drive are precisely what make possible unlimited adjustment to changing environments within the sensory and motor capacities of the organism.

Trial-and-error behavior is the intelligent organism's only means of *actively* generating new cognitive sets. For conditioned reflex learning is merely a passive mode of learning, in which the organism is left to the mercy of whatever may catch its attention in its surroundings. And inventive learning, as we shall see, is only a more subtle form of trial and error. Active intelligence is based on trial and error.

## 5. SCIENTIFIC METHOD AS SYSTEMATIZED TRIAL AND ERROR

The inductive methods of experimental science are essentially systematized trial and error. And, incidentally, the inductive leap, that 'scandal of pure logic,' which deductive logicians have employed every ingenuity to close, is no scandal at all, but the gap of novelty between a drive and a goal which man's active intelligence fills by means of methodized trial and error. If there were no leap, there would be no intelligence. To try to convert induction into a species of deduction is like trying to convert appetitive purposive behavior into a species of chain reflex. The justification for anticipations of regularity lies in the very biological constitution of any animal like man whose life depends on such anticipations. Our drives and instinctive trial-and-error mechanisms with which in the course of evolution we have been endowed, and by which we have successfully adjusted to our environment, indicate that our environment is such as to justify the predictive anticipations we refer to it. For whenever our predictions are in error our appetitions are unfulfilled, and if this happened often we should (we do!) soon perish.

So there is, in one way, nothing very remarkable in our ability to make true predictions about regularities in our environment. If we could not, we should not be here to see our error. The very fact that we are here to wonder how we are justified in inferring regularities in nature is the overwhelming justification for our belief in their existence. This is not a logical justification but (much better) a factual one for the legitimacy of the inductive leap.

Very briefly, the leap is intuitively justified by the instinctive trial-and-error mechanism with which we are endowed, to handle novel situations in our environment. It is factually justified by the survival of our species, which depends on the reliability of its cognitive sets developed by trial and error for the prediction of means to satisfy the drives.

Trial-and-error learning is the pivot about which all our intellectual life turns. It is the means by which we attain virtually all that we have learned about our environment. And as an instinctive endowment in a surviving species which survives mainly by its intelligence, it is a mute guaranty of the cognitive soundness of its method of getting results.

To the question which troubled both Hume and Kant—How are regularities in nature possible?—the answer is that we are innately endowed with dispositions which anticipate regularities, and that if our environment did not fit the regularities we come to anticipate, we should not be here to ask such a question. The question would be even more urgent for an organism like the digger wasp, which is endowed with a highly specialized chain reflex sequence and would cease as a species if the environment did not regularly on the whole conform to the wasp's implicit predictions. The world is categorized for the wasp as a sequence of causally connected events from the appearance of a grasshopper to a well-stored hole in the ground. The wasp does not wonder at the miracle of how nature should conform to these special categories. She does not, like Hume, introspectively examine each articulation of her chain reflex and find in it no ground of necessity why nature should confirm any successive link, and so doubt if there are adequate intellectual grounds to believe in the regularities of nature. Nor, like Kant, does she say, "I must believe nature is necessarily connected in a succession of links between a grasshopper and a hole in the ground, because I am mentally so made with a series of dispositions that I cannot act or think otherwise." The wasp just acts and on the whole perpetuates her species. The wasp's chain reflex categories, of course, were generated by an environment which had the regularities to support them. Kant, in a way, was right. The inability of the wasp to act otherwise was the guaranty of the wasp's trust in the causal regularity of nature—but this was only because the wasp would not even be alive if her mode of behavior were not supported by the regularities of nature.

And so with man, who really is able to wonder how nature comes to satisfy his drives and his cognitive anticipations. The answer for man is more complex than for the digger wasp. For man is endowed with docility and trial-and-error technique, and he can be aware of his errors and of failures of his environment to conform to his anticipations. But again the fact that he is innately endowed with these techniques for acquiring novel anticipations, and that with this endowment he has survived long and successfully by means of beliefs in regularities which were confirmed by his environment, is evidence of the soundness of his beliefs in such regularities.

The logician interested in the theory of induction is wasting his time when he seeks a universal postulate, or a deductive calculus of probability, to justify inductive conclusions. His task is to describe the methods of prediction which experience shows to be dependable. These methods probably vary with varying conditions. There may well be different sorts of regularities, and there is no antecedent reason for believing that a method suitable for uncovering regularities in one field will prove suitable for another. Just as the method for solving a maze is not suitable in all details for escaping from one of Thorndike's cages, the methods suitable for physics are not entirely suitable for sociology or psychiatry. Probably the only common element in all these methods is the process of trial and error itself.

6. INVENTIVE LEARNING

As trial-and-error learning is based on conditioned reflex learning with certain significant additions, so inventive learning is based on trial and error, and is properly regarded as the sign of the highest intelligence. Here the organism performs an extremely active part and develops an anticipatory set without previous experience with the pattern of that set in his environment. In short, he invents a hypothesis. This presupposes what we call *thinking*.

Thinking consists in a process of detaching cognitive sets (or, if you will, thoughts or hypotheses) from their linkage in a sequence of behavior, giving them a sort of freedom and life of their own, so that a man without explicit action can look over the possibilities of action before deciding how to act. This kind of behavior is most characteristic of man, though some higher animals are capable of it. In its simplest form, thinking is a mere substitute for acting, mere trial-and-error activity going on in terms of thought or cognitive sets instead of in terms of explicit action. A man tries out one idea after another in his mind, as we say, instead of trying them out in his environment. Thinking is a great saver of energy and time. Where a cat in confinement struggles with walls and bars, a man sits down and thinks the situation over. Whenever we see a man, or an animal, stop in the course of action and look around, and perhaps scratch his head, or simply stop, we say, "He is thinking." In this interval he is running over the possibilities of action. The cognitive sets he runs over are the possibilities. And, in terms of purposive behavior, such intervals of thought are the realm of possibility, which has fascinated the world's great thinkers from Plato to Santayana. These possibilities, these 'forms,' 'essences,' cognitive sets, are for that interval lifted out of the overt dynamic drive of action and viewed in the light of their own intrinsic patterns and implications. Most of them will never be acted upon, but when one is chosen it descends from the realm of possibility and becomes actualized as a dynamic causal factor in the temporal progress of a purposive act and participates in its achievement.

In its simplest form, thinking is a remarkable enough process. But in its simplest form it does not constitute a new kind of learning. It is only a more economical way of carrying on trial-and-error learning. It becomes a new kind of learning when it creates a new idea or anticipatory set. Thinking performs this almost miraculous feat by taking to pieces old ideas and putting them together again in new ways. It analyzes old ideas into their elements and then forms new ideas by synthesizing the elements. In its simplest form, however, inventive thinking consists merely in putting two or more old ideas together to make one new idea.

The classical experiments for inventive learning, corresponding to those with Pavlov's dogs for conditioning and Thorndike's cats for trial and error, are Köhler's apes. The following experiment with the young ape Koko is typical:

> On the third day of his residence at the station, he [Koko] was given a small wooden box as a toy. (Its dimensions were forty by thirty by thirty centimeters.) He pushed it about and sat on it for a moment. On being left alone, he became very angry, and thrust the box to one side. After an hour had elapsed, Koko was removed and his chain fastened to the wall of a house. On one side, one metre from the ground, the objective was suspended from the wall. The box had been placed between three and four metres from the objective, and two metres from the wall while rope allowed him to move freely about the box and by the wall where the objective hung. The observer withdrew to a considerable distance (more than six metres from the box, and the same side), and only approached once in order to make the objective more atttractive. Koko took no notice of him throughout the course of the test. He jumped upwards several times to begin with, perpendicularly beneath the objective, then took his rope in his hand and tried to lasso the prize with a loop of it, could not reach so far, and then turned away from the wall, after a variety of such actions, but without noticing the box. He appeared to have given up his efforts, but always returned to them from time to time. After some time, on turning away from the wall, his eye fell on the box: he approached it, *looked straight towards the objective,* and gave the box a slight push, which did not, however, move it; his movements had grown much slower; he left the box standing, took a few paces away from it, but at once returned, and pushed it again and *again with eyes on the objective,* but quite gently, and not as though he really intended to alter its position. He turned away again, turned back at once, and gave the box a third tentative shove, after which he again moved slowly about. The box had now been moved ten centimeters in the direction of the fruit. The objective was rendered more tempting by the addition of a piece of orange (the *non plus ultra* of delight!), and in a few seconds Koko was once more at the box, seized it, and dragged it in one movement almost up to a point directly beneath the objective (that is, for a distance of at least three metres), mounted it, and tore down the fruit. A bare quarter of an hour had elapsed since the beginning of the

test. Of course, the observer had not interfered with either the ape or the box, when he 'improved' the objective. The improvement of the objective by the addition of several items is a method which can be employed over and over again with success when the animal is obviously quite near to a solution, but in the case of a lengthy experiment, there is the risk that fatigue will intervene and spoil the result. It must not be supposed that before the exhibition of the orange, the animal is too lazy to attain its objective; on the contrary, from the beginning, Koko showed a lively interest in the fruit, but none—at first—in the box, and when he began to move the latter, he did not appear *apathetic, but uncertain;* there is only one (colloquial) expression that really fits his behavior at that juncture: "It's beginning to dawn on him!" [5]

When Koko got the idea that the box could be used as an instrument on which to stand to reach the fruit, he had *invented* a new anticipatory set. He did not discover the use of the box as a result of random trial-and-error activity which happened to get the box under the fruit so that he could step up on it. Koko thought it out and in one deliberate act brought the box from a distance for the purpose. He put together the idea that standing on the box gave him extra height and the idea that extra height directly under the fruit would permit him to reach it. These two old ideas united produced the new idea of the box as an instrument for reaching the fruit. Köhler calls this 'insight'; Tolman, 'inventive learning.' Logicians would call it 'inference.' In its highest manifestations among scientists and artists, it is called 'creative imagination.'

A characteristic of this kind of learning is that one successful performance is sufficient to teach the organism the connection involved. Obviously, an invented hypothesis is not always successful. Trial of the hypothesis—and if it is in error and fails to verify, trial and trial again—applies to inventive learning as well as to regular trial-and-error learning. Science and art exemplify many unsuccessful invented hypotheses to one that proves successful. It is the method of invention that distinguishes inventive learning from simple trial and error. In a sense, this is merely a supremely effective species of trial and error.

All the factors involved in conditioned reflex learning and in trial-and-error learning are involved here also, with certain additions. The additions have to do with an organism's inventive or imaginative capacities: the relations among stimuli in the environment that facilitate invention (proximity, for instance, of objects which if connected in thought would produce the new idea, as the box within Koko's field of vision which included the suspended food), and the relations of thoughts in the sequence of time that facilitate their coming to mind together when the occasion requires.

In man, assisted as he is by the extraordinary instrument of language, an enormous amount of thinking is inventive in some degree, and often it is hard to draw the line between genuine invention and that part of a man's thinking which is mere trial and error among old established ideas. Nevertheless, so characteristic is inventive learning for human behavior that a man or a child who cannot invent a hypothesis when the occasion demands is open to ridicule from his fellows as somebody who does not use his brain.

## 7. CONCLUSION

These, then, are the ways by which anticipatory sets, or cognitive sets in general, are developed. The basic principle is conditioning. But even the simplest process of conditioning is not so simple as many psychologists have assumed. Mere recency and frequency are not enough. Other equally important factors are involved. When a new anticipatory set is acquired by conditioning, it is something that has been learned through the agency of a drive, and, apart from latent learning, is acquired in the service of the drive. A theory of conditioning which does not take account of the drive as a major factor in the process of learning overlooks the central dynamics of the process.

Conditioned reflex learning is relatively passive. An organism with a drive in action discovers correlations between objects in the environment and objects already charged by the drive.

Trial-and-error learning requires of the organism an active role in the environment. The trial-and-error form of activity is an instinctive technique which goes into action when an organism is faced with a gap between a drive and its quiescence. Its function is to discover an anticipatory set which will bridge the gap. It is at once a sign of complete ignorance regarding a situation at the point where it has to go into effect, and of docility and intelligence. For, by trial and error, the organism acquires knowledge of the means of satisfying drives in a variable environment. And if a particular acquired anticipatory set appropriate to one situation proves inapplicable to another, the organism, by trial and error again, can acquire a new set appropriate to the changed situation. This innate technique renders an organism adaptable to a wide range of environmental changes—and, incidentally, makes it possible for the organism to learn a great deal about the correlations of objects in his environment.

So it appears that knowledge is founded on ignorance. For consider again the digger wasp. If *per impossibile* she could become self-conscious, she would discover that all she could possibly know about the surrounding world would be the chain of fixed relations between the articulations of her chain reflexes. She would be bigoted in the certainty that the world was categorized throughout according to her little repertory of chain reflexes. If something apparently went wrong, she would reassert her firm convictions by again putting her chain reflex into operation just as she did before. And if the sequence went through this time to the end, that would prove to her that the world was indeed categorized as she had believed. If the sequence failed to go through, she would simply die with her categories and her firm dogmatic beliefs, still unconvinced that the world was not constituted to fit her chain reflexes.

But organisms like rats and men that are capable of gaps of ignorance are compensated by being capable likewise of a wide knowledge of their environment. In proportion to their capacities for adjustment they can shape their categories to take account of errors as well as successes. And when man through the agency of language, tradition, and the written word can transmit his knowledge from generation to generation, as rats cannot, his capacity to learn about his environment becomes almost unlimited. But all this knowledge is based upon man's capacity for ignorance and the technique of trial and error to overcome it.

Inventive learning is a further development of trial-and-error learning derived from thinking, which is trial and error among cognitive sets without the effort of overt action. Thinking turns into invention when a new cognitive set is created out of a combination of old ones or out of a combination of parts of old ones. The new set is then open to verification through overt trial-and-error action.

For value theory, the importance of learning is in the value mutation that it entails. When a new anticipatory set is developed and charged by a drive in the belief[6] that it will lead to a goal object which will lead to the quiescence of the drive, this anticipation and its object, previously devoid of value, become objects of value. This is the *conditioning mutation*.

Reciprocally, when an anticipatory set suffers extinction through lack of reinforcement, an object which previously had value through being charged by a drive now ceases to have value. This may be called the *unconditioning mutation*.

In addition to these two mutations derived from the process of conditioning, there is another mutation resulting from the factor of fusibility or mechanization. When a cognitive set or sequence of cognitive sets is uniformly verified in an organism's environment, it tends to drop out of consciousness and to turn into what is known as mechanized habit. Whatever pleasure or displeasure is attached to the sets disappears in consequence.

The habit mutation then is pertinent in the consideration of the affective values of pleasure and displeasure. But the pertinence of the conditioning mutation consists in the development of anticipatory sets and of the subordinate acts which fill the gap between a drive and its quiescence pattern. It is through these that instrumental values are generated. And these, as they apply to appetitions, are the subject of chapter 6.

# 6

# Subordinate Acts

## 1. The Relation of Subordinate Acts to the Drive

The main structure of an appetition consists of a governing propensity, subordinate acts, and the goal. We have examined the first of these three main divisions, which was subdivided into a drive and an anticipatory set.

Our next task is to examine the nature and operation of the subordinate acts. The function of these acts is to fill the gap between the drive and its quiescence pattern. Actually, the anticipatory set of the governing propensity, together with its goal object, is the first of these subordinate acts. But if this first anticipatory set—consisting in the organism's prediction of an object that will produce the quiescence pattern—is one which the organism cannot immediately put in action because the object is not present to be acted upon, then a new gap appears between the anticipatory set of the governing propensity and its goal object. This gap calls for another anticipatory set for a subordinate goal object which is expected to produce the super-ordinate goal object of the original anticipatory set, and so on until a set is found with a goal object in the immediate environment which can be acted upon. These subordinate sets with their goal objects are the subordinate acts we are concerned with here. They are the succession of means for obtaining the end of quiescence for the drive.

Consider the example of the thirsty geologist in the desert. His drive was thirst. When he became aware of his situation he began to think (that is, he ran over his ideas relevant to the drive) and developed the anticipatory set of finding a water hole. This functioned thereafter as the governing directive idea for the rest of his behavior. A succession of subordinate anticipatory sets then developed in his thinking; these were calculated to guide him from an appropriate action in his immediate environment to the attainment of a water hole. If he were to find water, he must find evidence of green in some depression of the hills. To see a green patch he must get up on an elevation which would command a view over the country. He noticed a ridge just above him. To get there he must walk up the slope. The beginning of the slope was at his feet. Thereby the gap was closed, and action could begin on the succession of subordinate acts leading to water.

The relationship among the acts can be diagramed as follows:

Let $I$ = impulse pattern of drive (thirst)

$A^N_1$ = anticipatory set of governing propensity (idea of a water hole)

$A^N_2$ = next subordinate anticipatory set (idea of a green patch)

$A^N_3$ = next subordinate anticipatory set (idea of an elevation from which to see a green patch)

$A^N_4$ = next subordinate anticipatory set (idea that the slope starting at his feet would lead to such an elevation)

$O^G_1, O^G_2, O^G_3, O^G_4$ = goal objects referred to by series of anticipatory sets

$Q^P$ = quiescence pattern of drive (satisfaction of thirst)

Then:

Governing propensity      Subordinate acts        Terminal goal      (1)

$$I \quad A^N_1 \qquad A^N_2 \qquad\qquad O^G_2 \qquad O^G_1 \qquad Q^P$$
$$A^N_3 \qquad\qquad O^G_3$$
$$A^N_4 \; O^G_4$$

We say the geologist walked up the slope $A^N_4\, O^G_4$ because he anticipated that this act would bring him to an elevation, $A^N_3$, which would bring him in sight of a green patch, $A^N_2$, within which he could find a water hole, $A^N_1$, which would satisfy his thirst, $I$. Each subordinate act is a means to the superordinate act above it, and each goal object is judged to be a means of producing the goal object above it, all ultimately to the end of satisfying the geologist's thirst. Each of these acts acquires value as a means of attaining the terminal goal, which itself has value through the impulse of the drive.

If any one of these anticipatory sets seemed to the geologist to be in error either as a result of his thinking over the evidence for its correctness or from actual trial, it would cease to have value for him, and so would all the anticipatory sets subordinate to it. Of course, the corresponding goal objects would likewise lose their value. Suppose, for instance, the geologist became convinced that the elevation above him would not give him a view into a promising valley beyond, because there seemed to be a higher ridge behind it. Then his desire to climb that ridge would cease. His anticipation of standing on that elevation, $A^N_3$, would lose its value, and likewise his anticipation of climbing its slope, $A^N_4$. He would instead begin seeking means of getting around to the slope of the higher ridge behind.

It also becomes clear that as soon as a subordinate act is carried out and the superordinate goal object has been attained, the subordinate act is no longer of value. It is no longer needed. It is no longer instrumental to the acts above, or to the terminal goal of the drive. It has performed its function and its value has ceased. This obvious fact is, for some reason, frequently overlooked. After the geologist has climbed the slope and reached the elevation, the slope is no longer of any instrumental use to the geologist for quenching his thirst.

If another person in the same predicament happened to become aware of his thirst at the same spot at the foot of the ridge, and developed a similar hypothesis for finding water, the slope of the ridge would again acquire instrumental value as a means of getting to a promising elevation. But this would be a completely new act of valuing.

Similarly it becomes clear that the whole series of subordinate acts and their goal, including the terminal goal, cease to have value when finally the drive is satisfied. When the geologist has reached his water hole, quenched his thirst, and filled his canteen, all the subordinate acts and goals, including the goal of the impulse itself to satisfy the geologist's thirst, cease to have any value. When the geologist's thirst is quenched, he clearly does not want to quench his thirst any more. That desire has ceased, and the value it conferred upon the series of goals that led to its satisfaction no longer obtains. This fact also is often overlooked.

To be sure, we know that the geologist will become thirsty again. He has a disposition to become thirsty in predictable cycles. But when he is not thirsty, he does not desire to have his thirst quenched. Each emergence of the thirst drive is a separate desire for the satisfaction of that particular drive. And when that particular drive is satisfied, that particular value activity is terminated. In short, there are ultimate goals in value activity. There are final quiescences and satisfactions which bring a sequence of valuings to a conclusive end. Some contemporary writers seem to deny this fact, and to assert that every end is at the same time a means to something else. They talk as if the relation between means and end were entirely relative and arbitrary and as if there were no final satisfactions of desires. This error is so persistent and its correction so vital to sound judgment regarding values that we must give special attention to it even at this stage of our study.

## 2. Errors Regarding the Means-End Continuum

The error arises from three distinct facts. The first is the cyclic or recurrent character of many drives like thirst and hunger. A man has a continuous innate disposition to become periodically thirsty or hungry. It is thus possible to speak of the total disposition as a single interest which is periodically brought to quiescence only that it may become active again. The satisfaction of thirst is simply a means of replenishing the organism so that the desire for this satisfaction may arise again. This is, of course, a totally different sense of 'means' from that of the relation between the subordinate act of a purpose to its superordinate act which it serves. This is 'means' in a sense of 'cause' which has no connection with the requirement that a 'means' be a factor in an act instrumental to the quiescence of a drive. I propose that in this inquiry we use the term 'means' or 'instrument' only in the latter sense, *as an act or factor in an act believed through a mediating judgment to be productive of a superordinate act that is desired.* This definition signifies that an anticipatory (or apprehensive) set is required as a mediating judgment for the determination of anything referred to as a means or instrument. If the judgment is mistaken, the object or act is thought to be a means to something wanted, but erroneously. If the judgment is correct, the object or act is truly a means to the end desired. The point is that even if the mediating judgment is false, still the object of anticipation is sought as a means: that is, a means is not a cause.

In this precise sense of 'means,' it is clear that the satisfaction of the geologist's thirst was not a means to his being able to become thirsty again. The satisfaction was terminal. The various subordinate acts leading up to the quiescence of his thirst in the act of drinking the water were instrumental because they were all mediated by anticipatory judgments to the effect that they were steps to the satisfaction of the drive. But the satisfaction of the drive was not mediated by any anticipatory set to the effect that it would lead to something else. It was final. It was the end desired.

This particular difficulty is dissolved by clearing up the ambiguity in the word 'means.' But it brings out another ambiguity in the term 'interest.' This term has become so hopelessly ambiguous that it would be better to discard it as a technical term. Since, however, many authorities, including Perry and Dewey, use it as a pivotal term for value, something must be said about interest in this connection.

The principal aim of our study of single purposive acts is to describe precisely what an actual interest is. Toward this aim an interest (in the sense of a unit of value corresponding to Perry's basic usage) is a single appetition or a single aversion. The behavior of the geologist in the pursuit of water represented a single interest. We can speak of a dominant interest in water generating a succession of subordinate interests in climbing to an elevation, looking for a green patch, digging a hole, and so on. There are terminal and there are subordinate interests.

But we should not speak of a disposition as an actual interest in this strict sense. A disposition, such as the capacity for thirst or hunger or for baseball or business or social service or music or art, is still a *potential* interest, but not, if we stick to the first use of the term, an *actual* interest such as the geologist's active desire for water. So, when someone speaks of an interest in baseball or music, we should be careful to find out whether he means a disposition for these objects or an actual appetition in action in pursuit of the objects. Only the latter would represent an actual valuing. Yet many writers speak of 'an interest' ambiguously in both senses at once, both as a disposition to desire something and as the actual desiring of it.

Worse still, we shall find writers (and this applies particularly to Dewey) referring to the 'labor interest,' the 'shipping interest,' the 'family interest,' and the like, as if these were technically single interests. These, of course, are meaningful references, and it would be hard to find a good substitute for these terms. But clearly the 'labor interest' is not an appetition in action like the geologist's interest in finding water, nor is it an organism's disposition for valuing like thirst. It refers to a value situation without question. It is a *social disposition* of some complexity, capable of controlling the actual purposive activity and individual dispositions to belief and action of many persons. But it is not any one individual's interest in either of the previous senses.

'Interest,' then, may mean: (1) *an actual act of valuing* as it is going on, an appetition or aversion in action; (2) *a disposition in an individual organism* for a type of appetition or aversion; (3) *a disposition of a social group* for certain ends. All three meanings are in good usage, and colloquially it would be hard to find convenient substitutes.

So, on the whole, we shall avoid the term 'interest,' except where the context makes it clear and where circumlocution would seem pedantic. For its ambiguities have much to do with the contemporary vagueness in value theory, including the current tendency of many writers to blur the distinction between means and end.

A second reason for the confusion is the fact that, within a single extensive and highly articulated appetition, each superordinate act of a succession of subordinate acts is the proximate end of the act leading to it. The geologist climbed the slope to the end of reaching an elevation, but this end was a means for seeing a green patch, and so on. Observing this fact, we could easily be tempted to generalize that all ends are relative, and when achieved will be found but means to something further. But such a generalization overlooks the striking fact that subordinate acts are charged by a drive and mediated by judgments which terminate in the quiescence of the drive and that this terminating act is the unique act on which the whole sequence is based. This terminal act is not itself charged by any drive but its own, which is consummated in its own quiescence pattern.

The activities of Richter's rats, whose lives were regulated almost solely by the emergence and quiescence of hunger, with sleep between, show how final purposive activities can be. When the rats had had enough to eat, that was the end of that activity and they quieted down and slept. No continuity of relative ends and means in their lives. And human lives are not so totally different as to have no terminal purposive acts.

This leads to the third reason for the confusion of means and ends: the great complexity of human life and the multitude of purposes every man is carrying out simultaneously. Many of these purposes are interrelated, and many or all of them may be integrated into a life plan. The consummations of purposes thus tend to be conceived as relatively incidental to the total sweep of the integrated plan.

But complexity and integration of purposive actions do not involve the loss of consummations. In fact, the value of integration among purposes is to render their consummations more frequent and complete. But the complexity does bring it about that the consummation of a particular purposive activity may at the same time mediate some wider purpose. Yet the consummation of that particular drive is actually the full quiescence of that drive, with all the satisfactions it may entail. It is terminal for that drive.

The geologist's purpose of studying the desert rocks was interrupted by his thirst. That purpose was still potential as a disposition of his mind. But for the period of the emergency his research aims probably passed entirely out of his thought. If, however, the thought had come up, he might very well have connected his need for water with his research purpose. It might have occurred to him that in order to bring his research to its conclusion he must live, and in order to live he must find water, and through this mediating judgment connecting his desire for water with his desire to finish his research, the drive motivating his research might have added more energy to his search for water. If the search had been difficult, this added drive might have been just enough to carry him on to success. By this means the two drives become integrated, and the one does become a means to the other. But the thirst drive still remains a complete purposive act in its own right; when the water is found and the thirst quenched, that drive has attained its consummation and attendant satisfaction. This marks a period for a sentence of the geologist's life history—not a comma or a semicolon but a period —even though the sentence happens to be part of a paragraph, and that part of a chapter in a highly integrated life. Integration and complexity of purposive activity are not incompatible with final consummations of purposes. On the contrary, it is the function of integration to maximize such consummations.

The complexity of human activity, therefore, is not good evidence for a sweeping relativity of means and ends. In a subordinate act charged entirely by a superordinate drive, the goal object of that act is indeed only a relative end, an end for that act only in virtue of its being a means to a superordinate act which can bring quiescence to the drive. But any act that actually brings quiescence to a drive is a terminal end for that drive —an absolute end for that drive and not relative to any superordinate activity. If some other drive can utilize this drive as a means to its own end, that is another matter, the matter for this other drive.

When we are tempted to flatten out human experience into a never-ending plane of ends continually changing into means and never attaining final consummation, it will be salutary to reflect on Richter's rats. Their history ran in simple cycles of eating and sleeping. There was no complexity or overlapping; each cycle was complete, and its consummation absolute. A relativity theory of means and ends could never be made to fit their behavior. Nor, when we look closely, can it be made to fit human behavior.

## 3. The Dynamics of a Subordinate Act

That the source of the energy for a subordinate act is the superordinate drive has already become abundantly clear. But it has not perhaps been brought home to us just how this energy is channeled down from the generating drive through the series of subordinate acts. Surprisingly enough, it appears upon close scrutiny that each subordinate act has the structure of a complete appetition. We find literally a hierarchy of appetitions all with the same structure like a succession of double mirror images, all originating from the basic drive.

Suppose we amplify diagram 1, representing the geologist's hierarchy of subordinate acts, in such a way as to bring out exactly how the charge of the drive is transmitted down the series. It will come out like this:

$$
\begin{array}{llcccc}
 & \overbrace{\begin{array}{c}\text{Governing}\\\text{propensity}\end{array}} & & \overbrace{\text{Subordinate acts}} & & \overbrace{\text{Goal}} \\
\text{A:} & I \quad A^{N}{}_{1} & & & & O^{G}{}_{1} \quad Q^{P} \\
 & \quad \| & & & & \quad \| \\
\text{B:} & I_{2} & A^{N}{}_{2} & & O^{G}{}_{2} & Q^{P}{}_{2} \\
 & & \| & & \| & \\
\text{C:} & I_{3} & A^{N}{}_{3} & & O^{G}{}_{3} & Q^{P}{}_{3} \\
 & & \| & & \| & \\
\text{D:} & I_{4} & A^{N}{}_{4} \quad O^{G}{}_{4} & Q^{P}{}_{4} & & (2)
\end{array}
$$

Interpreted, this diagram means that the geologist's thirst $I$ stimulated the thought of water and charged it with energy through the mediating belief that water would quench his thirst. So far it is an old story with us. $IA^{N}{}_{1}$ is the governing propensity of the system; $O^{G}{}_{1} Q^{P}$ is the goal; and between are the subordinate acts needed to bridge the gap from the drive to its goal.

But now note the next level of the subordinate acts. $A^{N}{}_{2}$ is the geologist's idea of a green patch. But this anticipatory set generating a desire to reach a green patch arises through the mediating belief that a green patch in the desert will have water in it. That is to say, the anticipation for the green patch $A^{N}{}_{2}$ has the same relation to the anticipation of water $A^{N}{}_{1}$ that the anticipation of water $A^N_1$ has to the originating drive $I$. The geologist wants a green patch because he wants water, and believes the green patch will produce water. This sequence is exactly parallel to the previous one in which the geologist wants water because he wants to quench his thirst and believes that water will produce that result. But this signifies that the charged superordinate anticipatory set $A^N_1$ is functioning as the drive for the next subordinate anticipatory set $A^N_2$. In its function of transmitting its charge to $A^N_2$ through the mediating belief of $A^N_2$, $A^N_1 = I_2$ (the superordinate anticipatory set *is* the functioning drive for the next subordinate act). And this would be equally true of $A^N_2$ in relation to $A^N_3$, and $A^N_3$ in relation to $A^N_4$. Every superordinate anticipatory set functions as the drive for the next subordinate anticipatory set, which is connected with it by a mediating judgment.

Why not say that the original drive $I$ is the drive for each of these successive subordinate acts? It is the energy of the drive that is channeled down through them. $I$ is the only source of energy for the whole sequence. But it is not the *unqualified* original drive that motivates the subordinate acts. It is only that drive as mediated by the belief implicit in the subordinate anticipatory set that the subordinate act will produce the goal object of the superordinate anticipatory set. The mediating judgment of the subordinate act $A^N_2$ connects this act with the superordinate anticipatory set $A^N_1$, but not directly with the drive. The energy of the drive is channeled into $A^N_2$ only via $A^N_1$, not directly from $I$. The originating drive cannot directly motivate the subordinate act. The direct motivation for the subordinate act is the superordinate anticipatory set charged by the drive. So, literally, it is the charged superordinate anticipatory set that functions as the drive for the next subordinate anticipatory set, and not the governing drive $I$.

By way of exemplification, the geologist does not desire the green patch in the belief that it will quench his thirst. A green patch, of course, would not. The geologist is motivated to seek a green patch because he believes it will produce water. Thus the charged expectation of water is the direct drive for the desire for the green patch, not thirst. This fact comes out clearly if we conceive the geologist's thirst arising in some other environment, say a large city. The desire for water would remain the same in the governing propensity, but in that context a green patch would hardly suggest itself to the geologist as an appropriate way to get water. He would look around for a drinking fountain or a restaurant. The proximate drive for a subordinate act is never the unqualified governing drive of the appetition, but is that drive channeled through the superordinate anticipatory set.

Thus a subordinate act has the complete appetitive structure of the total governing act. It has its own governing propensity with its drive and anticipatory set, its correlative goals, and subordinate acts. Level A of our diagram gives the structure of the total act as we have been describing it from the beginning. Descending now to level B, we find $A^N_1$ (charged with $I$) functioning as the drive $I_2$ for level B, whence $I_2 A^N_2$ constitutes the subordinate governing propensity for this level. The goal object for $A^N_2$ is, of course, $O^G_2$ corresponding to $O^G_1$ for $A^N_1$, and (here is the interesting and conclusive point for our analysis) $O^G_1$ functions as the quiescence pattern for $I_2$. Thus $O^G_1 = Q^P_1$. If the green patch $O^G_2$ actually produces water, $O^G_1$, that will bring to quiescence the charged anticipation of water, $A^N_1$, just as the thirst drive $I$ will be brought to quiescence if water, $O^G_1$, actually quenches the thirst. Thus $A^N_1$ and its goal object $O^G_1$ function as proximate drive and quiescence pattern for $A^N_2 O^G_2$. And then between this subordinate governing propensity at level B and its subordinate goal are its own subordinate acts functioning, just as at level A, to bridge the gap between the subordinate drive and its subordinate goal. Thus level B has exactly the same form as level A, and the same for level C and until we reach level D, where no subordinate acts and further mediating judgments are necessary because the anticipatory set finds its goal object in its immediate environment and can go directly into action upon it.[1]

Furthermore, this detailed description shows just how each appetitive level is bracketed within the level above, and so on till the final governing drive is reached with its correlative quiescence pattern. It must be stressed, however, that the governing level (level A) is the only one that has an independent self-energized drive.[2] All the other subordinate drives derive their energy solely from the ultimate superordinate governing drive.

This fact is what holds the system together and binds every level to the level above. Moreover, the bond is tight. The moment any level proves to be incapable of producing the goal object anticipated by the level above, that level ceases to be energized by the level above, as well as all the levels subordinate to the one rejected.

Here we can see exactly the dynamics of the means-end relationship as it operates in appetitive acts.

# 7

# The Problem of the
# Independence Mutation

## 1. THE PROBLEM

We have already considered the conditioning mutation by
which objects previously neutral acquire value as means through
a mediating judgment which connects them with objects already
having value. We are now on the threshold of another, possibly
even more significant, mutation, by which objects previously
valued as means come to be valued as ends. We shall call this
the *independence mutation*. An object or act previously valued
because of its dependence through a mediating judgment upon a
superordinate act acquires independence and sallies forth on its
own.

There is not much question that this sort of thing does occur.
But the dynamics of the mutation is puzzling and even paradoxical. It is as if level C, for instance, in diagram 2, chapter 6,
detached itself from the level B above and started out on its own
power. The geologist suddenly discovers that he has a spontaneous drive to climb up to elevations, whether or not there is
any reason for doing so, such as looking for a green patch. The
desire to climb is no longer dependent on a mediating judgment
such as that connecting $A^N{}_3$ with $A^N{}_2$ whence $A^N{}_2$ could function
as the drive for $A^N{}_3$. That drive is eliminated and the mediating

connection cut. The problem now is whence comes the energy which charges the anticipatory set $A^N{}_3$ after it has lost its charge from $A^N{}_2$.

As an example of the independence mutation, let us consider mountain climbing. This strenuous activity, so eagerly engaged in by those who enjoy it, is clearly not an innate drive, and to many this fascination is incomprehensible. Similarly, skiing, snowshoeing, horseback riding, all originally means of transportation, are now pursued for their own sake. Possibly in our times driving a car is a better example, since it is primarily utilitarian in most families and yet nearly everyone comes to enjoy it for its own sake.

The mutation often passes from a general activity to the instruments used in performing it. A fisherman comes to enjoy a well-balanced rod for its own sake, and will cast when there are no fish to catch or even on dry land. A golfer cherishes his golf sticks, a smoker his pipes. Many men entering a profession, craft, or trade as a means of making a living come to enjoy it for itself. Unless this happens we tend to question the quality of the work. Even the manners and mores of a culture, which a child originally learns out of love or fear of his parents and teachers as a means of getting along with them, become ends in themselves. There seems to be no activity or thing employed as a means which under certain conditions may not be converted into an end. This is the principal way in which new drives and interests are generated. It is the source of practically all derived[1] drives (some would say of all), and since man immersed in cultural institutions is motivated in his daily actions much more frequently by derived drives than by basic innate ones, it becomes very important to know what are the conditions for producing them, and also for eradicating them if they prove undesirable.

Too little attention has been given to the motivations for derived drives. Writers have indicated that the mutation from means to end takes place, and frequently stop there as if further explanation were superfluous. Or they have referred to one of the simpler theories about the mutations without seeing its difficulties.

A knowledge about the mutations is extremely important in ethical considerations, however, not to mention other areas of value. For it is often assumed in ethics that the solution of a personal or social conflict must be sought in terms of the interests involved. Given the drives bearing on a situation, how is the maximum satisfaction to be obtained from this collection of drives in their interrelations? It is assumed that the drives are fixed, and the solution must be found in terms of satisfactions of all the drives. But the best solution might come from the elimination of one of the drives or in the generation of a new independent drive. This solution is always a possibility with derived drives —though not, of course, with innate drives. It is the usual psychiatric solution for persistent neurotic problems. But it is often available in simpler cases. And one of the principal aims of education is the development of new derived drives which will be socially useful. So the determination of what drives are innate and uneliminable, and what are derived, and how the latter come to be derived, and once derived how they may be extinguished if they prove persistently disruptive are matters of great ethical significance.

At this stage we do not have sufficient data to be able to describe the mechanisms generating independence mutations. There are probably several such mechanisms. But we can, at this time, point out the inadequacies of the two commonest theories. And it is advisable to do so, for it will show us exactly where the problem lies, and it will keep us alert for data that can contribute to an adequate theory.

## 2. THE DIVERTED IMPULSE THEORY

One of the commonest conceptions of the mechanism of the independence mutation is that the source of the energy is the original drive. This drive is conceived as rechanneled. The connection between the subordinate act and its superordinate act is, according to this theory, severed; the energy of the original drive is said to be diverted directly to the subordinate act, which then moves independently. The mutation is diagramed on page 130.

From:

$$I \quad A^N{}_1 \qquad\qquad O^G{}_1 \quad Q^P$$
$$\| \qquad\qquad\qquad \|$$
$$I_2 \quad A^N{}_2 \qquad O^G{}_2 \quad O^G{}_2$$

To:

$$I$$
$$\searrow$$
$$A^N{}_2 \quad O^G{}_2 \tag{1}$$

When the proposed mechanism is clearly described in this manner, its impossibility is obvious. It actually involves a contradiction. Utak's fishing, let us imagine, begins as a purely practical matter of obtaining food to satisfy his hunger and that of his family. With repetition of the activity, fishing becomes something he likes to do for its own sake. It becomes a sport. He may not even care for the fish he catches. It is the catching of them that intrigues him. The activity has acquired an independence of its original practical meaning.

$A^N{}_1$ would refer here to the anticipation of eating fish and $O^G{}_1$ the eating of them. $A^N{}_2$ would be the anticipation of catching fish and $O^G{}_2$ the catching of them. The mutation consists in the fact that the activity of catching fish has become an independent activity carried on without any connection with the eating of the fish, which was the original motivation. There is no question that such an independence mutation occurs for many people. But that the drive for it is the basic hunger drive diverted from its former channel through the anticipation of eating fish is out of the question. For the hunger drive requires as its goal its quiescence pattern—the digestion of food and the quieting of the stomach contractions. This drive will continue until it is satisfied, barring death or interruptions from stronger conflicting drives or fatigue or some artificial way of stopping hunger by intravenous feeding and the like. The mere catching of fish will not satisfy this drive. If hunger were the direct impulse for Utak's fishing trip and catching fish was his idea of how to satisfy that impulse, either Utak would be disappointed after he caught the fish and found he was still hungry, and then would look around for some better idea for satisfying his hunger; or he would change his anticipatory set back to that of eating fish, whereupon catching fish would become a subordinate act and no independence mutation would have occurred.

This conception of the independence mutation is self-contradictory, for it both does require and cannot require the quiescence pattern of the diverted impulse as the terminal goal of the activity. If hunger is the drive, then the hunger must be satisfied by eating the fish. But if the goal of the activity requires eating the fish, then catching the fish is not an end in itself.

When we become aware of its absurdity, we wonder whatever led anybody to propose such a mechanism. Paradoxically, quite possibly the conditioning mutation—the idea that a subordinate act appearing regularly in the context of a governing impulse could become directly associated with the impulse. But the consequences with respect to the goal of the impulse are neglected. The conditioning mutation is postulated on the expectation of the satisfaction of the governing impulse.

Moreover, there seems to be at least one type of independence mutation in which part of the drive comes from the original governing drive. This seems to be what happens in sublimation, for instance. But for this to happen, the governing drive is greatly modified by other inhibiting drives. The net result could be called a modified drive. We shall discuss this form of the mutation later (in chap. 11, §5).

But a pure diverted impulse theory is impossible.


## 3. THE IDEOMOTOR THEORY

The other common theory, which has been aptly called the ideomotor theory, considers the source of energy for the independence of a subordinate act as deposited somehow in the act itself. The idea, on this view, is its own motive—ideomotor. The theory may be diagramed like this:

From:

$$I \quad A^N_1 \qquad\qquad O^G_1 \quad Q^P$$
$$\| \qquad\qquad\qquad\qquad \|$$
$$I_2 \quad A^N_2 \qquad O^G_2 \quad Q^P_2$$

To:

$$A^N_2 \quad O^G_2$$
$$\| \qquad \|$$
$$I_2 \qquad Q^P_2 \qquad\qquad\qquad (2)$$

According to this diagram, we proceed *from* a condition in which a governing drive charges a superordinate anticipatory set that functions as the drive for a subordinate anticipatory set, which, set in action, attains its goal object, which object in turn produces the goal object of the superordinate set and brings quiescence to the governing drive; *to* a condition in which the subordinate anticipatory set goes spontaneously into action on its own initiative and finds quiescence in its own goal object. Literally, on this view, the anticipatory set *is* its own drive. $A^N_2 = I_2$ literally. Then, naturally enough, the goal object of this anticipatory set is the quiescence pattern of the act: $O^G_2 = Q^P_2$.

This seems to be a perfectly straight description of what happens in the change from valuing an activity as a means to valuing it as an end—from fishing as a means of satisfying hunger, where the fishing activity is motivated through a mediating judgment connecting it with eating fish so as to produce the quiescence pattern for hunger, to fishing as an activity for its own sake, self-motivated. What is the mutation from means to end but the change from a mediated action to a self-motivated action?

The difficulty with this description is the failure to distinguish between a drive and an anticipatory set. For all of our data so far indicate that an anticipatory set has a purely cognitive function in an appetition, that it has no energy of its own, but serves to channel the energy of the governing drive to the final quiescence pattern. The evidence consistently shows that when an anticipatory set in a subordinate act fails often enough to prove to an organism that its goal object cannot be expected to produce the superordinate goal object, it ceases to be charged by the drive. All the drive goes out of it, and there is no motive left to act on it. This is the very principle of conditioning. The ideomotor theory, in short, violates the law of extinction connected with the laws of conditioning. The bell for Pavlov's dogs soon ceased to stimulate the saliva flow when meat ceased to appear on the conditioned stimulus.

The ideomotor theory is not self-contradictory like the diverted impulse theory, but it runs counter to one of our best-established laws concerning the motivation of behavior in docile animals.

At the very least, the theory must offer a plausible explanation of why some conditionings suffer the normal extinction when the mediating judgment is severed and why some do not but become independent acts. Why do some acts go on of themselves after they no longer serve their original ends, whereas most acts serving as means suffer extinction when they no longer lead to their ends? This is the problem.

Deeply ingrained habit, often appealed to, will not do. This will account for the need of a longer period of unconditioning. But unless some new drive enters in, a deeply ingrained habit is still motivated by the drive it serves. Most people have a deeply ingrained habit of tying their shoes, but we do not hear of many people tying shoes just for the fun of it. What is the difference between tying shoes and fishing or collecting stamps?

The first man to bring the ideomotor theory of action into prominence was William James. Here are a few of the main passages in which he describes the theory:

> We think the act, and it is done and that is all that introspection tells us of the matter. Dr. Carpenter, who first used, I believe, the name of ideo-motor action, placed it, if I mistake not, among the curiosities of our mental life. The truth is that it is no curiosity, but simply the normal process stripped of disguise. Whilst talking I become conscious of a pin on the floor, or of some dust on my sleeve. Without interrupting the conversation I brush away the dust or pick up the pin . . . The mere perception of the object and the fleeting notion of the act seem of themselves to bring the latter about. Similarly, I sit at table after dinner and find myself from time to time taking nuts or raisins out of the dish and eating them. My dinner properly is over, and in the heat of conversation I am hardly aware of what I do, but the perception of the fruit and the fleeting notion that I may eat it seem fatally to bring the act about. . . .
>
> We know what it is to get out of bed on a frosty morning in a room without a fire, and how the very vital principle within us protests against the ordeal. Probably most persons have lain on certain mornings for an hour at a time unable to brace themselves to the resolve. We think how late we shall be, how the duties of the day will suffer; we say, "I must get up, this is ignominious," etc.; but still the warm couch feels too delicious, the cold outside too cruel, and resolution faints away and postpones itself again and again just as it seemed on the verge of bursting the resistance and passing over into the decisive act. Now how do we *ever* get up under such circumstances? If I may generalize from my own

experience, we more often than not get up without any struggle or decision at all. We suddenly find that we *have* got up. A fortunate lapse of consciousness occurs; we forget both the warmth and the cold; we fall into some revery connected with the day's life, in the course of which the idea flashes across us, "Hollo! I must lie here no longer"—an idea which at that lucky instance awakens no contradictory or paralyzing suggestions, and consequently produces immediately its appropriate motor effects. It was our acute consciousness of both the warmth and the cold during the period of struggle, which paralyzed our activity then and kept our idea of rising in the condition of *wish* and not of *will*. The moment these inhibitory ideas ceased, the original idea exerted its effects.

This case seems to me to contain in miniature form the data for an entire psychology of volition. It was in fact through meditating on the phenomenon in my own person that I first became convinced of the truth of the doctrine which these pages present, and which I need here illustrate by no farther examples. The reason why that doctrine is not a self-evident truth is that we have so many ideas which *do not* result in action. But it will be seen that in every such case, without exception, that is because other ideas simultaneously present rob them of their impulsive power. But even here, and when a movement is inhibited from *completely* taking place by contrary ideas, it will *incipiently* take place.[2]

Perry carries on the same view, applying it specifically to the sequence of subordinate acts in an appetition.

In the type of mutation to which we now turn, we suppose an activity to be induced by an interest, and then as a consequence of its interested exercise to become an interest on its own account. . . . A certain response occurs because it promises an ulterior response in which a governing propensity is consummated . . . Accepting this analysis, it would be improper to speak of the subordinate response as an interest, or of its object as an end, unless it functioned itself as a governing propensity selecting anterior subordinate responses in their turn. The fact is, however, that subordinate responses *tend* to *become* governing propensities, and means to become ends.[3] . . .

Subordinate propensities, organized under the stress of a dominant propensity, tend to persist, or to become permanent dispositions, ingrained in the higher neural centres. The very tentative character which they assume implies that the higher centres are engaged, and their pattern persists as a mode of activity that may in the future come into control of the organism. In propor-

tion as they engross the subject the ulterior control which gave
rise to them tends to be relaxed and they acquire a relative independence . . . One may come to acquire the special interests of
the money-maker or the locksmith as *interests in themselves,* which
require no ulterior motivation from love or hunger.[4]

What can we gather from such statements? The intention is
clear enough. For James every idea is a dynamo and carries its
own motivation with it. For Perry something similar seems to
be implied. At least as regards the independence mutation, the
view seems to be that since an anticipatory set in a subordinate
act is tentative in character and therefore cognitive in function,
this "implies that the higher centres are engaged, and their
pattern persists *as a mode of activity* that may in the future come
into control of the organism." The cognitive pattern becomes a
mode of activity; the idea becomes its own drive, ideomotor.
There is some suggestion that, even in the state of dependence
upon the superordinate governing propensity, the subordinate
set had acquired a relative independence, which *tends* to become
complete. It is as if Perry conceived of an anticipatory set as
intrinsically ideomotor from the moment it arose, an 'interest'
in its own right even while in a state of dependency, and as if
the connection with the superordinate act were rather external
in nature and not necessary for its drive. This would be a thoroughly ideomotor conception. Perry, as we shall see in detail
when we come to analyze his treatment of the appetitive goal,
is ambivalent on this subject. But there is no question that his
description of the independence mutation implies an ideomotor
conception of a subordinate act that has acquired independence
as an 'interest on its own account.'

Do James and Perry adduce any compelling evidences for
this view? None that can stand up against the overwhelming
evidences for the law of extinction derived from the conditioning
experiments. The law of primacy and the evidences for latent
learning show that a pattern of behavior once learned does indeed persist in the higher centers as a *potential* anticipatory set.
After you have learned to tie your shoestrings, that anticipatory
set is ready for use at any time when there is a drive that calls
for that channeling of its energy. It is ready even after you have

been wearing buckled shoes for many months. But such a pattern of response does not persist 'as a mode of activity,' in Perry's words. It has to acquire a superadded drive from somewhere else before such a statement can be true.

Perry does have a point when he asserts that "in proportion as they [the subordinate acts] engross the subject the ulterior control which gave rise to them tends to be relaxed and they acquire a relative independence." This happens whenever a strong blockage comes in the way of a subordinate goal. In such a situation a person often becomes so absorbed in overcoming the obstacle that he nearly forgets his reason for wanting to attain the goal in the first place. I start chopping up a block of wood for my fireplace. The block is exceptionally tough, and soon I find I am intent on breaking up that block no matter what. The act has acquired a relative independence, and may even become for a few minutes 'an interest on its own account.' This sort of thing is common enough and occurs in much wider contexts. We shall want to keep it in mind, for it promises to be highly pertinent to our problem. But clearly what has happened is the infusion into the act of a new drive (an 'injective,' as we shall later call it) not to be beaten by that block of wood. The relative independence of the act of chopping up the block of wood is far from ideomotor. Similarly with the love of chopping for its own sake, which many men possess.

Turning to James's examples, we find on scrutiny that they are not so convincing as they superficially seem. Brushing dust from his sleeve and picking a pin off the floor are rather obviously well-motivated acts beyond the mere sight of the objects. All that his description shows is that he was not conscious of his own drives for these acts at the moment. A gardener showing a friend his flowers pulls out a weed as he is talking. He may scarcely realize that he has done so. Would anyone assume that the sight of the weed motivated the act rather than an aversion to weeds in his garden stimulated by the sight?

Besides, there is plenty of evidence that what we see and even think is motivated by the drives in ascendancy at the time. The question is not that the sight of the dust on his sleeve induced him to brush it off, but what induced him to notice the dust at all. Was he perhaps expecting a caller? Or was he on his way to class?

The illustration of getting out of bed on a cold morning is a classic. No one would question the veracity of the description. But James's notion that it yields any evidence for his ideomotor theory is mistaken. What keeps him in bed is not the mere *idea* of warmth in bed and of cold outside but the actual warmth of the bed and its consummatory comfort and an actual aversion (fear, dislike) charging the idea of the cold outside. Those were strong drives to hold him in bed. Then he runs over the various duties that should induce him to get up. But these duties were not mere ideas either. Presumably they were his college lectures and the means by which he made his living. All the drives that motivated his profession were charging those ideas. Taking these drives into consideration, we can simply accept on his own authority James's very perceptive description of how he did happen to get up that morning:

> A fortunate lapse of consciousness occurs; we forget both the warmth and the cold; we fall into some revery connected with the day's life, in the course of which the idea flashes across us, "Hollo! I must lie here no longer"—an idea which at that lucky instant awakens no contradictory or paralyzing suggestions, and consequently produces immediately its appropriate motor effects.

Exactly. His "revery connected with the day's life" with all the strong drives charging it and momentarily inhibiting the intensity of his desire for warmth and his aversion for cold, and also, no doubt, intensifying the charges on the day's anticipated goals, charged strongly the mediating judgment "I must lie here no longer," and the act followed.

There is no difference in principle between this act and the geologist's starting up the slope of the ridge in search of water. It was not the idea of climbing the ridge that motivated the geologist but the thirst drive channeled down to that particular mediating judgment. Nor was it just the idea of getting out of bed that motivated James's act but the drives of his profession channeled down to that particular mediating judgment which he reports.

There is just this important truth in the ideomotor theory—a truth that needed emphatic expression when James was writing in the midst of a rationalistic atmosphere of thought—namely, that every idea has a motor element connected with it. There is more and more evidence that no thinking or perceiving goes on except as it receives energy from some accompanying drive. If this were all that James meant—and sometimes it seems to be—there would be no issue. But so far as he implied that an idea was automatically the source of a drive, that an idea was literally self-motivating, he started a theory which has become widespread and influential and is contrary to some of the best-established evidence regarding purposive motivation.

Two curious consequences of the ideomotor theory literally interpreted have never been pressed as they should be. The first is the great multitude of drives that would be competing for action if the theory could be maintained. If every idea is its own dynamo, then every perceptible object stimulating the eyes and the ears and the other senses, and all associated images and concepts should be competing for action simultaneously, all the time. According to some of James's statements, apparently all that keeps an idea from starting action in its behalf is other inhibiting ideas. This would mean that most of these hundreds of self-driven ideas were in a state of suppressed action held down by the few that got out. That would seem to imply a state of high (even neurotic) tension in any man's normal waking hours. It would also seem to blur the useful and now rather well-evidenced distinction between suppressed and latent ideas. Of course, on our view so far developed, what selects the object of perception and the ideas before the mind is primarily the governing drive in action. We just do not perceive or think of anything we are not interested in, anything that is not charged by a governing drive.

The second damaging consequence of the ideomotor theory is that it makes no provision for the waxing and waning of the degree of interest in a derived act. Variations in the intensity of basic drives like hunger and thirst are easily understood in terms of their underlying physiological conditions. These presuppose impulse patterns, such as stomach contractions and dehydration of the organism, distinct from the anticipatory sets charged by them. If there are no distinct impulse patterns, it would follow that there could be no variation in charge upon an anticipatory set. There could be variations in general tone, caused by fatigue or sickness, which affect the whole organism, but no specific variations like the fluctuations of hunger and thirst. Hence the intensity of a derived drive like fishing or running a car or chopping wood or cooking should be constant. They should act like the knee-jerk reflex, which is a self-driven mechanism. When released they should go off with the specific constant intensity of their self-stored energy. At the very least, the intensity of the reaction should vary only with that of the stimulus. A big chunk of wood might stimulate a stronger desire to chop than a small one! But that does not seem to be borne out by the facts. The desires for fishing and chopping and cooking and shopping fluctuate a good deal. Not so much as hunger and thirst, but enough to suggest that the drives for these patterns of action are distinct from their anticipatory sets. A craving for fishing or hunting or sailing may come over a man much like sex. It seems unlikely that these desires are ideomotor—not denying, however, that the sight of fishing tackle in a store window or of a sail on the bay may set off the craving.

The latest variation in the ideomotor theme is Allport's concept of *functional autonomy*. It is just possible that Allport does not intend to commit himself to an ideomotor theory by this term, but only wishes to have a name for the independence mutation and to stress its independence. But an overemphasis on the independence of derived drives without due attention to their mode of derivation from basic drives, and particularly the distinction between their impulse patterns and their anticipatory sets for goal objects, can have all the effect of an ideomotor theory. For the effect of an ideomotor theory is to identify the terminal goal of a purposive act with the goal object of its anticipatory set. It leaves out the impulse and its satisfaction or quiescence, and tries to telescope these into the anticipatory set—goal object pair. The result is extremely distortive of human action, and leads to false and possibly dangerous ethical conclusions.

What may be the more nearly true descriptions of the independence mutations we are not prepared to attempt until later. But this discussion has exhibited the two commonest and, as it happens, diametrically opposed conceptions, neither of which on scrutiny is at all acceptable. The one would have all derived activity directly motivated by the original basic impulses diverted to new ends. The other would somehow cut loose entirely from basic impulses; derived activity would be motivated by the mere thought of it. The one ties derived acts so closely to their original impulses that their derivativeness becomes impossible to make out. The other cuts off the derived acts so completely from the basic sources of motivation that it becomes impossible to conceive how they can be motivated at all. The truth evidently lies somewhere between. In chapter 11 we shall be in a position to present a more adequate solution.

# 8

# Superordinate Acts and the Problem of Instincts

## 1. WHY PURPOSIVE BEHAVIOR PRESUPPOSES INSTINCTS

In chapters 6 and 7 we have been following down the hierarchy of subordinate acts in appetitive behavior, tracing the course of the dynamics of their drives. In this chapter we shall look in the opposite direction and follow up the hierarchy of superordinate acts to their ultimate dynamic sources in the instincts. For the tenor of our analysis so far indicates that the ultimate source of all appetitive activity is to be found in innate impulse patterns, or instincts. If we take any purposive act and follow it back through its superordinate acts, we reach either an instinct or a derived independent act. If we follow the latter back through its origin as a subordinate act to the superordinate acts on which it once depended, again we come upon an instinct. The whole structure of an organism's purposive activity ultimately rests upon its instincts.

With this assurance we might think that the instincts of an organism would be easily discernible and well defined. Exactly the opposite is the case. There are few more controversial subjects in psychology than that of instincts, and especially human instincts. A few decades ago it was fashionable to affirm that there were none.

The issue divides into three main schools: the reflex school, the single impulse school, and the multiple impulse school. The last of these is the one which the evidence so far has led us to assume. It would be accepted without question if there were agreement on what constitutes an instinct. But since agreement is lacking, we must seek our own conclusion from the evidence available.

## 2. THE REFLEX THEORY OF MOTIVATION

In an earlier passage (chap. 3, §4) we ventured to define instinct as either a chain reflex or an innate drive. In regard to the chain reflex there would be no issue. The reflex school,[1] which ordinarily denies instincts, simply would not call a chain reflex technically an instinct. They would merely call it a chain reflex. But they would have to deny that there were innate drives.

Of course, there is a sense in which the reflex school is making a very important point. Just as the cell is the anatomical unit for describing in detail any part of an organism's body, so the reflex is the physiological unit for describing in detail any act of an organism's behavior. All purposive behavior as well as all the rest of an animal's behavior can be physiologically analyzed, at least in theory, into sets of reflexes. An instinctive drive theory does not deny that. The issue arises at the next level. The reflex school seems to deny that there is anything between a chain reflex structure and the conditioning of innately unconnected reflexes. In opposition, the instinct school affirms that docile animals including man are endowed with a number of innately connected sets of reflexes or drives, not so tightly connected from start to finish as a chain reflex sequence, nor yet so loose and unconnected as the reflex school's conception of a mere repertory of innately isolated reflexes would require.

The evidence against the reflex school seems to be very great and steadily increasing. The likelihood that the characteristic impulse patterns of hunger, thirst, and sex and their complementary quiescence patterns are results of learning through conditioning is becoming weaker the more these are studied. Even the notion of prenatal conditioning will not suffice. A docile organism seems to be born with certain sets of reflexes already disposed to go into systematic action as a group. And that is precisely an innate impulse pattern. If the reflex school can accept the chain reflex as consistent with their theory, it is difficult to see any good reason why they should not accept the conception of a broken-down chain reflex, which is just the sort of thing an innate appetitive drive and quiescence pattern appears to be.

The reflex school seems to have been chiefly anxious in its denials to reject romantic ideas about instincts which made them out to be a kind of semimiraculous teleology in nature. But the conception of innate drives described here has nothing inconsistent with physiological conceptions of causal action. It is even possible that most exponents of the reflex school would not raise any serious objections to the conception of innate drives as we have described them.

## 3. The Single Drive versus the Multiple Drive Theory of Motivation

The issue between the single drive and the multiple drive theory of motivation may well turn out to be the more serious one. We have been assuming so far a multiple drive theory—the theory that docile animals are endowed with a number of distinct drives having functionally independent sources of energy which go into action in response to stimuli specific for each drive.

As opposed to this view, the single drive theory assumes that there is one source of energy that can be channeled in different directions according to the needs of the organism. The principal evidence for the latter theory is the capacity of a single urgent drive to draw off apparently all the energy of the organism in its behalf during an emergency. There is also evidence of a large amount of interconnectedness among drives, especially in human behavior. On the single drive theory, what we have been calling separate drives would be regarded as diverse channels through which the energy from the single dynamic source could flow according to the needs of the organism.

How serious is the discrepancy between the two views? What

difference does it make whether you adopt a single drive or a multiple drive theory? At first sight it may not appear to make much difference. If an organism is both hungry and thirsty, what is the difference between thinking of these as two sources of energy or as two channels drawing on one common source of energy? Both views agree that behavior channeled through the thirst pattern is different from that channeled through the hunger pattern. Both agree on the innate character of the patterns and the innate source of the energy.

Before proceeding further, it should be pointed out that there is a sense in which everybody must agree that only one sort of energy is available to motivate human or animal action—the energy made available to the organism through its metabolic processes as the physiologist describes these. In times of sickness or lack of nourishment the quantity of energy available to the organism is plainly much reduced. The available energy fluctuates as a whole. And this energy is a single sort of energy whether it is all available to the various channels indiscriminately, according to the single drive theory, or is parceled out in some determinate manner, according to the multiple drive theory.

The issue between the two theories thus seems to be not so much over the source of the energy as over its mobility. On a single drive theory, there should be an indefinite amount of substitutability of one channel for another in reducing the tension of the drive. On a multiple drive theory, there should be no substitutability at all for basic drives. Here is a matter for crucial experiment. And on this issue the multiple drive theory appears to be the verifiable one. But it is important to be as precise as we can about what is verified.

The crucial evidence is that the basic drives can attain quiescence only in terms of their own quiescence patterns. Thirst cannot be satisfied by the quiescence pattern of hunger, nor vice versa. Eating crackers will not quench thirst, and drinking water will not permanently stop the pangs of hunger. Nor is eating or drinking a substitute for the need of sleep, nor any of these for the need of elimination. Sex seems to permit a considerable degree of substitution, but this is a drive that apparently matures through a series of stages, and whether to regard some of the earlier modes of sex satisfaction as substitutes for the complete sexual quiescence pattern or as actual modes of partial satisfaction is a matter requiring careful interpretation. But in general the evidence is clear that the quiescence pattern of one basic drive cannot be substituted for that of another. This is the crucial evidence in favor of the multiple drive theory.

For, on a single drive theory, there would presumably be just one quiescence pattern, and the problem of living would consist merely in finding the most suitable means of channeling activity for the maximum satisfaction of this one terminal goal. To appreciate the form of behavior on such a theory, we have only to observe the behavior of a man when a single drive takes complete and extended control of all his actions. Our illustration of the thirsty geologist in the desert is a good example. The striking characteristic of this sequence of behavior is that, apart from the terminal consummatory act of quenching the thirst, every act is entirely instrumental and substitutable. So long as an act is only a means, some other act can always be found as an alternative means. If the elevation just in front of the geologist is inaccessible, perhaps another elevation can be found. If he cannot find a green patch, perhaps a dark sheen on rocks in a gully will show where water is dripping. If all else fails, perhaps a signal fire in the night will attract men to his assistance. Even water itself may not ultimately be necessary. Possibly he could live long enough on the juices of cactus to get back to camp. But the one thing for which there is no substitution is the quiescence of the thirst itself. According to the single drive theory, there would be only one thing in life for which no substitution could be made, and that would be the quiescence of that one dominant drive.

Obviously, this is not the pattern of human or animal behavior. As soon as the geologist's thirst was satisfied, he would surely discover that he was hungry, and in due time he would have a desire for sleep, and all the other basic organic drives would come up in their turn. Many of these must have their terminal satisfactions or the organism perishes; others are not so urgent, though failure to satisfy them fully can have disruptive consequences.

All this seems so obvious that we now begin to wonder what a writer could have in mind for a single drive theory. The most common single drive theory today is the libido theory, though not all who employ the concept of the libido commit themselves to a single drive. The plausibility of the libido as the source of all the energy and all the goals of human activity seems to depend on a writer's being somewhat vague in describing its nature. Conceived as the generalized sex activity, it is one drive among others. Even if it is shown that sex in its various manifestations is the dominating drive in human living and shapes the pattern of a man's whole life, still we do not have a single drive theory but a multiple drive theory with the thesis that one drive is prepotent over the others. Hunger and thirst still require their terminal satisfactions. The consummatory quiescence of a drive which can be utilized as a means to the quiescence of another drive does not cease to be the consummation it was for the original drive. The geologist's satisfaction of his thirst when attained was as terminal for that drive as if it were not also a condition for the consummation of the research drive and all the other potential drives of his organism.

In summary, the plausibility of the single drive theory seems to depend on just two things: a vagueness in the nature and manner of functioning of a drive, and the evidence for a high degree of mobility of energy in the organism for the service of the various drives.

In regard to the first, we have just seen that one basic drive cannot in fact function for another. Even derived drives cannot function for one another, though they can sometimes be extinguished. The necessity of each drive to attain its specific kind of quiescence is the crucial argument against the single drive theory. Superficially, there may seem to be a good deal of substitution of one drive for another, but only subordinate and instrumental acts serving superordinate goals are fully substitutable. There is no substitution of the terminal quiescence pattern of one basic drive by another, though the satisfaction of one drive is often a condition for the satisfaction of others. Only vagueness of description can conceal this crucial fact, which definitely establishes the tenability of the multiple drive theory as against the single drive theory.

However, this fact does not dispose of the positive evidence stressed by the single drive theory regarding the mobility of the total energy available for the needs of the various drives. In stressing this evidence, the exponents of the single drive theory have performed a definite service for the general theory of motivation. Whatever the form a multiple drive theory takes, it must account for the high degree of mobility of energy in action.

This fact cuts off one of the commonest conceptions of the multiple drive theory, which conceives the various drives as so many separate reservoirs of power or potential charge. Each drive, on this view, has not only its specific pattern of action but also its private reservoir of power. Some drives have larger reservoirs than others. In a system of subordinate acts, the power from the main reservoir is conceived as channeled down from subordinate act to subordinate act till overt action can take place. Upon quiescence, the power from that drive is drained and has to accumulate again through the organic processes of the body. It is assumed that the power from the private reservoir of one drive is not ordinarily available to another drive. The power of the thirst drive is not channeled into the hunger drive. The two could, however, supplement each other through a subordinate act which served them both. Two weak drives meeting a common obstacle might together motivate a subordinate act to overcome the obstacle where neither alone would suffice. But the power in the private reservoir of one drive would not literally flow into the reservoir of the other drive. In short, on this conception, not only is the quiescence pattern of one drive not substitutable for that of another, but neither is the energy of one drive transferable to that of another.

This last idea appears to be contrary to the evidence, and this is the evidence stressed by the single drive theory. Apparently almost any drive, and certainly all, or nearly all, the basic drives in emergency, can drain off singly the total available energy of an organism. In the illustration of the thirsty geologist in the desert, this was evidently the fact. All other interests were set aside and were emptied of power in the one absorbing interest of finding the means of satisfying his thirst. A tenable multiple drive theory must be modeled to permit transferability of the organism's energy even while it insists on the nonsubstitutability of the quiescence patterns of the several drives.

Some writers have substituted a sort of atmospheric analogy for this private reservoir metaphor. The organism is conceived as a volume susceptible to various pressures, which produce areas of disequilibrium. Wherever there is an area of disequilibrium, the organism goes into action according to the structure existing in that area. These areas of disequilibrium would be something like low-pressure areas in the earth's atmosphere generating winds and storms. The nature of the activity depends on the amount of the pressure and the contours of the land over which it occurs.[2]

This analogy does account for the distribution of the organism's energy at various points according to the needs of the situation, and for the possibility of all the energy being drawn to one area if there is a high degree of disequilibrium at that spot. And the idea of an energy disequilibrium as the condition for action is a useful one to keep in mind. But the analogy underemphasizes the structural firmness and articulation of purposive behavior. It mirrors the behavior of an amoeba rather than that of a vertebrate animal. A purposive structure, such as the appetitions we have been studying, admits of a large amount of adjustment and mobility of adaptation, but it is firm in its impulse pattern and its conditions of quiescence and the structure of its hierarchy of subordinate acts. This firmness of structure is projected into the derived drives also, as we shall see later. A personality is a stratification of such structures. The psychiatric problems of neurotic conflicts are tacit testimony to the rigidity of some of these structures when suitable adjustments have not been made. The atmospheric pressure analogy, likening human activity to disequilibrium states in a viscous medium, may actually disintegrate into a kind of single drive theory with the typical inadequacies of that hypothesis.

A closer analogy—since we are rather obligated to find one in order to hold off more distortive metaphors—is that of credit within the structure of a bank. Each drive is like a depositor who has credit on the total capital of the bank. There are larger and smaller credits applicable to each drive. These are not private reservoirs of potential power. All the power available is in the common pool, the capital of the bank. The total amount of this common capital fluctuates partly as a result of the drafts upon it by depositors, and partly as a result of the management of the bank. But there is a normal limit on the drafts intrinsically available to each depositor depending on the character of the depositor. Hunger can draw on a great deal of capital if it has not drawn for some time. But if it has drawn off all that it needs, it is incapable of drawing off any more till its needs accumulate. An after-dinner appetite for salted nuts (noted earlier in a quotation from James), as distinguished from hunger based on stomach contractions, can never acquire the huge credit that intense hunger can. It has only an after-dinner intensity as a drive, and so only an after-dinner credit on capital of the common energy of the organism.

This analogy accounts for the separateness of the drives, and for their intrinsic potential intensities or charge, without compartmenting the energy into isolated reservoirs, which is contrary to the evidence.

If we may elaborate the analogy a bit further to include the concept of injectives, which we shall soon encounter, we may add that among the depositors are certain directors of the bank, who have unlimited credit. Sometimes, when the community of depositors is drawing rather conservatively on the total capital and there is a surplus of energy in the system, the directors may spontaneously draw on their credit just for the fun of it. But usually they watch carefully over the welfare of the whole community, and if any one of the depositors has not enough personal credit to satisfy his requirements, and the need is great, the directors will inject some of their own credit into his account; if the need is an emergency, possibly involving the very existence and solvency of the whole bank, they will inject the total energy of the system into this one account. These injective credits are normally held in reserve, and are used only when obstacles come in the way of other drives whose normal credits appear insufficient to attain their ends under the circumstances.

This energy bank is clearly a beneficent and not a profit-making institution. It is conducted for the good of all and for the survival of the whole, in the manner of a consumers' coöperative. But we must not embroider the metaphor too intricately or it will begin to disintegrate.

Nevertheless, it may help to vivify our more literal descriptions of the structure of purposive motivation. According to the evidence we possess, a multiple drive theory is the only hypothesis conformable with the facts. But it is only the patterns of these drives that are unsubstitutable and their liens on the energy available to the organism. The energy itself is highly mobile, and is distributed according to the demands of drives called into action.

Finally, the ultimate determination of these demands is often the result of deliberate human decision. This is where the value element particularly enters into the picture. This is why it is necessary for us to be as clear as possible about the nature and structure of human motivation.

## 4. THE INSTINCTIVE DRIVES

So, with an increased assurance of the tenability of the multiple drive theory, we are free to look into the question of what the instinctive drives may be. This proves to be a very difficult question. Especially in human behavior, the origins are so covered over with cultural layers of derived drives, many of them acquired early in infancy, that it is hard to disentangle what is innate from what is acquired.

However, we now have the advantage of knowing fairly precisely what we are looking for. The recent work in animal psychology can be called to our assistance, since instinctive behavior is more clearly discernible there than in human action, and it is fairly safe to infer that man has about the same types of instincts as are discovered in animals that are biologically similar to man and exhibit similar purposive behavior.

Turning again to Tolman's writings for information to build on, we discover in his *Purposive Behavior in Animals and Men* a carefully considered list of first-order drives. Ten years later, in *Drives toward War,* he lists the basic drives again and introduces a number of revisions. These revisions are mute testimony to the fluidity of the subject, and of the difficulty of spotting and classifying the basic drives. Here is his second list:

A. *Appetites*
   Hunger drive
   Thirst drive
   Sex drive
   Maternal (suckling of young) drive
   Nurturance (giving aid and protection) drive
   Infantile dependence drive
   Nest-building and nest-using drive
   General activity drive
   General exploratory drive
   Rest or sleep drive
   Elimination drives (urination and defecation in specific types
      of locale)
   Play and aesthetic drives
B. *Aversions*
   Fright (injury avoidance)
   Aggression (obstruction avoidance)
   Gregariousness (isolation avoidance)

This list must strike anyone not conversant with recent animal studies as peculiarly haphazard. It seems more like a collection of chance discoveries than a systematic survey. Is this really what the foundations of purposive values look like? The list is, in fact, a list of the motivations which experimenters in animal behavior have empirically discovered they could rely upon in their experiments. In introducing it Tolman says, "The first and most basic needs of the human being are those which come from his biological drives. Man shares these drives with the lower animals. In fact, most of our precise knowledge concerning such drives comes from experiments on rats, monkeys, and chimpanzees." [3] The merit of the list is its simple empiricism. It is the catalogue of the innate drives as these have appeared to date in the work of animal psychologists. It is not final, but is open to revision, as Tolman himself has already shown. For all these reasons it is a good list to start from.

## 5. EXAMINATION OF TOLMAN'S PROPOSED APPETITIVE DRIVES

As we examine the list carefully, we notice that the appetitive drives are by no means all of a kind. They roughly divide into three groups: cyclical drives (hunger, thirst, sex, nest building, maternal suckling, rest, elimination), noncyclical drives (nurturance, infantile dependence, general activity, general exploratory), and consummatory activities or gratuitous satisfactions (play and aesthetic drives).

By 'cyclical' is meant the periodic emergence and gathering intensity of a drive, due to metabolic processes, continuing till satisfaction is attained in the consummatory act or quiescence pattern, after which the drive subsides until the organic need emerges again. The cycles are clearly described in Richter's rat experiment. It is the hunger cycle he is particularly observing here. But the rest and sleep drive cycle is also well exemplified. It is characteristic of the cyclical drives that normally they are internally stimulated. The geologist became aware of his thirst through the intensity of his internal need, which overpowered his absorbing interest in the rocks. The drive was not aroused by any external stimulus, though the sight of a brook when he was mildly thirsty would undoubtedly have reminded him of his thirst.

A noncyclical drive is a state of tension or potential tension (a lien on the general energy of the system) which is constantly ready to go into action when an appropriate stimulus presents itself. The nurturance drive is a constant readiness to act for the aid and protection of the young when occasion arises. The same with infantile dependence. A noncyclical drive is not internally stimulated by metabolic changes, as hunger and thirst are, though it may be stimulated by association of ideas. A mother may suddenly remember that she left a hot electric iron within reach of her baby in another room, and that idea will release the nurturance drive. The idea (cognitive set), however, is here acting as a substitute for the actual sight of the iron. A noncyclical drive is normally stimulated by external objects. The instinctive unconditioned stimulus in nurturance, for instance, is presumably the crying and other signs of distress of an infant.

The third group of play and aesthetic drives are (with certain qualifications to be considered later[4]) free quiescence patterns. They are innate readinesses to have consummatory satisfactions without the necessity of seeking them. They are the delights of warmth and coolness, of a pleasant odor, a shimmer of light over the water, ripples in the sand, the murmuring of a brook, that come unsolicited and are not ordinarily based on cyclic metabolic changes. They are more or less constant readinesses for consummatory response, and do not necessarily involve a previous demanding need.

Since they are innate consummatory acts without impulse patterns demanding them for quiescence, another characteristic of gratuitous satisfactions is that they do not call for subordinate acts for their attainment. An intelligent organism, having experienced gratuitous satisfactions, may remember them later and develop anticipations for more of such satisfactions and so begin to seek them with appropriate subordinate acts for attaining them. But there is no innate impulse pattern attached to a gratuitous satisfaction setting up a gap that has to be bridged by a system of subordinate acts. There is nothing in man that innately requires him to seek a delightful odor, as the impulse pattern of thirst requires him to seek the delight of drinking.

Because there is no innate impulse pattern or gap to be bridged for gratuitous satisfactions, their inclusion in the field of appetitions is sometimes questioned. But there is no question of their inclusion among the terminal values of an intelligent organism, nor about their being deliberately sought once they have been experienced. A person enjoying the gratuitous satisfactions of lying on a sea beach within sound of the waves, watching the movement of the water, and feeling the soft air and the gentle warmth of the sun on his skin, may long prefer these satisfactions to the growing demands of a hungry stomach. The gratuitous satisfactions clearly fall within the field of purposive choice. If we did not wish to include them among appetitions, we would have to make a separate heading for them as instinctive sources of value. The descriptive facts about them and their relation to appetitive structure are clear enough. It seems simpler to include them among the varieties of appetitions as the limiting case where the appetitive structure is telescoped into its terminal segment. The justification for this disposition of gratuitous satisfactions will be still more evident after we have examined the forms of aversions and can survey at once all the varieties of purposive structure.

So it is probably well to accept Tolman's inclusion of aesthetic drives among the appetitions, though his reasons and ours may not be quite the same.

This leaves among Tolman's appetitions his 'general activity drive' and 'general exploratory drive.' The latter is, of course, another name for the instinct of curiosity. Without denying that these activities are unlearned, and in that sense instinctive, they are sufficiently different in nature to raise the question whether they are distinct appetitive drives on a level with the others listed. The qualification 'general' makes them suspect. The typical appetitive drives we have so far been considering have all been specific in their impulse patterns and particularly in their quiescence patterns, which determine their conditions of quiescence. What would be the conditions of quiescence for a general activity drive?

We have already at hand a good instance of general activity behavior in Richter's rats. While the hunger drive was weak, the rats exhibited general activity behavior. Would not *any* drive at an incipient stage, before it became strong enough to marshal the energy of the organism toward the achievement of its quiescence pattern, break out in the restless aimlessness of general activity behavior? Is it not often incipient trial-and-error behavior in which, so to speak, the organism is trying to find out what the drive is that is stirring it up? At other times the behavior appears to be a spontaneous overflow of the surplus energy of injectives, to be described presently. In short, general activity seems to be a by-product of other drives rather than a specific drive in itself. It is instinctive but not a specific instinctive drive.

There are, of course, many forms of unlearned activity that are not purposive drives. Trial-and-error activity is the most conspicuous of these. Purposive behavior would be impossible without the innate capacity of an organism to throw trial-and-error activity into gear whenever there is an unbridged gap between an impulse pattern and a goal. Trial and error is an innate technique. But it is not an instinctive drive.

So I should question Tolman's inclusion of general activity as a distinct appetitive drive. Somewhat the same sort of question can be raised about Tolman's general exploratory drive. But recent work by H. F. Harlow and others on this drive has definitely shown it to be a distinct basic source of instinctive motivation. Its presence and strength vary from species to species, but it seems to be especially pronounced in monkeys and men. Harlow's best-known work was carried on with monkeys. It appears that a hungry monkey given a choice of receiving food through one door or of looking through another door at a circulating toy train will make the latter choice. His curiosity drive proves stronger than his hunger drive.

The curiosity drive is clearly a noncyclic appetitive drive. In that respect it falls in the group with the nurturance and infantile dependence drives. Its impulse pattern can be inferred from the range of stimulus conditions which arouse it. Objects and movements in the environment which are familiar do not arouse the drive, nor those so foreign that the organism has no cognitive sets approximating them. The drive seems to be evoked by environmental occurrences which partially conform to the organism's available cognitive sets, but not completely. The drive is satisfied when a cognitive set is found or created which the environmental conditions can adequately fulfill. If the environmental conditions are complex in terms of the organism's available concepts, or constantly changing in unfamiliar ways, the curiosity drive may be stimulated to activity for a very long time. Harlow has verified this fact.

From this description it is evident that the curiosity drive rests on the results acquired by the dynamics of other drives. For it depends on cognitive sets being already formed in order that it be stirred into action; and, for cognitive sets to have been formed, other drives must have instituted them as elements of subordinate acts leading to the satisfaction of their drives. The curiosity is in this respect similar, as we shall see later, to the injective drives of fear and aggression. It is a pattern of tensions aroused by factors connected with other drives, not by direct stimulation from within or from outside the organism.

Since it is conditions among cognitive sets that both arouse and ultimately satisfy the curiosity drive, this is the cognitive drive par excellence. For this reason it is often spoken of as the drive particularly motivating the scientist and the philosopher. This is, however, only partially true. A blockage of any drive can stimulate intellectual activity on the motivation of the drive blocked. And, by the operation of the independence mutation (cf. chap. 11, §§1-5), investigative and competitive intellectual activities begun as subordinate acts instrumental to any of a number of drives may acquire the status of independent derived drives. The basic motivation of a scientist or a philosopher for knowledge for its own sake may be quite different from man to man, may often be complex in its origin, and frequently, as in scientists and philosophers of the genius type in whom we sense a compulsive element, may be based on mechanisms of repression. We must be careful not to confuse the full wide connotation of the popular word 'curiosity' with the curiosity drive. There is nothing neurotically compulsive about the curiosity drive. It is as natural and open to the voluntary integrative control of the personality as, say, the parental nurturance drive. It is an instinctive drive that obviously offers survival advantage to a docile organism and could be expected to be favored in the process of natural selection.

As an appetitive drive it has a distinct impulse pattern in the tensions aroused by incomplete fulfillment of acquired cognitive sets (and possibly of certain sets of innate readinesses which come to function as cognitive sets in a completed purposive structure). It has its distinct consummatory act or quiescence pattern in the satisfaction that comes from final comprehension, or the attainment of cognitive sets which are fulfilled by the environmental situation stimulating the drive. And subordinate acts are performed to fill the gap between the curiosity impulse aroused and its terminal goal of satisfactory comprehension.

The earlier discussion of whether to include among drives certain types of admittedly innate behavior, such as gratuitous satisfactions and general activity, brings out the reason why it is so difficult to make up an unequivocal list of instinctive human drives. The conception of an appetitive structure as a broken-down chain reflex comes to our assistance here. There is no difficulty in distinguishing a clear-cut instinctive structure when it is all tightly linked together in a progressive chain reflex sequence, as with the digger wasp. But when the links have become disconnected and some have disappeared entirely, and new innate mechanisms have sprung up to fill the gaps between the missing links, how do we identify an instinct or decide how many separate instincts there are?

In this study we have a practical criterion that somewhat simplifies the problem. We have found our interest centered in those factors which determine human decisions. The significance of instinctive drives is that they are the basic (or at least the most primitive) determinators of motivation and so of decision making. Now, an innate technique like trial and error, essential though it is for purposive activity, is not a source of motivation or a ground for decision. It does not, therefore, count as an instinctive drive. We have been arguing similarly in regard to general activity. But we do have to include gratuitous satisfactions because these are terminal acts which have an intrinsic positive weight in decisions of preference.

In short, any remnants of a chain reflex scattered along the path of an appetition or any activities which intervene, like trial and error, and function solely as innate techniques for bringing quiescence to a drive, will not be considered as instinctive drives. The reason is that these would not act as either positive or negative motives for action or preference in their own right. But any innate elements which do act as positive or negative motives for action or preference will be considered as instinctive drives. On this ground we concur with Tolman in including gratuitous satisfactions among the basic appetitive drives. But, on the same ground, we question the inclusion of general activity.

What comes out of this discussion is that an appetitive instinct must have the essential structure of an appetitive act: an impulse pattern, a quiescence pattern, and a gap between to be filled with acts instrumental for getting from one to the other. The only exception is that of gratuitous satisfactions which are in the nature of telescoped appetitions, where the quiescence pattern is directly induced without the necessity of a preceding impulse pattern to bring it about.

If we are clear about this descriptive criterion, it is immediately possible to reject a variety of suggested human and animal instincts, of which the most persistent is probably the so-called 'instinct' of self-preservation. Obviously, on the evidence of our description this is not a basic drive. If it were, it would be an appetition, something the organism positively wants. But we do not find it among Tolman's experimentally observed drives. And rightly so. There is no such drive to be observed. There is no specific impulse pattern for it, no specific consummatory act or quiescence pattern. As soon as we are asked to show these structural traits of an appetitive instinct for the proposed instinct of self-preservation—something corresponding to the impulse pattern of hunger and its quiescence pattern of eating and digesting food—we begin to have an inkling that something is wrong with the idea of an 'instinct' of self-preservation. This concept does not conform to the descriptions of observed appetitive instincts.

Nevertheless, the concept does refer to something highly significant. It refers to the fact that the whole repertory of instinctive drives and techniques is so selected as to tend to further the survival of the organism and its species. It refers to a tendency for survival to be found in the repertory of actions characteristic of organisms of surviving species. If this were not so, obviously these organisms would not be present to exhibit the tendency. The survival factor is, we shall surely discover, an important one for certain phases of value theory. The exponents of evolutionary ethics have persistently thought so. And we shall consider its bearing later.

The bearing of the factor is misplaced, however, if it is lodged as a specific instinct among the basic appetitive drives of an organism. There is no such instinct. But the totality of an animal's instincts does exhibit a tendency toward the self-preservation of the animal. This is an evolutionary biological tendency, however, for the preservation of the species, not an individual motivation for specific behavior. Every time an animal eats or drinks it automatically acts for its self-preservation and exhibits that much of the result of the survival principle, but it is not motivated by an impulse pattern or even an anticipatory set for self-preservation. Only self-conscious man, and he only occasionally, develops anticipations of the preservation of his life or that of his group, and makes deliberate choices to that end. This is highly derived intelligent activity, however. It is far from instinctive.

For similar reasons we can easily reject proposals for basic instincts of self-interest or altruism.[5] Many of the instincts have either altruistic or self-centered effects, but these characteristics do not constitute specific drives. The first thing to ask about a proposed appetitive instinct is what specifically are its impulse and quiescence patterns. If these cannot be indicated, the proposed instinct is suspect.

Tolman's list with the emendations proposed is not final, but at least we see what sort of thing an instinctive appetition is. From the discussion it is plain that the evidence for a number of distinct innate drives as the primitive sources of purposive behavior and of the values embedded there—the evidence, in short, for some form of multiple drive theory—is pretty well established.

So far we have examined Tolman's list of appetitive drives only. Now let us look at his aversions.

## 6. Examination of Tolman's Proposed Aversive Drives: Discovery of Injectives

Though we have not yet studied the structure of an aversion, Tolman's little list of basic aversions calls for a preliminary examination because of the very strangeness of it. After the long list of basic appetites, only three basic aversions are suggested.

And these three are not coördinate. In fact, it is questionable that any of them are, strictly speaking, aversions. But in examining them we may come upon something profitable and unexpected.

Let us look at gregariousness first. Tolman describes it as 'isolation avoidance,' exemplified by the South African ox, which shows no affection for, and scarcely notices the existence of, his fellows while among them, but displays great distress when separated from them, and then hastens to bury himself in their midst. Does not this seem like a kind of fright? Why pick out this one instance of fright to put on a par with fright and aggression? And if this attention is given to gregariousness, why not a basic instinct of loud-sound avoidance, and falling-from-height avoidance, which are at least as well-evidenced aversions as isolation avoidance? Something is odd about this list. Suppose, then, we do the obvious thing and tentatively lump gregariousness under fright.

We are now left with the other two aversions, fright and aggression. It seems strange to list these as aversions parallel to the appetitions. For one thing, they are not normally autonomous. This is clear from Tolman's description of aggression as 'obstruction avoidance.' Obstruction to what? Naturally, to the attainment of some goal already in action.

Our first thought with regard to aggression is, therefore, that it is not an instinct at all, but, like the general activity behavior, a readiness to act in a certain way on the basis of another drive. But there is this very important difference between aggressive behavior and general activity behavior: there is no evidence that the latter has any lien on energy of its own, nor any impulse pattern of its own; whereas aggressive behavior clearly throws into an activity a large amount of energy on its own, and has a specific, easily recognizable impulse pattern. We recall that the Eskimo Utak became furious when the anthropologist Poncins began walking about the fishing hole. Utak's fury at Poncins' interruption had a distinctive 'fury' pattern which Poncins quickly recognized as quite different from Utak's behavior in the face of an obstruction met purely on the basis of the fishing drive. Compare Utak's behavior toward Poncins in this instance with his reaction to the wind, which also interfered with his fishing and motivated his subordinate act of building up a wind barrier. The latter subordinate act derived its energy solely from the fishing drive, but the subordinate act directed at Poncins contained an accretion of energy derived from a very different source. Aggression definitely has an impulse pattern of its own, and therefore its own source of energy and its own quiescence pattern. When Poncins obediently stood still, Utak's fury subsided. Aggression is definitely an instinct having its own drive and its full complement of impulse pattern, innate readinesses, conditions of quiescence, and quiescence pattern. It accordingly develops its own anticipatory set, and specific subordinate acts. What is peculiar about it is that it normally enters appetitive behavior as a subordinate act within the course of the activity of some other drive. For its usual stimulus situation is, as Tolman says, an obstruction. Its function is like that of reserves in an army to back up any division at the front that needs more power. It can throw in the whole power of the organism if necessary. It has a lien on the total energy available in the system. Its function is to inject energy into any drive that needs it over and above the latter's normal powers. Therefore, I propose to call aggression an *injective*.

An injective is an instinct in conformity with our definition. It is an innate drive. But it is not an instinctive appetition, since its goal is always (except in the special condition when it acts independently) a subordinate goal within some other purposive activity. Neither is an injective an aversion, for the same reason. It functions in an instrumental role, backing up another impulse. Nevertheless, wherever it functions, it has an original contribution to make which is in the form of a distinctive innate drive. An injective is a class of instincts all its own, not to be confused with instinctive appetitions or aversions.

Fright is also an injective. It is closely allied with aggression. W. B. Cannon's studies, described in his *Bodily Changes in Pain, Hunger, Fear, and Rage,* show that the impulse pattern for the two is nearly identical. The chief difference is in the innate readinesses, which in these instincts tend to merge with the impulse pattern. The innate readinesses for aggression are of a type to remove an obstruction from the path of a goal-seeking organism, whereas the innate readinesses for fright are of a type to remove an organism from the path or proximity of a noxious obstruction. These are the two possible ways of handling a noxious object or obstruction. Their joint biological function is evident. They are the organism's ultimate means of avoiding injury or death and of carrying on life's functions. Which of the two on any occasion will be thrown into action depends on the situation in relation to the powers of the organism. If the organism believes it is strong enough to overcome the obstruction, or is desperate, aggression normally comes into action; otherwise, fright.

One of the consequences of fright is that by its means appetitions, even powerful instinctive ones, are frequently blocked entirely from their goals. Biologically this is done to save the organism's life, or to prevent it from incurring serious injuries that would outweigh any gains to be derived from attaining the goal. Of course, aggression does not always attain the goal either. But aggressive behavior does not block off a goal from within the organism, whereas fright does precisely that. Fright, accordingly, is the great inhibiting agent in animal behavior.

One of the most serious practical problems in behavior is to determine when fright is appropriate in an emergency and when aggression; and, we may add, when neither is appropriate, if there is no emergency to justify such an expenditure of energy. A large proportion of man's social and personal problems arise not so much from maladjustments among his appetitions as from those due to inappropriate use of his injectives. This is a rather important point to note.

Moralists and social reformers have generally sought to cure social ills by attempting to regulate man's appetitions. In their normal action these are probably in no great need of regulation, but, on the contrary, for the health of the organism, are in need of release. The behavior that needs adjustment and control is that arising from inappropriate use of injectives. If our fears and aggressions were in proper proportion to the actual obstructions in the path of our instinctive appetitions, we might have little need for drastic inhibitions on most of our appetitions. The traditional moral indictment of the passions would be converted into a discrimination between the appetitions and the injectives, and the indictment would then be restricted to badly adjusted injectives.

## 7. INJECTIVES AS SPONTANEOUS DRIVES

Normally, injectives are stimulated by obstructions in the path of other drives. But on occasion, usually when the organism is not seriously engaged otherwise and is in high spirits, an injective will go off spontaneously. Then its role is reversed. Instead of overcoming obstacles for the sake of attaining the goals of other drives, it now seeks out obstacles for the sheer satisfaction of overcoming them. And then the character of its quiescence pattern comes out most clearly. The popular name for it is 'triumph,' and introspectively the satisfaction is the feeling of triumph. For spontaneous fear, as in the shoot-the-shoots, the quiescence pattern is relief.

Sports and play are in large degree motivated by spontaneous injectives. Originally men chased foxes and rabbits to get rid of them because they damaged their property; but later, for the sheer fun of it, and to use up an excess of energy, men sought out foxes and rabbits in a country with plenty of walls and fences to jump horses over so that they could experience the triumph of the chase. On a fine fresh morning, when the sun is out and the air clean, and the body is tingling after a full night's sleep and a good breakfast, the body craves a mountain to climb or a boat to row. If nothing better is at hand, even mowing the lawn may quiet the desire to use up this surplus of energy in some sort of achievement.

'Aggression' is an unfortunate name for the injective when it functions spontaneously. Yet this spontaneous impulse to use up an excess of reserve energy is the same drive and has the same impulse pattern as aggression against obstruction, but free of the quality of hostility due to the blockage of some other drive. The term 'initiative' is more appropriate for this manifestation of an injective, but it does not suit the hostile manifestations. We shall probably need both terms to fit different situations.

Suppose, then, we employ the term 'injective' for the drive in question. Its impulse pattern, described in detail by Cannon, has the function of drawing on the reserve energy of the organism. When stimulated by a blockage which prompts the individual to escape, the injective appears as fear or fright, and employs the innate readinesses appropriate for escape. When stimulated by a blockage which prompts the organism to attack, the injective appears as aggression, and employs the innate readinesses appropriate for destroying or overcoming the source of the blockage. When spontaneously stimulated from sheer excess of energy, it appears as initiative, and generally seeks an outlet by looking for obstacles to overcome. But it may make use of some practical activity already in progress, simply augmenting the energy employed beyond necessity—mowing the lawn when the lawn does not really need it yet, or washing the car, or perhaps even offering to wash a neighbor's car.

Initiative as a spontaneous overflow of energy is quite different from internally stimulated, displaced aggression due to inner blockages. Such aggression seeks an object upon which to vent its suppressed hostility. A bully seeks somebody to torment or fight because he is inhibited from attacking the source of his frustration. Here is a venting of energy internally aroused and seeking an object and an occasion to give it outlet. But it is hostile and malicious in intent, not the carefree exuberance of high spirits. Some degree of pent-up aggression can be mixed, of course, with genuine high spirits. A man may have some pent-up hostilities and a surge of high spirits at the same time; a good boxing match or game of tennis may serve both phases of the injective at once. In a competitive culture, a degree of aggressive hostility is nearly always present in manifestations of initiative. But pure good spirits do occur. And initiative may add itself to other-regarding impulses like sex and maternal love without involving the least element of hostility.

But if the injective may be spontaneous in the way described and if it has a quiescence pattern of its own, felt as relief for fear and triumph for aggression and initiative, why is it not to be regarded as an appetition? When an injective is spontaneously aroused, it has unquestionably the structure of an appetition. If we had to restrict ourselves to just two categories of innate drives, we should probably be compelled to treat injectives as appetitions. The determining reason for this decision would be (as will come out clearly when we have described the structure of aversions) that an injective has a positive terminal goal in the form of a quiescence pattern of relief or triumph. (An aversion does not intrinsically have a positive goal.) And yet the primary function of an injective is not to attain its goal but to rid the organism of blockages in the way of other drives. This is a function of negative intent, and in this respect more characteristic of aversions. In fact, a blockage of a drive is always a source of aversion; so the primary function of an injective is to serve aversions. This is what leads Tolman and others to think of the injectives as aversions.

In order not to be forced to a decision which would distort some feature of an injective whatever choice were made, it seems best to consider it as a separate class of instinctive drives. It partakes of an appetitive drive in having a quiescence pattern and a positive consummatory goal. But it partakes of an aversion in having as its principal biological function the negative one of ridding the organism of blockages in the way of progressive activity.

Moreover, at least introspectively, the quiescence pattern of an injective has a different quality from that of the basic appetitive drives. Satisfying as relief from fear may be, or triumph over an obstacle, it is a thinner kind of consummatory feeling than is characteristic of the typical appetitive drives of hunger, thirst, sex, or the maternal suckling of a child. The sort of satisfaction derived from the successful course of an injective lies halfway between the fullness of sensuous delight to be found in consummations of the typical appetitive drives, and the emptiness of mere riddance of pain characteristic of pure aversions. Perhaps not too much should be made of this introspective point, but it grows in significance when we see what an enormous proportion of civilized appetitive activity attains only the satisfactions of triumph and relief, and how starved of sensuous and emotional delight a highly successful man's life may be. Introspectively, the quiescence patterns of the injectives feel intermediate between the sensuous fullness of the consummation of innate appetitive drives and the emptiness of the terminus of a pure aversion.

Accordingly we shall place the injectives in a separate category.[6]

But now what has happened to Tolman's list of instinctive aversions? We questioned gregariousness and found that fright and aggression are not aversions but injectives. Apparently there are no instinctive aversions. On the basis of Tolman's classification, apparently there are not. The reasons for this paradoxical outcome will appear when we take up the subject of aversions. But we have yet to complete our description of the appetitive structure. There is still the appetitive goal to consider, which will be the topic of chapter 9.

Up to this point, our list of instinctive drives is as follows:

*Appetite drives*

Cyclical
- Hunger
- Thirst
- Sex
- Maternal (suckling of young)
- Nest building, etc.
- Rest and sleep
- Urination
- Defecation

Noncyclical
- Nurturance (giving aid and protection)
- Infantile dependence
- Curiosity
- Gratuitous satisfactions of many kinds

*Injectives*

- Fright (escape from obstacle)
- Aggression (attack on obstacle)
- Initiative (when a spontaneous overflow of surplus energy)

(Added later, in chap. 10, §5, will be:
*Aversive drives*
- Riddance patterns of many kinds)

# 9

# The Goal and the Problem
# of Terminal Value

## 1. GOAL OBJECT AND QUIESCENCE PATTERN

The reader may wonder what more there is to be said about the
goal of an appetition. Our analysis has already described the goal
in some detail as the complement of the drive and the anticipatory set. The goal divides into two parts: the quiescence pattern,
which is the reciprocal of the impulse pattern of the drive and
the actualization of the conditions of quiescence; and the goal
object, which is the object of reference of the anticipatory set.
We have repeatedly diagramed the goal in various contexts as
follows:

Goal

Goal object | Quiescence pattern

What more is there to be said? There really would be nothing
more, were it not for a confusion and a rumbling controversy that
has never quite broken out into the open. It is the controversy
over which of these two factors in the goal of an appetition is
to be taken as the final locus of value for an appetition. Common
speech and Perry tend to place the terminal value of a purpose
on the goal object. Tolman's analysis of the appetitive activity
and ours place the terminal value on the quiescence pattern. This
is an issue of major importance for the theory of purposive value,

and one for which there should be a definite answer. In the
present chapter we shall seek that answer. If, however, the
reader accepts Tolman's view and ours, the rest of this chapter
may be skipped; for it is simply a detailed analysis of the sources
of Perry's confusion.

Let me add that if the reader has accepted the analysis of
appetitive behavior up to this point he may skip this chapter
without interrupting the argument. This chapter is occupied
wholly with removing some errors.

## 2. TOLMAN'S INDICATION OF THE QUIESCENCE PATTERN AS THE TERMINAL GOAL

Let us begin with one of Tolman's unambiguous statements of
the quiescence theory of terminal value.

> The ultimate purpose of a rat in a maze, discrimination-box or
> other problem-box situation is in the last analysis, it would seem,
> one of getting *to* a final physiological quiescence or *from* a final
> physiological disturbance, or both. The rat is getting to hunger-
> satiation, or it may be to thirst-satiation, or he is getting from
> physiological injury, or from an electric shock, or the like. That
> is, rat experiments are, in fact, always so arranged as to arouse in
> the animal one or more of what may be called the first-order
> drives—i.e., the appetites and aversions. These first-order drives,
> appetites and aversions, are to be conceived as due to initiating
> physiological excitements, as their primary 'initiating causes'
> which, once they are aroused, keep the animal in a condition
> of 'demand for' the final presence of some physiological quies-
> cence, e.g., hunger-satiation, thirst-satiation, sex-satiation, etc., or
> in one of 'demand against' the final presence of some physio-
> logical disturbance, e.g., injury, physiological blocking, etc.
> These first-order drives are, that is, demands for the presence
> of specific physiological quiescences (appetites) or against the
> presence of specific physiological disturbances (aversions) which
> result from initiating organic excitements. A more detailed discus-
> sion of such appetites and aversions will have to be reserved for
> a later chapter. For the present it suffices to assert their ubiquity.
> It is such demanded physiological states of quiescence and dis-
> turbance which constitute the final goal-objects [quiescence pat-
> terns, in *our* terms] which the rat, and all other animals, are to
> be conceived as persisting to or from.[1]

On the basis of the available evidence and of our analysis, what else could be chosen as the final goal of an appetition? Everything else that appears as a goal—the goal object and all the subordinate goals—is subject to error and modification under the control of the impulse pattern persisting until it attains its quiescence pattern. What else, in view of the facts, could be chosen as the final goal, and the ultimate locus of value for a purposive act, than the quiescence pattern?

If Perry disagrees, it must be due to some inadequacy either in his analysis or in ours. Naturally, our conviction is that the error is his. But the error is made so often and involves such a complication of issues that we must trace it to its roots. Let us follow Perry's analysis through so far as it bears on this problem. We have two things to show regarding Perry's treatment of the goal: first, that he does place final value on the goal object and omits the quiescence pattern; and second, that this omission is falsifying and leads to difficulties.

## 3. Perry's Espousal of the Goal Object

At the very start, Perry's general definition of value implies the omission of the quiescence goal. His first definition proposes 'value as any object of any interest.' 'Object' here appears to connote something picked out by an act (our goal object) rather than the completion of an act (quiescence pattern). This surmise is further substantiated within the body of the chapter that has this definition as its chapter heading. The chapter begins:

> It is characteristic of the living mind to be *for* some things and *against* others. . . . To be 'for' or 'against' is to view with favor or disfavor; it is a bias of the subject toward or away from. It implies . . . a tendency to create or conserve, or an opposite tendency to prevent or destroy. This duality appears in many forms, such as liking and disliking, desire and aversion, will and refusal, or seeking and avoiding. It is to this all-pervasive characteristic of the motor-affective life, this *state, act, attitude or disposition of favor or disfavor,* to which we propose to give the name of '*interest.*' This, then, we take as the original source and constant feature of all value. That which is an object of interest is *eo ipso* invested with value. Any object, whatever it be, acquires value when any interest, whatever it be, is taken in it;

just as anything whatever becomes a target when anyone whoso-
ever aims at it.[2]

The tenor of the passage is to identify the object of value with
our 'goal object' as something deliberately and clearly aimed
at like a target; as an object clearly marked for a goal by an idea
of it (anticipatory set) and then shot at.

But a wider interpretation might be given to the phrases so
as to include our 'quiescence pattern.' This is a goal, too, the target aimed at by the 'impulse pattern,' somewhat blindly previous
to experience, to be sure, but nevertheless definitely aimed at.
In his first general definition of interest which had to include all
objects of value, subordinate goals as well as final goals, perhaps
Perry was purposely making the conception as easy as possible
for his reader to catch, and so stressed, by way of example, goal
objects as most familiar to the reader, not intending to exclude
quiescence patterns.

## 4. PERRY'S BIOLOGICAL ANALYSIS OF THE GOAL

Keeping this possibility in mind, we proceed to Perry's next
chapter, "The Biological Approach to Interest." There he runs
over a series of suggested conceptions of teleology, or purposiveness, to find just where the line should be drawn between purposiveness in the sense of value and other tangential or meta-
phorical uses of the term. So he excludes purposiveness in the
sense of mere causal determination like gravitation, or mere
physical tendency like growth, or evolutionary adaptation in the
survival of the fittest, or automatic compensatory or complementary adjustment such as a thermostat and many purely
physiological life processes. In the last, however, we are getting
close to purposiveness in the sense of value. And here Perry
comments:

> That complementary adjustment is important and distinctive
> in principle, is not to be denied. It would appear that in its more
> complicated 'progressive' and 'preparatory' forms it is peculiar
> to living organisms. There is no absolute ground for rejecting
> this as an interpretation of teleology. The important thing is to
> distinguish principles, and not to label them. It certainly would
> not be nonsense to speak of the interior temperature for which

the thermostat is set as 'good' since the heating plant tends to maintain it; or to speak of a cold wind or open window as 'bad' since it needs to be offset by a restorative mechanism. Still less would it be nonsense to speak of the maturity of a plant as good, since the organism's responses tend to bring the organism to that form; or to speak of food as good since the organism's responses utilize them. The propriety of such a use of terms will depend on whether or not there is a more restricted use which is more convenient for purposes of theory of value. That there is such a more restricted use is evident. These terms can be reserved for *modifiable* or *inventive* adjustment as distinguished from adjustment of the *automatic* type.[3]

This passage is highly revelatory, for it gives us a clue in regard to what Perry is steering away from in his definition of purposive value. He wishes to exclude automatic compensatory adjustment. In a way, as he says, the exclusion is a matter of definition. But the distinction between automatic adjustment and modifiable adjustment is by no means arbitrary and a matter of mere definition. The distinction is structural. It differentiates two structures or plans of behavior having quite different effects. The action of a thermostat, or of the circulatory system of a vertebrate organism, or of a typical chain reflex, is distinct in structure from that of modifiable behavior of the sort we have been describing in the foregoing chapters. The term 'purposive,' or 'purposive value,' could be ascribed to both of these structures of behavior or to only one. There is no logical difficulty if the two concepts of automatic adjustment and modifiable adjustment are kept distinct. Common usage allows both. To avoid issues over words, Perry suggests that it would be more convenient to identify purposive value with modifiable behavior, and most people on reflection would probably agree with him. When all ambiguities are cleared away, most people would not regard automatic behavior of the type of a thermostat as a kind of purposive behavior. Tolman's use of 'purposive value' and ours, of course, agree with Perry's on this point.

But the passage is significant in its bearing on our immediate question of defining the final goal of value, for it indicates an anxiety on Perry's part to avoid any element of automatism within his field of purposive value. In short, we see why he might swing too far away from automatic adjustments and so fail to do full justice to the biological roots of modifiable adjustments. He might fail to note essential factors of automatic adjustment which lie within the structure of purposive modifiable behavior.

Passages which immediately follow the one just quoted show this is exactly what Perry does.[4] Speaking of systems of automatic adjustment, he writes:

> Their action is adaptive . . . in relation to specific circumstances and a specific result. Such systems might be said to constitute the limit of strictly biological achievement. But nature has evidently transcended this achievement, in producing organisms which are adaptive in an undetermined variety of situations to an undetermined variety of results. This occurs in what appears, on reflection, to be the only possible way. Systems cannot be *constitutionally adapted to nothing in particular,* but they may conceivably possess a constitutional capacity to *adapt themselves as contingencies arise.* Nature here rises to that level which we recognize as characteristic of mind or intelligence. . . . The crucial difference which marks this advance, and which is the contribution of mind, is *control by anticipation;* which constitutes the essential meaning of what is variously known as prescience, prospicience or foresight.[5]

It becomes more and more evident that Perry is working toward regarding the differentia between automatic adjustment and modifiable adjustment to be the presence of an anticipatory set which clearly sees ahead the goal object it is aiming at. This is apparently what he means by 'prescience,' 'prospicience,' 'foresight,' and also 'intelligence.' "In the case of intelligence it seems necessary, or at least appropriate," he writes, "to refer to the sequel as being somehow in prospect at the moment when the action occurs." [6] And since the differentia which defines modifiable adjustment will also be that which defines purposive value, it follows that if the presence of an anticipatory set is the defining characteristic of the one, so will it be of the other. And if he makes the anticipatory set the defining trait, he will almost inevitably be led to locate final purposive value in the goal object which is the object of reference of that set.

Still we are not quite sure, for it seems obvious from our analysis that it is not the presence of an anticipatory set and a goal object that constitutes modifiable adjustment but rather the presence of what lies behind these and makes them possible: namely, the impulse pattern and the quiescence pattern and the open gap between. So we wonder whether the thing that bothered Perry about these factors of the drive and quiescence may not have been that their action is automatic. What he perhaps failed to note is that, though the action of these factors is automatic, the behavior resulting from their action is not automatic but modifiable. As we saw in the description of the behavior of Richter's rats or Thorndike's cats, the impulse pattern set the organism automatically in motion which continued automatically until the quiescence pattern was attained. The quiescence pattern might be reached blindly (or relatively so) through trial and error, or else by way of the mediation of an acquired anticipatory set and a correlative goal object.

Perry apparently turns his attention to the latter method, and neglects the former. But the differentiating characteristic of modifiable behavior, we hold, is not the presence of an anticipatory set (which may be absent), but of a drive and quiescence pattern *with a gap as to the mode of connecting the two* (which gap, in some sense, we believe is always present). It is the openness of this gap that opens the way to *modifiable* as opposed to *automatic* adjustment. The generation of anticipatory sets and goal objects is one method of filling the gap, and the only method that preserves the results of experience in learning, but this method is not the differentia of purposive behavior, since the earliest acts of purposive behavior are wholly or partially blind and must perforce do without it. As for intelligence, if we have no idea what to do, the intelligent thing is to try and try again. Intelligence does not presuppose an idea of what to aim at, but it does presuppose a method of action to escape distress.

Perry, we suspect, leaped too soon and too far toward a restricted definition of purposive value in terms of goal object and anticipatory set from an overanxiety to escape from the level of automatic behavior. In doing so he leaped over the drive and correlative quiescence pattern, without which the dynamics of purposive behavior becomes a mystery.

## 5. PERRY'S PSYCHOLOGICAL ANALYSIS

When we enter Perry's next chapter, "The Psychological Definition of Interest," our hypothesis regarding the nature and reasons for his oversight is still further strengthened. After contrasting the lower with the higher level of adjustment, Perry summarizes it in the difference between adaptation and adaptability: "It [adaptability] consists not in an equilibrium between the existing organization of the species and the constant features of its environment, but rather in a capacity to form projects, deal with novel situations, overcome difficulties and *plan ahead*."[7] He obviously has the anticipatory set, with its definite aims and its target, its goal object, foremost in his mind.

Perry's first carefully phrased definition of interest is given in italics: *"An act is interested in so far as its occurrence is due to the agreement between its accompanying expectation and the unfulfilled phases of a governing propensity."*[8] Another form of the same definition occurs on page 209, but offers no further enlightenment. In terms of our previous analysis, this definition leaves us in suspense on most of the main issues of purposive value.

Let us compare Perry's definition with the diagram of our completed analysis of purposive value:

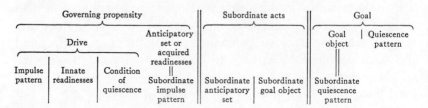

Now, referring Perry's definition to our diagram, what does he mean by 'governing propensity'? Does he mean the whole system of control of the purposive act, as we do, or the drive, or the anticipatory set? What does he mean by 'accompanying expectation'? Does he mean the anticipatory set or the governing propensity? What does he mean by 'the unfulfilled phases'? Does he mean the innate readinesses, the conditions of quiescence, or even the anticipatory set? Or, since these phases are in agreement with the 'accompanying expectation,' does he mean factors further along in the purposive act, such as the agreement of the subordinate acts with the demands of the anticipatory set, or the agreement of the goal object with the references of the anticipatory set, or possibly the agreement of the goal object with the conditions of quiescence and hence its efficacy in producing the quiescence pattern and so bringing the purpose to an end? What does 'the agreement' mean?

We do not find a clear answer to any of these questions. In the section following his definition Perry alludes to Thorndike's cat and says, "The situation involves two levels: the controlling or inciting propensity, on the one hand; and on the other hand, the subordinate responses or 'trials,' among which occur both the errors which are eliminated and the success which survives." [9] This sounds as though his 'propensity' were our 'drive.' He continues, "This higher or selective propensity controls the whole process. It excites the animal to efforts that continue *until* a certain subordinate act occurs; and it determines what specific character that subordinate act shall possess in order to become recurrent." [10] But now we are all mixed up again. For, in our account, the drive generates subordinate acts only when a superordinate anticipatory set is blocked. In our analysis of the primitive trial-and-error behavior of Thorndike's cat there was no anticipatory set and therefore no subordinate acts. The drive was directly blocked, and what was selected by the drive was not a subordinate act, but the superordinate act which directly produced or failed to produce quiescence. To be sure, the goal object of this superordinate act is, in a sense, subordinate to the quiescence pattern. Does Perry, then, recognize our quiescence pattern as the final value of a purposive act?

We might for a moment think so, but, in the pages following, Perry is puzzled about the mechanism of learning in a way that practically verifies our original hypothesis that he does not recognize the action of the impulse and quiescence pattern. After rejecting several theories of learning, he adopts the anticipatory reaction theory. Why should a chick, he asks, "not learn to pick up and reject orange peel rather than to pick up and swallow yolk of egg?" Our answer would be simply that the orange peel does not produce quiescence, whereas the yolk of egg does; the set for orange peel would never acquire a reference to quiescence, whereas the set for yolk of egg would.

But Perry apparently fails to see the connection with quiescence and, looking backward instead of forward for an explanation, finds it in the reinforcement of some anticipatory reaction already present. Swallowing, he says, is already part of a pecking reaction.

> If pecking is a part of eating, then it will be accompanied by a partial excitement of the swallowing reaction, . . . by a 'getting ready' to swallow. This anticipatory reaction will be brought to completion by certain stimuli such as the yolk of egg, inhibited by others, such as the orange peel. In the future the former will awaken these anticipatory reactions more strongly, and so reinforce the pecking reaction; whereas the latter will partially excite the rejecting reflex, which will diminish the force of the pecking reaction by inhibiting the anticipatory swallowing with which that reaction is normally correlated. This would not be the case unless swallowing were in some sense the natural sequence to pecking, or unless the two were part of one total act.[11]

Undoubtedly this account is true of any act having a sequence of innate readinesses or an anticipatory set once acquired. But it does not account for learning where these two factors are absent. It does not account for the behavior of Thorndike's cat, for instance. There is significance, however, in Perry's finding it so necessary to account for learning in terms of anticipatory reactions. It means that he thinks they are necessary to purposive activity. Since innate readinesses quickly amalgamate with anticipatory sets, it evidently means that he considers an anticipatory set essential to purposive activity. If every purposive activity in fact, on his view, has an anticipatory set, he can easily conceive the act as coming to an end with a goal object. Impulse pattern and quiescence pattern can then, apparently, be ignored. The more so if the writer also holds an ideomotor theory of action.

By this time we are almost certain that Perry is trying to develop a theory of purposive activity without any drive or quiescence pattern. It is symptomatic that, apart from the references to Thorndike's cat and the pecking chick, all of Perry's constructive illustrations of purposive activity in this crucial chapter are of *acquired* acts derived from an independence mutation. When we ourselves were describing these acts and the independence mutation, we noticed that they did give a superficial appearance of having no drive. If Perry were heading for a descriptive definition of value that excluded a drive, he would naturally collect derived purposive acts as illustrations from which to generalize. So he refers to a chess player, a foresighted housewife, a football player, a host planning to meet a visitor, a professor desiring a book who finds his study door locked. The trial-and-error behavior of the professor is of the thoughtful type; he looks about till he sees a key hanging on a nail. "Being a person of intelligence," the professor does not "as a baffled kitten turn to playing with its tail" or start "kicking, pounding, shouting or running back and forth." [12] In view of this tendency of Perry's to identify intelligence with derived purposive acts where ideas or anticipatory sets have already become well established, we are anxious to see how he would interpret a primitive purposive act with an obvious drive like hunger.

## 6. Hunger Treated as an Aversion

To our surprise, but still in conformity with what we now begin to sense is Perry's desperate attempt to get rid of drives, he breaks up a primitive hunger appetition into two separate acts, with the effect of denying that there is such a thing as a hunger appetition. He begins by referring to Cannon's distinction between appetite and hunger:

> Careful observation indicates that appetite is related to previous sensations of taste and smell of food. Delightful or disgusting tastes and odors, associated with this or that edible substance, determine the appetite. . . . Among prosperous people supplied with abundance of food, the appetite seems sufficient to ensure for bodily needs a proper supply of nutriment. We eat because dinner is announced, because by eating we avoid unpleasant consequences, and because food is placed before us in delectable form with tempting tastes and odors. Under less easy circumstances, however, the body needs are supplied through the much stronger and more insistent demands of hunger. The sensation of hunger is difficult to describe but almost everyone from

childhood has felt at times that dull ache or gnawing pain referred to the lower midchest region and the epigastrium which may take imperious control of human actions. As Sternberg has pointed out, hunger may be sufficiently insistent to force the taking of food which is so distasteful that it not only fails to arouse appetite, but may even produce nausea. . . . Hunger may be satisfied while the appetite still calls . . . On the other hand, appetite may be in abeyance while hunger is goading . . . Although the two sensations may then exist separately, they, nevertheless, have the same function of leading to the intake of food, and they usually appear together.[13]

Cannon's observations are extremely pertinent, and we have no reason to question them, except to observe that hunger need not be painful. On our interpretation, they show that men eat for a variety of reasons besides being hungry. Especially among well-fed people, the hunger drive with its attendant appetition for food is a less prominent source of motivation than a number of others such as the acquired acts of answering to the dinner call, being well-mannered and punctual, avoiding hurting other people's feelings, and so on, together with certain immediate aesthetic reactions, gratuitous satisfactions, to pleasant odors and tastes. Cannon gathers all these motives together, and especially the last, into the term 'appetite.' And he reserves the term 'hunger' for the appetition for food on the basis of the hunger drive with its impulse pattern of stomach contractions, its correlative emotional quality, and its quiescence pattern. This is how we should interpret these observations.

What does Perry do? He converts the hunger drive into an aversion! The appetitive element in the desire for food he gives entirely to 'appetite.'

The hunger pang, a sensation so peremptory, so disagreeable, so tormenting as to induce suicide or crime [compare this exaggerated description with the observations on Richter's rats] . . . is unmistakably an organic sensation. The sensory factor in appetite, on the other hand, is olfactory or gustatory. This difference is further accentuated by the fact that hunger is negative, while appetite is positive. Both are interests in a sense conformable with the definition already adopted; but while the organism is 'goaded' by hunger, and seeks *relief,* it is 'tempted' by appetite and seeks *satisfaction.*[14]

Having thus sharply distinguished hunger and appetite, and made the one negative and the other positive, Perry is apparently not quite satisfied with what he has done, and half draws them together again—we suspect in order to return that positive element to hunger which he has taken away from it. "Hunger has, then," he says, "three important characteristics: (1) it is a negative interest; (2) it is initiated by a somatic sensation; (3) it is associated with a specific appetite which supersedes it and converts it into a positive interest." [15] Nowhere, however, does he explain how hunger, a negative interest, actually gets converted into a positive interest. It might be superseded by another interest, but hardly converted by association with another interest into the opposite of itself.

The nearest he comes to an explanation is when, after generalizing from food hunger to a number of others, he says: "In these . . . the stimulating physiological state is so closely associated with the appetite that it borrows the name of the appetite and is ordinarily accompanied by ideas that induce a mild incitement of it." But there is no conversion in his process. The hungers are still aversions. Perry, indeed, is doing his best to get rid of them. These hungers obviously include all of Tolman's basic appetitive drives. Here are Perry's sentences:

> Hunger being so conceived, it can be extended to other functions than food taking. Thirst is a negative interest stimulated by a dryness of the mouth and pharynx; asphyxiation by a lack of oxygen. Employing the conception in this sense, there may be said to be a 'sex-hunger,' in so far as there is an impulse to be rid of a sensation occasioned by an excess of seminal fluid; or perhaps a hunger for exercise stimulated by a sluggish circulation.

This anxiety to get rid of drives in appetition now even begins to appear funny. The sex drive turns into an aversion for an excess of seminal fluid, and a sluggish circulation is suggested as comparable to the impulse patterns of hunger, thirst, and sex!

The final sentence of the paragraph we are considering is an extraordinary summary of all these efforts to escape drives: "Appetite, on the other hand, is a positive interest, initiated by an extra-organic stimulus, and giving rise, when 'starved,' to cer-

tain physiological changes which induce a correlative hunger." [16]
This is, on our view, a complete reversal of the facts. An impulse
pattern ('certain physiological changes') is not initiated by an
appetition, but an appetition is initiated by an impulse pattern.
Yet once more we find Perry trying to establish a theory of purposive activity with no distinct drive or quiescence pattern, a
theory in which the anticipatory set and goal object are supposed to be sufficient.

This sounds like an attempt to generalize the ideomotor theory
of action in order to make it cover all purposive activity. This
theory, which merges the drive with the anticipatory set and
makes the anticipatory set autonomous, came to our attention as
a possible but dubious hypothesis for explaining the dynamics of
the independence mutation. But there we were thinking of it as
applying only to derived acts—acts which had been subordinate
acts previous to the independence mutation. We had not dreamed
of applying the ideomotor theory to the superordinate instinctive
acts from which the latter were derived. The effect of the trend
of Perry's view and of such an analysis of instinctive 'hungers'
is to push the ideomotor theory of action back into the instincts
and so make it cover all purposive activity.

If, then, the ideomotor theory is to be all-explanatory (i.e., the
theory that the anticipatory set, idea, judgment, is self-propel-
ling), we should think all judgments, on Perry's view, would be
purposive acts. We should think that there would be no difference between a cognition and an interest. For what else does
the ideomotor theory mean but just that? What else would the
ascription of autonomy of action to an idea mean but that the
idea not only referred to its object but pursued it as its goal? Or,
to reverse the phrasing, how could the goal object be the final
goal of a purposive act unless the anticipatory set (the idea of
the goal) were the ultimate basis of impulse? In an ideomotor
theory of action, every idea is by definition a purposive act, and
the goal of the act is the object of the idea. Or, vice versa, if the
goal object is set up as the final goal of purposive activity, then
it would seem that every anticipatory set (idea of a goal) is an
ultimate source of impulse for the activity—that is, ideomotor.
Consequently, on a generalized ideomotor theory of purposive

activity consistently carried through, there would be no difference between cognition and interest. A judgment of an object would automatically be a desire for it and vice versa. From the trend of Perry's statements so far and his apparent attempt to dispense with a drive, we should expect him to develop such a view.

## 7. Cognition versus Interest: A Conflict of Purposive Dynamics

Perry takes up the relation of cognition to purposive value in his two chapters, "Analysis of Cognition" and "Role of Cognition in Interest." Here the issue that we have been following comes to a climax.

Again we are surprised, for he does not identify cognition and interest, but on the contrary is at great pains to contrast them. He recognizes a distinct dynamic factor in interest over and above the cognitive expectation of the anticipatory set. He is explicit in attributing to this dynamic factor the propulsive force that directs the interest through the anticipatory set to the goal object. But he neglects to give this dynamic factor a goal of its own. This dynamic factor is, apparently, our drive minus a goal of quiescence.

Consider the following typical passage:

> Expectation is an anticipatory response correlated with a contingent object. It implies no disposition to bring its object into being, but only a readiness to deal with it when and if it occurs. Interest, on the other hand, promotes its object. To expect an event signifies only a disposition to act on it; while to be interested in an event signifies a disposition to act for it, or to provide an occasion for acting on it. This supplementary dynamic factor which distinguishes interest, lies in the governing propensity which renders the anticipatory set prepotent, and which gives a peculiar eligibility to any antecedent performance which affords promise of it. An expectation becomes an interest when the anticipatory response in which it consists, is in demand.[17]

In our terms this conception would be exhibited as follows:

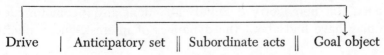

Drive    | Anticipatory set ‖ Subordinate acts ‖ Goal object

The anticipatory set refers to the goal object, as with us. It apparently has no propulsive force of its own and derives this force from the drive, as with us. But the drive has no quiescence goal of its own. The drive seems to be conceived of as simply giving propulsive force to the anticipatory set, which directs the activity to the goal object, which is final.

The term 'governing propensity,' moreover, is here confined to, and identified with, the drive. This identification is a little perplexing because on this conception the governing of the activity is given entirely to the anticipatory set, and the dynamic factor provides only the force or propensity. Moreover, the identification is contrary to the use of the term in Perry's original definition of interest: "This definition involves a *governing propensity*, or determining tendency, or general 'set' which is at any given time in control of the organism as a whole." [18] This inclusion of a determining set in the 'governing propensity,' according to some of Perry's earlier implications, we have followed throughout, applying the term to the whole governing system of a purposive act—that is, to the drive and the anticipatory set both as a group. Perry's present limited use of the term has the effect of casting the anticipatory set into a limbo that is neither subordinate act nor superordinate act. The set is thereby loosened from its integrated relationship with the drive (as we have described it) and this contributes to some of the strange results of Perry's analysis which we shall soon see.

So here we have a nonideomotor theory of purposive value in which the final goal is identified with the goal object. The issue upon which we launched—whether the goal object or a quiescence pattern was the locus of final purposive value—here comes to a definite head. The essence of Perry's argument seems to be that there is no goal or no need of another goal beyond the goal object. We could understand this if Perry were developing a generalized ideomotor theory of purposive activity. We should then have questioned the adequacy of the theory in view of the facts, but we should not have questioned the superfluousness of a quiescence goal beyond the goal object in an ideomotor theory. But here Perry definitely abandons any ideomotor ideas he may have had about the dynamics of interest, and explicitly supports a drive theory of interest. Now, we maintain that a drive theory of purpose requires a quiescence goal for the drive and that this automatically becomes the final goal of the purpose. How does Perry avoid this consequence? Or does he avoid it?

First, let us assure ourselves that he does make the goal object—that is, the object of reference of the anticipatory set—the final object or goal of interest. Such a sentence as this seems to clinch the matter: "This cognitive factor which is essential to the interest as such, or which mediates the interest as a whole, may be termed the *interest-judgment;* and its object is the object of the interest as a whole, or the end." [19]

How could such a theory be made to work? Would an independent drive stop merely at the attainment of a goal object? On the ideomotor theory, the drive stops at the goal object because an anticipatory set contains its own drive. When the object of the set is attained, of course the drive contained in the set ceases. But, on an independent drive theory, why would the drive stop when the object of an anticipatory set was attained? Our answer is: It would not, unless the goal object of the set also produced the quiescence pattern of the drive; and if the attained goal object did not produce the quiescence pattern, then the drive would not cease, but would call for another anticipatory set and goal object to attain the quiescence goal which had not been reached by the first goal object. In fact, the drive does not stop on the goal object.

How does Perry try to explain the stopping of the independent drive of his interest on the goal object? Perhaps he actually has an ideomotor theory of interest anyway. Since his 'governing propensity' in the limited sense is given no structure, no impulse pattern or anything like that, but is simply the dynamic force in the anticipatory set, possibly he means that the force is contained in the set and that the pattern of the force is the pattern of the set itself—an ideomotor theory after all.

But the whole atmosphere of these two chapters is contrary to this solution. Perry really intends the 'governing propensity' to be an independent dynamic factor. A specific way in which this comes out is his emphasis upon the fallibility of interest. On an ideomotor theory of interest, the anticipatory set or interest-judgment cannot, of course, be in error. There is nothing in reference to which it could be in error. A self-propelled anticipatory set might fail to reach its goal object, but by definition the goal object is the object of its self-propulsion, and error as to the goal object is impossible.

If there is an independent drive, however, the goal object of the anticipatory set may be in error in reference to the quiescence pattern of the drive, for the object may not be of the proper kind to produce quiescence. Now, Perry is explicit that the anticipatory set, the interest-judgment, may be in error. "As all judgment is liable to error," he writes, "so all interest is by virtue of the interest-judgment liable to failure or disappointment." [20] This would be impossible on an ideomotor theory. If to think of an apple is to want an apple, no disappointment is possible by virtue of the thought of an apple, but only by virtue of an unpropitious environment that does not provide the apple. If the apple appears, the thought and the want are both, by the theory, automatically fulfilled and no disappointment is possible. If, however, the thought of an apple is motivated by an independent drive of hunger with a quiescence goal of its own, then the thought of an apple might be erroneous, and might cause disappointment. The disappointment would be due to the error in the mediating judgment to the effect that this goal object would bring quiescence to the drive. But Perry cannot avail himself of this explanation because he admits no goal for his drive with reference to which the goal object of his mediating judgment might fail.

How, then, does Perry explain the situation? Instead of trying to solve the difficulty by looking forward to a quiescence goal beyond his goal object, he looks back to the region of the mediating judgment. He overhauls the structure of cognition.

Now, on our view, cognition arises under the impetus of a blocked drive. It is entirely motivated by the drive and consists in the generation and application of anticipatory sets. The process of making workable sets does, of course, become a derived purpose and an end in itself exfoliating into all the branches of science and philosophy familiar to our culture. But on our view all this is derivative and the result of independence mutations.

Basically, on our view, cognition functions in a subsidiary role in purposive activity; it functions in the service of the drive to bridge the gap between the impulse pattern and the quiescence pattern.

The one aspect of Perry's analysis of cognition that follows ours (as closely as his treatment of interest will allow) is that which puts the dynamic element entirely into his 'governing propensity' (in the limited sense), and regards cognition as serving the demands of this propensity. It might be said to be the prevailing view wherever Perry is not faced with the difficulty of accounting for the demands of a 'governing propensity' (limited sense) when that propensity is given no goal of its own. But he has another very different view of cognition which serves him from time to time in escaping from the dilemma about the quiescence goal.

This is an ideomotor theory of the process of verification, which he comes to identify with cognition. His chapter "Analysis of Cognition" is chiefly occupied with this view. It amounts to setting up another description of purposive activity side by side with that of interest. And now the contrast between cognition and interest is not that between the dynamic and the consciously directive factors in a purposive act; but that between two different sorts of purposive activity, the one ideomotor, the other motivated by a separate 'propensity.' This contrast now takes on the aspect of a possible conflict. On this ideomotor view of cognition a cognitive activity might easily conflict with an interest.

Such conflict is, of course, impossible between cognition and interest, so long as cognition is regarded as a factor within interest and subservient there to a 'propensity' drive. The latter cognitive factor (conceived as the anticipatory set and goal object) then either serves the drive and is integrated into the total purpose, or fails to serve it and is dropped out of the purposive act. No activity can conflict with a drive that does not itself contain another drive to produce the conflict. I shall consequently offer Perry's explicit statements of the conflict he conceives possible between cognition and interest as evidence that his description of the process of cognition is definitely a description of a type of purposive activity, and that Perry conceals this fact from himself only because the drive he puts into the cognitive process is absorbed into the acts of judgment them- selves—that is, because he conceives of cognitive activities as ideomotor. Since now he is conceiving interest as motivated by an independent drive, the ideomotor conception of cognition appears by contrast as if it lacked a drive. But the ideomotor drive in Perry's treatment of cognition reveals itself whenever he exhibits it in *conflict* with the drive of an interest.

The use he has for this ideomotor theory of cognition is pre- cisely the conflict it renders possible with interests. He attempts, by these conflicts between cognition and interest, to account for some of the difficulties he gets into because of the lack of a quiescence goal. He has, we might say, brought in two drives as a substitute for our two goals. Where we account for a value error by calling attention to a discrepancy between the two goals, Perry often tries to point to a conflict between the two drives. This method, of course, does not actually solve the prob- lem, because two drives make two purposes and the problem about the final goal has to do with each single purpose.

For the correctness of this interpretation of Perry's analysis of cognition, we must examine his statements and the way in which he uses his concepts. But the following passages are suffi- cient to show the trend. In a footnote he comments, "Mention of suggestibility, and the question of 'ideomotor' action present no special difficulties for the present view. . . . According to the view here presented ideas *are* actions, more or less completely executed." [21] And in another footnote to a paragraph expanding on the idea that the "conversity of interest and belief implies that the two may be in conflict," he comments emphatically, "That cognition acts as a compelling force which may contend with interest, is recognized in all studies of the genesis of opinion." Footnotes, being more casual than the text, perhaps reveal most clearly the drift of his thought toward an ideomotor theory.

Now to show how this method of handling the issue does not solve anything, but only makes it more confusing. In the follow- ing passage Perry is trying to illustrate the relationship between cognition and interest:

To judge that there is money in my purse, signifies that the act of dealing with money (seeing it or handling it) is so connected with the act of opening the purse that the former is released by the latter. If when I open my purse my anticipatory dealing with money is thereupon executed, my judgment is fulfilled or proved true. To desire that there shall be money in my purse signifies that the act of dealing with money is in agreement with a governing propensity such as avarice or need, which predisposes me to its performance independently of my response to the purse. The opening of the purse, possessing the function of releasing the money-response, may then occur because of this fact, or because of what is expected of it. If when I open the purse I see or handle money, my judgment is fulfilled because what I expected has happened; and my interest is satisfied, because what has happened also harmonizes with my governing propensity. While I can judge that there is money in my purse without desiring it, I cannot desire it without judging it. I cannot open the purse because of what I expect of it, unless I expect something of it. The money in the purse can fulfill without satisfying, or its absence can surprise without disappointing; but I cannot be satisfied without fulfilment of expectation, or be disappointed without being surprised.[22]

This is about as complete an inversion of our explanation of the facts adduced as could be conceived. So far from asserting that "I can judge without desiring but cannot desire without judging," we should say, "I can desire without judging, but cannot judge without desiring." A purposive act can be initiated by a drive without an anticipatory set. Whenever we have a driving need but do not know how to satisfy it, we are desiring without judging. When we are forced to resort to primitive trial-and-error behavior like Thorndike's cat, we have a desire of that sort. And it is inconceivable on our study and analysis of the facts of behavior that a person could judge without some drive for judging.

Here Perry is describing two different purposive acts having different drives and different goals. If I open the purse to see if my expectation that there is money in it is true, the drive is in the nature of curiosity or a wager on my power to predict correctly, and it is satisfied on seeing that there is money in the purse. If I open the purse to find out if I have money there to spend or to hoard, the drive, as Perry says, is something like need or avarice or perhaps the fear that it might not be there, and it is satisfied in the relief or the assurance that it is there. It just happens that these two purposive acts have nearly the same goal object and corresponding anticipatory set. Actually, the goal object is not quite the same, for it is essential for the second goal object that the money should be *my* money, which is not a property essential to the first goal object.

As to the difference between surprise and disappointment or between fulfillment of expectation and satisfaction, both purposive acts had both. For both, on our view, had a quiescence goal to be satisfied and an anticipatory set to be fulfilled. But notice the use to which Perry puts these 'feelings.' By means of them he gives the effect of accounting for the difference between the attainment of a goal object and the final satisfaction of the drive in quiescence without, however, admitting a goal of quiescence. The feeling of fulfillment of expectation is, for him, the feeling of the conformity of the goal object with the anticipatory set; the feeling of satisfaction is for him the feeling of the harmony of the goal object with the drive: "My judgment is fulfilled because what I expected has happened; and my interest is satisfied because what happened also harmonizes with my governing propensity." By means of these feelings of fulfillment and satisfaction referring backward from his goal object to the anticipatory set and the drive, he gives the impression of having explained the demands of both by one goal. The goal object is the object of the judgment by fulfilling the anticipatory set, and it is the goal of the desire by satisfying and harmonizing with the drive. These words almost take the place of an explanation.

But we need only think of Richter's rats to perceive how unrealistic these words are. The goal object of food fulfills the anticipatory set, but only the eating of it and digesting of it in the quiescence pattern satisfies the drive. Besides, if the goal object is wrong, does not the demand of the drive to be satisfied and harmonized with still remain? Perry, by distinguishing between 'fulfillment' and 'satisfaction,' thereby admits implicitly what he never recognizes explicitly—the quiescence goal.

## 8. SUMMARY OF PERRY'S DIFFICULTIES

To point up our argument of the inadequacy of such a theory of purpose without a goal of quiescence, let us briefly review Perry's handling of his theory. For I fear that the exposition of the evidence has been so long that the full impact of the difficulties may have been missed.

Perry begins with a rough definition of purposive value as 'any object of interest.' This definition has the effect of focusing his attention on the goal object as the *object* of value, from which he rarely allows his attention to stray. Right here is the beginning of the trouble that follows. He defines himself into trouble.

Having made this rough definition, he proceeds to make it more precise in a detailed description of interest. If value is a relation between a subject and an object, and if it is the interest of a subject taken in an object that endows the object with value, naturally the elaboration of such a theory would consist in the elaboration of the description of interest.

His first step is to determine the exact line between interested behavior and behavior on more primitive biological levels. He draws this line between behavior consisting in automatic adjustments and that consisting in modifiable adjustments. Interest is purposive behavior aiming deliberately at a goal involving a modifiable plan of action as a means of reaching that goal. Drawing the line, however, just above automatic adjustments and in terms of the exclusion of automatic behavior has the unfortunate effect of leading his attention away from the functions of the drive and quiescence pattern in purposive behavior, which are partially automatic.

This effect shows up in the next chapter, where Perry offers a more precise definition of interest in terms of two levels, or two springs of action.[23] The definition itself analyzes interest into a governing propensity and an expectation, and an agreement between the latter and unfulfilled phases of the former. This would seem to distinguish the governing propensity from an anticipatory set (expectation) and so to recognize the drive in the governing propensity. Ambiguously it does, but in the succeeding passages expanding on the definition, the expectation is either absorbed back into the governing propensity or forward into the subordinate acts. There is no telling which. But Perry is definite in reiterating that "the situation involves *two levels of response:* the controlling or inciting propensity, on the one hand; and, on the other, the subordinate responses or 'trials.' " [24] His 'governing propensity,' therefore, may be either the drive alone, or the drive plus the anticipatory set, or the anticipatory set alone conceived as ideomotor.

The definition itself seems to separate the governing propensity from the anticipatory set by saying that they can partially agree with one another. But all the explanatory comments on the definition shift the contrast to that between the governing propensity and the subordinate acts, and give the control over the subordinate acts to the governing propensity. But since the subordinate acts are directly controlled only by an anticipatory set, this would force the anticipatory set back into the governing propensity. Hence, so far as the comments are concerned, the governing propensity must consist either in the drive plus the anticipatory set (as we maintain in our analysis) or in an anticipatory set alone, conceived as ideomotor.

The tenor of Perry's next three chapters is toward a generalized ideomotor theory of interest. This amounts to the exclusion of the drive as a distinct factor in a purposive act. Consequently, we are particularly interested in Perry's treatment of hunger, which to us appears obviously as an independent drive. Perry interprets it as an aversion, and ascribes the appetitive side of eating to another source more easily interpretable according to ideomotor theory. He generalizes this analysis in such a way as to imply that all the instinctive appetitions would have their drives explained away in the same manner.

We are then ready to expect a generalized ideomotor theory of interest which would virtually amalgamate interest and cognition. On the contrary, in the two chapters dealing with cognition and its relation to interest Perry contrasts and even opposes the two. He gives an ideomotor account of cognition, without ever letting us be quite sure, however, whether or not the cognitive process is a self-sufficient cognitive act; and then gives an independent drive theory of interest, without, however, granting the drive an independent goal of quiescence. The dynamic element or drive is here definitely identified with his 'governing propensity,' and his 'expectation,' or anticipatory set, is consequently placed in a very ambiguous position. The involvements and confusions and inconsistencies now multiply rapidly.

His failure to recognize the goal of quiescence leads him to develop two distinct theories of purposive activity—one for cognition and one for interest. To only one of them, however, does he attribute value. This leads to the inconsistency of admitting a type of modifiable adjustable behavior (i.e., a type of interest) which does not institute value (i.e., which is not interest). Some awareness of this inconsistency leads to a second inconsistency, that of admitting a compelling force, or drive, imminent in the ideomotor cognitive process, and yet asserting also that the cognitive processes lack a dynamic factor and receive this factor only in interest through an independent drive or governing propensity. And since this governing propensity is not granted a goal of its own, this second inconsistency leads to a third, that of admitting a possible incompatibility between the governing propensity and the expectation, or anticipatory set, whence the separateness of the two; at the same time he renders this incompatibility impossible by his assertion that the governing propensity and the expectation have an identical goal.

All these inconsistencies arise from a failure to admit the presence of the independent quiescence goal for the drive. They all vanish and the whole analysis straightens out and becomes simple as soon as this goal is admitted as the final goal of a purposive act beyond the goal object of the anticipatory set. I offer this examination of the difficulties into which Perry got in his attempt to identify final purposive value with the goal object as evidence that this attempt is in principle erroneous. The terminus of purposive value must be located in the quiescence goal of the drive.

The surprising thing is that these inconsistencies and the erroneousness of the view do not show up on the surface, and come to light only as a result of searching analysis. The conformity of Perry's view with a common conception of the matter may account for part of it. But the principal explanation lies, I think, in the fact that Perry constantly implies, and in some of his illustrations actually describes, the goal of quiescence. Referring to Thorndike's cat, Perry says in one place, "The hungry kitten's pawing at the button which fastens the door of the box in which it is confined, is interested in so far as the sight of the button arouses expectations which cause the pawing owing to their congruence with hunger." [25] Here 'congruence with hunger' sounds like our 'quiescence pattern,' not like a goal object. And we are confirmed in this idea when Perry speaks of "the propensity . . . *completed and brought to rest.*" [26] I am even inclined to think that I derived the idea of the quiescence pattern as the final goal of purposive value from Perry as much as from Tolman, for I was surprised, on closer study, to discover that fundamentally Perry had no place for it.

But, apart from inconsistencies, the basic objection to Perry's view is that it is incompatible with the empirical facts. However plausible the elimination of a goal of quiescence may be made for derived acts, original acts motivated by an instinctive drive can only be described as terminating in the quiescence of the drive. In these ultimate purposive acts a goal object is clearly only a way station to the final goal of quiescence.

## 9. Conclusion: Goal Object Not Terminal

Our conclusion that the goal object cannot be the final goal for all purposive value has a bearing on Perry's general definition of value as 'any object of any interest.' Says Perry, "X is valuable = interest is taken in x," value being thus "a specific relation into which things possessing any ontological status whatsoever, whether real or imaginary, may enter with interested subjects." [27] The 'things' referred to here are obviously goal objects. This general definition of purposive value becomes, in view of the foregoing criticism, untenable.

We are not yet ready to formulate a general descriptive definition of purposive value. But we have gone far enough to see that it cannot be offered in terms of a dyadic relation between a subject and an object. This simple relational theory of value will not do for purposive value. Many objects, it is true, do acquire value as goal objects in virtue of interest taken in them. But these objects acquire their value only in virtue of their service to the quiescence of a drive. Whatever our general definition of purposive value will be, it cannot be in terms of an object related to a subject, but must be in terms of an activity brought to completion.

## 10. A Subsistent Objective as a Goal

There are other aspirants for the final goal of a purposive act besides those we have been considering. One of these is the so-called subsistent 'objective.' Perry has a leaning toward this goal,[28] and its influence crops up every now and again, though he intends to suppress it for the sake, as he explains in a footnote, of avoiding metaphysical questions.[29] It crops up, for instance, at the very beginning in the passage explaining his general definition of interest as "a specific relation into which things *possessing any ontological status whatsoever, whether real or imaginary, may enter.*"[30] Or consider the following sentences in the very heart of his discussion of the object of interest:

> The object of interest is *never* a datum during the life of the interest, but is always the objective of the interest-judgment, or the object of an anticipatory rather than of a consummatory response. But the object of interest at any given moment is primarily the objective of the *agent's* interest-judgment.[31]

The idea of making a subsistent 'objective' the final goal comes very near having the effect of making the anticipatory set the final goal of a purposive act. But according to Perry's intention, the 'meaning' of the anticipatory set, not the set itself, is the goal; and the 'meaning' is given a special ontological status of subsistence to provide for the possibility of its not being realized in the goal object.

The anticipatory set for the quest of Ponce de Leon, for example, was an expectation of the Spring of Life. The meaning referred to by this set, accordingly, it is claimed, was the Spring of Life as an integral whole, and this meaning, it is then maintained, was the objective, or goal, of Ponce de Leon's subordinate acts in the pursuit of the goal, whether or not the goal physically existed. But this objective did not, as it happened, physically exist. Therefore, since it was still what Ponce de Leon was aiming for, and thus his real objective unquestionably, it must have a non-physical status of being, which may be called 'subsistence.' It is therefore maintained that the goal of a purposive activity is a subsistent objective.

We might diagram the proposal in this way:

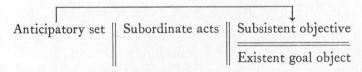

The anticipatory set has an existent status in the mind of the agent. (It is, for instance, Ponce de Leon's idea of the Spring of Life.) This set refers to a subsistent objective which is its meaning and also its goal. (That is, the idea of the Spring of Life means the objective Spring of Life conceived as an integral whole which has a subsistent status. Presumably, the content of the existent idea actually is the subsistent objective. And this content is the goal which Ponce de Leon seeks to realize.) This objective governs the subordinate acts, which have a physical status and are supposed to bring about the goal object, which, in turn, would be the physical realization of the subsistent objective. But whether or not the objective is physically realized in the goal object, the objective is still the goal and indeed the final goal of the purposive act. (Though Ponce de Leon never found the Spring of Life, and though, in fact, it did not physically exist, nevertheless this was his final goal.)

Superficially, a subsistent objective covers up a number of the difficulties that a man gets into while trying to make the goal object the final goal. It is almost a substitute for the quiescence goal that is missing. But actually it solves nothing. For the function of a quiescence goal is to be the goal of the drive, but the objective is simply another goal for the anticipatory set beside its goal object. The drive is still left floating—unless we accept an ideomotor theory, in which case a second goal becomes superfluous.

Moreover, it is questionable if a subsistent objective can

legitimately be regarded as a goal at all. The word 'goal' is ambiguous. It may signify, on the one hand, conditions to be satisfied (like the conditions of quiescence for the impulse pattern) or an idea or plan to be fulfilled (like an anticipatory set); and, on the other hand, it signifies the consummatory satisfaction (quiescence pattern) or fulfillment (goal object) itself. Strictly speaking, only the latter is the goal. The latter is what is aimed at. Our diagram makes this very clear. It is because the latter is the goal that we can properly speak of an anticipatory set being in error because of the nonexistence of the goal, or of a drive being frustrated through the failure to attain its quiescence pattern. It is essential to an adequate description of purposive action that provision be made for both the possibility of the presence and of the absence of the goal.

Now, the odd thing about the subsistent objective in the functioning of a goal is that it never fails. Whether or not the physical goal object appears, the objective is still the goal. The goal, in fact, through its role as the meaning of the anticipatory set, is achieved at the very moment the set is instituted. Since the objective, then, in the role of a final goal is achieved before ever the purpose gets into action, why act at all? If the objective of the Spring of Life is really Ponce de Leon's final goal and the ultimate locus of purposive value, Ponce de Leon had attained it in the very thought of it.

Of course, that is ridiculous. The notion that an objective may be literally a goal springs only from a verbal ambiguity. An objective is at most just the meaning of an anticipatory set. If it is to be distinguished from the anticipatory set at all, it should be considered as a factor in the description of that set, and not as in any proper sense a goal. To regard it as a goal is tantamount to regarding the anticipatory set as its own goal, which is absurd.

Once all ambiguity is removed, and the objective is lodged where it belongs right with the anticipatory set, there remains very little inducement to continue it in separate subsistent being. The set itself as a pattern of references, or readinesses to act in specific ways, is sufficient for its own meaning. The 'subsistent objective' is, we believe, a fiction. Many motives have gone into its creation. But the evidence for its subsistence melts away under analysis—as in the present instance, where it is proposed as a way of avoiding certain difficulties in value theory, which all arise from trying to get along without a quiescence goal.

## 11. Pleasure as the Goal of Appetitive Purpose

Another aspirant to the final goal of a purpose is pleasure. The idea that pleasure or the avoidance of pain is the goal of all desires is a popular one, and has many exponents in the history of ethics and value theory. It constitutes the typical hedonistic interpretation of purposive value.

There is no question that pleasure (unless it can be proved nonexistent) is an item of positive value. We debated early in this study (chap. 1, §5) whether we should begin our examination of values with the analysis of pleasure or of purpose. We decided on the latter, promising to return to an analysis of pleasure as a value if this question had not already been fully explored in the course of our analysis of purpose.

The suggestion at this point is that pleasure is the terminal goal and locus of value in all positive purposive behavior. We are not yet really prepared to attempt a final answer to this suggestion. We do observe that up to this point pleasure has not emerged as a distinct and essential factor in the behavioristic description of the appetitive structure. This is not, however, a serious objection, seeing that we have not yet had occasion to attach introspective data to the behavioristic description of the appetitive structure.

Some relevant preliminary remarks may, however, be made at this time. If pleasure is involved in purposive activity, it must find its place somewhere among the articulations of the appetitive structure we have been describing. That this may be done does not seem unlikely, particularly since it is noticeable that people commonly associate pleasure with the consummatory phases of a purposive activity—with what we have been calling the quiescence pattern. The most conspicuous occasions of pleasure are those associated with eating and drinking, sex consummation, aggressive triumph, and the like. The correlation of the introspective quality of pleasure with some phase of the quiescence pattern of an appetitive purpose seems not unlikely. The hypothesis is bound to spring to mind that the correlation is that of pleasure quality with tension reduction. This is indeed one of the prevailing theories about pleasure at the moment. We shall, in fact, find ourselves drawn to a qualified form of this very theory.

Suppose, however, the theory were accepted in an unqualified form, by which tension reduction is directly correlated with pleasure quality. The introspective feeling of pleasure would then be the qualitative aspect of what we have been behavioristically describing as tension reduction. It still would not follow that pleasure or tension reduction is the final goal and locus of appetitive value. The terminal act of value for any particular appetition is still the particular quiescence pattern for its particular drive. The terminal goal for a thirst drive cannot be the same as that for a hunger drive. This is a crucial fact of appetitive value. The terminal act for thirst is drinking, and for hunger, eating. This difference must be preserved in any verifiable theory of purposive value. If, then, something is suggested as the terminal goal of an appetitive purpose which is the same for all purposes, this cannot verifiably be described as the terminal goal of any purpose. But this is just what pleasure identified with tension reduction would be. Every quiescence pattern is characterized by tension reduction (or, on the tension-reduction theory, pleasure). Every appetition then has the same terminal goal—tension reduction (or pleasure).

But this conclusion is empirically false. Appetitions with different drives require different terminal goals. That fact is precisely what compels us to accept a multiple drive theory of purposive behavior. In short, the terminal goal of a drive is not tension reduction (or pleasure) in the abstract, but the specific mode of reducing tension supplied by the specific quiescence pattern for the particular tension of a specific drive. Pleasure, or tension reduction, in the abstract cannot then be considered as the terminal goal or ultimate locus of value for an appetitive purpose. Tension reduction does in fact accompany the terminal act of every appetition. But tension reduction is not specifically what the drive was seeking. It was seeking its specific quiescence pattern, which does in fact reduce the tensions of that drive and bring it to quiescence.

This does not mean that pleasure is not a value, or perhaps even the ultimate criterion of value. These are matters to be examined later. All it means is that the evidence supporting our description of an appetitive structure shows that pleasure cannot be taken as the terminal goal of each and every appetitive action. The terminal goal is the actual quiescence pattern for the drive in action.

We shall have much to say about pleasure and its relation to purposive activity in the chapters ahead.[32] All that was needed here was to correct a widely prevalent notion that the terminal goal of an appetition is necessarily the pleasure it gives. This is, from our evidence, impossible.

Sometimes 'satisfaction' (as mere tension reduction distinct from pleasure) is suggested as the terminal goal of purposive activity rather than pleasure. The same considerations as those brought up against pleasure would obviously obtain here—and, in fact, even more strongly, since satisfaction is customarily attributed to the terminations of aversions as well as to those of appetitions. And, as we shall see, there is no terminal act of quiescence, no actual consummatory event, in the quiescence of an aversion. An aversive drive just stops when the object of aversion is disposed of or evaded. Nor is there ordinarily any pleasure at the termination of a simple aversion, though the tensions of the aversive drive are reduced (which is an objection to the unqualified correlation of pleasure with tension reduction). Nevertheless, the termination of an aversion is said to satisfy the drive. Satisfaction, in the strict sense of the satisfactory termination of a drive, cannot, then, be identified in its meaning with pleasure, or with the consummatory quiescence pattern of an appetition, or with anything positive at all (even though pleasure does accompany it in the quiescence pattern). It means simply the release or nullification of tension. Satisfaction in this sense is not an appetitive goal.

## 12. FINAL RESULTS

So, after this long but necessary digression, we are back where we were at the beginning of the chapter. What seemed simple and obvious to begin with has proved to be obvious and correct after all. The goal of an appetition consists of two parts: a goal object and a quiescence pattern. The function of the former is to produce the latter, whence it follows that the quiescence pattern is the final goal and locus of terminal value for an appetition. It is possible, however, that if pleasure can be identified with the release of tension of a quiescence pattern, then pleasure can also be regarded as a necessary element in the terminal goal of an appetition. The latter possibility, however, we shall soon find we cannot admit without a large qualification.

This completes our description of the positive purposive act, or appetition. We turn next to the description of the negative purposive act, or aversion.

# 10

# Aversions

## 1. What Is an Aversion?

Now we come to one of the most perplexing topics in the field of purposive value. What is a negative purposive value? The answer seems simple. An aversion, of course. But when we were studying Tolman's list of instincts we discovered, after critical examination, no instinctive aversions. We discovered a number of instinctive appetitions and some injectives, but no instinctive aversions. And if there are no instinctive aversions, how can there be derived ones?

As a way of entering the problem, let us take a hint from Tolman's classification of injectives as aversions. The function of an injective is to mobilize the energy of an organism in reference to some noxious object or situation. In an appetition, we observed, the injectives enter in whenever an obstruction rises above a certain threshold. Here the stimulus for the release of an injective is an obstruction to an appetitive goal. But injectives may be released also on the stimulus of certain primitive reactions. Burns, cuts, blows, stings, and the like, when suddenly received and fairly severe, produce what may be called *riddance patterns*. These primitive reactions are biologically so designed as normally to remove the source of stimulation, and they frequently stimulate an act of fright or aggression. Such acts in which a riddance pattern is followed by fright or aggression would be recognized by everyone as unquestionable aversions. Let us call them 'injective aversions,' and begin our analysis by describing them, subsequently expanding our descriptions once we are sure of the nature of at least these aversions.

## 2. THE SIMPLE INJECTIVE AVERSION

I once had a cat in the family that leaped onto the top of a hot oven with intentions upon a platter of meat. As soon as he felt the intense heat on his paws, he jumped clear of the stove, ran through the kitchen and the dining room, and did not stop till he was in the living room, where he began licking his paws. There was no question that he had an aversion to the burning heat of the stove, and that he exhibited a kind of purposive behavior quite different from any we have been describing up to this point. Just what was going on in this succession of acts? Anyone describing it in ordinary terms would say that when the cat felt the burn on his paws he got a fright and ran till he felt he was out of danger.

In more technical terms we would say that the cat was stimulated by the heat to respond in a riddance pattern which took his paws off the oven, and that the arousal of the riddance pattern was so sudden and intense that this stimulated the injective of fright, which caused him to run from the stove till his fear subsided. Then his paws were evidently still stinging, which set off a new, gentler riddance pattern of licking them. Neglecting this last act, the general form of this type of aversion can be diagramed thus:

| Riddance pattern | Injective | Quiescence of riddance pattern | Quiescence of injective |
| --- | --- | --- | --- |
| | | | |

Or, letting $R$ stand for riddance pattern, $J$ for injective, and $Q$ for quiescence, then:

$$R \mid J \mid Q \text{ of } R \mid Q \text{ of } J$$

Let us call this a simple injective aversion. There is no question that this is an act of aversion. The cat obviously had an aversion to extreme heat, and acted with energy and effectiveness to get away from it. Moreover, as very soon became apparent, it was a docile purposive act, because from this time on for many months the cat never attempted to jump on the oven again, and was afraid of it. The cat had *learned* to be afraid of the oven. This mode of learning is somewhat different from conditioning, and is called *avoidance learning.* The experience was so intense that one instance was enough to set the association. But the result of it was to create a new type of aversion having a totally novel structure.

## 3. The Simple Apprehensive Aversion

This new form of aversion may be called the *simple apprehensive aversion.* It describes the behavior of the cat in being afraid of the stove, and, in fact, for a while, of the whole kitchen. It introduces a new descriptive concept, the *apprehensive set,* which functions in this form of aversion much like the anticipatory set in an appetition. An apprehensive set is a set of references to an object of aversion. The references are negative in intent in regard to something not wanted, and in this respect just opposite to an anticipatory set, which is a set of positive references to something wanted.

For quite a while the cat would not go into the kitchen. But since he was customarily fed under the stove, there was a strong inducement to try out the kitchen again, and he soon got over his fear of the room, but for months he did not make another attempt to get on the stove, much less to jump on the oven, which was elevated on one side of the stove. How do we describe this type of aversion? In ordinary terms, we would say that the cat was afraid of the oven and even of the stove and the whole kitchen because he had once got his paws burned there and had a fright and was afraid of being burned again. Moreover, as came out in time, these apprehensions were stratified after a fashion. The cat feared the kitchen because the stove was in it, and he feared the stove because of its oven, and the oven because he got his paws burned on it. In short, these three apprehensive sets were connected by a succession of mediating judgments, and each depended on the other very much like a succession of anticipatory sets leading to the terminal goal of an appetition. The riddance pattern in this aversion functions somewhat like the quiescence pattern of an appetition. It is the terminal object of reference that is being avoided through the succession of mediating judgments incorporated in the successive apprehensive sets.

Putting these results into diagrammatic form, allowing $A^P$ to stand for apprehensive set, and $O^A$ for object of apprehension, we can symbolize the structure of this behavior.

| $R$ | Subordinate apprehensions | | $A^P{}_R$ | $J$ | $Q$ of $J$ |
|---|---|---|---|---|---|
| | $O^A{}_1$ | $A^P{}_1$ | | $J$ | |
| | $O^A{}_2$ | $A^P{}_2$ | | $J$ | |
| | $O^A{}_3$ $A^P{}_3$ | | | $J$ | |

$R$ = riddance response to burn on paws

$O^A{}_1$ = top of oven

$O^A{}_2$ = stove

$O^A{}_3$ = kitchen

$A^P{}_R$ = apprehensive set for riddance pattern of being burned

$A^P{}_1$ = apprehensive set for top of oven

$A^P{}_2$ = apprehensive set for stove

$A^P{}_3$ = apprehensive set for kitchen

$J$ = injective of fear

$Q$ = quiescence

(1)

That is to say, from the fright at burning his paws on the oven, the cat acquired a whole series of subordinate apprehensions based on the fear of burning his paws. Consequently, when later he started to go into the kitchen, he was afraid and retired elsewhere. The sight of the kitchen $O^A{}_3$ stimulated the apprehensive set $A^P{}_3$ and the injective of fear $J$, which motivated a response to get away from the kitchen to a place where the apprehensive references were no longer stimulated and the fear stopped, $Q$ of $J$.

Observe that there is no $Q$ of $R$ because $R$ is not usually an actual dynamic agent in an apprehensive aversion. The whole function of this structure is to shield the organism from the arousal of $R$.

The important point to notice here is that the motivating agent was the injective $J$, not the original source of the aversion $R$. The cat was not literally responding to a burn, but to a fear aroused by apprehensive references to a burn. The *purpose* of this behavior was precisely to avoid a burn. The whole structure of the aversion was designed to protect the organism from the burn. The layers of apprehensive sets were extended like a thick shield to ward off the noxious stimulus of the riddance pattern. This shield is represented by the succession of subordinate apprehensions descending from the primary apprehension of the riddance pattern.

Of course, in a cat or even in a man these successive apprehensive references are not ordinarily so clearly articulated as the diagram indicates. They may be jumbled and fused, with many extraneous references thrown in besides. But something of a hierarchy does emerge, with mediating judgments connecting the sets. Some of the judgments may be correct and some incorrect, just as with the linkage of mediating judgments in a hierarchy of anticipatory sets.

In describing the action of apprehensive sets, we run into the same problem about the mode of description as with anticipatory sets. In order to be clear about them we have to treat them as clean-cut articulations, and almost as if they were verbal judgments—which they rarely are in man and never in animals. Everything stated in chapter 4, §§4 and 5, on the anticipatory set and verbal expressions of it applies at this point equally to apprehensive sets. If that can be understood, we can talk about them in terms of verbal judgments without danger of being misunderstood.

If the cat's apprehensive references to the kitchen were articulated and formalized they would come out essentially as diagramed. The fear of the kitchen was mediated by the fear of the stove, which was mediated by the fear of the oven, which was mediated by the fear of a burn. Everything that we discovered earlier about the operation of mediating judgments for anticipatory sets in relation to superordinate sets and the terminal goal of an appetition applies to apprehensive sets in aversions. The negative value, the aversion, that an organism has for an object of aversion referred to by an apprehensive set is mediated by a judgment that this object will lead to another object which is an object of aversion. The cat presumably valued the kitchen negatively (feared it) on the implicit judgment that entering the kitchen would bring him in proximity to the stove, which might hurt him. As long as the cat believed that it was dangerous to be near the stove, he would stay out of the kitchen. That his action was mediated by such an implicit judgment was later demonstrated when the cat was induced by food and hunger to risk entering the kitchen and eating under the stove. He found that no harm came to him, and so lost his fear of the kitchen. The same mediating judgments held with the relation of the stove to the oven, and the oven to being burned. The superordinate apprehension of being burned, $A^P_R$ charged by the injective $J$, was charging each successive subordinate apprehensive set by way of the mediating judgments connecting the sets.

There is, however, this big difference between the structure of an appetition and that of an aversion. In an appetition the mediating judgments connecting the anticipatory sets with the terminal goal are constantly being tested for their correctness. For the appetitive structure is designed to lead the organism through a succession of subordinate acts to a goal. But in an aversion the subordinate apprehensions and their mediating judgments are not automatically tested. For the aversive structure is designed to create a safe distance between an organism and noxious objects in the environment. The result is that men and animals learn to be afraid of many things they do not need to be afraid of. Many negative values are based on erroneous mediating judgments which are never brought to a test. Even the terminal object of apprehension may be misjudged. The object may no longer exist, or not with the degree of harmfulness believed, or not with the constancy of dangerousness believed. Indeed, this was the condition with the cat. The top of the oven was not hot all the time, but for months the cat never tried to test it, much to the comfort of his mistress. The cat implicitly believed that the oven top was a continuous source of harm. And not only the oven: he also implicitly believed that the whole top of the stove was a source of harm. These beliefs (negative charges on the apprehensive sets) induced unqualified negative references and avoidance reactions to those objects of apprehension.

Furthermore, as long as the interdependence of the apprehensive sets through the succession of mediating judgments is maintained, the loss of belief in a superordinate apprehensive set will lead to a loss of belief in every subordinate apprehensive set below it. The motivating charge flows down through the mediating judgments, and if a charge ceases to flow into any superordinate level, it ceases to flow into every level below it. If the cat is afraid of the kitchen because of his fear of the stove, then a loss of fear of the stove will automatically relieve him of a fear of the kitchen.

If this does not take place, it shows that a mediating judgment is no longer functioning and that an independence mutation has occurred. A subordinate apprehensive set and its injective charge now go off on their own, independently of their origin. The object of the apprehensive set is now feared for itself. It has become an independent acquired aversion. This mutation can very easily occur in an apprehensive aversion because the drive motivating the behavior is not the original riddance pattern but an injective. And the injective is thrown into action on the stimulus of any object of any subordinate apprehensive set. The subordinate acts are already partially independent, because their charge no longer comes from the riddance pattern but from an injective stimulated by an object connected only by a chain of mediating judgments with a final reference to the riddance pattern. The references and linkage of mediating judgments can easily begin to weaken and drop out, and the injective attach itself directly and exclusively to the acquired object of apprehension.

Here, in fact, is the first time we have been in a position to see clearly what may be the mechanism of an independence mutation. With this clue we can get to work constructively on the problem of the independence mutation, which we had to leave unresolved in chapter 7. What makes an independence mutation possible is the intrusion of a new drive that can take over the dynamics of a subordinate act and so detach the act from its original motivating source.

Apart from this mutation, the subordinate apprehensions of an aversion depend on their superordinate sets for their charge; as soon as the mediating judgment which connects them is proved to be incorrect, the subordinate sets lose their drive and drop out. Like anticipatory sets that have dropped out through lack of reinforcement, however, they are not totally forgotten by the organism. They are latent and readily reactivated if some new mediating judgment connects them with a new charge.

The next time the cat jumped up on the oven was many months later. He landed on a plate of turkey containing some tableware that fell off with a loud clatter. The riddance pattern this time was not a burn but a terrifying sound. The subordinate objects of apprehension, the oven and the stove, were the same, however, and his fear of these was strongly reinforced; again it was months before he made another attempt to jump onto the oven. Meantime, platters of meat and fish remained quite safe there.

The simple apprehensive aversion in conjunction with the simple injective aversion give us the essential structure of all acts of aversion. They constitute the central model for the study of aversions, just as the simple anticipatory appetition served as our model for appetitive behavior. But of course there are other forms of aversion.

### 4. The Compound Apprehensive Aversion

The next in complication, and the most complicated that we need consider, is a type that may be called the *compound apprehensive aversion*. This is the type of behavior in which an organism is blocked from getting away from a riddance pattern or object of apprehension and has to seek positive means for overcoming the blockage. An appetitive element has to be introduced into the structure of the aversion in order for final quiescence to occur. For this reason I am calling it a compound aversion. Though basically an aversion, it is partly appetitive.

Most of the striking examples of negative purposive activity among men are of this type. I shall select a rather extended illustration, for it will serve to bring out a number of points about aversions besides that of the particular structure under discussion. A characteristic example of a man exhibiting such an aversion is given in *Kabloona*, the book from which the example of Utak fishing was taken. The author, Poncins, reports his terror at being caught in a blizzard from which he could be saved only by getting back to his cabin.

I was out trapping. It was an escape from the excessively oppressive atmosphere of the Post. But as white men are not allowed to trap here, I was watching certain traps for an Eskimo. He had set them, and I used to go out to visit them. One day, taking advantage of the couple of hours of dusk that remained to us, I went off in the wind, a sack of bait slung across my chest in Eskimo fashion. It was one of those days when you look around and say to yourself, "Not too good, but it will do," and you chance it anyway. I was bound for a trap-line about half a mile from the Post. I reached it, reset two traps, stood up and looked round to make certain of my bearings. Behind me the wind was blowing harder. I was in a situation which makes people like me a bit nervous but in which also they say, invariably, "Just one more and I'll turn back." Already I was having trouble with the shavings of fish which constituted the bait. They would blow off the trap, and I would run after them to put them back where they belonged. I knew well enough that I was playing the fool, but I was stubborn, and I hummed a tune to let myself know that I was perfectly sure of being able to look after myself. I did turn back, though, and I came finally in sight of the cairn that marked my first trap. By this time the blow was stiff, I was worried, and I had stopped humming. I couldn't fool myself any longer. There was no comfort in this situation. I was fidgety, exasperated; and wherever I looked I saw snow-filled space and nothing else. I started to run, stumbled, panted as I ran, and then fell heavily, as if I had been tripped up. By the time I was on my feet again things looked really bad.

I got as far as the cairn and drew breath. Ahead of me, in the direction of the Post, was a bare patch of rock, and with my eyes riveted on it I went forward. I knew that if I took my eyes off it I should never in my life see it again. The thought bothered me. It is absurd, I said to myself, that a man's life should hang on a thing like this, on keeping his eyes glued to a black dot in a gray cloth. But I was less than half a mile from the Post, I knew where I was going, and in ten minutes all danger would be behind me.

It was ahead of me. Suddenly the snow was whirling round me, encircling me, and the whole landscape vanished.

I shouldn't have started to run. Running is the worst thing a man can do. It makes him perspire, and when he stops he freezes. But I ran nevertheless. I said to myself that my life was a matter of seconds, that each second was priceless, and that if I did not reach my objective immediately I was gone.

I ran back where I had come from. This is how men get lost, for they always arrive at a different point from that which they were running to. They think they have spotted a landmark. It is on the right. But it is not on the right; it is not on the left; it is nowhere. Then they go round and round in a circle, out of breath. Damn! There goes a glove! And it means that the hand . . . under an axe . . . will follow the glove. They stop, try to catch their breath, and feel that the end is near. Their *attige,* or inner coat, is frozen with sweat; and as they no longer know what they do, they do the maddest things. They strip to take off this coat of ice, and then freeze without it. They tramp backward and forward for two days in order not to freeze to death; and then they topple over. Not far from where I stood trembling, the grave of Luca was dug after he had been found gloveless and frozen stiff.

I did not want to become one of those men: it was too stupid. I wanted to be calm. But there were no landmarks. I had no notion where I was. The stones I had only just seen had disappeared as by enchantment. I was somebody's plaything, and I knew now that Death had his own peculiar sense of humor.

Visibility was barely five yards. I sat down. This looks like the end, I thought. I am a dead man. An Eskimo would have built an igloo in this blizzard: I couldn't. I hadn't had enough practice. I thought of those men on Herschel Island who had been playing football just outside the settlement when a blizzard had sprung up. They had crawled into icehouses to escape it. Five had frozen to death. I tried to dismiss the thought, saying to myself that I must keep my head. Still, here I was, ten minutes from the Post and already dead. A living dead man! The idea amused me and I thought, I must make a note of it. But how, being dead, could I make a note of it? This little humorous passage was useful: it furnished me momentary relief.

.   .   .   .   .   .   .   .   .   .   .   .   .   .

Suddenly I thought I saw something and hurried towards it. A black dot. But no. A single swift gust of wind erased it from this grey blotting-paper. Death was playful. There are people with whom Death plays for three whole days.

I gave up the notion of direction. I began merely to roam. If there was a chance in a million that I should come out safe, I was taking it. I do not know what happens to the brain, or if eyes are capable of going mad, but everyone who has been lost like this will tell you of extraordinary optical effects. You rush towards a landmark a quarter of a mile away, sure that it is one of the beacons round the Post: it is four yards off and is a tuft of blackened weed. This time I really saw a curiously black spot and my heart jumped as I recognized it. It was one of another set of traps I was serving. But could it be? For it meant I was out at sea! How could I, in a radius of half a mile, have wandered so far off my course?

The shore line. "I follow the shore line!" Stubbornly, afraid that if I do not cling to the word I should lose the thing, I repeated to myself, "The shore line!" It might easily have slipped away from me: I had already proof enough that things were as malicious as people. And I knew the shore line should curve: why was it not curving, confound it!

It curved, thank God! I was safe. Up there at the Post Gibson must have been thinking that I too would be good for five foxes a season. Not this time! There was the beacon straight ahead of me, and I was going straight towards it. A gust. The snow blinded me. I looked again. Where was that beacon? This was really too much! Fortunately, my retina if not my mind knew in what direction I should be going. I sprang forward . . . and a form emerged from the blizzard close enough to touch me. It was Gibson.[1]

Here is an aversion on a big scale, but in a sufficiently condensed space of time for us to see the whole of it. The riddance pattern is mainly reaction to cold and snow. This might stimulate fear or aggression of itself. But a number of apprehensive sets stimulated by the situation conspired to raise Poncins' fear to the highest possible pitch. The succession of his fears, that is, of his apprehensive sets, is graphically described, and the acts that followed upon them. The situation was so desperate that the acts are mostly of the trial-and-error type. And it is also revealing of a point I have been making all along about the essential identity of emotional source for fear and anger. Though this experience of Poncins' is dominantly one of fear, spurts of anger spout up every little while. "I was fidgety, exasperated" —that is, worried fear grading over into worried anger. "Damn! there goes a glove"—even though this was only a thought, it gives anger a chance. "And I knew the shore line should curve: why was it not curving, confound it!" The sources of anger and fear are the same, but their outlets are opposite. They are opposite emotions precisely because they have the same dynamic source.

But the particular point I want to bring out in the illustration is how quickly Poncins' aversion to the blizzard projected itself into an appetition for the Post as a means of escaping from the blizzard. The steps of the act of aversion turned into the steps of an appetition toward a goal which if attained would remove the riddance pattern and all the apprehensions. Our task now is to describe clearly the connection between the appetition and the aversion on which it is based.

Considering the act as a desire to get to the Post, we see it has all the characteristics of an appetition except a spontaneous drive. There is the anticipatory set to get to the Post, there are subordinate acts with their subordinate sets and goal objects, and there is the terminal goal object of the Post. But what takes the place of the drive and its correlative goal? Obviously the injective. The dynamics of the act comes mainly from the injective— fright in this instance. But the injective presupposes a system of apprehensive sets and an original riddance pattern behind it. It dawns upon us that the whole system of a simple apprehensive aversion which we outlined in diagram 1 occupies the function of the drive in this appetition of Poncins' to get to the Post.

Since the action of the injective with its inherent readinesses did not suffice to remove the object of apprehension and bring quiescence to the injective, an appetitive system of anticipatory sets and goal objects was interpolated to attain that quiescence. Diagram 2 represents this situation. Notice that $O^{G}_1$ is the only substantial element in the goal. $Q$ of $R$ and $Q$ of $J$ are nothing, simply signifying the ceasing of the tension of the drives $R$ and $J$. In short, there is no $Q^P$, or consummatory act, required for this purposive structure. *That is what makes it an aversion.* Its function is to escape the objects stimulating the drives, not to attain objects stimulating a consummatory act. It has the superficial appearance of an appetition because it contains anticipatory sets and goal objects which are genuine appetitive structures. But it lacks the pivotal element of an appetition, a positive consummatory act.

Diagram 2 is what we mean by a compound injective aversion. If we compare the structure of this total act with that of a simple apprehensive aversion (diagram 1) we see that it consists merely in interpolating an anticipatory set, subordinate acts, and a terminal goal object between the injective and its quiescence. The expected function of the goal object is to cause the quiescence of the injective by removing the organism from the stimulation of the riddance pattern and the various objects of apprehension. Just as a simple apprehensive aversion consists of the interpolation of a system of apprehensions between the riddance pattern and the injective of a simple injective aversion (compare diagram 2 with diagram 1), so a compound injective aversion consists of the interpolation of a system of anticipatory acts between the injective and the quiescence of a simple apprehensive aversion. The method of interpolation is the same, but the aim in the one case is to keep the organism away from an object of aversion, whereas the aim in the other is to bring the organism into the presence of an object of appetition as a means of escaping from an object of aversion.

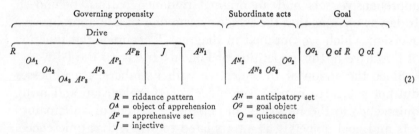

$$R = \text{riddance pattern} \qquad A^N = \text{anticipatory set}$$
$$O^A = \text{object of apprehension} \qquad O^G = \text{goal object}$$
$$A^P = \text{apprehensive set} \qquad Q = \text{quiescence}$$
$$J = \text{injective}$$

(2)

But the final outcome of a compound injective aversion is to produce a total act that has the general structure of an appetition with, however, a very peculiar and complex sort of drive. The 'drive' is in essence a simple apprehensive aversion minus quiescence. The dynamics of the 'drive' is predominantly the injective, though some of the dynamics may come from the riddance pattern if this is actually a stimulating agent in the act. In Poncins' aversion, of course, withdrawal reactions to the cold and snow were going on continuously along with the much more powerful reactions of the injective of fright. The dynamics of his act was consequently very complex. But the net result was to cause the whole system of aversion factors (from the riddance pattern through the injective) to function very much like the drive of an appetition instituting an anticipatory set for the Post as terminal goal object. This complex 'drive' and the anticipatory set it generates thus acquire the form of the governing propensity of an appetition. This governing propensity then controls a succession of subordinate acts in the pursuit of the goal object, which, if properly chosen, brings quiescence to the 'drive.'

Here, then, in this compound aversion is the apparent structure of an appetition. Is it any wonder that aversions have proved very difficult to describe? For whenever an aversion seeks objects as means to escape from other objects, it incorporates elements of an appetition in it, and even takes on the general appearance of an appetitive purpose. We must consequently examine the compound aversion with great care. Within its structure lies the source of many of the confusions of value theory, and also, once it is understood, the source for the solution of many paradoxes. For here is a negative purpose which takes on a positive form. How is this possible?

The importance of having a good strong instance of a compound aversion now is evident. No one would describe Poncins' actions as instances of a positive desire. The purpose was throughout intensely negative. Poncins wanted to get out of the blizzard, was terrified of it every minute, and desperately wanted to reach the cabin as a means of escaping death. This is very important to notice. For the cabin also had positive attractions. It was warm and dry and secure against the storm. These could also be inducements to reach the cabin. If they were, they would be genuine consummatory acts of an appetitive purpose. There are almost always some such positive consummatory acts at the termination of a compound aversion. Consequently, it is often possible to make it look as if these were the primary motivations for the act. One of the reasons for selecting this instance of intense fear is that such an interpretation would obviously be ridiculous. In Poncins' vivid account he never mentions the prospective delights of the cabin. The cabin is his objective solely as a means of getting out of the storm. But even if he had thought of those accruing delights, the essential structure of the aversion would not have been altered. He wanted to get away from the storm. If he had also happened to want to get warm and dry, this would not have obliterated his negative desire to get out of the storm. In short, we have here a definite act of aversion, and it does not cease to be an aversion if some characteristics of an appetition are found within it, or if genuine appetitive drives happen to accompany it.

Now, let us look carefully at the structure of the compound aversion to determine just why it should not be described as an appetition in spite of its superficial resemblance to one. The reason is that its 'drive' is centered on a riddance pattern with negative conditions of quiescence, not on an impulse pattern with positive conditions of quiescence. A positive purpose is one so constructed as to direct the organism to a positive consummatory act or quiescence pattern. A negative purpose is one so constructed as to lead the organism away from a riddance pattern to a condition of mere quiescence of the riddance pattern or mere quiescence of apprehensions of it. The definitive difference is whether the act is so organized in its dynamic structure as to terminate in a $Q$ (mere quiescence) or in a $Q^P$ (a specific consummatory act or quiescence pattern like eating or drinking or gratuitous satisfaction). If the former, it is an aversion, for its aim is to avoid a certain stimulation; if the latter, it is an appetition, for its aim is to attain a certain pattern of stimulation.

What makes Poncins' act an aversion, despite the fact that it took the form of trying desperately to get to a goal object, the cabin, is that his motivation for reaching the cabin was the quiescence of his fears and discomfort. The cabin was simply a means for final quiescence. It was not a means for a quiescence pattern, not a means for a positive consummatory act.

But, it might be said, what about the quiescence pattern of an injective? We noticed earlier that injectives have consummatory acts—a positive feeling of relief for fear and of triumph for aggression. Unquestionably Poncins felt greatly relieved when he met Gibson and finally reached the cabin. He mentioned his relief a little earlier, when he found the shoreline curved: "It curved, thank God!" So this purposive act did have a positive quiescence pattern for its injective at the end. Why does this not convert the act into an appetition? Because the injective is subservient to objects of apprehension and riddance. The injective is bound into the act by the mediating judgments of the apprehensive sets which refer ultimately to acts of riddance. He is terrified at the danger of being frozen to death. His fear is based on the mediating judgment that the storm is likely to kill him. His primary motivation is accordingly to get out of the storm. It is not that of attaining the delights of relief. So far as we can see, he never thought of these delights any more than of those of the warmth and dryness of the cabin. Put the matter another way: even if there had been no feeling of relief on the termination of his fear, Poncins would have been just as frightened of the storm and would have acted just as desperately. The quiescence pattern of an injective is a sort of gratuitous satisfaction superadded to its motivating function in the structure of an aversion.

This is why, in diagraming the dynamic structure of aversions, it is proper to describe the termination of the purposive act as mere quiescence of the injective ($Q$ of $J$). The superadded relief or triumph (which would be a $Q^p$ of J, a positive quiescence pattern for a spontaneous overflow of injective energy, as described in chapter 8, §7) is irrelevant to the motivation of an aversion containing an injective drive. Once this point is understood, an aversion can be unqualifiedly described as a purposive act which terminates in mere (negative) quiescence of the drive, in contrast to an appetition, which always terminates in a positive quiescence pattern or specific consummatory act.

And yet the positive quiescence pattern of an injective is not to be ignored. It has an important bearing on the development of independence mutations. We shall stress its significance then. But at this point, where we wish to become clear in regard to the contrast between the dynamic structure of an aversion and that of an appetition, it is important to notice that feelings of relief and triumph are irrelevant to the dynamics of an aversion. An aversion containing an injective depends heavily, and often entirely, on the drive of the injective, and terminates only with the quiescence of the injective. But it does not depend at all on the feelings of relief or triumph which ordinarily follow the quiescence of the injective.

I dwell on this important point because failure to notice it is one of the reasons for the almost universal failure to distinguish the striking contrast between the structure of an aversion and that of an appetition. Nearly all accounts describe an aversion as if it had the same structure as an appetition, as if it were a species of appetition with a somehow different goal. My point is that the structure of an aversion is diametrically opposite to that of an appetition. The structure of an aversion is such as to avoid objects of riddance and apprehension, whereas the structure of an appetition is such as to attain a specific act of consummation. Accordingly, the satisfaction of an aversion consists in the mere quiescence of its drives ($Q$ of $R$, or $Q$ of $J$), but the satisfaction of an appetition requires a specific quiescence pattern ($Q^p$). Or, again, the conditions of quiescence for the drives of an aversion are negative, merely the nonstimulation of the aversive drives (the riddance patterns and injectives)—merely getting away from the burning or the cold or the objects of apprehension. But the conditions of quiescence for the drives of an appetition are the attainment of specific patterns of acts like eating and drinking for hunger and thirst.

Briefly, the contrast between the two kinds of purpose can be summarized thus: *an aversion is characterized by having drives which require only negative conditions of quiescence; an appetition, by having drives which require specific positive conditions of quiescence.*

The structure of Poncins' purposive behavior is, accordingly, an aversion. All its articulations are subordinated to certain negative conditions of quiescence, to escape from the cold and the fear of freezing to death. But since it incorporates appetitive anticipatory sets and goal objects as means of escaping the stimuli of its aversive drives, it may be considered compound in structure—a purpose that is dominantly an aversion but incorporates some appetitive elements in its service.

## 5. Samples of Other Forms of Aversion: Riddance Aversions

We are now well introduced to the subject of aversions. After examining two kinds of purposive acts which common speech would unquestionably classify as aversions—the simple injective and the simple apprehensive—we ventured to investigate a highly complex type which led us into a whole nest of issues connected with the relation between aversions and appetitions. Having worked through that analysis, we shall find other forms of aversion that fall easily into line with the preceding analyses and serve to confirm the points we established concerning the distinguishing traits of aversive structures in contrast to appetitive.

All the forms of aversions so far considered have involved injectives. We began with them because they provide the most striking illustrations of negative purposes: a cat scared of a hot oven, a man terrified of a blizzard. No initial argument is necessary to show that these are instances of negative purposive behavior. They are obviously designed for avoidance. But many common aversions involve no fright.

We may begin with *simple riddance:*

| Riddance pattern | Quiescence of riddance pattern |
|:---:|:---:|
| R | Q of R |

I am pricked by a pin and pull away, feel a draught and move to another chair, notice a glare in my eyes and turn my head, feel my leg going to sleep and uncross my legs. These are all simple riddance acts, instinctive or nearly so. In fact, so far as they are unlearned, they make up the list of instinctive aversive drives which seemed to be lost in our study of Tolman's classification of instinctive drives in chapter 8. They were missed because they are so common and obvious, and partly too because they are so simple. For the question can be raised whether they should be included in the field of purposive behavior when they are practically nothing but reflexes.

This question is quickly answered by considering the slightly more complex form of aversion which may be called *simple riddance with trial and error:*

| Riddance pattern | Trial-and-error activity | Quiescence of riddance pattern |
|:---:|:---:|:---:|

Suppose I get a splinter in my hand and, after two or three tries, pull it out with my fingers—which would be simple riddance with trial and error. That would clearly be a purposive act achieving, through a number of attempts, the riddance of an irritating object. But suppose I got the splinter out at the first pull—which would be an act of simple riddance. Would I have to declare that this was not a purposive achievement? That is to say, an imperfect achievement of a riddance drive would be an acknowledged purposive act, but the perfect achievement would not! The absurdity of this dilemma lies in the fact that simple riddance, when it works, is the most efficient achievement of a negative purpose conceivable. The irritating object is removed by a single act. All other forms of aversion require a whole system of acts to get the same result. Simple riddance is a negative purposive activity reduced to the simplest possible terms, to a single act of the drive which is immediately successful. All other more complex forms of aversion are the result of the inadequacy of the drive to achieve satisfaction on the first try. Simple riddance is, in fact, the ideal of aversive achievement, and all other forms of aversion are degrees of approximation to this ideal. When this is grasped, the place of simple riddance in the field of purposive activity is clear to see.

Simple riddance may even appear as a mechanical reflex act, such as the eye-winking reflex to avoid a cinder. For if the cinder got into the eye, and one had to visit a doctor to have the cinder removed, it would be a very extended purposive act. The mechanical eye-winking reflex then shows itself to be the ideal form of aversion for keeping foreign matter out of the eye. It is just so simple and effective that it is not noticed until occasionally it does not achieve its aim. Even a mechanical reflex falls within the field of purposive acts if it functions as a riddance pattern— if, in other words, it is capable on occasion of directing subordinate acts or of having weight at any time in comparison with other drives.

Coughing, for another example, is most efficient as simple riddance in the form of a mechanical reflex. But when on occasion it develops into a coughing spell it shows itself plainly as an aversive drive capable of directing an extended series of subordinate acts. Also one often has to consider whether to cough at a concert, or try to hold one's breath, or leave the hall. The reflex act functions as a drive that has to be weighed with other drives for an evaluative decision. We cannot therefore draw the line of purposive values so as to exclude all reflex acts. If a reflex act functions as a riddance pattern, it must be considered as within the field of purposive values.

The next stage of complexity beyond simple riddance and simple riddance with trial and error is the *compound riddance aversion:*

| Riddance pattern | Anticipatory set | Subordinate acts | Goal object | Quiescence of riddance pattern |
|---|---|---|---|---|
| $R$ | $A^N{}_1$ | $A^N{}_2\ O^G{}_2$ | $O^G{}_1$ | $Q$ of $R$ |

(3)

Suppose the splinter in my hand was too small to pull out with my fingers; so I had to turn to the idea $(A^N{}_1)$ of getting a needle $(O^G{}_1)$ and of putting on my glasses $(A^N{}_2\ O^G{}_2)$ in order to see what I was doing with the needle to remove the splinter $(Q$ of $R)$. Here, the blockage of simple riddance stimulated elements of an appetition to attain an instrument to remove the stimulus of the riddance pattern.

Apropos of our discussion of the irrelevancy of relief or triumph (the $Q^P$ of $J$) for the dynamics of a compound injective aversion, notice that there is nothing in the nature of a positive quiescence pattern even available for the compound riddance aversion just described. A riddance pattern simply ends when the irritating stimulus is removed. So here. The drive to remove the splinter has brought in subordinate anticipatory sets and goal objects as means to that end. But having got the splinter out, the drive stopped and that was all. There was no feeling of relief because there had been no injective fear or strain.

I might have approached the issue over the difference of structure between appetitions and aversions by way of the compound riddance aversion. For here the issue does not even arise. There is patently no positive consummatory act of any sort attached to this form of aversion, even though it incorporates anticipatory sets and goal objects. But it seemed to me the contrast would come out most strongly if it were first demonstrated where it seemed least plausible; and then the other forms of aversions, where the issue could not possibly arise, would put the seal of confirmation on our earlier analysis. All forms of riddance aversions, where the drive is supplied solely by riddance patterns, lack any semblance of positive quiescence patterns. In these forms, accordingly, the aversive structure shows itself in greatest purity. These are the forms, therefore, to be particularly considered by writers who try to force both aversions and appetitions into a single structural mold.

The three forms diagramed in this section are all samples of pure riddance aversions. Their drives are solely from riddance patterns. Clearly a riddance aversion may take on a much more complicated structure. A whole succession of means may be needed to do away with an object of riddance, and trial-and-error activity may enter in at any point where a blockage occurs in the progress of the purposive act. And an organism can learn effective means of getting rid of a specific object of riddance just as he can learn how to attain an appetitive goal. Getting a needle for a small splinter is a good example of a learned series of subordinate acts adapted to a typical aversive need.

Moreover, an organism acquires apprehensive sets. Having got a splinter from an old rake handle, I use the rake more carefully thereafter, or throw it away and get a new one. Apprehensive sets may follow on the stimulus of any riddance pattern, and are almost sure to follow if an injective is added to the motivation. Any blockage of a response to an object of apprehension leads to the pursuit of goal objects as means to overcome the blockage, to trial and error if necessary, and possibly to new accretions of injective energy. The structure of an aversion in the face of serious obstructions may become very extensive and intricately stratified.

However, all these forms of aversion will be found to have this trait in common: their conditions of quiescence are negative. All that they require for termination is the removal from stimulation of the object of riddance or apprehension (the mere $Q$ of $R$ or $Q$ of $J$). In this respect they differ from an appetition, which requires a positive consummatory act for its terminal goal ($Q^P$).

The crucial distinction between an appetition and an aversion was clearly, if somewhat too simply, described by Wallace Craig as early as 1918. His statement makes a fitting conclusion to this section of our analysis:

> An appetite (or appetence, if this term may be used with a purely behavioristic meaning) so far as externally observable, is a state of agitation which continues so long as a certain stimulus which may be called the appeted stimulus is absent. When this appeted stimulus is at length received it stimulates a consummatory reaction after which the appetitive behavior ceases and is succeeded by a state of relative rest.
>
> An aversion is a state of agitation which continues so long as a certain stimulus, referred to by us as the disturbing stimulus, is present; but which ceases, being replaced by a state of relative rest, when the stimulus has ceased to act on the sense-organs.[2]

## 6. PERRY'S TREATMENT OF AN AVERSION AS AN APPETITION FOR A NEGATIVE GOAL

In the light of the foregoing analysis of positive and negative purposes, what do we find when we turn to Perry and Tolman? Any divergences between their careful treatment of the subject and ours will illuminate the issues involved.

From our survey of Perry's treatment of the goal of an appetition in the last chapter, we would expect him not to define the distinction in terms of the presence or absence of a consummatory act $(Q^P)$. He never clearly perceived the function of the impulse pattern with its correlative quiescence pattern as distinct from that of an anticipatory set referring to its goal object. Since he never recognized the consummatory act $(Q^P)$ as the terminal goal of an appetition, he naturally was unable to see that this would be the distinctive mark of an appetition in contrast to an aversion. Moreover, not noticing the function of the consummatory act, he failed to be clear about the distinction between a drive and an anticipatory set. From this it followed that he would not be in a position to discriminate between a riddance pattern and an impulse pattern, or between an anticipatory set and an apprehensive set. In view of all these limitations, it appears that his only recourse was to try to describe the difference between a positive and a negative purpose in terms of some character of the goal object.

Accordingly, Perry offers the classic attempt to conceive the structure of all purposive behavior as essentially appetitive, and to find the positive or negative character of the purpose in a positive or negative character of the goal object. Since this is a conception widely held, at least implicitly, by many writers within the value field and by a considerable body of common sense opinion, it requires explicit consideration.

Perry's position is the more surprising in that he quotes with approval the passage from Wallace Craig given at the end of the last section. He starts his analysis with it. But he immediately interprets both of Craig's definitions in appetitive terms—that is, in terms of 'expectations' (anticipatory sets) of goal objects. And he ignores the definitive function Craig ascribes to the consummatory act. Perry writes:

> Positive interest will then be a response determined by a positive expectation; and negative interest a response determined by a negative expectation. Just as in our previous analysis it is the object of expectations which is the object of interest, so here it is the sign of the expectation rather than that of the original or stimulating situation that defines the signs of the interest.[3] . . . The difference lies not in any character possessed by the response itself, viewed as movements of the organism, nor in the character of the actual results of such performance either within or without the organism, but in the *expected results so far as such expectation determines the performance.* The general form of interested action is the same, whether positive or negative; the difference lies in the positive or negative sign of the governing expectation . . . Unless negative interest is to mean non-interest, a negative interest in *a* must be the same thing as a positive interest in *not-a*.[4]

If there was any doubt about Perry's intentions in the first passage, it is dissipated in the second. "The general form of interested action is the same, whether positive or negative," he says. But according to our findings the general form of an appetition is quite different from that of an aversion. And then he says that a negative interest in *a* is the same as a positive interest in *not-a*, which signifies that a negative interest in *a* is an appetitive structure directed upon *not-a*. The context also shows that *not-a* is supposed to be a goal object. And all notice of the consummatory act of an appetition has vanished.

But this conception of an aversion as an appetition for a negative goal object will not do. An appetition for a negative goal object is not an aversion at all. It is precisely what the term signifies, a positive desire for the absence of something. When a musician indicates a rest in the course of a composition, he wants the absence of sound as a goal object for a consummatory satisfaction at that point just as positively as at the next moment he wants the presence of sound for a similar consummatory satisfaction. In the same way a person may positively want a noiseless room at times without any implication of aversion to noise. He wants at that time the positive satisfaction of silence, as at other times he wants the positive satisfaction of sweets without any implication of aversion to nonsweets. A man may often desire solitude without any aversion to company. The choice of the one or the other will be a choice between two positive desires that cannot both be satisfied at the same time, like the choice between eating and drinking at a certain point in a meal.

Not only is an appetition for *not-a* a genuine appetition, as these illustrations show, but a genuine aversion can never be twisted into the characteristic basic structure of an appetition. The cat leaping off the hot stove was not seeking a *not-a* but was negatively responding to a very substantial and logically positive *a*, the actual hot oven. And in the cat's apprehensive aversion that followed, he was not seeking a not-kitchen, and a not-stove, and a not-hot-oven, but quite the opposite. If this system of apprehensions had been anticipations, then the line of mediating judgments would have to be read off in the opposite sense from that which it actually takes. That is, if the hierarchy of apprehensions were to be turned into a hierarchy of anticipatory sets, then we should have to say that the cat was positively desiring the not-hot-oven as a means to his desire for the not-stove, which he desired as a means to his terminal goal of a not-kitchen! Of course, the whole conception is absurd, because the function of a system of apprehensive sets is precisely to shield an organism from response to the terminal object of reference (namely, the riddance pattern)—just the opposite of a system of anticipatory sets, which has the function of guiding an organism to the terminal objects of reference (namely, the goal object and quiescence pattern). The difference between an appetition and an aversion lies in the total structure and function of the two acts. The most convenient definitive feature is that of the presence or absence of a consummatory act $(Q^p)$. But the idea of trying to mold aversions into the form of appetitions will not conform to the facts. The more we enter into the details of purposive activity, the more repugnant the hypothesis becomes.

The only reason Perry's account seems at all plausible is that he deals in his examples with apprehensive sets which he and the reader are induced to accept as anticipatory sets.

> The father, who is middle-aged, apprehensive, and lightly shod, selects his footing in one way; while his son, who is youthful, adventurous, and equipped with a new pair of rubber boots, selects his footing in another way. In describing the two performances we say that the son steps in all the puddles, while the father steps *anywhere but* in a puddle.[5]

Here the father is responding through the references of an apprehensive set; the son, through those of an anticipatory set. Perry's description in the concrete is accurate and charming, but his conception that these acts both have the general structure of an appetition with forward anticipatory references is erroneous.

## 7. COMPARISON WITH TOLMAN'S TREATMENT: HIS CONCEPTION OF A POSITIVE-NEGATIVE DRIVE

So far as I can see, there is no essential difference between our conception of negative purposes and that of Tolman in his *Purposive Behavior in Animals and Men.* Not being primarily interested in value in this book, he does not carry through an analysis of negative purposive value in detail, as we have done. He does not seem to distinguish between what we have called the 'apprehensive set' and the 'anticipatory set.' But he speaks often about 'threatening' objects and the negative subordination of these to 'a final state of physiological disturbance,' which is our riddance pattern.

> We hold that the ultimately to-be-got-from entity is, not the 'disturbing stimulus' *per se,* but rather a final state of physiologi-

cal disturbance (e.g., injury, physiological blocking, or the like), which is threatened by that disturbing stimulus. That is, we should hold the avoidance of the disturbing stimulus is, in most cases . . . docile in the sense that, if it is demonstrated to the organism that nothing 'bad' will actually result from the disturbing stimulus, he will eventually cease to avoid it.[6]

All this is in agreement with our analysis. Particularly to be noticed is the agreement of the two accounts regarding terminal negative value. For both of us this is the riddance pattern, the 'final state of physiological disturbance' itself. This is what is ultimately bad, and it is also intrinsically bad, just as in an appetition the quiescence pattern was ultimately and intrinsically good.

In a number of his more recent studies, however, Tolman employs a novel conception of a drive that requires comment at this point. He now apparently thinks of a drive as having intrinsically both negative and positive components.

A hungry individual is considered to have acting within him (as long as he is hungry) two complementary stores of drive tensions or charges . . . One of these . . . , the positive one, is conceived to endow (primarily as a result of learning) certain types of objects (i.e., types of food objects) with positive values. And the complementary negative store of charges tends to endow the individual as an immediate 'behaving self' in the behavior space with a special set of negative charges which I shall call a negative hunger 'need-push.'[7]

Tolman applies this type of conception to aversive drives as well. This leads him to describe a child's fear of a bear as also a drive for security, as if the fright were due to the negative tensions of the drive, and the desire for security to the complementary positive tension. Positive and negative drives are thus alike in possessing positive and negative tensions in their basic impulses.

Tolman here seems to be yielding to a common sense tendency to force positive and negative purposes into a single mold. His recent conception is novel, however, in taking as the mold not the form of an appetition but a new construction having both appetitive and aversive elements. It has the same effect as the older conception, nevertheless, in that it blurs or breaks down the important structural differences between an appetition and an aversion. It conceals the important difference of biological function between the positive purpose designed to attain something beneficial for the organism and the negative purpose designed to protect the organism from something noxious.

Tolman's new conception of a drive as containing intrinsically both positive and negative charges seems to be unconfirmed by the available evidence. A good many appetitive drives have no observable negative charge. All gratuitous satisfactions are of this sort: the pleasantness of fresh air when you open the door, the odors of a garden, the warm welcome of the sun. Moreover, the emergence of an anticipation for any one of these and an impulse to attain it—the thought of how nice it would be to go out into the garden—does not seem to depend on any negative charge of aversion to remaining in the positive comforts of the house. A realization that some subordinate acts are required for the consummation of the impulse does not imply an aversion or an avoidance of something else. The comfort of the house is nice, but at the moment the delights of the garden may seem nicer. The evidence indicates that many purely positive anticipatory appetitions contain no negative or aversive component whatever.[8]

Moreover, all riddance patterns of aversion seem to be purely negative, without the least evidence of positive components. This would clearly be true of all simple riddance aversions—responses to cuts, stings, burns. It would be true also of all simple injective aversions so far as their dynamics is concerned. To be sure, on our hypothesis, an injective has a quiescence pattern (triumph or relief) which is a positive value when attained. But a typical injective aversion, like the cat's to the hot oven, contains no evidence whatever of its being motivated by any desire to attain a positive sense of relief in the parlor. Whatever positive feeling of relief the cat had in believing himself out of danger of the stove was something gratuitously added on the termination of the act. It was not a component in the dynamics of the drive.

Even compound aversions, which gather up appetitive elements into their structures, employ these elements (and whatever positive drives emerge among them) solely in a subordinate role, and base their dynamics on purely negative motivations. Poncins, terrified by the blizzard, was basically motivated by riddance patterns and the avoidance factors in his injectives of fear and aggression. Whatever moments of relief and triumph he enjoyed in obtaining subordinate goals along the way were incidental, and so was even the great terminal relief of seeing Gibson. He was not engaged in a spontaneous act of seeking relief. He was trying desperately to get out of the storm. There were positive as well as negative values scattered along the path of his aversion, but the basic motivation was entirely negative. In aversions this is always true: the basic motivation is entirely negative.

In certain appetitions, however, Tolman's conception of a drive containing both positive and negative components can be substantiated. Strong hunger is a clear instance, and this is the one Tolman employs. Since strong hunger is painful and even moderate hunger uncomfortable, it is evident that the hunger drive above a certain intensity contains a negative value. The impulse pattern then somewhat resembles a riddance pattern. The organism is trying not only to get food, but also to avoid the discomfort of his intense stomach contractions. This interpretation is confirmed whenever an organism develops apprehensive sets against the danger of intense hunger. If he is a man, he lays in provisions to prevent its occurrence.

It is probably true of all instinctive appetitive drives, except those based on gratuitous satisfactions, that above a certain threshold (which I shall call the pain threshold) they take on a negative value and become avoidance impulses as well as appetitive. Apart from introspective reports, however, it is often difficult to find evidence of this fact. On a strictly objective basis, such as Craig maintains for his description of an appetition (p. 221), all that is remarked is a state of agitation which continues until an appeted stimulus produces a consummatory reaction. If this state of agitation is a positive drive at one intensity it is so for all. That is, in our terms hunger is a positive drive (at any intensity) because it carries positive conditions of quiescence ($Q^p$). So it remains a positive drive (a desire for something) no matter what other characteristics it may take on besides. But now it is called to our attention that it does take on negative characteristics above a certain threshold of intensity. From introspection there is evidence of a desire to avoid the discomfort of an intense appetitive drive as well as the desire to attain the consummatory act. Moreover, objectively, a number of typical avoidance reactions may accompany a painful appetitive drive. A nursing mother whose breasts are overfull may cry with the pain.

But it still remains doubtful whether a mild appetitive drive has any negative component. Is mild hunger even uncomfortable? It induces restlessness, as was observed in Richter's rats. But this is scarcely evidence of discomfort. Mild hunger, or thirst, or nurturance, or love seems introspectively to be pleasant, if anything. It prompts the pursuit of an appropriate object, usually with pleasant anticipations if there is any previous experience with the consummatory act. If not, the restlessness or trial-and-error behavior seems to start automatically. It does not introspectively seem to be either pleasant or unpleasant, and seems to be based on a desire somewhat vaguely to find something, rather than to get away from something. Objectively it would be clearly positive and appetitive, since it ceases with the quiescence pattern and there is no evidence of accompanying riddance patterns.

Tolman's new conception of a drive has thus served to bring to our attention an important point which we shall have to go into carefully later. That is the possibility of a number of different values distributed through the structure of a purposive act. An aversion may have positive values spread through its structure, and an appetition may contain negative values. But it still remains true that an appetition is structured for a positive function, and an aversion for a negative function, and that their basic dynamics reflect this opposition. Moreover, there appear to exist some purely positive drives and some purely negative ones.

An attempt to mold all drives into a single form containing both positive and negative components is thus probably untenable.

## 8. Treatment of an Appetition as an Aversion with a Positive Goal

Perry tried to reduce an aversion to a kind of appetition; Tolman tried to reduce aversions and appetitions to a kind of "push-me pull-you" which is half one, half the other. It would be strange if the third possibility had not also been tried, of reducing an appetition to a kind of aversion.

It has. And it is fairly common. An oversimplified tension theory of drives falls easily into this form. Let physiological tensions be regarded as states of disequilibrium, and equate disequilibrium with negative value, then a drive as a system of tensions is intrinsically negative, and all purposive action is in the form of the avoidance of the drive tensions to recover the quiescence of a state of equilibrium. It is a very neat and attractive theory. It almost works. That is to say, it directly fits half of the evidence, and by ingenious interpretations can be made to fit a great deal more. A clear statement and application of the theory can be found in *The Development of the Sexual Impulse* by Money-Kyrle.

The grounds for rejecting it are the same as those for rejecting the two previous attempts to reduce purposive structures to one common form. The facts do not justify the reduction. The structure of an appetition and that of an aversion are observably different in form. The one pivots on its consummatory act or quiescence pattern ($Q^p$), and its drive is linked to this terminal act by its conditions of quiescence. The other pivots on its drive or riddance pattern, and terminates in bare quiescence ($Q$) when the organism has got out of the range of the source of stimulation. The one is organized for the attainment of a certain act and its stimulating object; the other, for the avoidance of a certain act and its stimulating object. In spite of all the intricacies of purposive action, the basic structural difference can never be eradicated. Writers who try to reduce the differences away are forced sooner or later into denying some of the observable facts.

An attempt to reduce appetitions to aversions has to ignore the specific properties and function of the consummatory act ($Q^p$), and turn it somehow into a means for avoiding tensions and reaching bare quiescence ($Q$). It has to make all appetitive drives negative. Even gratuitous satisfactions must be turned into riddance patterns. The positive function of a hierarchy of antici- patory sets for the attainment of the consummatory act charac- teristic of the structure of an appetition must appear as an in- cident in an aversion. A hungry workman's anticipation of his savory evening supper would have to be considered dynamically the same as his anticipation of the end of his day's monotonous labor. It would have to be said that he wants to get through being hungry just as he wants to get through his work—to avoid the tensions! There is no provision for terminal delight.

It is unlikely that any of these reductive views will prove tenable. We can proceed with a fair assurance that there are distinct positive and negative purposes, basically distinct both in structure and in function.

# 11

## Solutions of the
## Independence Mutation and
## Other Value Mutations

### 1. The Role of the Injective in the Independence Mutation

Earlier in this study (chap. 7) the question arose how derived purposes developed. For it is evident, especially in complex human behavior, that much of man's purposive life is motivated by acquired drives far removed from instinctive appetitions and aversions. It is generally acknowledged that these derived drives result from an independence mutation by which a subordinate act breaks loose from its dependence on superordinate acts and operates on its own power. An act performed as a means becomes an end in itself, and an object valued as a means becomes something good (or bad) in itself.

The dynamics of this mutation is very puzzling. The diverted impulse theory and the ideomotor theory, which are the usual suggestions, have proved to be inadequate. Among the components of the simple anticipatory appetition we found no promising solution. So the problem was temporarily dropped. But now that we have studied the structure of aversions, and discovered the action of injectives in the dynamics of purposive behavior, a solution for the dynamics of the independence mutation begins to appear. We are at last in a position to develop a descriptive hypothesis of the way in which this value change takes place.

The probable solution emerged when we were describing the dynamics of the apprehensive aversion. Here we found that the original drive for this type of purpose, its riddance pattern, was supplanted by another drive, an injective, which directly motivated the subordinate acts of apprehension. Moreover, it was the function of this injective drive to motivate the subordinate acts so that the original riddance pattern would never have to operate again. This shift of dynamics did not, however, constitute in itself an independence mutation. For the injective charge was mediated by the judgment (or cognitive association) which connected the subordinate object of apprehension with the original riddance pattern. As long as the subordinate act depended on this mediating judgment, it lacked independence. But all that was necessary to effect the independence of a subordinate act of apprehension was for the mediating judgment to drop out while the act continued. This would not be ideomotor, because the dynamics of the injective was prepared to motivate the set. And it would not be a diverted impulse, because a new drive had taken over the motivation in place of the old drive. The injective drive seems to offer the clue for the dynamics of the independence mutation.

Since the injective enters the structure of purposive activity in a number of different ways, a corresponding number of different forms of the independence mutation arise. After briefly describing these, we shall examine some forms of activity that operate in practice much like an independence mutation, but are actually different. This analysis should give us a good deal of detailed understanding of the manner by which means become converted into ends.

## 2. INDEPENDENCE MUTATION FOR SUBORDINATE OBJECTS OF APPREHENSION

A subordinate act in a simple apprehensive aversion may acquire independence by merely dropping off the mediating judgment to the superordinate act. The injective charging the apprehensive set is adequate for the motivation. The object of apprehension then becomes an independent (though derived) object of aversion. This form of the independence mutation may be diagramed thus:

From:

$$R \qquad A^P{}_R \mid J \mid Q \text{ of } J$$
$$O^A{}_1 \; A^P{}_1 \qquad \mid J \mid$$

To:

$$O^A{}_1 \; A^P{}_1 \qquad \mid J \mid Q \text{ of } J \tag{1}$$

Anything that would lead to the disappearance of the mediating judgment connecting the subordinate apprehensive set with the set above it would lead to this form of the independence mutation. Apart from instinctive objects of riddance (as with a child's fear of being dropped) and repressions (chap. 11, §5), all objects that directly stir us to fear or apprehension without our knowing why, are presumably derived in this manner. Even when the reason for the fear is obvious, the mutation may have taken place. Stormy clouds, breakers on the shore, jagged mountains, all the typical symbols used by poets for the so-called sublime, seem to be culturally predictable objects of independent apprehension. The objects referred to are dangerous, but they continue to feel so even when they are not actually so to us, and that is why artists can use them with predictable effect.

It is hard to say just where to draw the line between a dependent and an independent derived object of apprehension. The test would be in the amount of proving necessary to convince the organism that the object was no longer dangerous. If it takes more than the ordinary amount of unconditioning to break down an established apprehensive conditioning, that would be evidence that an independence mutation had taken place. When a person realizes that his fears are ungrounded but he is still afraid, he may be sure that a mutation has occurred. As the saying goes, he is intellectually but not emotionally convinced. It may take a great deal of emotional convincing to overcome an acquired apprehension.

Ideally, of course, our fears should fit the occasion, neither more nor less, allowing only for a fair margin of safety. But biologically they tend to operate with a very wide margin of safety, and the independence mutation for objects of apprehension is a case in point. When the object is always or frequently dangerous, the mutation has an obvious biological utility. It throws the organism into effective action with a minimum of delay. But often the object is only occasionally dangerous or has ceased to be dangerous long ago. How to handle such unnecessary fears is one of the great cultural problems.

## 3. Independence Mutation for Subordinate Goal Objects in Aversions

Another way in which an independence mutation may develop out of an aversion is through the anticipatory sets of a compound aversion. This is a particularly interesting form of value mutation, for it is a process by which an independent positive purpose is derived out of the structure of a negative purpose. An aversion gives birth to an independent derived *appetition*.

Take the following instance. A poor boy who must help support the family after the father's death begins selling papers in a big city. Obstructed by the competition of other newsboys, he meets the challenge, and through his energy and need learns the techniques for successfully competing. He then acquires a liking for the competitive activity itself, and on the wave of this new drive finds a more lucrative business, and, in short, sets out on the career of a businessman.

No doubt the motivation here is quite complex, but its general frame is an independence mutation from the appetitive segment of a compound apprehensive aversion. It can be schematized thus:

From:

$$R \quad \underset{O^{A}{}_1\ A^{P}{}_1}{A^{P}{}_R} \ \Big|\ J\ \Big|\ A^{N}{}_1 \quad \underset{A^{N}{}_2\ O^{G}{}_2}{O^{G}{}_1} \ \Big|\ Q \text{ of } J \text{ and } Q^{P} \text{ of } J$$

To:

$$\Big|\ J\ \Big|\ A^{N}{}_2\ O^{G}{}_2\ \Big|\ Q^{P} \text{ of } J \tag{2}$$

Through apprehensions of suffering in his family and of his mother's disapproval if he does not find a way of earning money, he seeks a job to neutralize these fears, is stimulated to aggressive action to overcome obstructive opposition, learns the techniques for successful competition, and thus acquires the means of neutralizing his apprehensions ($Q$ of $J$) but also the triumph of successful aggression ($Q^P$ of $J$). Presently, he finds that he values the competitive activity itself ($A^N_2 O^G_2$) charged with the injective ($J$) for its own reward of the triumph of success ($Q^P$ of $J$). From an original compound aversion there has developed an independence mutation to a derived appetition.

In a competitive society, a large proportion of purposive activity probably consists in appetitions of this sort. It should be noticed that the drive of such an appetition operates very differently from that of an instinctive purpose. It is not cyclical and self-generative like hunger and thirst. The energy of an injective is always available in some degree. It is always ready for discharge when a proper stimulus appears. So, any competitive sales situation becomes a stimulus for our newspaper boy, or even any competitive situation whatever.

Introspectively, or even objectively, the drive and its quiescence pattern are not so clearly distinguishable from the anticipatory set and its goal object as they are in hunger or thirst appetitions. The perception of the goal object is the immediate stimulus which arouses both the injective charge and the anticipatory references all at once. The positive satisfaction of success in the quiescence pattern comes like a postscript, and the significance of its relation to the drive as its consummatory act is easily overlooked. That is to say, the perception of a chance to sell a paper sets the act in motion; and the triumph of the successful sale looks almost superfluous.

It is now easy to understand the persuasiveness of Perry's widely accepted description of value as simply 'interest in object.' It seems to fit this derived act exactly. Nearly all of Perry's illustrations are taken from such acts. An anticipation of selling a paper (interest) is satisfied in a paper sold (object). But this description telescopes into two the following four factors: the drive $(J)$ charging an anticipatory set $(A)$ with references to a goal object $(O^G)$ which produces a positive consummatory satisfaction $(Q^P$ of $J)$. And yet in the act itself these factors are fused in the occurrence. The fusion of them in the occurrence, however, does not eliminate them as distinguishable factors in the act. It merely accounts for the plausibility of the over-simple 'interest in object' definition of value.

This form of derived appetition accounts also for the prevalence of the ideomotor theory. The impulse pattern of an injective does not draw attention to itself, especially at low intensities. It does not stand out as a distinct articulation of a purposive act as the introspective feeling of hunger does, or the objectively observed restlessness of Richter's rats. The idea of selling a paper seems automatically to sell the paper. The operation of an injective drive comes to light only after more careful observation.

## 4. Independence Mutations for Subordinate Goal Objects in Appetitions

Now that we have a clue to the mechanism, it is clear that an injective can develop an independence mutation in a compound appetition as well as in a compound aversion. A compound appetition would be one in which elements of an aversion were incorporated. This happens whenever a serious obstacle blocks the path of an appetitive drive evoking an injective (fear or aggression) to circumvent or overcome the obstacle. An injective that is so aroused in an appetitive act, and that is regularly successful in overcoming an obstruction of a certain sort, would tend to detach this mode of getting satisfaction from the purpose it served, and lead to the pursuit of this act for its own sake.

If the newsboy had happened to come from a well-to-do family he might have been impelled to sell papers for extra pocket money to buy a bicycle or a rabbitry. On this appetitive drive he might have met the challenge of competition much as the poor boy did, and similarly developed an independent drive for sales competition. This mutation would be schematized thus:

From:

$$I \mid A^{N_1} \qquad\qquad O^{G_1} \mid Q^P \text{ of } I \mid Q^P \text{ of } J$$
$$A^{N_2} \qquad O^{G_2}$$
$$J \mid A^{N_3} \; O^{G_3}$$

To:

$$J \mid A^{N_3} \; O^{G_3} \mid Q \text{ of } J \qquad\qquad\qquad (3)$$

In fact, so far as the poor boy was motivated originally by the hunger drive (neglecting the aversions to the deprivation caused by poverty) he also developed an independence mutation from an appetitive drive. In actual life, a derived appetition is likely to have very complex motivational origins. Diagrams 2 and 3 show that often an aversion and an appetition can be simultaneously served by the same injective-charged subordinate act, and so can mutually help to produce an independence mutation upon this act. In other words, the poor boy had a dozen or more motivations for selling papers—some of them aversions, some appetitions. All these drives conspired to put pressure on the subordinate acts which served them all and so mutually augmented the aggressive drive on that act, and so also intensified the condition favorable to the production of an independent injective drive upon that act.

This observation indicates that the last two diagrams represent simply the subspecies of the same form of independence mutation (the development of a derived positive drive by means of a positive injective), whereas the first diagram represents the contrasting form (the development of a derived negative drive from a negative injective).

## 5. INDEPENDENCE MUTATION DUE TO REPRESSION

A form of independence mutation which has been given much prominence lately as a result of psychiatric developments is fixation due to repression. The structure of this mutation is easily understandable in terms of our schemes. It consists in shutting off through fear the mediating judgment which connects a subordinate act with its superordinate drive and quiescence pattern. The connection, however, is blocked only to consciousness; it is still there for unconscious behavior. Thus a subordinate act which serves the basic drive emerges in consciousness as independent.

This is, so far as the total personality is concerned, a pseudo-independent drive. Unconsciously, it is still mediated by a cognitive set and would lose its charge if the connection were disproved. In the Oedipus complex, which has frequently been uncovered in psychiatric treatment, a boy's infantile love of the mother leads to jealousy of the father, which the boy fears to display. The fear is so great that the very suggestion of the thought of this hostile attitude toward his father is a stimulus to the fear which immediately inhibits the thought. But the impulses toward both the father and mother are still as active as ever. In fact, the frustration may even increase the fear. The conscious connection (i.e., the integration of this judgment with other judgments which regulate the child's voluntary behavior) is cut off, but an unconscious connection (i.e., an isolated and unintegrated judgment relating to the two parents) still holds. This *complex* of connected impulses amounts to a new derived drive in the child's personality. It seeks quiescence in any of a variety of means which would be effective in removing the father as a rival: it may take the form of seeking to become powerful as a military man, or a businessman, or a scientist. When the means is socially useful in this way, the result is called a *sublimation*. Not infrequently a man's choice of an occupation appears to be determined at least in part by such a derived drive.

But repression often operates in much simpler ways. It has been pointed out that the acceptance of rumors is partly dependent on repressed desires. People do not like to think of themselves as having impulses for illicit sex relations, for instance. These impulses, as soon as they emerge, are repressed. But when an opportunity arises to project these impulses on others with impunity, it is welcomed—whence the ready acceptance of the widespread rumor about the immoralities of the WAC's in the last war. The rumor seems to have had no objective justification, but it was very persistent.

Race prejudice seems likewise to be fed largely by the projection of repressed desires. A scapegoat is found for hostilities which one does not dare to direct upon the object which is their true source. Statistically it has been found that people who are self-critical and willing to admit having desires they do not approve, are much less addicted to race prejudice than those who are unable to admit such impulses.

A derived drive due to repression may take either a positive or a negative form. If it is some form of the sex drive that is repressed (and some authorities say that at least in part it always is), this provides an appetitive impulse in the complex, whereas the inhibiting fear impulse is aversive. Consequently, if the appetitive impulse dominates in the derived drive (as, for example, quite conspicuously in many perversions) the result is essentially appetitive; but if the injective dominates (as in race prejudice), the result is essentially aversive.

Such derived drives due to repressions can never attain complete satisfaction, however. So far as it is the sex impulse that is repressed, this generalization is obvious: the repression automatically keeps the impulse from attaining unqualified consummation. Not but that the impulse may attain full quiescence under certain conditions, but not under those which call out the derived drive embodying the repression. That is why these drives are often the cause of neurotic conflict. Even in the most successful sublimations there is a residue of unsatisfied impulse. Even the greatest triumph of election to high office, or the attainment of honors or fame, does not wholly compensate for that unsatisfied residue. Perhaps that is what Milton darkly meant in his tantalizing reference to fame as "that last infirmity of noble mind."

And that is why it is a half truth to say that society owes its greatest achievements to its neurotics, and that it would lose many of its most valuable men if all men were mentally healthy. Some artists are known to have refused psychiatric help for fear they would lose their creative drive. For a successful cure of a neurotic consists essentially in removing the repressions, thus integrating the repressed impulses with the rest of a person's voluntary behavior. Inevitably, this breaks up the derived drive due to the repression. It may not, however, change the person's profession if this is socially useful and is supported also by other independent injective drives such as were described earlier in this chapter. It will remove the frenetic intensity of the pursuit, but may well increase its effectiveness by the release of all the energy that was wasted in the efforts at repression.

This form of independence mutation is the source of the conception of the impossible diverted impulse theory so widely held. Through repression an original impulse is diverted to accept partial satisfaction in some instrumental activity which would remove an obstacle in the way of the activity. Innate readinesses, possibly even portions of the consummatory act, also become activated and produce a sort of partial consummatory quiescence. The forms of sublimated acts are often analogous to phases of the consummatory act of the drive repressed. But in any case the charge of the original drive is diverted into the subordinate act and endows the goal object of that subordinate act with a terminal value. This happens because the drive is blocked by the repression from continuing through to the complete quiescence pattern of the consummatory act. So to speak, the drive continually tries to attain its quiescence pattern, but is blocked at the goal object of the subordinate act. Thus the goal object of the subordinate act gets the appearance of the terminal goal of the impulse. To all appearances an independence mutation has occurred. The personality has acquired a new drive for which that instrumental object has become an end in itself. As long as the repression is frozen into the personality, this is an independent derived drive and often a very intense one. But it is not a completely independent act, because the repression conceals a mediating judgment which connects the derived drive with its original impulse, which is still functioning, though incompletely.

Nevertheless, there is considerable relief from such acts: the partial relief or triumph of the injective in successfully carrying through the subordinate act, even though it does not lead to the end for which it was designed; and also whatever partial release the original impulse may gain from quiescence of some of its innate readinesses. The mutation may be schematized thus:

*Positive form*, as in sublimations and perversions:

From:

$$I \mid A^N{}_1 \qquad\quad O^G{}_1 \mid O^A{}_1 \; A^P{}_1 \mid J \mid \text{Frustrated} \mid \text{Frustrated}$$
$$A^N{}_2 \; O^G{}_2 \qquad\qquad\qquad\qquad\quad Q^P \text{ of } I \quad\; Q^P \text{ of } J$$

(This overt act is blocked and never occurs.)

To:

$$I \mid \overbrace{A^N_1 \qquad O^G_1 \mid O^A_1 \ A^P_1}^{\text{Repressed}} \atop A^N_2 \ O^G_2 \qquad\qquad \Big| \quad J \ \Big| \ \begin{matrix} \text{Partial} \\ Q^P \text{ of } I \end{matrix} \ \Big| \ \begin{matrix} \text{Partial} \\ Q^P \text{ of } J \end{matrix} \qquad (4)$$

(This act with a repressed complex occurs as a substitute.)

*Negative form,* as in race prejudice and similar displacements and phobias:

From:

$$I \mid A^N_1 \ O^G_1 \mid O^A_1 \atop O^A_2 \ A^P_2 \quad \Big| \ A^P_1 \ \Big| \ J \ \Big| \ \begin{matrix} \text{Frustrated} \\ Q^P \text{ of } I \end{matrix} \ \Big| \ \begin{matrix} \text{Frustrated} \\ Q^P \text{ of } J \end{matrix}$$

To:

$$I \mid \overbrace{A^N_1 \ O^G_1 \mid O^A_1 \qquad\qquad A^P_1}^{\text{Repressed}} \atop O^A_2 \ A^P_2 \quad \Big| \quad J \ \Big| \ \begin{matrix} \text{Partial} \\ Q^P \text{ of } I \end{matrix} \ \Big| \ \begin{matrix} \text{Partial} \\ Q^P \text{ of } J \end{matrix} \qquad (5)$$

These should not be regarded as the only forms of the mutations, but as two typical forms. Actually, the repressed complex energized by the original drive and the injective practically amount to a novel derived drive frozen into the personality of the agent. It motivates the search for subordinate acts to bring about its quiescence. The variety of subordinate activities open to such a repressed drive is as great as that open to an unrepressed drive. Consequently, the variety of forms the pseudo-independence mutation may take because of repression is almost unlimited.

These repressed drives are possibly the pivot of our most serious social and ethical problems. For, unlike the instinctive biological drives, they are incapable of complete satisfaction and quiescence. Yet, at the same time, like the instinctive drives, they are incapable of modification by learning through voluntary conscious behavior. That is to say, they are irrational in their demands and, as we commonly say, not subject to the control of reason.

The usual ethical solution is to accept them as part of a personality structure—accept them as interests or needs which have to be taken for granted in any problematic situation in which the person is involved. They can, however, be modified by psychiatric means which operate on the causes of the repressions and bring the repressed mediating judgments back into the voluntary conscious control of the agent. This is obviously another ethical solution.

The important ethical point here is that the repertory of interests which a person has at any period does not necessarily constitute the ultimate base of ethical decisions for that person. His repertory of interests may be intrinsically self-defeating, and the appropriate decision may be that of taking measures to change the person's interests.

For instance, some moralists take the position that if a person has an independent interest in self-humiliation or self-annihilation, this is an ultimate value judgment for that personality and nothing can be done about it ethically. It is most unlikely, however, that a drive to commit suicide, whether piecemeal or all at once, is an instinctive basic drive. For organisms so endowed would long ago have eliminated themselves and left the world to those inheriting repertories of drives tending to self-preservation. A suicidal drive is thus almost surely one that is derived, and one most probably derived from a complex of repressed mediating judgments. Psychiatric practice has steadily confirmed this conclusion. For repeatedly it has been observed that after a repression has been removed, the agent ceases to have his suicidal impulses. The agent wants to act as he does only because he is inhibited from knowing the grounds of his impulses, which he recognizes as the farthest from his desires as soon as these grounds are uncovered.

The ethical problem, therefore, even in terms of an individual and apart from social consequences, cannot be assumed to be limited to that of satisfying the given interests of the agent concerned. The repertory of the agent's interests itself may be subject to ethical scrutiny. This point is especially pertinent in respect to drives based on repressions.

## 6. Various Forms of Pseudo-independence, and Other Mutations Sometimes Confused with Independence

Whether to consider a drive based on a repression as a genuine or a pseudo-independence mutation poses a problem, because, though the drive is frozen into the personality as long as the repression endures, still it is there only as a result of an inhibition upon the voluntary control of a mediating judgment which continues to connect the subordinate act with a superordinate drive. But there are instances of subordinate acts entirely open to conscious mediation which nevertheless behave virtually as independent drives. They definitely exemplify pseudo-independence mutations. They are easily confused with genuine independence mutations, and for that reason, if for no other, should be pointed out.

*Multiple instrumentality* is perhaps the most conspicuous of these. When any object has a great variety of uses, and is thus in constant requisition in the service of a variety of drives, it ceases to be identified as an instrument suitable for any one purpose, and comes to be seemingly prized for itself because it is so widely useful.

Money is a striking instance of multiple instrumentality. There is almost nothing that money will not buy. Consequently, in any society in which this is true, money is always desirable, and the sight of a coin on the sidewalk is an immediate stimulus to pick it up. There is no thought of what we may use it for. It is a thing we continually have use for. A specific mediating judgment is not needed to motivate the act. And yet, if money suddenly loses its purchasing power, it quickly ceases to be an object of value at all. This is easily verifiable wherever currency has been repudiated. Hence, money is not the object of a genuine independence mutation. It is mediated by a judgment of multiple instrumentality, which gives it the appearance of an object of independent value.[1]

Many objects in our environment have a pseudo-independent value resulting from multiple instrumentality. A fair test is that of what objects we would pick up if we saw them on the road. Probably any common tool would be picked up: a screwdriver, a hammer, a saw. Even if there is one in the house, it is always handy to have another. Likewise, pencils and pens, articles of clothing. Perhaps an even more reliable test is objects that are likely to be stolen. But there is no point in trying to be precise about determining such objects. All of them are actually objects of instrumental value in some sense and not actually objects of independent terminal value at all.

The psychological mechanism of *identification* is another source of pseudo-independence mutations. We all have a tendency to identify with someone we admire greatly—a parent, a teacher, an actor, a public figure, or anyone outstanding in our profession or social environment—to take on his characteristics and value what he appears to value. This is a pseudo-independence mutation, at least in its origin, because the value given to the traits ascribed to the worshiped hero are mediated by the judgment that they belong to the hero and therefore are desirable. When a new hero arises, the traits lose their desirability like a devaluated currency. But as long as the hero has ascendency, the traits maintain their value.

The reason for their value may not be immediately obvious to the hero worshiper. He often finds himself acting in certain ways, approving and disapproving of certain things, and only after self-scrutiny discovers that these are the traits of his hero. They seem like things valued for themselves. And sometimes, in fact, they become so, but not as a result of identification alone. The mechanism of one of the genuine forms of the independence mutation described above must be superimposed on that of identification in order to bring about the complete disappearance of the mediating judgment. In the child-parent relationship, this result is almost inevitable, since the relationship is shot through with injectives. The often-noticed resemblance of children to parents is probably due as much to the action of identification by which children take over the parental attitudes and patterns of action as it is to heredity.

Third, mention should be made of the mechanism by which we learn to *anticipate gratuitous satisfactions*. This process is so commonly recognized that little thought is given to its anomalous nature. But the question may well be asked whence comes the drive that motivates an anticipatory set like this even when the references of the set are to consummatory satisfactions. The usual answer is that the pleasantness in the anticipation of pleasure motivates the pursuit of the end. But this seems unlikely, since the pleasures of anticipation are themselves consummatory. It would be more plausible to ascribe the motivation to the unpleasantness of the present deprivation of anticipated pleasures.

Let us consider an instance. We respond to odors as gratuitous satisfactions. But to make the problem the more emphatic, consider first an unpleasant odor, such as that from a garbage pail. The very thought of the smell brings up an apprehensive set motivated by an injective which increases in intensity the more we think about it. The motivation that keeps us away from the smell of garbage is thus easy to explain. Now what is the parallel motivation that impels us, on the thought of the pleasant odor of lilac or phlox, to walk from one end of a garden to the other to enjoy it? Would there be an annoyance or frustration if we found we could not get to the odor? Is that then the drive? Is it an injective emerging to overcome the gap between the anticipation and its consummation? This hypothesis seems hardly adequate for so positive a mode of action.

But whatever the correct hypothesis (and we shall return to the problem in chap. 14, §7), there is no question of the fact that a consummatory or gratuitous satisfaction once experienced becomes a goal for the anticipation of its attainment. A drive charges the anticipation of a consummatory satisfaction.

This fact accounts for another group of apparent independence mutations. An activity first entered upon as a means to an ulterior end becomes something performed for itself if it incorporates gratuitous satisfactions in its own right. A walk through woods and fields to our daily work, which is first used as a means to get to the work, may become a delight in itself, and the object of a Sunday stroll, because of the many immediate pleasures along the way.

A value mutation is involved in these derivative anticipations, but it is not exactly an independence mutation. The consummatory value of the instrumental act was inherent in the act itself and needed only to be discovered by the person performing it. The mutation is in the development of a charged anticipation for the act as a terminal goal: the gratuitous satisfactions could not be anticipated until after they had been experienced.

An effect easily confused with the preceding but actually quite different comes from the action of *affective diffusion*.[2] The pleasure that suffuses a consummatory act or gratuitous satisfaction tends to spread out over neighboring and similar objects and acts. A man in love projects his happiness on everything about him. A gift from his beloved, or her photograph, becomes an object of diffused consummatory delight. There is a mediating judgment (an association) which directs the pleasure upon the associated object, but there is unmistakable consummatory satisfaction in the object itself. An object that was previously neutral becomes a source of consummatory delight.

This is not a genuine independence mutation, because the mediating judgment (an association with the beloved) is essential to the result. But it is a genuine value mutation, for an object previously neutral comes to have consummatory value. It becomes incorporated, so to speak, into the consummatory field. Neither must this effect be confused with the simple conditioning mutation by which an object previously neutral comes to be valued as a *means* through a mediating judgment connecting the object with the appetitive goal. For here the object comes to be valued partially as an *end* through a mediating judgment.

The consummatory satisfaction of the original goal is spread out over some of the subordinate acts. This consummatory spread is affective diffusion.[3] If, owing to the persistent action of a mediating judgment, the affective diffusion is constant, it takes on a strong but deceptive appearance of an independence mutation. Many emotive symbols probably have this character. Religious symbols seem obvious examples. Our cultural life, secular as well as religious, is full of such emotive objects. Many emotive words have acquired semi-independent values through affective diffusion. That is one reason why profanity can give so much relief.

Affective diffusion can, of course, be negative as well as positive. In a depressed mood, things become suffused with unpleasantness and dread through association with objects of riddance and terror, just as in a mood of exhilaration objects become suffused with joy.

A mutation which has great importance in the aesthetic field but which has not been sufficiently studied I have called *habituation*. It is not to be confused with habit, for habit is mechanical conditioning. Habituation is a mutation of aesthetic taste in terminal values—in the liking and disliking of things in themselves. It seems to have nothing to do with mediating judgments, and so nothing to do with learning in the sense of conditioning. The cultivation of taste (which is, of course, a matter of value mutations guided toward an increase in the capacity for aesthetic enjoyment) is developed partly by the habituation mutation.

Illustrations of this mutation may be found in the changes in appreciation for consonance and dissonance in music. In the earlier periods of Occidental music only octaves, fourths, and fifths were considered consonant intervals and regarded as intrinsically pleasant. Subsequently, thirds and sixths were admitted. Today the cultivated ear is expected to find pleasure even in seconds and sevenths. The fully habituated ear will now accept any interval in the scale as pleasurable musical material. The simple intervals may seem a little tame and the complex ones tangy, but all are intrinsically likable for themselves.

Similarly, some color combinations are easier to like than others. Close intervals of strong warm hues like purple and orange, yellow and cerise, are disliked by many people. But with experience, all color combinations are intrinsically acceptable and the more difficult combinations are the most exciting ones when they first come to be liked.

All sense qualities appear to be susceptible to habituation in this way. In the field of savors, the uncultivated taste dislikes the dry wines and the harsh cheeses, and in fact has many dislikes. The cultivated taste finds delight in both sweet and dry wines, in gentle and harsh cheeses. The cultivated taste is more discriminating but less finicky.

The way in which habituation occurs is apparently simply through stimulation, through much experience or exposure to the full range of sensory materials. The adage about olives seems to be sound: if you don't like olives, eat a dozen and you will discover that you do like them. The one proviso is that you have no ulterior prejudice against them other than a present dislike for them.

Habituation accounts in large measure for the fact that the ablest artists are usually in advance of the taste of their contemporary public. An artist, by virtue of his more intensive experience with the materials of his art, is always more highly habituated than the public of his time. The public needs time to be exposed to these materials and to catch up with the artist. When the public does catch up, as today's public has to Cézanne and Gauguin and Van Gogh, by that time a new set of artists is offering a new set of materials, which is to this present public as mystifying as the works of last generation's artists were to their public.

The habituation mutation appears to indicate that our dispositions for liking and disliking sense materials are interconnected in such a way that a change of liking for certain sensory materials produces a change of liking in others also. Thus a change from the disliking of thirds and sixths among musical intervals to a liking for them was accompanied by a less intense liking of octaves, fourths, and fifths (these began to feel a little tame) and a less intense disliking of seconds and sevenths. After having come to like a moderately dry wine, a sweet wine begins to seem a trifle cloying to the taste and a very dry wine seems less puckery.

The habituation mutation goes on entirely in the field of gratuitous or consummatory satisfactions. It is a mutation from negative to positive terminal likings, or from positive to negative. It is not a mutation of means to end. But since it is a way of obtaining new terminal likings, it is sometimes confused with an independence mutation; or, at least, attempts are made to explain it in terms of conditioning as if it were a means-to-end mutation.

The habituation mutation may be diagramed as follows:

|  | Intense pleasure | Neutrality | Intense displeasure |
|---|---|---|---|
| Stage 1: | $a$ | $\mid b$ | $c$ |
| Stage 2: | $b$ | $\mid c$ | |
| | $a$ | | |
| Stage 3: | $c$ | $\mid$ | (6) |
| | $b$  $a$ | | |

Let $a$, $b$, and $c$ represent dispositions for terminal likings of sensory materials of a given sort. Thus $a$ might stand for octaves, fourths, and fifths among musical intervals, $b$ for thirds and sixths, $c$ for seconds and sevenths. At stage 1, $a$ is much liked, $b$ somewhat disliked, and $c$ very much disliked. Then, as a result of experience and exposure to these materials, such as musicians have in composing with them, $b$ begins to seem less unpleasant, indeed seems to acquire a tang of novelty, and suddenly emerges as exciting musical material. When this change of attitude toward $b$ has occurred, we have attained stage 2. Here $b$ appears as the most delightful material for auditory enjoyment. But, as a result of this change to $b$, certain changes have been induced also in $a$ and $c$. There is a certain insipidity and hollowness now in $a$, still pleasant but not as intensely so as it was before $b$ was liked. And now $c$ is not as jarring as it used to be. Finally, at 3, $c$ becomes liked very much, and then $b$ becomes a little tame, as $a$ was before, and $a$ becomes still tamer.

With more habituation, $a$, $b$, and $c$ may come to be regarded as having about equal capacities of liking. Just as for a person with a mature taste for wines there are occasions when port is most suitable and others when Riesling is, so with the intervals of fifths and seconds. It is then not a question of these aesthetic materials being intrinsically liked or disliked, but of their fitness for certain aesthetic occasions and in the company of certain other materials.

Certain cyclic effects, also, seem to be due to the habituation mutation. But these would lead us too far into the details of aesthetics.

Apart from the intrinsic interest of this value mutation to value theory, the reason for alluding to it at this point is to indicate that it is not in any sense an independence mutation.

But what about *habit,* which is the traditional mechanism for explaining the independence mutation? Habit in the sense of mechanized learning is indeed a value mutation. But it is a special value mutation in its own right. When an activity sinks completely into mechanized habit, it is no longer conscious. It becomes a sort of chain reflex activity. All terminal value goes out of it. It becomes an automatic instrument like a dial telephone or an adding machine. Certain initial stimuli set it going in a desired manner and, if it is functioning smoothly, it delivers the desired result.

Habit is thus to be clearly distinguished from habituation, on the one side, and from the independence mutation on the other.

Habit is not in any way to be confused with habituation. Habit operates purely on instrumental acts, while habituation operates solely on terminal acts. Habit is a mutation from imperfect to automatically perfect instrumental action. The mutation is complete when every articulation runs without error from the initial act to the terminus desired, and goes off unconsciously. As a change in behavior rendering action unconscious, it does produce a change in values. For where there is uncertainty among the articulations of a succession of subordinate acts, there is suspense and occasional frustration and the satisfaction of stages of achievement along the way. These satisfactions and dissatisfactions are all smoothed out and eliminated in mechanical habit. It is a mutation from positive and negative affective values to neutrality. All that is left is the purely instrumental value of the act to some ulterior end which the total habit system serves.

For this reason, habit is a mutation to be avoided in the aesthetic field. Many aesthetic techniques are designed to hold the habit mutation off, or to break it up once it has started. The warnings against clichés in literature are of this sort, and the devices like metaphor for maintaining the vividness of experience in a work of art. But in the field of instrumental techniques, habit is beneficial. For the stenographer, for the mechanic handling his tools, for the tennis player or the skier with his skills, for the musical performer, the more highly perfected and automatic the basic techniques the more accurate the performance and the more attention can be given to the ends for which the technique is used.

But, at the same time, habit does not of itself institute an independence mutation. It does not inaugurate a new drive. To institute an independence mutation, two things must happen: first, the mediating judgment between the means and the end must be broken off so that the means can act independently; and second, a drive other than that for the original end must be accounted for to activate the means independently. Now, habit does apparently have a good deal to do with the first condition, but it is utterly incapable of satisfying the second condition.

There is nothing about habit in itself that can institute a new drive. Being an instance of extreme conditioning, habit does connect a succession of responses to be ready as a system whenever they are needed. Thus the skill of a trained stenographer is always ready whenever there is a motive to use it. Typing is of use for a variety of ends: a source of livelihood, or a means of filling out an income-tax form, or of writing a personal letter, or of giving expression to a poem. Many drives can be served by the automatic skill of typing. But the perfecting of the skill does not of itself make it an independent derived drive. On the ideomotor theory, this should occur, but the ideomotor theory is inadequate precisely because this does not occur. There is nothing about conditioning or habit in itself to institute a new drive. One does not usually hear of a typist just typing for the fun of it.

A skier skis for the fun of it, but that is because something more than habit is involved in the technique. There is affective diffusion from the occasions when a man skis, and anticipated gratuitous satisfactions, and as a competitive sport there is probably a genuine independence mutation resulting from an injective attached to the skill. But these accretions of drives that attach themselves to the technique of skiing rarely attach themselves to techniques like typing.

Such a comparison shows that it is not habit, not conditioning alone, that institutes an independence mutation. All that habit can do is to weaken and eventually break the mediating judgment that connects a subordinate means activity with its super-ordinate end activity, and so prepare the way for an independence mutation if an injective or some other drive is present to motivate the subordinate activity independently. Habit and conditioning have no drive in themselves. They are simply mechanisms for channeling drives into new acts in docile behavior. A derived independent drive must obviously have some drive actually in it. The drive cannot come out of nowhere. Yet that is what the ideomotor theory implicitly proclaims. It declares that just the repetition of a series of subordinate acts under an original drive will somehow generate a new drive for the series, independent of the original drive. There is no reliable evidence that such a generation of something out of nothing occurs in this field of natural events any more than it does elsewhere in nature.

Once more we are confirmed in our belief that the ideomotor theory will not work. And if what Allport calls 'functional autonomy' is also something of the same sort, then that idea will not work either.

However, habit is nonetheless a value mutation. For the change from tentative nonautomatic to automatic activity neutralizes all the satisfactions and frustrations along the way. It is a mutation from whatever positive or negative values lie along the path toward value neutrality.

## 7. The Fatigue Mutations and Satiation

There is still another group of value mutations, different from those already observed, by which objects at first valued in certain ways lose their values. They lose their values not through habit or through simply attaining the normal quiescence of a drive. These mutations are due to physiological changes which affect the gratuitous satisfactions. Consequently, like habituation, they closely concern aesthetics. There are probably a number of them. But the most conspicuous ones are the result of the fatiguing of the sense organs and of the attention. They are the sources of monotony. As a result of repeated stimulation, objects that are at first valued intensely lose their values by the loss of their stimulating powers.

In *sensory fatigue,* continuous or repeated stimulation gradually tires the sense organ so that it ceases to respond as actively as at first. After wearing blue glasses for a few minutes, we notice that the intensity of the blue is greatly diminished. The first few tastes of an orange, the first whiffs of an odor, are the most intense. Now, normally, if we like a sense quality, the more it loses its stimulating power the less enjoyment we can get from it. Thus sensory fatigue tends to reduce the value of the sensory stimulus.

*Attentive fatigue* does the same thing even more effectively. It can completely eliminate a stimulating object. Thus the ticking of a watch on the bureau, or the whirr of city traffic out the window, soon ceases to be heard. As with sensory fatigue, it is continuous or repeated stimulation that produces the result. But in attentive fatigue it is not the sense organ that is affected but the neural functioning of the brain. Hearing is a good sense in which to note the effects of attentive fatigue, because hearing is not, like color vision, taste, smell, and touch, susceptible to sensory fatigue—or, at least, not much. But the effect is just as monotonous.

The aesthetic principles of variety are developed precisely to offset the devaluating effects of monotony. Contrast, gradation, and theme-and-variation are three aesthetic devices by which artists counteract monotony. An artist wishes to keep interest in his work steadily at a rather high level throughout its duration in a temporal work of art, or over the whole surface in a spatial work of art. The principles of variety direct him to keep changing the stimuli to hold the interest, but in an orderly fashion so as not to produce confusion.

Superficially, fatigue looks like habit. Both act upon value materials in a manner that reduces their values toward neutrality by making them less conscious and vivid. But the mechanisms involved are totally different. Habit is a long-term value mutation requiring hours and weeks to get established. Sensory and attentive fatigue are short-term value mutations, effective in a matter of seconds and minutes, and as quickly over when the stimulus is removed.

Fatigue mutations operate on unpleasant sensory materials, of course, as much as on pleasant ones. A disagreeable smell soon loses its worst intensity, and an irritating continuous noise will cease to be heard if it is not too irritating. This aspect of these mutations is often a blessing, and is possibly their biological function—to shield us from the hundreds of minor irritations of daily life by the muffling action of monotony.

Another value mutation, somewhat analogous but with a much longer span, goes under the name of *satiation*. It is not well understood. It acts as if men were susceptible to some sort of long-term fatigue operating upon their whole pattern of living. This mutation seems to be the reason why men need vacations, and also why vacations can be too long. We can understand why a day of sightseeing leaves us willing to rest in the evening from ordinary physical fatigue. The total energy of the body has been drained off, and needs replenishing. But why is it that after a month or so of delightful sightseeing we may have had quite enough of it, and may even welcome a return to office work? This is not sensory or attentive fatigue, for it is a long-term affair; and it is not physical fatigue, for we may be physically fit; not habit, for there has been constant variety, and, besides, habit does not call for relief; not habituation, for there is no alteration of our dispositions for terminal values. Why, if we like to travel, or ski, or sail, or fish, or teach, or study, or run a business, or operate a truck, or an engine, should we not wish to continue these activities indefinitely? Ordinarily, satiation sets in when any of these activities are carried on too continuously. This is recognized in the accumulated wisdom of tradition by the institution of Sunday, and of feast days, and gala days. It is an important value mutation to keep in mind, whatever may be the mechanism behind it.

Having called attention to these mutations, and particularly having found a hypothesis to account for the independence mutation and the vast number of acquired drives characteristic of behavior in human societies, we are now ready to bring our results together for a comprehensive descriptive definition of purpose. This will be the subject of chapter 12.

# 12

## What Constitutes a Single Interest, or the Types of Structure Available to Purposive Behavior

### 1. THE IMPORTANCE OF A SUMMARY OF TYPES OF SINGLE INTEREST

One of the common deficiencies in contemporary discussion about values is the frequent assumption that the ascription of value is a simple isolable act. R. B. Perry cannot be sweepingly accused of this failing, though even he oversimplified the variety of purposive structures, or 'interests,' as he called them. Most of his followers, however, who have been espousing the prevalent interest theory employ a very cursory conception of an interest as if it were the bare attachment of an emotive element to an object, and as if the value problem were simply a matter of identifying the sort of emotive element to be used, whether desire, pleasure, satisfaction, or what not, and then, from there on, a matter of the algebraic addition and multiplication of interests. An interest treated in this way is so oversimplified that it becomes little more than an abstract counter.

Many remarkable inferences about value are drawn as a result of this oversimplified treatment. Some of these are half true, and generate fictitious problems because only half of the relevant factual material is made accessible. The best answer to most of these problems lies in the presentation of the factual material in its entirety. The problems dissolve in the exhibition of the total situation. Here lies the importance of our detailed study of the structure of a single purpose, of a single interest. An interest is not, as we have seen, a simple, isolable emotive occurrence attached to an object—except in the special cases of isolated riddance patterns and gratuitous satisfactions. Characteristically, a single interest is an articulated structure of interconnected acts. It has a beginning, a middle, and an end. Moreover, these structures are not all of a kind, nor are they indefinitely variable, for they follow definite laws of internal connectedness. The various emotive elements exclusively considered by some exponents of the interest theory of value find their places within these structures. The emotive elements are not, therefore, isolable (except by arbitrary abstraction from their empirical relationships), but are interconnected and functionally related to the other articulations of the total structure.

It turns out, moreover, that there is an evaluative element in the internal operation of these structures. A description of these structures and the ways in which they operate turns out to be also a description of the emergence of norms of value and of the ways in which these norms evaluate acts and institute choices. Accordingly, in these purposive structures we have complete evaluative situations on a small scale. They may, therefore, serve as models for evaluative activity on a larger scale. From a close examination of the structure and functioning of a single interest, we may be able to find out the grounds for empirically justifiable modes of evaluation that will prove suggestive for the whole range of human decisions.

The extreme emotive judgment group of writers in the interest school of values affirm that a single interest, being emotive, is beyond the sphere of cognitive judgment, and hence beyond the sphere of true or false evaluations. (See chap. 1, §3.) In our detailed examination of the structure of single interests we have implicitly accepted the challenge of this school. Virtually we have been saying, "Very well! Let us suppose that it is interest with its emotive charge that institutes value, but let us take interest really seriously and see in detail exactly how interest works and what it is. Let us get right down to the biological and psychological facts, and not be satisfied with the superficial clarity of an abstract noun or a linguistic phrase the full meaning of which is never examined."

The phrase 'interest in an object' is an excessively thin phrase to be ascribed to the whole wide range of appetitions and aversions, with all their varying structures. If this phrase is taken as a literal description, as if an appetition or an aversion were a simple relation between a simple entity 'interest,' and another simple entity 'object,' the phrase would be highly distortive and often false, in view of our study of the material up to this point. If, however, it is taken as a rough general symbol which means, when its references are fully expanded, the articulated structures we have been describing, then it appears that these structures contain not only emotive but also cognitive and verifiable evaluative elements. In short, then it appears that an interest is not purely emotive and devoid of cognitive features. The pure emotive theory of value (including the paradoxes of the 'emotive judgment') then evaporates, or at least becomes so qualified as to be no longer formidable. For every actual imperative act is supported on a declarative mediating judgment and may be false. Pure imperatives that are neither true nor false exist nowhere in behavior, but only on paper.

Our close study of the nature of a single interest is going to repay us in many ways. It automatically estops, by the direct exhibition of relevant evidence, many logically possible but factually impossible conceptions of value. And it may offer us a model in a small, easily controlled situation for the solution of some of the central problems of value in their application to the whole range of human decisions.

Let us, therefore, proceed to collect the characteristic structures of single appetitions and aversions that we have described at length in the foregoing chapters, and spread them out for a comprehensive view.

# TABLE 2

## APPETITIONS

**1. Simple anticipatory appetition**

| Governing propensity | | | | Subordinate acts | | Goal | |
|---|---|---|---|---|---|---|---|
| Drive = $I$ | | | Anticipatory set = $A^N_1$ | Subordinate anticipatory set = $A^N_2$ | Subordinate goal object = $O^G_2$ | Goal object = $O^G_1$ | Quiescence pattern = $Q^P$ |
| (a) Impulse pattern | (b) Positive conditions of quiescence | (c) Innate readinesses | | | | | |
| Physiological need \| Neuromuscular tension pattern | Quiescence pattern = $Q^P$ | | | | | | |

**2. Gratuitous satisfaction**

| Positive conditions of quiescence for subliminal tension pattern | Quiescence pattern = $Q^P$ |
|---|---|

**3. Simple trial-and-error appetition**

| Drive = $I$ (a) (b) (c) | Trial-and-error activity | Quiescence pattern = $Q^P$ |
|---|---|---|

**4. Compound trial-and-error appetition**

| Drive = $I$ (a) (b) (c) | Trial-and-error activity | Injective = $J$ | Quiescence of injective = $Q$ of $J$ | Quiescence pattern of drive = $Q^P$ of $I$ |
|---|---|---|---|---|

**5. Compound anticipatory appetition**

| Governing propensity | | Subordinate acts | | | | Goal | |
|---|---|---|---|---|---|---|---|
| Drive = $I$ (a) (b) (c) | Anticipatory set = $A^N_1$ | Subordinate anticipatory set = $A^N_2$ | Injective = $J$ | Subordinate goal object = $O^G_2$ | Quiescence of injective = $Q$ of $J$ | Goal object = $O^G_1$ | Quiescence pattern of drive = $Q^P$ of $I$ |

# AVERSIONS

## 1. Simple apprehensive aversion

| System of apprehensive references | | | Governing propensity | | Sequence of actions | |
|---|---|---|---|---|---|---|
| Riddance pattern = R | Subordinate apprehensions | | Apprehensive set = $A^{P_R}$ | Injective = J | Trial-and-error activity, if necessary | Quiescence of injective = Q of J |
| | Subordinate object of apprehension = $O_{A_1}$ | Subordinate apprehensive set = $A^{P_1}$ | | | | |

## 2. Simple riddance

**a) Without injective**

| Riddance pattern = R | Quiescence of riddance pattern = Q of R |
|---|---|

**b) With injective**

| Riddance pattern = R | Injective = J | Quiescence of riddance pattern = Q of R | Quiescence of injective = Q of J |
|---|---|---|---|

## 3. Simple trial-and-error aversions

**a) Without injective**

| Riddance pattern = R | Trial-and-error activity | Quiescence of riddance pattern = Q of R |
|---|---|---|

**b) With injective**

| Riddance pattern = R | Injective = J | Trial-and-error activity | Quiescence of riddance pattern = Q of R | Quiescence of injective = Q of J |
|---|---|---|---|---|

## 4. Compound aversions without apprehensive sets

**a) Without injective or trial-and-error activity**

| Riddance pattern = R | Anticipatory set = $A^{N_1}$ | Subordinate acts = $A^{N_2}$ $O^{G_2}$ | Goal object = $O^{G_1}$ | Quiescence of riddance pattern = Q of R |
|---|---|---|---|---|

**b) With injective but without trial-and-error activity**

| R | J | $A^{N_1}$ | $A^{N_2}$ $O^{G_2}$ | $O^{G_1}$ | Q of R | Q of J |
|---|---|---|---|---|---|---|

**c) Without injective and with trial-and-error activity**

| R | $A^{N_1}$ | Trial and error | $O^{G_1}$ | Q of R |
|---|---|---|---|---|

**d) With injective and with trial-and-error activity**

| R | J | $A^{N_1}$ | Trial and error | $O^{G_1}$ | Q of R | Q of J |
|---|---|---|---|---|---|---|

## 5. Compound apprehensive aversion

| Apprehensive references | | | Governing propensity | | Subordinate appetition | | | |
|---|---|---|---|---|---|---|---|---|
| Riddance pattern = R | Subordinate apprehensions | | Apprehensive set = $A^{P_R}$ | Injective = I | Anticipatory set = $A^{N_1}$ | Subordinate acts = $A^{N_2}$ $O^{G_2}$ | Goal object = $O^{G_1}$ | Quiescence of injective = Q of J |
| | Subordinate object of apprehension = $O_{A_1}$ | Subordinate apprehensive set = $A^{P_1}$ | | | | | | |

## 2. Types of Purposive Structures

The two main groups of purposive structures are the appetitions and the aversions. An array of typical purposive structures therefore naturally falls into these two groups. Having made this division, we might naturally be expected to proceed from the simplest to the more complex structures. But such a procedure fails to bring out the sort of complexity that is specially characteristic of purposive behavior. So, in order to stress the typical complex structure of an appetition or an aversion, we shall start, as we did in the exposition of the preceding chapters, with the simple anticipatory appetition and the aversive structure that corresponds to this—the simple apprehensive aversion. Then we shall be in a position to show why certain still simpler forms are properly regarded as purposive, even though they trespass on the borderline between docile and automatic behavior; and we thence proceed to make an intelligent sampling of some other complex types of purposive structures. Nearly all these structures have been described already. The reason for repeating them here is simply that we may see them all together, so that we can draw out more fully and conveniently their implications for the theory of value.

To make sure that the difference between a *simple* and a *compound* structure is clear, let me state the difference again at this point. A simple purpose is one that is either positive or negative throughout. A compound purpose is one that contains elements of its opposite within its structure. Specifically, if an appetition contains an injective, it is considered compound. For this means that the positive pursuit of a goal has run into opposition and that an injective has been brought in to help overcome the obstacle. The obstacle in such behavior is always an object of apprehension or a riddance pattern (something feared or actually annoying or painful), but in the diagrams I have let the symbol *J* stand for all this. I did not wish to make the diagrams unnecessarily confusing with a multiplicity of symbols.

Similarly, if an aversion contains anticipatory sets with their accompanying goal objects, the aversion is considered compound.

For this means that the acts of avoidance have run into difficulties which require the pursuit of an instrument, as an appetitive goal object, to overcome them. There is this much of a positive purpose incorporated into a dominantly negative purpose.

Now for some typical examples of these typical purposive structures. Mostly, I shall refer to illustrations already used:

## EXAMPLES OF APPETITIONS

*Simple anticipatory appetition:* the thirsty geologist and the sequence of his acts in pursuit of water for the satisfaction of his thirst.

*Gratuitous satisfaction:* sensing the odor of lilac or phlox in a garden; a sunset sky; receiving a caress, an unexpected gift, a compliment.

*Simple trial-and-error appetition:* the usual maze learning experiment for rats, particularly at the first trial; trying to open a jar of jam when the cover sticks; solving a crossword puzzle.

*Compound trial-and-error appetition:* trying to pull up a sapling by the roots, being angered at the resistance, and so redoubling one's efforts.

*Compound anticipatory appetition:* the boy who meets competition in selling his newspapers to purchase a bicycle and rises aggressively to the challenge.

## EXAMPLES OF AVERSIONS

*Simple apprehensive aversion:* the cat in the kitchen after he has learned to avoid the stove subsequent to burning his paws from jumping onto the oven.

*Simple riddance*

*Without injective:* winking the eyes to avoid a cinder; moving out of a draft; brushing off a fly.

*With injective:* the cat leaping from the stove frightened when he burned his paws.

*Simple trial-and-error aversions*

*Without injective:* trying to find a dry place in a leaky cabin; trying to find the rattle in a car.

*With injective:* trying to get out of a burning house.

*Compound aversions without apprehensive sets:* going to a dentist to get over a toothache. If the ache is intense, an injective enters in. And if it is Saturday and one has to hunt for a dentist, there will be trial and error.

*Compound apprehensive aversion:* Poncins out in the blizzard, terrified of being frozen to death, seeks his cabin as a place of safety. Here the riddance pattern, the avoidance of cold and wind, is present simultaneously with the injective and the apprehension of freezing to death. An example in which the riddance pattern is not active and is operating solely as the terminal object of apprehension would be the piling up of sandbags along a swollen creek to avoid the flooding of one's house. Purchase of fire insurance. Even such simple acts as carrying a raincoat on a cloudy day.

In all these instances a goal object is sought as a means of avoiding or escaping from something.

### 3. Some Comments on These Structures

When these two groups of purposive structures are drawn up in parallel diagrams, both the similarities and the differences of their structures and modes of functioning stand out. Let us take special note of some of these.

1. *The parallelism of the simple anticipatory appetition and the simple apprehensive aversion as typical model structures for positive and negative purposes becomes clear.* Each of them exhibits all the main structural features of their opposite purposive aims. Each has its drive, its cognitive sets, its hierarchy of subordinate acts, its pivotal object of terminal reference (the quiescence pattern for appetition, the riddance pattern for aversion), and its quiescence state.

2. From these central models, other types of purposive structures can be viewed as modifications either by simplification or by complication. The *simplification* may be brought about either by the omission of cognitive references, which thus produces the simple trial-and-error structures, or further by the omission of even trial-and-error activity, resulting thus ultimately in gratuitous satisfaction and simple riddance. These last two structures are thus seen to be purposive structures carried to the limit of simplification. The *complication* is brought about by the incorporation of negative elements into a positive purposive structure or positive elements into a negative purposive structure. The result is a compound structure (as explained in §2).

3. The ordering of the purposive structures in a compact array shows clearly that *gratuitous satisfaction and simple riddance are properly to be regarded as purposive structures in spite of*

*their simplicity*. They are purposive structures reduced and telescoped to their pivotal acts alone.

The only reason why these would be excluded as purposive acts is that they do not conform with obviousness to our earlier description of purposive behavior as docile behavior. According to our early descriptions, as we were working into the field, it appeared that purposive behavior should involve a gap between its drive and its goal, to be filled in with learned behavior, in order that it might properly be regarded as purposive. But this, of course, was only an early approximation toward an adequate descriptive definition of the field. It fits the anticipatory and trial-and-error appetitions admirably, but becomes somewhat strained when applied to the aversive structures, and does not fit gratuitous satisfactions and simple riddance at all.

Yet there can be no question that aversions are instances of docile behavior. An organism learns concatenated systems of subordinate acts for the avoidance of things just as truly as for the attainment of things. Moreover, in compound purposive structures these two modes of learning are incorporated into one another. And in derived purposes resulting from the independence mutation, the mingling of aversive with appetitive structures is carried even farther. That is to say, docile behavior cannot be limited to appetitive structures to the exclusion of aversive structures without gross distortion of the interrelations between these two types of structures. The very functioning and structure of these systems of behavior require that they should be described as interrelated and not as divided by an arbitrary definition. In short, if our earlier definition of purposive behavior in terms of drive, gap, and goal does not adequately fit the field of relevant facts when this field is more carefully examined, the proper thing to do is not to stick arbitrarily to a somewhat hasty and inadequately informed definition of purposive behavior, but to change the definition of purpose to fit the structural relationships of the field defined. The structure of the field of facts referred to demands the change in the descriptive definition to conform to the structural lines that appear there.

This may seem obvious to many readers—and indeed it should

to all—but some writers on value apparently think they can stipulate what they shall mean by value and can compel others to abide by their arbitrary definitions, irrespective of the relationships among the facts referred to. They may, of course, do so 'logically,' in the narrow sense of the term, meaning simply abiding by a verbal consistency, but not in a broader sense of the term, meaning the making of a fruitful objective examination of an empirical field.

Thus purposive activity could be limited to appetitive activity by an arbitrary definition which required a purposive act to terminate in a positive goal (a $Q^p$). This requirement of a positive terminal goal would exclude aversions. For, as we have seen, aversive structures do not ordinarily terminate in a positive quiescence pattern or consummatory act, but in a negative state of simple quiescence of the aversive drive (a $Q$ of $R$ or $Q$ of $J$). But the exclusion of aversions from the field of human evaluation would make a farce of ethics and of any of the traditional value studies. Temptations would fall within the field, but not the Ten Commandments!

To repeat, our definitions of the value field, and here of the field of purposive values, cannot fruitfully be determined by arbitrary stipulations which ignore close factual relationships. The definitions, to be fruitful, must follow the most nearly adequate descriptions we have of the structure of the field. So, if our preliminary definition of purpose in terms of drive, gap, and goal fails to accord with aversions which are structurally bound in with appetitions, we will alter our definition of purpose to conform to the relations exhibited in the facts.

Now the same considerations lead to the inclusion of gratuitous satisfactions and simple riddance within the field of purposive behavior and purposive values. These acts clearly fail to conform to the preliminary definition in terms of drive, gap, and goal. For there is no gap. In the one, drive and goal collapse into a simple happy consummation; in the other, there is merely drive producing at once its own quiescence. Nevertheless, these acts are drawn into the purposive field by the structure of the field itself. They are, we discover, the pivotal acts for appetitions and aversions. They are the acts with respect to which all learning goes on. A complex appetition is simply a search for a consummatory act that unfortunately is not gratuitously given. A complex aversion is simply a riddance pattern that unfortunately does not rid itself at once of its noxious object. All the complexities of the articulated structures of appetitions and aversions pivot on consummatory satisfactions and riddance patterns. To exclude these from the field of purposive behavior by arbitrary definitional fiat would thus gravely distort our information about the field.

Another way of reaching the same conclusion is to appeal to our guiding practical maxim: to regard anything as relevant to the field of values which bears on the making of human decisions. Clearly, in attempting to make correct decisions in the field of human purposes, it would be impossible to rule out of consideration the gratuitous satisfactions and simple riddances that are spread through human living. The prospect of getting into a position favorable for obtaining the one and evading the other is a major consideration in human decisions. Of course, not only ethics but also aesthetics are deeply concerned with these pivotal acts.

4. A comparison of the two sets of diagrams brings out *the defining characteristics for distinguishing appetitions and aversions.* The appetitions all terminate in a quiescence pattern $(Q^P)$ or consummatory act; the aversions all terminate in the mere quiescence of the drive ($Q$ of $R$ or $Q$ of $J$). The significance of this difference of termination is that the structure of an appetition is all directed upon the attainment of its pivotal act $(Q^P)$, whereas that of an aversion is all directed upon the avoidance of its pivotal object of reference (the riddance pattern $R$). Consequently, barring death or fatigue or the interception of a stronger drive, an appetition continues in activity until its consummatory act is attained; an aversion continues in activity until the organism has got completely outside the field of the riddance pattern and its subordinate objects of apprehension.

These two kinds of purposive structures are diametrically opposite in their functions and in the directions of their references and activity. They cannot be reduced one to the other without radical distortion and falsification.

It is true, however, that the injective drive has a quiescence pattern of its own, particularly in its positive aggressive role. This may become quite prominent in the feeling of relief or of triumph, and even of gloating after periods of vigorous or extended frustration from obstacles finally overcome. Consequently, when an injective becomes a strong drive in an aversion, the purpose may well end in a prominent consummatory act of triumph or gloating. This gives the appearance of an appetition to many aversions. But the structure of an aversion (e.g., any apprehensive aversion) is not affected by this really gratuitous termination. The injective drive is controlled by the riddance drive and ceases to operate when references to the latter cease to operate. Thus it is the quiescence of the riddance pattern or of the apprehensive references to it that bring an aversion to termination whether an injective enters in or not. If a positive act of relief or triumphal satisfaction accrues to the achievement of the injective, that is a sort of bonus to the act.

When Poncins finally reached his cabin after his battle with the blizzard, he undoubtedly had a tremendous feeling of relief. But the structure of his activity was directed to the avoidance of the blizzard, not to the attainment of a feeling of relief. The feeling of relief was a bonus to his achievement, an almost superfluous value not essential to the structure of the act but probably biologically adaptive in serving to reinforce learning.

Consequently, in describing the articulations of the aversions in the diagrams, I have set down simply the quiescence of the injectives ($Q$ of $J$) and not emphasized the positive quiescence patterns ($Q^p$ of $J$) that may accrue. The latter, however, become very important, as we know, in accounting for some forms of the independence mutation.

5. Lastly, it should be repeated that *these diagramed structures represent only a sampling of the possible structures of appetitions and aversions.* Especially the compound structures may be indefinitely complicated. Moreover, none of the derived appetitions and aversions generated by the independence mutation are exhibited here. Their structures are not essentially different, but neither are they exactly the same.

## 4. The Detailed Definition of a Purposive Act

Now that this summary is concluded, it may be pointed out that the array of diagrams just presented offers a detailed and more nearly adequate descriptive definition of a purposive act than the rough definition with which the study began. Purposive activity was then defined simply as docile activity. That definition guided our study and still holds, but it can now be replaced by the detailed specification of the structures of acts which constitute docile activity. Our new definition may now stipulate that *a purposive act is any act falling within the field of activity for which these structures diagramed* (tables 2 and 3) *are selected samples.* Or, if a generalized definition is desired, it may be said that *a purposive act is one in which a drive stimulated to action attains a state of quiescence by means of acts that are not wholly instinctive but learned, and also any act or acts that are capable of functioning as integral parts of such a system.* The second definition depends upon the first. For it is simply a general statement designed to cover the structures which our study indicated go together to make up this field of purposive behavior.

The last clause in the second definition is needed to provide for a variety of acts which fall within the field of purposive activity, but would be excluded by a literal reading of the first clause if this were left unmodified. The first clause of the general definition, literally interpreted, would cover only complete purposive acts in which already learned cognitive sets function as subordinate acts. It would include simple anticipatory appetitions and simple apprehensive aversions and combinations of these. But it would exclude any simpler purposive structures and any incomplete purposes. It would exclude simple trial-and-error appetitions and aversions, for these do not incorporate any already learned acts that lead to quiescence. For the same reason it would exclude simple riddance and gratuitous satisfactions. Likewise, but for a different reason, it would exclude incomplete and interrupted purposes, such as an interrupted journey or college education, because here the terminal quiescence is not attained by instrumental acts. Yet all such acts that would be excluded are structurally part of the field of purposive behavior. The second clause brings them back into the field defined, and likewise indicates their intrinsic structural relationship with more complex and complete purposive structures.

The second clause of the general definition does this by stating that these simple and incomplete structures are still purposive because they are capable under other conditions of functioning as integral parts of the complete and more complex structures which are unquestionably purposive. This is a rather roundabout formal way of saying a very simple thing: a purposive act is not only one that shows the results of learning for the attainment of ends, but also any act capable of being modified by learning for a terminal attainment. So, simple trial-and-error activity is purposive if it can eventuate in learning how to attain an end, even though no cognitive anticipations of the end are present. And simple riddance is purposive even when it performs its function perfectly without resort to trial and error and other clearly purposive forms, because with obstruction it automatically becomes the drive for one of these purposive forms. And gratuitous satisfactions are purposive even when they come unsought for, because if they are anticipated while absent they become the goal of appetitions. And an uncompleted purposive act is purposive because, barring frustration, it would be completed.

So with the coöperation of the two clauses the general definition covers the field indicated by the selected diagrams. This, then, till more information leads to still more adequate descriptions, can be accepted as a relatively adequate descriptive definition of purposive activity. With this as a base, we can now safely inquire where the values lie in purposive activity.

Let us remind ourselves of the procedure on which we embarked for this inquiry. We began with a common sense list of terms to which value, or 'good' and 'bad,' are frequently ascribed. We agreed that the list could be considerably shortened by legitimate uses of generalization and reduction. But it was not clear that it could be reduced to a single meaning or

property. So we suggested as a fruitful and undogmatic procedure the successive study of each of the areas of subject matter denoted by the principal terms to which value is frequently
ascribed. We chose 'purpose' as the first of these terms to investigate.

Theoretically, up to this point we have been simply describing purposive behavior. We have not been ascribing value to it,
except as we might recall that this was a term which appeared
in the list of value terms. Actually, of course, we have constantly had our eye on the prospective relevancy to our problem
of the structures we have been examining, and have not seriously tried to restrain ourselves from making remarks about
value features that appeared to be specially significant. But
theoretically all these remarks could now be expunged, and we
could regard ourselves as presented with a rather detailed factual description of typical structures characteristic of this field
of docile animal behavior—in short, a description of purposive
activity that is devoid of value terms. If, consequently, value
terms are attached to certain articulations, and relations within
these structures, nothing is changed in regard to the factuality
of these structures or the verifiability of descriptions of them.
Now this is precisely what we propose to do.

Let us see where the terms 'good' and 'bad' can be applied to
these behavior structures in ways consonant with the traditional
meaning of the terms. Where do the 'values' lie in these purposive structures? We shall be adding no new descriptive properties to the structures described. We shall simply be attaching
some names which have traditonal value connotations. Rough
traditional terms like 'desire,' 'conation,' and 'object of value'
can thus obtain a more precise denotation and definition. For
these terms, in their traditional references, signify activities going on in purposive behavior. And at least that much of their
meaning can be clearly defined by discovering just where they
fit into our relatively precise descriptions of purposive structures.
It is not, however, that we are so concerned about getting precise meanings for such terms as 'desire' and 'conation'; our main
concern is with the application of the over-all value terms 'good'
and 'bad' to these purposive structures. That is the next step to

be made, in order that we may begin to talk intelligently about purposive *values,* and *evaluations.*

But before we take that step it is necessary to consider some general matters about the principles of evaluation. We need information about the functions of definitions as criteria of value and of the relation between these and standards of value. This will be the subject of chapter 13.

# 13

## The Principles of Evaluation

### 1. THE GENERAL THEORY OF EVALUATION

The present chapter is offered as a general statement of the theory of evaluation. So far as the principles developed here are sound, they should be applicable to any conception of the specific nature of value. That is to say, they would hold whether a writer centered his theory of value on pleasure, or desire, or approval, or fitness, or integration, or evolutionary survival, or any of the other items in the original list drawn up at the beginning of this study to indicate the traditional and common sense area of our subject matter. They would hold even for a nonempirical treatment which took its departure from one of the devices of dogmatism, such as self-evidence, indubitable immediacy, or insight into the essence of some linguistic meaning. For these nonempirical devices are intended as cognitive justification for implicit belief in proffered principles or other elements of evaluation. So the principles would be the same whether they were supported on empirical or on nonempirical grounds.

For instance, whereas we should seek to ground our evaluative principles on empirical grounds of weight of evidence and probability, a nonempiricist might seek to ground his evaluative principles on self-evidence or indubitability. Nothing is actually gained by such a device. It simply blocks inquiry at that point, so far as the nonempirical writer is concerned. Those of us interested in his principles will go on anyway to see what empirical grounds can be found to support them. So, since dogmatism adds no cognitive weight to a statement, we shall proceed as heretofore on empirical assumptions. We shall seek to ground our principles of evaluation on the empirical evidence that can be adduced to support them.

## 2. CRITERIA OF EVALUATION

What then is an evaluation? *An evaluation is a judgment about the presence or the quantity of value of any sort in an object or event.* Not all judgments about value are evaluative judgments. Analyses of value situations and anthropological or historical statements about values are not necessarily evaluative judgments. An evaluative judgment requires some criterion with reference to which the judgment of the presence or the amount of value is made.

Ultimately, on an empirical view, these criteria are grounded in observable facts, and the dynamics of evaluation comes out of the facts. But in theories of value and in discussions about value the criteria are expressed in the instruments of speech. So it is necessary at the outset to distinguish between evaluative criteria in discourse and those among the facts outside of discourse. By discourse is meant symbolic expressions for communicative purposes—roughly, verbal expressions. It is theoretically just possible that there are no evaluative criteria outside of discourse. That would mean that the grounds of evaluation are to be found only in certain forms of speech. This would be one sort of empirical theory of evaluation. But it seems unlikely, in view of our study up to this point, that the criteria for evaluating purposive values, as at least one sort of values, would be grounded in forms of speech rather than in the purposive structures themselves. In fact, one of our chief concerns will be to show how evaluative criteria in discourse become cognitively responsible by their attachment to the evaluative criteria which operate outside of discourse. A cognitively responsible evaluative criterion in discourse, we shall hold, is one that is true to an evaluative criterion outside of discourse. Where this attachment cannot be made out, the evaluative criterion in discourse is cognitively irresponsible.

It can operate to give evaluative judgments, but there will be no rational grounds for accepting the judgments.

The two principal kinds of evaluative criteria in discourse are *qualitative* criteria, by which the *presence* of some sort of value is established; and *quantitative* criteria, by which the *amount* of some sort of value is determined. The qualitative criteria in discourse consist of definitions of value. The quantitative criteria consist of quantitative standards correlated in an appropriate way with the defining characters of the definitions. Quantitative standards are thus dependent on the definitions to which they apply. This result may strike many readers as surprising in view of the emphasis, in traditional ethical and aesthetic theories, upon quantitative standards in the treatment of evaluation rather than upon definitions. But we cannot judge the quantity of something until we have determined something that can have the quantity. We must know what a value is before we can tell how much of it there is. A qualitative evaluative judgment based on a definition of value, which determines that a value is present, is presupposed by every quantitative judgment stating the amount of value present. A definition of value is consequently the basic evaluative criterion in discourse.

This point is confirmed when we consider that the principal issues in the history of ethics and aesthetics and in value theory generally revolve about the definition of the value concerned. What is not always realized is that this is an evaluative issue, and the basic one.

The issue between a hedonist and a nonhedonist is over the definition of value. Once that is settled for a theory of value, the quantitative evaluations follow almost automatically. The issue between Meinong and Ehrenfels, which continues into our time, was whether affection (pleasure and pain) or desire should be defined as the basic value datum. This was an issue over the basic definition of value, the basic criterion for judging whether something is a value or not. Thus, on the definitional criterion of affection, a desire has value only as it contains or leads to feelings of pleasantness or unpleasantness; whereas, on the definitional criterion of desire, pleasure has value only if it is an object of desire. These are evaluative judgments, and basic ones, in comparison to which quantitative evaluations of pleasure or desire are quite secondary.

The basic evaluative function of a definition is so fundamental and so often passed over without adequate recognition that it will bear special emphasis. An amusing incident which occurred in 1927 illustrates the crucial importance of a definition for establishing the value of an object within the aesthetic field.

The works of the sculptor Brancusi are well recognized today, and particularly the bronze "Oiseau," which has become a classic of the abstract style. In the 'twenties, however, this style of sculpture was a novelty in America, and the tradition in the visual arts for representational treatment in painting and sculpture was strong and resistant. When it was learned that Brancusi was bringing a number of his works into this country to exhibit in New York, feeling ran high among the traditionalists against the modernists and vice versa. A group of conservative artists notified the customs officials of New York that Brancusi's sculptures were being brought through the customs under false pretenses.

The customs officials, on unpacking the objects, found it easy to agree with the art authorities who had warned them of an imposture. "Oiseau," a single modulated column of brightly polished bronze about four feet high, has no physical resemblance to a bird. But if it was not a work of sculpture, the customs officials were obliged to classify it as something else. The best disposition they seemed to find for it was under paragraph 499 of the Tariff Act of 1922, which included household and hospital utensils in metal. This disposition might not have been serious but for the fact that, though the customs officials could change a classification at their discretion, they could not change the declared value on an article. The duty on the amount of bronze used in "Oiseau" and the rest of Brancusi's works would have been negligible, but the duty on the declared value of these articles under the schedule of paragraph 499 came to $4,000. Brancusi sued the United States government for recovery of the duty charged.

The trial is a famous one. Witnesses for the plaintiff were

Edward Steichen (who by the time of the trial had purchased "Oiseau"), Jacob Epstein, Forbes Watson (editor of *The Arts*, then the principal publication supporting the modernist movement), and others. The witnesses for the defense, members of the National Academy, testified that "Oiseau" was not sculpture, nor a work of art, nor a thing of beauty. The plaintiff's witnesses testified to the contrary. The split was, of course, over the definition of a work of art, or aesthetic value.

Here is a bit of the testimony, in which Brancusi's attorney questioned a Mr. Robert Ingersoll Aitken of the National Academy:

Q. "How many works of art of Mr. Brancusi's have you seen?"
A. "I haven't seen any."
Q. "You haven't seen any works by Brancusi?"
A. "You said, 'works of art.' I have not."
Q. "Have you seen any of his works?"
A. "I have seen works like that [pointing to Oiseau] but I haven't seen any works of art."
Q. "In other words, you do not regard them as works of art."
A. "I do not." [1]

This incident emphasizes the pivotal role of a definition in evaluation. If it had been a question of the quantity of aesthetic value of "Oiseau" there would have been no issue with the customs officials. Suppose the traditionalists had notified the customs officials that "Oiseau" was exceedingly ugly and a thoroughly bad work of art. The officials would no doubt have agreed, but "Oiseau" would still have fallen under the definition of a work of art and could have passed the customs on Brancusi's declaration. This shows that there is an even greater insult to an artist's work than to assign it a very low quantitative rating and call it ugly. For it is much worse to assert that it is not a work of art at all, to assert that it does not even fall within the field of the definition, since on this judgment it is not given any aesthetic value whatever. It is not even given a *negative* aesthetic value. Better to be a bad work of art than not a work of art at all. At least the bad work of art has hit within the field of the target, though on the penalty fringe. But not to be a work of art at all is not even to have touched the target.

So when we hear it said of a contemporary nonobjective canvas that it may be called entertaining but hardly art; or that writers of free verse are often clever, but of course they are not poets; or that James Joyce may have produced some interesting psychological analyses but nothing that can be called a novel: we understand what is meant. No judgment of an object is so devastating as that it failed to meet the qualitative criterion of the sort of value it purported to have.

The reader will no doubt be curious to learn what happened to "Oiseau." It got through the customs. But how did the court decide? That is a matter we may well wonder about. Part of the absurdity of the case is that such a decision should have been left to a New York court of customs. The difficulty was not in the lack of evaluative criteria. The traditionalists had their basic qualitative criterion in the definition of sculpture as a type of representative art; and the modernists theirs as, let us say, an object of significant form which has no need of being representational. The basic evaluative criteria of the two groups are in conflict and each is a contrary of the other. What is the solution?

Here, in a simple instance, is the whole evaluative problem. And note particularly that the problem pivots on the qualitative or definitional criterion. A skeptic could suggest that there is no solution. It is simply a difference in the definitions employed. Definitions are arbitrary and one definition is as legitimate as another. The absurdity of the issue, says the skeptic, is that it is meaningless. Testimony is produced as if this were an issue of fact where evidence would have weight. But with arbitrary definitions it is not a queston of fact but only of how different people decide what they shall arbitrarily mean by a term.

But the man who takes this position must in consistency hold also that the customs schedule headed "Works of Art" is arbitrary. And incidentally, why not all the other schedules, since they are all definitions? The whole customs agency then becomes an absurdity and meaningless, since it imposes arbitrary definitions on things and imposes duties on the basis of such arbitrary definitions. Clearly something is wrong with the skeptic's position. For evidence does seem to be pertinent as to whether objects coming through the customs do fall under the government's definitions of them, and these definitions do not seem to be entirely arbitrary.

The nonskeptical position would find the absurdity of the trial over "Oiseau" in a very different quarter. On this position, the trial was an absurdity because a court procedure is an inappropriate way in which to marshal evidence for or against the legitimacy of a basic aesthetic criterion. It is as if a civil court should be called upon to decide whether the Newtonian or the Einsteinian conception of space and time were the justifiable one. The evidence for such a decision is too complicated and technical to be entrusted to a court of law. Suppose the court had decided that "Oiseau" was not a work of art. Would that have made any difference except to increase the ridiculousness of the procedure? For "Oiseau" is now, by some process, widely recognized as a work of art and a very beautiful one.

The conclusion forced upon a nonskeptic about values and upon an empiricist about evaluation is that the basic evaluative criteria gain their cognitive justification by close attachment to fact. That means that a cognitively responsible definition employed as an evaluative criterion cannot be entirely arbitrary. Or let us put it the other way round. An empiricist in value theory will see to it that the definitions he develops as basic criteria for evaluation are not arbitrary but are responsible to the relevant field of value facts.

We are thus led to the recognition of the importance in value theory of what may be called the *descriptive definition*. This is a definition which in its very formulation is responsible to the facts defined. Our next task is to examine the form of such a definition.

## 3. THE DESCRIPTIVE DEFINITION

For clarity's sake, the descriptive definition should be contrasted with the so-called *nominal definition,* for the latter is the kind of definition which is regarded as the model by many writers, and which has the traits of extreme arbitrariness that unfit it as a reliable evaluative criterion. There are actually many kinds of definitions. A definition may itself be defined as a rule or stipulation by which a meaning is given to a term.

Nominal definitions are of two kinds. Both consist of a two-term relationship between a symbol, S, to be defined and something else which defines it. In one of these kinds, which may be called the *equational definition,* the defining entity is a set of other symbols for which it is stipulated that the symbol defined may be substituted at any time:

$$S = MN$$

In its purest examples the equational definition is found in mathematics, where it is employed simply for economy of thought. When a complex of symbols is to be frequently used, the complex is equated with a single symbol which is defined by the complex and may be substituted for it in any place. The symbols may be words as well as letters, whence the definition of triangle as 'a plane figure bounded by three straight lines' is an equational definition. Thus it is possible to regard any verbal expression of this sort as an equational definition. The characteristic of the equational definition is that the defining entity (definiens) is itself a set of symbols, and there is no stipulation that these symbols either separately or as a set have any reference to fact. They may have a factual application or they may not. There may be actually existing triangles as defined above or there may not. It makes no difference in the formulation of the definition. An equational definition is thus entirely arbitrary in its stipulations. Any complex of symbols may be stipulated as the meaning for any selected symbol. Actually, however, an equational definition is almost always made with an eye to its utility. When constructed of verbal symbols it rarely strays far from some common usage or from some possible application to the factual world. But these references to usage or fact are not in any way stipulated, for, if they were, it would cease to be an equational definition.

The other form of nominal definition is the ostensive. In an *ostensive definition* the defining element is some fact referred to by some recognized operation, such as pointing:

$$S \rightarrow F$$

The symbol S is defined by what is pointed at. This is the original way of learning any language, and, when dictionaries are lacking, it is still the way in which a foreigner learns what a word means. A teacher points at an object and repeats the sound 'apple.' The student thus learns that 'apple' means that object. Or the teacher points at a number of white surfaces, and the student learns that 'white' means the quality indicated.

Neither of these forms of the nominal definition are suitable for a factually responsible evaluative criterion. The equational definition is in its mode of stipulation entirely irresponsible to fact. It does not stipulate any reference to factual matters. It simply stipulates the substitutability of one symbol for a set of other symbols. Consequently, it cannot be characterized as either true or false. That, indeed, is the feature that demonstrates its factual irresponsibility. The set of symbols on the right *may* have an application to matters of fact, but this is irrelevant to the stipulations and, so to speak, a matter of chance.

For another reason the ostensive definition is unsuitable for a factually responsible evaluative criterion. It does stipulate a reference to fact. But it does not stipulate any characterization of the fact. Therefore, it also cannot be characterized as true or false. It cannot be systematically tested in terms of its stipulation by reference to a description of the fact indicated.

Both of these nominal definitions are thus factually irresponsible because of the lack of any stipulated feature that could render them true to fact. The equational definition is factually irresponsible because it lacks any stipulated factual reference. Its right-hand set of symbols is potentially a description of some field of fact and often has an application, but this is not stipulated and so the definition is not responsible to the fact. The ostensive definition is irresponsible because it lacks any stipulated description of the fact indicated.

Now it may be pointed out that an ostensive definition could never find a fact indicated unless the person using it had an implicit description of the fact in mind. How would a person be able to distinguish the object apple from all the other objects in his environment unless he had a pretty clear descriptive concept of it in mind so that he would not at the same time name a peach or a plum an 'apple'? But if this description were stipulated, the ostensive definition would automatically become what we are calling a descriptive definition. And it could even be pleaded that there is no such thing as a nominal ostensive definition without a descriptive element implicitly stipulated, that an ostensive definition is, on careful analysis, always a descriptive definition with the description implicit instead of explicit. But it is unnecessary to press this point in the present context. All that should be noted is that an ostensive definition (as nominally defined) becomes a descriptive definition as soon as an explicit descriptive element is added to it by stipulation in such a way that its indicative reference can be tested.

And analogously with the equational definition. If its right-hand set of symbols is discovered to have a factual exemplification, then actually the right-hand set of symbols is a description of the facts it applies to. And if the definition is then employed for empirical purposes as a definition *of the facts* referred to, then it is actually functioning as a descriptive definition. All that is lacking is an explicit recognition of this reference as an element of stipulation. In other words, when an equational definition is used in empirical contexts as a definition of a field of facts, as in biology or psychology or elsewhere, it then clearly contains an implicit stipulated reference to those facts. The proof is that it would be discarded if the description were false, which shows that the implicit stipulation of a truth reference to the facts is present whether it is explicitly recognized or not.

In short, if an ostensive definition explicitly recognized the implicit descriptive element in it, and an equational definition when used to define an empirical field explicitly recognized the implicit descriptive element in it, then in both instances the result would be a descriptive definition. For a descriptive definition is nothing other than one which is explicit about such implicit descriptive references.

A descriptive definition stipulates that a symbol shall be defined by a set of symbols which truly describe a field of facts. The symbol is defined by a true description of facts. The expression is a definition because it consists in a stipulation regarding the meaning of a symbol. But it is also stipulated that what is meant by the symbol shall be a description true to fact. Such a definition by stipulation is characterized by truth to fact. This is, consequently, a factually responsible kind of definition, and hence is fitted to be a cognitively reliable evaluative criterion. It can be schematically exhibited thus:

$$S \rightarrow (D \rightarrow F)$$

A symbol, $S$, is stipulated to mean a description, $D$, which is stipulated to be a true description of a factual field, $F$. Whereas a nominal definition is a two-term expression without any stipulated truth reference to fact, a descriptive definition is a three-term expression with an explicitly stipulated truth reference to fact.

Some writers think that it makes for linguistic clarity if a definition is defined by stipulation to exclude a truth reference, so that a proposition may be universally defined as an expression that has a truth reference. This is, however, an arbitrary stipulation for a definition of 'definition'; and, though it provides a superficial clarity by permitting a sharp distinction between definitions as nominal and propositions as true or false, it has the great disadvantage of rendering definitions factually irresponsible. This is a serious deficiency, if not a falsification of the situation, when definitions are used on any empirical context to demarcate an area of study or summarize the findings in a field. Such definitions are intended to be descriptively true, and must be true to perform their empirical function. But the distinction denying truth reference to any definitions is utterly confusing when carried into the evaluative field. For, if a definition is by definition irresponsible to fact, and the basic evaluative criterion in discourse is seen to be a definition, it appears to follow that the basic evaluative criterion is irresponsible to fact. And so, too, with all other evaluative criteria which depend upon the basic definitional criterion. From this inference it is easy to pass to the conclusion that values are not facts but mere stipulations, or something of the sort, supposedly free from factual or cognitive control. Such conclusions hardly clarify the study of values. It would be an interesting inquiry to trace out how much of the recent trends toward irrationalism, apriorism, emotionalism, and general obfuscation of the empirical study of value emanated from the doctrine of the nominal definition, and the implicit denial of the descriptive definition with its stipulated reference to fact.

The only conception of definition that conforms to the actual procedures of empirical inquiry is that of the descriptive definition. For, apart from the occasional use of the nominal definition in an empirical inquiry to economize thought, the constructive employment of a definition there is to set the initial bounds and target for the subject matter to be investigated, and then to summarize the results of the inquiry in its terminal stages. The successive refinements of the initial definition constitute the *principle of successive definition*,[2] which serves to mark the progress of the inquiry. The definitions formulated in the course of such an inquiry are all supposed to be true to the facts investigated. It is their conformity to the facts that controls their successive refinements and dictates the acceptance or rejection of a definition in the progress of the inquiry. In other words, there is an implicit stipulation throughout that the definition shall not only give meaning to the term denoting the subject matter under investigation but also that this will be a true meaning for the term.

An investigator is not always explicitly aware of this stipulation or of the precise structure of a descriptive definition; nevertheless, his procedure indicates that this stipulation is carefully followed out and implicit throughout. The explicit expression of his implicit procedure would be his presentation of the descriptive definition with the twofold stipulation that the meaning of the term denoting his subject matter be a description of the subject matter and that this description be true to the best of his ability to make it so. But even without this presentation, frequently there is evidence that an investigator is explicitly aware of this twofold stipulation and consciously employs the form of the descriptive definition.[3]

Our investigation of the field of purposive behavior in the preceding twelve chapters may be referred to as an illustration of an empirical inquiry consciously employing the descriptive definition as a guide and finally as a summary of the findings. The symbol 'purpose' was first descriptively defined as 'docile adaptive behavior,' and this definition was explicitly offered as a first approximation to the facts. That is, the explicit stipulation was that the definition should be true to the facts. Then several successively more refined definitions of the field were offered, terminating in a final summary definition describing the field to the closest approximation possible so far, with the data on hand.

Tolman's *Purposive Behavior in Animals and Men,* to which we have been constantly referring for much of our data, would be a good example of the same sort of procedure, with implicit rather than explicit awareness of the nature of the descriptive definition. Yet his procedure is almost explicit, for he deliberately states that his definition of the behavior he is studying is in terms of the 'descriptive properties' of the behavior referred to by the definition. Throughout his treatise, definitions are in descriptive terms, and are defended by the observational evidence for them. Tolman's extended glossary is, with few exceptions, composed of descriptive definitions, and constitutes a rich source of illustration for that form of definition and its detailed mode of functioning in an extended empirical inquiry. But actually any of the classical treatises in the empirical sciences would supply abundant illustrations of the descriptive definition and its functioning.

Our serious concern with the descriptive definition in value theory, however, derives from the fact that the basic evaluative criterion in discourse is a definition of value. If such a definition is not factually responsible, no evaluative criterion in human discourse is. Consequently, it is extremely important to realize that the definition of value as an evaluative criterion should be a descriptive definition.

## 4. DESCRIPTIVE DEFINITIONS OF VALUE AND THE DISCOVERY OF NATURAL NORMS

Descriptive definitions are not confined to values. Any field of facts may be defined by a descriptive definition. How do we know when a descriptive definition applies to values and so functions as a basic evaluative criterion? The simple superficial answer is: When the definition is descriptive of value facts. But how do we know value facts when we observe them?

For the answer to this question we must refer again to the discussion in chapter 1. Value facts do not, of course, come into our field of observation labeled and licensed as such. At the same time, neither are we, as students in the field, wholly without clues for distinguishing value facts from others. The mode of entrance into the field which is least afflicted with question-begging assumptions is by way of the common sense definition of the field. In the very first few pages such a test definition, derived from usage and common sense, was spread out for our guidance. This constituted the first rough approximation to our field of subject matter, our first descriptive definition of the field. If there is no acknowledged tradition for a more highly refined definition, a common sense test definition is the most feasible means of locating the rough boundaries of a field of subject matter. Thereafter it is a matter of refinement through successive, more and more discriminating descriptive definitions.

Roughly, the field of value facts is descriptively located and set apart from other facts by the common sense definition of the field.[4] Now, since this is a descriptive definition, its descriptive content will be controlled by the properties discoverable in the facts referred to. Since, however, in this instance the facts are intricate, ill discriminated, and possibly heterogeneous, we have found it advisable to break down the inquiry into a number of more detailed inquiries regarding certain tentatively different kinds of value. One kind that looked promising was the area of purposive value, whence we embarked on a detailed examination of purposive behavior.

Now in this inquiry into purposive behavior, the facts (to the best of our ability) controlled the descriptions as they should in any empirical study. So far as these facts fall within those descriptively defined by the common sense test definition of value, they will automatically be value facts. The descriptive definitions of these value facts will thus be controlled, as they empirically should be, by the value facts referred to.

In some instances, however, we shall find that beyond this ordinary control of a descriptive definition by its factual field another sort of control enters in: a selective control of one set of value facts over another set. When this selective operation among the value facts is reflected back into the definitional criteria, it comes out in the form of the legislation through a definitional criterion of one set of values over another, or of one criterion over another. In other words, the value facts act as norms over their own field, irrespective of whether or not these facts are verbally described. So far as the facts are truly described, however, these descriptions will reflect the normative action of the value facts upon their field. By way of the descriptive definition, therefore, we come in touch with verifiably ascertainable natural norms of value in the field of value facts.

Probably the clearest example of the normative action of value facts upon themselves is in the area of instrumental values, which we have already analyzed sufficiently to present as a convincing illustration. The means-end relation in values turns out to be that of a subordinate act to its superordinate act in purposive behavior. The subordinate anticipatory set is charged by the same drive as the superordinate anticipatory set. The thirsty geologist was looking for a green patch in the anticipation that this would be a means of finding water to satisfy his thirst drive. His desire for the green patch was motivated by his thirst just as his desire for water was. Here it is clear that the superordinate anticipation of water was the norm for his subordinate anticipation of the green patch. The geologist valued the green patch for the sake of the water. If the green patch had failed to indicate the presence of water, he would have ceased to value the green patch. It would have been implicitly evaluated as a poor anticipation. But since it did lead to water, it was implicitly evaluated as a good anticipation. If later he had had occasion to describe his action in words, this is how he would have explicitly described it. In doing so, his description of his end would have functioned as a descriptive definition of his end value, his explicit evaluative criterion in accordance with which he evaluated the goodness or badness of the means.

The point particularly to be noted here is that the action itself with its superordinate-subordinate anticipatory set structure charged by a drive was the effective normative agent, not any verbal description of it. A verbal description could reflect these dynamic relationships, and reflect them truly. The geologist could even have carried on his action with the aid of verbal symbols, but the dynamic normative action of the end over the means was carried out by the drive in the appetitive act, not by mere words. The superordinate act through the dynamics of its drive normatively selects the good from the bad subordinate acts in terms of the success of these acts in achieving the superordinate goal. This is the sort of thing that is meant by a natural norm.

It is evident that a reliable formulation of evaluative procedure in the sphere of instrumental values would be one that truly described the action of a superordinate act as a natural norm over its subordinate acts.

Verbal formulations of means-end evaluation must conform to the actual facts of means-end valuing; otherwise they are fictitious and irresponsible, and there would be no evidential reason why anyone should follow them. And what has just been found true of means-end evaluation can be generalized for all evaluations. Descriptive definitions as basic evaluative norms are factually justifiable only so far as they truly describe natural norms which function independently.[5] That is why it was so important earlier to stress the fact that descriptive definitions are basic evaluative criteria in *discourse*. For behind these verbal criteria are the facts they describe; and the normative operations of these facts upon other facts constitute natural norms which are the actual basic norms that function selectively in the field of value facts.

As the illustration of evaluation in the means-end relationship already suggests, natural norms function only in certain structural relationships among facts. We might call these relationships among the facts, 'selective systems.' The stratified relationship of subordinate to superordinate acts in purposive behavior is one such system. It is only through the dynamics of the drive operating through this system that the superordinate act legislates selectively over the subordinate acts. So, always, a natural norm consists of a dynamic agency operating through a selective system which selects against some value facts and for others.

There seem to be a considerable number of such natural norms within the field of value facts as roughly marked out by our common sense test definition. In the chapters ahead, it will be our special concern to examine the principal ones, and discover what relation they have with each other. We shall probably find that they are all interconnected in somewhat complicated ways. Thus we shall find that these natural norms legislate not only over the common run of value facts within their own selective systems but over each other. And thus the empirical science of value discovers as its chief task that of describing these natural selective systems and the conditions under which they legislate over one another.

A characteristic trait of all selective systems is that the acts selected against can always be described as errors or failures or something of the kind. Fact is occasionally defined in such a way as implicitly to deny that a fact can go wrong. It is surely unnecessary, after the recent chapters describing characteristic structures of purposive acts, to consider a definition of fact that would have to deny the evidence for such factual structures. Every error in trial-and-error behavior is in fact a wrong act relative to the goal of the drive motivating that act. The act is performed by the agent in good earnest with a factual reference to a goal which in fact the act fails to achieve, so in fact the act is rejected by the purposive structure as an error. The whole process is factual, and also normative, and consequently such that acts selected against are in fact errors within the structure of the total process. There is nothing in the nature of fact to exclude normative processes operating there. And what reason would there be to concern ourselves with norms unless they could verifiably be described as things we truly should be concerned about?

From our discovery that the descriptive definition is the basic evaluative criterion in discourse we have been led to the discovery of natural norms which control descriptive definitions by virtue of being the facts that verify them. And these natural norms implicitly evaluate other value facts by positively and negatively selecting among them. In short, we have been led through our linguistic criteria to natural norms among the value facts. These natural norms are the ultimate empirical justification for evaluative judgments.

## 5. QUANTITATIVE STANDARDS

Up to this time we have been dealing almost entirely with the basic qualitative criterion of value which determines whether an object or event is a value or not and of what kind. There remain to be considered the quantitative standards—the criteria by which the amount or degree of value is estimated.

All sorts of quantitative criteria *can* be applied to a justifiably defined field of values. The problem is to determine which of these are relevant to the field defined. For instance, in evaluating the worth of a picture as an object of aesthetic value, we sense that the social standing of the painter, the political convictions he holds, the price the picture brings, its size, the popular vote it gets, and so on are all more or less irrelevant standards. Yet they are standards often applied and easily applicable. If they are relevant, or only partially relevant, how is their relevancy determined?

Very easily, as it turns out. Let us make a distinction between intrinsic and extrinsic standards. The *intrinsic standards* are the basically relevant ones. These consist in the quantification of the defining characters of the definitional criterion of value. If the definition of value contains among its defining characters any that are capable of quantitative differentiation, these quantitative features are the intrinsic standards. And the modes of measuring these characters are the ways of determining the quantity of value of the acts or objects possessing the characters. These standards are clearly relevant and intrinsic to the values defined because they are quantitative criteria of the values themselves as defined.

But these are not quite all. If there are any other characters of the values defined which might be used as defining characters, but which might not be included in a given definition because they are not necessary for practical identification, these also would be sources of intrinsic standards provided they are quantifiable. If the class of value items $M$ is defined by the characters $a, b, c, d$, and it is found that all items which have the character $c$ also empirically have the character $d$, and hence the class can be defined for purposes of empirical identification in terms of $a, b$, and $c$, with $d$ left out, nevertheless $d$ would be an intrinsic character of the class defined and its mode of quantification an intrinsic standard.

In practice, during the process of refining the definition of a field of values, following out the empirical connections of the objects in the field, we may come upon new intrinsic standards which were not at first suspected. And occasionally, too, some trait which we first thought was intrinsic turns out not to be so. If the descriptive definition of value follows the guidance of value facts, readjustments among the defining characters of the definition to conform to the contours of the field are to be expected.

By contrast, an *extrinsic standard* is not one of the defining traits, but is some feature that is more or less reliably correlated with the intrinsic characters of the definition. Thereby a high or low quantification of the extrinsic standard may be taken as a symptom or fairly predictable condition for the appearance of the value as defined. If there is no correlation, the standard is irrelevant.

To illustrate the principle for determining the intrinsic relevancy of a standard, the following passage from R. B. Perry states the matter with clarity:

> If one object is better than another, it must be better in respect to the same condition that renders it good, or worse in the same respect that renders it evil. . . . This would hold whatever the definition of generic value. If good is pleasure and evil pain, then the more pleasure the better and the more pain the worse; if good is wholeness and evil partiality then the more whole the better and the more partial the worse; if good is union with God, and evil fall from God, then the nearer God the better, and the remoter the worse; so, if good is favor, and evil disfavor, then the more favorable the better and the more unfavorable the worse.[6]

Let me illustrate still further in detail with respect to pleasure. If value is defined in terms of pleasure and pain, then, as Perry says, the more pleasure the better, and there are three respects in which pleasure is directly quantifiable: in *intensity*, in *duration*, and in *number* (since a single individual may have pleasure from several sources at once, whence the number of pleasures is not reducible to duration). Similarly with pain or unpleasantness. There are, then, these three intrinsic hedonic standards.

With respect to these three intrinsic hedonic standards, such standards as health and wealth would be extrinsic. Health would unquestionably be a relevant extrinsic standard, since health seems to have a high correlation with the capacity for joy of life. At the same time, it does not seem to be in perfect correlation; so it cannot be suggested for an additional intrinsic standard in its own right. For wealth the correlation with the intrinsic standard is so much lower that, even though it is often popularly regarded as a sign of happiness, its use as a relevant extrinsic hedonic standard is much open to question. But however difficult it may be in practice to determine the relevancy of this standard to the hedonic criterion of value, in principle the mode of determination is perfectly clear: namely, the degree of empirical correlation, if any, between wealth and happiness in hedonic terms. If the correlation is low or negligible, then the standard is irrelevant to hedonic value. Of course, people can still be measured for their wealth, just as they can be measured for their height, but this will be no indication of the hedonic goodness or badness of their lives.

It should not be assumed that all the defining characters of a definitional criterion are open to quantification. Santayana in his *Sense of Beauty* defines aesthetic value as 'objectified pleasure.' In this definition, pleasure is quantifiable, yielding intrinsic standards. But objectification as Santayana describes it seems to be incapable of quantification. In a given experience, pleasure either is or is not objectified. There are no degrees of objectification. Accordingly there are no intrinsic standards of objectification.

In terms of Santayana's definition of aesthetic value, the standards mentioned earlier for evaluating a picture would all be extrinsic and largely irrelevant. The artist's social standing would obviously be irrelevant to the capacity of a picture to give objectified pleasure. So also his political convictions, unless some correlation could be found between the conformity of an artist to the prevailing beliefs of his time and the hedonic aesthetic value of his production. Santayana does take up the standard of cost, and makes out a distant, highly qualified relevancy. The size of a work of art, also, may be shown to have some relevancy to its aesthetic value if carefully qualified; for as soon as it is shown that works of art have differing capacities for giving objectified pleasure, then there is some correlation between physical bigness and amount of intrinsic aesthetic value. A cathedral may be regarded as an object of greater beauty than a jewel box because of its size and inclusiveness and hence greater capacity for giving aesthetic satisfaction. The popularity of a work of art is, however, clearly irrelevant for Santayana, since it is based on an undiscriminating popular satisfaction, and objectification implies a highly discriminating satisfaction.

From the foregoing it can be seen that it is theoretically possible to define a field of values for which there would be no intrinsic standards. If all the defining terms of a definition of value were incapable of quantification, there would be a qualitative criterion for determining whether a value was present or not, but no intrinsic quantitative criterion. Croce's definition of the aesthetic field in terms of intuition is an instance of this. On his view, no measurement of the amount of an aesthetic intuition is possible. This is an immediate and unique qualitative experience for each occurrence. Whether a spectator has it or not can be determined, but not how much of an intuition it is.

So now we can see how the relevancy of a standard to a definition is determined. The relevancy of an intrinsic quantitative standard is determined directly by its consisting in the quantification of a character of the basic definitional criterion. A relevant extrinsic standard is one that is correlated in some degree with an intrinsic standard, thus constituting a gauge of the probable presence of the latter. Extrinsic standards lacking such a correlation are irrelevant. Irrelevant standards are very common in almost all spheres of value, and one of the tasks of value theory and criticism is to expose their irrelevancy as a fallacy of judgment in evaluative procedure.

Another relationship among evaluative criteria should also be mentioned here. One field of values may be subsumed under another. Thus Santayana's field of aesthetic values defined in terms of objectified pleasure is subsumed in his *Sense of Beauty* under the larger class of vital values defined in regular hedonic terms as any experiences of pleasure or negatively of pain. Objectification is an intrinsic character of aesthetic value for Santayana. It is not, however, a defining character of the field of vital values: only certain vital values (namely, the aesthetic) are for Santayana objectified. Now suppose objectification were capable of quantification (which it is not); then it would clearly be an intrinsic quantitative standard for aesthetic values. What would it be for vital values? To speak of it only as an extrinsic standard for vital values would obscure its intimate relationship with a particular class of vital values. Most pleasures, of course, are not objectified. Objectification would thus be a very poor gauge of the amount of vital value likely to be present in an experience. It would be a quite irrelevant extrinsic standard. It is significant for Santayana only in the aesthetic field, but there it is for him so significant that he believed it should be definitional. To bring out this significant relationship between the defining characters of one class of values and those of another under which the first is subsumed, we should allow for *subsumed intrinsic criteria*. If these are capable of quantification, they may be called subsumed intrinsic standards within the wider value field. Thus, for Santayana, objectification would be a subsumed intrinsic criterion of hedonic value, and, if it were capable of quantitative difference, it would be a subsumed intrinsic standard for quantitative evaluation.

A question often raised is that of the relevancy of ethical standards to aesthetic worth. This question can now be precisely answered in theory (though how it should ultimately be answered in terms of the value facts depends, of course, on the facts). If the definition of the aesthetic field subsumes the aesthetic field under that of ethical values, then ethical standards are *intrinsic* standards of the aesthetic field. For in this relationship every instance of aesthetic value will be an instance of ethical value, and the defining characters of ethical values will also be defining aesthetic characters. If the relation is reversed, and the ethical field falls within the aesthetic, then ethical standards will be relevant, but only as *subsumed intrinsic* standards for a limited range of aesthetic facts. If neither field is subsumed under the other, then the only question is whether there is any correlation between ethical and aesthetic standards, and this can determine only whether there is any *extrinsic* relevancy.

Some such extrinsic relevancy is usually admitted by empirical moralists and aestheticians. The relationship is often stated thus: if an aesthetic object is subject to a strong negative ethical evaluation, it is likely to receive a negative aesthetic evaluation also. But some writers regard the two sets of standards as totally irrelevant to each other. The answer, however, is determinate once the definitions are clearly formulated. And if these definitions are descriptive in type, the answer lies in the facts and will be given by the best hypotheses we have to cover the facts.

The subsumptive relation among fields of values is thus an important one to keep in mind for evaluative judgments. It brings out an intimate relationship between some standards that might otherwise be missed.

## 6. TYPES OF QUANTITATIVE RELATIONS

In developing the relevancy of quantitative standards to the basic definitional criterion of value, we have said nothing about the nature of the quantitative differences involved. Any relation that can be stated in terms of more or less is a quantitative relation. The three main types of quantitative relations, any of which may apply to evaluative standards, are the *extensive,* the *intensive,* and the *distensive.*

*Extensive measurement* is based on the relation of whole to parts. If the discrete parts are numbered, the size of the whole is determined by the number of parts. The parts themselves may or may not be divisible into parts of the same kind. In the measurement of populations, where the parts or elements are persons, the parts are not divisible into parts of the same kind. A person is not composed of lesser persons. Each person enumerated is an ultimate qualitative element in the whole. But in the measurement of space, as in the length of a line, whatever length is taken as a unit is itself divisible into lesser lengths or parts of the same kind. In this latter sort of extensive measurement, it is essential that the sizes of the parts measured be equal.

When extensive quantities fall within the span of a single perception, the parts or elements can be intuitively apprehended in the whole, which is composed of them. Thus we can see the separate marbles that make up a bag of marbles, or the inches in a foot rule that make up the foot. Intuitively we can estimate fairly accurately that one bag contains more marbles than another (even if the marbles are of different sizes), or that one stick is longer than another (even if they are not side by side). But if accuracy is wanted, or if the wholes are too large to come within the span of perception, then the operation of measurement is called for. Then the marbles in each bag are counted and the sums compared; or a unit of length is selected and the number of times this unit is contained in the lengths concerned is counted and the sums compared. The intuitive characteristic on which extensive measurement is based, however, is the perception of discrete units in a whole.

In *intensive measurement* the perception of separate units in a whole is impossible. A loud or intense sound is not intuited as a whole composed of many soft sounds. Yet a loud sound on a given pitch is intuitively heard as a greater sound than a soft sound on the same pitch. It is a quantitative, not a qualitative, difference. Differences in intensity can be judged with fair accuracy when they are not juxtaposed. We sense at once that a police siren is louder than a robin's song. But we might be in doubt whether one police siren were louder than another. Then we would wish to hear them in close succession.

For the greatest precision in intensive measurement, however, the device is employed of correlating degrees of intensity in any medium with degrees of extensity on a spatial scale. Then degrees of intensity become correlated with parts within an extended whole which can be subdivided into units of almost any degree of minuteness. This is the significance of pointer readings on a scale for precision of measurement in the natural sciences. Intensities of sound, for instance, are correlated with the energy of air vibrations; these in turn are correlated with effects on a mechanism which terminate in marks registered by a pointer on paper. The height of line designates the intensity of the sound.

Measurements of degrees of intensity do not depend, however, upon correlations with pointer readings. Rather the reverse; the significance of precise measurements of intensive quantities in terms of pointer reading correlations with extensive quantities depends upon the direct intuitive perception of degrees of intensity. Unless we intuitively heard one sound as louder than another, the readings of the energy of air vibrations would have no significance as measurements of the intensity of sound. The correlation of intensities of sound with the energy of air waves registered on a chart is simply an ingenious device for giving greater accuracy and permanence to measurements of the intensity of sound. The direct intuitive measurements of intensity are not reduced away by the device; they are still essential to the significance of the correlation. In short, the direct intuitive measurements of intensity are the basic measurements of intensive quantities whether or not these can be correlated with extensive quantities and pointer readings for greater precision.

This point is important to bear in mind for our present study, since most quantitative judgments of value have to be made by direct intuitive measurement. There are few devices for correlating degrees of value with pointer readings on scales. That means that the high precision expected of quantitative measurements in the natural sciences is not to be expected in the field of values— at least in any very significant way in the near future. But that does not mean that sufficiently reliable quantitative measurements cannot be made by direct intuitive comparisons in the value field.

By *distensive measurement* is meant the determination of the degree of difference between one thing and another. An example of distensive quantity is the degree of difference between one pitch and another in music, or between one hue and another in color.

Again by direct intuition, we sense that there is a greater difference between a tone at the bottom of a piano keyboard and a tone at the top than there is between any two tones within an octave. For greater precision, however, it is customary to dispose distensive quantities in arrays of increasing difference from some one quantity taken as point of origin. Often it is possible to extend them in an array of barely perceptible differences. Such an array can then be correlated with points on a line, and so reduced by correlation to a sort of extensive measurement. Thus pitches of sound can be disposed in a one-dimensional array along a length of line from the lowest perceptible pitch to the highest. Then the farther the two pitches are from each other on the line, the greater the difference or distensive quantity between them. Similarly, by just perceptible differences, hues can be arrayed in a circle: red, orange, yellow, green, blue, violet, purple, and back to red. On this circle, hues across the diameter will differ most from each other, and thence in either direction they become less and less different. Thus orange is less different from red than yellow is, and purple less different from red than violet or blue is.

Illustrations of these three types of quantities from some of the traditional standards of value may be helpful to bring out the pertinence of the distinctions. Pleasure and pain are generally regarded as being open to quantification in terms of intensity, duration, and number. Degrees of intensity of pleasure and pain are obviously intensive quantities. Duration and number, however, are extensive quantities. For time is an extensive quantity. To be sure, for convenience time is reduced by correlation with movements of a pointer over a dial to seconds, minutes, and hours in terms of distances on the dial. But we directly intuit the longer duration of a minute in comparison to a second, and, as with space, intuit the seconds as parts within the duration of a minute. The minute is perceived as composed of the seconds that add up to it, just as a foot is perceived as composed of its inches. So a pleasure that lasts five minutes is quantitatively more extended than one that lasts a minute.

As for number of pleasures, that is clearly an extensive quantity. There is more pleasure when we are enjoying warmth, and a cup of coffee, and a spirited conversation than when only one of these is present. Of course, it is well recognized that pleasures in different media do not add up like marbles in a bag. Some pleasures interfere with others and some add up to more pleasure in combination than they would if added separately; for the principle of the organic whole may come into action by which a whole may be greater than the sum of its parts. These effects of pleasurable media upon each other complicate the quantitative judgment and lead to the conception of the algebraic sum and other modifications of extensive estimates beyond that of the simple addition of discrete units. Still, whatever the details of combination of pleasures in different media or from different sources of stimulation, the result is a summation into a whole of which the various pleasures are parts or elements, whence the quantitative evaluation remains essentially extensive.

For a common example of distensive quantity among values, consider evaluations in terms of the degree in which objects or actions approach some model set up as an ideal. How the ideal itself acquires its value is a separate matter; but the evaluation of objects in comparison with the ideal, in terms of their nearness or remoteness from it, is in terms of distensive magnitude. The comparison is not made in terms of the number of elements or parts, nor in terms of degrees of intensity. It is made in terms of degrees of disparity. The ideal may be that of human beauty, or of heroic manhood, or of political greatness, or of moral integrity; or the ideal may be simply that of the man or woman one would like to marry. Evaluations by such ideals are rarely reducible to extensive or intensive quantities, and so provide ready instances of judgments of distensive magnitudes of value.

All three kinds of quantities thus have their applications in the field of values, and it may sometimes make quite a difference in the interrelations among evaluative judgments for a person to be aware of the type of quantity on which the judgment is based. Is the quantitative judgment that of the amount of some quality contained in a descriptive definition of value, or of the intensity of such a quality, or of the degree of approximation to or remoteness from such a quality?

In attempting to maximize values of any sort, it may become extremely important to distinguish these types of quantities, and to give some quantities precedence over others in order to attain the greatest over-all quantity of value. The problem of maximizing values is often oversimplified by the failure to observe what the effect of maximizing one value quantity may be upon other value quantities. Perry is one of the few writers who noticed these effects in developing his quantitative standards, and described them, and showed how the best results could be obtained in practice.

Perry has, besides 'correctness,' which for him plays a unique role in evaluation, three quantitative standards of interest. (It is in terms of interest, of course, that he descriptively defines value.)

These three standards are *inclusiveness, intensity,* and *preference.* The first is an extensive quantity, the second intensive, and the third distensive, for in his observation the third is not reducible to the other two.

Having discriminated these quantities, Perry then produces evidence to indicate that, in conformity with his descriptions of these quantities as he finds them operating in interested (or purposive) behavior, inclusiveness must be given priority over preference and preference over intensity if a maximum quantity of interest is to be attained in any given situation. His evidence is that if preference or intensity is given priority over inclusiveness, certain preferred interests will occupy the whole field to the exclusion of all others, with the result that the most harmoniously inclusive disposition of interests for the situation is blocked off. The initially preferred interests, like the dog in the manger, can take up all the energy of the organism in their limited enthusiasm and bring about much less than the potential maximum of interest. So first seek the maximum of inclusiveness of interests. The more interests that can be integrated and harmoniously combined, the greater the inclusiveness, and the better by that standard. Then introduce preference, taking in the most preferred of an array of alternative objects of interest which will at the same time most fully integrate with other interests in the situation. The object chosen might not be the one that would be most preferred independently, but it would be the most preferred of the alternative objects which could also harmoniously coöperate with the other objects of interest included. Then, finally, raise the whole organization of interests so selected to the maximum possible intensity. But if intensity had come into the evaluative procedure by itself earlier, it could, like preference, have played the dog in the manger, not only precluding a harmonious integration of many interests, but also precluding the operation of preference by impetuously raising to a maximum absorbing intensity some object of only minor preference.

Here, then, in Perry's theory we see all three types of quantitative standard in operation and can observe how, in his treatment, priorities of one standard over another emerge for the over-all maximization of interest. These priorities, of course, are descriptively justified by reference to the quantitative relations actually found in the facts of interested behavior, to the best of Perry's ability to describe them truly.

Our descriptions of the operation of evaluative standards will not exactly square with Perry's, since our descriptions of purposive behavior do not entirely correspond with his. But his three quantitative standards very neatly exemplify the diversity of intrinsically relevant quantitative evaluations under a single definition of value, and the importance of studying their effects upon one another for the maximization of value.

The same sort of problem about the priorities of standards which mutually affect each other's valuations will come out in an even more acute form as we uncover natural norms in the value field and see their effects in legislating over one another.

## 7. SUMMARY OF PRINCIPLES OF EVALUATION

Now we shall do well to summarize our findings about the nature of evaluation:

1. *The basic evaluative criterion in discourse is a definition of value* which determines what is or is not a value, and of what kind, whether positive or negative, instrumental or terminal, ethical or aesthetic, and the like. This is a qualitative criterion in that it establishes the quality of the value judged to be present.

2. If this definitional criterion is to be responsible to the facts and open to empirical verification, it must be a *descriptive definition* which stipulates that the meaning given to the value defined can be descriptively verified. Otherwise the definitional criterion is an arbitrary act of irresponsible volition. Its arbitrariness may be openly admitted by way of a frankly stipulated nominal definition. This is the road to skepticism in theory of value. Or the arbitrariness may be concealed under the various devices for an appeal to certainty, such as self-evidence, indubitable immediacy, incorrigible insight into the meaning of terms or forms of sentences, and the like. This is the road to dogmatism in theory of value. In the present study it is possible (though unlikely) that we should be driven to a skeptical theory by an inability to find any empirically verifiable definitional criteria of value. But then

we should not undertake to define value at all. We shall, however, deliberately avoid dogmatism except as we may fall into a bit of it now and then by inadvertence. This study intends to be an empirical theory of value, and protects itself in this regard by holding to descriptive definitions of value as the basic evaluative criteria.

3. *A common sense test definition of value* is the initial determination of what are value facts as the objects of reference for a descriptive definition of value. The function of this test definition is to locate roughly the field of value facts. Starting from this rough approximation to the field of value facts, then, by means of observation and analysis, we make refinements of description leading to closer and closer approximations, with the result that the descriptive definitions become more and more discriminating and precise. This is the *principle of successive definition.* The basic evaluative criterion in discourse is thus always in the making, always subject to further refinement in conformity with the value facts.

4. It follows (unless we are driven to the skeptical view that there are no value facts) that the value facts themselves are the ultimate evaluative criteria. For it is the selective operation of the value facts themselves that justifies the selective function of descriptive definitions as criteria of evaluation. The descriptive definitions of value are justified only if they are verified by the value facts they describe. The selective operations of the value facts are thus implicit evaluations which are explicitly described when expressed in terms of verifiable descriptive definitions and the evaluative judgments made by them. Hence the need to distinguish definitions of value as *basic criteria in discourse* from the relations or structures in value facts which by their selective action behave as *natural norms* and are the *ultimate evaluative criteria in fact.* So, evaluative criteria in discourse are subject to evaluative criteria in fact; descriptive definitions of value as the basic criteria in discourse are subject to verification by natural norms which are the ultimate evaluative criteria in fact; explicit evaluative statements in discourse are subject to confirmation by implicit evaluative acts which are the facts that verify the statements.[7]

5. *Quantitative standards,* by which quantitative evaluations of the amount or degree of value of any kind are made, depend for their relevancy on the qualitative definitional criteria.

*a*) *Intrinsic quantitative standards* are those which consist in the quantification of the defining characters of a definition of value. These are intrinsically relevant because they are themselves characters which determine whether the objects being judged for the amount of value they possess are values at all.

*b*) *Subsumed intrinsic standards.* If one definition of value is subsumed under another, the defining characters of the subsumed definition, if quantifiable, are clearly intrinsic standards of the subsumed field of values. They are also partially intrinsic to the larger field under which they are subsumed. For they are intrinsically relevant to the larger field for that limited area of the field in which they are defining characters. This partial but intimate relation of relevancy of the criteria or defining characters of a smaller field of values to the criteria or defining characters of a larger field of values that entirely includes the smaller field is acknowledged by calling the subsumed definitional characters *subsumed intrinsic criteria.* If these characters are quantifiable, they function as intrinsic quantitative standards.

*c*) *Extrinsic standards* are criteria which are not intrinsic as defined above, but which are applied to a field of values for quantitative evaluation. They are relevant in proportion as they are correlated with intrinsic standards—that is, with the defining characters of the definition of value concerned. They are irrelevant if the correlation is negligible or lacking. They serve merely as representatives of the intrinsic standards. They are used because they are often easier to apply than are the intrinsic standards. But they are frequently misused. The commonest fallacies of evaluation arise from using an extrinsic standard as if it were intrinsic, or an irrelevant extrinsic standard as if it were relevant. The relevancy of an extrinsic standard is entirely a matter of empirical testing to see how good its correlation is with the intrinsic standard it is supposed to represent.

*d*) The *types of quantification* open to quantitative value criteria are of all possible kinds, which resolve themselves into three: extensive, intensive, and distensive. Moreover, quantitative criteria are often related in complex ways; so, for an over-all maximization of value by several relevant standards, it may be necessary to apply them in a certain order. In this manner, some standards acquire a sort of priority over others, even though all are intrinsic. The determination of the priority is justifiable, of course, only by empirical testing to find out under just what conditions the over-all maximization of value can be attained through the application of diverse standards. Extrinsic standards are obviously always subordinated in application to the intrinsic standards they are supposed to represent.

With this survey of the principles of evaluation in mind, we are now ready to put these principles to work on the subject matter that has been occupying our attention in the twelve previous chapters. We opened our study with a test common sense definition of value, as by our principles an empirical theory of value should open. Since the field so located was very large and confused, we picked out one promising sample (purposive activity) for intensive study. At the present stage of our study we are able to present a relatively adequate descriptive definition of purposive activity. Now we wish to convert this definition of purpose into a definition of value or possibly definitions of a number of varieties of value. To this task we turn next.

# 14

## Values Found in Purposive Behavior: Conation, Achievement, Affection

### 1. How Values Are Found in Purposes

From our study of the principles of evaluation in the last chapter it becomes clear that the way to find out the values contained in purposive structures is to find out what selective systems or natural norms are embedded there. By this means, descriptive definitions of purposive structures yield descriptive definitions of purposive values.

What selective systems, then, are there in purposive behavior? How do they show up? They show up in dynamic polarities of positive versus negative characters intrinsic to the descriptive definitions of the structures indicated. The common sense test definition, with which our inquiry opened, indicated that purposes lie within the field of values. It follows that the positive and negative features of purposes resulting from the latter's selective action constitute positive and negative values. More specifically, now that we have a relatively refined descriptive definition of purposive activity, it follows that whatever positive and negative features appear among the defining characters of this refined definition will constitute our best-evidenced description of positive and negative purposive values. These will constitute the values intrinsic to our descriptive definition of purposive action.

What features of this sort, then, are intrinsic to the descriptive definitions of purposive structures? What selective systems, or natural norms, are embedded in that subject matter?

The major polarity that springs to the eye is the opposition of appetition to aversion. The whole structure of an appetition is designed for the attainment of a terminal goal, and that of an aversion for the avoidance of a terminal object of riddance. These total structures are selective systems, natural norms, dividing an organism's environment, wherever they go into action, into terminal objects of positive value purposively sought after, and terminal objects of negative value purposively avoided. This molar opposition of the essentially positive value function of an appetition and the essentially negative value function of an aversion is of ultimate significance. It is the first thing to catch the attention of the common sense observer, and it will be the last and most significant thing about purposive activity which we shall come back to in the end. But in the meantime our detailed study of purposive structures has brought to light other selective activities within these total structures. The molar opposition of appetition to aversion that first strikes the eye may turn out to be in the nature of a resultant effect from the interaction of these other selective activities which operate inside the total purposive structures.

## 2. SEVERAL VARIETIES OF VALUE WITHIN PURPOSIVE STRUCTURES

There appear to be three selective polarities, in addition to the molar opposition of appetition to aversion, operating within purposive structures. They seem to constitute three kinds of value (i.e., three different ways in which purposive action makes selections pro and con). These three kinds of value are not apparently reducible to one another, though circumstances can be described in which priorities are set up among them. They are not new to the student of values. All that may appear novel is the discovery that all three of them emerge from purposive behavior when the structures of such behavior are described in detail. They are *conative value,* colloquially known as desire (favor or liking versus disfavor or disliking), *achievement value* (success versus frustration), and *affective value* (pleasure versus pain or unpleasantness).

The discovery of these diverse values within purposive structures as intrinsic features, involved in the very descriptions of purposive structures when the descriptions are detailed, comes, at least to the present writer, as something of a surprise. For, in the common sense indication of the value field, these were all separate items, and purposive value was possibly a fourth, though perhaps identifiable with achievement. But now we find them all gathered together in articulated purposive structures which bid fair to show the factual intercommunications among these diverse values without, however, reducing any one of them to another. The issue between the exponents of desire versus the exponents of feeling (Ehrenfels versus Meinong, Perry versus Prall) will perhaps be resolved in the detailed facts of purposive action without either side being wrong. The only trouble with both sides was that they did not get far enough into the details of the relevant facts to discover the interconnections among the values indicated.

But we have gone a trifle ahead of our evidence in drawing these conclusions. The next matter before us is to make clear to ourselves that conation, achievement, and affection (as distinct selective activities, each with its peculiar mode of polarity pro and con) are indeed intrinsic features of the purposive structures we have been describing.

## 3. The Distributive Principle

If we begin on the assumption that an integral purpose has a single value which perhaps is conceived as the value of the goal at which the action is directed, we are suddenly brought up short with the realization that every purposive act has a history, and that within this history both good and bad things may happen. There are likely to be minor triumphs and frustrations in the course of the major achievement attained by the total integral purpose. An aversion is not altogether and throughout negative, nor an appetition altogether positive.

In fact, within the very structure of a compound aversion is a *positive* appetitive act. That was why we called such aversive structures compound. And wherever an injective enters into an appetition, there is evidence of a riddance pattern with its *negative* value as an intrinsic articulation of the total appetitive structure. Even when we are dealing with simple appetitions and aversions, their mere duration and the number of their subordinate acts have a bearing on the amount of positive or negative value to be attributed to them. The total quantity of negative value in a complete act of aversion, like Poncins' fright in the blizzard, consists, in any estimate of it, in the amount of negative value spread over the total act minus any moments of positive value intrinsic to it.

It is useless to say that such estimates cannot be made. They actually are made, and it is on the basis of such estimates that we intelligently order our lives and determine what risks we shall take. If Poncins could have been rescued half an hour earlier, his suffering would have been that much less. The negative values in Poncins' long aversive activity increased with the duration of the act.

All this goes to show that, while in some overarching sense (not yet very clear) a total appetitive act is a positive value and a total aversive act a negative value, in a more intimate and obvious sense positive and negative values accrue to a purposive act segment by segment as they occur; and the total value of the act is a sort of algebraic sum of the positive and negative values of these segments. This principle of the distribution of values through every segment of a purposive act requires a name. I suggest it be called the *distributive principle*.

The application of this term is an abstract way of indicating something very simple, which is nonetheless not always taken to heart: an actual value occurs only in an actual act. Utak does not get any actual positive value from spearing a fish till he actually spears it. Before he has speared it, he may have positive value in the anticipation of spearing it, and negative value in the fear that he may miss it, but these segments of the total appetition are very different from that of spearing the fish—each segment having its own intrinsic value, positive or negative. No actual intrinsic value is attributable to the spearing of the fish, except in the actual spearing of it. And so with every other intrinsic positive and negative value in the appetition. In some over-all sense the total appetitive structure from the initiation of the drive to the spearing of the fish is a positive value. But for the specific actual values of the act we must examine the value of each segment as it actually occurs. And in this sense the total actual value of the act is found in the summation of the values distributed through its successive segments. I am giving explicit recognition to this fact by naming it the distributive principle.

The action of the distributive principle comes out in a particularly striking way when we consider what happens in frustrated purposes. What happens when an animal dies of starvation or an athlete loses a race? Obviously, these acts have purposive value, though their positive goals are not attained. The starving animal went through agonies of wanting before he died; and during the race the athlete who lost had his moments of exhilaration as he caught up to, and perhaps passed, the winner, and the winner incidentally had his moments of anxiety. There are values of various kinds in all these moments. The total value of the act spreads over all its segments. The actual intrinsic values of a purpose are the values contained in acts actually performed within the total structure of the purpose.

The fact that the actual experienced values of a purpose are those experienced in each segment of the total act as it occurs is what is meant by the distributive principle. The distributive principle is a correction of a not uncommon assumption that the whole value of a purposive act is somehow concentrated upon its goal.

## 4. APPLICATION OF THE DISTRIBUTIVE PRINCIPLE BRINGING OUT THREE VARIETIES OF VALUE

As soon as this distributive principle is recognized, we are led to examine in detail the nature of the values of each segment of a purposive structure. And now we can safely enlist the assistance of introspective reports to augment the preponderantly behavioristic descriptions of the preceding chapters. It was early pointed out (chap. 2, §1) that introspective data are quite reliable if they can be located in previously established objectively described structures. So it was with the work on sensory discrimination after the physiological structures of the sense organs were well established. For local details, introspective reports could then give reliable evidence that would be very difficult to obtain otherwise. So, now that we have fairly detailed objective descriptions of appetitive and aversive structures, we can safely fit available introspective data into the segments of these structures, and obtain information about the inner character of these segments that would be difficult to get otherwise. From now on we shall not hesitate to make use of this information whenever it is pertinent.

So, right now, by way of a preliminary application of the distributive principle to purposive structures, let us see how conative, achievement, and affective values spread out over the segments of a purpose, and let us make as free use as we wish of correlated introspective data.

A purposive theory of value traditionally tries to confine value to desire or conation. It is likely to identify positive value with wanting and negative value with not-wanting (avoidance). This is virtually what Perry does.

Suppose we begin with this proposed identification. It will be found that every segment of an appetition or aversion does in fact contain either wanting or not-wanting. For, according to our descriptive analysis, every segment of an appetition or aversion is charged by an impulse pattern or a riddance pattern or an injective. In any extended appetition (like that of the geologist in search of water), the seeker wants not only the superordinate terminal goal (water), but also each subordinate goal of each subordinate act. In Utak's fishing expedition, which was a compound appetition, there were segments of negative conation (things he did not want), such as his acts in building a windbreak to avoid the wind, but no segments that did not exhibit either positive wanting or negative wanting. And so of any of our purposive structures. Thus conative value, either positive or negative, is distributed through every segment of an appetition or aversion.

But if we look still more closely at the distribution of values in our purposive structures, we find that conative activity is not the only selective activity at work there. Look at the geologist's simple appetition again. In all the subordinate acts and even in the ultimate attainment of the goal object, the energy of the drive keeps up a strong conative value of positive wanting. Finally the goal is attained and the climactic act of the appetition, the consummatory act with its quiescence pattern, comes to actuality, and suddenly the wanting drops off rapidly and the conative value melts away. Yet this is the culminating act of the purpose. Consider any typical consummatory act: a thirsty man quenching his thirst, or a hungry man eating his meal, or an affectionate mother suckling her child, or a sex orgasm. In terms of conative value these are low in value compared with many subordinate acts that precede them, yet, in the structure of an appetition, here is the crowning segment of the whole structure containing a very intense value—*but the intense value is affective*, not conative. Though there is conative value there, the typical consummatory act is high in pleasure but low in wanting. True, there is some sort of correlation between the two. But the intensity of the pleasure is not directly correlated with the intensity of the wanting. The correlation seems rather to be one between pleasure and the *quiescence of wanting* in the consummatory act. In short, since the consummatory act contains high value and this value accrues to it by virtue of its place and function in the structure of an appetition, this value is intrinsic to it. It happens that this high value is affective, not conative. Accordingly, affective value is intrinsic to the consummatory act of an appetition, and must be reckoned among the values of a total purposive activity.

Once this is grasped, we see that pleasures of lesser degree spread along through the minor consummations of the subordinate acts of an appetition. Utak was undoubtedly pleased at finding a suitable place to start cutting a fishing hole, pleased at the completion of the hole, pleased at attracting a fish to his decoy, as well as pleased at the final spearing of a fish. These affective values are intrinsic to these acts too.

Similarly with pain or unpleasantness. The pain of a riddance pattern is actually more conspicuous in immediate perception than the negative conation that accompanies it. So much so that pain, rather than the burn or the cut or the bruise, is popularly regarded as the object that is not-wanted. Sometimes pain is even identified with not-wanting. But though they are closely correlated, we shall presently see reasons for questioning their identification. Nevertheless, pain is unmistakably an intrinsic character of a riddance pattern, and, since pain is negative affective value, it follows that affective values are intrinsic to aversions too.

Then we are reminded that pain or unpleasantness normally accompanies all blockages or frustrations in purposive activities, with the result that negative affective values get spread widely through the segments of appetitions as well as aversions, and are intrinsic to these segments.

In sum, affective values are found scattered all through the structures of appetitions and aversions and are as intrinsic to these structures as are conative values.

Might the two be identified or reduced to one another? Not very obviously, and probably not at all, though some sort of correlation is to be expected. This matter will be treated in detail later (§8). But right now it can be pointed out that the most striking obstacle to identification is the fact that pleasure is at its intensest in the consummatory act when the wanting is going down.

Are pleasures and pains perhaps not values at all but just sensations like sounds and colors to which conative values may become attached? Pleasures may be wanted and pains not-wanted and so be objects of value, as consonances of sound may be wanted and dissonances not-wanted, yet not literally be values in themselves. This thesis is a common one. In fact, a common description of hedonism (generally preparatory to an attempted refutation) is that it is the theory in which pleasure is the only object of wanting (desire) and pain the only object of not-wanting. But this theory would be only a cousin of pure hedonism (a hedonism once removed), for the strict pleasure theory identifies pleasure with positive value directly, not indirectly by connection with conative value. In the latter conative interpretation, pleasure would not itself be value at all, but only an object of value (even if the *only* object of value).

But what our analysis of purposive structures brings out is not that pleasure is an object of conation necessarily, but that it does regularly characterize the consummatory act of an appetition as an intrinsic character of it. Once this is observed, and the well-known polarity of pleasure and pain remarked as intrinsic characters attributable to purposive structures, then automatically, by our principles of evaluation, these become intrinsic purposive values just as clearly as wanting and not-wanting. They constitute another selective polarity intrinsic to purposive acts making positive and negative determinations concerning items that enter into their sphere of action.

But we have not finished yet. There is still another sort of value that emerges from a detailed scrutiny of purposive activity. This sort does not come to light till we begin to consider questions of maximizing values. Since conation is a value, it would follow from our study of evaluative principles that the greater the amount of positive conation the better, and the greater the amount of negative conation the worse. If wanting is good and not-wanting bad, then the more wanting the better and the more not-wanting the worse. As Perry puts it in a passage quoted earlier, "If good is favor and evil disfavor, then the more favorable the better and the more unfavorable the worse." [1]

As regards total conative acts, this selective polarity is confirmed in the behavior of the organism. An appetition is preferred to an aversion. The development of an apprehensive aversion on the basis of a simple injective aversion is mute testimony to this fact. The organism learns a way of avoiding the original riddance pattern altogether, and of shortening the aversive series to a minimum. The cat learned to keep off the hot stove. That is, the cat reduced the segments of the not-wanting series to the minimum by keeping out of the area of apprehensive and riddance response. In general, an organism avoids aversions and welcomes appetitions. People wish to avoid burns, cuts, blows, and insults, or the risk of these, but they wish for food and the appetite for food, for love and the capacity to love.

If, then, aversions are avoided and appetitions are sought, we would think the more aversion the worse and the more appetition the better, without exception. And so it is for aversions. Not only are aversions generally avoided by an organism, but the shorter an aversion the better. On this basis, we would conclude: the shorter an appetition the worse, and the longer an appetition the better. But here the organism behaves in reverse. The shorter the appetition the better. Intuitively we all sense that. With just a few important exceptions, the quicker we can get to the goal the better. Not only the less not-wanting the better in an aversion, but also, paradoxically, the less wanting the better in an appetition. A man positively values an appetition as he negatively values an aversion, but having got an appetition he negatively values the extension of it, and acts so as to attain the goal as quickly as possible.

Evidently another, selective activity is in operation on top of the conative impulse, determining the organism to pursue the shortest path once a purposive action is initiated. It institutes a value very familiar to us—the value of achievement, the opposite of which is frustration. The aim of achievement is the attainment of the shortest path to an appetitive goal as well as the quickest avoidance of a riddance pattern. So here we have to distinguish a third value operating among the structures of purposive behavior.

Are any other kinds of value besides these three working within the purposive structures? What about the instrumental value of a subordinate act in relation to its superordinate act? Certainly this relationship institutes a selective system. But it can without distortion be regarded as part of the structure instituting achievement value. A subordinate goal is good if it leads to a superordinate goal, not only as an instrumental value conducive to the goal but also as a part of a total achievement in process. If it fails to lead to the superordinate goal, it is not only a bad instrumental value but also a frustration to the total achievement. So we need not regard instrumental value as a fourth type of value.

No other selective polarities seem to show up besides conation, affection, and achievement, if instrumental value is amalgamated with achievement value. This does not mean that there are not other selective values operating upon purposive acts, but only that these three appear to be the only ones operating within a single purposive act. These appear to be the only kinds of value attributable to a purposive act as intrinsic characters of it in virtue of its purposiveness. Other values may be attributed to purposes in virtue of the incorporation of purposes in larger wholes having their own selective systems. But these three appear to be the values intrinsic to these particular wholes which we have called purposes and which are the source of docile behavior.

In the remainder of this chapter our task will be to describe each of these values in more detail and to show their interrelationships as far as present evidence goes.

## 5. CONATIVE VALUE

Conative value is what is commonly known as desire or wanting. Desire is either pro or con, positive or negative. But strangely there is no recognized pair of words to express this opposition except the rather weak pair favor-disfavor and the ambiguous pair liking-disliking. To have something more precise and expressive of the dynamics of conation I shall use wanting versus not-wanting as the technical terms for positive and negative desire or conation.

1. *The conative references.*—The two definitive characteristics of desire are its intensity and its direction, or reference. The intensity of desire comes from a purposive drive. The reference comes from the patterns of action characteristic of the segments of a purpose charged by a drive. These constitute the *conative reference*. This reference determines the terminal object of desire and whether the desire is positive or negative. It tells whether the desire is for something or against something, and precisely what it is for or against. It becomes a matter of major importance, in defining conative value, that we should be clear about the nature of the conative reference.

This reference is often assumed uncritically to be cognitive. If the pattern of purposive action charged by a drive happens to be a cognitive set (either an anticipatory or an apprehensive set), then the conative reference is indeed also a cognitive reference. It is true that cognitive references are more conspicuous than noncognitive ones. But the assumption that all the references of conation are cognitive is brought up short by the concept of 'blind drive.' The instinctive drive (impulse pattern) of an appetition previous to experience of its goal (or quiescence pattern) is, in fact, cognitively blind. The appetition has not acquired an anticipatory set cognitively referring to the goal object productive of its quiescence pattern. In that respect the drive is blind. Nevertheless, as we have seen, this does not mean that the drive does not have a definite reference to its terminal goal. Unless there were such a reference, there would be nothing to determine the consummation of an appetitive purpose. The reference for a cognitively blind drive lies in its conditions of quiescence, which are implicit in the very pattern of the drive. There are verifiably different conditions of quiescence for hunger and thirst, for instance, and these differences are implicit in the different impulse patterns for the two drives. A conative reference is thus not necessarily cognitive.

Our initial task in deepening our understanding of conative value is to examine in detail the nature of conative references derived from the various kinds of drives and cognitive sets.

The variety of conative references in table 4 is impressive, and the error of the assumption that these references are all cognitive is now glaringly apparent. Even the cognitive references are not homogeneous (as the assumption often further assumes). The references of a positive desire with an idea (anticipatory set) of what is wanted are directed upon a goal object and are positive in intent. But the references of a negative desire with an idea (here an apprehensive set) of what is not-wanted are directed upon an object of apprehension and are negative in intent. In the former, the cognitive references are the dispositions guiding action to the attainment of the object referred to. In the latter, the cognitive references are directed upon the center of a field of avoidance, and some action separating the organism from this center is designated.

But even more marked differences in the nature of conative

TABLE 4

KINDS OF CONATIVE REFERENCES WITH THEIR SOURCES AND OBJECTS

| Segment | Nature of references | Sign of references | Object of references |
|---|---|---|---|
| Impulse pattern | Positive conditions of quiescence | Positive | Quiescence pattern or consummatory act |
| Anticipatory set | Cognitive | Positive | Goal object |
| Riddance pattern | Acts of riddance | Negative | Object of riddance |
| Apprehensive set | Cognitive | Negative | Object of apprehension |
| Injective (as reinforcing other drives) | Acts of riddance (by aggressive action or fright) | Negative | Object of riddance or of apprehension |
| Injective (as spontaneous drive) | Positive conditions of quiescence | Positive | Quiescence pattern: <br> a) Triumph over obstacle for aggression <br> b) Relief from object of fear for fright |

references are seen in the contrast between the cognitive and the noncognitive references. For an impulse pattern the conative reference is its conditions of quiescence. An impulse pattern (without a cognitive set) is not aimless. The reference to its quiescence pattern is as definite as that of an anticipatory set to its goal object. In fact, it is the former that determines ultimately the correctness of the latter and evaluatively legislates over it. For the sole purposive function of an anticipatory set is to lead to an object that will produce the quiescence pattern of the drive.

For a riddance pattern the conative references are different again. They consist in the acts of riddance themselves: retracting the hand from a flame, retreating from the smoke of a campfire, brushing off a tickling insect, coughing up a fishbone. These acts of riddance are in direct commerce with the object of riddance and have reference to it as the center of riddance. They are not cognitive, however, for they are instinctive, or partially so. They may be inadequate, like coughing to get rid of a fishbone when the bone is too deep to be dislodged, and so may need to be supplemented by cognitively directed action. But unlearned acts of riddance are not subject to cognitive error. Coughing refers to a center of stimulation that is not-wanted whether the coughing itself can get rid of the object or not. Acts of riddance thus constitute direct negative conative references to the objects which stimulate them, and these references are not cognitive.

The injectives present a peculiar case, because in different roles they exhibit different conative references. In their distinctive role as agents for the reinforcement of other drives on occasions of blockage or intense noxious stimulation, they act directly on the object concerned with their special, very effective pattern of riddance. For the frightened cat that had jumped on the hot oven, the riddance pattern of fright reinforced the direct riddance reaction to the heat on the paws. The reference of both of the riddance patterns—the instinctive leap from the stove and the fright riddance pattern superimposed—was to the heat stimulus. At that point both riddance patterns converged on the identical stimulus. But then the fright riddance pattern continued on to react to a succession of associated objects in the environment—the oven, the whole stove, and the whole kitchen. The fright riddance reaction was in commerce with these associated objects, instituting a fear of them well after the heat stimulus was removed by the instinctive leap off the stove.

The same reaction will be seen in respect to all the objects of fright and apprehension with which Poncins was dealing in his panic in the Arctic blizzard. Whatever his fright pattern acted upon became, by that very act of commerce with it, an object of negative wanting—not only the cold and the snow and the buffeting wind immediately stimulating him, but the cognitive apprehensions, too, of being lost, being frozen, being dead. The latter were cognitive objects of apprehension. But what made them objects of fright was the immediate fright riddance reaction at the time to the thought of them. The negative conative reactions of fright are always originated by the fright riddance reaction itself.

Similarly with aggression as a reinforcing agent. If we are hit, we strike back. If the door sticks, we are likely to bang it. Here the object of riddance is also the object of aggression. The riddance pattern of aggression directly reinforces that of the simple riddance, and in both instances the riddance reactions constitute the conative references to the unwanted object.

If the blockage is in the guise of an object of apprehension, then the aggressive riddance reaction is to the object of apprehension. Thus, when Utak was afraid that Poncins' walking on the ice would scare away the fish beneath, he attacked Poncins with words. The attacking response itself constituted the reference to the object of attack. That is to say, the riddance reaction of the injective gave the reference to the object of negative conation.

So, when used for the reinforcement of other drives, both the positive and the negative injectives (both aggression and fright) institute negative references through the riddance reactions characteristic of these drives. In common sense terms, a person does not want an object that is obstructing a drive or an object that he fears or apprehends. A riddance reaction of attack or withdrawal shows the attitude to the object.

But when injectives are acting as spontaneous drives in periods of high spirits and play and sport, the conative references are reversed. Then aggression seeks objects of obstruction for the consummatory exhilaration of triumph over them, and fear looks about for fairly safe objects of apprehension in order to indulge in a consummatory feeling of relief. In a sport like mountain climbing the two kinds of consummatory satisfaction are combined. The dangers are considerable, and consummatory relief is gained after each cliff is scaled and each chasm crossed; the triumph of success in attaining the chosen peak is proportional to the seriousness of the obstacles met and overcome along the way. But every act is positively wanted, whether aggressive or fearful, because of the consummatory goals of relief and triumph. Here the references are all positive, and the source of these in the injective drives would be their positive conditions of quiescence, and the objects of reference for these drives are the quiescence patterns of relief or triumph which would satisfy those conditions.

Of course, in mountain climbing, as in other sports, accidents may occur. Then the sport is spoiled by the practical problems of averting injury. There is a threshold in every such sport at which the matter ceases to be fun and becomes practical and serious. The recognition of this threshold is marked by a concept which has justly received a good deal of attention in the aesthetic field. It is known as *psychical distance*. Psychical distance is maintained as long as conative activity is directed primarily toward the consummatory satisfaction of an injective drive. It is lost when the conative activity is directed primarily at the riddance reactions.

All these discriminations bring out still more emphatically than we were able to demonstrate earlier the peculiar nature of these injective drives as intermediate between the purely appetitive drives of hunger, thirst, and sex, and the purely aversive drives initiated by specific riddance patterns. The drive of an injective behaves as a riddance pattern when it is stimulated by segments related to other drives for purposes of reinforcement. When so stimulated, the consummatory results of successful achievement in relief or triumph are irrelevant to the structure and motivation of the total activity. They come as a welcome aftermath, as in Poncins' relief when at last he found he was safe from the blizzard. Still, they are not essential to the purposive structure of these acts. But when these same drives are spontaneously aroused, they function as impulse patterns with positive references in terms of their conditions of quiescence to the consummatory quiescence patterns of relief or triumph which give them terminal satisfaction.

Neither pure riddance patterns nor impulse patterns have this bipolar mode of functioning. A specific riddance pattern is always negative in its conative references, and there is no consummatory relief from its quiescence. When a pebble has got into your shoe, and you shake it out, there is no consummatory triumph or relief unless the irritation had become intense enough to stir up an injective. You just felt comfortable in your shoe again after getting rid of the irritating object. And an appetitive impulse pattern never ceases to set its ultimate goal on its quiescence pattern. An impulse pattern always has a positive conative reference. Intense hunger or thirst can become painful and disliked, but this does not stop the positive reference to the appetitive goal. The pain actually augments the inducement and desire to reach the positive goal. The negative conative reference to the pain is superimposed upon the positive conative reference of the impulse pattern to the consummatory goal. It has the effect of teaching an intelligent organism not to allow an impulse pattern to continue so long unsatisfied that it produces unnecessary pain. The appetitive drive still maintains its positive reference all the time. It is only an injective that has the peculiarity of changing the sign of its conative references under certain changes of conditions.

2. *The definition of conative value.*—After this extended examination of the varieties of conative reference—necessary, nonetheless, in view of the widespread assumption that the reference is homogeneous and always cognitive—we are prepared to give a workable *definition of conative value.*

In somewhat dangerously abstract terms, the relationship involved in conation is ordinarily set down as 'interest-in-object,' or something equivalent, where 'interest' stands for the charge of the drive, 'in' for the conative reference, and 'object' for the object of the conative reference. This could be symbolized $I(R)O$. On this formulation, three abstract possibilities can be offered for the definition of conative value:

To define conative value as the total relationship, thus stressing $R$:

$$\text{Conative value} = I(R)O \tag{1}$$

To define conative value as the property of an object in virtue of an interest taken in it, thus stressing $O$:

$$\text{Conative value} = O^{(R)I} \tag{2}$$

To define conative value as the dynamic reference of an act to an object, thus stressing $I$:

$$\text{Conative value} = I^{(R)O} \tag{3}$$

Formulations 1 and 2 are the traditional and current ones. I believe, however, that the third is the advisable one.[2] Theoretically they should be intertranslatable. But the third keeps a firmer hold on the pivotal element of conative selectivity—the drive. The object of interest is actually determined by the drive through the references charged by the drive. The object does not even need to be mentioned if the pattern of action charged by the drive is indicated in sufficient detail. The danger of the other two formulations lies in overstressing the object, which often gets rather lost in its surrounding environment and confused in its status; it is then very hard to bring it back again into the dynamic conative act. Even to treat conation as essentially a relational entity, in line with formulation 1, and so elaborate a relational theory of value, may turn out to distort the facts of actual conative behavior. The relational formulation is not so much false as unilluminating, for it deëmphasizes the active selective operation of the drive. Conation is essentially a dynamic selective activity of an organism in the midst of its environment. It is primarily an act. A formulation which makes the object selected by the act as important as the act of selection throws the facts out of balance and tends to direct study on the less enlightening term of the relationship.

So I suggest defining conative value in the manner of the third formulation as being more in conformity with the facts referred to. We desire a definition that indicates the dynamic action of the drive together with the specific selective action of the references it charges (see table 4). I suggest the following: *Conative value is the charge of a drive on an impulse pattern, a riddance pattern, or a cognitive set.* Or still more simply, it is *the charge of a drive on a pattern of references.* In introspective terms, conative value is either a desire for what we believe will satisfy the desire or a blind impulse for whatever the state may be that would satisfy the impulse. The pattern of the impulse, or that of the charged cognitive set, determines by the direction of the references whether the value is positive or negative, and also determines the terminal object of conative value.

Conation is a selective agency in that it determines what an organism will avoid and what it will seek. The environment ceases to be neutral through the agency of conation, and takes sides for or against the organism. Not only the outer environment is so affected, but whatever stimulates the conative reference of a drive. Conation thus functions as an evaluative norm making implicit judgments of good and bad through the conative references charged by drives. It also makes implicit judgments of better and worse through its quantitative evaluations.

3. *The intrinsic standards of conative value.*—Now let us consider the quantitative standards that are intrinsic to the definition of conative value. The defining characters resolve themselves into two: the charge of a drive and the pattern of references charged. The charge of a drive is clearly quantifiable in terms of *intensity, duration,* and *number.* There is more drive charge if you increase its intensity, and its duration, and if the number of drives present is greater. And the same introspectively with desire. So there are three intrinsic standards of conative value.

These standards are more easily indicated, however, than applied. There is no trouble about duration. But it is not always easy to tell how many drives are operative. In simple situations, a number of different drives can often be discriminated. If you are chilly and are being bitten by mosquitoes and have a splinter in your hand, you clearly have more negative conation than if any one of the drives was operating alone. But complications arise from the fact that one drive can inhibit another. Intense fear can drive away hunger, and a very intense drive augmented by an injective can take over a whole organism and inhibit most of the other drives that were present previous to the onset. Another complication arises from the integration of a number of drives for a total organized effect. When there is an integration of purposes there is a fusion of incentives, and usually it is not illuminating to treat an organic structure of action additively as if its conative charge were the sum of the charges of the drives that compose it. If, instead of number, we could refer to the extensity of active conative charge in an organism, this would clarify some of these complications. So, wherever the context makes it more suitable, we shall speak of the *extensity* of conative charge instead of number. These will be synonyms for this same quantitative standard of conation.

Although intensity of conation seems transparent enough introspectively, as the immediately felt intensity of desire, it is difficult to indicate its specific denotation behavioristically. And this behavioristic difficulty is ultimately reflected in the introspective report. We sometimes have objective evidence of intense desires that use each other up in an internal conflict, with the result that the superficial report is of only a very weak desire for something. But when the evidence of the conflict comes home to the person concerned, he frequently becomes introspectively aware of his conflict, and then his introspective report will agree closely with the objective evidence.

For the handling of these difficulties the concept of *conative tension* has emerged. On first thought, we are tempted to identify the intensity of a drive with the physical energy expended. There is a rough correlation between them: when a drive exhibits itself in full muscular action, the energy expended is an indication of the intensity of the conative charge behind it. In other words, expenditure of energy in purposive action is a fairly reliable extrinsic standard of conative intensity, but not the intrinsic standard. For there can be very intense desire without a movement of a muscle. Think of a runner waiting for the signal to start, or of an outpost watching a machine-gun nest. Conative intensity cannot be directly correlated even with muscular tension, though again this is a fairly good extrinsic standard where it exists. The common expression 'pain in the neck' is a popular recognition of the significance of a type of muscular tension that shows intense hostile desire held in check.

The best literary term expressing the precise nature of conative intensity is probably 'eagerness.' If a person has a strong desire, he is eager to do something. But circumstances may be such that, for all his eagerness, there is no evident expenditure of physical energy. So eagerness is not actual expenditure of physical energy either in muscular action or in muscular tension preparatory to action. It consists in a readiness to expend energy, and the intensity of this eagerness is somehow proportional to the quantity of energy actually available for action. The degree of eagerness seems to be proportional to the amount of potential energy available for an act at the moment. It is as if the intensity of desire were a direct report of potential energy of an act, as if it were introspectively the feeling of that potential energy. This is the conative tension from the introspective angle. From the behavior angle, it is the particular physiological disposition which holds a portion of the physical energy of an organism immediately available for action. During action this potential energy may not diminish (being constantly replenished out of the physiological system) until the consummatory act is reached, when, as we say, the tension is released. And then the feeling of the intensity of desire goes down and disappears.

The concept of tension as the gauge of the potential energy of a drive has proved a very useful one. But it should be frankly admitted that at the present stage of information it is in the nature of a conceptual hypothesis. It is a unifying and fruitful concept. Like some of the subatomic elements of physics, it would account for a wealth of data; and the data which are systematized by reference to it have a confirmatory effect, indicating that it may well be as clearly indicated and described some day as the synapse in physiology is now. But at present it is only a promising hypothesis. I shall, however, take the risk of accepting it as explanatory of conative intensity.

Following a large number of contemporary writers from different schools, I shall identify intensity of conative value with degree of physiological tension: the greater the tension, the greater the intensity of conation.

Behavioristically, the intensity of a drive is measured by a number of methods. They are worth calling attention to, because they help to confirm the view that intensity of drive is an energy manifestation. And, what is even more convincing, the different methods agree on the whole in their results about the relative strength of drives wherever comparisons are possible though none of the methods appear to be entirely trustworthy.

The most direct way of testing the strength of a drive is by the obstruction method. In the usual laboratory apparatus for animals, an electric grill is placed between the animal and its goal object. In proportion to the voltage on the grill, the animal gets an electric shock, which stimulates a riddance pattern of an intensity increasing with the voltage. The strength of the drive can thus be measured by the amount of shock necessary to keep the animal from crossing the grill. The energy of an aversive drive is thus balanced against that of an appetitive drive, and the intensity of the latter (the potential energy available under the circumstance) is measured by correlation with the voltage on the grill. The animal will cross the grill for some goal objects when it refuses to cross for others. In more complex forms, men's drives are similarly tested. The commonest test is how much we are willing to pay for an object we want. It hurts to spend our money; the more we have to spend for something the more it hurts, and so we can see, by the amount we are willing to pay, how much we want it.

Another way is the method of choice. Of two goal objects equally accessible, which is selected? The object chosen is the one most wanted. Preference series can be arranged by this method. Of itself, this method does not necessarily prove that the preferred object is the object of a more intense drive. But when the method of choice checks with the method of obstruction in its results, there can be little doubt that intensity of drive is the basis of preference. In human monetary terms, we will pay more for the object we prefer. The two methods check.

A third way is the learning method. The assumption here is that the speed of learning is correlated with the strength of a drive. If a problem has to be solved, such as learning a maze or getting out of a cage, in order to attain a goal object, the quicker it is solved the stronger the drive. As with the previous test, this would not necessarily prove that it was the intensity of the drive that made the difference, but when this test also correlates in its results with the obstruction test, it becomes pretty convincing.

Closely correlated with speed of learning is the number of errors made in learning. When we are less eager we are not so careful or alert, and the errors increase as well as the time of learning.

A variation of this test is the shift-of-motivation method. When a new goal object is set up as a reward for learning, a striking change in the learning curve often occurs. This change is fairly reliably correlated with what the preference test would show was the changed degree of preference for the object. With a less preferred object as goal, learning slows down and errors increase. And vice versa for a more preferred goal object.

To the same effect, the addition of a moderately wanted goal object to one already moderately wanted will often augment the total attractiveness of the goal. This would be hard to explain except as the addition of the energy of one drive to another so as to increase the total energy of action. Again, in human bargaining, a store can capture purchasers if it advertises a bonus of crockery or canned goods with every purchase over a certain minimum.

All these methods of testing the intensity of a desire seem perfectly natural to our common sense feeling, which is another way of saying that they check with our introspective reports. Why, of course, if I want something intensely I will go to a lot of trouble to get it! Also, I would prefer it over anything I would not go to so much trouble to get. And, being eager to get it, I would be quick to learn how it could be got, much quicker than if it were something I did not want very much. In fact, in the early days of animal psychology, when these laws were being verified by controlled laboratory experiments, one of the trials animal psychologists had to put up with was the reproach that they were not proving anything that everybody did not know. But one fact these experiments have steadily confirmed, which the common man has not yet fully realized, is that the feeling that he wants something intensely is the index of his willingness to make a great effort to get it.[3] This feeling is his introspective registering of the degree of tension present, the amount of potential energy available to that particular end.

So once more we may affirm the fruitfulness of identifying the intensity of a drive with the degree of tension attributable to the drive, which in turn may be correlated with the amount of potential physical energy of the organism available to the drive at that moment.

To return, then, to the point of origin of our discussion of conative standards: We observed that the two pivotal characters in the definition of conative value as the charge of a drive on a pattern of references were the drive and the pattern of references. We found that drive was quantifiable in three respects: intensity, duration, and extent (or number). These are, accordingly, intrinsic quantitative standards of conative value. And we have just examined these with some care. The next question is whether or in what respects the character 'pattern of references' may be quantifiable. For if this also is quantifiable, some additional intrinsic standards will be attributable to conative value.

The 'pattern of references' of a conative act is quantifiable. It is quantifiable in terms of the extent or number or massiveness of the references, and in terms of their correctness.

The extent of drive pattern is not quite the same as drive extensity, considered earlier, for the one quantifies references and the other drives. But in practice the two amalgamate into what we may regard as one standard, that of conative extensity. More conative value is involved in starting to run a city than in starting to run a car. We say the performance of the duties of a mayor is more significant than that of taking a turn in a car for the fun of it. The one involves an institution; the other, just one's own immediate satisfactions. And in the greater depth and scope of conative value of the one over the other is included a much larger system of conative references and many more drives enlisted to charge them. Let us then amalgamate drive extensity and referential extensity into one, and hereafter refer simply to the standard of *conative extensity*. Conative extensity, then, will consist in the amalgamation of drive extensity and pattern of reference extensity.

Correctness—that is to say, the truth or probability of the mediating judgments among the references of a charged conative pattern—is a distinct intrinsic standard, however. The appropriateness of this standard is commonly recognized whenever it is affirmed that a realizable desire is better than one that cannot be realized. In fact, this brings to light another standard which is generated out of correctness, namely, speed of realization. It is also true that a desire is better if it can be realized speedily, and this follows in proportion as the mediating judgments are correct through all the subordinate acts of a projected series of purposive references.

But these two closely allied standards of correctness and speed are the characteristic standards of achievement. Yet earlier (§2) we saw reason to believe that achievement value was a kind of value distinct from conative value, and that it was capable of being differently defined. How do we harmonize this fact with the discovery that these standards intrinsic to achievement value are intrinsic also to conative value? The answer is that the *potentiality* of a degree of achievement value is an intrinsic standard of conative value. And this relationship gives the connection between the two sorts of value—and a very close connection it is.

Nevertheless, a conation is not an achievement. A conation is, so to speak, a potential achievement, and an achievement an actualized conation. Conation institutes values by charging patterns of reference with drives. Achievement institutes values by bringing drives to quiescence. The values are different because the selective action of the two agencies is different. But the materials on which the two agencies operate—drives and their patterns of reference—are the same. We shall have more to say about this relationship presently (in §7).

Our conclusions about conative value may now be summarized. *Conative value is a pattern of references charged by a drive.* Its intrinsic standards are the intensity and duration of its drives, the extensity of its charged references, and the correctness and potential speed of realization of these references. The objects of conative value are the references charged by the drives and the objects to which these references refer.[4]

## 6. Achievement Value

Achievement value comes to light as something distinct from conative value when we see the effects of maximizing conative value. If positive conation is good and negative conation bad, then the more of the former the better, and the more of the latter the worse. Speaking precisely and within the domain of conation, this is true. The more of positive wanting there is, the more of good wanting there is; and the more of negative wanting, the more of bad not-wanting. Moreover, the organism welcomes the good positive wantings as a whole and avoids the bad not-wantings. A man with foresight works up an appetite for a Thanksgiving dinner, and develops his taste for the arts; but he kills poison oak on his property so that he will not have to keep avoiding it, and has a doctor periodically check on his health to prevent ills from getting started. The organism does naturally select for positive and against negative conations—*so long as these do not begin to realize themselves in achievement.*

But the moment the process of achievement begins, the paradox occurs that the organism favors the quickest achievement whether it be aversion or appetition. The organism in achievement seeks to minimize both negative and positive conation. Poncins sought to get out of the blizzard as quick as he could, in order to minimize his positive conations. Utak showed by his actions that he *thought it good* to have *as few good* conations as possible in his appetitive pursuit! Obviously there are two senses of 'good,' two different selective principles at work. The process of achieving quiescence of a drive legislates over the selective process of conation as soon as the latter begins to realize itself in action. Achievement seeks the shortest route whether the drive be negative or positive.

For achievement is the building of the bridge over the gap from impulse to quiescence. It is the norm of learning, of docility, of intelligence. And so it is at the heart of purposiveness, of docile adaptive behavior. Its implicit aim, or norm of selectivity, is the efficiency of the bridge over the gap, both in the building and the maintenance of it. Consequently, the selection is for whatever tends to increase the speed and security of passage over this bridge, and against whatever tends to block the passage. Roughly, the norms of achievement will be found in the laws of learning. And that is why the recent careful study of the learning process in psychology provides so much that is illuminating to value theory.

The complete achievement of an appetition consists in the succession of acts from the incipience of the drive through the subordinate acts charged by the drive to quiescence in the consummatory act. But there are also partial achievements along the way as each successive goal object is reached. Similarly, for an aversion a complete achievement consists in the succession of acts from the initiating riddance pattern or charged object of apprehension through the succession of subordinate acts to final quiescence of the riddance pattern or the injective. Here too there are partial achievements along the way as each subordinate act attains its quiescence.

An achievement is thus primarily a succession of acts within a purposive structure initiated by a drive and terminated by the quiescence of the drive. But the definition of achievement activity in preparation for a definition of achievement value requires a little care, in order to provide for partial achievements and for frustrated and incomplete achievements. The definition to be fruitful must, of course, conform as closely as possible to the actual mode of selection (the natural norm) operative in this area.

The natural norm operative in this area is the complete achievement. This, then, should be descriptively defined first, and thereafter provision should be made for partial and incomplete acts of achievement. *A complete achievement is a succession of acts by which a pattern of conative references charged by a drive attains the terminal object of the references if they are positive, or terminal quiescence of them if they are negative.* By referring to a pattern of conative references, we compendiously include all the varieties of purposive acts which can initiate achievement: impulse patterns, riddance patterns, anticipatory sets, apprehensive sets, and injectives.

From this definition of a complete achievement, we can now define *achievement activity* as any portion of a complete achievement, whether or not the terminal object or the quiescence of the charged conative references is attained. Then a *partial achievement* is the attainment of the object referred to by the conative references of a subordinate anticipatory set if the references are positive, or the attainment of quiescence of the charged references of a subordinate apprehensive set if these are negative. In a partial achievement the quiescence of a drive-charged subordinate cognitive set is attained. What has occurred is a subordinate achievement. But the drive is still active and charging the superordinate act with its pattern of conative references. It is a partial achievement on the way to the complete achievement.

An *incomplete achievement* occurs when the succession of acts required for a complete achievement fails at any point to attain its terminal goal or quiescence. The failure may occur for a variety of reasons: blockage, emergence of a stronger drive, discouragement, fatigue, death.

In order that an act should contribute to a complete achievement (or even a partial achievement), the quiescence of the drive charging the conative references must be due to acts of the organism in the manner referred to by the conative references. In ordinary terms, we do not consider that a man has achieved his aims unless he did it himself by his own acts and got what he aimed for. We expect him to find the correct acts by his own efforts. This does not mean that he necessarily knows beforehand what the correct acts are. He may not yet have learned the way to get what he wants. He may have had to use trial and error. And, having hit upon the correct act, he may not yet have learned just why it was correct and may make an error at the same point again. But if he hit upon the correct act by his own trial-and-error activity, this act along with the errors counts as part of his achievement activity and as finally yielding a complete achievement. If, however, some other agent—a parent, or a teacher, or an experimenter manipulating the goal— gave the answer, that act would not be part of the man's achievement activity. He would have *ob*tained his goal, but would not have *at*tained it. The obtaining of the quiescence of his conative references (getting what he wanted) by sheer luck or by *deus ex machina* would not constitute achievement. The act has to be linked to the purposive structure in operation in order to fall within the sphere of achievement activity.[5]

But more important still, if quiescence of the drive comes because the organism has given up, or has become so fatigued that there is no drive left, or finally may have died, such eventualities do not constitute a complete achievement. For in such instances the quiescence of the drive is not the result of the attainment of the object referred to by positive conative references, nor of an act of the organism bringing about the avoidance of the object referred to by negative conative references. In order to count as a complete achievement, the terminal quiescence of the charged conative references instituting the purposive act must attain the specific type of quiescence indicated by those references. An impulse pattern must attain its characteristic consummatory act; and a riddance pattern or apprehensive set must attain freedom from conditions of commerce with its object of riddance or of apprehension. If the quiescence of the drives comes about by any means other than the actual attainment of the conditions of quiescence indicated by the conative references, the achievement is incomplete and a failure.

Nevertheless, an incomplete achievement is still within the sphere of achievement activity. There was an attempt at achievement, but it was unsuccessful. It generates a negative achievement value.

With all this understood, we may now profitably present a definition of achievement value. *Positive achievement value is success and consists in the attainment either of the object or else of the quiescence of a set of conative references charged by a drive. Negative achievement value is frustration and consists in the delay or failure of such attainment.*

The intrinsic quantitative standards can readily be derived from the three defining characters found in this definition: the process of attainment, the conative references to objects of appetition or avoidance, and the drive. All these characters are quantifiable.

1. *Speed and correctness of attainment.*—The process of attainment consists in the passage from the initiation of a purposive action to its terminus by way of a succession of subordinate acts. In the learning process an organism selects its acts so as to reduce the time of attainment to a minimum. That is, it maximizes the speed of attainment. So the quicker the attainment the better. For if speed of attainment is good, the speedier the better.

Moreover, our earlier descriptions showed that the selection of subordinate acts in the learning process is guided by the correctness of the mediating judgments. Errors in the learning process are systematically eliminated. In appetitions, all errors must be eliminated for final attainment to occur. And the fewer the errors the quicker the attainment. So correctness is essential to speed of attainment. In aversions, errors of mediating judgments are not so easily detected, since attainment consists in the avoidance of an object of aversion. But as soon as an organism is convinced that a subordinate object of apprehension is erroneously connected with the terminal object of aversion, it eliminates that subordinate act, thereby shortening the attainment of quiescence. The more correct the sequence of acts in the process of attainment, the quicker and better the attainment.

How can there be degrees of correctness? For many details here I must refer to our earlier discussion of the mediating judgment (chap. 4, §§4–10). The correctness of a mediating judgment is a matter of probability, and there are degrees of probability. Absolute correctness would be ideal, but an achievement is a process subject to unforeseen contingencies, and a highly probable mediating judgment is the most that can practically be demanded in the way of correctness in linkage between a subordinate and a superordinate act. The worst condition for effective achievement is that of total ignorance of connection, the absence of any mediating judgment, or, even worse, belief in a false mediating judgment; for these conditions constitute the inner aspect of frustration. When there is a complete gap at some point between a drive and the attainment of its conditions of quiescence, achievement is blocked till trial-and-error activity can find the correct act to bridge the gap. So there are degrees of correctness in terms of degrees of probability of the truth of a mediating judgment, with absence of any judgment counting as zero probability.

There are also degrees of correctness in terms of the number of correct as opposed to incorrect judgments in the sequence of acts leading to a complete achievement. This is easily seen in maze learning. As errors are gradually reduced, this signifies that some acts in the sequence are correctly connected and some are not. Usually the acts nearest the goal are correctly learned first, and gradually the whole sequence is learned. The same is true of learning a part for a play, or how to run a car, or establishing a policy for manufacture and sales in a business enterprise, or training students in a professional school. Such skills and functions require a succession of acts for the achievement of a definite goal. The greater the number of correct judgments connecting the successive segments of the achievement, the quicker and more secure the success.

These two applications of correctness—that of the degree of probability of a mediating judgment, and that of the proportion of correctly learned to unlearned connections among subordinate acts—can be combined in one, which may be described as the degree of correctness in the mediating judgments connecting the acts of a total achievement. The greater the correctness of these judgments, the better the achievement.

But is it not a good achievement if the correct acts have been performed, even if they were made by trial and error and there were no correct mediating judgments? In judging the success of an achievement in terms of correctness, should we not judge the acts rather than the judgments mediating the acts? Here, I think, we have come upon a seldom-noticed ambiguity in the standard of correctness. It is really two standards, not one. There is correctness in the sense of the proportion of erroneous *acts* performed in a total achievement, and there is correctness in the sense of the proportion of true (or probable) mediating *judgments* in the performance of an achievement. The first is a quantitative standard of the efficiency of the performance; the second is a quantitative standard of the degree of insight in the performance. Since both the acts themselves and the mediating judgments connecting the acts are intrinsic to a purposive structure, both standards are intrinsic standards of achievement.

The distinction between them is more technical than practical, however, because, in the learning process, correctness of insight is essential to efficient performance in the long run. Without insight into the correct connections in a series of acts for the attainment of terminal quiescence, a chance efficient performance cannot be repeated. Nearly everyone at some time has chanced to solve a mechanical puzzle in a few moves, and then taken hours with many errors to work out what he had done. The original performance was efficient, for it actually put together the correct sequence of acts without many errors. But it totally lacked insight into the correct sequence of acts to be anticipated; there were no correct mediating judgments. So the bridge across the gap from drive to goal had not after all been efficiently learned.

Unless an occasion calls for the distinction between correctness of performance and correctness of insight, I shall employ the latter as the standard of correctness for achievement value. This amalgamates the degree of probability of a mediating judgment with the proportion of correctly learned to unlearned connections among subordinate acts. Drawing all these elements together, we may regard the standard of correctness for achievement value as the degree of correctness in the mediating judgments connecting the acts of a total achievement.

2. *Extensity of conative references.*—The more extensive the correct conative references actualized in an achievement, the greater the achievement. It is a greater achievement to climb a high mountain than a small hill, to build a house than a hencoop. It makes no difference whether references gain their extent through time and the longer sequence of acts required for the final attainment, or through simultaneous spread in the broader texture of acts required for a performance. But all the acts must be necessary (i.e., correct) in order to count as increasing an achievement value. An unnecessarily long path up a mountain does not increase the achievement of attaining the height. It decreases it by reducing the speed. A specious extensity can be given an achievement by increasing the number of erroneous acts. There will be much more effort in the achievement, but much less achievement value. The learning process itself makes this elimination by selecting against the errors. We are all familiar with this selective process, but do not always notice that the laws of learning here act as a natural norm of achievement value.

The only apparent exception to the norm of the shortest path for achievement value is in tests of strength and endurance, where the aim is to show how much energy one has. Then the longer the path the better. But the goal in such instances is the longer path, that is, the greater extent of actualized conative references, acts carried out. The acts are all correct. So there is no real exception here. A man who outwalks another man in an endurance test performs more correct acts, has a more extensive achievement.

3. *Intensity of drive.*—An achievement performed with great intensity of drive has a greater achievement value than one per-

formed at low intensity. There is more achievement value in finding the means of satisfying an intense thirst than a mild one, even though the sequence of acts performed was the same. It is more of an achievement to avoid poison oak than a thistle, though a step off the path suffices for each. If there were any question about this, the selective action of the organism, when the two apprehensions are simultaneously in competition, would settle it. If the poison oak were on one side of the path and the thistle on the other, and the avoidance of the one meant getting into the other, a person would accept the consequences of the lesser fear for the sake of relief from the greater. Whether the drive be positive or negative—the attainment of a goal or the avoidance of an object of aversion—the value of the achievement is proportional to the intensity of the drive motivating the act.

The same is true of frustration or negative achievement value. The greater the intensity of the drive that is blocked, the greater the frustration. It follows that the degree of frustration mounts as the energy of an injective is drawn in to support an appetition or an aversion that is blocked. The greater the tension, the worse the frustration.

A somewhat paradoxical result develops from this situation: an increase in the amount of positive achievement value can be generated from a negative value base. Suppose a person has made a bad mistake in some purposive undertaking. He was crossing a stream on a tree that had fallen over it, and through carelessness (an inadequate mediating judgment) slipped and fell into the stream. His crossing the stream was, of course, blocked and frustrated by his misjudgment, and the achievement value of the crossing when he finally came out dripping was very low. But, having fallen into the stream, his positive achievement in getting out of his difficulty could be high. Thus the total achievement value accruing to the crossing of the stream could be increased by the mistake!

The paradox is partly resolved by considering the crossing of the stream as one act and the getting out of the water as another. The one had low achievement value as a much delayed success; the other a high achievement value as a prompt success in escaping from the water as speedily as possible once having fallen in. Furthermore, the second was a distinct aversive act on its own, despite the fact that it developed from a misjudgment in the course of an appetitive act in progress. A man who slipped into a river would want to get out of it under almost any circumstances.

But this observation only partly resolves the paradox. For there is some kind of selective process at work that sets a negative value on the generation of *some* positive successes. It would have seemed better to the person falling into the stream if he had not fallen in at all. Yet not to have fallen in would have denied him the success of getting out. Then, in terms of success, it must have been good that he fell in! For if success is good, the more successes the better. In terms of achievement value there is no question of this. Accordingly, why not multiply mishaps in order to maximize successes? But something in us says, "No, this is not a good way of increasing values." Clearly some other selective system is legislating in this area over achievement value. And once we begin to examine the matter we see that this other selective system is that which favors positive against negative conation. It is good to multiply positive desires, but bad to multiply negative ones. That is to say, conative value legislates over achievement value in the initiation of achievements. Aversions are bad and appetitions good, and the more aversions the worse. So an organism minimizes its aversions in spite of the added successes that might accrue.

Here is another close connection between conative value and achievement value, though they cannot be reduced to one another. Conative value legislates over achievement value in regard to the initiation of a purposive value, but achievement value legislates over conative value in regard to the realization of a purposive value. The one is a screening process; the other, an actualizing process. The two natural norms, whatever they are, operate in a reciprocal relation with respect to one another. Conation dominates in the initiation of values to be realized in achievement, and selects for positive conations and against negative ones; but achievement dominates in the realization of values initiated in conation, and selects for success and against frustration whether the conations be positive or negative. Once more the intimate relationship between conation and achievement comes out. A conation is a potential achievement, and an achievement the realization of a conation. As a selective agency, conation rules over the starting of purposes trying to minimize aversions, but achievement rules over the realization of purposes trying to minimize frustrations.

Because of this reciprocal relationship, the intrinsic quantitative standards of the two types of value are closely bound together. First, the intensity of the drive is exactly the same; the more intense the drive, the greater the value for both conation and achievement. Second, the extensity of the conative references is the same, except that for conative value it applies to each segment of a purpose as it comes, at a single time only, whereas it consists in the total summation of these references as they are progressively realized for achievement. Figuratively speaking, conative references at any time are a vertical slice through the extended structure of an achievement's total system of references. Third, the speed and correctness are the same, except that these are actualized in achievement and only potential in conation.

## 7. The Convergence of Conation and Achievement as Phases of a Single Selective System

The close reciprocal relation between conation and achievement, and the near identity of their standards, raises the question whether we are actually dealing with two different norms or with phases of the same norm.

There is no question that the two can be linguistically defined as two distinct descriptive definitions. We have already done so. Conation is defined as a drive-charged pattern of references positive or negative; achievement, as the attainment of the goal of positive drive-charged references or the quiescence of negative drive-charged references. According to the principles of evaluation worked out in the previous chapter, these two definitions constitute qualitative norms of value in discourse. Since they are descriptive definitions referring to verifiable modes of selection in behavior, these modes of selection would be referred to as natural norms of selective systems. These selective systems, so far as they are truly described, would constitute the empirical justification for the definitions functioning as evaluative norms in discourse. Since there are two definitions in discourse, we superficially assume that there must be two natural norms or selective systems justifying these definitions in behavior.

But our suspicions are aroused when, as the final result of our analysis, it looks as if there were just one total act of behavior referred to, and that conation, roughly speaking, refers to the beginning of the act and achievement to the end. What both the descriptive definition of conation and that of achievement seem to refer to as the effective selective structure is a purposive structure. Conation indicates the initial dynamics and directive references of a purposive act; achievement indicates the realization of these dynamic references. But is this enough to account for the selective action of conation over the initiation of purposive acts?

To bring this query to a head, let us ask just what are the selective agencies for both conation and achievement, and what are the values, acts, or objects selected by these agencies. The natural normative structure controlling achievement is easy to discern. It is the total purposive structure, whether appetitive or aversive. In this structure the superordinate act or governing propensity functions as a selective norm rejecting or accepting subordinate acts on the basis of whether or not they satisfy the conative references of the superordinate drive. Here the dynamic structure of a natural normative selective system is revealed with transparent clarity. The dynamics of the superordinate drive splits and charges not only its own superordinate conative references for its terminal goal but also the subordinate conative references for a trial act toward the satisfaction of the superordinate references. This split dynamics in a purposive structure is what renders the structure intrinsically normative over the trials initiated by its own dynamics. Here we obtain an insight into the essential requirements for a natural norm, or selective system. There are two such requirements: one is that such a system shall exhibit a split dynamics; the other is that trial acts, which may be in error, are made within the system and are subject to correction. A result of these two characteristics of a selective system is that such a system defines a tendency, which is that of eliminating the errors of the trials performed within it. The terminus of such a tendency is the correct trial. If a range of alternative trials is available, the correct trial may well be called the perfect trial, and may be properly referred to as the ideal for that dynamic tendency.

Not all tendencies, of course, are controlled by selective systems. A selective system is an intrinsically normative tendency. Other tendencies are not intrinsically normative. A west wind tends to blow leaves eastward. But there is nothing normative about this tendency. For a wind does not split its dynamics with the leaves. It just pushes them before it. But a superordinate drive actually splits its dynamics, charging not only its own references but also the conative references of its subordinate act. The subordinate act thus becomes vitalized from within the system, and is still bound to its superordinate drive and conative references; for the source of all its dynamic activity is this very drive. This one drive is what sanctions the normative function of the superordinate act in its governing selection of the subordinate act in a purposive structure. This is what makes such a structure a selective system in our restricted technical sense. A selective system is one that determines a normative tendency in virtue of its split dynamics and its capacity to initiate trials which may be in error with reference to its own controlling dynamics.

Now there is no question that achievement value, as we defined it in discourse (§6), refers to the action of a purposive structure functioning as a natural normative selective system. A negative achievement value is the failure of a subordinate act to satisfy the conative references of its superordinate act. A positive achievement value is the success of such an act in satisfying those references.

But what about positive and negative conative values? What is the natural norm with its split dynamics and trials open to error sanctioning the selection of positive conative acts over against negative ones? A negative conative act is a drive with negative references; a positive conative act, one with positive references. These references are selective of objects in the environment, which automatically become objects of disfavor or of favor with the emergence of the drive and its references. But this selection does not of itself involve a split dynamics and potentially incorrect trials. It is a flat selection pro or con in terms of the drive-charged reference active in the organism's behavior. Some of these selections will be subject to correction, but not through the mere conative distribution of judgments of favor or disfavor about the environment. Those that are cognitive sets will be corrected by their success or failure in yielding achievement value. For them the purposive structure for achievement will be the selective system in action. But what system selects positive conations against negative ones?

Perhaps there is a distinct selective system unique for conation performing this function. Many will think that we have no need of a selective system to justify the maximizing of positive conations and the minimizing of negative ones. Intuitively we feel the evaluative positivity of wanting something and the negativity of not-wanting it, the qualitative difference between an impulse pattern and a riddance pattern, just as we intuitively feel the evaluative positivity of pleasure and the negativity of pain. But these qualitative oppositions would have no objective evaluative sanction unless they were somehow susceptible to normative action by trials and corrections. If no selective systems were available to try out these oppositions and to show up errors of action and correct them, these oppositions of contrasting qualities of drive and of appetition would appear as neutral in evaluation as the opposition of contrasting qualities of warm and cool or of light and dark.

There is indeed a selective system which operates on *affection* —or perhaps I should say two systems: the consummatory field for pleasure and the riddance field for pain. In the consummatory field an organism (if not pressed for speedy achievement) maneuvers for the optimum location for consummatory satisfaction. A consummatory field functions as a genuine selective system. The drive for the optimum satisfaction is the same as that for the less satisfactory trials, and through the structure of the field the organism is drawn to the optimum location. Likewise in the riddance field, an organism is motivated to move out of the field; an error is registered at once as an increase in pain and is corrected. It is these selective acts of the organism in the affective fields of consummation and riddance that give the evaluative dynamics to pleasure and pain.

Now I am going to suggest that it is the selective action of these affective fields that institutes the evaluative motivation for maximizing positive conations and minimizing negative ones. This action is clearly evident in the negative conations of riddance patterns. The riddance field, in selecting against the continuance of painful activities in that field, automatically selects against the continuance of negative conations there. The selective system for affection here functions as a selective system for conations also tending toward minimizing negative conations. Indirectly, the consummatory field for affection functions similarly for positive conations. For the terminal goal of an impulse pattern is its consummatory field (its quiescence pattern), and the selective action for prolonging activity in that field would have the effect of maximizing positive conations. It is the dynamics of the selective systems for affection that sanctions the selective evaluation of conative acts. If we have an opportunity to choose between positive and negative desires in purposive action, we prefer the positive ones. This seems so obvious that a layman might wonder what could be the problem. And this conclusion should go far to confirm the suggested hypothesis. But the result of the hypothesis is something quite significant: in the evaluation of conative acts, the natural norms of affection have a legislative role over conations.

It does not follow, however, that the natural norms of affection necessarily legislate over achievement values. The appetitive and aversive structures of purposive behavior constitute the natural norms (or selective systems) for achievement, selecting for the positive achievement values of success and against the negative values of frustration. Achievement values have their own selective system.

But conation has no unique selective system of its own. When conations go into action they enter the course of achievement and are evaluated by the natural norms (the purposive structures) of achievement value. If conations are evaluated outside their realization in achievements, they become subject to other norms, particularly to the natural norms of affection (the consummatory and riddance fields). It is the latter which sanction the evaluation of positive conations above negative ones in the initiation of purposive acts.

Of course, both of these norms, the affective and the achievement norms, operate within the articulations of purposive structures, as do also the affective, conative, and achievement values. They are all very closely connected, but nevertheless irreducible to one another. What we have found is three types of values, subject to two selective systems. And the conative and achievement values are so closely connected that hereafter we shall generally refer to them as the *conative-achievement values*. Total purposive structures constitute their specific selective systems. Nonetheless, conation and achievement are distinguishable values. Conative values are the values of potential achievements (positive and negative desires). Achievement values are those of conations carried into realization (successes and frustrations). Each type is complemented by the other, but is not reducible to the other.

The evaluative selection of positive conations as better than negative conations, however, is sanctioned by the natural norms of affection (the riddance and consummatory fields of purposive behavior).

According to this analysis, the over-all achievement value of the man who fell off the log into the river was high in terms of the natural norms of achievement. He blundered in slipping off the log, but he made a fine recovery. (By the same criterion, an alcoholic who keeps sober attains a much greater success than a nonalcoholic who avoids overindulgence.) But by the natural norms of affection the man's total activity was greatly lessened in positive conative value, since he let himself in for a great deal of discomfort in the riddance field. And it is to be supposed that the man would not in the future desire to slip off the log, even though it could increase his achievement values.

At the end of §6, we said that conative value legislates over achievement value in the initiation of achievements. Now we find that this means that the natural norms of affective values legislate over conative values whereby the latter legislate over achievement values in the initiation of achievements.

This particular legislation of affective values over conative values extends only far enough to account for the selection of positive over negative conations in the initiation of purposive acts —to account for the intuitive feeling that a life of positive desires is better than one filled with aversions. There is much more to be said about the legislation of purposive values over one another, as we shall see in §9.

We now turn to a consideration of affective values, which do have their own unique selective systems in their riddance and consummatory fields.

## 8. AFFECTIVE VALUE

1. *Affection, a natural norm but not an exclusive one.*—As we saw when we were applying the distributive principle to purposive structures, a positive achievement normally culminates in a consummatory act or quiescence pattern which is prominently characterized by the distinctive feeling of pleasure. And the opposite feeling of pain characterizes the riddance pattern, which is the pivotal segment avoided in a negative achievement. And these two feelings generate a new type of value polarity that is not reducible (at least not obviously) to either conative or achievement value.

Exponents of conative and achievement theories have frequently tried to reduce affection (pleasure and pain) away, or to find means of plausibly denying its existence. Thus there is the view that pain is correlated and so identifiable with frustrated activity and pleasure with unfrustrated activity. The correlation holds roughly but not the identification, because, for one thing, the correlation is not precise. Pleasure is particularly pronounced in the consummatory act of an appetition, and here there is frequently a delay in achievement, which is a sort of frustration of achievement. It is as though pleasure blocked the speediest achievement. Besides, introspectively the feeling of pleasure is distinct from the feeling of desire or the quiescence of desire in achievement.

The two principal sources of evidence for pleasure as something that exists in its own right are, first, the slowing up that frequently occurs in the consummatory area of an appetition; and second, the introspective report of a distinctive feeling in that area that is qualitatively different from other sensations and feelings. Either of these evidences alone might lead us to seek an explanation through some form of reducing away, as many writers have attempted. But both of these together confirm each other so neatly—the one as objective evidence of the truth of the second, and the second as subjective confirmation of the interpretation of the first—that it looks useless to try to simplify them out of the picture.

It is theoretically possible to develop an adequate motivational theory without pleasure—entirely on a pain basis or even without pain on the basis of a mechanical negative conation. This is practically what Money-Kyrle does in *The Development of the Sexual Impulse*. For him any drive signifies a want, and a want signifies a pain or a discomfort. The structure of a purposive act is to remove the discomfort. Aversive and appetitive achievement can both be plausibly handled in this way. There may actually be organisms so formed as to act in this way, simply reëstablishing an equilibrium of the body temporarily upset by either internal or external changes. Once the equilibrium is reëstablished, that act, whether purposive or reflex, is over. Pleasure is not required at all, nor even perhaps pain.

The plausibility of such a theory as a possible way in which an organism might be motivated to make purposive adjustments to its environment is an added testimony to the existence of pleasure and pain as effective agents in behavior. Such a purely conative-achievement theory describes the way in which organisms could have been motivated, but the descriptions of actual behavior indicate that this is not the way in which organisms resembling man actually are motivated. Just because the consistent following through of a strictly conative-achievement theory does not take care of certain observed facts, it is necessary to admit some other agent into the mechanics of purposive behavior, and this agent is precisely what is ordinarily spoken of as affection.

It is particularly in regard to the action of an organism in the consummatory field that we are induced to admit the agency of pleasure (and reciprocally of pain) as a distinct selective system legislating at times over achievement and conation. In strict consistency an achievement should realize its conative references with the greatest speed possible to the drive in action. In fact, however, in the consummatory area the organism frequently draws out an action to last as long as possible. This is the objective fact, and the introspective report about this segment of behavior is that a man draws out the consummatory act so as to get the greatest possible enjoyment from it. A man here is maximizing his pleasure in opposition to a possible maximizing of achievement. He reports that it is better to get all the pleasure he can out of his consummatory act than to get it over as quickly as possible so as to maximize his achievement. Here the natural norm of affection legislates over that of achievement.

Perry tries to get over this difficulty by distinguishing between progressive and recurrent interests. His progressive interest corresponds closely to what we should call an appetitive achievement. It is a progressive realization of a succession of *different* conative references through a series of subordinate acts until terminal quiescence is achieved in the attainment of the goal object. Then Perry describes a recurrent interest as a succession of *similar* conative references (wanting more of the same thing) until quiescence is achieved. But a recurrent interest, by his description, is still in the mode of an achievement. It is still something to get over with as speedily as possible. On the hunger drive this would lead to gulping, not to savoring the delights of an excellent meal. The progressive interest accounts for the speed with which a man gets to a restaurant. The recurrent interest would account for the speed of his consumption of soup and a sandwich in order to catch a train. It would not account for his taking a full hour out of his evening for the delights of a four-course dinner. *In spite of* other fairly pressing drives, he will often choose to spread out the pleasures of a savory meal for as long as he can make it last.

It is this sort of fact that has led hedonists in ethics and aesthetics to set up pleasure as the one and only intrinsic value— the only intrinsic positive value—and pain as its reciprocal intrinsic negative value. For the hedonist all other values are extrinsic and derive what value they have only as they lead to pleasure or away from pain. This uttermost reduction of all values to the hedonic we cannot accede to. This is simply the reverse of the attempts at the reduction of affection to conation and achievement. Our descriptions of the capacity of drives to institute conative and achievement values independently of pleasure and pain would hardly support this. But the attractiveness of the pure hedonistic theory of value, and the large number of adherents the theory has gained from man's earliest reflections on these matters to the present decade,[6] is strong evidence for the actuality of affection as an effective natural norm in human conduct and probably in all purposive behavior.

After having safely avoided the Scylla of reducing pleasure and pain out of existence, we now find ourselves ironically faced with the Charybdis of a theory that these are the only intrinsic values. Why, it is argued, is not affection to be regarded as the one and only source of intrinsic value? Considering that the consummatory act is the terminal goal of every appetition and that this is prominently characterized by pleasure, why is it not true that pleasure is the one positive intrinsic value which the whole purposive structure is designed to achieve, and the quality without which the structure would have no positive intrinsic value at all? And why not the same for its polar opposite, pain, as the determinant negative character avoided in the pivotal riddance pattern of an aversion?

It will be clarifying to show at once just why. Take pleasure first. Referring to our descriptions of appetitive behavior in the earlier chapters, we see that it is not pleasure but the drive that is the primary motivating agent in an appetition. It is hunger, thirst, and the like, not the pleasure in the quiescence of these, that sets appetition in motion. Even if there were no pleasure in the quiescence of these drives, an appetition would still be a positive purpose in its selective action, and would still be contrasted with the avoidance structure of an aversion as a negative purpose. It is this fact that gives a firm empirical basis to conative and achievement theories of value like Perry's. Unquestionably, the *anticipation* of pleasure may become a drive or augment a drive already in action, *after* the organism has had experience with the pleasure of a consummatory act. But pleasure is not the sole original and primary motivating agent. Herein lies the fundamental error of the view known as *psychological hedonism.*

Pain and pleasure seem to be relatively independent feelings correlated (but not directly correlated) with conative tensions or drives. Biologically, these feelings seem to function as intensifiers, the one negatively and the other positively. Pleasure is a sort of bonus to successful achievement, and in gratuitous satisfactions a pure bonus. Life becomes that much the more worth living by all the pleasures it gives out. But biologically life is worth living without them, and quite possibly is being lived without pleasures or pains by some whole species differently endowed from ourselves. Conative and achievement values do not depend on pleasure or pain. It would be dogmatic to define value, and so analytically to identify it exclusively, as affection. Introspective reports indicate that even in man some motivating acts are free from affection (as reflexes like coughing and appetitive impulses below the pain threshold). But it would be equally dogmatic to define value exclusively in terms of conation and achievement, on the plea that affection is unnecessary to a pure conative-achievement theory of value. It remains a relevant fact that among purposive structures pleasure can operate as an independent selective agent maximizing itself under certain conditions in dominance over the natural norm of speed of achievement. So the evidence seems to be that pleasure (with its opposite, pain) is present, and is effective, as a distinct natural norm within purposive structures, but this fact is insufficient to justify a pure hedonistic theory of value.

2. *A modified tension theory of pleasure and pain.*—Having justified the highly probable existence of affection as a natural norm among purposive values, we are next led to ask what sort of thing it may be. There is no established theory of affection. It is widely agreed, however, that the so-called pain receptors—the free nerve endings in the skin—are not to be mistaken for sense organs of the feeling of unpleasantness. The term 'pain' is thus ambiguous. But unless otherwise stated, I shall always mean *negative affection* by pain, and will distinguish the sensa-

tion coming from the free nerve endings as 'prick.' Prick may be pleasant, but is usually painful. As for pleasure, there are no sense organs with sensations even remotely to be confused with the feeling quality of pleasure. So pleasure and pain pretty definitely are not connected with sense organs specific to them, and are not sensations.

The problem, then, in the theory of affection is to seek out what physiological activities may be correlated with them. There are many such theories. I am going to take the risk of accepting a modified form of one of the most widely held of these theories— the *tension theory of affection*. This theory seems to me the most probable on the basis of evidence available and of its compatibility with our descriptions of purposive structures.

We shall, I believe, gain more clarification of the relations between affective value and other forms of value by working into the details of a tentative theory of affection, with the risk that these details may require modification, than by retiring into the safety of wide generalizations and the protection of the respectable ambiguity these afford. Pleasure and pain in most contemporary hedonistic value theories are treated as insulated counters carefully wrapped against all contact with the other vital mechanisms of animal behavior. This makes for a most logical systematization, but also for a sterilization. The important thing in value theory is to find out how values truly operate in human desires and achievements and in a man's vital relations with his environment. A tension theory of affection gives the details of such relations. Even though many details so arrived at may have to be modified, it is better to see the sort of things they probably are than to blur them in noncommittal generalities.

In the simplest statement of the tension theory, pain is directly correlated with the occurrence of tension, and increase of pain with increase of tension; and pleasure is directly correlated with release of tension, and the intensity of pleasure with the speed of the release of tension. This, however, is too simple a correlation to fit the facts as they appear in our earlier descriptions. Low intensities of appetitive conation do not seem to be painful or even uncomfortable. Mild hunger, thirst, and sex desire, and most derived appetitive desires, like the desire to go sailing, or to write a book if you are an author, or to make a sale if you are a salesman, or to plead a case if you are a lawyer, do not seem to be unpleasant. They may even be pleasant in the imagination of their attainment and gratification. They will become unpleasant if blocked, whence the source of the theory that identifies pain with frustration; but an unfrustrated appetition at low intensity is not considered painful, as is strikingly evidenced by the common view that pleasure may be correlated with unfrustrated achievement. However, we did find it true that very intense appetitive drives ordinarily are painful—great thirst, hunger, and so on—and continue to be so even in the process of unfrustrated achievement, and even well into the consummatory act. So, though the simple tension theory covers many of the facts, it needs to be qualified to fit all the details of our earlier descriptions.

I therefore suggest a modified tension theory by bringing in the concept of a *pain threshold*. If it is recognized that every drive has a pain threshold, above which increase in intensity is correlated with increase in pain, then pleasure may be correlated with decrease in tension below the pain threshold. Accordingly, increase in tension below the pain threshold increases conation but not pain, for no pain is felt. Increase in tension above the pain threshold is accompanied by increase in pain. Decrease in tension above the pain threshold is accompanied by decrease in pain. Decrease in tension below the pain threshold is accompanied by pleasure, and the greater the speed of the release of tension (or, more accurately, the amount of tension released) the greater the intensity of the pleasure. These relations are schematized in table 5.

In riddance patterns set off by stimulation of the free nerve endings (prick) the pain threshold is practically at the point of stimulation, very low. In other drives like thirst and hunger it is fairly high, and considerable tension of conation is necessary before pain is felt. The range of pleasurable satisfaction below the pain threshold in the latter and in the other basic appetitive drives is therefore considerable. And in most of the gratuitous satisfactions—delight in odors, colors, tastes, touch—the pain threshold seems to be very high once they fall within the field of positive habituation (cf. chap. 11, §6).

Is the pain threshold fixed at a precise degree of tension for any one drive? This would have to be experimentally determined. We know that in the area in which the habituation mutation operates, the pain threshold moves in a fairly predictable way. It could well change for any drive as a result of long-term changes in the

TABLE 5

RELATIONS OF TENSION, AFFECTION, AND CONATION

| Tension | Affection | Conation |
|---|---|---|
| Increase in tension above pain threshold | Increasing pain | Increasing conation |
| Increase in tension below pain threshold | Neither pleasure nor pain | Increasing conation |
| Decrease in tension from above pain threshold | Decreasing pain | Decreasing conation |
| Decrease in tension from pain threshold down | Pleasure | Decreasing conation |

organism. Furthermore, release of tension may yield pleasure at a degree of tension above that where increase of tension begins to be accompanied by pain. But here we are probing into a precision of detail beyond what is needed for our purposes. Introspective reports are always fairly reliable if we know how to attach them to segments of purposive structures, and the key to these correlations is given by our tension theory.

3. *Intrinsic standards of affection.*—Now we are prepared to inquire about the *intrinsic standards of affective value.* If positive affective value is defined as pleasure and negative affective value as pain, then the intrinsic quantitative standards are (1) the intensity, (2) and duration, of pleasure and pain, and (3) the number of the affective experiences occurring. These are the traditional standards accepted by virtually all exponents of hedonistic theories of value. The testimony of these writers

amounts to a consensus of judgment in terms of direct introspective observation. Through the tension theory, these observations are confirmed in relatively objective terms. Above the pain threshold, the negative affective value of pain is increased in intensity with increase in tension. Below the pain threshold, the positive affective value of pleasure is increased in intensity with the amount and the speed of release of tension. Also, the longer tension lasts above the pain threshold, the longer the duration of the pain as a negative affective value. And the longer the period of release of tension below the pain threshold, the more extended the pleasure as a positive affective value. Lastly, the greater the number of drives in action with tension above the pain threshold, the greater the amount of pain being suffered by the organism and the greater the negative affective value. Also, the greater the number of drives actively releasing their tensions in an organism, the greater the amount of pleasure experienced by the organism as positive affective value.

From this description it is evident that the intrinsic standards of affective value are generated solely from correlations with the drive element in purposive behavior, and have nothing directly to do with conative references, or the objects with which an organism is in active commerce during purposive behavior. These latter do indeed, as we shall see in chapter 15, supply the objects of pleasure and pain. We speak of the painful thorn and the pleasant honey, and these objects derive affective values from the pain and pleasure they produce, but the value is not *intrinsically* in the objects, only in the pains and pleasures themselves. Introspectively, it is the feelings of pain and pleasure themselves that are quantified for the standards of intensity, duration, and number. And objectively, it is the tensions and release of tensions of drives correlated with the introspectively reported feelings that yield the standards. The quantifications of the drive tensions are theoretically as intrinsic to affection as are the introspective feelings of intensity, duration, and number, because we are inferring that, with respect to the pain threshold as point of origin, these constitute strict correlations. (It may even turn out that the tensions are identical with the feelings of affection, and that it is only the units for objectively measuring the tensions that are different from the introspective reports, and so correlated with them.)

No further comment is needed at this time on the standards of duration and number. In regard to intensity, however, a question could arise on the applicability of its correlation with the amount and speed of release of tension. If pleasure is good, a more intense pleasure would evidently be better. So, if intensity of pleasure is correlated with speed of tension release, would not this lead the organism to pass through the consummatory act as rapidly as possible so as to intensify the pleasure available in the act? Then why does the organism often slow down in the consummatory field, and why do introspective reports often agree in declaring that more pleasure is obtained by extending the consummatory period? There can be little doubt about the fact that usually more pleasure does accrue from extending the period of consummatory delight, even with some diminution of intensity. In aesthetics this is well known, and has been called the principle of restraint. It is perhaps equally important in ethics. Overimpulsiveness in the gratification of a person's drives lessens the amount of gratification obtained. Why is this, if apparently speed of gratification tends to increase intensity?

There are at least two reasons. One is that the consummatory area of all our basic drives includes many closely connected gratuitous satisfactions. Thus, if you swallow a liqueur too quickly, you lose its exquisite taste. The connoisseur takes a sip, allows it to spread widely over his tongue, and savors its taste completely. The same in various degrees with all delicious edibles. Connected with the satisfaction of the hunger drive are all the gratuitous satisfactions of taste and smell, and these are lost for the man who gulps his food. Consequently, as soon as these tastes are stimulated, they tend to slow down the speed of the consummatory act of the hunger drive. And with experience and learned anticipation of these gratuitous satisfactions, the speed of release of the basic hunger drive is still further slowed down. More delight is obtained from spreading out these varied gratuitous satisfactions of eating than from an intense quick gratification of the basic hunger drive.

But, in addition to this consideration, more pleasure is obtained for the basic hunger drive itself from spreading out the duration of its quiescence pattern than from impulsively gratifying it quickly. This comes from the fact that the energy of a drive is not like that of water power from a tank of limited capacity, but rather like that of credit on a bank account with income constantly flowing in. The available energy for a drive (even neglecting the role of injectives) may be quite great. A man may have worked up a large appetite and be very eager to eat. If he eats quickly, he gets an intense pleasure proportional to the speed of release of the tension below the pain threshold. But the tension is quickly used up and there is no more tension to release. If, however, the release is restrained, the tension is then held with steady increments of energy flowing in which continue the longer the duration; so there is a larger amount of total release of energy tension over a long duration than over a short one. That is, more energy develops for release in a longer quiescence period than in a shorter one, even given the same amount of eagerness at the start. With experience an organism learns the advantage of moderate restraint. Of course, such restraint can be overdone and introduce actual frustration and pain. If the suspense of a narrative is carried too far, the story becomes irritating and tiresome.

What is being done through restraint is a balancing of the standard of intensity with that of duration of pleasure. Introspectively, we sense that often there is more over-all pleasure in a longer but less intense experience. It has sometimes been objected that we have no precise way of measuring the difference, and so no way of telling whether the evaluation is true. The point of the objection is to cast doubt on the possibility, or at least the verifiability, of such quantitative hedonic evaluations. The situation, however, is like that of measuring heat by thermal feelings without correlating with thermometers and other physical measures. Yet we could judge with fair assurance that there was more heat from the gentle warmth of a slow fire lasting all day than from the intense heat of a pile of excelsior lasting a few minutes. But the final confirmation would depend on a correlation of heat with energy units. Much the same with pleasure, and here also, theoretically at least, the final confirmation would depend on a correlation of pleasure with the expenditure of energy through release of tension.

On a tension theory, pleasures and pains are theoretically measurable by correlation with objective units in terms of the three traditional standards of intensity, duration, and number, whence these three standards become intercommunicable. The validity of quantitative hedonic evaluations does not depend, however, on such intercommunication of standards. Even if there were no way of balancing a longer duration of low' intensity of hedonic value against a shorter duration of greater intensity, we could still say that, given the same intensity of pleasure, the longer it lasted the better, or, given the same duration, the more intense the better.

On a tension theory, however, it becomes theoretically understandable how a longer duration of pleasure at less intensity can be directly compared with a shorter duration of greater intensity. On the basis of our feelings we make such comparisons and choices regularly, and have a pretty good idea of how much added duration will compensate for so much reduced intensity. Shall we eat six chocolate peppermints one right after the other or spread them out through the evening? Will you have your whisky "on the rocks" or with soda? Will you have your dessert first or wait till the end of the dinner? Shall we look up all our friends in New York on the day we arrive, or shall we spread them out through the week of our visit? Our decisions will not always be the same, depending on our states of mind (i.e., drives), and we shall not always consider that we have decided wisely. But in all such decisions, we are making direct comparisons of durations against various intensities of possible hedonic values. And we check our decisions against the hedonic values realized.

4. *Psychological hedonism and the natural norm of affection.*—We have mentioned the error of psychological hedonism several times. But unless there were some truth in the view, it would scarcely have been so persistent in ethical theory. The error has been in regarding pleasure and pain as the exclusive motivating agents in human conduct. The truth in the theory is that pleasure

and pain are motivating agents under certain conditions, and, unless they were, they would be utterly fictitious sources of value.

From the evidence that has come to light in the previous pages, it appears that pleasure is a direct motivating agent in the consummatory area of an appetition slowing up the achievement propensity of a drive so as to maximize pleasure in that area. And since there are partial consummations in the attainment of goal objects in every well-articulated subordinate act of an appetition, this tendency to maximize pleasure over against speed of achievement can be distributed to some extent over the whole course of many appetitive acts. That is to say, there is a tendency to maximize pleasure whenever pleasure emerges in a purposive act. And it is common knowledge that whenever pain emerges, the direction of activity is to minimize the pain. So, in regard to pain, the aims of affection and of conative achievement become identical: to get rid of the negative tension as quickly as possible.

It may, therefore, be truly stated that whenever pleasure or pain actively appear within a purposive structure, the tendency is to maximize the one and minimize the other. It is precisely this very well-known and commonplace fact that makes pleasure and pain values at all. If there were not such a selective activity in human conduct for maximizing pleasure and minimizing pain, these would not commend themselves to the human mind as values. When a pleasure comes, we relax into it as something immediately and intuitively positive—not because we *want* it (for that would convert it into a conative value, which it is not) but because we *have* it. And when a pain comes, it is correspondingly something immediately and intuitively negative. And, similarly, it is negative not because we do not want it, though this also is true. It is affectively negative in the mere having of it. And it is rather because it is affectively negative in its own right that we do not want it.

So, first, there is at least this much truth to psychological hedonism: wherever pleasure appears in a purposive structure it tends to be maximized there, and wherever pain appears it tends to be minimized. We may call this the *immediacy principle* of affection. Wherever pleasure and pain immediately occur in purposive behavior, there is a selective tendency to maximize the one and minimize the other within that purposive act.

But, second, there is another sphere within which affection is in some sense a motivating agent. For we have seen evidence that men, at least, and probably some other animals, can be motivated by the anticipation of pleasure and the apprehension of pain. We may call this the *anticipatory principle* of affection. After experience of the pleasure of a consummatory act, the anticipation of the pleasure can move a man to action as well as the appetitive drive which is the originating motive. And in the pursuit of gratuitous satisfactions the anticipation of pleasure becomes the sole motive.

But how can the anticipation of pleasure be a motive? For, of course, the anticipation of pleasure is not itself the pleasure anticipated. Pleasure being immediately felt is not a motive for anything but its own continuance and maximization, as we have seen in the immediacy principle. Then why not just continue to enjoy the anticipation of a pleasure rather than make the effort to realize it? If we look for the motive in the anticipatory reference, that does not seem helpful either. Such a reference is just an anticipatory set or mediating judgment and has no drive in it. How, then, can the mere anticipation of a pleasure motivate its realization? The problem is to account for the drive that charges a mediating judgment for an anticipated pleasure.

The problem comes out most clearly in the anticipations of gratuitous satisfactions. Why should I cross the garden to sense the odor of a rose? Why do I want to lie in the sun on the beach or go in bathing? Why do I go to a movie or a musical concert or a picture gallery? Why do I put a record on the phonograph? Why do I turn on the radio? The usual answer is, "Because these things give me pleasure." But just how can a future pleasure motivate a present act? Introspectively, we feel quite sure that in some indirect way it does. And we also know that one of the most effective means of persuading a person to a desired action is to point out to him the pleasures he will get from it. But literally, of course, a future pleasure that does not exist cannot motivate a present act.

One tempting solution is in effect to deny the anticipatory

principle, to say that there is always some other drive than that for the anticipation of pleasure which motivates the acts in question. If I go into the sun, it is because I was cold in the shade —a compound riddance reaction. If I turn on the radio, it is because I was bored. If I go to a concert, it is because it is the social thing to do. And so on. These motivations are not to be denied. They may often be the determining motives. And perhaps generally in the complexity of human situations, they can be found in operation.

But in numerous situations such drives seem to be secondary or absent, and a drive to maximize pleasures in the future seems to be predominant. There are two ways in which the anticipatory principle seems to work: by *imaginative foretaste,* and by *cognitive estimate.* For imaginative foretaste, suppose we are considering whether to take a vacation in the mountains or at the seashore. Ordinarily we imagine what we would do in each instance and weigh the pleasures that come in fantasy. The alternative that seems pleasantest will determine the decision. But sometimes we make such decisions without the use of fantasy. In selecting between steak and chops on a menu, I may well choose on the consideration that I had steak last night and chops will be more of a novelty and probably give me more pleasure today. This is, so to speak, a scientific judgment about my probable consummatory responses based on my own past experience. There is no imaginative foretaste, but only a cognitive estimate of probable results. Something of a mixture of both ways is no doubt present in most such decisions.

It is still not clear, however, what motivates the decision. Imaginative foretastes and cognitive estimates are not in themselves drives. Why not go on enjoying the fantasy of being at the beach and in the mountains without precipitating action to go there? And what is there in a computation of possible effects to precipitate action? A drive or tendency set in motion by these processes needs to be accounted for.

We learn, it is said, from past experience with pleasures how to anticipate them. The drive in the anticipatory principle is evidently a derived one, and has its source in the immediacy principle. Taking a clue from this suggestion, let us work out from the immediacy principle. Having seen and smelled a rose, thereafter I associate the sight of the rose with its odor. Then the pleasant sight of the rose will lead me to smell it just on the immediacy principle of maximizing pleasure in the consummatory area. I shall be led to smell it at the best distance and see it at the best distance.

When I enter a gallery and see a picture that intrigues me in the distance, I walk to the point of optimum enjoyment and there feast my eyes. Suppose I am in the next room and the image of the picture arises in my mind. Now I am only imagining the picture, but, since this image is associated with the perceived picture that can be seen in the next room, I am drawn again to where I can see the picture and see it to optimum advantage. The pleasure, such as it is in the image, is broadly speaking still within the consummatory sphere, and on the immediacy principle seeks to maximize itself and so guides me to the optimum location. And so with all imaginative foretaste.

The immediacy principle works on a gradient that draws an organism to the optimum consummatory point. But the organism has to learn the lines of approach to that point or area of activity. Thus wherever pleasures are connected so that the immediacy principle can operate upon them, a lesser pleasure behaves as a drive in the direction of the optimum pleasure derivable in the field.

This accounts for the paradox often raised against the drive theory, that sometimes the tension of a drive is increased during its consummatory period. Start eating salted almonds and the appetite for a while increases. The consummatory pleasure once started sets up its own gradient and institutes its own drive on the immediacy principle.

But this is only the beginning. So far the anticipatory principle appears to be only a sort of extension of the immediacy principle. The next point to notice is what happens if a blockage occurs in the course of the consummatory action, either in the consummatory field proper or during an imaginative foretaste. As with the blockage of any drive, an injective comes in. Now what the injective reinforces on such an occasion is the maximization of anticipated pleasure blocked in the consummatory field. What it charges is a reference to the goal of the pleasure drive, which was generated from the immediacy principle. Since such blockages are fairly frequent, the scene is set for a regular independence mutation by which an injective takes over as its goal the goal of another appetitive drive (cf. chap. 11, §4). When this happens the organism has acquired a derived drive for the maximization of anticipated pleasure totally independent of the immediacy principle. This would be the dynamics of the anticipatory principle working on the basis of a cognitive estimate of expected affective value.

On our view, then, there are three ways in which behavior may be motivated for the maximization of affective value:

By the *immediacy principle*, which is the tendency for pleasure to maximize itself wherever it occurs, but particularly in the consummatory area of appetition.

By the *anticipatory principle*, an extension of the immediacy principle, which generates what may be called a *pleasure drive*. This consists in the tendency for pleasure, whenever actually experienced, to guide the organism toward conditions of optimum gratification.

By the *derived anticipatory principle*, which is a derived drive generated as a value mutation from the immediate anticipatory principle. Here the drive is an injective, and has nothing to do with pleasure, but it charges a mediating judgment for a terminal goal object, which leads to a maximization of pleasure. In the operation of the derived anticipatory principle, pleasure is not the motive, but it is the intention or goal of the act.

A word should be added about the range of the pleasures affected by these three principles. In the first two, where the immediacy principle operates, the pleasures maximized are only those resulting from releases of tension actually going on. The range is limited to purposive activities in process at the time. The organism is trying to get the most out of the pleasures it is actually having. The range of the immediacy principle is thus highly constricted.

By contrast, the range of pleasures affected by the derived anticipatory principle is as wide as the mediating judgment that determines the goal of the activity. It differs according to the individual and the circumstances. At its origin its range presumably would not extend much farther than that of the immediacy principle. But in the very nature of its dynamics as a derived activity freed from the restrictions of the immediacy principle, its range can spread as far as one desires. How far, in fact, may the hedonic consequences of an act extend when such consequences are taken into account? If it is a choice of vegetables on a menu, probably the pleasures considered do not extend beyond the period of dining. But if the man who is making the choice is allergic to tomatoes he is thinking of consequences running over several days. If he is buying a suit, the range of hedonic consequences spreads over many months and many possible occasions. If he is thinking of marriage, the range is still greater. Moreover, the range may be enlarged to consider not only his own pleasures and displeasures but those of others—his family, his country, mankind. One of the problems in hedonic value theory is to determine the empirically justifiable range of application of the derived anticipatory principle for the maximization of hedonic value.

But this much can be said at once. The immediacy principle sets a lower limit to the range of application of the derived anticipatory principle. Whatever pleasures and pains are going on in the present experience of an organism will not be ignored. And the laws of learning see to it that an organism takes into consideration the pleasures and pains which he can be conditioned to expect within his life span. The latter is the range of individual prudence. A man is easily persuaded to do what he can see is to his own best advantage. So the range of the anticipatory principle can be expected to expand for men, at least, to the area of individual prudence. Beyond that the dynamics become more complex, as nearly all recent hedonists have recognized.

For right here is the gap between individual and social hedonism. An individual easily recognizes the equal claims of his own pleasures and pains present or to come. But he finds it much more difficult to recognize that another person's pleasures and pains should be considered on a par with his own. And what defines the gap is the limits of operation of the laws of learning. These laws operate only within a given organism. If the consequence of my act gives me pain, I feel the punishment and learn to rectify my behavior. But if the consequence of my act gives another man pain, I do not feel his pain nor receive any punishment unless it comes from an outer source of resentment, from the other man or from his society.

The laws of learning automatically work to bring corrections of affective value within the range of a single individual's responses. They automatically set up a natural norm of individual prudence. But some other sort of sanction is required to force consideration of other persons' pleasures and pains on a level with one's own. Hence the problem of the gap in the ethics of hedonism between individual prudence and social justice. But for a comprehensive solution of this issue we must wait till the end of this study.

Holding the foregoing points in mind, we can now, however, assess the traditional hypothesis of psychological hedonism. It contained a core of truth. But it was vague. When, for instance, Mill writes, in his *Utilitarianism,* "Desiring a thing and finding it pleasant . . . are phenomena entirely inseparable, or rather two parts of the same phenomenon . . . and to desire anything, except in proportion as the idea of it is pleasant, is a physical and metaphysical impossibility," what precisely does he mean?

The first phrase would seem to commit him to our immediacy principle, and he seems to be saying here that all human motivation is carried on by that principle alone. But the last phrase seems to commit him to something like our derived anticipatory principle, and he seems to be saying that all human motivation is carried on by that principle alone. Both statements cannot be true. Moreover, Mill apparently does not have an inkling that the latter statement is incompatible with the idea that pleasure motivates, for here pleasure is only an end, and it is still a mystery what motivates for that end. Mill, like most hedonists of the past, does not even seem to be aware that a problem exists here. Besides, his bland assumption that the desire for anything but pleasure is an impossibility turns out on further evidence to be most probably false. For appetitive drives are not ordinarily for pleasure, but to attain the goal designated by their conditions of quiescence.

Such a completely generalized doctrine of pleasure and pain

as exclusive motivating agents will not, accordingly, hold. And yet the psychological hedonist was making a very important point. For unless pleasure did motivate in a crucial area, as indicated by the immediacy principle, pleasure would not be a value that could be sanctioned at all. The psychological hedonist erred only in overgeneralizing that important point, and usually also in a vagueness and lack of discrimination among the facts of motivation.

Since pleasure and pain are not exclusive motivating agents, nor the only natural norms of value, the question arises how far the pleasure criterion can be justified as legislating over other norms of value.

### 9. The Legislation of the Natural Norms of Conative, Achievement, and Affective Values over One Another

On our view there is no empirical justification for a value criterion that cannot be shown to be an effective agent in making selections within a field of value facts. A criterion is unrealistic that is not empirically based. To this extent, at least, an 'ought' depends upon an 'is.' Such an empirically justifiable criterion appears in discourse as a descriptive definition truly describing a natural norm or selective system through which choices are made in actuality.

Now, in the domain of purposive behavior we have discovered three kinds of value (conative, achievement, and affective) and two kinds of selective system (affective fields and purposive structures). And we have worked out the intrinsic standards belonging to each of these values. Whence, at this point, the question arises how these sets of standards legislate in respect to each other.

For a single purposive act performed freely without pressure from other external sources, the answer is simple and decisive. The answer springs out of the very evidence which led us to discriminate the three kinds of value. It springs out of the facts. It is, namely, that achievement legislates over conation, and affection over achievement. When appetitive achievement conflicts with a maximizing of positive conation—stretching out the duration of wanting a thing over against the quickest possible attainment of it—the achievement value takes precedence. And when a conflict arises between a maximizing of pleasure in the consummatory area and the speediest possible achievement, the affective value tends to take precedence. These are the facts we observe as they become summarized in the laws of learning for achievement and in the immediacy principle supplemented by the anticipatory principle for affection.

However, this order of priority for these values holds only under conditions of relative freedom of pressure from outside sources. When there is pressure there is a reversal, and achievement tends to have a priority over affective value.

Pressure may come from a number of sources, but one of the commonest is that of other purposive acts competing at the same time for the energy of the organism. Thus a man cannot spend time enjoying his dinner if he has a train to catch, or a lot of business to get done, or is apprehensive and worried about financial or family affairs. Under such conditions, achievement value tends to take precedence over affective value. If the objective conditions justifiably require a man's concentration upon a set of achievements, then achievement value properly takes priority over affective value. It acquires this priority, however, not in its own right but in serving some pressure outside the appetition in which achievement is being maximized over affection. That is to say, achievement value acquires priority over affective value only when an appetitive purpose is no longer performed freely but is under external pressure.

This point is important because it shows that in respect to single freely performed purposive acts affective value is prepotent. Here is the great strength of the hedonistic theories. It explains why they have persisted with such tenacity in spite of all the criticisms that have been heaped upon them. Pleasure is the central positive value for an individual freely performed act. Some external compulsion is involved wherever other values take precedence. Consequently, individualistic theories gravitate toward hedonism.

On the other side, however, it can be maintained that freely performed purposive acts are the exception rather than the rule, that an act is always in the context of other acts and other agents and rarely to be considered as a thing to be evaluated entirely in its own right. As will come out more clearly as we go on, a purposive structure is only relatively independent. It is involved in other selective systems, which bear down upon it. But the degree in which these other selective systems bear down upon a purpose varies greatly with the context. Yet, this much can always be said: however great the pressure of selective systems external to the structure of a purposive act, there is a continuous counter-demand for the hedonic satisfactions that are being denied. Under certain conditions, such as those of war and famine, very little enjoyment of life can be expected. Minimum pain with maximum of achievement in contexts of want and hostility is the most that can be hoped for. Achievement value inevitably takes precedence. There is no time and little desire in the pressure of such living to seek or indulge in pleasures. But the tendency to maximize pleasure is still there in human behavior, and ready to reassert itself under more favorable conditions.

In short, though affection legislates over achievement under conditions of relatively free purposive action, achievement legislates over affection under conditions of pressure for achievements instituted by certain external selective systems.

The question may still be raised whether there are any conditions under which conative value has a priority over achievement and affection. We did notice that in the *initiation* of purposes conative value has priority over achievement. An organism selects against negative and for positive desires (chap. 14, §6 at the end). Conative value has a priority in sifting out the conations presented, and in minimizing and shortening the negative conations. An organism definitely prefers positive desires to negative ones. But we noticed that when a desire gets started, achievement value takes over and seeks to realize the desire as quickly as possible. But can that priority sometimes be reversed? Does it ever happen that an organism not only shows a preference for positive conation over negative, but also, barring consummatory satisfaction, shows a tendency to prolong positive conation rather than attain the speedy achievement of the goal wanted?

Apparent instances of this sort do occur among men. Browning's recurrent theme that the struggle counts for more than the achievement of the goal looks superficially like such an attitude. The attitude could develop as a way of making the best of a life of constant frustration. When the achievement of the things a man most wants seems unlikely, he can make a virtue out of perseverance in wanting them and persistently trying to get them—perhaps even, when the attainment of a goal seems near, to throw in some new obstacle to keep the goal at a distance! To prefer to live on hope! But the point to notice here is that it is the constant frustration of achievement that throws the man back on a prolongation of conations. The prolongation of the conations is taken not in lieu of a positive achievement but of the frustration of achievement. Positive conation is not maximized in preference to positive achievement, but only as better than no final achievement at all. So this is not an instance of positive conative value acquiring a priority over positive achievement value.

As for the man who perversely throws in obstacles to keep an achievement from success, psychiatric information indicates that his attitude is based on fear, and so again on the frustration of achievement. Such a man is not increasing his positive wantings in preference to a positive achievement. He is blocking off an achievement which he fears to have. He is exhibiting a negative conation which turns into a not very successful achievement of his aversion for success—not very successful because the natural tendency for success is working all the time. That is just why it is accurate to call such action perverse. It is self-conflicting; it is acting *against* the very tendency which it is acting *for*. It is trying to make a success of nonsuccess.

It does not appear likely that any clear instances will be found in which conative value (except in minimizing negative conations) legislates over achievement or affective value. This further confirms our earlier conclusion that there is no separate selective system for conation.

In sum, the normal line of priority within a freely operating purposive act runs from affective value through achievement and conative value. But if there is strong pressure for achievement, which is generally indicated in the intensity of the drive and generally due to some external norm of value demanding achievement, then achievement value will legislate over affective value. In simple human terms this means that if a man is given absolutely free choice, he prefers pleasure to achievement, but if a situation urgently calls for achievement he can quickly adapt to the situation.

## 10. An Empirical Description of Obligation: An 'Ought' as a Kind of 'Is'

The operation of the natural norms or selective systems just described generates a factual basis for an empirical definition of obligation. The two characterizing features of a selective system were brought out in §7: first, that the system exhibits a split dynamics, with the result that the same energy that activates the corrective agency in the system likewise activates the trial act under correction; and second, that incorrect trial acts occur within the system. These two features institute an empirical relation of obligation. The relation of the trial act to the corrective agency is a relation of obligation. The trial act *ought* to conform to the requirements of the corrective agency. This 'ought' is sanctioned by the dynamics of the system, because, if the trial act fails to conform, not only will it be rejected by the normative agency in the system but also it will lose all the dynamics it contained, since the only motivation it had was that split off from the normative agency.

The important point to notice is that all the features here referred to are descriptive features of a selective system. The relation of a trial act to its normative agency in a selective system is a descriptive relation, and at the same time it is a normative relation exhibiting an obligatory requirement.

We have just observed this relationship in two selective systems: in that of the purposive structure and in that of the affective field. In the appetitive structure the impulse pattern provides the dynamics which is split in its channeling between the conditions of quiescence for its superordinate act and references of the anticipatory set for its subordinate act. The latter is a trial act which *ought* to be such as to produce the quiescence pattern required of the superordinate drive. The superordinate drive here functions as the normative agency in this selective system. The relation between the subordinate act and the superordinate drive is here clearly a relation of *obligation*. Yet all the relations are purely descriptive relations open to verification within the selective system.

Similarly with the consummatory field. For this selective system the dynamics is again that of an appetitive drive, but now in its consummatory phase where the tensions are being released in a field of consummatory satisfactions. The dynamic structure of this field, with its affective conditions and conative references directed toward the locus of optimum satisfaction, is here the normative agency. The trial act is an act of maneuvering in the field. The drive that motivates the trial act is again the very drive that is demanding the optimum satisfaction, and will correct the maneuver if the trial act lessens the affective satisfaction. The trial act *ought* to be the one for optimum satisfaction. The relation between the trial act and the dynamic requirements of the field is again a relation of *obligation*, and is purely descriptive.

Likewise the relation of the legislation recently described, of one selective system over another, is a relation of obligation. Actually it is exactly the same sort of relation as those just described. When, in a free purposive act, it is observed that the selective system for affection legislates over that for achievement, what is meant is that in such a situation a drive entering its consummatory phase is nowise inhibited from maximizing the satisfaction available in the field and hence dynamically tends to do so, and in view of the affective structure of the field *ought* to do so.

When, however, there is pressure upon a purposive act, this means that the act is an element in a wider situation which requires speedy achievement. Here the wider situation constitutes an overarching selective system with its own normative requirements. The act of achievement is now the trial act, and the wider situation supplies the norm requiring speed. It becomes perhaps *prudent* to reach the goal quickly and proceed to the next purpose. Then it is that achievement legislates over affection, because of the requirements of a wider norm for which the achievement is a trial act. So again the legislation of the norm of achievement over that of affection is an obligatory relation based on the requirements of a situation[7] functioning as a natural norm. And again all this is purely descriptive and at the same time normative.

And so, we shall maintain, it is with all empirically justifiable 'oughts.' They are all 'is's' of a special kind, all descriptively verifiable. They are all of the nature of a dynamic relation that *exists* in those natural structures which we have distinguished as 'selective systems.' And our view is that if an 'ought' cannot be empirically justified in this way as a kind of 'is,' it is not something upon which reliable human decisions can be based.

In these last paragraphs I have been illustrating this point by reference to the selective system of the appetitive purpose and that of the consummatory field. Having studied both of these structures (and particularly the former) in great detail, we are in a position to see just how such a structure works to produce the relation of an 'ought.' In principle the same sort of relation holds for any selective system operating as a natural norm. The dynamics of any such system will require a certain conformity, and all acts performed within the system will be inherently subject to those demands for conformity because such acts share in the dynamics of the system. It is important to see how this works within the relatively simple structure of an appetitive purpose, for then we know what to look for in the much more complex structures that lie ahead.

# 15

## The Object of Value

### 1. VARIOUS SORTS OF OBJECTS OF VALUE

One more important question remains to be answered before we leave the simple purposive act to find the natural norms that apply when purposes interact on one another. This is the question of the object of value. Most interest theories make two very dubious assumptions: that every value has an object, and that there is just one object for that value. These two assumptions generate a relational theory of value.

Perry developed such a view in the form: value = interest in object $[I(R)O]$. We have had occasion to consider this formulation in several contexts, especially where we were concerned with the goal of an appetition (chap. 9) and the problem of conative references (chap. 14, §5). From these earlier considerations, we are prepared for certain complications and the need for making careful distinctions in the solution of this problem of the object of value. It is one of the most confused topics in the whole field of value. Perry was fully aware of its difficulties. It is, consequently, surprising to see how cavalierly many later writers seem to treat the subject. They often just assume an interest theory and just assume that this would be a relational theory. They proceed as if some difficulty might be admitted in describing an interest (though not always even that), but as if there were no difficulty, given an interest, in finding its object. As if the object of an interest were transparent!

It is, I am sure, wisest to assume nothing in regard to the object

369

of the three kinds of value we have so far distinguished. Allow it to be possible that there may be values without objects (object-less values), and values with a plurality of objects, as well as values with unique objects. Let us divest ourselves of preconceptions and just follow the facts as they come.

A preliminary distinction that will vastly clarify the problem is that between an *actual* object of value and a *potential* object of value. The two are very frequently confused. *An actual object of value is one that exists at the time when and in the place where the valuing is going on.* The valuing going on can thus be observed as directed upon or as accompanying the object with reference to which it is going on. Both the object and that which endows the object with value must exist at the same time with some active transaction going on between them which constitutes the endowing of the value, in order that the relation 'actual object of value' should hold.

*A potential object of value,* in contrast, *is one that does not exist at the time when the activity which endows it with value exists.* Thus if we are interested in building a house, the house that we are planning is a potential object of value. It is something wanted that does not exist. The act of wanting endows this object with value, but the object is potential only. The goal of an appetition is thus always a potential object of value until it is actualized and until a person is having immediate commerce with it. When the house is built and being used, it becomes an actual object of value in virtue of the use actually being made of it.

Within the domain of potential values a further preliminary distinction comes to light. For here a very common confusion arises between *a potential object of value* and *an object of potential value.* It is the failure to make the distinction between a house that is wanted but does not yet exist, and a house that exists and may be, but is not yet, wanted. It is the difference between a house being planned and a house on the market. The house is the potential entity in the former instance, but somebody's wanting the house is potential in the latter. The two instances are just opposite. The term in the potentiality relation that exists for the one is potential for the other, and the term that is potential for the one exists for the other. In the potential object of value, the valuing act exists which endows the value, but not the object endowed with the value. In the object of potential value the object exists but not yet the valuing act which would endow it with actual value.

The distinction is easily confusing, and the term 'potential value,' which applies to either sort of potentiality, adds to the confusion. I shall therefore use the term 'conditional object' for object of potential value. This is an appropriate name because an object of potential value is one to which 'value' is ascribed only on the condition that it might be actually valued at some time.

These three distinctions will go far to keep us out of the commonest of the confusions attendant on descriptions of the object of value. They will constitute the main headings for the analysis in this chapter. And under each of these three headings we must consider each of the three types of value. So, to begin with, what is the actual object of value for conative value, for affective value, and for achievement value?

## 2. The Actual Object of Conative Value

The relational theory of value has its most plausible base in conation. For every conative act has a conative reference (chap. 14, §5). These references terminate in objects referred to. Accordingly, when acts of conation are accepted as value acts, the objects of conative reference become value objects. More than that, it may be asserted that in the broad field of values the particular function of conative references is to indicate objects of value for purposive action. Not that all objects of value are objects of conative reference. As we shall soon see, objects of affective value are otherwise defined, as well as still other value objects. But if an object of value is to become an object of purposive pursuit or avoidance, it must necessarily become an object of conative reference. The relational theory of value marks, therefore, an important though not all-sufficient insight into the functioning of values in human behavior.

Since every conation has a conative reference, every conation as an act of value endows the object of its conative reference with value. But this is only the beginning of the matter. What is the status of the object thus endowed with conative value? Is it an actual or a potential object of value? The very term 'endowed' is trouble-bearing. It suggests that in some way the object exists and is an actual object already, only awaiting a conative act to become invested with conative value. There were fish in the lake before Utak wanted them. The notion is a common one that these fish were swimming about without value till Utak in his igloo had the desire to catch them. Then, so to speak, his conative references spread out like tentacles to all these fish, suddenly endowing them with value. The notion is that all these fish in the lake became actual objects of value in virtue of Utak's desire.

I mention this illustration because it is of a very common sort; yet it is a nest of confusions. Some of these confusions were encountered in the chapter on the goal of an appetition, and were partially cleared up there. We must now try to clear them all up. The instruments for clearing them up have only just been brought to our attention: namely, the distinctions between actual object of value, potential object of value, and conditional object. A little time spent now in a closer examination of Utak's desire will more than repay us later.

When Utak in his igloo experienced a desire to catch fish, the object of his conative reference was not literally the fish in the lake. Quite possibly there were no fish in the lake at all. The object of his conative reference would be just the same whether there were or were not any fish there. For the reference instituted a mediating judgment, which might or might not be true, and which his fishing trip was designed to verify. The object of his fishing trip—the speared fish—would be just the same whether the trip were successful and verified his judgment that fish may be caught there or not. Moreover, we now see that the object of his conative reference was not fish in the lake but fish on his spear. Finding evidences of fish in the lake would be only subordinate acts to the achievement of fish on his spear. He did not ultimately want the fish in the lake. He wanted them on his spear. This brings out the fact we have been heading for: the object of his conative reference when in his igloo he wanted to catch fish was a *potential* object. For clearly there were not any fish on his spear at that time. His conative reference designated only a potential, not an actual, object of value.

But what about the fish swimming in the lake? Were they not actual objects, and were they not valuable to Utak in virtue of his desire to catch them? Of course, but only as *conditional* objects of value. They were objects in existence truly capable of becoming terminal objects of conative value for Utak. As such, they were all properly to be considered as potential speared fish. But an actual free swimming fish is not the desired speared fish, much less an actual speared fish in Utak's grasp. These are three quite different objects, easily confused with one another, because they all have some relevance to Utak's conative activity. The first is a conditional object of conative value; the second, a potential object of conative value as the object of Utak's conative reference through all his preparatory activities. Only the third would be an actual object of conative value, and would become so only when Utak's conative act had become realized in a successful achievement.

These three objects are quite distinct. They are all, though each in a different sense, objects of conative value. The first question, therefore, to ask an exponent of a relational theory of value is: Which one of these does he mean to indicate as $O$ in the relation $I(R)O$? He generally wishes the relation to be a through-and-through factual one. In some sense, then, he wishes $O$ to be an actual object of value. Perry, fully aware of the problem, describes $O$ as an 'objective.' This 'objective' is not the object indicated by the conative reference, for that does not exist. It is, he suggests, the actual meaning of the reference, that is, the actual proposition '*that* he have a speared fish' which is the *meaning* of the reference. Perry gives this 'objective' a special ontological status of subsistence which is a kind of Platonic being independent of space, time, and change, a realm of possibilities. Most exponents of a relational theory of value, however, have not entered into the situation far enough even to see the problem. They make a vague gesture toward the three conative objects and think they have made themselves clear.

Perry's underlying assumption that the actual object of conative value is the meaning of the references, the actual proposition or judgment, seems to me the proper approach to the problem. Only I would suggest that the references themselves (as behavior readinesses, neural dispositions, of the body) be taken as the judgment. Nothing is gained by setting up an 'objective' or subsistent proposition parallel to the references as an independent meaning for them. Or, if anyone thinks there is, let him add it systematically to every conative reference, or at least to every mediating judgment that enters into our description of conative values. As for myself, I shall take the low nominalistic road for the present study, and shall maintain that a cognitive set (a pattern of bodily readinesses) constitutes the meaning of the references that make it up. One part of the meaning of these references is, of course, that they are actively referential, that they are guides to action leading to conditions for verification or confirmation. On my view a conative reference *is* a meaning, and a cognitive set composed of conative references *is* a meaningful judgment.

Now, as our descriptions of purposive structures have shown, the cognitive set is an actual object whenever it is functioning as a guide to purposive action. It is therefore always available as an actual object of value in a conative act. It is, in fact, as we shall presently see, *the* actual object of conative value (being the object actually charged by the drive) wherever it is actively functioning in a purposive act.

With the preceding remarks as preparation, let us now fully face the question of the actual object of value in conation. When Utak wants to catch fish, what is the actual object of his want? The question is likely to be stated in this way. But if it is so stated, we get the idea that the actual object of his want is a single and perduring object throughout the course of his purposive act, and that this is the terminating goal of achievement for that purpose. Literally this is impossible, since the goal does not yet exist and may never exist. Nevertheless, the question expresses a basic insight: there is something in a purposive act that guides a want steadily to, or toward, its achievement. Naïvely the ordinary man assumes that this is the goal. Actually it is the set of conative references to the goal. If, then, the actual object of a want is what is steadily guiding it, that object is the goal-directed set of conative references itself.

But this is only part of the story. When Utak had attained his goal and was actually spearing his fish in a consummatory act, what was the actual object of conative value then? Clearly, the speared fish. But up to this moment the actual object of Utak's want had been his anticipatory set for the fish. At the act of spearing, however, the anticipatory references ceased and were replaced by actual commerce with the fish. The actual conative references now become the consummatory acts of commerce with the fish. The actual object now is the consummatory goal itself, the actual fish functioning in its role of fulfillment of the quiescence pattern.

We are not quite through yet. There were a number of subordinate acts in Utak's catching of the fish. These were not irrelevant to his want. Each act had its anticipatory set and consummatory fulfillment. These must not be lost sight of.

Also, there is in all underived appetitions the instinctive impulse pattern, whose conative references are not an anticipatory set but the conditions of quiescence of the impulse pattern itself. Here the actual object cannot be the conditions of quiescence in the abstract, for these are nothing apart from the impulse pattern in action. The actual object is the impulse pattern itself carrying its conditions of quiescence which are its pattern of conative references.

And in aversions there is the riddance pattern to consider, in which the actual object of conation is the object of riddance in commerce with the appropriate acts of riddance. Where there are apprehensive sets, the situation would be the same as with anticipatory sets. The apprehensive sets themselves, as the guiding instruments of purposive action, would be the actual objects of conative value.

The determination of the actual object of conative value varies, accordingly, with the segment of the purpose in action. And now perhaps we get the clue to its determination. It consists in whatever pattern of action is being charged by a drive. The drive provides the dynamics of the value; *the pattern charged by the drive provides the actual object.* The actual conative object is the object of the drive, that which is actually charged by the drive. The actual object varies with the segment of a purposive act charged at any given time. When many subordinate acts are involved, the number of charged sets will be numerous and the actual object will be the whole system of these acts. So Utak from wanting fish wanted the sled and dogs and all the instruments needed for cutting through the ice, decoying, and spearing. These all (as bodily sets) became actual objects of conative value, all interconnected into one structure, and all wanted at once, though, to be sure, in due order.

To determine the actual object of conative value at any time, we have to consider the total structure of a purposive act in relation to the segment in operation at that time. Take, for instance, the usual simple anticipatory appetition. Let it be an act motivated by ordinary hunger.

At the emergence of such an instinctive drive previous to experience of how to satisfy it, we have what is ordinarily called a *blind drive,* one that has conditions of quiescence but no cognitive references. Introspectively, it is a wanting without knowing what one wants. There is the drive, the wanting, but no idea of what one wants, no anticipatory set. Such blind drives are rare in mature persons, though the restlessness of a sexually inexperienced young person is often noticed. The best way to get a notion of the inner feel of a blind drive is to recall occasions when you started off for something and then momentarily forgot what you went for. You start upstairs for a pair of scissors, talking to someone as you go. At the top of the stairs, "What was it I wanted?" You have a sense of the room that you headed for, and the height at which the object was to be found. The conditions of quiescence are there in vague outline. But what will satisfy them? Perhaps you see the scissors on the bureau: "Aha! that was what I wanted!"

The importance of noticing the blind drive is the evidence it gives that a cognitively known object of wanting is not needed for a genuine instance of wanting. Conative valuing sometimes occurs without any cognitive reference to an object of conation. Nevertheless, an actual object for the wanting is still seen to be supplied for a blind drive in the very pattern of the conative act (the impulse pattern) whose implicit conditions of quiescence constitute a conative reference. This pattern with its implicit references is charged with energy by the very fact of its being an appetitive drive.

When such a drive charges an anticipatory set with explicit cognitive references, however, the set with its references becomes an actual object of conative value. In strictness, there are now two actual objects of conative value: the impulse pattern, with its conditions of quiescence referring to the consummatory act; and the anticipatory set, with its cognitive references to a goal object. But ordinarily the impulse pattern is taken for granted when a drive is also charging an anticipatory set, and lost from explicit notice. This neglect adds to the confusion attendant on common conceptions of the object of conative value. When there is (1) an impulse pattern for a drive charging (2) an anticipatory set, the actual objects of conative value for both segments should be recognized. For the latter leads to the goal object and may be in error, and the former to the quite distinct consummatory act. The only exception is a derived appetition generated by mutation from a goal object originally incorporated in a compound aversion (cf. chap. 11, §3); for here the goal object is structurally terminal and incapable of error, and the consummatory satisfaction of the injective drive incorporates the pattern of the goal object as part of its specific quiescence pattern for that drive. A large proportion of our independent derived drives, however, seem to follow that pattern. And this circumstance has also added to the confusions regarding the object of conative value.

Proceeding next from the superordinate to the subordinate act of an appetition, the anticipatory set of that act becomes still another actual object of conative value for the drive charging it. And so on from subordinate act to subordinate act. When Utak wanted his dogs to pull his sled, to get him onto the lake, so as to chisel a hole, to decoy a fish, to spear it, all these anticipatory sets were actual objects of conation for the drive in action.

Lastly, when the consummatory act is reached, what is there charged by the drive is the quiescence pattern itself in commerce with the terminal goal object which stimulated it. The quiescence pattern itself (in commerce with its object, of course) is here the actual object of value.

Similarly with an aversion. To find the actual objects of conative value for an aversion, its structure must be examined segment by segment. In a riddance pattern, the pattern of riddance in commerce with the object of riddance is the actual object of negative conation. For an apprehensive set, the set of cognitive references constitutes the actual object of negative conation. If there are subordinate acts of apprehension, their apprehensive sets are also actual objects of negative conation.

In sum, *whatever is charged by a drive is an actual object of conative value for that drive.* It is the object of that drive, the object charged by it. The sense of the conative reference determines whether it is a positive or a negative object of value.

This solution may sometimes sound strange in terms of common sense. To speak, for instance, of the idea of catching a fish as the actual object of Utak's desire may sound strange. But when it is realized that the idea in Utak's mind is directed upon actually catching a fish, not on simply imagining the catching of one, then the conception will perhaps be found not so far from common sense. Utak was vigorously acting on the anticipatory references of his idea, trying to achieve them, not possessively contemplating them. Besides, where common sense is vague and confused, we cannot expect that a more discriminating analysis will exactly square with it. The utility and correctness of our solution will, I believe, become more and more evident as we proceed. People commonly confuse the *object of cognition* of the anticipatory set with the *object of conation* charged by the drive. The former is usually potential; only the latter is always *actual*.

These various kinds of objects connected with conation may become very confusing. Let me list them in series for clarity's sake:

1. *Actual object of conative value =*
   the set of conative references, which are a set of neural or bodily readinesses charged by a drive. For instance, Utak's drive-charged anticipation or set for fish. This is the actual object of the *drive*.
2. *Potential object of conative value =*
   the quiescence pattern for the conditions of quiescence or a

goal object for an anticipatory set, as referred to by the conative references previous to actualization. For instance, the would-be fish that would reduce Utak's drive. The would-be fish exist only in the conative sets of readinesses.

3. *Cognitive object of conative references* =

the goal object of an anticipatory set that would determine the truth or falsity of the mediating judgment contained in these references. It becomes *actual* only in the act of verification. For instance, the would-be fish that would verify Utak's anticipations for catching fish. Or, in the verificatory act, the actual fish transfixed on Utak's spear.

4. *Cognitive linguistic object* designated by *linguistic* signs uttered or 'thought' by the agent =

either (1) or (3) or both. For instance, the meaning of Utak's word 'fish' (in his language) would be either his idea of fish, which would be his anticipatory set, or what his idea cognitively referred to, which would be the would-be fish that would verify his idea, or both. The linguistic object (1) would be my interpretation of Perry's 'objective' (chap. 9, §3); the linguistic object (3) would be the pragmatic meaning of the linguistic signs in terms of their verifiability.

5. *Conditional object* =

object of potential value (to be discussed more fully in §6). This is an existing object that is judged to have a likelihood of being valued. For instance, the fish swimming in the lake, since Utak might spear one or more of them in a consummatory act of his appetition.

## 3. The Actual Object of Affective Value

We have now to consider the actual objects of affective value. In some respects this is a simpler problem than the preceding. For one thing, there is not the same traditional demand that pleasures or pains should have objects in order to be considered values as that desires should. Pleasures and pains are intuitively accepted as positive or negative values whether objects can be found for them or not. And for another thing, there is much less question about the locus of an object of affection, assuming there is one.

An actual object of pleasure or pain is rarely conceived as miles or months away from its feeling, as an object of conation often is. It is assumed to be in close proximity, rarely farther away than the immediate field of perception.

The problem of an actual object for affection is not so much to find one as to get used to the idea that a simple pleasure or pain may simultaneously have several objects. This is, to be sure, just another way of saying that an object is not essential to affective value. The essential thing is to have the pleasure or the pain. That alone is what is affectively good or bad. What it is attached to as an object is relatively incidental, and has only a tangential or consequential significance. The ache is what is bad. That it is a *tooth*ache has significance only in showing me the object on which to direct my action in order to get rid of the ache. It is as though an object of affection were of no concern to affection but only to conation, as though an object of affection only became important when an organism wanted to do something about his pleasures and pains. If this is true, as I believe it is, we come upon the very significant fact that objects of affection act as links of connection between affective and conative values; so, through the objects of these values, judgments of affective value can be coordinated with judgments of conative value and vice versa. Distinct as feelings of conation are from feelings of pleasure and pain, the two modes of valuing come together in a single system through sharing some identical objects.

However, in the hedonistic tradition it seems to be taken for granted that if a pleasure or a pain does have an object (which is not, to be sure, always implied) this object is the unique object of that specific pleasure or pain. The hedonistic tradition does not seem to be very insistent that there should be an object of affection, but when it does ascribe an object to pleasure or pain, the assumption seems to be that this is the one and only proper object of the affection. The weakness of this assumption, however, comes to light as soon as we inquire specifically what the proper object is. We find ourselves faced with four distinct possibilities, each having good grounds for acceptance.

The commonest idea of an object of affection is that the object has something to do with the cause of the affection. The object of pain probably is generally thought of as the proximate cause of the pain, and the object of pleasure as the proximate cause of the pleasure. But it is left ambiguous whether the object actually is a cause or one which the organism ascribes as a cause.

According to the first interpretation, the relation between an affection and its object is a factual one of causal dependence and no error is possible. According to the second interpretation, an object is ascribed to an affection by an act of judgment and an error is possible.

When I am bitten by a mosquito or enjoy eating an apple, what is the affective object? I say unreflectively, "Of course, the mosquito is the painful object; and the apple, the pleasant one." But suppose the mosquito I strike at is not the one that bit me! Which, then, is the painful object, the one which actually bit me, though I did not see it, or the one I saw but which did not bite me?

And now in the presence of this option, the third possibility appears: that the consideration of cause may be altogether irrelevant to the question; and it is the object on which an organism projects his feelings, cause or no cause, that is the actual object of affection. On this view, the first mosquito disappears entirely from the picture, since no feeling is projected upon it; and the second mosquito becomes the actual object of affection, but not because it is mistaken for the first mosquito which actually bit me, but only because I do not like the looks of it. I find it disagreeable in my sight, project my displeasure upon it, whence it automatically becomes an unpleasant object. The fact that I thought it bit me no doubt contributes to my disliking it, but that is not what makes it a disagreeable object. It is the object of my feeling simply because I direct my feeling upon it. This is a pure matter of fact, and, as with the first view, there is no error about the object of affection on this view either, so far, that is, as the person who projects the feeling is concerned.

On this third view, a diffusion of affection makes all objects within the field on which an affection radiates, objects of the affection. So a young lover who in the exuberance of his emotion radiates his joy over all that he sees—flowers, birds, children, and passers-by, and even inanimate things—makes all these into objects of his delight, for he finds a pleasure in them which he himself has projected there. He may even be aware that he is making them pleasant, and not they him. Certainly we know that many objects which give us pleasure do not cause the enjoyment we find in them, but only crystallize it. We pick up a chair and dance with it, throw a hat in the air and catch it and squeeze it. They draw our joy to them, but we do not imagine that they cause it.

Diffusion of pain or negative affection is, of course, just as common as that of positive affection with or without the person being aware of the projection of his pain. So it is when a man pounds a pillow after stubbing his toe in the dark, or berates his secretary because a competitor outwitted him in a business deal. The man who pounds his pillow knows perfectly well that it was the rocking chair that hurt his toe, and that it was he himself who did it by his own carelessness, but for the moment he can actually see the pillow as a hateful object in lieu of the chair and himself. On this third view, the pillow would then be an actual object of negative affection.

But there is still a fourth view, which is in a way the most relevant of all, though it is least often alluded to in discussions of the subject. On this view the actual object of pleasure or pain is the sensuous pattern in which either of these is embedded. In our terms, the affection is a property of, or is correlated with, the riddance or quiescence pattern itself. On this fourth view, the actual object would be not the mosquito but the bite, not the pillow or the chair but the bruise, not the secretary or the business competitor but the anger and fear, not the apple but its taste and the eating of it, not the sexual mate but the orgasm.

Now I am proposing the unorthodox hypothesis that all four are actual objects of affection whenever they actually occur in connection with pleasures or pains, and that, moreover, they are all objects of purposive value, for they are all contained within the field of individual values defined by the structures of appetition and aversion. The first, second, and fourth, in fact, are objects with which we have already become well acquainted in our previous descriptions of appetitions and aversions. The third is not so familiar to us, but from now on it will become so. It indicates a diffusion of the energy of purposive drives beyond the strictly efficient pursuit of goals. Of these, however, only the fourth could remotely be regarded as an intrinsic object of affection, implied in the descriptive definition of the term.

We shall need names for these four kinds of actual objects of affection. Let us call them: (1) the actual stimulus object, (2) the imputed stimulus object, (3) the object of diffused affection, and (4) the immediate sensuous object. The connection between these objects of affection and those of conation is now of considerable interest, particularly as this connection seems to be the principal source of significance for specifying objects of affection.

1. The actual stimulus object of negative affection is identical with the actual stimulus of a riddance pattern, which, as we have seen, is the terminal object of aversion. It is this object which the whole structure of an aversion is designed to avoid or escape. It is the actual conative object of riddance whenever an organism has commerce with it, which is also just the occasion when it is an actual object of negative affection. Its great practical significance is that through our knowledge of this object we obtain the means of avoiding pain.

In parallel fashion, the actual stimulus object of positive affection is the correct terminal goal object of an appetition—the object that actually stimulates the quiescence pattern with its accompanying pleasure. Through our knowledge of this object we control our pleasures.

2. The imputed stimulus object of affection is identical with an object of apprehension in an aversion, or the goal object of an anticipatory set in an appetition. It is what the organism *believes* is the cause of his pain or pleasure when he is engaged in a painful or pleasure-giving act. It is an actual object of affection, however, only while the organism is having pleasure or pain which is imputed to it, at which time it is also an actual object of conation. It differs from object 1 in that it presupposes an apprehensive or an anticipatory set which object 1 does not. The pleasure or pain is actually taken in the set, which is believed to be true of the stimulus object. If the set is correct, the object will be the same in both cases (for both 1 and 2). But if the set is in error, then the objects will differ. So far as pleasure is taken in subordinate goal objects in the achievement of their subordinate goals, these would be imputed objects of pleasure. So, too, with the pleasures of

foretaste in anticipatory objects. And conversely with painful objects of apprehension. All these also would be imputed stimulus objects of affection.

The significance of this affective object is that by its means the organism *tries* to control his pleasures and pains. But actually he will not succeed, except by coincidence, until the imputed stimulus object becomes identical with the actual one.

All rationalizations indirectly involve a discrepancy between actual and imputed objects of affection. The basis of the error here is mistaken motivation. Such a mistake in a person's idea of the drive that gives him satisfaction, however, entails mistakes in the stimuli that produce that satisfaction. When a man expresses intense indignation over a salacious novel that he has read from cover to cover, he indicates not only his ignorance of the drive that impelled him to read the book so thoroughly but also his inability to control his behavior by that or similar stimuli. When he can correctly impute his satisfaction or dissatisfaction to the stimulus which produces it, he will no longer be deceiving himself about his motives.

It is by means of this relation between the actual and the imputed stimuli of affection, trying to make the latter conform to the former, that we are rationally able to control most of our behavior and its values.

3. The object of diffused affection involves a phase of our study that has not received its share of description yet. When a painful purpose is frustrated in achieving quiescence it tends to spread out in a trial-and-error manner to environing objects, even when the organism is well aware that these are not correct stimuli for furthering the attainment of quiescence. Likewise when there is a great release of tension in excess of that which can immediately be taken up by the consummatory activities of the quiescent pattern underway, there is a tendency for the organism to diffuse this energy and have commerce with environing objects in partial consummatory acts as far as the nature of the objects will allow.

The objects which gather up this diffused energy are in some degree analogous to the correct objects of those activities. A man who diffuses his rage over a bruised toe in beating a pillow chooses an object that can take a blow of the fist without risk of further pain. The lover who diffuses his joy over flowers and children selects something sweet and bright in appearance which he can happily gaze at or even touch and kiss.

These are all in the nature of partially incorrect objects of apprehension or goal objects whose degree of incorrectness is, however, properly gauged by the organism; so they are not strictly incorrect at all. But the pain or pleasure is nevertheless projected and fully felt in them. They are actual objects of conation just as much as other incorrect objects of apprehension or appetition.

4. The immediate sensuous object of affection corresponds to the riddance or quiescence pattern, which, as we have seen, is an actual conative object charged by whatever drive is activating the pattern. The pleasure in the sensations of a quiescence pattern is the feeling of release of tension going on in a succession of physiological activities correlated with those sensations. The quiescence pattern of thirst is the drinking of water, and pleasure is felt in the sensations of drinking it.

In every one of these four instances an object of affection is also an object of conation. The conative object, moreover, is of great practical significance in the attainment of a pleasure or the avoidance of a pain. We are suggesting that this is the whole significance of the search for objects of affection. Pleasures and pains do not of themselves call for objects. They are positive and negative values intuitively accepted as such regardless of any objects to which they may become attached. They have no inherent references toward objects, as conations always do even when the latter are cognitively blind and groping for their objects. The only reason for ascribing objects to pleasures and pains is that frequently we *want* pleasures and *want to avoid* pains, and for these conative acts we require objects which are causally related to, or correlated with, these affections.

It follows that we need not be concerned about the large number of alternative objects to which pleasures and pains can be ascribed. None of them, except perhaps the immediate sensuous object, are strictly inherent in the affections. But all of them have some bearing on the conative control of our affections.

## 4. THE ACTUAL OBJECT OF ACHIEVEMENT VALUE

Positive achievement value is success in a purposive activity. The success consists in the speedy termination of a purposive act. We speak of a purposive act as 'good,' in the sense of successful, when it goes through smoothly and quickly. Now just what is it that is characterized as good in this sense? There seems to be some ambiguity in terms of common opinion. Is it the act as a whole or the termination of the act?

When Utak spears his fish, after making his expedition onto the lake and going through all the necessary preparations, we spontaneously remark, "That's good! That makes the whole expedition a success, its having such a successful ending." The whole expedition is a success, and the termination is a success. And it sounds also as if the successful termination made the expedition a success. What, then, is the actual object of success? Is it the terminus or the whole act? There are difficulties with either alternative.

Take the alternative of the terminus first. Consider the terminus of an aversion. It is characteristic of the structure of aversions that they terminate not in a consummatory act (a quiescence pattern) but simply in the quiescence of the drives motivating them. This is particularly clear in the simple riddance aversions. Suppose something is tickling my nose, or a window has blown open letting in a rush of wind, or an alarm clock starts clanging unexpectedly. The terminal success consists in merely stopping the annoyances. There is no terminal consummatory act to celebrate the success, like Utak's spearing a fish. The success lies simply in the ceasing of the annoyance. In a typical aversion there is no actual terminal act to function as an actual terminal object of success. The aversive purpose was successful and so generated a positive achievement value without any terminal act that could be endowed with that value. Since, then, an aversion can be successful without any terminal act to function as an actual object for that success, it appears that a terminal act is not required for a successful achievement, and so, by extension, cannot be regarded as the actual object of positive achievement value either.

Thus when, in the context of appetitive, in contrast to aversive, behavior, the attainment of an appetitive goal is called a good successful terminal act, all that can justifiably be meant is that *unless* the consummatory act of an appetition were attained, the appetitive activity would not be a success. It is apparently the appetitive purpose as a whole that is properly characterized as successful.

May we then say that the purposive structure as a whole is the actual object of achievement value? With a certain liberty in the use of the term 'actual,' we might. But it must be realized that a total purposive act may stretch over hours, months, years. Utak's fishing expedition was carried through with expertness and success, but it took most of a day. We defined an 'actual object of value' as one that exists at the time and in the place where the valuing is going on. How widely do we care to stretch existence? Apparently we must let it stretch as far as it actually goes.

The determination of the actual object of achievement value brings out prominently something that was only latent before. This is that an actual object of value is always an event. It is actual not at a knife-edge present but through a 'specious present,' as James calls it. The actual object of conative value is always some charged segment of a total purpose. No matter how brief the segment, it stretches over a certain duration for the very realization of its pattern of references. Similarly with the various objects of affective value. But the actual object of achievement value, as the total purposive act itself, brings the duration of an actual object into prominence. We cannot be called upon in a work on value theory to enter into the whole problem of time and duration. All we can do is to note that the descriptions of purposive activity, on the evidence at hand, show actual objects of value to be events spreading over a certain duration. Probably whatever is actual has a certain duration. The trend of our descriptive analysis leads us to accept as an actual object of value whatever at a given time is indicated as the structural unity exhibiting the value in question. If the structural unity spreads the duration of a given act over a considerable period of historical time, we must evidently accept the total time it took as its actual duration. If this act is designated as an actual object of value, then the object clearly has the same duration the act has. Accordingly, if our descriptive analysis leads us to designate a total purposive act as an actual object of value, there is no objection in consistency why this should not be done.

The actual object of achievement value is, then, to be taken as the total purposive act so far as it has gone. If the act has been completed, it is a success. If it is partially completed and still in process, it is a partial success. If it is blocked, it is frustrated, and so is characterized by negative achievement value. The object of frustration is thus the purposive act in progress, not, it should be noted, the frustrating object. The frustrating object is an object of negative conation. It enters into the frustrated purposive act as a segment of the frustrated purpose, but it is not itself the object frustrated. If Utak had come to an open channel on his way to the fishing grounds, the channel would have been an actual object of negative conative value for him. But the actual object of negative achievement value for him, the object actually frustrated, would have been his purpose to go fishing, which was blocked at that point.

If any doubt remained whether achievement value could be reduced to conative value or vice versa, these last disclosures should pretty well dissipate it. For the object of frustration (which is the blocked achievement) could not possibly be identified with the object of aversion which produced the frustration.

In summary, the actual object of achievement value is the total purposive act in progress up to the moment of evaluation. If the act is completed, it is an object of positive achievement value. If it is blocked, it is an object of negative achievement value. However, should the concept of an actual object of achievement appear too strange, it may be dropped with impunity, for there is no distinction between a historically enacted purpose and an actual object of achievement.

## 5. The Potential Object of Value

In the preceding sections we sought out and examined the actual objects of conative, affective, and achievement value. Many objects dignified in the tradition of value did not find their accustomed place there. We shall now find that most of them turn out to be potential objects—either potential objects of value or those objects of potential value which, to avoid confusion, we are calling conditional objects. In fact, in the history of culture potential objects function more prominently than actual ones. And in an individual purposive act the goal, which is generally taken as the controlling object of the total act, is a potential object for all the earlier and progressive phases of the act.

The concept of potentiality is thus a crucial one in the theory of value. We must examine it with care and determine as precisely as possible its application to the various segments of purposive activity.

1. *Potentiality, inherent and hypothetical.*—Let us first ask what potentiality in general means, and then work down to its applications in the field of values. In a very general sense, an object is said to be potential if there is a probability that it may become actual. The potentiality is said to lie in the conditions which provide the evidence or grounds for the probability of the object's becoming actual. These conditions justify the probability only, however, through the mediation of something in the nature of a statistical or causal law or a dispositional character or process which connects the present condition with the presumptive future actuality of the object.

Thus three factors are involved in potentiality: present or given conditions; a future state or object; and a law, disposition, trend, or other principle connecting the first with the second. Then the future state or object is said to be potential in the given conditions. Let us call the conditions in virtue of which an object or state is potential the 'generating conditions,' and the connecting law, disposition, or trend the 'connecting principle.'

So an egg is said to be a potential chick, a worm a potential butterfly, an acorn a potential oak, a low-pressure area a potential storm, and so on. Notice that as soon as the connecting principle for any of these objects ceases to be attached to the generating conditions, the potentiality vanishes from the situation. If an egg is unfertilized, it ceases to be a potential chick, or if it is boiled, or if in any other way the law of hatching ceases to apply to it. If there is no connecting principle leading from certain conditions to an object or state, then there is no potentiality in the situation.

Thus potentiality is a relation between a conditioning state or object and a potential state or object. The relation between the two is set up by the connecting principle. Once such a relation is set up by a connecting principle, either term so connected may in common speech be denominated a potential object, to the great confusion of the general situation. Someone may, for instance, speak of a prominent citizen in a town, a Mr. Smith, as a potential mayor. He presumably means the actual Mr. Smith who is not yet a mayor but whose qualifications show that he possesses the generating conditions for a mayor. To avoid serious ambiguities, let us agree to call the first term in a potentiality relation a 'generating object or state' and reserve the phrase 'potential object or state' for the second term only. It then follows that in the potentiality relationship the generating object is conceived as existing and the potential object as not yet existing whenever the relation holds. So, when Mr. Smith is considered as a potential mayor, Mr. Smith, as an actual citizen and not yet a mayor, is a generating object (an object of potential mayorality), but the potential object, Mr. Smith as mayor, does not yet exist.

The distinction is easy to make when the terms have different names—the egg and the chick, the acorn and the oak. The egg as a potential chick is not itself the potential object, but the generating object for the chick. When, however, the generating object and the potential object get the same name, and no pervasive metamorphosis occurs between the initial and the terminal state, there is great danger of confusion. Mr. Smith the mere citizen can easily be confused with Mr. Smith the possible object of a successful election. In the potentiality relation the generating object in our terminology exists or is conceived as existing, whereas the potential object of the relationship does not exist.

By this characteristic it is possible to distinguish a potentiality relation from other relations. In all other relations, all the terms related exist (or are conceived as existing) in the same status. In 'the car is on the road' both the car and the road exist at the same time. In 'three is greater than two,' both of the numbers thus related exist in the same status, however that may be described. But, in 'egg is a potential chick,' 'egg' exists in a given present while 'chick' does not. And as soon as 'chick' exists or is conceived as existing, the potentiality of chick to egg evaporates. It is essential to the potentiality relation that one term exist at a given time (or at least be conceived in that way) while the other does not.

Now, a potentiality relation may actually be in operation in some natural process, or it may be merely conceived and hypothetical. An egg may be under a hen or in an incubator in the process of becoming a chick; or, contrariwise, a farmer may be entertaining the hypothesis of putting an egg in an incubator to hatch an additional chick. In either instance there is a potentiality relation. But it is an actual relation inherent in the situation in the one instance and a hypothetical one in the other. *An actual inherent potentiality relation is,* of course, *an instance of becoming.* But *a hypothetical potentiality is a hypothesis about the possibility of something.*

There is the same difference between an inherent potentiality relation and a hypothetical one as anywhere else in the difference between actual fact and hypothesis about fact. An actual fact is neither true nor false. It just is. But a hypothesis about a fact is true or false. So a hypothesis about a potentiality relation is true or false. It purports to be true but may be false. An inherent potentiality relation, however, is neither true nor false. It is a process actually going on. It may be blocked but not falsified. The distinction is that between potentiality developed in a causal process actually in operation and potentiality as a judgment about such a process.

Think of an egg in an incubator in the process of turning into a chick. Or think of an artillery shell that is just fired and traveling along its trajectory toward its target. These are actual instances of potentiality relations in operation. They are instances of change according to a determinate law. These actual processes of change through time according to natural law are, accordingly, inherent potentialities. They are factual in the sense that they will go on according to the natural law in process whether or not anyone observes the processes, or whether or not anyone makes hypotheses and probability estimates about them.

But a rancher who looked at an egg or thought of an egg and estimated its probability of hatching would be imputing a hypothetical potentiality to the egg. Similarly with a gunner who

picked up a shell and judged its capacity to follow a certain trajectory and land upon his target. Such hypothetical potentialities
are hypotheses subject to truth and error. The inherent potentialities to which they refer are factual processes of change or becoming, and, though they may be blocked, are not subject to error
and cannot be either true or false.

Many writers try to make out that a process extending through
time according to a predictable law, and thus exhibiting an inherent potentiality relation, can be reduced either to a succession
of existential facts exhibiting only existential relations, or else to a
matter of human calculation and hypothesis, that is, to pure
hypothetical potentiality. The idea is that if anything is a fact it
must exist with all its terms in a momentary present. Though
this is a widespread conception of fact, its consequences are not
usually followed through, nor likely to be acceptable.

If a causal process is reduced to a succession of disconnected
momentary states, then no causal ground for prediction remains
in the succession. If, for instance, the trajectory of a shell is
broken down into a succession of disconnected positions of the
shell with no recognition of a specific temporal relation of the
earlier to the later segments of the path described by the shell
according to a law of ballistics, then there is no cause, ground,
reason (whatever you wish to call it) why the shell should follow just that path, and consequently no ground for prediction.
Either the shell in following the path of its trajectory is determined by a potentiality relation (a natural law of ballistics), or
it is totally undetermined. Since our gunners do make predictions
on the assumption that potentiality relations (causal determinations) do hold on the firing of shells, and the shells do hit their
targets, the natural assumption is that the shells were terms in
potentiality relations and were determined in their flight. If so,
the potentiality relations were among the factual relations in the
process of firing these shells upon their targets.

But this conclusion is often evaded by the argument that the
predictions of the gunners are not based on an inherent potentiality in the trajectory of a shell, but simply on the gunners' past
experience with similar shells. The gunners have confidence and
believe in their shells, it is said, because they have fired shells so

often to good effect. This is essentially the Humean argument. It pretends to complete ignorance about any inferred facts of unobserved shells in trajectory moving upon a target, and recognizes as facts only momentary existential relations. But on repetition (or by other methods acquired by experience), men, on this view, come to expect observations that have been conjoined to be conjoined again. By a process of conditioning or habit, men make predictions. The path of a shell, therefore, is a human habit of thought and the gunner's predictions are informative of his conditioning with shells, but not of any relations between shells and targets apart from the gunner's training. In short, on this view a shell that is fired might, for any relations the shell itself is known to have, go in somersaults and spirals and nestle in the gunner's arms. But the gunner does not from his training expect this, and so, purely on the basis of his habits of thought about shells, he fires the gun.

On this view, it is argued that the only meaningful question we can ask about a gunner's behavior is on what grounds he *believes* his shell will reach the target. The answer then accepted is: "The gunner bases his belief on the frequency of his observations of the firing of a gun and the hitting of a target." This does, no doubt, pretty well account for the psychological causes of his belief. The belief is doubtless a case of conditioning. But the question of the grounds for the frequency of the observations still remains. Why this constancy in the observations? There are two possible answers: first, that the constancy in the observations is due to a constancy in the facts which stimulated the observations; second, that there is no constancy in the facts, and that the constancy in the observations was coincidental or the result of a willful selection on the part of the observer, as in superstitious beliefs, and that the expectation that the shell will hit its target has no grounds other than the expectancy of the observer. When confronted with this pair of alternatives, most people will immediately reject the second. The rejection is based on a great amount of evidence distinguishing between expectations based on coincidence and superstition, which sooner or later break down, and expectations based on factual relations, which do not similarly break down—in short, on evidence distinguishing between error and truth in man's anticipations and apprehensions.

The effect of the second alternative, which rejects constancy in the facts, is to deny that there is any essential difference between a gunner's expectations in firing a shell at a target and a primitive magician's expectations in weaving a spell for rain. There would, of course, be no difference if there were not some sort of relation holding in fact between the shell at its firing and the target, whereas no such relation holds in fact between a magician's spell and rain. Granted the many difficulties in discriminating between the two sorts of cases, nevertheless we seem to have been pretty successful in sorting them out, and the degree of this success is precisely the measure of our evidence against the view that there is no relation in fact, apart from human expectancy, between a present cause and a future effect of that cause when a causal law is in action.

Moreover, the view which identifies causal relations with human expectancy seems to presuppose what it denies. For what is the basis of the constancy of human expectancy, habit, conditioning, and the like, which is supposed to account for the gunner's belief in the destructiveness of his shell? This expectancy is assumed to have a constancy in fact which is not based on an expectancy of it. It assumes a psychological law of stimulus, anticipatory set, and response. By this causal law the gunner in fact acts on the visual stimulus of the shell, which with his present anticipatory set causes him to load it into the gun, aim it, fire it, and watch the effect on the target. If it is only the gunner's habit of expectancy which justifies him in believing that the shell will reach its target, is it only some theorist's expectancy of the gunner's habit of expectancy which justifies the theorist's belief in the habits of the gunner, and so on ad infinitum?

And, finally, is the evidence so weak, even though most of it is indirect and inferential, that eggs do hatch into chicks, that beans do grow into plants, that shells with given charges do follow definite trajectories under definite conditions, that the planets do follow definite orbits, that animals do respond to certain stimuli in certain ways, do acquire habits, do even exhibit goal-seeking behavior—without benefit of human expectancy or probability estimates to justify the specific causal relations involved?

Do not these actual causal processes with their inherent relations of present to future go on whether or not anyone knows that they go on?

It must appear strange to some readers that there should be any need to make this point. But it is necessary to make it in order that a causal process as an actual fact containing an actual inherent potentiality relation, some of whose terms do not exist at the moment when others do exist, should not be ignored and lightly interpreted away. Purposive behavior is a striking example of such a causal process, and unless a relation of inherent potentiality is observed between the initial and terminal stages of such an act, a complete description of such behavior and the values it contains becomes very difficult if not impossible.[1]

In arguing for the factuality of an inherent potentiality relation (in contrast to a purely hypothetical one), I am not arguing for any particular theory of causality, but only against any theory that reduces this relation to a purely hypothetical one. I am certainly not arguing that the nonexistent potential object is existent or exerts an actual pull on the generating conditions. I am only insisting on the evidence that a causal process in action exhibits some actual reference to the future, which is an inherent property of whatever is going on in the present, and constitutes the factual ground for true prediction. The usual term for this reference to-day is 'dispositional property.' Whatever a dispositional property turns out in truth to be, this is what I am indicating as an inherent potentiality. Whenever such a dispositional property is exhibiting itself in action, that would be a potentiality relation in operation.

To summarize the findings of this section on potentiality in general:

A. A potentiality relation is one that holds between terms some of which exist at a given moment (or are conceived as so existing) and some of which do not exist.

B. The relation may be analyzed into:

    1. Generating conditions or the *generating object*.

    2. Future nonexistent state or object, the *potential object*.

    3. Law or disposition connecting (1) and (2), or the *connecting principle*.

C. An *inherent potentiality relation* is to be distinguished from a *hypothetical potentiality relation.* The former is a process in factual operation; the latter, a hypothesis about the factual possibility of something.

2. *Potential objects of conative and achievement value.*— There are hypothetical and also inherent potential objects of conative and achievement value. The two kinds of value are here considered together because inherent potential objects of conative value depend upon the inherent potentiality of purposive achievement. Moreover, hypothetical potentiality of conation and achievement would have little significance unless it were based on a process having inherent potentiality. So the heart of the present problem lies in the inherent potentiality of purposive achievement. In fact, what else would be the biological or human significance of a purpose unless it were its inherent power to achieve its aims?

The inherent potential object of achievement is the completed purposive structure. For the object characterized by success in evaluating an achievement is not the state of quiescence following success, but the whole purpose successfully brought to its inherently determined end. In an appetition, success lies in the attainment of the desired goal objects and the final consummatory act. In an aversion, success lies in the riddance of the object of riddance and of such objects of apprehension as provoke fear or aggression. Whatever segments of a purposive structure remain uncompleted while a purpose is in process, these constitute the nonexistent and still potential terms in the potentiality relation. Whatever segments have been completed and are charged with the drive, these constitute the generating conditions for the potentiality relation. The structure of the purpose as a whole constitutes the connecting principle.

In the nature of purposive activity there would not be an inherent potentiality of frustration. A purposive structure is so organized as to be conducive to success. It may be blocked and so frustrated. But its tendency, its inherent potentiality, is for success. Whether the purpose is positive or negative, an appetition or an aversion, it is so constructed as to lead inherently to success. So we have inherent potential objects of positive achievement value, but none of negative achievement value.

This does not mean that there are not inherently self-frustrating personalities which have developed from certain neurotic conditions. But these arise out of conditions of internal purposive conflicts, and it is the personalities or the complex of purposes that are inherently frustrating rather than any single purpose. Any single purposive structure is designed to be successful either for appetition or avoidance.

Now it is out of this inherent potentiality of successful achievement that certain inherent objects of conative value are generated. For an inherent potential object of conative value is one that has an inherent potentiality of being actualized. In practice this observation entails that a conative reference is actually charged by a drive within a purposive structure which is in process of trying to bring the object of that conative reference into actualization. This would be true of all *positive* conative references—specifically for all references to goal objects and quiescence patterns. Whenever an appetition is in action, therefore, the quiescence pattern for its drive is an inherent potential object of the drive in virtue of the positive conditions of quiescence characterizing the drive; and all the goal objects referred to by anticipatory sets charged by the drive are inherent potential objects of conative value for those sets. The reason is that the structure of the purpose in its actual process is tending toward the actual attainment of these potential objects.

In contrast, the objects of the *negative* conative references characteristic of aversions are never inherent potential objects, but only hypothetical ones. An object of apprehension referred to by the cognitive references of an apprehensive set is a potential object of negative conative value only on the basis of a mediating judgment which evaluates it as a probable object of riddance and pain. Successful achievement in an aversion is to avoid, not to actualize, potential objects of negative conative value.

This observation about mediating judgments in aversions leads us to consider again and amplify what was just said about the mediating judgments of appetition. Are not these also probability judgments, and in the nature of hypotheses? Would they not then institute hypothetical potential objects of conative

TABLE 6

POTENTIAL OBJECTS OF VALUE FOR APPETITIONS AND AVERSIONS IN ACTION

| Type of value | Generating conditions | Inherent potential object | Hypothetical potential object |
|---|---|---|---|
| Achievement value | Charged segments of purposive structures | Unrealized segments of purposive structures | Goal objects and objects of apprehension |
| Conative value | Impulse pattern | Quiescence pattern | None |
| | Anticipatory set | Goal object | Goal object |
| | Apprehensive set | None | Object of apprehension |
| | Riddance pattern | None | None |

value? Would not goal objects then be hypothetical potential objects of value? Yet it was just stated that goals were inherent potential objects. They are, of course, both. A mediating anticipatory judgment in virtue of its role as a hypothesis about a goal institutes a hypothetical object of value; but at the same time, in virtue of its role as a dynamic segment of an appetition tending to actualize its cognitive references, it institutes an inherent potential object of value.

The conative references of an impulse pattern, however, not being cognitive in nature, do not of themselves institute a hypothetical potential object of value. The consummatory act of an appetition is always (in reference to its drive) an inherent potential object of conative value. Once the quiescence pattern of a drive has been experienced, it may be anticipated and so become also a hypothetical potential object of conation, but only, be it observed, in virtue of an anticipatory set which emerges parallel with the impulse pattern and is not essential to the dynamics of the act.

A riddance pattern, being an actual act of riddance going on in the present, generates no potential object of conative value. As an act of aversion, however, the uncompleted phases of the riddance act, however short, would be its inherent object of achievement, just as with any more extended purposive act designed for success.

These observations about the potential objects of value for achievement and conation are summarized in table 6.

One more distinction needs to be made. The value objects listed in the table are the potential objects of value generated within appetitions and aversions with respect to certain future segments of their own structures while in action. These must be carefully distinguished from descriptions of potential objects of value generated outside the act in question. The latter are judgments *about* values as distinct from mediating judgments operating within a purposive structure. This distinction is not difficult to make with respect to inherent potential objects, but it is sometimes confusing with respect to hypothetical objects.

It is the difference between my being restless and thinking I want a walk, on the one hand, and, on the other hand, your seeing me restless and thinking I want a walk. The walk becomes a hypothetical goal object, to be sure, in both instances. But for me it is a mediating judgment within my purposive activity charged by my own restlessness. For you it is a judgment about my restlessness and its probable goal object. Your judgment is motivated by a very different drive: your professional interest as a psychologist, or some personal interest in my comfort, or perhaps irritation at my fidgeting behavior. But of course you have generated a genuine potential hypothetical object of value quite as truly as I have. The generating conditions are much the same: my restlessness in both instances, though I can feel it while you can only observe it objectively. The connecting principle is the same, the appetitive structure in action. The evidence for the probability of verification is the same. But the big difference is that my judgment is not only a probability judgment about a choice I might make, but is also the mediating judgment that enters into the dynamics of my choice. Your judgment about my possible goal lies completely outside the structure of my act. I may have no cognizance of it. Even if I do, it enters into my act simply as a contributory item in making up my mind (that is, toward commitment to my mediating judgment).

In short, a hypothetical goal object generated by a mediating judgment is in a very different status from one generated by an external judgment about value. The one enters into the dynamics of a purposive act; the other not (or only by indirection). It is only the former with which we need be particularly concerned. In other words, judgments about potential objects of value need concern us only so far as they are true of potential objects actually generated within the dynamic structure of a purposive act.

One reason for bringing out this distinction is that our study may be relieved from considering every hasty hypothesis about human motivation. Men can imagine all sorts of potential objects for other men's actions. My friend who thought I wanted a walk may have misconstrued my restlessness. His hypothesis may have been much more revelatory of his own state of mind than of mine. It showed what he would have wanted if he had felt restless. For possibly I have an aversion to walking. But, having exhibited the foregoing distinction between a hypothetical potential object based on a mediating judgment and one based on a judgment about a mediating judgment, we can reject the latter as subject matter for our study except so far as it truly describes the former. Since we are here studying values, not theories about values, we need have no concern with theories about values except so far as they appear to be reasonably true of values, or in some other way are revelatory of value facts.

3. *Potential objects of affective value.*—After the previous analyses, this topic can be quickly covered. It is first necessary to distinguish between (*a*) affective value as itself an object of conative or achievement value, (*b*) the objects of affective value as also objects of conative and achievement value, and (*c*) potential objects of affective value strictly considered without conative or achievement references.

*a*) Pleasures which lie ahead as inherent consummatory qualities of the unrealized segments of a purposive structure in action would clearly be inherent potential objects of the achievement process. Since pleasure is correlated with the release of tension which regularly occurs in the quiescence pattern of an appetition, the pleasure, as well as the other characteristics of the quiescence pattern, is an inherent potentiality of an appetitive drive in action. This makes the pleasure definitely an *inherent potential object* in virtue of the impulse pattern as its generating condition. But it does not make the pleasure necessarily an *inherent potential object of value.* For the potential object of conative value here is the quiescence pattern, not pleasure. And the potential object of achievement is success, not pleasure. Pleasure becomes an object of conative value only when (after experience of a quiescence pattern) it becomes an object of cognitive anticipation in an anticipatory set. Then it becomes a goal object and takes on the inherent potential value of any goal object.

This situation sounds paradoxical at first, but it is simply the reflection in this context of some of the issues over psychological hedonism. A drive is not necessarily for the sake of the pleasure of its achievement. But pleasure nevertheless is inherent in part of the appetitive process, and does accrue with success, and *may* (after experience) become an object of deliberate appetitive pursuit.

Of course hypothetical judgments *about* the possibility of obtaining pleasures can be made at will.

*b*) Much the same situation holds regarding the four kinds of actual objects of affection when viewed in a potential status. So far as any of these objects enter into an appetitive process, they become inherent potential objects in respect to the process, but not inherent potential objects of affective value. For instance, the immediate sensuous object of affection (the fourth kind of actual object, mentioned in §3) is the quiescence pattern of an appetitive drive. As such it is the inherent potential object of conative value for that drive. But this does not make it an inherent potential object of an *affective* value, since that accrues only after the object is actualized. By a sort of coincidence, one of the actual objects of affection is identical with a potential object of conation. But the inherent potentiality relates this object to the conative drive, not to the pleasure which comes later and only upon the quiescence of that drive. The sensuous object of a pleasure is not potential to the pleasure, but actual and contemporaneous.

*c*) Now, in regard to potential objects of affective value considered entirely apart from conation and achievement, Does affection generate any inherent potential objects of affection? The simplest answer is to say No, and this is practically true. All the various objects of affection are in its immediate field and contemporaneous. The sensuous object of pleasure is the sensuous medium of the consummatory act in which it arises. It is all actual. No future reference is involved. True enough. And yet, in considering the problem of psychological hedonism, we found that there was a pleasure drive coming out of what we called the *immediacy principle,* the tendency to maximize pleasure within the consummatory field. This tendency would, of course, institute an inherent potentiality. It institutes a sort of reference to the optimum condition for pleasurable satisfaction in that field. This would have to be admitted as an inherent potential object of affective value.

Beyond this, however, potential objects of affection would all be hypothetical. They would be based on judgments about means for maximizing pleasures and minimizing pains. In practical action these would function as mediating judgments according to the anticipatory principle (cf. chap. 14, §8, 4). They are hypotheses based upon our previous experience with pleasures and pains regarding the conditions likely to produce them.

This completes our consideration of the potential object of value. There still remains the important subject of the conditional object.


6. THE CONDITIONAL OBJECT OF VALUE

We found it necessary earlier to distinguish between the potential object of value and the object of potential value. To avoid ambiguity we decided to call the latter the *conditional object.* This is an existent object that would be valuable on the condition that someone found a value in it. The object is actual, but it is the valuing of it that is potential.

There are both inherent and hypothetical conditional objects of value. It is said, for instance, that a low-priced well-made commodity tends to capture the market. This apparently means that there is a tendency for such an object through the economic process to become valued. If this is so, it indicates an inherent potentiality of value in such an object. Nevertheless, we shall find that it will suffice for our purposes to restrict our attention to hypothetical potentialities so far as conditional objects of value are concerned. The main matters here of interest for us circulate about human judgments of the probability of certain objects being valued—that is, about their hypothetical potentialities of being valued.

In the broadest sense, there is probably nothing in the world that is not a conditional object of value, nothing that might not be conceived as possibly being valued by somebody. But, in practice, conditional objects become significant only when some person judges that they will be valued by himself at some other time or by other people, and for that reason he values them himself immediately. The geologist filled his canteen after he had drunk his fill. He did not want any more water then. But he judged that he would want water later, and through the mediation of that judgment he valued the extra water then as a conditional object of value and took the trouble to fill his canteen. Utak's fish were all conditional objects. Utak was not hungry when he caught them, but he judged he would be if he did not have a store of food for the future. It was on the mediation of that judgment that he loaded up his sled. In general, when a person judges that he *may* want something sometime, he is likely to want it *now*.

This is value on credit, value on the grounds of a belief in value—*credit value*.

The correlate of credit value is *cash value*. It was William James who established this term in the broad context of values. Credit value is tested by seeing whether the conditional object valued actually yields the value it is credited with. Cash value is the actual valuing that verifies the value credited. So cash value as well as credit value are derived from the conditional object of value. If I give a man a loan and accept a note for it, I do so on the belief that the note is good and that the borrower will return the sum to me on the promised date. The note is thereby a conditional object and has credit value. I may be able to pass it on to somebody else who also believes it is good. It keeps its credit value as long as people believe it will yield its cash value at the promised date. The belief may be right or wrong, like any other mediating judgment. People may lose faith in the note, and it may lose its credit value when, as a matter of fact, the borrower is perfectly solvent. Or again lenders may keep their faith in it and give it full credit value when actually the borrower has become incapable of paying. The final test comes when the date arrives and the holder of the note asks for his money. If the cash is forthcoming, the credit value accorded the note is justified. The potential value of the note is then actualized in its cash value.

Here we have a literal application of the relation of credit value to cash value. But James had the insight to notice that this relation extended much farther in the field of values. It extends wherever conditional objects are to be found. I pick up a log to get me across a stream. The log becomes a conditional object with credit value as long as I believe in its intended utility. If I lose faith in it upon noticing a streak of dry rot, it will thereby lose its credit value, and I will drop it. But its cash value appears in its fulfilling the expected utility which gave it its credit value. Cash value thus means for general value theory the actualization of any credit value, or the degree of actualization if the credit value is only partially justified.

The credit value is ultimately tested for its justification by the cash value it refers to. But judgments may be made about the relation of a given credit value to its prospective cash value. So people speak of a house being overvalued, or the price of a piece of furniture being out of line. This means that somebody judges that the seller's judgment of the potential value of the object is exaggerated. The seller's credit value is thought not to correspond with the object's cash value. Similarly someone may judge that a certain university is going on its reputation. This means that its credit value no longer corresponds with its cash value in teaching and research. When somebody is called a "stuffed shirt" it has a similar significance. It is a judgment on the relation between the man's reputation and his performance.

A man who attracts high credit value on the basis of his judgments about credit values is known as an *authority*, or an *expert*. He is a conditional object whose credit value lies in people's belief in his capacity to make true judgments about the credit value of objects of a sort that they desire. Theoretically, an authority is one whose judgment can be trusted on some subject, irrespective of anyone's having a use for the matter. But actually there always is a use of some sort, even if this is attenuated to that acquired drive in the truth for its own sake.

So an appraiser is an expert on the justifiable credit value of an object in relation to its financial cash value. A literary critic is an authority on the justifiable credit value of a book in relation to its aesthetic cash value. A doctor is an authority on the justifiable credit value of a person's symptoms and of the cures for them. Anyone in whom we have confidence for certain services, however casual, becomes a sort of authority in this sphere and a conditional object with credit value. So with the pilot of the plane we ride in, or the engineer of the train, or even the taxi driver. We not only have confidence in their capacity to get us to our destination, but confidence in their judgment to make the decisions necessary to get us there safely.

As is well known, credit values can pyramid on one another. They pile up through successions of mediating judgments in an amazing way. Gold has some intrinsic value, but it is valued today mainly in the *belief* that anyone will take it in exchange for almost anything we want, and therefore we accept bank notes in the belief that these will give us gold and whatever gold would buy, and we accept checks in the belief that they will yield bank notes, and we accept stock certificates in the belief that they will yield dividends in the form of checks, and so on up to investment trusts and holding companies.

A military organization is another such credit pyramid. The private obeys his officer in the belief that he has authority to command, and so for each officer up to the supreme commander. Similarly for any social organization where there are lines of authority or of trust. People follow or obey in the belief that their leaders have good judgment or power to enforce obedience. Not only systems of men but systems of thought and feeling develop interdependent credit values. The very terms 'a faith' or 'a creed' testify to the dependence of these values on credit.

And thus not only things and men become conditional objects but traditions and symbols, and symbol systems like books and legal instruments and constitutions. Of course, science as an organization of hypotheses is a system of credit values, as is any religious faith.

It is curious how long a time a system of credit values may stand without actual trial of its soundness in terms of its cash values. Often, the more suspicious people become in regard to the validity of their beliefs, the more strongly they resist the testing of their systems of credit values. And sometimes it is not easy to decide just what are the cash values which would verify the credit values—occasionally there are not any.

When, however, a mediating judgment in a credit system is proved false or ceases to be given credence, all the judgments in the system that depended upon it lose their validity and all the conditional objects of those judgments lose their value for the men who credited them, and the whole credit system crashes to a level below any belief depending upon the discredited judgment. That is what happens in a financial panic and economic depression, in the collapse of a nation at war when confidence in its armies or its leaders is lost, or in the disappearance of religions when their faith grows dim.

To avoid these disasters, it is important to keep credit systems sound, and as close as possible to their cash values. Therein lies the need for constant social criticism, and for the most complete knowledge available about man, society, and the world in which he lives. Not only does society need to keep its credit systems sound, but the individual man as well. For each man builds up his own system of beliefs to which he gives credence and by which he lives; if these are not realistic, he lets himself in for a great deal of unnecessary frustration.

Credit values are as often negative as positive. Objects believed to be sources of pain and aversion are as much conditional objects of value as are objects of pleasure and benefit. Many of these negative objects are important economic commodities. Poisons for insects, traps for skunks, and similar objects are negative credit values that men positively value for that reason. Such also are the instruments of war, including the armed forces. Such too, for the most part, are the police, law courts, and all the other agencies of law enforcement.

Conditional objects of either positive or negative value occupy so much of man's attention that some writers on value place them in the center of consideration. C. I. Lewis, in his *Analysis of Knowledge and Valuation,* virtually defines value as a property of an object. What he calls 'inherent value' is the value an object has in virtue of its being a possible object of what he calls 'intrinsic value,' which is a felt satisfaction. And he gives his major attention to inherent values. The final result is an empirical theory not very different in principle from the one we are developing. But the focus of emphasis is almost reversed. I would be tempted to say that his treatise was on the conditional object of value rather than on value proper.

One consequence of his treatment, however, is to show the need of a much more careful analysis of the nature of a conditional object than has been customary among writers on value. So far I have not raised that epistemological problem. I have been speaking rather loosely of the conditional object as that actual object, presumably continuously existent, which may at some time enter into commerce with a valuing organism. The reader has probably assumed that this is the perceptual object —the chair, the apple, the flower at the other end of the garden as perceived. The continuity of a perceptual object as perceived is, however, a very dubious hypothesis. The problem of perception is another problem all its own. And yet a fully adequate treatment of the conditional object of value would require among other things an adequate treatment of the perceptual object to determine in what degree it is fitted for the role of a conditional object of value.

One of the significant contributions of Lewis' book is that it brings this problem into the prominence it deserves. Several different kinds of objects appear in the role of conditional objects, some of them in great need of more adequate analysis and description. The most conspicuous are these: (1) the perceptual object, (2) the scientific object, (3) the commodity, (4) the moral agent, (5) the social group, (6) the social institution, (7) the work of art, (8) the man of taste, (9) the personality or character.

Each of these kinds of conditional objects of value deserves a book to itself. Books, of course, have been written on many of them. All are commonly accepted conditional objects that are capable of being objects of actual value. Some of them make demands on others. A work of art is a perceptual object and in its physical continuity a scientific object. It requires a reference to the man of good taste and also to the social group and institution. As an object of criticism it is composed mostly of hypothetical and inherent potentialities—that is, of dispositional properties. It is this complex thing that we call beautiful or ugly. A man's personality or character is hardly less complex. Nor, for that matter, is the commodity, the perceptual object, or the scientific object. In the end, the description of these objects will draw on a writer's complete theory of nature—on his basic presuppositions, the categories of his world hypothesis.

Lewis, with his emphasis on the conditional object, thought it necessary to analyze the grounds for beliefs in objects in general as a preliminary to his study of value. The same necessity does not bear upon us. With our attention centered on the value act and on the grounds for evaluative decisions, we can note, as we have, where the conditional object impinges upon the valuing activity, and leave the precise description of that object, for the most part, to another occasion. I do not mean that the precise description is not of great importance for value theory.[2] But we shall have enough to do here in tracing out certain selective systems and their ways of legislating over one another.

The various special value sciences, as we know them, seem to have been divided roughly on the basis of the kinds of conditional objects they concentrate upon. Thus economics is roughly the study of commodities, ethics the study of the moral agent and his acts, sociology the study of society and institutions, political science the study of governments, aesthetics the study of the work of art and its appreciation. The natural place to expect to find careful descriptive analyses of these objects is in those special disciplines. But if this has not always occurred, perhaps the reason is that a more adequate description of those objects is waiting upon a more adequate description of the valuing activity. And the latter is the particular responsibility of a general theory of value to supply.

So, turning aside from this tempting vista into the analysis of the various special kinds of conditional objects of value, let us resolutely follow the path of the valuing activity. Up to this point we have been dealing essentially with the single purpose. Now we must ask what happens when a number of purposes enter into a situation. First we shall consider such situations within a single individual (personal situations). This will lead us into an examination of personality structure. Then we shall consider situations which involve several individuals (social situations). And this will lead us on to look into cultural patterns for their value significance. And thence to life itself and the evolutionary process.

# 16

## The Mutual Encounter
## of Purposes in an
## Organism's Life-Space

### 1. LEWIN'S CONCEPT OF LIFE-SPACE

Up to this point we have been dealing with the structures of single purposive acts. Now we must ask what happens when a number of purposes come together. What new values emerge, what new selective systems? After the foregoing detailed study of the way values arise and are interconnected in single purposes, the sequel should proceed much faster, for we know what to look for. The remaining chapters will be concerned with the discovery and description of these other selective systems and their interrelationships.

What happens when two or more separate purposes come up in the same organism at the same time? Of course, if the two do not happen to compete for the same avenues of response and for the available energy of the organism, no selective problem will arise. A man can do many different things simultaneously without any mutual interference occurring—or not much. He can sip coffee, read a newspaper, and smoke his pipe all at once, merely adjusting the periods of sipping coffee to those when he is not drawing on his pipe. He can run his car and carry on a conversation with a companion. He can be weeding a garden, whistling a tune, and working out the details of a professional problem. There is no conflict in carrying on such activities simultaneously. Conflicts arise when a person needs his hands or other avenues of response as means for the achievement of two purposes occupying him at the same time (he cannot weed his garden and type a letter at the same time), or when one activity is taking up all his attention (he cannot carry on much of a conversation with a companion if he is just learning to drive a car).

The most fruitful detailed work so far in the study of simultaneously competing drives within the individual organism appears to be that of Kurt Lewin.[1] In dealing with this particular problem, I shall lean heavily on his methods of analysis. To schematize the area of potentially competing action, Lewin developed the concept of a *life-space*. Through this concept he was able to work out a field theory of motivation and purposive response. Some such conceptual expansion was necessary in order to describe clearly the complexity and spread of alternatives open to an intelligent organism acting, as he usually is, in a widely stimulating environment which is of interest to a variety of simultaneously active drives.

This life-space, in terms of our preceding analysis, is the field of cognitive sets as these are envisaged by the organism at any one time in relation to their potential paths of action. Often these paths of action are possible literal acts of locomotion from one point of physical space to another in the pursuit of a goal, avoiding barriers along the way. But often the barriers in Lewin's life-space are not physical barriers, nor the distance between them physical distance. It would be physical distance in my life-space if the anticipated act was to get a loaf of bread at the grocer's, and the barriers would be the physical ones of intervening houses which force me to keep to the roads. But if my purpose were to be elected to the city council, the distance in my life-space would then not be literally physical, nor would the barriers—such as the incumbents who have to be defeated and the voters whose prejudices have to be gauged. Nevertheless, the distance from where I now am to the goal of being elected can be mapped out with all its alternative open paths, and the sequence and extent of the barriers along the way, just as precisely as if these were all physical. This is what Lewin's concept of a life-space makes possible.

Life-space is not, then, a literal physical space. But, as Lewin often emphasizes, neither is it entirely a conceptual fiction. It is descriptive of actual relations holding among anticipated sequences of acts, and of the degrees of freedom or of obstruction for these acts. Our schemes for the structures of appetitions and aversions can easily be amalgamated with Lewin's life-space. The limitation of our schemes is that they are linear, whereas his life-space is two- or three-dimensional as the conditions require. The linear formulation, I believe, is clearer as long as we can confine our study to a single purposive structure, for it clearly shows the flow of the charge of the drive. But a multi-dimensional schematization is clearer (and necessary) when a number of appetitions and aversions are simultaneously in action: such a scheme brings out the structure of the organism's anticipated and apprehended field of action.

## 2. SOME ILLUSTRATIONS OF LIFE-SPACE

Let us consider a few very simple illustrations of the concept of life-space. Imagine a Mr. Jones who has come to a busy intersection of two streets, Main running north and south and Market running east and west. He is on his way to a store on the west side of Main Street, south of Market, to get a loaf of bread. He has just reached the northeast corner of the intersection, and a red light has gone on for the Main Street crossing and a green light for Market Street. There is a mailbox in front of him on the corner, and a lady beside the mailbox, and at an interval a newsstand by the edge of Market Street.

As a modern citizen conditioned to city living, the space before him becomes structured immediately in a pattern of positive and negative potential values. He has a vigorous group of apprehensive sets against crossing streets with red lights showing, and against jay-walking. So all of Main Street is negatively valued. So is Market Street except for the pedestrian crossing. This crossing, however, is positively valued, as are all the sidewalks so far as he thinks of them. The mailbox in front of him and the lady, who does not appear to be moving, are obstacles in his way and so are negatively valued. (They would jar him, or make him feel badly, if he bumped into them.) So is the

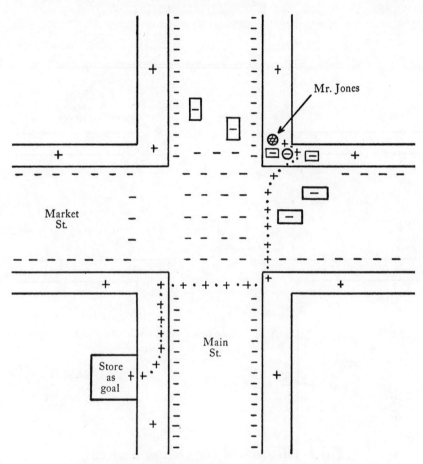

Fig. 1. Life-space of man crossing a street.

newsstand farther to his left. The cars waiting to cross Main Street on Market, one of them butting into the pedestrian zone, are potentially dangerous and objectionable, and so are negatively valued. And the car just moving into the intersection from Main Street is very dangerous, for it might take a whim to turn east on Market. The anticipated path indicated by a dotted line is positively valued, with the expectation that the traffic light will change when Mr. Jones gets across the street.

This field structure of positive and negative values (fig. 1) is the life-space of Mr. Jones at the moment we have been

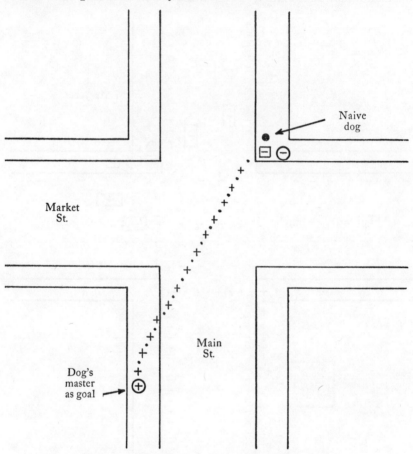

Fig. 2. Life-space of dog crossing a street.

describing. And it brings to light that the seemingly simple appetitive act of crossing the street to get to the store is actually a resultant of a large number of more or less conflicting purposes.

Imagine a dog unaccustomed to city traffic placed where our Mr. Jones was. Sighting his master at the location of the store which was Mr. Jones's goal, the dog would try to take the straightest path, jay-walking right to the store, and might well get run over in the attempt.

The naïve dog's life-space would have been much simpler than Mr. Jones's in this situation. It would have indicated only one line of purposive references—one appetitive goal with its subordinate acts in direct line with the goal object. It would have looked like figure 2. In the dog's life-space no conflicts in getting to his master would have been anticipated.

### 3. VALENCE AND VECTOR IN LIFE-SPACE

From these two examples we can bring out the main features of Lewin's concept of life-space and its clarifying power in exhibiting the interaction of purposive drives in complex situations.

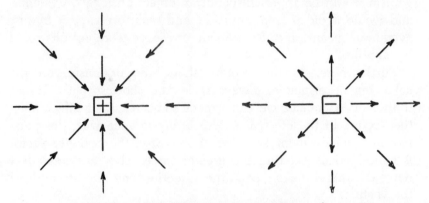

Fig. 3. Contrast in field structures: an object of appetition and an object of aversion.

Lewin calls the value which an organism places upon an object in its life-space the *valence* of the object. If it is an object of appetition, the valence is positive $\boxed{+}$ ; if an object of aversion, the valence is negative $\boxed{-}$ . The relation of the object to the organism in the organism's life-space he calls a *vector*. A vector has the properties of direction and strength. The length of a vector is proportional to the strength of a valence.

Amalgamating these concepts with ours, we may identify his vector with our conative references, and the strength of the vector with the intensity of the drive charging a set of references. His positive or negative valence indicates whether the drive is appetitive or aversive in character. The object to which the valence is attributed is our *actual* object of conative value. It is the object actually charged by the drive which is directed upon it. It is, accordingly, our anticipated goal object, or our dreaded object of apprehension, or our conditions of quiescence, or our object of riddance.[2]

Through these concepts the contrast between the field structure of an object of appetition or positive valence and of an object of aversion or negative valence is striking (cf. fig. 3). The one is a convergent, the other a divergent, field of vectors. An organism would expect to approach an object of positive valence from any side, by any avenue or means, and if cut off from one approach would seek another. Contrariwise, an organism would be apprehensive of an object of negative valence, and would avoid it from any side, and seek to escape it by any avenue or means, and if one mode of escape were cut off would try another.

Furthermore, as the vectors show, the organism, on the achievement principle, always seeks the shortest path. Hence if there is a conflict we can expect some resultant effect upon the vectors in the life-space. Also in accordance with the conative and achievement criterion of intensity, the stronger vector is conceived as exerting the greater force. The resultant effect depends, therefore, on both the direction and the strength of the vectors.

## 4. THREE BASIC TYPES OF CONFLICT

With these concepts, Lewin describes the three basic types of purposive conflicts.

1. There is the conflict between two positive valencies. A child has a choice between going on a picnic or playing with his friends. This sort of conflict is easy to solve if one attraction is much stronger than the other. If they are about equal, oscillation may occur. It is the theoretical dilemma of Aesop's ass, which, according to the story, starved between two equal heaps of hay. Adult men develop techniques for forcing a decision

under such circumstances, even if it comes to the ultimate resort of tossing a penny. The guiding maxim that mediates the quicker decision is that indecision under such conditions is itself a deci-

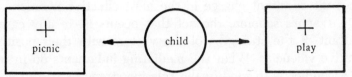

Fig. 4. Conflict between two positive valencies.

sion, and usually the worst one. The maxim, together with whatever device is employed to throw the decision one way or the other, amounts to an inhibiting force on one of the drives, which automatically gives preponderance of strength to the other one. Then action proceeds in the direction of the stronger drive.

2. The second type of basic conflict is that in which an object is at the same time positively and negatively valenced. This is the condition of ambivalence. A child wants to climb a tree but

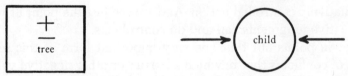

Fig. 5. The condition of ambivalence.

is afraid. If his fear is much greater than the attraction, he retires; if the attraction is stronger, he climbs the tree. Here for adults the problem of commitment is often focal. Even if the positive and negative valencies are unequal, it is often better practice to give full commitment to one choice or the other. If one is on a high springboard contemplating a dive and afraid of it, it is better, having to dive, to act with full commitment and inhibit the fear. For the halfhearted dive is the most dangerous. In contrast, a certain amount of fear in a child climbing a tree may make the act safer.

All that we discussed earlier about inertial and intelligent commitment and the mediating function of the probability judgment and the feasibility judgment (chap. 4, §§4–10) comes in for a more extended application here. These mediating judgments are the experienced person's instruments for evaluating a situation involving conflict and arriving at a rational decision. They function as inhibiting agents on one vector or another so as to direct the resultant charge in the most effective manner.

On Lewin's scheme, the act that occurs is, in any case, the resultant of the strengths of the vectors with their positive or negative valencies. What the mediating judgments do in resolving a conflict is to modify the relative strengths of the vectors. This is what makes the difference between acting impulsively and acting on the basis of learning and experience after judgment and reflection. A child who climbs a tree thoughtlessly may not notice a rotten branch, but a child who climbs with a sense of the danger (that is, under the control of a mediating probability or feasibility judgment) will be on the alert for the sources of danger. The resultant act is the resultant of the strengths of the vectors, in Lewin's terms, in either instance. But now we can clearly see, through Lewin's mode of analysis combined with ours, just what makes the difference between impulsive and evaluatively controlled action. And we see just the point at which evaluative judgments can and do control acts.

Lewin points out that one very important form of this second type of conflict is that in which a barrier or other negative valence is interposed between the organism and an object of positive valence. This is the situation of reward for an unpleasant task. It is one of the devices of teaching. If a dog does his trick, he gets a bone. The attraction for the bone is sufficient to overcome the negative valence for the trick. There must, however, be no other way to get his bone than by the performance of the trick. It is as if the attractive bone were surrounded by the irksome obstruction of the trick (fig. 6). If the dog wants the bone strongly enough, he will do the trick to get it. The coaxing of a reluctant dog to do a parlor trick takes the form of adding to the bone's attraction by dangling it and turning it to show the meat; or it takes the form of reducing the felt obstruction by bringing it close to the dog's nose; or, lastly, it may take the form of adding other inducements to those already present, such as harsh words or words of encouragement. It is much the same in teaching a child to ride a bicycle; much the same again in surrounding a coveted

A.B. or Ph.D. degree by a barrier of courses with units and grades, or surrounding an intrinsic interest in a subject matter with the techniques required to master it.

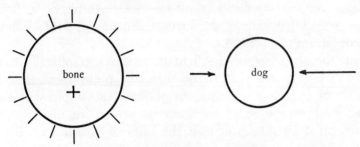

Fig. 6. Negative valence interposed between organism and object of positive valence.

3. The third type of basic conflict is that between two negative valencies. Lewin's example is that of a child who is threatened with punishment in order to induce him to perform a task he does not want to do (fig. 7). As Lewin points out, the tend-

Fig. 7. Conflict between two negative valencies.

ency in this situation is for the child to abandon the field. The structure of the life-space of a child caught between two negative valencies is represented in figure 8. The vectors tend to push

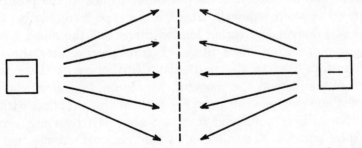

Fig. 8. Life-space of child caught between two negative valencies.

the child out of the field at right angles to the line joining the two negative valencies. This represents the shortest path of escape from the distasteful situation. This is, of course, simply a more complex application of the fact exhibited in figure 3, that a negative valence produces a centrifugal field of forces in an organism's life-space.

From the structure of the field it becomes graphically clear, as Lewin points out, that if the threat of punishment is to be effective in inducing the child to perform the unpleasant task, the lines of escape must be rendered still more disagreeable. Barriers must be set up against the lines of escape (fig. 9), so

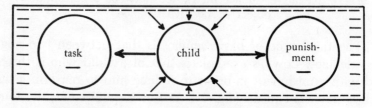

Fig. 9. Barriers set up against lines of escape.

that the least disagreeable thing to do in the totally disagreeable situation is to perform the task.

In almost any actual situation all these basic types of conflict are combined in various ways. For Mr. Jones at the street crossing (fig. 1) there was a type 1 conflict between the two positively valenced opposite sidewalks, but the green light for Main Street gave greater strength to the Market Street crossing. There was a type 2 conflict between the negative valence of passing in front of the dangerous cars in order to get to the positively valenced opposite sidewalk. There was a type 3 conflict between the lesser danger of crossing Market Street and the much greater danger of crossing Main Street. Figure 1 represents the field relationships due to the particular distribution of these three types of conflicts at the moment. Mr. Jones, of course, did not figure these out pair by pair. He took in the situation with an intuitive glance, perceived it as a whole. His response was to the total pattern. Nevertheless, in this glance he made the discriminations which can be made analytically explicit only by

diagrams and comparisons such as we have been spreading out
in these half-dozen pages. His resultant response showed his
discriminating insight regarding the dynamic structure of the
situation, just as the dog's jay-walking (fig. 2) showed his total
lack of insight into the potentialities of that very situation.

## 5. COMPARISON OF THE STRUCTURE OF LIFE-SPACE AND PURPOSIVE STRUCTURE

These illustrations of the nature of life-space and the types of
conflicts arising therein have prepared us to consider the difference between the structure of a life-space and its mode of selective action and the structure of a purposive act and its mode of
selection. A purposive structure shows the dynamic relations of
the various means to an end, and the way in which a means is
accepted or rejected; a life-space shows the dynamic relations
among a variety of ends and the way in which one of a number
of competing ends is selected. Purposive structures deal with the
selection of means; life-spaces, with the selection of ends.

If we look closely into the details, we shall see that this distinction does not, to be sure, hold absolutely, but it is essentially
correct. A life-space deals with means also, as the diagram of
Mr. Jones's life-space at the street crossing abundantly shows.
Most of the objects there are valued positively or negatively in
terms of their being means toward his getting to the store. And
a purposive structure frequently incorporates conflicts of ends.
Whenever there is a blockage of a drive due to some object in
its path, a competing drive in the form of a riddance pattern or
apprehension charged by an injective is automatically indicated.
Most frustrations encountered in the course of a purposive act
are, on a broader view, conflicts of ends. Purposive structures
do, in this manner, deal with conflicts among ends, also. But it
is nonetheless true that purposive structures are the selective
systems for means, and life-spaces the selective systems for ends,
in a man's actions.

Neither can be reduced to the other. This can be shown by an
example of the contrast of dynamic effects between a conflict
of means and a conflict of ends. For a simple choice of means,

consider a hungry man's choice between two meats on a menu. For a conflict of ends, consider a man who is both hungry and thirsty and has to choose which drive to satisfy in advance of the other. The first is basically a choice of means; when the man has made his choice and taken steak, for instance, he has no appetite left for chops. Just one drive was operative, and either goal object would have been a means of fully satisfying it. One might be a more effective means than the other, and there are realistic grounds of choice. But the conflict is not among drives, but only over the most effective way of satisfying a drive.

As between satisfying hunger or thirst, however, there is a conflict of ultimate consummatory ends, and the satisfaction of the one leaves the other unsatisfied. This kind of conflict a purposive structure cannot resolve. And it is precisely this kind of conflict that Lewin's life-space is designed to resolve. Consequently, the life-space selective system cannot be reduced to that of a purposive structure. A choice between two or more drives is not the same as a choice between means for the satisfaction of a single drive.

But neither can the choice of means be reduced to a special case of a choice of ends. The dynamic interrelations of subordinate to superordinate acts in a purposive structure are lost sight of in life-space, and show only in their momentary tension effects. It is the purposive structures that bind the successive life-spaces into a living whole. This is why our earlier diagrams of appetitions and aversions cannot be absorbed without residue into Lewin's life-space diagrams. Purposive structure and life-space are two distinct selective systems: one is primarily explanatory of choices of means for the satisfaction of a single drive; the other, primarily explanatory of choices between competing drives or the terminal potential objects of such drives. Neither selective system is reducible to the other.

Three important corollaries follow from the foregoing observation. First, any hypothesis involving a complete relativity of means and ends is untenable. This position is held by many pragmatists. It amounts to a denial of the distinction we have just observed between a purposive structure's selection of means toward the terminal satisfaction of a single drive, and a life-space's selection of a resultant act to reduce the tensions among a number of competing drives. It amounts to a reduction of purposive structures to life-spaces or vice versa. It amounts to a denial of the distinction between (1) a choice among alternative goal objects to satisfy a single appetitive drive where any correct choice would bring quiescence to the drive, and (2) a choice among competing drives where a choice that satisfies one drive leaves the other unsatisfied. For the satisfaction of a drive is a terminal end so far as that drive is concerned, and is not a means at all.

The quiescence of an aversion and the quiescence pattern (consummatory act) of an appetition are ultimate terminal values —absolute ends of achievement with respect to the purposive drives charging these acts. This fact is what the doctrine of a general relativity of means and ends implicitly denies. The doctrine is consequently untenable in failing to take account of this crucial fact.

The rejection of the doctrine as a general hypothesis does not, however, deny relativity of means and ends in limited ranges. Where there is a succession of subordinate acts directed toward the attainment of a terminal satisfaction, the goal object of each act in the series is an end for the acts subordinate to it, and a means for those superordinate to it. It is means or end relative to its role in the purposive structure. But the final consummatory act of the series which brings the drive to quiescence is the absolutely terminal end for the series, and within that purposive structure not a means at all. Similarly with aversions and their objects of apprehension.

Nor does the rejection of the doctrine of general relativity of means and ends carry with it an implication that the terminal satisfaction of one drive may not be a means to the satisfaction of another drive. The terminal enjoyment of a meal can serve also as a means toward doing the day's work. A terminal satisfaction may have many value relations with other acts in a person's life-space. The act is nonetheless terminal for its drive whatever other value relationships may also appear.

The second corollary from the fact that life-space cannot be reduced to purposive structures or vice versa is a confirmation of a multiple drive theory (see chap. 8, §3) as against a single drive theory. For a single drive theory of motivation consistently carried through amounts to an assertion that all conflicts involve choices of alternative ways of releasing energy from a single source. They are all choices among alternative means of satisfying that one drive. It is conflicts of drives that are here denied. So, on the single drive theory, it should follow that hunger could be satisfied by drinking and thirst by eating. Saltines, then, should quench thirst, and plain water satisfy hunger!

This corollary is roughly the converse of the first. The first says that conflicts over means must not be confused with conflicts over ends; this one says that conflicts over ends must not be mistaken for conflicts over means. If life-space selects primarily among ends (and purposive structures among means), then there must be a plurality of drives to generate a plurality of ends among which life-space can make a selection. So the selectivity of life-space confirms the multiple drive theory.

The third corollary has to do with another typical feature of pragmatic value theory, in this instance confirming it. It confirms the interconnectivity of values and the effect of means upon ends in life-space, in contrast to the strict subordination of means to ends in a purposive structure.

In the complexities of human life we rarely act under the motivation of one drive only. Several purposive structures are usually operating simultaneously in our life-spaces, and so the total situation has to be considered. Then a means for one drive may prove an obstruction for another; hence an end may have to be given up because of the means involved. This is a common enough observation. I should like to smoke, but find I do not have a match. To obtain a match, however, would interfere with my present reading; so I give up the idea of smoking for the nonce. Many pragmatists assume that such facts show that ends may be subordinated to means as well as means to ends—and thus again lead to a breakdown of the contrast between their respective modes of selection. But clearly the facts do not justify any such conclusion. The conflict is not between a means and an end but between one drive (reading) and another drive (smoking) for which the need of a match happened to be a means and so precipitated the conflict. The dynamics of the two purposive structures proceeds as usual, with the charge flowing from end to means—superordinate to subordinate act. The match was wanted as a means to smoking; the smoking drive charging the subordinate need of a match came into conflict with the reading drive; and the reading drive, in this conflict of *ends*, proved stronger.

Yet the pragmatic insight is true that means may often alter ends in life-space conflicts, but only because the means are charged by other ends and the conflict of ends causes a frustration of one or the other end. The insight is an important one. For it brings out the fact that purposive structures have to adjust to one another when they come into contact in life-space. And the mode of adjustment is a resultant act effected by a life-space as a selective system.

Having thus become assured that a life-space is a selective system in its own right and is not reducible to purposive structures, we must next examine its mode of action in somewhat the same detail that we used in describing the operation of purposive structures. The two main features for determining the selective operation of a purposive structure, we found, were its dynamics and its mediating judgments. Taking these features as a clue, we shall investigate what constitutes the dynamics and what the mediating agents for a life-space. These will be the topics of the next two sections.

## 6. The Dynamics of Life-Space

1. *Dynamics of personal situation versus dynamics of social situation.*—All the dynamics of life-spaces comes from drives of purposive structures. (This statement will have to be qualified later, in chap. 21, §4, but not in a manner that affects the present argument.) It consists, however, not in these drives severally but in their simultaneous interactions within the confines of a single life-space. It consists in a resultant effect. The resultant effect is not simple in most instances, however, but is highly channeled by mediating judgments which can often alter the total dynamic configuration of a life-space. The difference

between Mr. Jones's life-space and that of the naïve dog at the corner of Market and Main streets was due primarily not to the differences in their drives (though these were different) but to the differences in their mediating judgments. So, in describing the dynamics of life-space, it is very difficult not to trespass on the subject of the mediating agents which channel the drives. But for clarity's sake we shall do our best to keep the two apart.

The statement that the dynamics of life-space comes from the drives of purposive structures has a far-reaching consequence. Since these drives have their seat in individual organisms, the direct resultant effects of these drives upon one another also have their seat in individual organisms. The field in which these drives operate directly upon one another is the field of individual response. The resultant effects we are now describing, which constitute the selective action of life-space as a selective system, all go on within the reaction systems of single organisms.

Consider the three types of basic conflict described earlier with their characteristic field structures. These are all conflicts between drives within a single organism. A child is faced with a choice between two attractive positive goals, or between a positive and a negative goal where the latter must be accepted in order to attain the former, or between two negative goals of different intensity one of which must be accepted as the lesser of the evils. These are all conflicts of a single individual's own drives within the arena of his own responses. The life-space, the conflict of drives, the resultant solution, the whole selective system, goes on within the individual organism.

Something quite different occurs in a conflict between individuals. We have then stepped out of the field of an individual's life-space. Another selective system comes into play involving factors which are not included in the present field of action. It is the difference between *my* choice whether I shall drink a glass of water first or eat a slice of bread, as against *a* choice whether you or I shall drink a glass of water first. The first choice is determined within my individual life-space, and the resolution is found and the selection is made by my own drives in their own field of mutual interaction. The second choice is made in a field that extends beyond my drives and on the pressure of forces that lie outside my drives. The second is, of course, the field of social obligation. It poses special problems not involved in the first, which can fitly be identified with the field of individual prudence.[3]

The empirical school of individualistic moralists from Butler down have, with ample justification, been worried about the gap between these two selective systems: the field of prudence within which choices are made with inner intuitive clarity, in accord with the motivating interests of the individual; and the field of social obligation that often demands choices of the individual for the social good which the individual is reluctant to accept.

The issue is serious if a moralist tries to limit value to individual life-space, or, in other words, to prudence or enlightened self-interest. But the issue evaporates if we follow the operation of selective systems wherever they lead. A thoroughgoing empiricist cannot deny that social situations do make themselves felt as selective agencies, and do induce individuals to conform to their demands. If the selective action of a drive within a single purposive structure institutes a value, and the selective action upon conflicting drives within an individual's life-space institutes a resultant value, it is hard to see why the selective action of a social institution upon men in a social situation should not also institute a value. The only question would be the empirical one whether and how far one of these selective systems could be shown to legislate over the other. So, by our manner of approach, we do not have to worry about the gap that opens up between the values of individual impulse and those of social obligation. Two different selective systems are observed here. There is indeed a gap between them. But both systems, as grounds for decisions, institute values. The only question (which will occupy us in chap. 21) is which selected value should have priority over the other, and under what conditions.

Let me amplify a little, for this is an important contrast. Individual life-space is to be viewed as one selective system clearly distinguishable from that of the social situation, which is another. This distinction empirically justifies the further distinction between the individual and his personal values, and society and its overindividual values. The evidences for the distinction come mainly under two heads. First, the dynamics of the two systems is different. The dynamics of the one comes entirely from the drives of a single individual; that of the other involves the impact of drives from outside the individual. Second, the effects of the two systems and the ways in which they correct errors are different. For life-space the resultant effects arise from the simple projection of the dynamics and mediating structures of the very appetitions and aversions we have been studying, and errors are corrected by increased tensions within the individual's dynamic field. But for the social situation the effects involve new channels through the structures of social institutions which are not simple projections of the mediating judgments of appetitions and aversions, and corrections are made by social sanctions. Thus, in both the dynamics and the effects, the selective process is quite different in the two systems.

Since the dynamics of individual life-space is that of the drives themselves instituting their own resultant action, it follows that the individual goes along with these results and finds them intuitively satisfying, reasonable, and internally compelling. The resultant action is spontaneously arrived at inside the individual and without external social compulsion.

Now it dawns upon us that what we are here describing is the dynamics of free will or free choice. What is traditionally called individual choice and individual freedom is nothing other than the selective action of life-space. And when moralists and political theorists speak of the values of individual freedom, they are referring to the unimpeded action of individual life-space as a selective system. Individual freedom is encroached upon whenever some other selective system, such as a political institution operating in a social situation, brings pressure upon certain elements within an individual's life-space requiring a resultant effect which would not arise from the spontaneous activity of the individual's own drives in the situation. The individual is then forced to make a decision in acquiescence to a social demand. It may be evaluatively justifiable that he should do so. But some of his freedom and resultant satisfaction are lost thereby.

This is not to deny that every act a man performs in a society is performed in his own life-space as a resultant of the appetitive and aversive drives in action there. But it is emphatically to point out that a social demand which an individual violates will bring its sanction to bear on the individual and induce him to conform —or else!

A social demand requiring a response to a situation which is not a response spontaneously evoked by any of the drives possessed by the individual at the time will be felt as an overindividual compulsion. It requires an act he would not naturally perform apart from the social compulsion. He may act anyway, in defiance of the social demand, just as he wants to, whereupon, if the social pattern is vigorous, he will meet the unpleasant impact of the social sanctions. There will be disapprovals, fines, deprivations or threats of these—all riddance patterns evoking aversive actions which as a rule finally bring him into conformity and a reluctant willingness to do what he did not want to do.

Social compulsion usually makes itself felt by modifying the resultant action in the life-space of a docile individual. It injects a new drive or an increased incentive into a given life-space. The individual *learns* to respect and respond to the social demand. (Of course, social compulsion may act in a purely physical way by bodily removing an individual from an objectionable place— lifting him off the street into the police wagon, imprisoning him, or, in the last resort, executing him.) But social compulsion usually works not entirely outside of but *through* the individual life-space. Social compulsion operates largely by *teaching* the individual to conform.

This fact leads to the ideal of a perfect conformity between social pattern and individual desire. It is a little early to discuss this. But since it has come up, we should perhaps touch upon it, particularly as it suggests the obliteration of the gap between the social selective system and the individual. Is that gap perhaps somewhat fictitious or unnecessary? [4]

2. *Problem of harmony between life-space and social situation.*—The gap is certainly not fictitious, but is it necessary? Theoretically a congruence can be brought about by adjusting the social system to conform to the individual, or the individual

to the social system, or a combination of the two. The first is in practice impossible because of the diversity of men's interests and the scarcity of means to satisfy them. But it can be approximated through mutual compromise and tolerance, and in this form constitutes the ideal solution for political individualism.

The second is also probably impossible in practice except for brief periods (if even then) because of the constant pressure of the instincts for full satisfaction. But it can be approximated by means of persistent social pressure through the development of derived drives guided so as to conform to the social pattern. This is the ideal of political socialism. So educate every individual in a society, particularly in his youth when his habits are in a formative stage, that he acquires a repertory of derived drives in conformity with the social pattern. Then the individual would spontaneously do what the channels of his society require him to do. So far as the society is successful in this program, the individual's actions would be free, since they would be resultants of his own drives; at the same time they would be conformist, since they would be the actions required by the social pattern.

This solution, however, appears better in theory than in practice, though there are many examples of its being carried out to a fairly high degree of approximation. The difficulty is that many of the acquired drives most essential to high morale and social solidarity (when not based on individual tolerance and compromise) are in the nature of sublimations based on repressions (cf. chap. 11, §5). This leaves an uncontrolled residue of frustration; the actions of the individual turn out to be not as free as they seem. There is a continuous smoldering rebellion, and hence a continuous individual pressure to escape from the demands of a socially disciplined society, even for highly indoctrinated individuals.

To offset this constant pressure of the instincts, such a society must constantly keep in view of its members the reasons (true or fictitious) justifying the discipline. The very fact that this sort of justification needs to be kept up shows how far the practice falls short of the ideal. For in the ideal conformist solution, every individual should find the same spontaneous satisfaction in following the customs of his society that he would find in following

his own instincts and desires. Indeed, the two should have become indistinguishable. Then there would be no need for social
discipline or the parading of social sanctions, even if this be only
the authority of the elders. But every human society has its
unindoctrinated babies continuously flowing into its midst, and
these keep arriving with the old original repertoire of instincts
not conforming to the social pattern. To mold these into conformity, the social sanctions will always be required.

So the socialistic ideal is not humanly attainable either. Indeed,
the very conception of the docile individual might suggest that
a perfect adjustment between his impulses and his environment
would be "not for him." That is a solution open to nondocile
organisms such as ants and bees, if the description fits even them.
Their instincts could exactly conform to the demands of their
social organization. But not so for docile man, whose special gift
of intelligence and exceptional learning capacity signifies exceptional readiness to be restless in an environment not congenial to his drives. He is the animal notorious for not being
satisfied with his conditions, and conspicuous for changing conditions to suit him better. He has never been content to take his
physical environment as he found it. In consequence he has
changed the face of the world. It would be surprising if he were
ever content to take his social environment as he finds it. He will
always be looking for ways to make it more satisfying to his
desires. As long as he persists in looking, and thinks he might
find something better, he will not be an ideal conformist.

So, in practice, something between the individualistic and
the socialistic ideal is the lot of man, and this means that there
will never be a complete congruence between the values of the
individual and of society, or, in our terms, between the selection
of acts made in life-space and the selections made in a social
situation. The two selective systems will never completely coin-
cide. And that is why man will always have to consider the
peculiarly ethical problem of which of these selective systems
will legislate over the other and under what conditions.

We cannot, then, expect an individual's judgment of values to
become merged and absorbed into an overindividual field of
values. A man's life-space, his personal decision resulting from

the spontaneous action of his impulses under the guidance of his experience and his own best judgment, has an indefeasible title in the realm of value. This is the seat of his free will. And his decision, when thus freely made and carefully considered, goes by the name of prudence.

3. *Prudence.*—A man has prudence who acts according to his own best interest. Such action may be impulsive and implicitly evaluative, or reflective and deliberately evaluative. Either way, an evaluative criterion is implicitly or explicitly involved. The criterion is, of course, the selective system of life-space itself.

It is widely recognized that a person does not need much persuasion to be prudent. So much so that it is often questioned as a moral criterion. For prudence does not take into consideration the interests of other persons except so far as they bear on the individual's own interests. But for us as students of value it is a matter of some moment, and very revealing of the dynamics of evaluation that prudence is not usually regarded as needing much external sanctioning. A person tends to be prudent of his own accord. That is to say, a person tends to maximize the values of his life-space, and of the sequence of his life-spaces without artificial inducement, such as social approbation, laws, police, and the like. This is rather astonishing if it is not simply taken for granted. How does it happen?

Prudence would not be surprising on a single drive theory. A man with a single drive naturally, from the very structure of a purposive act, seeks to achieve its satisfaction as quickly and fully as possible. But on a multiple drive theory, which our studies of purposive motivation impel us to accept, why should an individual try to maximize the values of all the drives he has in a life-space or over a span of time rather than to favor one drive and let the rest go? So far as the dynamics of any one drive with its purposive structure is concerned, our descriptions indicate that this drive would be completely egoistic in its action. Each drive on its own, unless blocked off and inhibited by some other drive, undertakes to achieve satisfaction in a consummatory act if it is an appetition, or through quiescence of disturbance or apprehension if it is an aversion. Now, why does a person prudently consider all the drives competing for his favor and try to get the maximum amount of satisfaction possible in view of the total situation? Of course, this is just what the resultant act achieves in the structure of a life-space. But how is this motivated?

On a naïve multiple drive theory, with every drive possessing its own private reservoir of nontransferable energy, there would be nothing to prevent cutthroat competition among the drives, with each drive using up its energy battling obstructing drives and trying to achieve its sole satisfaction. The organism would be in a continual state of turmoil and indecision. In fact, something very much like that happens occasionally in an acute state of depression. Why is this not a man's usual state?

The ordinary answer is that men are intelligent and reasonable enough not to waste their energies in that way. But how do they use their intelligence to make sensible decisions between ends and among ultimate competing drives? It is not exactly the same as among the subordinate acts of a purposive structure. Here it is not merely a matter of channeling a drive through a succession of true mediating judgments: it is a question of adjudicating among a group of competing drives.

The adjudicating requires judgment, clearly. In adjudicating among drives, mediating judgments will be needed to facilitate some drives and inhibit others. But, as we have seen, mediating judgments do not have in them any drive of their own. That would lead to an ideomotor theory with all its problems. Hence there must be some drive source to charge the mediating judgments which are employed to adjudicate among drives in a life-space.

These reflections lead to another confirmation of the modified multiple drive theory we developed in chapter 8, §3. There we contrasted the naïve multiple drive theory on the analogy of separate unconnected reservoirs of power with a modified multiple drive theory on the analogy of depositors with credit on the central capital of a bank. Each appetitive and aversive drive has its credit on the central store of energy and can draw on that energy up to the amount of its credit. In addition to these is the injective drive, held in reserve, ready to act whenever an emergency calls for more energy than some particular drive, in difficulty, has credit for. The distinctive feature of our hypothesis is that it provides for a unitary distributing center of energy along with a multiple claim on portions of that energy. It combines certain characteristics of the single drive theory with the distinctive characteristics of the multiple drive theory.

Such a modified multiple drive theory is needed to account for the natural prudence of men and animals in a complex personal situation. For the organism is not simply pitting one drive against another in the resolution of the tensions within a life-space. It is also distributing its energy for the most effective action within its view of the situation. The resultant act is the shortest path for relieving the complex of tensions in view of the *total* situation.

Moreover (a very important point to notice), the injective, when resorted to, is always on the side of the strongest drive—the drive presumably most pressing to be satisfied for the quiescence of the tensions. For what, in terms of life-space, is the blockage of a drive? It is a counterdrive. It is the bruising resistance of a barrier or the fear of it. It is the hard climb up the hill or the dread of it. And when an injective comes to the assistance of a blocked drive, it is assisting the stronger drive. It comes to the geologist's thirst drive, not to the pain of climbing the ridge. If a gust of wind suddenly blows Mr. Jones's hat into the street as he stands on the corner, the injective pours into his drive to recover the hat, not to his fear of the open street. But if a car seemed to be coming too fast, the injective would switch to the fear of the car and stop him from pursuing his hat. An injective adds conviction to an act that might otherwise be weak and ineffective. But notice that it always comes to the stronger drive (stronger partly because it is considered most feasible) to add more strength to it.

This means that the injective drive acts very much in the manner of the supposititious single drive theory. It steers the reserve energy of the organism into the channel making the strongest claim. And this means, further, that there is a central reserve drive available to strengthen action in the midst of a multitude of conflicting drives favorable to that act which appeals to the organism as most feasible in view of the total situation.

An organism therefore tends, as we say, to be naturally prudent according to his lights. According to the modified multiple drive theory, the rival claims of the multiple drives receive their energy from a central common store; so they all share in the same energy, and consequently share in the tendency of the system as a whole to attain over-all quiescence. The various drives are not insulated from one another. In spite of their rival claims, a large expenditure of energy in the satisfaction of one drive diverts action away from other weaker drives. And then very little inner conflict develops. This is particularly true in situations in which drives are severely blocked and injectives are called into action. For an injective when aroused throws all its energy into whatever channel seems, in view of the total situation, to be most demanding.

The dynamics of life-space or the personal situation is thus intrinsically prudential. A man naturally tends to look after his own interests. We can now see why, in terms of the dynamics of his drives. And perhaps we can see also why the same cannot be said of man in his relations with the social or interpersonal situation. For a man is not disposed by the inner functioning of his drives to act in the same way for the general interest of his society. Individual men in a society are insulated energy systems. They do not draw on a common store of social energy. The power of a society is the result of the organization and the contribution of the powers of the individuals that compose it. Individuals in a society have to be persuaded or compelled to consider the interests of society as a whole. In a society we have dynamically what amounts to an insulated multiple drive system, every individual functioning as a separate dynamic center with his own private store of energy in no way literally transferable to another. This is not the dynamic setup within an individual organism. A man's drives are not insulated energy centers: they are nontransferable claims (barring certain mutations) upon a common energy source. Accordingly, an individual organism seeks by the very structure of his dynamic system to maximize the values of the total system.

This contrast between the dynamics of a social system and of an individual organism accounts for the appearance of the gap at this point between the individual and society. The motivation of a resultant act in which the claims of diverse drives are adjusted to bring about the maximum reduction of tension within an individual's life-space can, through our previous analysis, be easily followed. The drives themselves, in their relations with the central energy source, generate this resultant solution. But why an individual should be expected to sacrifice his interests to the interests of others is not accounted for in the same terms. It cannot be accounted for in terms of an individual's own system of drives. The sacrifice of individual satisfactions to social interest consequently seems irrational in terms of the dynamics of the individual. Such sacrifice from the point of view of the individual appears always as an evil—though no doubt a necessary one—unless a man is indoctrinated to repress it.

This result is not to be lightly viewed either. It constitutes the dynamic base of individualism, the entirely justifiable ground for the individual's bias for the individual. It forces a society to justify its demands in the long run against the pressures of individual satisfaction.

A social situation is not simply an expansion of the life-space of a personal situation into interpersonal proportions. In a personal life-space the tensions are all generated out of one common energy system with drives making their several claims upon it. But in a social situation when a number of different persons are in conflict, each person is his own dynamic center, and there is no common store of energy on which each person draws. The dynamic structure of a social situation is therefore quite different from that of a personal situation. Its mode of functioning is through the agency of all the social sanctions, such as religion, custom, law, police, and armies. By these social sanctions a society compels individuals to expend their energy for the welfare of society. The energies of individuals do not spontaneously coördinate for social welfare.

Dynamically, therefore, the gap between the personal situation, or life-space, and the social situation is descriptively justified. The ethical writers who called attention to it were in effect making a discrimination between two distinct selective systems with distinct dynamic structures. And they were quite right in showing that this gap posed an evaluative problem of major significance as to which should legislate over which, and when.

But just now let us simply note the gap: the fact that there are two distinct and irreducible selective systems with very different dynamic structures and modes of selection. And, having clearly noticed the distinction, let us study with some care each selective system alone before we try to consider the evaluative interrelations of the two systems.

Having thus brought into view the peculiarities of the dynamics of life-space, let us now turn to the closely connected topic of the mediating channels characteristic of it.

## 7. THE MEDIATING JUDGMENT IN LIFE-SPACE OR THE JUDGMENT OF REALITY

So far we have been considering an organism's life-space mainly as a distribution of drives in a behavior field. Our attention has been upon its dynamic side. Now we must consider the cognitive side as well. For an organism's life-space may be egregiously in error in respect to the environing situation in which he is acting and to which his action refers. When this is the condition, the organism's action is sure to be blocked and his purposes frustrated. The cognitive system embedded in life-space is thus just as important as the dynamic system. It is often referred to, quite appropriately, as the organism's sense of the *reality of the situation*.

This leads to a distinction between the organism's judgment of the reality of a situation and the actual reality of a situation. And we shall find it convenient to distinguish further between actual reality as relative to the capacities of the organism, and this reality irrespective of the responses of any particular organism.

The *judgment of reality* is the mediating judgment for life-space. It is the connecting link which channels the system of drives in action toward the realization of their satisfactions. Its reference is to actual reality through which the drives can attain their satisfaction. It may be in error (which is our reason for calling it a judgment), and if so this indicates a discrepancy between the judgment of reality and the actual reality. This means further that actual reality functions as the criterion of correctness for the judgment of reality in life-space.

We have then to consider in this connection (1) the judgment of reality for life-space, (2) the actual reality relative to an organism's capacities of response, (3) some further indicated reality not relative to an organism's limited capacities, and finally (4) the actions of both relative and ultimate reality as criteria of correctness for the reality judgment. We shall take these up seriatim.

1. *The judgment of reality.*—To illustrate what we are talking about, compare Mr. Jones's life-space as it was diagramed in figure 1 with that of the naïve dog in figure 2. The two organisms are at the same actual street crossing, with spatially similar goals in view. And yet the structure of the life-space for the one is quite different from that for the other. The dog perceived an open, positively valenced path diagonally across the intersection. Mr. Jones perceived a much more circuitous path including some delays and careful timing. That the perceptions of each were highly mediated by judgments would be clear to anyone after the preceding analyses of purposive structures. But if there were any doubt, it is sufficient to note that the naïve dog's response proved to be *in error*. The dog was not able to run across an open diagonal path, but was forced to dodge among a number of cars in jeopardy of his life. The dog had to correct his judgment of the reality of the situation to avoid frustrations and frightening objects he had not anticipated. As a docile animal he would learn from the experience and would approach the crossing with a different conception of the reality of the situation at another time. The fact of error demonstrates the judgmental character of a docile animal's life-space.

That is to say (and this is the added point in regard to mediating judgments that emerges in this chapter), an animal learns to modify his acts not only in order to make a subordinate act correct in relation to its superordinate act, but also *to make a total life-space correct in relation to the reality of the situation in which it occurs.*

We speak of a correct perception of the total situation. Such a perception is implicitly a correct judgment of the reality of the situation. This judgment is, to be sure, just the resultant of having correct mediating judgments for all the purposive activities combined in the situation. When the mediating judgment for life-space as a whole is correct, then automatically all the mediating judgments of the various drives involved in the situation are also correct. But should anyone construe this conclusion to mean that if all these correctly mediated drives were taken in isolation, and then brought together into a single life-space, the total act would be correct, this, of course, would be quite false. It would be like saying that a correctly rowed eight-man scull was just the same as a collection of eight correctly rowed one-man sculls.

It is not enough that each man be a good oarsman in his own right, but he must row on the crew of eight with a view to how all the others are rowing. It is not only the relation of means to the end, but that relation with a view to the total situation. It is true that a good oarsman, finding himself in a crew of eight, would inevitably adjust his rowing to the rowing of his neighbors in order to attain the highest speed. Each good oarsman wanting to attain the highest speed for himself adapts his movements to the others so that the highest speed is attained for the crew as a whole. But that is just the point: each man has the total context in mind and adjusts his action to what is most efficient for the total situation. The resultant effect is a function of the crew as a whole, and not a mere summation of the insulated efforts of each. So also with the teamwork exhibited in the reality judgment and its resultant act in life-space. The mediating judgment of life-space (the reality of the situation judgment) is not to be reduced away as a mere sum of the mediating judgments of subordinate acts.[5] It is the mediating judgment of another selective system. Moreover, a special function of this judgment is to regulate the release of the injective. It is the correct sizing up of a total situation that determines the time and amount of release of reserve energy appropriate to a situation.

The function of the judgment of reality, then, is to mediate between drives present in life-space and the reality of the situation. Its function is to channel these drives in the most effective manner to attain a maximum of purposive value for them in the light of the actual situation within which they arise. To repeat our main point at this juncture: the reality judgment does not mediate between a subordinate and a superordinate act (as simple cognitive sets do); it mediates between a total life-space and the reality of the situation in which this life-space must find fulfillment.

2. *The reality of the situation relative to life-space.*—We are thus led to consider what is involved in the reality of the situation to which the reality judgment of life-space refers. The first thought is that the reality of the situation is whatever actually is the case—the complete actual situation in which the organism is making his decision and his response. We shall need a name for this conception, for it will come up prominently later. Let us call it the conception of *ultimate reality,* and the reference to it the reference to ultimate reality.

This is not, however, the reality reference ordinarily involved in an organism's life-space. Ordinarily the reality of the situation referred to is a *relative reality*—relative to the capacities of the organism to make discriminations in his environment and to learn by experience. This is so commonly the case that unless I qualify the reality reference as 'ultimate,' I shall be signifying the relative reality reference.

That the reality of the situation referred to by life-space is ordinarily relative can be strikingly brought out by comparing the life-spaces of different docile animals and determining the nature of the reality of the situation to which these life-spaces could refer. Take any of the experiments designed to bring out the comparative learning capacities of different animals.

If, for instance, a chick is placed in a three-sided wire enclosure with the fourth side open, and food is placed outside the wire opposite the open side, the chick cannot solve the problem. He just runs up and down the wire fence in front of the food. A dog or a man before such a barrier sizes up the situation quickly and solves the problem.

Can we say that the reality of the situation is the same for the chick and the dog and the man? Evidently not. For the situation is unsolvable for the chick but easily solvable by dog or man. In terms of the chick's capacities, he was not making an erroneous response in running up and down before the food: it was all he could do. An observer aware of a chick's capacities would no more expect a chick to run back and around the barrier than to fly over the top. The one was as behavioristically impossible to the chick as the other was physically impossible.

A man with a wider range of discriminations can see that the chick's set of discriminations is just a small selection from his own. But the chick has no way of knowing this or of enlarging his range of discriminations. The cognitive references from his life-space are limited by the selection of details he can discriminate. These are the only details that would correct or verify his references. Consequently, they are the only details that can be included in the chick's life-space. Since the chick cannot discriminate the open path in the rear, he can make no anticipatory reference to it in his life-space, and, since he can make no references to it, he cannot verify its existence, and so for him it does not exist. It is not part of his reality for that situation. The situation turns out to be a truly frustrating one for the chick.

This illustration makes us suddenly aware that beyond the threshold of an animal's powers of discrimination there would be no life-space. Because of his limitations of response, the chick could not see the open path although his eyes were open. His life-space would stop at that threshold: beyond that point his perception would be blank.

Carrying on the same line of reasoning, it becomes clear that an organism which had no cognitive references would also have no reality judgment, and therefore no sense of either reality or unreality. Such an organism, if her behavior really is entirely reflex, is our old friend the digger wasp. Since she is incapable of learning, she has no cognitive references. Each link of her chain reflex has its conditions of quiescence in the link ahead. Wanting can be ascribed to the wasp. But if the next link required is missing, the wasp's outlook is blank and blind. No life-space of a variety of possibilities spreads out before her, just one of blank frustration. She is incapable of perceiving a variety of objects of different valencies relative to a temporarily blocked goal. All she can do is to start the chain over again from wherever a stimulus appears for the initial link. For a varied life-space cannot spread out before an organism unless it is capable of learning and so of filling in a gap between a drive and its quiescence by acts with which it was not innately provided. The digger wasp thus has no corrigible life-space, no freedom of decision, no sense of error, and finally no mediating reference to reality. There could be no sense of the reality of the situation for the digger wasp.

This outcome sounds paradoxical. But it stresses emphatically the relative character of the reality of the situation to which the ordinary judgment of reality refers. If there are no cognitive references, there can be no corrigible life-space, and hence no reality referred to which may confirm or correct the references of such a life-space. It would not be denied that there is a reality beyond the wasp's wanting which either fulfills or blocks the linked responses of the chain reflex. But this would have to be that ultimate reality which is not relative to any cognitive references subject to error. Noncognitive conative references are actually (as we shall see later) references to this ultimate reality. Such would be riddance pattern references[6] and those involved in the conditions of quiescence. But, then, all the more reason to distinguish clearly between ultimate reality and the relative reality of the situation which is that to which cognitive references must ordinarily refer. And the reality of the situation is thus seen to be definitely relative to the cognitive references which an organism is capable of making.

Since cognitive references are thus connected with the capacity to learn, then without this capacity no cognitive references; and no cognitive references, then no corrigible life-space; and no corrigible life-space, then no reference to a reality of the situation (distinct from some ultimate reality) relative to an organism's capacity for learning. *The greater an organism's powers of discrimination and capacity to have insight into the relation holding among things, the more extensive and articulated his life-space and correspondingly the reality of the situation* to which his cognitive references refer.[7]

Another point comes out now. The scope of the reality of the situation relative to an organism's capacities for differentiation extend not only widthwise spatially but lengthwise temporally.

Lewin brings this out in comparing the capacities of a child and an older person. He indicates the difference in the degree of differentiation between a younger and an older child by a diagram[8] (fig. 10). The compartments represent the cognitive sets

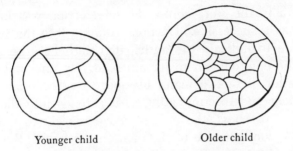

Younger child                    Older child

Fig. 10. Comparison of organism's capacities for differentiation.
(After Lewin.)

that the child has acquired and that are available for anticipations and apprehensions. Incidentally, Lewin points out that the rigidity of the compartments differs also. A younger person can learn and unlearn more easily than an older one. But the important point for us here is Lewin's observation that along with an increase in differentiation in an older person's life-space comes an increase in perspective past and future. An older person is much more aware of the consequences of his acts than a younger one, and of causal relations running far beyond the immediate field of perceptual stimulation.

> An infant lives essentially in the present. His goals are immediate goals; when he is distracted he "forgets" quickly. As an individual grows older more and more of his past and his future affect his present mood and action. The goals of the school child may already include promotion to the next grade at the end of the year. Years later, as the father of a family, the same person will often think in terms of decades when planning his life.[9]

A man's life-space at any moment includes a time dimension, and so also would the reality of the situations relative to it. It may be so short as to be negligible, or it may be so long as to stretch over many years. With experience and maturity it tends to get longer and longer. The older person is more aware of the consequences, and has these spotted along in anticipation, or apprehension.

A chart of a man's life-space should provide for the time perspective also. Actually, the time dimension was implicit in our plotting of Mr. Jones's life-space (fig. 1). For Mr. Jones's intended path to the store across the intersection was indicated, and this was a succession of actions running into the future. It was possible to indicate the anticipated path here because we expected the environment to remain relatively unchanged.

As a matter of fact, a man's life-space tends to become less and less clear and discriminating as it extends into the future. Like a game of chess, the present move is clear and discriminated in the configuration of the men on the board. But in estimating the effect of a present contemplated move we cannot precisely predict future moves because so much depends on our opponent. And the farther off the effects of a move lie in the future, the more uncertain the prediction because of the cumulative action of uncontrolled effects. Nevertheless, the more skillful a chess player is, the farther ahead he looks, and the more detailed his anticipations.

The successive references into the future are all present and contemporaneous in any one life-space. The picking up of the loaf of bread which Mr. Jones anticipates doing in the store across the street five minutes hence is present now in his life-space spread out before him at the street corner. But that act is actually five minutes later in the reality of the situation to which his life-space is referring. Thus the reality of a situation is not just a man's present environment; it is also as much of his future and past environment as he is capable of differentiating. For it is the future with its causal relations connected with the present and the past that is going to verify his reality judgment. Time relationships are just as much a part of the reality of the situation as spatial and qualitative relationships.

So, if an organism has a limited capacity for following out consequences into the future, the reality of the situation for him will shrink in the time dimension accordingly. A chick's blindness about certain relations in the future would be exactly parallel with his blindness to the open path behind him in the barrier situation. This consequence has nothing to do with the question whether the future is fully determined or not. If it is not fully determined, that would be part of the reality of the situation for a mind that could look that far into the future.

The shrinkage of the time dimension for organisms with limited capacities for thinking of the consequences simply means that beyond the threshold of their limitations their perception of the future is a blank. When Lewin says that an infant lives essentially in the present, that does not mean that the infant perceives the future as undetermined, but that he does not perceive it very much at all. We call a person who does not think about the consequences 'thoughtless.' That is just it. And observe the attitude we take toward such a person. For that is quite revealing. If he is an infant, we make allowances for his thoughtlessness because he is not old enough to be expected to learn. But if he is older we hold him responsible. We say he is old enough to know better, meaning that at his age he should have the learning capacities to perceive the relationships in question. And this in turn means, in our technical terms, that we expect his life-space to be wider in scope and more articulated, and consequently that we expect him to be responsive to a correspondingly extensive and articulated reality of the situation.

Now let me call attention to another thing. In passing from the behavior of the wasp through that of the chick and the dog to man, and in passing from the human infant to the adult, we find the scope and articulation of the reality of the situation steadily expanding. Moreover, we can see that the more limited realities are simply selected portions of the wider realities. The dog in the wire barrier perceives all that the chick does in the situation, but more too. The dog has a wider sense of reality.

The wasp is at one end of this expanding sense of reality, the chick in between, and man at the other end. Now man has an extraordinary capacity in this regard, which comes near to justifying his traditional arrogance in setting himself apart from all other animals as a qualitatively distinct and superior sort of being. This is his tool-making capacity, including his linguistic powers. Just what the significance of this capacity is in terms of values and behavior has not always been fully grasped. Its sig-

TABLE 7

LIFE-SPACE REFERENCES

| References | Object |
|---|---|
| Conative but noncognitive (riddance reactions and conditions of quiescence) (neither true nor false, may be blocked but not in error or open to correction by learning) | Ultimate reality (of actual object of riddance or conditions producing quiescence) |
| Cognitive references dependent on limited capacities of discrimination (true or false, because open to correction by learning) | Relative reality of situation (relative to limited capacities of discrimination; beyond these capacities, situation is in fact flatly frustrating for individual) |
| Cognitive references with unlimited capacities of discrimination (true or false, because open to correction by learning) | Ultimate reality (which is also reality of situation given unlimited capacities of discrimination) |

nificance is that man is not limited in his capacities of discrimination to the biological endowment with which he is born, but can extend them indefinitely by inventing instruments—instruments to detect, to manipulate, and to clarify relations. As a cane extends touch to its ferrule, these instruments extend the rather limited human senses to the ends of the universe.

These instruments make it possible for man to extrapolate from the series of relative realities of the situation of ordinary perception to a reference to ultimate reality. It is very difficult to resist the attractiveness of the extrapolation, and probably it is cognitively correct. For with human instruments and the control techniques of the laboratory, and the logical techniques of language and mathematics, there seems to be no theoretical limit to the discrimination by man of any detail in his environment. This amounts to a reference to reality without limitation of any kind—that is, to ultimate reality.

3. *The reference to ultimate reality.*—From the preceding paragraphs it appears that under certain conditions a reference to ultimate reality is involved in life-space. In table 7 the scheme for the various types of references involved in life-space is spread out, and also the objects of these references, whether directed to an ultimate or to a relative reality.[10]

That noncognitive conative references have for their object elements of ultimate reality develops from the fact that these references cannot be corrected by learning, and so cannot be relative to learning. Yet something is referred to, and, if the reference is not to a relative reality, it must be to an ultimate reality. Or, more simply, a riddance reaction just takes place and that is that—an ultimate fact of nature. It is a primitive act of rejection with a reference to something actually rejected. Whatever the stimulus of the reaction, that was the object of riddance. That stimulus, whatever it was in ultimate fact, was the object referred to by the act and conatively disvalued, and the direction of response to the stimulus was the reference itself. No cognitive references, which could be considered true or false, could squeeze in. Moreover, whether the organism knows cognitively what the rejected object was is immaterial to the riddance reaction, or to the negative conative reference, or to the conative disvalue thereby registered. It would take additional cognitive references for the organism to possess cognitive and verifiable awareness of the object of riddance. The latter emerge immediately for a docile organism as apprehensive sets. Any object of apprehension is, of course, cognitive, open to error and correction through learning. But not so an object of riddance.[11]

The conditions of quiescence as the referential properties of an appetitive drive likewise refer to a condition of ultimate reality. For these also are not subject to correction through learning. They may be blocked but are not cognitively in error. Suppose an organism were born with a drive demanding conditions of satisfaction that did not exist in the world. Animals born with defective organs are virtually born in this state. Consider a baby born with defective lungs. The impulse to breathe is there, but not air concentrated enough in the environment to satisfy his craving. The conditions of quiescence, the conative references, are blocked and testified to by the hopeless struggle of the organism. The conative references are not in error, however. A natural selection occurs and the child dies. As we shall maintain later, this is a value act in the environment performed by the selective system of the evolutionary process. But it is not a cognitive act within the life-space of the defective organism. The conditions of quiescence for this child's breathing drive just did not exist in the child's environment. That was an ultimate fact of reality. In this instance the ultimate fact entailed a permanent blockage of the drive. But in an infant with normal lungs the conditions of quiescence for the breathing drive refer to ultimate reality conditions yielding satisfaction. Whether blocked or satisfied, then, the conditions of quiescence of a drive refer to ultimate facts.

As with the object of riddance, it is immaterial to these references whether or not the organism ever becomes cognitively aware of the consummatory objects. An intelligent organism does ordinarily with experience acquire cognitive references for the character of the quiescence patterns of his drives. But these are cognitive references superimposed upon the conditions of quiescence inherent in the drive. They emerge as anticipatory sets referring to the consummatory acts.

Whatever conative references occur in life-space, therefore, that are noncognitive in character have as their objects of reference objects of ultimate reality. These objects constitute much of what is meant by 'the stubborn facts of nature.' We must not assume, however, that they are easily cognized in their true nature. An apprehensive set is liable to error, even in the direct wake of an intense riddance reaction. Nevertheless, the 'shock,' as Santayana calls it, or the riddance effect of a stubborn blockage across a cognitive reference that is proved thereby false, comes as strong testimony for the ultimacy and determinateness of ultimate reality, even when we do not truly know just what the ultimate fact may be.

Most cognitive references refer not to ultimate reality but to a reality of the situation relative to the discriminating capacities of the organisms responding. Outside the threshold of the organism's powers of discrimination the environment appears as simply frustrating in nature. With the organism's given limitations of response, the reality of the situation truly is frustrating. But in the view of better endowed, more discriminating organisms, the reality of the situation does not necessarily have an ultimate frustrating character. This means that an organism cannot be held responsible for a correct judgment about the reality of a situation beyond his powers of discrimination. Where these powers are limited, he can have cognizance of reality only relative to these powers.

For all docile animals, so far as we can judge, the reality of the situation to which their life-spaces refer is relative to their limited biological endowments—with the exception of man. The exception arises from the fact that man's discriminations do extend beyond his biological endowments. By microscopes, telescopes, thermometers, electrometers, and so on, he extends his sensory discriminations. By language, mathematics, and logic, he extends his relational discriminations. By tractors, ships, dynamos, telephones, radios, he extends his motor coördinations. He leaves his biological limitations far behind.

To be sure, most men most of the time, even though they wear glasses, speak a language, and ride in cars, still make their cognitive references under considerable limitations. Men do not ordinarily hold one another responsible for wide ranges of incorrect or plain slipshod judgment. And they are usually tolerant of the limited capacities of their children. Men protect themselves by guards, police, signs, rules, ordinances, and all sorts of devices against their own bad judgment. They count on their cognitive references being ordinarily directed only to a relative reality of the situation.

But in the end, men do not submit to such cognitive limitations. They hold themselves responsible for the facts just as they are, whatever they may be. And if they do not yet have the instruments to detect the facts, they proceed to invent them. Is it yellow fever? We do not know what it is? We do not know how to cure it? Then we will experiment till we know what it is. And then experiment further till we can cure it. And whatever instruments we may need to increase our discriminations, we will invent. And so with cancer and poliomyelitis and so with social disturbance, and so with the difficulties in finding out about values! There may be intrinsically indeterminate and frustrating areas in ultimate reality. But cognizing man, when he is really serious about knowing, does not take these for granted. At least, frequently he does not. The cognitive function of the concept of the uniformity of nature, for instance, which guided the scientific attitude of the nineteenth century, was a way of keeping scientific judgments directed upon ultimate reality. It was a way of telling a scientist that, if he failed to discriminate a regularity by one hypothesis, he should not hold nature responsible for the failure, but his own incapacity to discriminate with the hypothesis and apparatus he was using, and that he should bestir himself to figure out another. It was a maxim urging him to increase his powers of discrimination.

So, because man has the power to increase his powers of discrimination apparently without theoretical limit, he can have cognitive references to ultimate reality.[12] This does not ensure the entire correctness of any of these references. But he can make them nonetheless, and do his best to render them correct.

How extensive these cognitive references of men to ultimate reality may be in factual judgments it would be hard to say. But most philosophical and scientific judgments probably have them at least implicitly. For even on an extreme pragmatic position of a general relativity of all things to their contexts, and large areas of unpredictable novelty, and the need for a completely operational approach—even on that view there would still be a hypothesis with a cognitive reference to an ultimate reality in which this was precisely the state of affairs. (And indeed it may be so.) But as long as man recognizes in himself a capacity to enlarge his discrimination for the correct cognizing of nature, whatever it may turn out to be, he will find himself legitimately making cognitive references to ultimate reality.

4. *Relative and ultimate reality as criteria of correctness.*— What is the bearing of this discussion of relative and ultimate reality upon values? These are criteria for the correctness of the judgment of reality which channels the resultant act in the dynamics of life-space. Given an organism's capacities of discrimination, and a set of drives with their mediating judgments in life-space, then a reality judgment with correct references to the reality of the situation would be the most feasible channel of response for the next act of the organism. The reality of the situation is a selective norm for the act. For if the organism has sized up the situation incorrectly, he will encounter frustrations to the drives involved. And if he gets another chance at the

situation, he will learn to act (by trial and error in the last resort) more nearly in conformity with the reality of the situation.

Actually, we are not entirely unfamiliar with this mode of action. Reference to the reality of the situation is involved in the feasibility judgment of each component drive in a life-space. The most feasible act for maximizing the value of every component act in a situation will be exactly the act that maximizes the value of the situation as a whole. It is the act which conforms to the reality of the situation. This result is quickly apparent if we remember that the time perspective, as far as it can be predicted, is part of the reality of the situation. Where one individual as a center supplies all the energy for an act in a situation (which is the way it is in life-space), the act which will release most tension for the situation as a whole is the very one most feasible for the tension release of every component drive as well.

Ultimate reality is the criterion for determining the degree of discrimination to be found in relative realities. It is essentially a theoretical ideal, though the references to it are actual enough. Actually, men gauge the degree of discrimination they have attained by looking back at the stages of relatively undiscriminating cognition that lie in their past. Then, regarding these as successive approximations to an ideal ultimate reality, men refer to this as the criterion of criterions of reality. Man can make this reference with considerable justification because of his proved capacity to improve his cognition in problematic situations. He is not blocked by a biological limit to his powers of discrimination.

## 8. Values and Evaluation in Life-Space

What are the values that life-space produces as a selective system, and what are their criteria of evaluation? The answer is simple: the dynamics of life-space is the dynamics of the component drives that enter into it. The selective activity of life-space is of the resultant type. Hence the values of life-space will be resultants of the values of the drives that are in the field. Since the values of the component drives are the conative-achievement and affective values examined earlier, the selective effect of the life-space field is simply to maximize these for the field as a whole.

There is nothing to add concerning these values and their quantitative criteria except their resultant effects due to their being in one organism's behavior field. The values and their evaluative criteria were discussed in chapter 14. Even their mode of legislating over each other remains the same. Actually, much of the discussion in that chapter spilled over into life-space —which is another reason why we find little more to say about them. For a number of drives are always interacting upon one another in the field of an individual's response. To maximize the values of any one drive, we must consider its effects on other drives in the field, and automatically we are considering how to maximize the values of the total field prudently, and not simply the values of one isolated drive.

In regard to the legislation of one sort of purposive value over another in life-space, the only question that might arise would be the resultant effect when the situation was such that for one drive achievement value would be in ascendancy and for another affective value. Which type of value would then legislate over the total field? Actually, this is probably the usual setup; we intuitively sense that if a very strong drive has reached the consummatory phase and is maximizing its affective values, all the lesser drives in process of achievement move off on the side lines. And this is probably the answer. Whatever drive is conatively the strongest and would dominate the resultant effect in an achievement field, that drive will legislate over the others when one of the drives is in a consummatory phase and the others are not.

Under emergency conditions, achievement value legislates over affective value. Otherwise the reverse. Dynamically an emergency condition is one in which a strong drive for urgent achievement overpowers a weaker drive ready to maximize pleasure. So the dynamic ground for our principle above is further confirmed.

In this connection, it is well to turn our attention to the complete contrast in the configuration of the life-space field when it is dominated by an achievement process and when dominated by a consummatory condition. If achievement value is being maximized in the field, everything is ordered for the greatest speed and economy of action. If a single instrumental act can serve several different ends at once, this act is utilized. Action is carefully planned into the future so that a minimum of means in the sequence of acts will serve a maximum of ends. So a housewife making out her shopping list sets down all the things she can get in one store, however diverse their terminal destination, and similarly for every other store she has to visit, and then arranges these stores in a sequence that will not require her to backtrack.

But if affective value is being maximized everything is changed, and consummatory values are ordered so as to increase the time spent on them as much as possible short of monotony and fatigue. Thus a composer planning a symphony offers a theme and repeats it or varies parts of it as long as he can count on continuous interest, then shifts to a contrasting theme which he dwells on for a while, then changes his mode of handling the themes in the development section till this might become monotonous, then shifts back to the original two themes in something like the original handling in a recapitulation, which may be followed by still further contrasting treatment of the material in a coda. The technique of a composer is to exploit the same pleasant material and multiply and spread out the consummatory responses as far as possible. Not economy but richness is his aim. He channels the multitude of tonal responses to keep the listener, so to speak, walking back and forth over the same fascinating paths as long as he can. The more backtracking the better as long as monotony is avoided—just the opposite of the shopping lady.

All this brings it about that the most distinctive thing to notice in the evaluative judgments of life-space is not any new values to be found there, but the channeling of them. In a field of many converging and intercepting values, what is the correct way of channeling these to obtain the maximum value result in view of the reality of the situation? Clarity in regard to the reality of the situation is the essential thing for correctly maximizing the values there. The reality judgment is the most distinctive feature of life-space.

We are then reminded that we have only half considered what renders a reality judgment correct or incorrect. We have considered it only in terms of degrees of discrimination. We have assumed that the reality judgment improves with increase of discriminated details. Weakness in the reality judgment would then derive solely from privation of discrimination. But reality judgments may be incorrect additively as well as privatively.

Among animals, incorrectness of response in sizing up a situation seems to be primarily of the privative sort. In man, it is quite as likely to be of the additive sort. This is presumably due to man's unusual powers of imagination and symbolism. For he is as likely to misjudge a situation by seeing things in it that are not there, as in not seeing things in it that are there. I am not referring primarily to the sensational instances of sensory illusions and hallucinations, but rather to common run-of-the-day instances of rationalization, displacement, identification, and the like, which are familiar to clinical psychologists. By these mechanisms men project into their view of a situation all sorts of entities and relationships that are not there. So much so that to say of a man that he has a firm sense of reality is tantamount to saying he has great capacity for happiness.

But now we are beginning to talk about a man's character. This is something different from life-space or a purposive structure, and leads us into a new chapter and the discernment of yet another selective system—that of the integrated personality.

# 17

## Personality Integration

### 1. Two Kinds of Selections Performed through Personality Structures

Up to this point we have been concerned with the goodness of an individual's acts. Now we must consider the goodness of the man who performs them.

For so far we have been studying the selective action of purposive structures and of life-space. Both of these selective systems operate upon individual acts. The selective action of a purposive structure is mainly that of choosing a subordinate act that properly serves its superordinate act. And the selective action of life-space is that of choosing a resultant act from among a variety of drives in action which will maximize achievement or affection in conformity with the reality of the situation. In both systems what is selected is a specific act. These acts are subject to correction in a docile organism through the very dynamics of their selective systems. But it is always specific acts upon which these selections work.

Now we must examine another sort of selection which bears not upon acts in process but upon attitudes of action. The name ordinarily given to a man's system of attitudes is 'personality,' or 'character'—the repertory of instinctive and acquired drives and their interrelationships which make up personality structure.

A man's personality structure faces two ways. In one direction, it determines the drives that are released in a given situation. It determines what at any given time interests a man, and so forms

455

the pattern of his drives in life-space. When we say that a man's character controls his acts, this is the sort of thing we are referring to. The resultant acts of a man's life-space depend upon the drives the man releases on the stimulus of the situation, and what will interest a man on the stimulus of a situation depends upon his personality structure. In this way a man's character controls his acts. In the long run his acts must conform to his personality structure, for this consists precisely in the repertory of his drives and their interrelationships, and these demand satisfaction whenever they emerge in life-space. So, on this side, a personality structure is a selective system determining what drives are released into life-space and what satisfactions will be demanded of a situation.

But, in the other direction, a personality structure makes its own demands upon its own internal organization. It develops a selective system for its own internal equilibrium. The result, when successful, is commonly called the *integrated personality*. This process of selection may then be aptly called an *integrative process*. Its distinctive trait is that it operates not on acts but on dispositions to act—that is, on drives and their interrelationships. The dynamics of the process is the drives themselves, through the mechanisms for value mutations studied earlier (chap. 11). But in the earlier chapter we were examining the mechanisms individually and each sort of derived drive separately. We were not looking at them collectively, and so did not notice the integrative tendency that runs through such mutations toward the development of a personality structure.

This collective action, we are now prepared to see, constitutes a distinct mode of selection in its own right. Very roughly, it works like this. If the personality acquires a disposition (a derived drive, or, in everyday terms, a habit) which proves to be continually frustrating in its encounters with other dispositions of the personality, then a tendency emerges to throw this disposition out of the personality structure or modify the structure so as to reduce the frustration. This reduction of frustration within the personality is the integrative process. The positive side of integration is harmony, for the reduction of frustration is the production of harmony in the personality.

The integrative process is thus a kind of resultant act. It arises out of the same dynamic tendencies which produce the resultant act in life-space. But here the effect is fed back into the system of attitudes which release the drives for action in life-space. The resultant effect of a system of attitudes upon an attitude that is persistently in conflict with the system is for the system to encapsulate the attitude or throw it out.

The most striking instance of this process is the recovery from neurotic disturbances by simply exposing repressions. As soon as the repressed drive is brought out in the open, and is no longer protected in its position in the personality by the mechanisms of repression, the drive has to confront the conscious personality system, its frustrating character is revealed, and the system automatically throws out the disturbing elements. The psychiatrist here performs the mainly negative task of removing the repression, and thereafter the integrative process completes the recovery by its natural selective dynamics.

Here the *integrative action* of the personality as a selective system for the acceptance or rejection of drives as dispositions of the personality can be clearly distinguished from the *distributive action* of the personality as a selective system for the pattern of drives released in any given life-space. Let us accept the terms 'integrative action' and 'distributive action' for the two modes of selective activity carried on by the personality as a selective system.

The distributive action need not occupy much of our time. The ways in which it works were implicitly described as the background for the action of life-space as a selective system. The stimulus elements of a situation and the state of the organism as it enters a situation determine the drives released for the life-space at that time. And the correctness of the pattern of cognitive references and the resultant response depend upon the reality of the situation relative to the organism. It amounts to the description of the distributive action of the personality. The act is good for this person in this situation if it maximizes the affective and achievement values released by the personality in that life-space. The distributive action of a personality and the resultant act of a life-space set up by that personality are two aspects of the same selective process. The one determines the pattern of drives released in the situation; the other, the resultant act. But the resultant act requires the pattern of drives, and the pattern of drives demands a resultant act. This is what makes it the act of this particular personality. So the distributive action of the personality is absorbed into an aspect of life-space as a selective system. It is part of the process of action in a personal situation.

Not so with the integrative action of a personality, however. This concept, not encountered before in our study, presents us with another type of value as different, it would seem, from affection and achievement as these are from each other—indeed, more widely different. For those are both values of acts. But integration of personality is a value of a potentiality of acts. It determines the value of attitudes, of dispositions. We have a contrast here between the value of an act and the value of a system of dispositions to act. To clarify this contrast it is necessary to formulate a descriptive definition of personality.

## 2. DESCRIPTIVE DEFINITION OF PERSONALITY

Personality has proved a troublesome concept to define. Sometimes it is identified with the succession of a man's acts, his history from birth to death. Then, at the opposite extreme, it is called an abstraction, a conceptual fiction, a conventional working hypothesis, or something equally artificial and unreal. What various writers have found difficult to describe is the status of a disposition, for a disposition is a potentiality to action. It has an actual existence in the object to which the disposition is attributed, and yet it is not simply an event or process occurring at a particular time or place.

If you say of a man that he is courageous, you attribute to him a disposition. This is not some particular courageous act of his. It is not even the collection of all the courageous acts of his life. These acts are the evidence of his disposition, which is something different from the acts. With the knowledge that a man has a courageous disposition, you predict such acts. But the courage he possesses as his disposition is not your hypothesis about it. His courage is not a mere verbal hypothesis. It is a fact that can be tested and verified and about which your hypothesis is made. His courage is a characteristic of his personality and an actual existing property of his.

A personality, then, is an actual object and is not reducible to a succession of events or a linguistic construction.

A personality is a set of dispositions. In the broadest sense, a personality consists in the total set of behavior capacities of a particular organism: his capacities to discriminate, to manipulate objects in the environment, to learn and to retain in memory, as well as his dynamic capacities of appetition and aversion and satisfaction and achievement. It is only the latter dynamic capacities that will particularly concern us in our value studies, however. Not that the other capacities are negligible, but they have significance for the personality as a selective system only because of their bearing on the dynamic capacities. When we refer to a man's personality, we generally refer only to the latter. We generally mean his particular set of interests, and these are precisely his aesthetic tastes, his hobbies and enthusiasms, his beliefs, his desires and ambitions, his aversions and fears, and his habits of serving these.

In the more specific terms of our previous study, these dynamic capacities are a man's capacities for gratuitous satisfaction, his instinctive and acquired drives, his anticipatory and apprehensive sets, and his habits of achievement in carrying out his appetitions and aversions. Roughly we may speak of these dynamic capacities as a man's particular set of drives, instinctive or acquired. The purposive structures within which these fulfill themselves are taken for granted as part of the dynamic capacities of the drives. In speaking hereafter, then, as I often shall, of a man's personality as his particular set of dynamic capacities or even as his particular set of drives, I shall not wish it to be thought that all the other capacities involved in his behavior are not also part of his personality. But on the whole we shall not need to concern ourselves in this study of value theory much beyond the dynamic capacities of an individual.

Note that, as a result of this compendious identification of a man's personality with his system of drives, our term 'drive' acquires a broader significance. Not that it did not implicitly have this significance throughout the earlier descriptive analyses, but now this implicit meaning becomes explicit. Heretofore a drive has been treated as an initiating pattern of action in process. Now we explicitly note that as a personality trait a drive is a disposition of an organism. As a disposition it has perdurance in an organism and is available for repeated activation as a motivating agent upon appropriate stimulation. Hunger and fear, for instance, are the motivating agents in certain specific appetitions and aversions; but they are also permanent dispositions of the organism, available periodically to activation under appropriate conditions.

The hunger drive is a cyclical disposition of the organism. This identical disposition motivates many appetitive acts. But each time that hunger arises, it functions as the particular appetitive structure. So, on the one hand, hunger is a perduring cyclical disposition of the organism, and, on the other hand, it is also, by virtue of that very fact, the particular motivating agent of particular purposive acts occurring at different times. So far we have been concerned mainly with a drive as a particular motivating agent. But now, in examining the selective functions of a personality, we shall be concerned with a drive mainly as a perduring disposition.

How is a disposition to be described? In the present context, a disposition may be regarded as a configuration of characters in a given object causally productive of certain other characters under specific conditions. The object having the characters capable of producing the characters in question is said to have a disposition for the latter characters. Thus water, through its character of being a liquid of a certain sort, has the dispositional property of dissolving sugar. The object with the productive characters is said to be the *seat* or vehicle of the disposition, and the characters produced are said to be the *character* of the disposition. Thus water, by virtue of its liquid quality, is the seat of its disposition to dissolve sugar, and the character of dissolving sugar is the character of the disposition.

Ordinarily we learn about a disposition through an occurrence in which it has been actualized. Observing sugar dissolve in water, we can ascribe that disposition to the water. The existence of a disposition, however, is not dependent on an occurrence of its character. The existence of a disposition depends only on its seat. Thus to a glass of water we should unhesitatingly attribute the dispositional property of dissolving sugar, even though no sugar were ever deposited in the glass. That is to say, a disposition may legitimately be inferred without anyone ever observing its character in an actual occurrence. And where dispositions have a quantitative character, it is possible that a disposition may never be fully exhibited, even though we may justifiably infer what it would be at a maximum. It is important to notice that a disposition is not to be reduced to its seat alone, to its character alone, or to an observer's observations or descriptions or hypotheses about it. It is a verifiable entity in its own right. It has its locus of existence in its seat, and it has its character through the dynamic potentialities of the configuration of characters in the seat.

Now the seat of a personality is clearly the physical organism with all those physiological modifications which are required for its specific modes of behavior. And the character of a personality is that exhibited in the actual behavior of the organism or inferable from it. The character, let it be clear, is not the observations or the inferences of a spectator. It is that which these observations and inferences refer to as their object—namely, the dispositional character of the system of drives and drive structures which have their seat in the organism. Though no spectator described or inferred it, that man's personality would be just what it was as the dynamic capacities of the organism over a certain spread of time.

In general, the character of a personality disposition is periodically exhibited in action when the appropriate environmental conditions call it forth. But some dispositions never exhibit themselves to their full capacity, and yet constitute traits of the personality and can often be legitimately inferred. Thus the full capacity of a person to endure hardship or suffering may never be brought to the test; yet that person's reliability in these respects can often be fairly well predicted, and, whether or not the predictions prove true in the event, that person's capacity was just whatever it was, as with any other verifiable fact.

The particular seat of a particular personality trait is commonly believed to be associated with a particular physiological modification of the organism. This, if adequately known, would literally be the seat of that trait. This would be the view of all who take seriously the correlation of a personality with the physical structure of an organism. The evidences for such a correlation are very strong. They include all the evidences of the dependence of a personality on neural and glandular functioning, not to mention transitory changes produced by drugs, temperature, humidity, and the like. Such a complete correlation will be the assumption of the present chapter, at least as a working hypothesis. This does not mean that we should regard a personality as a hypothesis (except in that last metaphysical sense in which even factuality itself is an object of cognitive criticism and is treated hypothetically). A personality is a fact about which certain descriptive hypotheses are made. As one such hypothesis we accept the evidence for a complete correlation between personality dispositions and physiological configurations in the organism. On this hypothesis, the seat of a personality disposition would always be found in a physiological configuration describable in physiological terms.

Thus we have regularly described the structure of an appetition in such a way that physiological correlates could be found for it. Whatever is the neural basis for a well-learned system of anticipatory sets leading to a terminal goal, that would be the seat of this anticipatory phase of the disposition. And whatever is the physiological source of the tension patterns generating the dynamic element for the act, that would be the seat for the dynamic phase of the disposition. The two physiological conditions together constitute the seat of the appetition as a personality disposition of the organism.

Any changes affecting the seat of the disposition would obviously change the disposition. This is obvious for cyclic drives like hunger, thirst, elimination, and the like. To take care of these, we customarily include the normal phases of the cycle in the description of the disposition. Moreover, the whole tone or energy level of the organism affects nearly all dispositions, and this is a dispositional trait of a personality, too. So one disposition can affect another, and the degree and manner in which this occurs are also personality traits.

But all these changes and interrelationships are stabilized and controlled through having their seat in the physiological organism. The stability of the personality is founded on that of the physiological organism. It cannot change faster than the organism can, and, though changes are going on in the organism all the time, these are not so rapid or so haphazard that a degree of constancy in a personality cannot be counted on. So much so that we can speak of a personality structure. And what we refer to as an *individual* person—as our friend or acquaintance, husband or wife, son or daughter, father or mother—is his or her personality. This retains an individuality and a certain constancy across the years. It matures rather than alters, and the saddest thing next to death is to see it disintegrate, as it sometimes does, in disease or senility.

Our next concern, now that we have a conception of the general nature of a personality, will be to examine the broad outlines of its structure and its mode of development. As a general descriptive definition, we may regard a *personality as a system of dispositions for purposive behavior having its seat in a biological organism.* And we may regard a person as a human organism with a personality. By the foregoing definition only purposive dispositions are explicitly included in a personality. This, I believe, runs fairly close to usage, but, more important, these alone generate the selective system which institutes the values of a personality. However, all other dispositions for action, and the whole reflex structure of the organism, enter indirectly into the personality, since these activities underlie most purposive behavior and ultimately need to be integrated with it.

3. CONSIDERATIONS RELEVANT TO THE GROWTH
   OF A PERSONALITY

A newborn child has very little personality. We expect the child's personality to develop. And much of the parents' and of society's

concern with the child is to guide, educate, cultivate his personality toward the prevailing ideals. At the same time the child's
instinctive endowment of dispositions, which have their own
indigenous capacities for growth and maturation, insist on spontaneous realization. So there is a continuous struggle between
the child's instinctive impulses and the social environment in
which he is placed. This struggle is not imposed entirely from
without. As a social animal the child is endowed with many
socially directed impulses. These begin with the sucking instinct,
which demands a mother, and the need to be loved, which has
lately been prominently brought out in observation of infants
under hospital care.

The child needs society and, because of the exceptionally long
period of infant dependence in the human species, he needs it
badly. At the same time he is liberally endowed with self-regard-
ing impulses. So the struggle goes on mainly within the child's
own personality—the struggle amid frustrations to obtain as
much satisfaction as he can for his multitudinous impulses in a
restraining physical and social environment. In the course of
this struggle, his personality is developed. Each time that he
learns a new way of handling a situation, he lays down a new
personality trait, a new disposition incorporated into his personality.

It will be rewarding to break off this train of thinking for a
moment and consider a totally different kind of animal, a paramecium. So far as we can observe, this simple organism has a
regular life cycle endowed with a small number of reflex actions
suited to a limited range of environmental conditions. It has no
capacity for learning. It has accordingly no personality problems.
This is not simply a matter of definition, though we did define
the personality in terms of docile behavior. But we defined it
in this way because of the factual difference we are here noticing. The dispositions of a paramecium involve no conflicts.
With each situation, it performs the reflex evoked; if the situation is one for which no reflex is provided, it makes no response,
and either nothing happens to it or perhaps it is destroyed.
There is no problem of fitting together a multitude of acquired
dispositions. There is no integration problem. Even if a situation

evokes more than one reflex, either both can go off at once or one is prepotent and that ends the act. The paramecium, without effort on its part, is endowed with a completely integrated system of dispositions, but not a personality, for it has no docility. Never do these dispositions literally conflict, since it is impossible for the organism to respond otherwise than it does. Its dispositional structure is not, in other words, a selective system. The paramecium cannot make a mistake in its responses. It cannot lay down a wrong disposition which must afterward be corrected, because it cannot lay down any new dispositions at all. There is thus no possibility of choice, no 'can' and so no 'ought.'

So far as their behavior is instinctive and nondocile, the same would be true of much more complicated organisms like ants and bees, which have an intricate social organization. Whatever docility they have is clearly very much limited. Their social organization appears to be congenitally fixed in their instinctive dispositional structure. Thus insect societies are very different from human societies. Among insects we find complex and highly integrated dispositional systems. If social insects are capable of a little docility, we could even consider them literally, in contrast to a paramecium, as having integrated *personalities*. But, so to speak, this integration is very little to their credit: they can hardly help being integrated. The intricate details of social interrelationship and mutual functioning are all embedded as an instinctive dispositional system in their physiological structure. Their docile acquisitions just fill in some interstices. Since for them too there is very little 'can,' there is very little 'ought,' very little choice, and hence very little personal value.

Now with man the conditions are entirely different. His personality is almost entirely of his own making. Man's instinctive repertory, apart from his internal organic functions of respiration, circulation, digestion, and the like, consists of riddance patterns and impulse patterns, mere triggers of terminally aimed action; the filling in of the gaps, in order to deal with the physical and social environment, is left entirely to learning. There is practically no act of his that may not be a mistake. From birth to death his acts are almost wholly the result of choice. The choice may not be entirely his own. It may be his parents' or the tribe's, but the choice has a human origin and might have been different, and may be correct or incorrect, and so either ought or ought not to have been made. Man, more than any other animal, because of the extendedness of his docility, lives in an enveloping atmosphere of personal values.

That is why a man's character is such a thing of worth. It is the repository and monument of all his choices. It is he himself who has made it, or, if not he alone, other men about him. He and his society are completely responsible for it; and but for the choices he and his community have made on the basis of his constitutional endowments, his personality could have been quite different. The responsibility of society for the character of its members we shall deal with presently in the study of cultural patterns. But just now we are concerned with the responsibility of the man himself in building up his character.

The aim of a person unhindered by outer tendencies is the attainment of an integrated character. There is a great deal of evidence for this. It has long been noted, and constitutes the central insight of the self-realizationist school of ethics, a school which traces its ancestry back to Plato and Aristotle and includes the Stoics, Spinoza, and most of the modern idealists. But just how this integration takes place has not in the past been altogether clear. Recent work in the psychology of the personality has shed much light upon it, and we begin to see fairly definitely what makes for an integrated personality.

The process of integration is not literally an act of purposive behavior. A person may, however, assist the process by making it an appetitive goal. The process is in the nature of a directional tendency, and unfortunately we have no common word for a directional tendency involving selection and correction except 'purpose.' Where there is an aim, we commonly attribute a purpose. But the integrative tendency of the personality is not an appetitive or aversive structure. The aim of rendering a person's system of dispositions mutually harmonious is not the goal of an instinctive appetition or the object of an instinctive aversion, though it is just as innate to the organism as are these instinctive drives. It is a resultant effect of the operation of these drives as this effect is fed back into the dispositional structure of a docile organism.

This tendency goes on all the time whether a person knows it or not. But if a person has some conception of how the process goes on, and some notion of its selective criterion, he can assist it greatly and ward off possible personality disintegration or even destruction. When the self-realizationists speak of the importance of living in harmony with nature, this is their insight. Observing the way in which a personality is trying to achieve a harmonious integration of its dispositions in relation to its environment, they set up this aim of integration, harmony, or adjustment as their ethical ideal, as the over-all appetitive aim of ethical behavior. Then a man's impulses as they arise may find themselves already guided toward integration, instead of being given temporary head, having to be knocked down in frustrations and personal crises, and finally being forced into adjustment the hard way.

The integrative process is a selective system in its own right. It is not intrinsically an appetitive structure. A person may make this natural norm his ideal and appetitive goal and so facilitate the process, but the norm operates whether or not a person is astute enough to recognize its operation within him.

In the early development of a personality, the person has no opportunity to control his destiny. This is in a way unfortunate, since evidence is rolling up that a very large part of a person's character is formed in infancy. The saying is attributed to a certain church that if they can have the child for the first four years, anybody can have him after that. In the first few years a large part of the dispositional structure of a child has been laid down, and can be altered only with great difficulty later. However, the process of personality development never ceases. In the early years a foundation is laid down on which the developments of later years are built up. Thus, in the personality structure, time shows up as a sort of depth. The metaphor is that of stratification. Later dispositions are laid down over earlier ones. And in order to change an earlier, deeply laid disposition, it may be necessary to work first upon the superficial ones that overlie it.

It becomes very important, then, in understanding human personality, to consider its stages of growth.

## 4. STAGES IN THE GROWTH OF THE HUMAN PERSONALITY

A human personality is a slow growth built up layer upon layer over an extraordinarily long period of infantile dependence amounting to fifteen or more years. The human instincts emerge into prominence at different stages during this period, and some of these instincts, moreover, are undergoing a maturating process. The broad outlines of the development are matters of common observation and general common sense. Shakespeare has depicted them as the common man conceives them, only more vividly:

> And one man in his time plays many parts,
> His acts being seven ages. At first the infant,
> Mewling and puking in the nurse's arms.
> And then the whining school-boy, with his satchel
> And shining morning face, creeping like snail
> Unwillingly to school. And then the lover,
> Sighing like furnace, with a woful ballad
> Made to his mistress' eyebrow. Then a soldier,
> Full of strange oaths and bearded like the pard,
> Jealous in honour, sudden and quick in quarrel,
> Seeking the bubble reputation
> Even in the cannon's mouth. And then the justice,
> In fair round belly with good capon lin'd,
> With eyes severe and beard of formal cut,
> Full of wise saws and modern instances;
> And so he plays his part. The sixth age shifts
> Into the lean and slipper'd pantaloon,
> With spectacles on nose and pouch on side,
> His youthful hose, well sav'd, a world too wide
> For his shrunk shank; and his big manly voice
> Turning again toward childish treble, pipes
> And whistles in his sound. Last scene of all,
> That ends this strange eventful history,
> Is second childishness and mere oblivion,
> Sans teeth, sans eyes, sans taste, sans every thing.
> > *As You Like It*, Act II, scene 7

This may be taken as a fair beginning.

In recent years, however, much expert attention has been given to the stages of human personality development, especially to the early years of dependence and maturation. Remarkable discoveries have been made, some of which run contrary to popular opinion, particularly that of the early emergence of the sex instinct even though in a very immature stage. Common sense belief had vaguely held that the sex instinct somehow emerges full blown at puberty, as with Shakespeare's "lover, sighing like furnace." The cultural pattern conveniently ignored the manifestations of early sex interest in the growing child, or, if they were too obvious to be ignored, denounced them with the illogic that is typical of common sense.

Other instincts, also, have periods of immaturity and culmination that had not been precisely observed and described. The exact manner in which these dispositions come to maturity and their times of culmination are extremely important in character development and in understanding personality structure and its operation as a selective system.

Though more information about the development of human character has been gained in the last fifty years than during all the centuries before, there is much uncertainty and disagreement among experts in the field. It would be sheer confusion to scramble the numerous schools of theory in the hope of getting a composite picture of the present state of thinking on the subject. I shall take the chance of following mainly the school that conforms most nearly to the views of the man who has unquestionably contributed most to this subject. For Freud is to personality theory what Darwin is to evolutionary theory. Though there have been modifications and reactions, no studies in these fields can neglect the contributions of these men. So, on the whole in this chapter, I shall follow the details of personality development and structure as these are presented by the Freudian school. Whatever the future accumulation of evidence may bring out, I venture to think that it will not greatly disturb the main contributions of Freudian theory, just as Darwin's main concepts of evolutionary theory still hold, though much modified and amplified.

At least, in following the Freudian theory of personality fairly closely, we have before us a substantial model of the way in which personality structure can function as a natural norm in the value field. Whatever the correct theory may turn out to be, it will be some sort of structure operating in much this way in determining a man's daily decisions and his destiny in life.

Anyway, it will serve as a concrete rejection of one theory of the self that the data on hand render forever untenable—the theory of the self as a collection of externally related impressions and impulses. At the very least a personality is a dispositional structure with an integrative tendency.

The following account of the early growth of the human personality is taken almost entirely from an essay by Eric Erikson:

> Personality can be said to develop according to steps predetermined in the human organism's readiness to be driven toward, to be aware of, and to interact with, a widening social radius, beginning with the dim image of a mother and ending with mankind, or at any rate that segment of mankind which 'counts' in the particular individual's life.[1]

Erikson introduces a diagram to symbolize dispositional relations

| | | | |
|---|---|---|---|
| First stage (about first year) | Basic Trust | Earlier form of Autonomy | Earlier form of Initiative |
| Second stage (about second year) | Later form of Basic Trust | Autonomy | Earlier form of Initiative |
| Third stage (about fourth year) | Later form of Basic Trust | Later form of Autonomy | Initiative |

during a child's first three stages. The purpose of the diagram is to indicate graphically

> (1) that each item of the healthy personality to be discussed is systematically related to all others, and that they all depend on the proper development at the proper time of each item; and (2) that each item exists in some form before its decisive and critical time normally arrives.[2]

The name Erikson gives to each item is that which he feels most fully connotes the disposition developed in the personality once this disposition has been brought to fruition in a normal growth. Each disposition, however, develops around the focus of an instinctive drive already familiar to us. Basic trust is developed around the sucking instinct. This is the infant phase of the hunger drive directed upon a quiescence pattern of sucking at the mother's breast. It draws into it all the characteristics of nursing: the warmth, the support, and the comfort of it, and most importantly the affection. The ingredient of affection includes the first elementary appearance of the sex drive. This last is somewhat surprising, especially to those who had been brought up to think that infants were sexually neutral and that the sex instinct first emerged at puberty. But the evidence for infant sexuality is extensively confirmed, even though it may perhaps be regarded as a discovery of the last fifty years. This sexual ingredient fused with the hunger drive in the development of the attitude of basic trust is what for Freudian theory justifies the classification of this attitude as a psychosexual one. The infant's life immediately following birth is centered on sucking. His life literally depends upon it, and there is little else that he is initially coördinated to perform. The pattern of this disposition, in fact, spreads over all his activities. Nearly all have a receptive, incorporative, oral significance. Thus the stage has become technically known as the *oral stage.*

As the newborn is separated from his symbiosis with the mother's body his inborn and more or less co-ordinated ability to take in by the mouth meets the breasts' and the mother's, and the society's more or less co-ordinated ability and intention to feed him and to welcome him. At this point he lives through, and loves with, his mouth; and the mother lives through and loves with her breasts. For the mother this is a late and complicated accomplishment, highly dependent on her development as a woman; on the way she has lived through pregnancy and delivery; on her and the community's attitude toward the act of nursing—and on the response of the newborn. To him the mouth is the focus of a general first approach to life—the *incorporative* approach. In present-day psychiatry this stage is therefore generally referred to as the 'oral' stage. Yet it is clear that, in addition to the overwhelming need for food, a baby is, or soon becomes, receptive in many other respects. He is willing and able to seek an appropriate object and to swallow whatever appropriate fluids they emit, he is soon also willing and able to 'take in' with his eyes whatever enters his visual field. His tactual senses, too, seem to 'take in' what feels good.[3]

The infant, of course, has very little that he can do if these needs for love and food are denied him. He can struggle and cry. He can suck his thumb. That is about all. An attitude of helplessness, depending upon the degree of frustration, is what could be expected as a result of insufficient care, and statistically this seems to be just what happens. A group of traits associated with a generally pessimistic attitude appears to characterize persons who have been seriously frustrated in the oral stage; contrariwise, children who have not met undue frustration at this stage normally develop an open, optimistic, and outgoing approach to life.[4]

Each stage has its particular crisis that a child has to meet and work through. That of the oral stage is weaning. Sooner or later it must occur. This first great inevitable frustration is unavoidable. But it can be eased by a loving and understanding parent. The loss is not simply that of an accustomed way of feeding but of a form of intimacy with the mother.

A drastic loss of accustomed mother love without proper substitution at this time can lead (under otherwise aggravating conditions) to acute infantile depression or to a mild but chronic undertone of mourning which may give a depressive undertone to the whole remainder of life.[5]

The second stage, that of autonomy, centers upon the elimination drives, and is technically known as the *anal stage*.

The whole procedure of evacuating the bowels and the bladder as completely as possible is, of course, enhanced from the beginning by a premium of 'feeling good,' which says in effect 'well done.' This premium [our quiescence pattern or satisfaction in a consummatory act] at the beginning of life, must make up for quite frequent discomfort and tension suffered as the bowels learn to do their daily work. [That is, there is a maturation in the elimination instincts which, coming to completion at about two years, institutes the anal stage.] Two developments gradually give these 'anal' experiences the necessary volume: the arrival of better formed stool, and the general co-ordination of the muscle system which permits the development of voluntary

release, of dropping and throwing away. This new dimension of
approach to things, however, is not restricted to the sphincters. A
general ability, indeed, a violent need, develops to drop and to
throw away and to alternate withholding and expelling at will.[6]

As, in the oral stage, the pattern of the consummatory act of
incorporation spreads over nearly all the other activities of the
child, so now the pattern of the controlled consummatory act of
elimination spreads over all the child's behavior. With muscle
control, the child begins to discover his 'will.' The positive injective of aggression is constantly brought into play to back up
the child's newly acquired capacities for muscular coördination
and overcome the blockages that occur in doing what he wants.
The child becomes capable of focusing his affection and hostilities upon determinate objects. "This stage, therefore, becomes
decisive," writes Erikson, "for the ratio between love and hate,
for that between co-operation and willfulness, and for that between the freedom of self-expression and its suppression."[7]

This is the stage in which the child first gets the sense of
himself as a person, an agent with a will of his own and capacities for choice, for autonomy in short. He finds himself often in
conflict with other persons and discovers the alternatives of
coöperation or opposition.

The typical crisis likely to be met at this stage arises from the
social mores of toilet training. Cultures differ greatly in their
demands on this matter. In some cultures little attention is paid
to it. But Western civilization in most areas takes it very seriously, and insists on a time and a place and points of cleanliness.
The whole process acquires the connotation of 'dirty.' To be sure,
sanitary measures are advisable in large societies. But the frustrations entailed in the training can be extreme. For they amount
to no less than converting an instinctive appetition into an object of aversion. Faulty handling of this stage by parents or
society leads to a variety of typical compulsions for excessive
cleanliness, orderliness, miserliness, stinginess, that may acquire
neurotic intensity and rigidity. In their milder forms they may be
simple independence mutations, where an injective has taken
over a dispositional pattern found by the infant to be the only
means of handling a persistently frustrating situation, but in the

acuter forms it may be inferred that a repression has occurred sinking the drive complex below the level of immediate voluntary control.

Yet this stage can be worked through in a healthy way even within a rigorously constraining cultural pattern. It requires only a solid foundation of basic trust in parental affection combined with firmness in regard to consideration of other persons and of social demands.

> To develop autonomy a firmly developed and a convincingly continued stage of early trust is necessary. The infant must come to feel that basic faith in himself and in the world (which is the lasting treasure saved from the conflicts of the oral stage) will not be jeopardized by this sudden wish to have a choice, to appropriate demandingly and to eliminate stubbornly. *Firmness* must protect him against the potential anarchy of his as yet untrained sense of discrimination, his inability to hold on and let go with circumspection. Yet his environment must back him up to stand on his own feet.[8]

In this stage emerges the *sense of shame*, often confused with conscience because, like conscience, it is an effective instrument of social control over individual conduct. Some cultures make more use of it than others. 'Saving face' as a motive is a symptom of it. But it is dynamically different from conscience, which normally develops at the next stage.

> Shame is an infantile emotion insufficiently studied. Shame supposes that one is completely exposed and conscious of being looked at—in a word, self-conscious. One is visible and not ready to be visible; that is why we dream of shame as a situation in which we are stared at in a condition of incomplete dress, in night attire, 'with one's pants down.' Shame is early expressed in an impulse to bury one's face, or to sink, right then and there, into the ground.[9]

Shame lacks the element of command that conscience has, and so the sense of guilt from disobedience. It is more immediately emotional, and less dynamically complex. It is a fear of social disapproval and a desire to escape from its glare, but it involves no sense of self-discipline, as conscience does. Consequently, the effectiveness of shame breaks down if a society pushes it too hard. "Too much shaming," Erikson points out, "does not result in a sense of propriety but in a secret determination to try to get away with things when unseen, if, indeed, it does not result in deliberate shamelessness." [10]

This second stage runs from about two to four years of age. Then at four or five comes the third stage, the so-called *phallic stage,* which is the first to center definitely on the sex instinct. But this instinct and its mechanisms for consummation are still in an immature state, and the human organism is still greatly dependent on his parents for sustenance and protection. These circumstances render the crisis characteristic of this stage particularly difficult and severe. This is the stage at which the so-called Oedipus complex and castration complex are likely to emerge, or possibly always do emerge, and when the principal repressions that become embedded in the personality are almost sure to occur.

In the first stage the child is in a state of horizontal relaxation; in the second stage he is sitting up and just learning to walk and run. By the third stage he is upright and can run about and coördinate his acts without thinking about them. If he wants an object, his muscles automatically coördinate to reach it. He can talk. "His sense of language becomes perfected to the point where he understands and can ask about many things just enough to misunderstand them thoroughly." [11] With freedom of locomotion and language his imagination expands. And at the same time he becomes aware of his sexual organs and the rudiments of sexual relationship. For the first time the child has a sense of his full potential capacities as a person, and the gathering initiative to make a success of himself, an initiative "for the selection of social goals and a perseverance in approaching them."

But the very intensity of this initiative aggravates the characteristic crisis of frustration at this stage.

Psychoanalysis verifies the simple conclusion that boys attach their first genital affections to the maternal adults who have otherwise given comfort to their bodies and that they develop their first sexual rivalry against the persons who are the sexual owners of those maternal persons. The little girl, in turn, becomes attached to her father and other important men and jealous of her mother, a development which may cause her much anxiety, for it seems to block her retreat to that self-same mother, while it makes the mother's disapproval ever so much more magically dangerous because unconsciously 'deserved.' [12]

Just at the period when these tensions are developing, the child is subjected to the educative influences of his social environment. In our culture he is sent to school.

This often demands a change of personality that is sometimes too drastic for the good of the child. This change is not only a result of education but also of an inner reorientation, and it is based on a biological fact (the delay of sexual maturation) and a psychological one (the repression of childhood wishes). For those sinister Oedipus wishes (so simply and so trustingly expressed in the boy's assurance that he will marry mother and make her proud of him, and in the girl's that she will marry father and take much better care of him), in consequence of vastly increased imagination and, as it were, intoxication of increased locomotor powers, seems to lead to secret fantasies of terrifying proportions. The consequence is a deep sense of *guilt*— a strange sense, for it forever seems to imply that the individual has committed crimes and deeds which, after all, were not only not committed but also would have been biologically quite impossible . . . Jealousy and rivalry, those often embittered and yet essentially futile attempts at demarcating a sphere of unquestioned privilege, now come to a climax in a final contest for a favored position with one of the parents; the inevitable and necessary failure leads to guilt and anxiety. The child indulges in fantasies of being a giant and a tiger, but in his dreams he runs in terror for dear life. This then is the stage of fear for life and limb, including the fear of losing (or on the part of the girl the conviction that she may have lost) the male genital as punishment for fantasies attached to infantile genital excitement. All this may seem strange to readers who have only seen the sunnier side of childhood and have not recognized the potential powerhouse of destructive drives that can be aroused and temporarily buried at this stage, only to contribute later to the inner arsenal of destructiveness which is ever ready to be used when opportunity provokes it.[13]

The crisis here must be very severe, for at about this time a child usually manages to forget, in terms of voluntary recall, everything that has happened to him previously in his life. Very few persons can spontaneously remember things that happened to them before the age of four, and yet their neural apparatus was well developed by the age of two or earlier. Under clinical treatment, memories from as far back as the age of two can be revived, which is evidence that the forgetting is not physiological but psychological. It is as though the emotional shock from the fears of the child's wishes and fantasies at that time repressed not only the fantasies themselves but all the surrounding content of his thought.[14]

Along with these repressions develop conscience and the sense of guilt. It is important here to make a distinction between conscientiousness, or the open conscience, which means well-considered action with a due regard for the requirements of others, and the rigid irrational conscience which is an inner command and the source of guilt feelings. The open conscience is relatively free from guilt, though a person will feel badly and kick himself for his stupidity if his act proves wrong from hasty judgment. But the rigid conscience punishes a person who violates it with feelings of guilt, often very intense. From its time of emergence, its irrationality, its rigidity, the quality of the guilt feelings, and the fact that the rigidity and the guilt feelings become relaxed by the same clinical treatment which releases a person's repressions, we are led to the conclusion that the rigid conscience is closely bound up with a person's repressions.

The rigid conscience, however, is an exceedingly important element in a personality. It institutes a selective system of its own within the personality. And ordinarily it reflects as in a mirror the social pattern. It is the incorporation into the personality of the authority first of the parents and then of all the other authorities who acquire an influence over the child's life— the teachers, the church authorities, and the civil officers. This is, as the classical moralists have pointed out, the internal sanction for moral conduct. The intuitionist and deontologist schools of ethics make this the basic concept of their theories. A rigid conscience implanted in a person is a most effective control of conduct—more effective than parents, police, or church, for it is always vigilant and always there.

Says Erikson,

It [conscience] is the great governor of initiative. . . . The child now feels not only ashamed when found out but also afraid of being found out. He now hears, as it were, God's voice without seeing God. Moreover, he begins automatically to feel guilty even for mere thought and for deeds which nobody has watched. This is the cornerstone of morality in the individual sense. But from the point of view of mental health, we must point out that if this great achievement is overburdened by too eager adults, it can be bad for the spirit and for morality itself. For the conscience of the child *can* be primitive, cruel, and uncompromising, as may be observed in instances where children learn to constrict themselves to the point of overall inhibition where they develop an obedience more literal than the one the parent wishes to exact; or where they develop deep regressions and lasting resentments because the parents themselves do not seem to live up to the new conscience which they have fostered in the child.[15]

The rigid conscience may be overdone in terms of the harmonious integration of the personality. It is a selective system in its own right, and may find itself in conflict with other phases of the personality. The evaluative question how far and under what conditions it should legislate over these other phases becomes a crucial one. On the intuitionist theory, its legislative prerogative is absolute. And so, of course, it feels to the self acutely pricked by the pangs of conscience. But if the rigid conscience is a source of personality rupture, or if a change of social condition sets the judgments of a man's conscience in conflict with his social environment—if, for instance, his conscience tells him that he cannot smoke or dance, yet all his present friends do these things and leave him out of their good times because he does not—then inevitably he is subject to the sanctions of other natural norms which operate on his decisions and on his life. But the point now is simply that a rigid conscience is a natural norm and yet clearly not an absolute norm, and that it ordinarily emerges in this third stage of personality development.

In the third stage, when the sex instinct first becomes oppressive, two important structures appear in the personality which were only rudimentary before: a system of repressed dispositions centered in sex impulses, and a rigid conscience rather closely connected with the repressed system. Both of these can be augmented, and there will be more to say about them later.

The crisis at this stage is almost as inevitable as weaning in the oral stage. It is doubtful if it can be avoided. The child's impulses cannot be satisfied at that time in the ways the child wishes. But the crisis can be softened by understanding parents or a favorable cultural pattern. It is said that there is very little evidence of the Oedipus complex among the children of the Hopi Indians. But this may actually be the sort of exception that proves the rule. In the early stages Hopi children are unusually uninhibited by their cultural environment, and are lovingly cared for not only by a mother and father but by a whole group of aunts and uncles and grandparents. After describing the family arrangements in Hopi society, one observer summarizes her findings thus:

> Even if we assume that the Oedipus situation is universal, the Hopi seem to have resolved a great deal of its conflict by diffusing authority and transferring much of it outside the elementary family; and also by directing childhood sexual inclinations to 'safe' objects outside the household—the father's sisters. Examining . . . the general sexual development of Hopi children, we find a minimum of repression.[16]

After the third stage of initiative, Erikson interposes two more stages: one stresses play and achievement; the next, which he calls 'ego identification,' stresses the integration of the self and the taking on of 'roles' (of which more presently), finding one's function, job, or profession in society. Then comes the classic fourth stage of the Freudian theory of personality development, that technically known as the *genital stage*. This is the stage of complete fruition of the sex drive. In a healthy person, who has passed without undue frustration and repression through the crises of the earlier stages, it represents

> [a] capacity to develop orgastic potency in relation to a loved partner of the opposite sex . . . [a] heterosexual mutuality, with full genital sensitivity and with an over-all discharge of tension from the whole body.[17] . . . Psychiatry, in recent years, has emphasized *genitality* as one of the chief signs of a healthy personality . . . The idea clearly is that the experience of climactic mutuality of orgasm provides a supreme example of the mutual regulation of complicated patterns.[18]

Just as in the oral stage the oral pattern spread over all of the child's activities, and in the anal stage the pattern of withholding and expelling, and in the phallic stage that of individual coördination and exploration and action, so in the genital stage the pattern and the rhythms of mutual coöperative consummation spread over all of a person's behavior as a sort of model of all ideal human action. As a person speaks, or moves in situations quite unrelated to the central one of this culminating stage, other persons will intuitively catch these rhythms and respond to them.

The attainment of his full capacity of mutual love seems to be the secret of personal happiness, for it represents the complete structural development of a person as man or woman. And, since the source of the value is the integrated capacity of the whole mature organism, a person carries this about with him wherever he goes and illuminates every situation with the light of his love in proportion to the reflective powers of the objects present. Such happiness does not have to wait upon the fortuitous occasion to add up little sums of pleasure, but carries consummatory satisfactions with it into all manner of occasions.

With the attainment of the genital stage a person has grown up. There are other stages to come. A person enters parenthood, passes into middle age, and into old age, and these carry with them dispositional changes. But a man's personality has been largely built up by the time he reaches the genital stage. His character has been pretty well set for the remainder of his life, and the new dispositions he acquires must be fitted in and superimposed on the broad outlines that have been laid down through his developmental stages.

That is why it is so important to have a rather detailed view of these developmental stages. From such a view it is clear that a later stage is conditioned by an earlier stage, with the result that a full development of a later stage is blocked or curtailed if there has been a serious distortion or inhibition of development at an earlier stage. We begin to see what is meant by an ideal normal healthy personality, and to see how it functions as a natural norm.

## 5. The Structure of the Personality

Having followed the growth of a normal personality, let us inquire into the structure of a mature personality. We shall then be dealing with a responsible person who has a place as a member of his society. What do we find are the main structural elements of his personality? Let us consider them with a view to their integrative action.

1. There are first the *drives,* instinctive and derived, with their purposive structures, and the learned *habits* of achievement wherever these have been formed. These drives and habits constitute the atomic elements of a personality, and other elements are constellations of these. Already, within the individual purposive structures, a good deal of integration has taken place. The learning process of an appetition is an integrative process. A subordinate anticipatory set is a disposition which if it serves its superordinate set is so far integrated with it; if not, it is disruptive and frustrating for the person as long as he mistakenly persists in it. And a well-learned habit serving a constantly recurring interest is already, so far as it operates in a man's living, an integrated structure. So we have already been dealing with the integrative process in describing the structures of appetitions and aversions. As selective systems they function through the learning process to lay down integrated dispositional structures of cognitive sets in the service of specific terminal goals or objects of avoidance. They are integrated dispositions to act so far as their mediating judgments are correct, so far as they protect the person from doing frustrating acts.

There is, accordingly, a good deal of personality integration on the atomic level, so to speak. Every well-learned habit is, so far as it goes, an integrated dispositional structure. Of course, the whole structure may be disruptive on a higher level, but no higher level can be well integrated if the purposive structures which enter into it are not sufficiently integrated themselves.

2. We enter upon a higher level of integration when we see the function of *roles* in a person's behavior. George Mead is probably to be credited more than any other writer for calling

attention to this important element in personality structure. A role is a cluster of dispositions which a person assumes for a specific sort of situation demanded by social structures in his environment. The concept of role is closely connected with that of the personal and of the social situation. Not that every situation in which a person finds himself calls out a role, but it is likely to do so. And the better integrated and more experienced the person, the more likely he is to have a role, or even a combination of roles, suitable for handling the situation. We shall expand upon this important function of roles in §6.

3. Then, in the succeeding sections, we shall consider three large constellations of dispositions which behave more or less as wholes within the personality structure: the group of repressed dispositions (in §§7, 8) the group of dispositions composing the rigid or irrational conscience (in §9) and the group of dispositions freely open to voluntary control, which we shall call the voluntary system (§10).

These last three groups cut right across the habits and roles. Roles are made up of habits, but we cannot say that the last three groups are made up of roles. They must be considered as another grouping of drives and habits besides that of roles, a vertical grouping in contrast to the horizontal grouping of roles in respect to drives and habits.

We shall now proceed to consider seriatim the nature and functioning of roles, the repressed system, conscience, and the voluntary system.[19]

## 6. The Integrative Action of Roles in the Personality

Mead is probably right in his conviction that a person becomes aware of himself as a person only when he perceives himself in a role that distinguishes his acts from the acts of others about him. This presumably begins to dawn on a child fairly early. But according to Erikson's account it appears with definiteness only in the second stage. And in children's play we can clearly see the taking on and off of roles. The child plays that he is a truck driver, a motorman, an Indian, a scout, a storekeeper, a father, a mother, a nurse. In taking on these roles—often to the amusement of the parents and sometimes to their revelation—the child is working out many of his own wishes and preparing for the serious assumption of some of them later, when he grows up.

The influence of his cultural pattern is apparent in the roles assumed by the child in play. Nearly all of a person's roles are culturally determined. This has been stressed by the anthropologists and sometimes overstressed to the point of leaving a person very little character of his own making. But it should not be understressed, and we shall give special attention to cultural pattern as a selective system in chapter 19.

A role functions in the personality as a norm regulating a person's actions in situations which call it out. And it is the usual basis for criticism of other persons' actions in similar situations. There is a role for practically every situation that comes up. A man takes on a role in his job or profession. He takes on another role as a father. He has a different role as club or church member. He has one role as a foreman and a superior, another as a subordinate. The same, with proper changes, for a woman. And there are, of course, the over-all masculine role and the feminine role, and the roles appropriate to different ages—the role of the child, the youth, the middle-aged man, and the old man.

Each role is a cluster of dispositions of the atomic sort. What, then, constitutes integration on the level of roles? First, the cluster of habits and drives making up the role must themselves be integrated. This is done usually through the action of tradition, since most roles are culturally determined and are the result of extended cultural experience, the wisdom of tradition. But tradition may lag, and it is not always wise. Hence, second, a person must know when it is appropriate to apply a role. Otherwise there is frustration in terms of the reality of the situation. Barring rigidity superimposed by repressions of some sort, a person usually learns with acute discrimination the cues for assuming a role. Third, there is in the integration of roles the problem of adjusting them one to another so that they will fit together without conflict. Situations which precipitate a conflict of roles give rise to some of the most serious frustrations a man has to meet. Sometimes the conflicts are unavoidable in the course of external events, but sometimes the conflicts arise from an incompatibility of roles embedded in a man's own character. These are the most important to resolve for personality integration.

A role thus draws upon a number of different drives, which converge and coöperate in its fulfillment. Such a fulfillment is a rather complicated achievement. It functions as a norm of conduct involving a set of duties or proprieties specific to the role.

Thus the role of husband in our culture draws upon a wide range of drives and a whole set of things is expected of a man in that role. He is supposed to be a good lover, a good companion, satisfied in his home relationships, a good provider, a good father, a good host, handy about the house, and so on. The role of husband is itself, we see, a constellation of other roles, and a certain proportioning of time and energy is required for the complete fulfillment of the role of husband. A proportioning that minimizes frustrations and regrets is what produces here an integration of roles in a personality.

For a man may be a jolly companion at the expense of being a good father, or a handy man about the house at the expense of being a good provider. His more than usual assiduousness in the fulfillment of these contributing roles actually disrupts his adequately carrying out the role of husband. The balance and distribution of duties required by a role immediately reveal themselves in an example like this.

And the sanctions emanating from the drives drawn upon, in conjunction with the reality of the social situation of a man within his family, are also immediately apparent. There is a constant pressure on a man to fulfill the role of husband as adequately as he can. A failure to adapt is a failure in personality integration.

In the foregoing we are assuming the preëminence of the role of husband over the contributory roles. Conflicts then arise only over the distribution of the contributory roles. A more serious conflict arises when one of the contributory roles acquires a genuinely competitive significance in reference to the reality of a wider situation. Suppose a man's profession makes demands on his time which conflict with the fulfillment of his duties as a husband and a father. Such a conflict of roles is sometimes very difficult to resolve. If a man's profession is one of public responsibility—an officer in the armed forces, a senator, a governor of a state, a president or prime minister—there is no question which role takes precedence. But if he is a businessman or a lawyer or a scholar and sacrifices his family to his profession, the choice is not so clear, and he risks the loss of a well-rounded personality and the suffering of much frustration. A career woman in our culture has a similar problem, and the sacrifice of the role of wife to that of a profession is usually at great personal cost.

These problems of the relative importance of significant roles bring out the supreme importance of the over-all conception a man has of himself, which in modern psychological lingo goes by the name of the *ego ideal*. This is the ideal a man sets up for himself. It may be a loose coördination of ideals, which shift more or less from situation to situation. But a well-integrated personality develops one such ideal which for him is the role of all roles. Only so does a man acquire complete stability of character. The original nucleus of an ego ideal is a person's father or mother or some other respected person in a child's environment whom he admires and with whom he tends to identify. The object of identification may shift or may graft on admired traits of other persons. It may be a fictitious or semi-fictitious character, the hero of a novel or a movie star. It may be several persons at once. But eventually, for a fully integrated ego ideal, it is a creation of the man himself—his own estimate of his capacities and desires and admirations, drawn up fairly close to the reality of his actual capacities. An ego ideal is not a man's actual personality. It is what he wishes to be. As such, it is just one disposition among others in his personality. But in a well-integrated personality it is the most important of all his dispositions, for it is the one in terms of which he tries to order them all. It is for him the role of roles. It proportions and therefore integrates all roles, just as the role of the good husband, within its more limited sphere, proportions its own contributing roles.[20]

A well-integrated personality will inevitably have a well-integrated ego ideal. One of the evidences of a personality lacking in integration is the lack of such an ego ideal. This may show up as aimlessness. A scattered diffusion of interests exposes a man, like a moth in a wind, to the mercy of every novel situation. He shifts roles at every change with no firm will for any steady accomplishment. Or perhaps he has two or three strong competing ego ideals with which he has never come to terms. In these contingencies a man lays himself open to much frustration—so much so that the lack of a well-formed ego ideal in a mature person is a sign of mental sickness. Some deep repression is blocking him from using the normal process of learning from experience with which he as a docile animal is amply endowed. For we are not thinking here of the mentally deficient.

Also, a man may be deceived in his own ego ideal. It may be a hollow front. Others watching his behavior can see that he is quite different from what he professes to be. If he has many repressions poorly integrated, he will actually be blind to his shortcomings, and not perceive the inconsistency of his actions with what he believes to be his character. He may think he is benevolent, and his actions show him selfish and self-centered. He may think he is a man of broad judgment and high ideals, and his actions show that he is rigid and bigoted.

This is a favorite area of rationalization. Such a man will find plausible reasons for his inconsistent acts to make them seem consistent with the ego ideal he aspires to maintain. Rationalization is a false mediating judgment which connects an act a person has a drive to perform with his ego ideal, which is itself a mediating judgment demanding fulfilment in order that the act may go through. Since the rationalization is false in terms of the act performed, frustrations are inevitable in view of the reality of the situation.

Actually, a brazenly selfish man may be better integrated than a man with a benevolent ego ideal who habitually rationalizes himself into selfish acts. A brazenly selfish man has set a low ego ideal for himself (so low we are likely to say he has none), but he lives up to what little he has and does not deceive himself. A rationalizing man has set a high ideal for himself, but fails to live up to it and systematically deceives himself about his failures. Both men for different reasons are lacking in integration, but the latter probably more than the former. Ironically, the trouble may be that the latter has set an unrealistically high ego ideal for himself—too high for fulfillment in the total reality of the situation.

This possibility brings up another concept pertinent to roles and personality integration, that of the *level of aspiration*. Kurt Lewin is responsible for bringing this important concept into prominence. Most roles make possible different degrees of achievement. Within limits a person can choose what he shall consider an adequate achievement for himself. This itself is a personality trait. A lazy man tries to get away with the lowest possible level of achievement in the roles he has to take, but an extremely lazy man makes more trouble for himself than he gets out of. And all laziness leads to frustration somewhere, otherwise it would not be considered a vice. At the other extreme, the over-ambitious man who overestimates his capacities and tries to do the impossible is likewise making unnecessary trouble for himself. This concept of the level of aspiration is a very fruitful one, and deserves expansion. It is obviously linked with group morale. It is linked with getting a person interested in what he is doing. But these details lie somewhat off the main line of our immediate concern with the integrative action of the personality as a selective system generating a distinct sort of value.

We have now reached a point at which we can see rather clearly what integration in the personality consists in and why it is so important. Its underlying dynamics is primarily the avoidance of frustration. But it has a positive side also in the maximization of satisfaction and of something else, too, which we cannot fully appraise till we have looked into the status of survival value—namely, adaptability. It turns out that the highly integrated personality is what has been extolled for generations as the well-balanced, well-rounded man. Negatively, he is a personality with a minimum of repressions, and so one that can be guided by true mediating judgments free from rationalizations. This will afford him insight into the reality of the situation. Likewise, it will free his drives for maximum satisfaction and a minimum of internal conflict. Positively it will give him what is commonly called 'vitality.'

The details of how the ground for such personality integration may be prepared through the healthy development of the child are schematically set forth in Erikson's account (§4). Thereafter integration consists in the selection of a man's roles in life. Many of these are assigned to him by the cultural pattern into which he is born. Others he can select for himself. For the latter he does well to consider his own aptitudes, since in doing what he is best fitted to do he gains most satisfaction. Here for most men comes the choice between specialization and breadth of interest. The path of personality integration leads between them. Too much specialization in certain roles places a man at the mercy of his immediate environment. Some slight physical or economic change and he is unequipped with a role for the new situation. Yet too little specialization produces the dilettante, who is not very good at anything. The notion of being good at things brings up the concept of the level of aspiration, and this in turn brings in the reality of the situation. If the level of aspiration is set too high, the achievements are too discouraging; if set too low, the achievements may be inadequate for the requirements of the situation. A well-integrated personality will find the proper level. Indeed, he will find it if he is flexible enough to perceive his errors and correct them—if, in short, his personality structure is sufficiently integrated to become even better integrated. This is just what we mean by describing personality integration as a selective system.

But what if he is not flexible enough to integrate himself further? What sanction determines his error? If his social pattern supports his inflexibility, he may have no trouble. It will be noticed only that his capacities for consummatory satisfactions are limited. But if the social pattern does not find a niche for his form of rigidity, then, being unadaptable, he is constantly in a state of frustration. He will in various degrees be socially ostracized; he may land in an asylum or worse. In short, if he cannot correct himself, he comes under social correction—of which we shall learn much presently. Eventually he comes under the demands for the survival of his species through social solidarity. The operation of an irrational conscience is also relevant to personality integration. But finally, as we shall see, the integrative process of the personality as a selective system calls for a rational conscience and full voluntary control of a person's actions in view of a man's actual environment and the reality of each situation as it arises. This yields the ideal of the well-balanced, adaptable man with a wide range of interests to apply to the situations he encounters both for achievement and for consummatory enjoyment. The traditional ideal of the self-realizationist for the most complete integration of the widest spread of interests gains confirmation here. This would be the ideal of ego ideals. It is the terminal aim (though not literally in our terms a purposive goal) of the integrative action of the human personality.

## 7. RATIONALITY AND IRRATIONALITY IN THE PERSONALITY STRUCTURE

We now have a fairly adequate impression of the way in which roles become embedded in a personality, and how, as clusters of dispositions for the handling of concrete situations, they acquire their integrative function. If it were not for man's peculiar susceptibility to repressions, our treatment of the integrative action of the personality could stop right here. And this is indeed where it does stop for many rational moralists of the past. For the integrative process of the personality that we have been following up to this point is an eminently rational procedure. Given the repertory of drives with which a man is innately endowed and the environmental objects of appetition and aversion appropriate to them, then the acquired habits as integrated purposive dispositions are the reasonable development for harmonious living in one's environment. And the superimposition over these of roles integrating a number of habits into dispositions well adapted for handling complex social situations is but a prolongation of the same reasonable development. The culmination of this process in an ego ideal as the role of all the roles in a well-integrated personality would seem to terminate the development. What else could rationally be expected for the integrative process within a single person?

Nothing rationally. But it happens that the human organism,

the most elaborately docile and reasonable of all animals, is uniquely provided also with an ample area of irrationality. It is as if this area of irrationality were given as a cushion to absorb the shocks and the strain of his excessive capacities for reason. The bases of reason are the capacities to anticipate and to be apprehensive. And these powers with man's range of foresight vastly increase his sources of anxiety. The keener a man's intellect, the more he can foresee to be worried about. All this is to his biological advantage, as the place he has made for himself in the world plainly shows—so long as the anxieties do not become overpowering. One way to take care of this danger is to provide a mechanism for shutting off excessive anxieties so that they will not interfere too seriously with the processes of adaptive foresight. This is apparently what has occurred in man's evolutionary development. The mechanism is that of repression.

This mechanism is far from being completely understood. By its very nature it is well concealed from rational scrutiny, and only recently has it been uncovered. I offered a diagram and a hypothesis which exhibit the mechanisms of repression as a kind of value mutation (chap. 11, §5), but this is patently a much oversimplified description. The mechanism is designed to escape the notice of man's reason and has done well in this respect. The human reason finally caught a clue to it and followed it up to its source, but only because there was a class of instances where the mechanism did not work adaptively for certain persons— namely, instances of emotional breakdown and insanity. These were a mystery to rational explanation. Insane persons were even said to be possessed by other persons (evil spirits), which was not far wrong except that the evil "persons" were not other persons entering the afflicted man but unintegrated parts of his own personality.

Plato came somewhat nearer the facts as known today when he ascribed insanity to an extreme state of conflict within the personality. But he pointed to the totality of a man's drives as the villain, calling them the faculty of appetency and setting over them two other faculties of will and reason. He was a self-realizationist in value theory (apparently the first in the Occidental tradition) and had an insight into the significance of integration as a focal source of values. The just man was the well-integrated man, and the just society the well-integrated one. He even had a surprisingly open perception of the repressed impulses and their nature, the way in which they worked out in dreams, and the mischief they could cause when they broke loose from rational restraint. In describing the character of the tyrannical man, for him the worst and most disintegrated type, Plato begins with these amazingly modern psychological generalizations:

> I think that the number and nature of appetites has not been satisfactorily defined, and while this deficiency continues, the inquiry upon which we are entering will be wrapped in obscurity. . . . Observe the peculiarity which I wish to notice in the case before us. It is this. Some of the unnecessary pleasures and appetites are, if I mistake not, unlawful; and these would appear to form an original part of every man; though, in the case of some persons, under the correction of the laws and the higher appetites aided by reason, they either wholly disappear, or only a few weak ones remain; while in the case of others, they continue strong and numerous. . . . I refer to those appetites which bestir themselves in sleep; when during the slumbers of that other part of the soul, which is rational and tamed and master of the former, the wild animal part, sated with meat or drink, becomes rampant and pushing sleep away, endeavors to set out after the gratification of its own proper character. You know that in such moments there is nothing that it dares not do, released and delivered as it is from any sense of shame and reflection. It does not shrink from attempting in fancy unholy intercourse with a mother or with any man or deity or animal whatever; and it does not hesitate to commit the foulest murder, or to indulge itself in the most defiling meats. In one word, there is no limit to its folly or its audacity.[21]

Then he contrasts the state of mind of such a man who has let down his restraints by indulging in meat and drink before going to rest with that of a man whose "personal habit is healthful and temperate" and who "before betaking himself to rest . . . has stimulated the rational part of him." By this means, he suggests, a man escapes bad dreams.

> Well, we have been carried too far out of our way, in order to make these remarks. What we wish to recognize is, that apparently a terrible species of wild and lawless appetites resides in every one of us, even when in some cases we have the appear-

ance of being perfectly self-restrained. And this fact, it seems, becomes evident in sleep.[22]

Plato proceeds to describe the growth of the tyrannical type of man, linking the causes with sex, drink, and insanity, and concludes: "So, my excellent friend, a man becomes strictly tyrannical, whenever, by nature, or by habit, or by both together, he has fallen under the dominion of wine, or love, or insanity." [23]

Here we have the frankest recognition of the repressed impulses and their disruptive power in the personality to appear, so far as I know, in Occidental thought until the middle of the nineteenth century. But, having noticed them, Plato promptly associated them with the whole group of man's drives, which consequently were, to him, contaminated with evil and disruptive tendencies. Then he set over all of man's impulses two controlling powers or faculties, which he called 'will' and 'reason.'

Plato thus brought into being the so-called *faculty psychology* (hypothesizing the three faculties of appetency, will, and reason), which dominated psychological thinking for many centuries. Its unfortunate effect was to disparage as something evil and disruptive the whole impulsive side of man's nature, and to present a considerably distorted conception of the dynamics of the personality. Reason in the faculty psychology was a dynamic agent capable of directing the will, which was a powerful force capable of standing off even the most tremendous impulses within a just and temperate character. Reason and will were thus set up in opposition to appetency, with its wild horde of impulses, and somehow were supposed to dictate the virtues of harmony to the otherwise unwilling horde.

The faculty psychology is now generally discredited except in Scholastic circles. But Plato came so near to working out a hypothesis to cover his perception of the action of the repressed impulses that his falling short of an adequate theory is the more to be remarked upon. We commented on how well the mechanisms of repression are designed to conceal the repressions themselves from observation, and what resistance a man has against becoming aware of them. They crop out obviously only in the irrationality of dreams and insanity, which are infrequent enough to be more or less neglected or rejected. But Plato did notice them and face them and describe them and mark their emergence in other emotional occurrences, as in the release of inhibitions produced by alcohol and by intense sex impulse. He noticed their disruptive tendencies and their opposition to the integrative demands of a healthy personality. He even described the Oedipus impulse. Why, then, did he not isolate them as the central dynamic disruptive agency in the personality? He did distinguish them as the 'unlawful appetites' in the foregoing and other passages. Why did he not take his cue from that and work out the dynamics of his personality structure from that basic division of 'unlawful' and 'lawful' appetites? Since all appetites are intrinsically dynamic, he would have found the source of dynamic opposition to his group of 'unlawful appetites' in the group of lawful appetites. Since all appetites shun frustration, there he would have found the source of his integrative values for the personality. But instead he veered away from the 'unlawful appetites' as a group, turned in the other direction, grouped all the appetites together, and indicted the whole group as intrinsically disintegrative and evil. How the mechanisms of repression must have smiled at this retreat! They had worked once more just when Plato had almost broken them down. And, having made this retreat, Plato had to manufacture some forces out of his imagination to explain the obvious tendency toward integration in a healthy personality, and to explain the obvious resistance of a healthy personality to disruptive impulses. So he invented the faculty of reason to account for integration, and the faculty of will to account for the dynamics of restraint.

I go into Plato's dilemma not only for its intrinsic interest in showing how near this exceedingly open and inquiring mind came to unlocking the door of the human soul's most carefully guarded closet, but also because of the enormous influence his faculty psychology, which he invented to take care of what he saw, had upon later theories of motivation and value. Even today, in the wake of a large accumulation of evidence that was not available to Plato and other men writing before the present century, man's impulses and emotions are looked upon with suspicion, and reason and will are still conceived as monitors delegated to keep them in order.

On the modern view, of which the multiple drive theory here recommended is one of a number of species, all the dynamics of human behavior comes from our impulses. Consequently it is only by our impulses that we can control our impulses.[24] Reason and will, on this view, cannot be separate dynamic powers opposed to drives. They are names for certain ways in which drives operate.

Reason can be satisfactorily identified with the sphere of cognitive references and mediating judgments, including, particularly in the present context, evaluative judgments. It follows as a corollary, since the function of the mediating judgments is to reduce frustration by correct mediating references, that reason is an integrative agency.

Cognitive references (pure reason as knowledge of true and false), as Spinoza knew, have no power to restrain an emotion. The power must come from another stronger emotion or drive charging the cognitive set. If the insights of Plato and Spinoza could have been combined, the solution for the problem of the integrated personality would have come in view.

Spinoza even got another relevant insight—the vagueness and confusedness of a person's attempts to describe impulses blocked by repressions. If the impulses can be brought into the clear light of conscious awareness and their motives and causes seen, then they can be rationally integrated in the personality by the regular dynamics of conscious or unrepressed purposive behavior. He writes: "An emotion which is a passion, ceases to be a passion, as soon as we form a clear and distinct idea thereof. *Proof.* —An emotion, which is a passion, is a confused idea. If, therefore, we form a clear and distinct idea of a given emotion . . . the emotion will cease to be a passion" (Part V, Prop. III). I do not think that Spinoza means, here, to give reason an active power like Plato's faculty of reason, though that is debatable, for presently he speaks of the power of the mind over the emotions (Part V, Prop. VI). He does not seem to have had Plato's vivid glimpse of the area of repressed impulses. But apparently he does notice one of the effects of repressions, and correctly points out that if an initially confused emotion is clearly and distinctly envisaged so that we know what it is and what it is directed upon, then the mind has power over it, or, as we should say, it can be taken up by the integrative activity of the personality.

Again, a man of unusual insight came very near to uncovering one of the mechanisms of repression, but in the end turned and looked the other way. He looked to reason to perform the integration. But reason has no dynamics of its own. Reason guides by its cognitive references. All the dynamics of integration comes from the drives of conflicting impulses operating to reduce frustrations.

Will, as Plato uses it, is not so easy to identify in terms of drive theory. But judging from Plato's examples, acts involving will power in his sense of will correspond for us roughly with acts involving injectives, or, better, with the positive injective of aggression. Plato's men of spirit and will and courage were those who would meet frustration and attack with aggressive action for the protection of the state. Plato's will, in our terms, is one of the drives—though, to be sure, a peculiar one, a reinforcing and emergency drive.

If, then, there is in the personality an intrinsically disruptive agency that has to be kept under constant control, this cannot be the impulses as a whole, but must be a group of impulses somehow constituted to produce a disruptive influence. And the dynamics for controlling this disruptive group of impulses must come from other impulses capable of this control.

Now the group of repressed impulses is precisely constituted to be such an intrinsically disruptive agency, and the mechanisms of repression just beginning to be understood are precisely calculated to render very difficult the integration of these impulses with other impulses. Consequently, this group has to be held in restraint by other dynamic forces, much as Plato realized. The restraining forces are the group of impulses constituting what has come to be called *the ego*—namely, conscience and the voluntary system.

## 8. The Group of Repressed Dispositions

What demarcates the group of repressed impulses? The simple answer is: they are the purposive structures cut off from the voluntary system by the mechanisms of repression. To understand just what they are, we should have a complete knowledge of the mechanisms of repression and of what these do to the purposive structures on which they act. Such complete understanding is still lacking, though a good deal is already known.

The repressed impulses are purposive structures or sections of purposive structure just like those open to conscious observation. That is to say, they are appetitions and aversions. The repressive mechanism is motivated primarily by fear. The fear is attached to the impulse itself as the object of the fear. A person is afraid of his own impulse. Or, more precisely, a person is afraid of his own thoughts charged with the impulse. For the impulse might not be repressed except so far as it is directed upon a certain object. It is the mediating judgment, the anticipatory or apprehensive set, the web of cognitive references charged by the drive, that ordinarily is repressed. The drive then becomes relatively blind. That is what makes repressions irrational.

Introspectively, repressions are characterized by being shut off from consciousness. We must ask ourselves presently what they mean in terms of purposive structures. But here are some familiar examples from Ives Hendrick:

> Many examples of human behavior can be cited where the effectiveness of a wish which is unconscious is obvious to anybody except the subject. The girl who vehemently criticizes the taste in clothes of a friend often cannot consciously admit the real motive: 'I wish I looked like her, and hate her because that man admires her.' The mother who consciously maligns a schoolteacher who justly punishes her son cannot endure the conscious thought: 'My son was bad, not so good as other children.' The real motives of the 'reformer' who consciously believes in protecting others' morality and unconsciously enjoys a mass of obscene literature in the role of public censor are usually recognized. In Eugene O'Neill's *Mourning Becomes Electra*, Lavinia contrives the death of Captain Brant, her mother's lover, apparently to defend her father and avenge her mother's turpitude. At the

height of angry passion, she suddenly cries: 'Brant' to her own lover. Every member of the audience realizes the mistake is not pure chance, but discloses her love of Brant, even though she has so persistently concealed it from herself. The significance of a similar 'slip of the tongue' in real life was immediately apparent when a man said to his childless wife: 'When you're sewing, I think of Penelope weaving at her *womb*.' [25]

In each of these instances, what is repressed is a cognitive reference. The impulse comes through a diverted channel and gets a partial satisfaction, but at considerable cost in terms of conscious rational behavior. The girl who criticized her friend's taste in clothes released her hate born of her frustration. That impulse was not totally inhibited, but only so far as it was channeled through her jealousy of her friend. It was the thought of being jealous of her friend—that set of cognitive references charged by the drive—that was repressed. So she became irrational about her friend's taste. This served no socially beneficial purpose. It probably offended her friend, and brought her no nearer to satisfying her basic wish to be attractive to a man like her friend's admirer. This is the sort of thing that is meant by the disintegrative action of the repressed impulses.

Now, what can be meant by the observation that repressions are unconscious? It means, if I am not mistaken, simply that the repressed cognitive references cannot be utilized as mediating judgments in the voluntary system of the personality. In other words, they cannot be integrated with the group of purposive structures which are docile and open to adjustment to the environmental demands upon the organism.

There are a number of striking corollaries to this condition. A repressed wish cannot be remembered. If by chance it bobs up into the conscious voluntary system at some uninhibited moment, as in a dream, it is promptly forgotten. That is why it is usually so difficult to retain a dream. Unless it is written down at once, it fades and by morning has entirely disappeared. This leads to the hypothesis that most forgetting is semipurposeful. The references are there but repressed. If you cannot remember a person's name, it is probably tied in with a repressed system. Sensitive people may have difficulty remembering the names of persons they dislike, possibly because of an underlying disposition to consider it immoral to hate anybody. And some are blocked from the names of persons for whom they feel a deep affection, from a fear of admitting anyone into close emotional intimacy.

Another corollary is the difficulty or impossibility of talking about one's repressions. If you can talk about an anxiety, it is no longer repressed, which shows—a thing clear enough anyway—that there are degrees of repression. Many anxious thoughts hover on the threshold of repression, and are hard to talk about; yet they can be shared with a sympathetic or socially authorized person, a priest or a physician, who can be trusted to keep a confidence. To talk about them is a relief and may keep them from becoming repressed.

But in saying that repressions cannot be talked about we are not saying that repressions cannot talk. They talk in dreams or blurt out words in embarrassing slips of the tongue, as with the unhappy husband's 'weaving at her *womb.*' But the talk is generally vague and in symbols and dreamlike. The crucial point is that it is not integrated with the talk that expresses the voluntary system of dispositions. It is disintegrated talk.

In general, the repressed group of impulses is a rather unorganized mass. On the Freudian theory, one of the deepest and earliest repressions, which may be unavoidable in some form or other, is the Oedipus complex and the closely related castration complex. But any unbearably fearful occurrence at any time of life may be repressed. Small children, however, are particularly vulnerable to traumatic experiences of fear. They are weak and helpless among beings who are to them huge and powerful and often unpredictable, and children have strong impulses for which initially they have no means of knowing the safe limits of indulgence. Presently, too, children develop vivid imaginations and are capable of wild fantasies without adequate knowledge of the reality of things to hold them within the confines of mature good sense. Consequently they are extremely susceptible to overpowering fears sometimes only too well justified, but often imagined; so, inevitably, most repressions in a man's personality are developed in childhood.

A deep repression, however, will propagate a litter of effects which amount to derivative repressions, and these can come out at any time in life. Nearly all displacements are of this kind (not all, for a man who has stubbed his toe on a chair in the night can get much conscious relief from a solid wallop at a pillow), and all rationalizations are of this kind, like that of the 'reformer' in the role of a censor.

Undoubtedly, no one is without a group of repressions. Nevertheless, an ideally integrated personality would theoretically be without any, since repressions are intrinsically self-frustrating, and are incapable of modification by the ordinary laws of learning. And yet the capacity for repression, at least on the scale for which men have the capacity, seems to be a peculiarly human trait. If we were conceiving a superman with the highest possible control of his own destiny for personal happiness and freedom from unnecessary anxiety, he would be a man unencumbered with repressions or the capacity to form them. But man so conceived would be of a different species.

To what degree the mechanism of repression is biologically necessary, it is very hard to determine. From the perspective of the individual it is an extreme escape mechanism. Because of man's intelligence and foresight and long infancy, repression may originally have been required for emotional balance. Or it may have a predominantly social significance. For, as we shall see, it is closely bound up with the rigid conscience, which is a force for social solidarity. The biological survival of man, as a social animal, depends in the last resort on group solidarity. A rigid conscience based on a system of repressions immune to learning may be (or may have been) the biological substitute in man for the rigid social instincts that determine the social solidarity of other social species such as ants.

For the great civilizations of the present, however, where rapid adaptability to constantly changing conditions is more important than unswerving adherence to custom, the action of a rigid conscience is perhaps more of a liability than an asset. We shall return to this question soon.

Repressions, then, are intrinsically disintegrative in the personality. Since, however, we probably cannot do away with them entirely, we must look to the best ways of integrating a personality with them. Three ways of minimizing their disruptive effects can be indicated. The best is to bring up the child in an environment that generates the least amount of repression at the lowest intensity. This means, on Erikson's account, so to handle the crises at the various stages of the child's development that no traumatic repressions occur. The child acquires the basic trust, autonomy, initiative, and the full capacity of mutual love. He then wastes no energy on inner conflicts—or not much. He is in control of his impulses. He knows what they are. He knows his motives. He knows himself. He is thus free to adapt himself to his environment in terms of the reality of the situation, for his own or society's greatest benefit.

This does not mean that he has no repressions but that he has had an opportunity to grow up *naturally* and the repressions are at a minimum in quantity and intensity. He has had an opportunity to develop under a favorable environment to the fullness of his capacities. Ideally, this favorable environment should be his whole society and its culture. And automatically an ideal for society is here laid out for us: the cultural pattern that provides a favorable environment for the growth of the integrated personality. It remains to be seen whether this may be a natural norm. If so, however, it will be evidenced as a tendency rather than an actuality, for no known societies measure up to this ideal. The favorable environment that is most nearly attained for the development of highly integrated character is that of the child's immediate family.

There is an easily understandable cultural contagion about personalities. Just as neurotic parents tend to pass on their neuroses to their children, so, fortunately, integrated characters tend to foster integrated characters in their offspring. The latter contagion, however, is the steadier tendency of the two, since men shun frustrations if they can find a way to avoid them. That is why the normal character is the integrated or harmonious character, and why the integrative action of the personality is a natural norm.

Every normal person of well-integrated character becomes a center spreading his healthy outlook on all who come in contact with him. And the most effective means of building up a favorable social environment for the development of well-balanced persons is probably from the normal individual outward.

The second way of minimizing the disruptive effects of repressions is almost the opposite of the first. It is by therapeutic treatment to remove repressions that have become noticeably disturbing. This is the psychoanalytic method, which has proved the richest source of information regarding the nature and origin of repressions and their pervasiveness in the personality structure. This method is likely to be employed, however, only on medical men training to use it, and on disturbed personalities that need assistance because of internal conflicts. Strangely enough, it is the only method that might be expected to free a personality completely from repressions. For it looks as though some repressions inevitably get laid down in infancy; normal favorable growth does not so much release these as redirect them in ways which render their effects negligible. These early repressions could be fully released only through psychoanalytic treatment. However, a personality without repressions would seem too perfect for human existence. Even psychoanalysts themselves, we are told, must sometimes have consultations to check on their own suspected blind spots.

The third and commonest way of minimizing the effect of repressions is to neutralize them. The method of natural favorable growth helps to keep them from being generated at all. The method of psychoanalysis removes them by medical treatment. The method of neutralization does not keep them away or remove them, but attains a sort of integration by redirecting them, or by counteracting them in some way, or by shoring them up with a variety of supports so that they do not break loose easily.

The most successful method of partial integration of this sort is that of sublimation. By this mechanism a potentially disruptive repression is actually turned to social use—or at least to some long-range personal use which is socially approved. There is likely to be an element of sublimation in most persons' hobbies and in their professions, particularly if there is something compulsive in the way they go about them. One should not, however, think that every independence mutation is a sublimation. And what is a sublimation for one person will be an independence mutation for another. The difference is that the former does and the latter does not involve a repression; the latter can be fully satisfying, while the former always carries an element of frustration. Of course, both mutations may be operating in conjunction. A man may be chopping wood to relieve a repressed aggression and, at the same time, chopping for the sheer fun of it. If the displacement of the repression is brought to his attention and he accepts it, the chopping may go right on but with a somewhat different quality to the act.

Conscience, social authority, identification with ideals, religion, and one whole side of art (the art of relief as distinct from the art of delight) are means of neutralizing repressions, and of helping to integrate otherwise troubled personalities.

In all these instances the repressions are either taken up, redirected, and the whole built into the personality structure, or else they are held in restraint by compensating dispositions that are built into the structure. Sublimation is clearly of the first sort, and is the most successful method of neutralizing repressions, since it actually produces a constructive form of integration.

Conscience is of the second type. It is a set of dispositions built into the personality with the express aim of holding the repressions in check. Religion and conscience are close allies. But religion adds many amenities to cushion the frustrations, anxieties, despairs, and rages due to the repressions. It gives faith and hope and the comfort of the church, and the relief of ritual and the support of an official priesthood or ministry. Part of this support is often in the form of myths and at the cost of beliefs which conflict with the reality of the situation, and so may add to a man's or a society's frustrations in the long run. But a great proportion of mankind has attained some degree of integration and found life bearable through this means of neutralizing repressions. At this point, of course, I am not thinking of religion as a social institution but as dispositions of belief and performance that neutralize the suffering from compulsions, remorse, and despair which have their source in repressions. And the arts of relief through music, sculpture, painting, and tragedy help toward the same end, and are often mixed with religion, and so these also have a medicinal function.

## 9. CONSCIENCE

This brings us to the group of dispositions composing conscience. The hallmark of conscience is the sense of *guilt*, together with the associated feeling of remorse and a need for expiation. It is often described as an inner voice which warns a person against evil impulses. As the offensive impulse rises, a person feels he ought not to succumb to it; a sense of guilt surrounds the act. And if he does not immediately reject the impulse, it appears as a temptation. If he yields to the temptation, the feeling of guilt carries over with an intensity proportional to the charge on the judgment as to the degree of evil in the act, and this is followed by remorse and a desire to do something to make up for the wrongdoing.

Here is a distinctive set of dispositions. It carries with it a good deal more than the simple evaluative 'ought' of other natural norms—for it is obvious that conscience is a natural norm, a verifiably describable selective system within the human personality. No other natural norm is sanctioned with feelings of guilt and remorse and the need of expiation, as conscience is. The negative sanction for achievement is frustration, which brings disappointment and perhaps redoubled efforts to succeed, but no guilt or remorse. The same is true of an error in judgment in sizing up the reality of a situation after a choice in a person's life-space. Even within a personality, the same holds true for instances of mere failure to reach a certain level of aspiration in a personal role—provided conscience has not got mixed up in it. These all involve 'oughts.' A person ought not to select a means that cannot serve his end, ought not to size up a situation wrongly for the purposes involved in it, ought not to fail in the performance of a role important in his life. But none of these 'oughts,' upon an error, necessarily makes a person feel guilty. And we shall find the same true of the natural norms of society —the social situation and the cultural pattern—provided conscience has not become incorporated in them. The feeling of guilt is not essential to the feeling of 'ought.' It is peculiar to one particular natural norm and one only.

The feeling is so intimate for the person experiencing it, however, and so poignant that it is inevitable that he should think that this is the 'ought' of all 'oughts,' if indeed there is any other 'ought' worthy of the name. Herein is the appeal of the deontologist and the moral intuitionist. It is a most natural intuitive judgment. In fact, that is just what the 'voice of conscience' is. The very mechanism of conscience is designed to produce in a person this conviction of immediate and absolute authority. In its immediacy it is at the moment of impact indubitable. That is indeed a fact. But, as we were careful to point out in our introductory chapter, a feeling of indubitability is not a reliable criterion of cognitive judgment and is one of the typical devices of dogmatism. And, on examination, the 'voice of conscience' proves to be as variable in detail as the cultures in which it originates, and can itself be controlled and even perhaps eliminated once we discover the mechanism by which it works.

As with everything else connected with personality structure, a description of the operation of conscience is in a theoretical stage and still controversial. But, with the evidence on hand, it can hardly any longer be conceived as an innate endowment. The problem is just how it is acquired and how it gets its peculiar and dominating character.

As in the discussion of the repressions, I shall here follow essentially the description of the Freudians. As Erikson pointed out, conscience usually becomes established in the child during the third stage, at about four or five years of age. In the second stage the child acquires a sense of shame, and a sense of guilt may be emerging. But the full development of a conscience and its inner sense of guilt seems to come with the development of initiative and the intensification of conditions of conflict and jealousy between himself and his parents and of imaginative idealization.

It is obvious that conscience is some sort of internalization of authority. At first we are tempted to explain it in terms of habit and the independence mutation. Conscience would then be simply a form of discipline. This would be the typical rationalistic way of accounting for its origin. It would be like army discipline. Strong authorities backed up by the power of punishment, which is promptly applied in case of infringement of orders, teach the agent to perform certain acts which eventually become automatic. Motivated as these are by the fear injective, the mediating judgment connecting the acts with the authority may fairly easily be severed and an independence mutation set up; thereafter, on the proper stimulus, the acts proceed automatically on their own motivation.

Such acts, of course, are common enough. But they lack the peculiar characteristics of conscience. They afford an internalization of authority, to be sure. The agent performs the acts without the external punishment or even the thought of it. But they lack the feelings of guilt and of remorse, the need of expiation, and the indubitable immediacy of the 'inner voice.'

These can be explained in part by the agent's assuming the role of the authority and incorporating it into his own personality. Suppose we bring into the light of overt action the sequence guilt-remorse-expiation, and see what kind of situation it reflects. It reflects a situation in which an impulse known to be forbidden was performed, disapproved, and punished. Take a simple instance. A child has an impulse to get the forbidden jam and, no parental obstacle being in sight, climbs for it. No signs of conscience here, nor yet if the parent discovers the child and punishes him. This is just ordinary conditioning.

But if, when the impulse again arises, the child begins to imagine himself in the parent's role, and the parent's disposition toward the jam between meals becomes incorporated in the child's personality as one of his own dispositions, then we find the quality of guilt emerging. The child now has within himself a disposition to punish himself for a forbidden impulse, which he himself is disposed to forbid. If he performs the act and gets away with it, he is still unhappy. For though his parent did not catch him, he in the parent's role caught himself, and from now on, as long as he keeps this role within him, he will always be caught. The feeling that he will be caught and should punish himself is the feeling of guilt. After the act, if the guilt is strong, he does punish himself with remorse, but even this may not be enough and he may seek overt expiation to ingratiate himself back into his own self-respect. Guilt shows itself in characteristic overt postures and facial expressions, as though the child were trying to conceal something. So, from his look of guilt, a child may be caught by his parent when otherwise he would have got away with it. And being caught and punished may be quite a relief and rather purposeful, since it provides the expiation that conscience requires.

But even this is not enough to explain the involuntary and oracular character of conscience. If conscience were merely the taking of a role, it would be as open to voluntary control and rational docility as taking on the role of a golfer or a gardener or a mayor or a lawyer. The role that speaks through conscience is no ordinary role. All one hears is the oracle, and all one feels is the guilt. The role itself is obviously repressed.

It is clearly the role of an authority that is repressed. Seeing how early conscience starts, it is evidently the role of the parent, the earliest authority, that is the original nucleus of conscience and is incorporated as a disposition within the child's developing personality. The parent is the child's earliest ideal with whom he identifies, and the original source of reward and punishment, approval and disapproval.

This ideal as the child's earliest ego ideal is obviously not always repressed. Under what conditions does it get repressed to act in the manner of conscience? It would be in circumstances of great fear, as we know from the mechanism of repression. No doubt there are many occasions when a strong impulse in the child evokes extreme disapproval from the parent and thus precipitates repression. The collection of these repressions could well form the nucleus for the repressed role of the stern parent and judge whose voice speaks as conscience and produces the feeling of guilt. But, according to the data gathered from psychoanalytical techniques, the central impetus for the repression of the stern parental role is the Oedipus situation. There is plenty of evidence that this is often the case. The only question would be whether it is universally so. The fact that the emergence of guilt normally coincides with the period in which the child is concerned with a sexual interest in his parents is, however, an impressive confirmation of the hypothesis.

Here is a summary of the typical Freudian view by a recent authority, Fenichel. The 'superego' is Freud's term for 'conscience.' Fenichel first describes what he calls the forerunners of the superego. These are the incorporation of parental dispositions which do not yet produce feelings of guilt but only of 'look out' or at most of shame, and are not ordinarily repressed. They accompany the positive and rewarding elements of the parental ideal.

> Originally the child certainly had the wish to do the things the parents do; his aim was an identification with the parents' activities, not with their prohibitions. The standards and ideals of the parent are an essential part of their personality. If children want to identify themselves with the parents, they also want to identify with their standards and ideals. Prohibitions are accepted as a part of the living up to these standards and ideals. The striving for the reward of feeling oneself to be similar to the parents facilitates the acceptance of prohibitions. The actual identification with the prohibitions becomes a displacement substitute for the intended identification with the parents' activities. . . .
>
> 'Internalized parental prohibitions,' the forerunners of the superego, are very strong in so far as they threaten the child with terrible punishment . . . but they are weak in so far as they can be easily disobeyed or circumvented whenever no one is looking . . . Policemen and bogeymen represent these 'externalized superegos.' The child fluctuates between giving in to his impulses and suppressing them; there is as yet no unified organized character in the prohibitions.[26]

Then comes the Oedipus situation, with its intense fantasies, jealousies, fears, inhibitions, and consequent repressions, all mingled with the parental idealizations and identifications.

> The identifications that resolve the Oedipus complex are, of course, not complete ones. They replace the sexual and hostile impulses toward the parents (at least the greater part of them); a tender object relationship with inhibited aims, however, continues along with the identification. . . . The newly introjected objects become combined with the parental introjects already present in the form of the previously described forerunners of the superego . . . The ego 'borrows' from its strong parents the

strength that enables it to suppress the Oedipus complex. In this way the resolution of the Oedipus complex brings about the marked and decisive step within the ego which is so important for subsequent ego development and which by its organization is differentiated from its forerunner—the superego.[27]

The superego is that part of the role of the idealized parents present in the child's personality that is needed to hold in check the repressed impulses involved in the Oedipus situation. Conscience thus originates in and is closely bound up with these repressions. The impulses to which conscience is tied are, of course, repressed, and also a large part of the parental role which maintains the repression; for conscience ordinarily appears as a quite impersonal voice, and only dimly does a person have any inkling of a personal role behind conscience, which usually appears, if at all, in the image of a personal God.

Fenichel summarizes some further findings on the precise source of the restraining role for conscience:

> If the superego were simply an identification with the frustrating object of the Oedipus complex, then one would expect that the boy would develop a 'motherly' superego and the girl a 'fatherly' one. This is not the case. It is true that in accordance with the 'completeness' of the Oedipus complex, everyone bears features of both parents in his superego. Under our cultural conditions, however, generally for both sexes the fatherly superego is decisive; in women, moreover, a motherly superego is effective as a positive ego ideal. Men who, contrary to the rule, have a pronounced motherly superego have regularly had a dominant mother. The outstanding identification takes place with that parent who was regarded as the source of decisive frustrations, which in the patriarchal family is usually the father but which in exceptional cases may be the mother.[28]

And it now turns out—which comports with the facts but is often overlooked—that conscience is a source of reward and self-satisfaction as well as of guilt and punishment.

> The superego is the heir of the parents not only as a source of threats and punishments but also as a source of protection and as a provider of reassuring love. Being on good or bad terms with one's superego becomes as important as being on good or

bad terms with one's parents previously was . . . Self-esteem is no longer regulated by approval or rejection by external objects, but rather by the feeling of having done or not having done the right thing. Complying with the superego's demands brings not only relief but also definite feelings of pleasure and security of the same type that children experience from external supplies of love. Refusing this compliance brings feelings of guilt and remorse which are similar to the child's feelings of being not loved any more.[29]

In short, let us not forget, in our concern with the source of guilt, which is the negative side of conscience, that it also has its positive side popularly equated with the calm and contentment that comes from a 'clear conscience.' [30]

But with all this, it remains true and significant for our study of the integrative action of the personality that conscience has its origin and its roots in the repressions, and is consequently ineradicably involved in the irrational elements of the personality. Conscience is essentially unintelligent, incapable of docility, hard and fixed. If it comports in its demands with its cultural environment, which in a static culture it usually does, it gives stability and helps to maintain an integration of the personality. But if it is carried over into another or a changing cultural environment or if it has become exaggerated and excessive even in a static culture, then it becomes an insidious source of inner frustration and a disintegrative factor in a personality.

Conscience is, to be sure, a definite moral norm and a selective system in its own right. It exhibits no reticence on this score. It claims through the intensity and intuitive immediacy of its judgment of guiltiness that it is the supreme norm of morality. Nevertheless, as just one element in the personality structure, it is steadily subject to the quiet pressure of the integrative action of the personality which accordingly legislates over it—unless some overindividual norm itself supersedes the personal.

The idea of conscience being sometimes immoral disturbs the sense of linguistic propriety for many people. For this reason I have followed Eric Fromm's lead in distinguishing between the rigid irrational and the docile rational conscience. In accordance with that distinction, what we have been describing in this section is the irrational conscience. In the next section, on the integrative action of the voluntary group of dispositions, we shall be dealing with the rational conscience.

## 10. The Group of Voluntary Dispositions

The group of voluntary dispositions constitute the responsible self. They are the core of the integrated personality. They may not all be integrated. There may be unresolved conflicts among them, and many of these may not yet have made the most satisfactory adjustment to their environment. But they are free to make these adjustments and resolve these conflicts among themselves. They are not blocked off from one another by mechanisms like those which close off the repressed dispositions.

The voluntary dispositions are, in fact, precisely those purposive dispositions which are not blocked by repressions. Or, more precisely, they are purposive dispositions *so far as* they are not blocked off from other dispositions by repression. For many voluntary dispositions in the complexities of human personality, and particularly as these become clustered and interconnected in roles, dip into the sphere of the repressions.

After the earlier detailed descriptions made of purposive structures and of the integrative activity among roles, not much more needs to be added concerning the integration of the personality within the voluntary system. In describing the integrative action of roles in the personality, we were actually describing the integration of dispositions in the voluntary system so far as these were free from the action of repressions.

Two further points need to be made regarding integration in the group of voluntary dispositions. The first is the manner in which they can, after a fashion, integrate portions of the repressed dispositions into their own system. An integral personality must succeed in doing this in large degree; otherwise a split personality results. The irrational conscience, our concern in the previous section, is a good instance to consider. It includes both repressed and unrepressed elements. The voluntary self can learn, if it does not already know, the sort of acts that produce the feeling of guilt. These can be consciously described;

the temptations can be anticipated and avoided. The dictates of conscience can thus in a manner be drawn into the voluntary system and respected as a physical barrier would be respected. The submerged repressed constituents of conscience may then never be suspected and may never produce a serious personality conflict.

It may even be possible to induce some modification of detail among the dictates of conscience by a cognitively justifiable rationalization. If conscience says "Thou shalt not lie," and reason says that on many occasions it is better to lie a little than offend with a distasteful truth, conscience may be assuaged by a distinction between white lies and wicked lies, and reserve its guilt feelings for the latter. It may even be weaned from details altogether and be directed upon the bare generalization, "Thou shalt do thy duty," leaving it to voluntary rational processes to fill in the details.

The repressions are great ones to fool the voluntary system into finding avenues of illicit expression under the guise of high morality—as witness the indignant censor of obscene literature mentioned by Ives Hendrick. But the voluntary system can sometimes reverse the process and fool the repressions into accepting a higher morality by some judicious rationalization. The repressions are not eliminated, but they are redirected into less frustrating avenues or even into socially satisfying ones. The most spectacular mechanism for doing this is, of course, that of sublimation.

But here we are touching again on the three ways of minimizing the disruptive effects of repressions: by keeping repressions, through proper child care, from being generated; by eliminating them through therapeutic means; by neutralizing them through redirection or mental support. So for this we shall simply refer to the earlier discussion.

The second consideration has to do with the relation of personality integration to the social and physical environment. The idea might have developed from our previous discussion that the integrative action of the personality was concerned simply with fitting the dispositions of a single organism together in a harmonious way. In a sense this is correct. But in a broader sense it neglects a crucial relation—the relation to the environment in which the person lives, his relation to reality. One of the most serious symptoms of insanity and extreme personality disintegration is the loss of contact with reality. Every disposition of the personality has one end in the organism, but the other end is in the environment. And when, by some gyration of repression, the channel to the environment is blocked, disruption of the personality begins and progressive deterioration sets in.

The more sedulously we examine the details of the harmonious integration of dispositions within the organism, the more it is made evident that this consists in the harmony of these dispositions to the environmental conditions outside the organism. One of the regular slogans of the self-realizationists, from the Stoics on down, is to live in harmony with nature, to integrate oneself with the world about one. We can now see how basically correct this was. The modern term for it has a biological connotation and is 'adjustment.'

An internally well integrated personality is well integrated also with the social and physical environment. His dispositions are so fitted to his environment that he meets the minimum of frustration and the maximum of satisfaction in his responses to it. This again is an ideal approximated under favorable conditions, never completely realized. But it can easily be seen, from our previous analyses of purposive behavior and the integrative action of the personality, that the tendency to approximate this ideal is involved in the very mechanisms of behavior constantly headed for the reduction of frustrations.

The most highly integrated personality, however, would not be one uniquely fitted for the particular environment in which he finds himself. This would be the ideal for a member of an instinct-structured society like that of ants or bees, but not for a member of a docility-structured society like the human. Apart from the rigidity produced by irrational conscience and the repressed dispositions, human personality integration is exceedingly flexible and adjustable. The ideally integrated human personality would be devoid of repressions and so also of an irrational conscience; consequently he would be free to adjust through his untrammeled docility to any type of physical environment. The

environments would be more or less favorable to man's repertoire
of innate dispositions. But beyond that the ideally well integrated
man would also be ideally adjusted to make the most out of
whatever cultural or physical environment he found himself
in—even to changing it to better fit his capacities for satisfaction.
So the modern self-realizationist slogan should be: not fit yourself to nature, but fit yourself for many natures or even fit yourself to make nature fit you.

But the important point is that the integration of dispositions
in the personality is at the same time the integration of a man's
personality with the world about him. This observation leads
naturally into the coming chapters on selective systems in the
social context. But before making that transition, we must consider the line of legislative priority among the several selective
systems that have come to light within the human personality.

## 11. Priorities among Norms within the Personality

The question of evaluative priority among the natural norms in
the human personality is a significant one because of the strength
and resistance of the repressed dispositions. Since these hold out
vigorously against the voluntary system, how do we establish the
evaluative priority of the integrative action of the personality
over the disintegrative action of the repressions? And, more
particularly, how is it possible to give an evaluative priority to
the voluntary system over conscience?

The evidences have all been given before, but let us review
them here so that there will be no question about the matter.
The three great groups of dispositions within the personality are
frequently in opposition to one another, and conscience is regularly opposed to the repressed system which it was instituted to
control.

In the repressed system, a group of genuine purposive acts
seeking satisfaction is blocked by conscience and the voluntary
system. Why should the latter two systems be given evaluative
priority over this group of bona fide purposive dispositions? The
immediately ready answer is, because, so far as the repressed
dispositions are not directed by the other two groups, they are

intrinsically frustrating to the personality as a whole. To this the reply is, Well, what of that? If a repressed impulse is seeking expression, does it not have the same claim for satisfaction as any other impulse? This reply is plausible, because in the nature of a repression only the impulse shows up in consciousness, and the frustration motivating it in part is concealed by the mechanism of the repression. Moreover, in a relatively integrated personality a sporadic derived drive based on a repression can generally be adjusted to the total personality structure. The issue becomes serious only when the group or the intensity of these impulses becomes massive and more than the voluntary system can assimilate by its regular integrative processes. Then we get the familiar neurotic effects and, in the extreme, insanity. The repressed system has, in that case, successfully captured the personality. And the reply of the repressed system to what remains of the voluntary system, or to some better-integrated observer outside, can still be, Well, what of that? Has not the repressed system here succeeded in legislating over the voluntary system and in setting its 'unlawful appetites,' as Plato called them, in judgment over the 'lawful' ones? What can the voluntary system now do about it?

If the disintegration has not gone too far, the voluntary system can reach outside into the social environment and seek medical assistance, or the assistance of a church, or of Alcoholics Anonymous, or of some other social group which may turn the balance in favor of the voluntary system. But the repressed system might consider this unfair. Just as it had almost manifested its evaluative superiority over the voluntary system, the latter squeals and runs for help outside the forces of the personality!

At this point it is worth remarking that one does not usually hear of a person in serious personality conflict asking for outside help toward becoming more disintegrated and having more insane wishes in order that the voluntary system may be definitely overcome and stop struggling. As Plato so early saw in depicting his unhappy tyrant, there is no surcease of struggle and frustration in that direction. Every increase in desire and strength in the repressed system simply increases the frustration and conflict within the personality. For the focal source of frustration is in the repressed impulse, itself derived from the very mechanism of repression which makes the impulse possible at all. That is to say, a repressed impulse is self-frustrating. The conflicts suffered by the repressed impulses, though due in part to the struggle of conscience and of the voluntary system to hold them in check, are due mainly to their own self-frustrating structure. So every increase in the size and power of the repressed system simply increases its own internal conflicts. And in the end it is very likely to become completely unbearable and result in the suicidal impulse.

Here the issue really comes to a head. Well, what of that? If a person wants to commit suicide, why is that not just as legitimate a wish as wanting to play golf or to discover another subatomic element? This terminal question comes up in any all-out discussion between an emotivist (cf. chap. 1, §3, for a summary of emotive judgment theory of value) and an exponent of a view like ours which holds that value norms are empirically describable and verifiable.

Our answer is of a sort already given. A descriptive analysis of the suicidal impulse (not, of course, voluntary death in line of duty, or as a rational choice in circumstances of irremediable physical suffering, and the like) shows that it is a self-frustrating purposive complex. And if the repression which blocks and exasperates the impulse were removed so that the person could be aware of his concealed motives, he would see its frustrating character and resolve the conflict in a rational way. The avoidance of frustration is a deep-seated natural norm in human behavior, and supplies the dynamics of the integrative action of the personality. A suicidal neurotic impulse represents an increase in frustration, not a decrease. If suicide is attempted it will simply add more conflict, count as an error, and increase the exasperation. Besides, recent study of these acts indicates that they are all blindly and mistakenly trying desperately to reduce the frustrations motivating them. Suicidal attempts are regular appetitive and apprehensive acts seeking satisfaction, but, because of the repressed segments, meeting inexplicable frustrations. In short, an empirical description of a suicidal impulse shows that it is a mistake in terms of the ends the impulse is seeking to satisfy.

The repressed system acknowledges in its very structure the legislation over it of the integrative action of the personality. As we say in common speech, a neurotic does not *really* want[31] to commit suicide. He really wants something quite different. Just as we would say of a thirsty man in the desert trudging toward a mirage, 'He doesn't really want the mirage; he wants water.' This, I believe, is the proper and fully adequate empirical answer.

But the emotivist may still object. He is likely to dismiss the distinction between what may be 'wanted' and 'really wanted' as meaningless verbal subterfuge. By doing so, he shuts his eyes to the evidence showing that man's wants do not all lie on the surface, but have many layers and complexities. But for the moment let that go. An emotivist will often insist that the man did in fact want to commit suicide. That is the plain and undeniable fact. And if the man succeeds, how does that increase his frustrations?

The tenor of this reply is to the effect that there are no norms operating on a man's actions after he dies. And this amounts to saying that there are no overindividual norms which can legislate over a man's individual purposes if he does not see fit to recognize them. This is an issue on another plane from that on which we have been working throughout the preceding chapters. In fact, however, we shall soon discover that such overindividual norms do exist. An ultimate norm relevant to the present issue is that of natural selection. A man with a tendency to neurotic behavior and suicide eliminates himself and all his personal standards of evaluation very effectively. His particular repertory of impulses drops out in the manner of a biological error. He no longer propagates his kind. A natural biological norm of evaluation has made its negative judgment and selected positively for the sort of man who has a greater integrative capacity for adjustment within himself and within his cultural and physical environment.

This biological norm of natural selection also is possibly dismissed by the emotivist as irrelevant to the evaluation of a neurotic's behavior. But the emotivist himself and his particular repertory of evaluations will meet the same negative judgment by the same selective norm if he elects too flagrantly to ignore its action. These natural selective systems are not fabricated out of men's wishes or even out of a theorist's stipulated definitions. On the contrary, men's wishes and definitions eventually get shaped to them.

A little neuroticism can be absorbed with no great harm. Even a good deal will be absorbed if it can be directed into socially approved and appreciated channels. But a seriously disintegrated personality, apart from his own terrible frustrations, meets the resistance of his social environment; and if that does not remove him from action, his own inability to survive will eliminate him by natural selection.

So the integrative action of the personality acquires ultimate evaluative priority over disintegrative tendencies. Impulses are not all on a par. The voluntary system of dispositions by virtue of the steady integrative action of the personality toward reducing frustrations legislates evaluatively over the repressed group.

Now, what about the rigid conscience? As a source of integration and control over the repressed system, it legislates over that system for the same reasons brought out for the priority of the voluntary system over the repressions.

But what about the evaluative relation of conscience to the voluntary system? We might think this should be an easy question to answer. If the voluntary system legislates over the repressed system by virtue of its freedom from the frustrations of repression, then, analogously, it should legislate over the rigid conscience, since this has its roots deep in the repressed system.

Purely from the point of view of the individual, this is undoubtedly the proper answer. But, as we have noted several times in this chapter, there is an alliance between the rigid conscience and the cultural pattern of the social environment, and beyond that there is a connection between the cultural pattern and the biological survival of man. The rigid conscience may have a survival value for man which under certain conditions may give it evaluative precedence even over the voluntary system. But we must find out more about the overindividual natural norms before we can unravel that relationship.

This is our project in the chapters that follow. Now for the first time we leave the individual organism with its purposive structures and personality dispositions, and move out into the social situation and the field of intersubjective values.

# 18

# The Social Situation

## 1. The Social Situation as a Selective System

A paradox appears in value theory, particularly in the sphere of ethical decisions, when we pass from the individual to the social context. There is nothing so personal as an ethical decision, and much stress is laid on its being the free choice of the individual. Yet unless it is made in view of the social situation and in terms of the social obligations it is scarcely credited at all as a moral decision. The decision must be our own and rise out of our own character; yet it must be a decision required by the nature of the social conditions within which we live.

The paradox is partly resolved by observing that the generating dynamics of action for every choice made in a social situation is contributed from the drives of the several individuals involved in the situation. Nevertheless, the correct resultant act which the social situation requires is no more the simple choice of any one person than the correct resultant act in a person's life-space is the simple satisfaction of any one of his drives. A social situation is a selective system in its own right.

The man who is most responsible for calling attention to the evaluative function of the social situation as a natural norm is John Dewey. This is his preëminent contribution to value theory. Any shortcomings in his view arise from his not giving sufficient weight to the significance of other selective systems surrounding it. He tried to make this one natural norm carry the burden of all of them. But in respect to this one norm, no other writer has such illuminating things to say as he has. So on this topic I shall depend largely on Dewey.

The social situation is in the social sphere what the personal situation or life-space is in the sphere of individual behavior. It is the particular theater of action in which a particular selective act or group of acts takes place. But in the social situation the component dynamic elements are the individual persons involved rather than the various drives of a single organism.

Why should a theater of action encompassing a number of persons generate a selective system? Very briefly, because every social situation presents a particular configuration of tensions among the individuals concerned, and ordinarily offers just one best solution for the reduction of these tensions. According to the general law of minimizing frustrations and maximizing satisfactions, action is directed toward a reducing of these tensions. Dewey's great contribution was to point out that the structure of a particular social situation determines a natural norm specific to that situation with reference to which acts are treated as good or bad. A bad act increases social tensions; a good act reduces them; and a best act is potentially implicit in the very structure of the situation. For any man astute enough to perceive what this act would be in view of the reality of the situation, this ideally best act would show him exactly how far short any particular act came from attaining the ideal. But more important, by way of sanctioning this ideal, the very dynamic structure of the situation actually guides acts toward that ideal and, much as in the personal situation, punishes with increased tensions the agents' failures to improve the total situation.

This, taken as a first approximation to be qualified later, is the gist of the matter, and the heart of Dewey's theory of valuation. Every situation, he shows, generates its own concrete specific norm, and the very dynamics of the situation generates the sanction for carrying it out. The main facts can hardly be questioned. Dewey is simply describing a natural norm open to any man's observation, but so commonplace that it escaped nearly everyone's attention.

The only questions that come up concern details of description and the scope of this natural norm. Some of these questions prove rather puzzling, but few of them are, to my mind, very serious, unless one tries, as Dewey does and we do not, to make the norm of the social situation legislative over all other evaluative norms.

## 2. THE BOUNDARIES OF A SOCIAL SITUATION

The one question of detail that brings out most of the pertinent issues is: What determines the boundaries of a social situation? The boundaries of a personal situation are rather definitely determined by the perceptual field of an organism at a given time. In terms of the environmental objects in his field of response and the objects of his cognitive sets, a man demarcates the scope of his personal situation. The definiteness of this field depends, in turn, on the definiteness that can be given to a description of the physiological organism as the seat of the personality. Now, what can be found in society to correspond with the physical organism? Dewey never satisfactorily answers this question. I shall venture to say that it is the seat of the cultural pattern. For a cultural pattern is to a social situation precisely what a personality is to a personal situation.

However, the whole cultural pattern does not enter into every concrete social situation that calls for a decision within the cultural area. Similarly, neither does the whole personality, or the organism which is its seat, enter into every personal situation that calls for a resolution. When Mr. Jones was crossing the street at a busy intersection, only a selection of his dispositions was engaged in the life-space that spread out before him. It was, of course, his individual personality as a whole that conditioned the selection, and determined what was of interest to him in the situation. But that situation evoked only that particular selection of interests as relevant to it. So, too, a social situation seldom affects the whole cultural pattern and all the men and women and artifacts which, as we shall later see, constitute its seat. Only a selection of these become involved—those relevant to the action which the situation demands.

Even for a personal situation the boundaries are not always

clear-cut. Those for a social situation are still less so. An unexpected object injected into a situation may immediately extend or constrict its boundaries to the point of changing the situation entirely from what it was in the beginning. If a fire truck with siren blowing bears down on the intersection in front of Mr. Jones and he apprehends that a building in the block is on fire, his life-space at that juncture becomes completely reoriented, and the boundaries of the situation (the objects he has to think of) expand continually. The same and more so with social situations. Nevertheless, the boundaries of a situation in either sphere can be approximately described, and, if errors are made, corrected.

Just as Mr. Jones's organism as the seat of his personality is the ultimate center of orientation and of the very existence of any personal situation of his, so also the social group which is the seat of a cultural pattern is the ultimate center of orientation and of the very existence of any social situation generated within it. The life-space of some other man is never Mr. Jones's own life-space. When Mr. Jones dies and his purposive acts cease, no more personal situations will be generated from his organism as a center. That is to say (what seems obvious enough), there is no personal situation unless there is a living organism with a personality to bring the situation into being. And so, too, with social situations. These cease to exist for any culture or society when the organisms and artifacts which are the seat of that culture cease to exist.

At this point, however, a crucial difference appears, which is one reason why the analogy of a society to a biological organism must not be allowed to go too far. A cultural pattern can be transposed bodily from one group of organisms as its seat to another group without major disturbance to the dispositional pattern. This is exactly what happens in any stable culture in the transition from one generation of men to the next. But there is no reliable evidence of a similar transposition of a personality literally from one physical organism as its seat to another. Moreover, when there is a major social revolution, the identical group of men who acted as the seat of one cultural pattern become the seat of another. That is how it happens that through conquest one social system can supplant another without necessarily destroying many of its members.

The bearing of these remarks on the question at hand is that only men embraced in a common cultural pattern are literally agents in a single social situation. Out of this fact springs the significance for value of the opposition of in-group to out-group: the opposition of man to animal, of civilized person to barbarian, of true believer to heathen. Animals, barbarians, and heathen are actually, when the opposition is supported by custom, regarded and treated as nonhuman. They are excluded from the circle of dynamic agents whose drives are channeled toward a resultant act, excluded from the circle of those whose interests have to be considered in working out what ought to be done in a situation. Through the dynamics of the cultural pattern, they are deposited outside the active in-group among the environmental objects of a situation, to be exploited as instruments if they can be found useful, and shoved aside or destroyed if they are found obstructive. In short, they become mere objects of anticipatory or apprehensive sets in the environment of the persons who are agents in the situation.

Thus a social situation is defined by its culturally determined in-group who compose its agents and the environmental objects of response for this group. The boundaries of a social situation accordingly tend to expand with the number of organisms included in the in-group. But the boundaries are not limited to the organisms which compose the in-group. The boundaries of a social situation extend to cover also the field of objects to which these organisms can respond in their purposive behavior. Another way of expressing this is to say that the field of a social situation is the sum of the personal behavior fields (or life-spaces) of the organisms composing the in-group of the situation. So, in describing a social situation, we must include both the individuals embraced in a cultural pattern who make up its in-group and also their environment of purposive response. The addition of new individuals to a group does not, however, necessarily enlarge their environmental field of response, since the newcomers may have the same field of response as the older members, but inevitably it alters the dynamics of the field. For it brings in a new set of interests to be taken into account. A similar comment is applicable in reverse when individuals drop out of an in-group through death, incapacity, or ostracism. The environmental field of response for the situation may not be greatly changed, but the dynamics of the field may be considerably reoriented.

We generally assume that a cultural group includes only a limited number of persons. However, it is true that modern civilized man, at least in his periods of best behavior, acknowledges that the interests of all mankind are included in his fully extended social situation. More to the point, whether he acknowledges it or not, the institutions of modern man have brought all mankind into a common cultural pattern of some sort which compels mutual consideration however unpalatable at times. But (barring certain religious sects) animals are still excluded, except a few pets, even though many of them are capable of very creditable purposive behavior. Which brings out another point: organisms may be mutually involved as agents in a social situation without one or both of them being aware of the fact. The social situation as a selective system will be working through them as agents nonetheless.

So now we get an idea of the outer boundaries of a cultural pattern and the social situations it generates. Most social situations in the concrete, however, have much narrower boundaries than those of the field of a cultural pattern. For the practical limits of a given social situation include simply those organisms within a society that are mutually affected and the objects in their field of response.

Consider an ordinary family situation. Son wants the car to take his girl to the Saturday game. What other needs are there for the car? Can Dad get to the golf course? Can Mother do her shopping without a car? Has the car been properly serviced? Will Son pay for the gasoline? Is he a careful driver? Is this game likely to be followed by a gay party? Has it been some time since Son had the car? Is the girl a mere date or is it an engagement? These considerations bear on the decision, but none of them extends very far into the environment. Theoretically, as Dewey has fruitfully brought out, there is a best solution for such a situation, and the structure of the particular situation itself is the criterion for that solution's correctness.

Furthermore, the solution is a purely empirical matter. If the method of solution is formalized (which in practice it usually is not), it consists in an analysis of the relevant interests involved, their importance and urgency, a hypothesis on how they may best be harmonized or compromised, a consideration of the probable consequences, and a decision what to do. The decision is in the nature of a verification of the hypothesis, for, if it was hastily or stupidly made, the consequences from the reality of the situation will rebound on all concerned, and particularly on those mainly responsible for the decision. After the event, nothing can usually be done about that particular situation, but similar situations are likely to arise again; so, in a delayed and rough sort of way, the structure of a situation does operate as a natural norm tending to require conformity to its demands.

The impact of a wrong decision upon the agents in a social situation is likely to be more diffused and slower in teaching the agents their errors than in a personal situation, where the individual has nobody to blame but himself. Nevertheless, the impact is there, and the dynamics of it much the same—the frustrations and diminution of satisfactions to all concerned.

The frustrations, of course, first show up in each individual's personal situation. As a docile individual he learns something, and this is laid down, so far as it is learned, as a new or modified disposition of his personality. The next time anyone wants to borrow the family car, everyone enters the situation with a somewhat different attitude. A family policy about the use of the car develops. This on a small scale becomes a cultural pattern for that family.

Incidentally, such a pattern was probably in the background of the very first decision, handed down to the parents from their parents' policy in these matters. And here, if this is so, we have a direct encounter with a cultural pattern on an extended scale. If this family then institutes a local reform in the policy of loaning cars to young sons which is at variance with the policy of the other families in the community, there is going to be a new source of pressure, the characteristically social one of conformity to the prevailing cultural pattern. This, clearly, is a powerful factor in any social situation, and more will be said about it later (§5). It is, however, so much taken for granted that we do not even think about it unless it develops a continuously frustrating effect and shows up as a cultural lag.

In the family situation above, though, there was no question of conflict with a custom of the community, and so it was not a community issue. The problem was confined practically to the family. An issue before a city council regarding the location of a new firehouse, however, affects a whole city. The building must be near the center of the district it serves. But will it require the purchase of a lot in a thickly populated residential area at the expense of the city, which will suffer a loss of taxes? Or shall the firehouse be placed on a corner of a small local park? How much should the councilmen be moved by the bitter protests of those near the park? Is there an obligation to respect an area formerly set aside as a park? Here is a situation with much wider boundaries than the last one. Yet again the situation is definitely local. An appeal to consideration of all humanity on the issue of the location of a firehouse would not seem very realistic. But if the councilmen make the wrong decision in view of the whole municipal situation, there will be repercussions and, if the damage can be remedied, corrections.

A national issue carries the boundaries of a situation out still farther, and today there are international situations which seem to involve all mankind.

The significant point that comes out of observing these expanding boundaries of the social situation is that a justifiable appeal to unbounded humanity is the exception rather than the rule in evaluating a situation. Most social situations are in various degrees local and confined, not because of selfishness or provincialism, but out of the very reality of the situation. As Dewey has eloquently stressed in a variety of contexts, a failure to observe this fact and to respect it can lead only to an unnecessary extension of periods of frustration. A father who denies his son the car on the thought of all the thousands of people in the world who have no cars and cannot ride, is not going to improve the situation.

Dewey's analysis gives rise, of course, to a form of relativity, and is entirely justified in respect to evaluations derived from social situations. The relativity, however, is itself relative and should not be exaggerated. The practical limit of a situation is a most healthy thing to stress in order to keep people to the relevant facts in making ninety-nine decisions out of a hundred thrust upon them. There is no rationalization so tempting as that of evading the boundaries of a difficult situation by vague diffusion. The father whom we imagined denying his son the car on high humanitarian principles just would not be facing the actual situation. The relevant facts in a social situation generally do not extend very far. But sometimes they do, and then it is just as unrealistic not to be aware of how far they do extend beyond our immediate circle. Just how far can they extend? The principle is evident from the examples described. The outer limits of a social situation are those of the cultural pattern acknowledged by, or better, dynamically sanctioned by, the persons involved in the situation.

Persons of completely diverse cultures, whose cultures encourage them to consider one another as barbarians and heathen, would not generate a social situation. Each would be an object in the other's personal situation with respect to whom it would be prudent to act in certain ways and not in others. But until or unless they entered into a coöperative understanding with each other, and their relationships became institutionalized in some way, with social sanctions accruing which would lead them mutually to increase the solidarity of their relationship, there would be no social situation functioning as a natural norm. Here is the element of truth in the contract theory of the state so frequently revived. And why, now, would there be no social situation in an encounter of two aliens? For the reason we have steadily maintained as fundamental to an empirical analysis of value: there would be no empirically discoverable *social sanction* to require the two to conform to anything between them.

But let one of them be a member of a cultural group which has instilled the doctrine of the brotherhood of man, in consequence of which he would encounter the disapproval of his society and the pangs of his own conscience if he did not treat an alien as he would treat one of his own number; then, on his side at least, a social situation is developed. Moreover, if the alien were approached in a friendly manner, he might well reciprocate, and the social situation would be acted out and perhaps even recognized on both sides. Otherwise it would have to remain a one-sided affair. The doctrine of the brotherhood of man is so deeply instilled in our present culture that many of us find it difficult not to take it as self-evident, or to hypothesize an instinct of general human sympathy to explain it. But anthropologists inform us to the contrary. This attitude is not contained in the usual cultural pattern. Antipathy for the alien or the out-group by the in-group is widespread, and even with us crops up persistently in opposition to our cultivated sympathy toward all.

But it is not so much antipathy to the alien as plain indifference to him that keeps a social situation from arising. Marked hostility among men is more often than not a symptom of a conflict within a social situation. But indifference is a symptom of an absence of social relationships.

To get a good idea of what it feels like to have an encounter with another organism that does not set up a social situation, think of meeting another animal in the wilds. Birds and squirrels cross our line of vision and we think nothing of them. A rabbit or a deer interests us, but not for any social contact. A bear might frighten us as we frighten him, but only as a dangerous object within a personal situation. These animals, with, incidentally, docile purposive behavior much like our own, may become objects of transitory interest or even of apprehension or appetition for food or sport or scientific curiosity, but they do not enter into a social situation. A wild man, if we came upon him, would be much the same, especially if we were not sure he was not an ape.

But let a man appear dressed like us, with the accounterments of our culture upon him, and particularly if we could understand each other's langauge, and immediately a social situation springs up between us. The thing that makes the difference is that we fall into each other's cultural pattern. Even if he turned out to be a bandit intent upon my wallet, it would still be a social situation.

Hebb and Thompson[1] make a point that is highly pertinent in the present context. They note that the two great types of social organization are those found among insects and those found among men. Insect societies are based on what the authors call 'sense-dominated or biosocial behavior,' which they describe as allowing of some slight learning and hence being a little less rigid than chain reflex behavior, but still essentially nonpurposive in that it lacks the flexible mediation of cognitive sets. Human society is based on the latter sort of behavior, which they call 'psychosocial' or 'under ideational control.' Then they point out the notable fact that, although many insect species have complex social organizations (bees, wasps, ants, termites), only man among the docile mammals has developed a social organization comparable in complexity to that of insects. To be sure, man has the most highly developed intelligent behavior, but the gap between human intelligence and that of a number of other mammals is nowhere near as wide as the gap between the very limited social relationships in these other vertebrate species and the complex organizations of man. What in human behavior could account for this big difference? The authors believe it is man's capacity for syntactical language, which permits him to combine and recombine his concepts or cognitive sets, and so to make plans, and enter into coöperative relationships with other men.

In the absence of a syntactical language, human culture patterns and social organization could never have developed, and a social situation would be rudimentary or absent. Man's persistent conviction that there is a wide gap, significant for values, between himself and other animals here finds much confirmation. The social situation described in this chapter is almost unique to man. It does not develop in insect societies because these are not based on docile adaptive behavior but on instinctive and sense-dominated behavior. And it does not develop among the vertebrates other than man because other animals lack the capacity for syntactical language. Language provides for intricate coöperative social behavior, and is the substitute in man's social structure for the intricate instinctive mechanisms of the social insects. Human society is the only highly organized *purposive* society. And it takes an articulated syntactical language to provide the communication of purposive aims that is necessary for a purposively organized social structure. This correlation seems axiomatic once it is formulated, yet the formulation presented by these authors with its full import exhibited comes perhaps as something quite fresh.

Expanding on the observation above, Hebb and Thompson write:

> The difficulty in identifying behavior as [purposive] is that it may have to be seen repeatedly in order to be sure that its objective is achieved neither accidentally nor mechanically; that it shows 'means-end readiness' [Tolman's phrase for our 'cognitive set'], or a variation with circumstances that tends toward the same end effect. A bird's 'warning' cry would be purposive, for example, if made only when the young were exposed and stopped when they got under cover, or if the warner approached the warned and called quietly, without drawing the marauder's attention also. The essence of the purposive communication is that the sender remains sensitive to the receiver's responses, during sending, and by modification of his sending shows that his behavior is in fact guided by the intention (expectancy) of achieving a particular behavioral effect, in the receiver. The 'broken wing' behavior of the grouse, for example, is purposive, since it is modified according to the marauder's behavior in such a way as to draw him away from the hiding chicks; but the warning cry of the gull, though it tends to produce a protective immobility in the chicks, seems quite reflexive. Carpenter points out that the alarm calls of a group of primates, startled by an observer, continue long after they have got away out of danger. The calls are therefore more emotional expression than purposive. Birds and animals do show purposive communication. It seems likely that the crow, for example, or the parrot may on occasion 'speak' with intent to influence another. A dog's bark, or a chimpanzee's begging gestures, may be unmistakably purposeful. This does not mean, however, that bird or subhuman mammal has language. It is important to recognize that language is something more.[2]
>
> From this point of view, the outstanding fact is man's capacity for a varied combination of symbolic acts, and we therefore propose to call language *syntactic behavior*. We thus have three classes of communication: (A) reflexive (not true communication) [like the gull's cry]; (B) purposive but nonsyntactic [like the dog's bark, etc. above]; and (C) syntactic (and usually purposive), or true language.[3]

The authors then describe a very crude coöperative act between two chimpanzees and observe:

> We know of no reliable report of coöperation by other animals that quite comes up to this, with its evidence of purposiveness. Yet it must be pointed out that there was hardly more than the barest beginning of teamwork as we know it in man, and that even this was achieved only in an artificial experimental setting which needed the planning of the human experimenter . . . What may be described as a 'one-sided coöperation' certainly occurs in the chimpanzee. An adult animal rescues an infant heading for trouble: A helps B, but B does not simultaneously help A. Teamwork at the human level is another matter. It involves a kind of prior understanding between coöperators that is impossible, perhaps, without a human capacity for communication. When X and Y coöperate fully, very complex mental processes are required. At each stage of action, X must anticipate not only his own next act and its effect, but also those of Y. . . . Teamwork, thus, makes intellectual demands of the same order as those made by language. Psychologically, it may in fact be hard to distinguish the two.[4] [For the spoken or written word is not the only vehicle of communication.]
>
> Let us then define three levels of coöperation, corresponding very well on the whole to the three levels of communication already proposed: (A) reflexive or non-purposive; (B) purposive, but one-sided; and (C) 'two-sided' or teamwork. [The first, expanded to include 'sense-dominated behavior,' is characteristic of insect societies.] The second of these is seen in higher vertebrates; the last seems to occur only in man, as far as one can tell from available evidence.[5]

As men, placing exceptional value on our powers of social organization, we must watch our step to see that we are not simply exhibiting once more our almost ineradicable bias for the in-group against an out-group, for man versus brute, Socrates versus pig. But the facts here do seem unassailable. Man through his linguistic powers alone among the docile animals can (barring a few exceptions of the simplest sort) perform two-sided acts of coöperation. Hence man alone has created a purposively organized society. Hence man alone (barring the few exceptions) generates social situations. The line between man and animals in the biological sphere thus parallels very closely the line between personal situations and social situations in the value sphere. Docile animals other than man are concerned with the standards of prudence but not with the wider standards of social coöperative relationships. The latter are almost uniquely the concern of man. Perhaps this explains why so many men are suspicious of studies like the present one that turn first to observations of animal behavior as sources for understanding human values. Their suspicions may herewith be allayed. As it happens, man is unique in the possession of instruments for coöperative purposive organization. Virtually alone he generates a social situation and the higher values that emanate therefrom. But these values would be very superficially comprehended if they were not followed back to their purposive sources in the purposive behavior of individual organisms. The social situation, however, is not reducible without residue to a collection of personal situations. It is a selective system in its own right, generating social values through its selective action.

That which determines the boundaries of a social situation is, then, ultimately the cultural pattern within which the interacting organisms are included. Furthermore, following the observations of Hebb and Thompson, we can risk going even farther and saying that among purposive organisms cultural patterns develop only through the agency of linguistic behavior. With allowance for a few rudimentary instances, a social situation seems to depend upon a common language as the medium of coöperation. The verbal expression of a cognitive set herewith acquires a value significance unsuspected when we were discussing the matter in an earlier context (chap. 4, §5). It then appeared simply as a personal convenience for economy of reference to a cognitive set. Now we perceive that it is the principal instrument for effecting social solidarity among docile organisms dependent on purposive behavior. It is because men can verbally express their thoughts and so convey them to others that they can coöperate, develop cultures, and enter into social situations.

## 3. ECONOMIC VALUE AND THE ECONOMIC SITUATION

The social value of an act as the resultant effect of the interaction of a number of persons in a social situation, and the manner in which it emerges and is corrected through the sanction of the reality of the situation, was brought out in the previous section. Perhaps the most conspicuous exemplification of this effect in our society is economic value. Accordingly, this deserves special notice here. The ramifications of economic value are numerous, but for the most part they stem from the concept of the value of an article in exchange, or, in the broadest sense, *price*.

Price is a typical social value generated by social situations, and so is an excellent instance of the overindividual character of a social value. Price is a sort of value that would never arise in a personal situation. It requires at least two persons in a peculiar kind of coöperative situation for the price or exchange value of an object to appear, and the proper price for the object lies in the nature of the situation, and the persons concerned in setting the price may be in error regarding it and pay too little or too much. Moreover, the situation sanctions the proper price and tends to bring it into existence in the actual economic process. Here, in relatively precise and quantitative terms, we can see how a social situation behaves as a selective system, producing a value that no single purposive act or personal situation would ever bring about of itself.

In the simplest conceivable situation, the price or exchange value of an object is what it will bring in terms of another object in a transaction between two persons motivated by prudence only to make an exchange. A has an extra cow and B has some extra chickens. A and B are neighbors and there is nobody else within miles. The boundary of the situation is thus limited to A and B. It is an economic situation in the broad sense because it operates with the understanding on both sides that if there is any transaction at all it will be exchange. A is not going to steal the chickens by sneaking in at night, nor is he thinking of threatening B with a gun if he refuses to trade with him. Thus an economic situation is one arising within a certain cultural pattern—that of voluntary exchange. For the same reason it would not be an economic situation if the two men exchanged the objects as gifts. To make it a clear-cut economic situation, both participants in the proposed exchange are supposed to be motivated on purely prudential grounds of self-interest without intent to plunder or to give in charity. And that is where the concept of the 'economic man' comes from. He is nothing more than the personification of the pure economic situation. It is doubtful if he was ever intended as a historical personality. But he can be quite useful as a representation of this concept of the pure economic situation. Something like him does appear in almost anyone (who has not been too well brought up) when faced with a typical bargaining situation. For then it is understood that each participant will, with self-interest and strict prudence, make the best bargain he can.

Return to A and B. How many chickens will B give for a cow? How few will A accept? The resultant act will depend on how eager each trader is to make the exchange. The bargaining that goes on between a couple of experienced traders is a succession of tentative acts feeling out the eagerness of each to make the exchange. I say 'experienced' traders designedly, for this everyday expression contains the implicit reference to the overindividual economic value potential in the situation. An inexperienced trader gets cheated by an experienced one and learns to do better when the next economic situation arises. He is punished for his incorrect anticipations and apprehensions relative to the situation. The reality of the situation is the criterion for his error, and directs the correction.

Each trader separately is involved in a personal situation, his own life-space, within which one of the central objects of interest is the other trader. As a prudent individual he feels out the other trader and makes his personal decision in terms of the resultant tensions of his interacting purposes. Thus the resultant act of the total social situation (the actual exchange of goods) is the convergence of the resultant acts of two personal situations (A's decision to give up his cow for some chickens, and B's decision to give up a certain number of chickens for the cow). Now, if the feasibility judgment (cf. chap. 4, §8) of the two traders is correct, then neither of them would have been cheated, and the exchange would represent the economic value of each article in terms of the other article—its exchange value or price in the broadest sense. That is to say, each man would have correctly estimated the eagerness of the other to make the exchange, and no relevant factors bearing on the exchange would have been neglected by either man. Each man might regard the other as a hard bargainer, but neither would have reason to regret the exchange later. That was just the exchange which the situation justified. Moreover, an economist describing the situation would agree that, all factors considered, that was the proportion of chickens to cow which the situation did justify.

It is this fact that renders economic value objective relative to the agents in an economic situation. Given the values each trader places on his own goods and on those of the other man, in terms of the intensity of desire to retain the one or acquire the other, the resultant exchange of goods in the situation is a describable fact independent of anybody else's wish or prejudice. This is the exchange sanctioned by that social situation; the sanction is effective and works, tending to bring that particular rate of exchange into being, for that is the very significance of those two potent expressions of trading: 'the experienced trader' and 'being cheated.'

Suppose A and B are 'experienced traders.' After the bargaining period, with the usual protestations that neither is interested in a swap but just to oblige will consider the idea—which is typical bargaining method for eliminating irrelevant emotion, and suggests 'bluffing' only to the inexperienced—they finally settle on fifty-two chickens to the cow.

This is the resultant social act of exchange, and we are regarding it, because of the method used in leading up to it, as the correct economic value for these articles for that situation. Now let us briefly examine some of the so-called economic factors concerned in reaching this resultant. My aim is not to suggest any particular basis for economic value, but only to show that right here (or with addition only of the concept of an 'open market') is the juncture in the general theory of value at which the specialized study of economic value takes off.

How did A happen to pick a cow to exchange and B some chickens? Because these represented a surplus. And why was A interested in getting chickens and B in getting a cow? Because these represented a need. A had a surplus of cows and a need for chickens; B, a surplus of chickens and a need for a cow. In short, here, in its most abstract form, is the relation of supply and demand. If this relation is examined in the light of the transaction of exchange, it appears that the transaction represents an increase in actual value on both sides. *Both* traders benefit from the exchange. The transaction would not take place if both did not benefit—or, rather, did not expect to, for we must allow for cheating and for disappointments after unwise exchanges.

The dynamics of the economic situation relies upon this increase in actual valuing as a result of exchange. A had a cow whose milk he could not use, or only for the pigs. The cow had some potential value in A's hands but little actual value, and vice versa with B's chickens. The exchange converts low values of the goods for their original owners into high values for their new owners. An economically justifiable exchange is thus a social benefit.

But to return to supply and demand. There is obviously an important relation between the two. If either changes appreciably, the situation changes and the economic value of the goods in terms of their exchange rate changes. Suppose B at the time of the bargaining had one hundred chickens, and with his large family could use seventy-five chickens, but had recently lost his cow. It was on this basis that he was willing to give up fifty-two chickens for the cow. Twenty-five of the chickens were of no immediate use to him anyhow, and he was willing to sacrifice twenty-seven more, incurring a period of scarcity, for the sake of getting a cow. Now imagine that he suddenly discovered twenty-five additional chickens that had hidden themselves in the brush behind the barn. With this added supply he would be justified in letting A have a larger number of chickens if A insisted; and if A could himself use seventy-five chickens, he should in all prudence bargain to get them, since the situation would justify his having many more if he needed the chickens as much as B needed the cow.

In short, the economic demand in this situation depends on the conative intensity of A's and B's appetitions for the cows and chickens to be traded. And the intensity of a man's desire for objects fluctuates. But if the two farmers have fairly stable personalities, these fluctuations would not be very great over a bargaining period. If one of them were unstable, and liable to unreasonable demands or sudden shifts of value, to the neglect of the reality of the situation, then either no trade would take place or he would surely be cheated. But within the framework of an economic situation like the one we have been imagining between two prudent men of stable personalities, the economic value of the objects in exchange is quite objective; even if a man is unwise in a bargain, his error can be demonstrated and usually is all too obvious to the victim anyway.

If this point has been made, the rest in regard to economic value is a matter of added complications. Up to a certain threshold in these complications, the added intricacy seems to augment the objectivity and the independence of economic value from other values. But when that threshold is passed, the economic situation gets more and more involved in other social relationships till the distinction between an economic situation and other sorts of social situations becomes confusing rather than helpful. We must expand the present abbreviated treatment of economic value just enough to make this very important point manifest. The substance of this point is that the social situation with *all* the factors it draws into it is the encompassing natural norm or selective system for all social values in process, and that the economic situation is just a phase or a species of social situation, though a very imposing one.

A transitional point requires mention before we proceed deeper into the complications. It has to do with an ambiguity in the economic term 'demand.' Is the demand based on the actual need indicated in a situation, or is it what the agent believes to be his need? Is the price of an article determined by some 'actual utility' or by the 'expected utility'? The problem here is the transfer to the wider economic social situation of the value problem posed in the means-end (subordinate-superordinate act) relationship that is found in every practical personal situation. Is the value of a goal object determined by the charged anticipatory set which channels action upon it, or by the impulse pattern which initiates the charge and terminates in the quiescence pattern? Is a key in a personal situation to be considered of value because it will open a door, or because we think it will?

There is no problem if the goal object happens to be based on a true mediating judgment and hence is conducive to the terminal goal of the drive charging the anticipatory set. Then the value attached to the goal object is its true value in accordance with the reality of the situation. But what if there has been an error and the mediating judgment is false? The goal object is then not conducive to the quiescence pattern. On our earlier analysis, it appeared that the goal object nevertheless possesses value because it is the object of an actively charged anticipation. It is the potential object of a set of anticipatory references; and this set is the actual object of conative value charged by the drive. The goal object and its anticipatory set retain conative value as long as a drive activates them. The value placed on these objects dissipates only when the agent becomes convinced that he was mistaken in his belief that the selected goal object would lead to his terminal goal. A key is valued as long as a man believes it will open the door, whether in reality it will or not.

So too with price. The price of an object is determined by the belief of the trader in respect to his need for it. It is a resultant of the beliefs of the traders involved in the transaction. There may thus be a discrepancy between the resultant price which the article brings in a given market and what may be called its 'proper price' based on the 'true value' of the article. The latter is what the article would bring if the beliefs of the traders about it were all true—and if they were all experienced traders. The 'proper price' is the price justified by the bedrock reality of the economic situation. The 'proper price' tends to become realized since it represents the reality of the economic situation in open exchange between prudent men. A trader who finds that he has been cheated learns to correct his errors like anyone else frustrated in his aims.

The actual price that an article brings, then, is the resultant of the 'expected utility,' not of the actual utility, of the object; but the actual utility legislates over the expected utility in much the same way in which an end legislates over its means. When we say that an object is priced too high, we may mean that its price is higher than we would be willing to pay, or we may mean that it is more than anyone *ought* to pay. If we mean the latter we are making a reference to the 'proper price' and indicating its legislation over the price asked or over the actual price paid if anyone is foolish enough to buy at that price.

So far we have been describing the very simplest economic situation—that of barter between two traders—and in rather abstract, ideal terms. But it serves to bring out the two social characteristics of an economic situation: (1) that the situation is bounded by the persons and objects embraced in its social pattern—the pattern in this instance being the mutually understood rules of bartering; and (2) that the value emerging from the transaction, the price, is a resultant of the situation. The dynamics of the social value comes from the drives of the individual persons entering into the situation, but the resultant value, the price, is determined by the overindividual structure of the situation.

The next stage comes when more than two persons are involved in a situation for exchange of goods. Suppose now we have a fair-sized community, and many of the farmers have cows and chickens. Then many persons are available to make the exchange of a cow for chickens. The supply of chickens and cows for exchange is widely distributed, and likewise the demand. The price will now be a function of the total supply and demand. If a good many people need cows and not many need chickens, and there is a fair surplus of chickens, the latter will be cheap in terms of cows. And the farmers will be eager to get rid of their surplus.

But a community that is carrying on a good deal of exchange soon finds it convenient to select one type of article as a standard object of reference for all articles to be exchanged. A widely valued article would be the natural one to choose. In a cattle community, cows would be the natural choice. Then cows become for that community the conventional medium of exchange. Cows become money. In fact, we are told, this is the derivation of the word 'pecuniary.' It came from a community that used cows as money. But a medium more convenient than cows is sure to be selected in time, and precious metals, silver and gold, were early put to this social use in many parts of the world.

Now, with a convenient medium of exchange, the relation of supply and demand becomes more flexible and fluid but also more complicated. Almost everything in the community now has its price, or exchange value, in terms of the accepted medium. But, also, almost everything has an effect on the price of almost everything else. If there is a scarcity of chickens, a farmer has reason to believe he will get a good price for them, but he may be disappointed because there happens to be a big surplus of ducks, and people are willing to buy ducks in place of chickens if the price of chickens is a little high.

This is the situation in the open competitive market. The generalization of this situation seems like an economic ideal. It is the ideal of *laissez faire*. The reality of the situation is relied upon to stop oversupply automatically, as the chicken rancher above would have discovered. Demand without adequate supply is an incentive to production, again through the reality of the economic situation. And, as we have seen in simple barter, every exchange transaction is one in which values are augmented for both parties in the exchange. *Laissez faire* then looks like an economic, not to say a social, heaven on earth.

This is just the point, however, at which other social factors enter into the economic situation. The pure economic relationship of value in exchange becomes so deeply fused with what would ordinarily be called moral or sociological values that often it is no longer profitable to try to make a distinction between an economic situation and a social situation.

As long as the price of an article is determined largely by the pure dynamics of exchange, as in barter between experienced traders, the situation is typically economic. But when the price reflects other factors involving social understandings and controls other than those of exchange, the resultant act including the price is a social value on a much wider scale. In the complexities of modern industrial conditions, most economic values are social values on a broad scale, determined by the structure of the total social situation rather than by that of the pure economic situation. Typical economic situations then become secondary rather than primary. They operate on the surface above a deeper social situation. Thus, in buying a house or a car, we may make a deal with purely economic motives, but the level of prices for real estate in the neighborhood, and the level of the wages we bargain from, will be determined by factors extending far beyond those of simple exchange.

What are some of these factors which enter in when money as a conventional medium of exchange becomes an institution in a large community? Perhaps the most important is the augmented ability to accumulate economic power through the accumulation of money. Money is an enduring object of multiple instrumental value (cf. chap. 11, §6). Any enduring object of multiple instrumentality will serve as a basis for an accumulation of economic power. But money is the most convenient and most fluid. Thus an accumulation of land will lay up economic power. But when a community is on a money standard, the worth of the land is itself translated into its money value.

Some of the social factors underlying the exchange value will come to light if we ask which has the more stable exchange value, land or money? If there is reason to think that the money of a community is stable in its exchange value, then an accumulation of money is a more fluid, extensive, and ready source of power than land, because land is susceptible to local fluctuations of value that money is not. Land may lose value through fire, lack of care, change of social conditions in the neighborhood. But money may lose value if changing conditions cause the community to lose faith in it. Then land would have a more stable exchange value, since it depends less upon credit.

But how does money depend upon credit? The simple exchange of a cow for chickens involves a minimum of credit because the farmers use the objects exchanged. But when objects are accumulated and kept solely for their anticipated value in exchange, then their value for the person holding them is solely their credit value.

What maintains their credit value? The answer is the confidence of the members of the community in the exchange value of their money. As long as this attitude is a part of their cultural pattern, the credit value of the money is stable.

But why is that credit not as stable as the flow of exchange in the open market? Here a variety of considerations spring up. Granted an open market, what maintains that? The governmental stability of social structure within which the flow of exchange goes on. That is to say, the economic exchange value depends on the cultural pattern of political rule and law enforcement which protects the credit value or the objects of exchange —protects property, in short, against robbery, breaking of contracts, flagrant cheating, and the like. The economic situation thus becomes embedded and fused in the general social situation.

But on the other side lies something even more disturbing to the purity of exchange value—the tendency of credit value to pyramid upon itself. Borrowing on credit is a simple instance of this. Thus a bond is an expansion of credit to the value of the bond. Then if somebody borrows on the bond there is an expansion of this expansion of credit. Thus bank loans, mortgages, installment buying are all in the nature of expansion of credit. The very bills we use as paper money in lieu of gold, for which they are supposed to stand, represent an expansion of credit, since they are printed far in excess of the gold available to the banks to pay them off if there were a run on the banks. And when a government makes it illegal to possess gold coin, it has virtually put its citizens off the gold standard and asked them to have faith in their government to maintain the exchange value of the bank notes they use. This tendency of credit to expand requires a degree of government control over banks and other sources of credit expansion. Without such control a community is subject to periodic financial collapse when the credit value rises so far above the observable cash value that somebody with a good deal of property on credit loses faith and demands the cash. Fear is contagious, and all the consequences of an economic depression follow if there is no social control to maintain the credit.

In spite of governmental devices to check undue expansion of credit, depressions or recessions do occur, which shows how much exchange value while credit is good depends upon the social situation within which exchange goes on and prices are set. A price then represents not only the exchange value of the article but also the level of credit stability at the time of the transaction. The proper price may then mean two quite different things. It may mean that this is the price the market warrants on present belief in the stability of the market. Or it may mean that this is the price the market warrants and that which the social stability underlying the level of credit warrants. Once more we see how the economic situation of value in exchange is dependent upon and can become fused with the encompassing social situation.

Even more disturbing to the purity of exchange value under a money economy is the tendency for wealth to accumulate in small groups and produce great concentrations of economic power. Then there is a gross disproportion in the advantages of an exchange. A poor man pays a large proportion of his week's income for a pair of shoes; a rich man pays a negligible proportion of his income for his shoes. The poor man's disadvantage is particularly evident when he is offering his own services for exchange. If the rich man offers to pay a certain amount and the poor man asks for more, the rich man with his ample resources can afford to wait. But the poor man without resources may even be unable to move to an area offering higher wages, and thus is forced to accept low wages.

In a certain hard sense, this is the actual exchange value of the man's services in that situation. But in a broader sense, it is the contemporary social structure of the society in which the two men live which permits the rich man to maintain his wealth and to make a hard bargain with the poor man.

Add to this the tendency for wealth to accumulate when it is protected and relatively uncontrolled, and the need of control for the sake of social stability becomes evident. Concentrations of wealth lead to monopolies restricting open competition, to indirect and even direct manipulation of the machinery of government, and to exploitation of labor. In short, *laissez faire* leads to its own destruction by converting an open market into a closed monopolistic and employer-managed economy unless there is some social control to keep the market open—which then is no longer a condition of *laissez faire*.

Again we see that an economic situation depends upon a broad social situation and, unless temporarily isolated in some way—as often happens in a bargaining situation of limited scope—becomes merged more and more with deep-lying social factors. The result is that attention in the economic sphere is forced away from considerations of pure exchange value to problems of the distribution of wealth. Then we find ourselves plunged into issues of the relative benefits to society of a capitalistic economy, of degrees of social control in a mixed economy, a socialistic economy, a fascistic economy, or a communistic economy. And we make no mention of economies of primitive peoples.

When such issues become paramount, we have passed quite outside the economic situation and are dealing with the social situation on the broadest scale. Moreover, these issues no longer have to do with the best resultant act in view of a given situation, but with the best total cultural pattern. Our consideration of this sort of problem should wait, therefore, until the next chapter.

In regard to the economic situation, the conclusion seems to be this: In a simple instance of bargaining, a pure economic situation can be demarcated within the limits of the transaction; and the correct exchange value for the participants can be rather definitely made out. Up to a certain point the same seems to hold true for the market value of an article under a money economy. But the complications of property relationships, of labor, of credit, of concentrations of wealth, gradually implicate the economic situation so deeply with a broad social situation that the two cannot be separated. In the end, any economic issue that goes below the surface of a local deal between a couple of men, or between certain groups of men bargaining for a price, becomes an issue within a more general social situation. And if the issue runs deep, it may extend the boundaries of the situation to the limits of the cultural pattern of the society.

## 4. The Temporal Limits of a Social Situation

So we come back to the social situation as the generic and fundamental process in interpersonal relationships. An economic situation is always a kind of social situation, and if the relationships involved in an economic problem raise issues that extend beyond those of bargaining for a mutually acceptable price of exchange, a more than merely economic situation is encountered.

The question sooner or later arises: What is the temporal spread of a social situation? In the simple situation of A and B bargaining for a price of exchange, the situation begins when the bargaining begins and ends when a price is agreed upon and the goods are delivered. Similarly, a beginning and an end can be set to local situations like that of whether Son shall have the car or whether the firehouse shall be constructed in the park. But the duration of broader complicated situations is often much more difficult to set.

The question of the temporal spread of a social situation seems to be more difficult to answer than that of its regional spread. The latter is determined by the number of persons implicated in the undertaking or problem which precipitates the situation. We might think that the same consideration would settle the question of temporal spread. Ultimately it does, but the determination is much less definite. The reason for the difficulty is the continuity of consequences among social events which makes natural stopping places harder to set.

In determining the temporal spread of a personal situation, the life of the organism sets a definite outer limit. No man knows just how long he will live, but he knows roughly, and individual prudence cannot realistically consider any consequences of his actions that would affect him after his death. Even considerations about his memory and provision for those he loves are not exceptions. These provisions must be made by him while he is alive. The life of the organism sets a natural time limit to all personal situations. In social situations nothing like this can be counted on. The termination of a cultural pattern does in fact bring to an end all expectations dependent on the institutions maintained through the pattern. And cultural patterns do come to an end. But no adequately authenticated prediction can be made for the end of a culture (not even Spengler's thousand years) that is comparable to the roughly predictable four score years and ten for the life of a man. Usually we assume—and quite properly—an indefinite duration for our cultural pattern, barring adjustments. Even rather violent social revolutions may not greatly disturb the cultural continuity. The uprooting of a whole cultural pattern is difficult and rare. Cultural continuity is the general expectation.

Again, in a personal situation each organism is the seat of the terminal satisfactions of the drives which mark the natural terminations of personal situations. Nothing exactly comparable holds in a social situation. There are no overindividual social drives demanding intrinsic social satisfactions. Only individual organisms experience drives and satisfactions. So the termination of a personal situation may be just an incident in a social situation—as the paid-off work of a stenographer hired to type the brief for a lawyer about to try his case.

Such considerations have led Dewey on the interpersonal level to stress the continuum of social situations, or, as he calls it, 'the continuum of ends-means.' He has greatly overdone the slurring of the means-end distinction, as our earlier analyses of purposive structures have made clear. But at the level of the social situation he makes some important observations that need to be brought out.

One of Dewey's classic passages bearing on this point occurs in a section headed "The Continuum of Ends-Means" in his "Theory of Valuation." [6] He opens the section dramatically with a reference to Charles Lamb's essay on the origin of roast pork. As the story goes,

> Roast pork was first enjoyed when a house in which pigs were confined was accidentally burned down. While searching in the ruins, the owners touched the pigs that had been roasted in the fire and scorched their fingers. Impulsively bringing their fingers to their mouths to cool them, they experienced a new taste. Enjoying the taste, they henceforth set themselves to building houses, enclosing pigs in them, and then burning the houses down.

On this Dewey comments:

> Now, if ends-in-view are what they are entirely apart from means, and have their value independently of valuation of means, there is nothing absurd, nothing ridiculous, in this procedure, for the end attained, the *de facto* termination, *was* eating and enjoying roast pork, and that was just the end desired. . . . The story throws a flood of light upon what is usually meant by the maxim 'The end justifies the means,' and also upon the popular objection to it. Applied in this case, it would mean that the value of the attained end, the eating of roast pork, was such as to warrant the price paid in the means by which it was attained—destruction of dwelling-houses and sacrifice of the values to which they contribute. . . . The maxim referred to, under the guise of saying that ends, in the sense of actual consequences, provide the warrant for means employed—a correct position—actually says that some fragment of these actual consequences—a fragment arbitrarily selected because the heart has been set upon it—authorizes the means to obtain *it*, without the need of foreseeing and weighing other ends as consequences of the means used.[7]

In this analysis we have to admit, I think, that Dewey is quite correct. He takes as his illustration, be it noticed, a striking (if fictitious) model of a *social* situation—the burning of a house and *all* its human consequences. Then he brings out the ridiculousness of viewing this situation from the perspective of one incidental group of consequences that happen to offer delight to some of the persons there. This little group of consequences is torn out of its context and given a preferential status out of all proportion to the reality of the situation. There was nothing in the social situation to single out these delights as the terminal value of the process. The consequences of the 'destruction of dwelling-houses' extend for long periods of time, adding up the 'sacrifice of the values to which they contribute.' And so, in social situations generally, the terminal values of individual purposes such as gratuitous satisfactions and quiescence patterns figure only as so many details within the continuing context of the situation.

But if individual terminal values are thus swallowed up in the resultant sequences of consequences, what is left to mark the terminus of a social situation? If every end is also a means in an endless continuum, where can a situation end and be bounded? Dewey is so anxious to show that personal ends may be irrelevant or only incidental to social situations that he creates a serious problem for himself concerning the evaluation of acts relative to a social situation.

Let us first be sure how serious he is about the relativity of the means-end relation in the continuum of social events. Here is a typical passage from the same section as the quotation above, giving the moral, so to speak, of the roast pig situation:

> We are thus brought back to the point already set forth. In all the physical sciences (using 'physical' here as a synonym for *nonhuman*) it is now taken for granted that all 'effects' are also 'causes,' or, stated more accurately, that nothing happens which is *final* in the sense that it is not part of an ongoing stream of events. If this principle, with the accompanying discrediting of belief in objects that are ends but not means, is employed in dealing with distinctive human phenomena, it necessarily follows that distinction between ends and means is temporal and relational. Every condition that has to be brought into existence in order to serve as a means is, *in that connection,* an object of desire and an end-in-view, while the end actually reached is a means to future ends as well as a test of valuations previously made. Since the end attained is a condition for further existential occurrences, it must be appraised as a potential obstacle and potential resource.[8]

In this passage he seems to be quite serious about the relativity of means and ends. By offering the parallel with the cause and effect continuum he seems to suggest there is no doubt in his mind that every end without exception is only an end in relation to what has gone before and is equally a means to what will be going on ahead. Nevertheless, the passage is tantalizing. Typical of Dewey's statements on this topic, it contains some qualifying phrases that give the effect of hedging. Why does he italicize '*in that connection*' in the statement: "Every condition that has to be brought into existence in order to serve as a means is, *in that connection,* an object of desire and an end in view?" Does this not imply that a means as an object of desire is a terminal end *in that connection,* that is with respect to that desire?

Does not a desire, then, institute a terminal end in respect to that desire?

To be sure, as we have seen in our analysis of the appetitive structure, a subordinate goal object is only relatively terminal to the drive charging the anticipatory set. But when the drive is finally satisfied in its quiescence pattern, there is in fact a terminal end to that desire. In the statement just quoted, Dewey seems to admit this fact, which is no whit neutralized by his statement that 'the end actually reached is a means to future ends.' This may also be true. After eating a good breakfast, a man is prepared for the morning's work at his office. For this overlapping desire to complete a piece of work at his office, the breakfast comes in as a means. But the breakfast was a means *in a quite different connection* from that in which it was an end. It was an end for his hunger drive, and presumably that drive was in fact terminated. The breakfast was a means to the man's drive to finish his work at the office, and that drive actually preceded his hunger drive, which entered as a temporary mild frustration to his office drive, delaying his getting to work. Dewey's error in regard to the flat end-means continuum lay in his beading ends and means along a single thread of events instead of noticing the stratification and complicated overlapping of desires in actual human behavior. Simultaneous desires may be running along and attaining their consummation at different times, often converging on identical goal objects as common means, and often having the consummation of one desire enter as a means toward the consummation of another. And yet has not Dewey here, contextualist though he is, neglected to take account of this stratification?

The passage quoted is typical, and the probable answer is that Dewey was puzzled, did not see a clear way out of his dilemma, and left the matter ambiguous. He may not even have clearly seen his dilemma.

The dilemma is this: On the one side, Dewey has described the social situation as a relatively self-contained unit which constitutes its own criterion for the correct act to resolve its inner tensions. On the other side, Dewey insists on an end-means continuum which seems to deny any natural terminals for social processes, and so makes it impossible to set temporal limits to a social situation. And if every social situation fades off indefinitely into the future, how can a situation function as a criterion for the value of actions?

The selective action of a situation, which was the first horn of Dewey's dilemma, was his great ethical insight, and we must keep that in mind. The dilemma itself falls away when an error in the second horn—the end-means continuum—is revealed. It simply is not true that every end is also a means. The means-end relation is not parallel to the cause-effect relation as Dewey conceives the latter. The means-end relation is a value relation and has to do with desires, as Dewey himself states, and the satisfaction of a desire is terminal absolutely for that desire.

Then how does Dewey slip into so great a misconception and make so plausible an argument for an end-means continuum? The answer is that his attention is so concentrated on the social situation that he neglects the personal situation, where desires and satisfactions are actually experienced. His official behavioristic approach to value problems makes this neglect the easier. And in the social situation it is often true that terminal individual values are instrumental there and, as personal satisfactions, partially irrelevant to the resolution of the social situation.

But it is not true that personal satisfactions are entirely irrelevant to the resolution of social situations. My point will be that the tensions in a social situation which bring it into action as a value criterion are tensions arising in the individual persons caught up in the situation, and the acts which are correct in the resolution of the situation are precisely those which reduce these personal tensions through terminal satisfactions or the nearest approximations to these possible.

When Son wants the car, a complex of tensions emerges in the family, and we have a social situation. The actual locus of the tensions is in each individual's personal situation relative to his organism as a center. The resolution of the tension of the social situation depends on the achievement of a substantial reduction of the personal tensions creating the complex. A marked relaxation of the tensions constitutes the temporal termination of the situation. This is an observable occurrence, and constitutes a natural break in behavior comparable to the termination of an appetition or aversion in the behavior of an individual organism. In the situation cited above, the tensions are ordinarily reduced when the parent has made his decision. If, however, the group tension increases after the parent's decision, then obviously the social situation is not over and the parent must look for some other way of resolving it.

The resolution and termination of a situation does not necessarily mean that everybody is fully satisfied. If the boy is denied the car, he will be disappointed. All things considered, it may well be the best decision. The boy's tensions are temporarily augmented, perhaps, though possibly not if he respects his father's judgment. But the anxieties of the parents presumably are much reduced and the question is closed.

Dewey himself sometimes suggests essentially this solution to his dilemma. In answering the objection to his view, 'that, according to it, valuation activities and judgments are involved in a hopeless *regressus ad infinitum*,' he makes the following statements:

> The 'value' of different ends that suggest themselves is estimated or measured by the capacity they exhibit to guide action in making good, *satisfying*, in its literal sense, existing lacks. Here is the factor that cuts short the process of foreseeing and weighing ends-in-view in their function as means. Sufficient unto the day is the evil thereof and sufficient also is the *good* of that which does away with the existing evil. Sufficient because it is the means of instituting a complete situation or an integrated set of conditions.[9]

The 'satisfying' of the 'needs or privations of an actual situation . . . is the means of instituting a complete situation.' Take those phrases literally and that is precisely what I am describing above as the termination of a social situation. But, taken literally, that situation really is terminated; the tensions which rendered it problematic are over. The end of a tension is its end for value. The end-means continuum is observably broken there. Dewey's solution, if this is it, is adequate. But then he should give up insisting on an end-means continuum.

One other ambiguity enters here. To deny that there is an end-means continuum is not to deny that there is a continuity of social processes wherever a society exists. Life in the family goes right on after it has been decided who has the car. And a point Dewey often makes: the resolution of one situation often precipitates another. If the boy is denied the car, he must find some other way of taking his girl to the game. But for one situation to precipitate another is not to render one situation a means to another. Every means is a cause, but every cause is not a means. Dewey often appears to make this illicit conversion.

The father's decision would have to take into account Son's difficulties in getting his girl to the game without the car. But if the situation produced by the boy's wanting the car was properly decided by his being denied it, then the consequence that the boy had a new problem on his hands constituted a new situation with its own tensions to be resolved.

Having thus found the boundaries of a social situation widthwise in the group of organisms and their life-spaces involved in a problematic or coöperative action, and lengthwise in a marked reduction of a group tensions resulting from action, we can now profitably make a few observations about the relations of situations to one another.

A personal situation may rise and end without ever becoming involved in a wider social situation. Such was the geologist's search for water in the desert; such would have been Poncins' battle with a blizzard if he had found his way to the cabin all alone. And many times a day little personal situations arise which affect no one else, and which we may notice so little as hardly to recall them at the end of the day: the nuisance about the shoestring that broke, the toothpaste that burst out too fast on the brush, the wonderful smell of the fresh morning air when we stepped out to pick up the paper, and the stroll through the garden before breakfast to greet the multitude of gratuitous satisfactions waiting there, and so on through the day.

Then there are the personal situations that do become involved in social situations. For every social situation gathers into it as many personal situations as there are persons concerned.

Then, too, there are personal situations that are mere contributory incidents within a wider social situation, like that of the stenographer engaged to type a lawyer's brief.

Likewise in the relations among social situations. Some social situations in which the participants are united by common customs are quite independent in their value relationships otherwise, or in respect to any other situations. Two solitary English-speaking fishermen meeting on a stream enjoy each other's company for a while and combine their resources for lunch over a campfire. The encounter with its brief interpersonal relationship is isolated from all other social situations in which either of the two men are involved, and they may never meet again.

At the other extreme are whole systems of social situations in which lesser situations are incorporated in wider ones. The termination of the wider situation depends on an orderly termination of the lesser ones. So it is in all large integrated social organizations, in the coöperation of teachers and departments and faculty and administration and students in a university, in the organization of an industrial plant, of an army, of a government.

Between the two extremes of a totally isolated social situation and an integrated interrelationship of social situations are all manner of intermediate relationships. And the extent of involvement can vary from a few to millions and the time span from minutes to years. There are enterprises in which a whole society becomes implicated in a single situation, as in the waging of a war, and the situation may continue without the sharp break that marks a terminus for years on end. But no situation lasts forever, though it may outlast the lives of many men.

One more observation should be made at this juncture. A social situation may be brought about not only through conflicts and problems among a group of men but also through coöperation and mutual gratification. A picnic is a social situation as truly as is a competition or a quarrel. Dewey has perhaps inadvertently stressed far too much the problematic character of social situations. They may arise from sheer abundance of good spirit and friendliness and love. When four musicians meet with their instruments at an appointed time to play a Beethoven quartet before an attentive audience, there occurs a complete social situation, with a definite terminus of marked release of group tensions, but all in the field of consummatory satisfaction and not generated by anything problematic or troublesome. Life is full of situations that are happy and exuberant throughout, well above the human pain threshold.

## 5. EVALUATION WITHIN A SOCIAL SITUATION

We have alluded frequently in this chapter to the selective power of a social situation by which it functions as a natural norm for the evaluation of acts performed within it. We now perceive fairly clearly what a social situation is. But just how does it operate as a natural norm? Roughly we have already indicated the mode of operation (§1). But now that we know more about social situations, precisely how do evaluations occur within them?

We saw earlier in detail how personal situations operate. Given a number of drives precipitated into an organism's life-space, and the physical and cultural environment within which action must go on, and given the tendency of the drives through their purposive structures to maximize achievement and consummatory satisfaction, then a resultant act is implicitly determined by the situation, which maximizes the purposive values available there. If the organism fails to perform this act, he meets frustrations which force him to become aware of errors in his mediating judgments. He learns from his errors and, if the situation permits, he tries again. Thus a personal situation tends to mold a person's actions through the dynamic aims of his own purposive drives toward the resultant act which maximizes the values available to him in the situation.

This implicitly correct act, it should be noticed, is the *ideal* act for that situation. It is an empirically verifiable act for anyone in command of the data descriptive of that situation. It is a dispositional property of the situation, a resultant act which the dynamics of the situation tends to realize. It is the act which the organism *ought* to perform as a prudent individual. If, however, the act is not performed, as often happens, there occurs the well-known gap between the occurrence and the ideal, between what happened and what ought to have happened.

However, what ought to have happened is pressing hard upon the erring person in the form of the frustrations and punishment entailed as a result of his performing the act he did. The ideal differs from the occurrence, but it is just as much an existential character of the field in which the act occurred as the act itself.

In short, life-space as a selective system or natural norm is a field of purposive forces which directs the acts occurring within it toward a resultant act that maximizes the purposive values. The forces within the field are the sanction for the field as a natural norm, and apply correctives to erroneous acts that occur within the field.

Very much the same sort of thing happens on a wider scale in the social situation. Here also is a field of purposive forces. But instead of a number of drives, a number of different personalities are precipitated into the field. Given these personalities, and the cultural pattern which distributes their aims and functions, and the environment within which these dynamic aims are operating, and given the evaluative tendencies of purposive behavior and cultural patterns, then a resultant act is implicitly determined which maximizes the purposive and cultural values available there.

Thus the social situation as a selective system points out an ideal resultant act for the persons concerned and guides them toward its realization, just as a personal situation does. But there are certain crucial differences which often have been ignored by writers in the past. Men like Lewin and the traditional hedonist, utilitarian, and interest schools of value tend to amalgamate the social situation into the form of the personal situation. Men like Dewey and the cultural relativists tend to amalgamate the personal situation into the form of the social situation. But at this juncture a new evaluative element (a new value, we may say) has entered into the selective process, which renders illegitimate the amalgamation of either of these forms of situation into the other. A failure to notice this accounts for some of the most serious issues in ethics and in general value theory as these have been inherited from the past.

Let us carefully compare the way in which a resultant act is determined by a personal situation and by a social situation. The

dynamic elements in a personal situation are drive-charged purposive structures. These are sifted and precipitated into the situation by the personality of the organism who is the center of
the situation. The agents in a personal situation, whose acts
may be wrong and subject to correction through learning better,
are the purposive structures in action and the personality of the
organism. The environment for these agents which constitutes
the reality of the situation is the physical environment of the
organism and the cultural environment in which the person is
living.

A personal situation divides itself rather neatly between the
personality and its purposive acts as agents in the situation and
the physical and cultural conditions as the corrective environment for the agents. The agents are the docile factors in a situation, and the environment constitutes the reality of the situation relative to the agents. They have to adapt their acts to the
reality of the situation in order to attain their aims. Given the
dynamic agents, the reality of the situation accounts for any
frustrations encountered and determines what the ideal satisfying act should be. This act is what is required of the situation.[10]

Now, in a social situation, what is agent and what is corrective
environment? The dynamic purposes of the persons involved are
clearly agents in a social situation. But so also is that portion of
a cultural pattern which distributes the functions of the several
persons involved. For in a social situation a cultural pattern performs the same sifting functions respecting the persons it precipitates into a situation that a personality does in a personal
situation. For instance, consider any social situation in which
the institutional pattern specifies the respective duties of the
persons concerned—the functions, for instance, of the judge,
clerk of the court, jurymen, lawyer for the defendant, lawyer
for the plaintiff, the defendant, the plaintiff, and all the others
involved in a trial. The cultural pattern within which a trial is
carried on distributes these functions, and the relative weight of
authority and privilege for each function in the social situation,
just as the personality of an organism distributes the relative
interests a person takes in the environing objects in a personal
situation. Moreover, if anything goes wrong in the carrying out

of these functions, this will be reflected back upon the cultural pattern, which is likely to be modified accordingly. The cultural pattern, in other words, is adaptable to change in a social situation relative to the reality of the situation. This means that in these respects a cultural pattern is an agent in a social situation, and in these respects is not part of its corrective environment.

We might suppose, then, that a cultural pattern would function in a social situation exactly as a personality does in a personal situation and would become completely an agent in that context. But that does not turn out to be true either, for a cultural pattern operates also as a corrective environmental factor for an act in a social situation, demanding conformity and inflicting punishment for infringement.

What makes this difference? In part it is due to the extensiveness of a cultural pattern and the time it takes for persons to encounter its sanctions or, as infants and also sometimes as adults, even to learn what the pattern is. If a person or a group of persons breaks a law or violates a custom, it may take quite a while for the social sanctions to catch up with the violators. This break between the act and its social consequences throws these consequences onto the side of the corrective environment. Sooner or later the malefactors come up against the reality of the situation and are required to conform.

But in larger part the difference is due to a new selective force that enters the social situation by way of the cultural pattern. This is the survival factor, which has its ultimate source in the evolutionary principle of natural selection. Human survival in biological competition depends upon man's social solidarity. As a solitary animal, man is remarkably weak and helpless. His survival, as cannot be too often noted in the study of values, depends upon his social relationships, which emerge in the form of cultural patterns. Cultural patterns are thus the principal biological instruments of survival for man. They are so effective that a great variety of cultural patterns serve this purpose, as we learn from the researches of anthropologists. In fact, the most serious biological competitor with man is now man himself. And the cultural problem is not any longer to develop cultural patterns that will permit man to compete successfully with other biological species, but to permit man to compete successfully with other men.

Within this more recent, though still primitive enough, mode of biological competition for men, there seems to be a considerable variety of cultural patterns suitable for human survival. The essential thing for human survival is conformity to some one of these relatively adaptable patterns. The particular pattern does not make much difference for survival, though it can make a great difference in personal comfort, as we shall see later. The new selective element that comes in with cultural patterns, however, is cultural conformity. As a selective element bearing on human decisions it is a new value. It enters into a social situation in a way that it does not enter into a personal situation, because a cultural pattern functions in social action as agent as well as part of the corrective environment of the situation.

The demand for cultural conformity thus enters into a social situation as another directive element along with the purposive aims of personalities involved. The resultant act that comes out of a social situation is thus not simply a resultant of the purposive drives precipitated into the situation, but a resultant of these plus the directive forces for cultural conformity.

Still more important, the forces for conformity are directed not solely toward maximizing the purposive values of achievement and consummatory satisfaction, but equally, and in an emergency far more, toward maximizing the security of the social group for the biological survival of the human species. An overindividual force is operating in a social situation that does not operate in a personal situation. Under emergency conditions this force for social security and human survival overrides the tendency of purposive values to maximize their own satisfactions, and utilizes purposive dynamics toward the maximization of social security values. This force for social security is attained by channeling purposive drives through cultural patterns which institutionalize them, hardening them into social forces strong enough to break down egoistic personal drives that might rise up to challenge them.

What natural selection seems to have done for the human species is to have endowed it with this mechanism for institutionalizing personal drives into overindividual social forces strong enough to control these drives in the direction of social solidarity. An important part of this mechanism appears to be man's biological endowment with a capacity to communicate by means of syntactical language.

But the significant thing to notice at this juncture is the emergence of a totally new value that is not, strictly speaking, a purposive value at all. Ultimately this value has its source in natural selection and is a survival value, but it makes itself felt in the social situation in the demand for cultural conformity. This survival value, or security value, as we are likely to call it in the social context, is properly called a value because it is a selective activity performed by a selective system determining the direction of human impulses, and that means human decisions. The selective system that ultimately operates to determine the correct versus the incorrect direction of impulse for social security is the evolutionary principle of natural selection, but that which proximately operates in any social situation is conformity to the cultural pattern.

A cultural pattern, however, may itself be out of adjustment and require changing in terms of the reality of the social situation. This fact brings to light a principle of social integration with which we shall be much concerned in the next chapter. The demand for social integration legislates as a natural norm over that of conformity to a cultural pattern. But how does this work out in any particular social situation? Social integration has to do with the adaptation of a cultural pattern to the purposive values of the individuals involved on the one side, and to the environmental conditions for the security of the society on the other.

Any social situation contains the following: the purposive interests of the persons involved demanding maximization; the institutions of the cultural pattern, demanding conformity; and the environing conditions, demanding adaptive adjustment for security. These demands may in a very favorable situation be harmonious. But generally there is some conflict. When a person's interests run counter to a cultural pattern, there is a conflict between impulse and duty. When the cultural pattern is out of adjustment with the environing conditions, either for the ensuring of survival or for the maximizing of satisfaction without endangering survival, there is a conflict between conventional obligation and moral principle. The moral principle here alluded to, which may legislate over conventional morality, is precisely the principle of social integration. And this can legislate over a cultural pattern either by relaxing the restrictions of institutions for more human satisfaction or by tightening them for greater security.

The dynamics of a social situation is thus split several ways among the personal impulses for purposive satisfaction, the demands for conformity, and the requirements for security. How, then, among these diverse forces, is the ideal resultant act determined in accordance with the reality of the situation? The determination depends upon the nature of the situation. For the present purpose we may distinguish three kinds of social situation.

1. There is the situation in which the appropriate act does not require an alteration in the cultural pattern. Under such conditions all the adjustments are in terms of purposive satisfactions of the persons concerned, in order to maximize these satisfactions in accordance with the reality of the situation. The cultural pattern here operates as a restraining or facilitating influence, as the case may be, to distribute the satisfactions in accordance with the institutionalized functions of the individuals involved.

Thus, in a simple economic situation of exchange through bargaining, the cultural pattern determines the rules of the game, which are recognized on both sides; the resultant act is that of reaching the proper price which distributes the maximum of satisfaction to both parties. The cultural pattern is an effective part of the situation present to guarantee fair play. Often it is not noticed because it is taken for granted on all sides. But its effectiveness becomes manifest when there is flagrant cheating and appeal is made to the cultural sanctions for fair play in the society in which the transaction takes place. The appeal may be to the courts, or to public opinion, or to both; and the offending party, if he is wrong according to the recognized standards of the society, is sooner or later brought into line.

A large proportion of social situations are of this sort. Superficially they appear to be just an extension of the maximizing principles that hold in a personal situation. The aim is to find the act which will yield the greatest satisfaction in view of all the purposive structures projected into the situation. Value theorists, however, do not always notice that the dynamic configuration of such an act in a social situation is quite different from that in a personal situation. In a personal situation the dynamics is directed entirely upon the satisfaction of the drives of the individual organism and upon the integrative action of his personality structure. But in a social situation in which a cultural pattern is present in a stand-by capacity, the cultural pattern is injecting a steady force for conformity to its requirements. It is this force for conformity to a society's institutions for justice and fair play that requires sacrifices from some individuals in such a social situation, and even the risk of death, and simultaneously metes out varying quantities of consummatory satisfaction to other individuals.

Consider the duties of a fire company in a city community or of a police force in an emergency that calls them into action. Or consider the requirements of team play in any coöperative sport like baseball. In the very nature of the game, some performers receive greater opportunities for personal satisfaction than others. 'Sacrifice' plays are often required. Although an expertly performed 'sacrifice hit' is a source of personal satisfaction to the performer and may evoke applause from the bleachers, he is deprived of the satisfaction of making the run himself. But by the rules of the game the sacrifice hit was required in that situation. If the player attempted to do something else that lessened the chances of his team to score, the social sanctions would come down upon him in the variety of ways which the cultural pattern sustaining the sport permit. He would not actually be 'murdered,' in spite of the judgments expressed from the bleachers! But he would be sufficiently humiliated to learn that in certain social situations a man suffers sacrifices of personal satisfactions in conformity with the institutionalized pattern of the game, and gives the glory of the run to another man.

In such a situation the only problem is that of maximizing the satisfaction potential to the total group of persons involved. The form of the resultant act is the same as in a personal situation. But the dynamics for distributing the satisfactions and the sacrifices is quite different. For with the individual the various drives all draw their energy from a common source in his physiological organism, and are so interrelated as to tend to reduce frustration and maximize satisfaction for the system as a whole. But the sources of energy for a social situation are scattered among the several organisms involved in the situation. There is no common pool of energy that is drawn upon and that tends to expend itself most advantageously on the whole. The dynamics for the distribution of satisfactions in a social situation must, therefore, be sought in part outside the sources of energy found in the organisms involved. It comes from the institutionalizing of behavior in cultural patterns. It comes from the force of social conformity, which is not an initiating force, but a powerful canalizing force. It imposes its directive force upon the energy of the drives quite as firmly as do the impulse patterns intrinsic to the drives themselves. On occasion it may impose on one or more of the organisms involved an entirely self-sacrificing role for the maximization of the purposive values of the community as a whole.

So, even when the problem in the social situation is simply that of maximizing the purposive values of the individuals involved, this is not to be regarded as a simple extension of the dynamics of a personal situation. Cultural conformity comes in as a demanding agent for the distribution of satisfactions in a social situation, whereas it appears only as a corrective environmental feature in a personal situation. Nevertheless, in a social situation which does not raise any problem demanding a change in the cultural pattern, the aim of the resultant act is to maximize, within the limitations required by the cultural pattern, the achievement and affective values of the purposes concerned. The problem is, *within these limitations which have definite requirements in regard to the distribution of the satisfactions,* to maximize the satisfactions in the resultant act.

2. The same principle holds when the problem generating the social situation does demand a change in the cultural pattern,

but a demand that comes from the pressure of the purposive drives themselves which are not able to attain maximum satisfaction as a group within the limitations of the prevailing cultural pattern. Think of an instance when some culturally established institution proves to be overrestrictive. The environmental conditions which originally justified it have changed. It is not justified on grounds of security. It frustrates rather than facilitates a distribution of functions serving to maximize the satisfactions available to the group. This is one form of cultural lag.

In such a situation the main concern is, as in the previous type, to work out a resultant act which will alter the cultural pattern in terms of the maximization of the achievement and affective values involved. However, it must not be thought that the restraining force of cultural conformity is entirely absent in such a situation. A change of cultural pattern occurs in the cultural context. It does not occur in a cultural vacuum. The change must not be so great as to disturb the beneficial effects of other institutions not sharing in the cultural lag. A type 2 situation is thus always in the context of a type 1 situation. When a social problem arises within a cultural pattern, there are always portions of the cultural pattern which need not be changed, but, on the contrary, for the very effectiveness of the cultural pattern in producing the changes envisaged, need to be left as they are. That is to say, an effective cultural change has to be embedded in a firm cultural context precisely in order to be effective.

Some exceptions to this principle may be found in the great social revolutions that occasionally rock a society. But the social disruption these produce and the reactions that commonly follow rather prove the rule.

For the most part the illustrations of this second type of situation that come to mind are mainly local in their application. They are instances of legislation for the benefit of groups of people, or deliberate minor changes of custom beyond the scope of legislation, such as public opinion regarding women's smoking, divorce, children's masturbation, attitudes toward insanity, prisons, capital punishment, and the like. On a still narrower scale, such situations confront city councils in problems of zoning ordinances, parking restrictions, transportation, and city planning generally. Every community builds up a set of communal assumptions and expectations which amount to a local cultural pattern. The intensity or the very presence of them can go unnoticed till something happens that conflicts with them. A proposal to enlarge a street in a certain section of a city may arouse a degree of protest unimaginable before the event. What comes to light is a group assumption that the householders' living habits in the area are immune to change. The threat of the disruption of a web of habits by a resistant group suddenly throws a glare of light on a latent social force.

As with the type 1 situation, the point to notice in the type 2 situation is that the problem is still simply one of minimizing dissatisfactions within the group of persons involved. In this sort of situation, however, the amelioration is sought not through the adjustment of individual purposive acts but through some alteration of a cultural pattern that has ceased to serve the purpose for which it was instituted.

3. The third type of situation is quite different from the other two. This type of situation requires a change in cultural pattern for the security or the very preservation of the society. This brings to light a second kind of cultural lag. In the type 2 situation, what is usually needed to resolve the problem is some relaxation of the existing cultural restrictions. In the type 3 situation, what is needed is a tightening of social demands. The advent of war in an individualistic society offers a striking illustration of this sort of situation. All sorts of novel social compulsions are instituted, not to increase people's satisfactions but to preserve their society.

Cannot these new restrictions be justified on socially hedonic terms? The advent of a war is like the coming of a storm, a change of environment that produces a new situation. How else would we determine the proper acts to resolve the problem but in terms of minimizing the anticipated frustrations so far as possible? Naturally the proper thing to do is to raise an army, institute draft laws, place restrictions on civilian consumption, and so on.

But here the basic consideration no longer is whether the members of the society will be less unhappy if they submit to these restrictions than if they do not. The question is whether the society will continue to exist at all.

It is pertinent to notice, too, that it is not a question whether more or fewer members of the society will be alive if they lose the war because of inadequate effort. Probably more will! It is not even likely to be a question whether the members of the society will not be just as happy under the institutions of the attacking society as under their own. They will ordinarily be persuaded of the opposite to augment their fighting morale. But that is not the point. They will ordinarily be all too ready to be persuaded, and to resist anything to the contrary. For another value is operating now, and is assuming priority over all personal values, however computed. This is the biological survival value.

It is in the social situation that personal purposive values and biological survival values first conspicuously meet. They do not meet in any mutually obstructive way in every social situation. They get on harmoniously together, and the presence of a survival value in the demands for cultural conformity is hardly noticeable in type 1 and type 2 situations. But in a type 3 situation the two sets of values have to face one another, and, in the event of a conflict, the personal values are subordinated. For human survival is ensured through social solidarity.

Assume that a rational group of men, faced with the alternative of surrender to an aggressive hostile group or resistance, resolve the situation by submission, on the ground that they would get more group satisfaction that way than through the miseries of war, even though they might win. What would be the result? They would be absorbed into the aggressive group and either exploited or amalgamated with their conquerors; in the latter case they would take over the more aggressive cultural pattern of their conquerors. The decision of our rational hedonistic society then results in more suffering than they had counted on, or, ironically, in the adoption of the very cultural pattern of firm social solidarity which they had decided against. So, in the event, they exemplify the error of their decision as decisively as if a man should decide to live on stones instead of bread. He would suffer and he would die, and leave the world to other men who resolve such situations by the choice of bread.

Such rational hedonists prove to be not so rational after all in that they omitted consideration of one of the most pressing features of the situation: the biological demand for human survival through social solidarity. In giving in to the group with a firmer grip on the human survival values of social solidarity, they confirmed the biological error of their choice and the correctness of the behavior of those who attacked them.

We shall have much more to say about this sort of situation when we discuss the principle of evolutionary selection as a natural norm for survival value (chap. 20).

Are there other type 3 situations besides those of war or the threat of war between social groups? These are the supreme examples, for there are no cultural restraints (or few) to control their mode of competition. It is one total cultural pattern against another, and in the decision one of the patterns is due for obliteration. But in a lesser way, with an encompassing pattern policing the mode of competition, the same sort of battle for survival is waged among economic groups. The more efficient business squeezes out the less efficient, and the organization and morale of the opposing groups have much to do with the outcome. The same is true of churches, and indeed wherever groups of men are bound together by a 'cause.'

But is not this an atavistic mode of competition, appropriate in the early stages of men in primitive tribes struggling for a living-space on earth, or in a civilized society defending itself against the pressure of encircling hostile hordes, but inappropriate among modern societies and in the prospect of world organization? So it would seem. But men will have to be realistic in the pursuit of this ideal. The force for group loyalty, especially under conditions of social pressure, is built into the human dynamic system. It shows up in the individual in the strength of his injective drives and his powers of identification and sublimation. His whole repertory of drives, his capacities for coöperation, for toolmaking, and for speech, are balanced to fit him for the power of social solidarity. Through this power, this balance of dynamic capacities, he has survived in the past. The force cannot be put aside for the mere wishing any more than the integrative tendency of the personality could be set aside. Moreover, if it could, it might not be humanly safe to do so. Man is never free from biological competition, even though he has so great an edge over his competitors other than man that he can now regard them as annoyances rather than threats.

The problem today of preventing the more and more devastating group competition of man with man hardly lends itself to solution in terms of changing the nature of man, but might be solved by changing the mode of group competition and enlarging to all humanity the object of group loyalty. This is simply the widespread current ideal of a world society. To achieve such a society, however, men must fashion a cultural pattern of worldwide scope which will have effective sanctions as reticulated as those which hold a modern nation together. Through the sanctions of a world culture, human competition could be limited by the cultural rules of the game, as economic and religious and political competition now is within any law-abiding national group. The reality of the world situation for man seems to point in this direction, provided he does not first destroy himself by his errors and leave the biological field to be taken over by his secondary competitors, the termites and other despised creatures.

In the formation of a world society, man would be employing his exceptional intelligence in the solution of his most serious survival problem, and would be using as the instrument for its solution the force for conformity and social solidarity which has been his chief instrument all along for survival in his struggle for existence. This is a feasible solution, for man does have exceptional intelligence and exceptional powers of coöperation under emergency conditions. The problem is to direct these powers upon a world society instead of upon a world war.

Let us now return to matters of general theory. It becomes evident that it is the type 3 situation that definitely marks an evaluative break between the selective action of a personal situation and that of a social situation. For when survival value enters as a factor in a social situation, it modifies the resultant act toward social solidarity and away from the maximization of satisfactions; it may take complete control of a situation and direct the actions of men to exhibitions of extraordinary consecration and personal self-sacrifice.

A social situation can thus be regarded as an extension of a personal situation for the maximization of satisfactions only if it is a type 1 or a type 2 situation. In a type 3 situation the survival factor has precedence in determining the resultant act, and the pressure for satisfaction becomes negligible except as it serves the values of social survival.

## 6. The Sanctions for Social Action

Before leaving this topic, I want to call attention to one more very significant fact. We observed earlier the peculiar dual function of the cultural pattern in the social situation. In part it is agent distributing the aims of the persons involved; in part it is corrective environment applying its sanctions to the resultant acts so far as these fail to conform with the culture. Is there nothing similar in the operation of a personality in a personal situation? We intimated that there was not, that a personality came to bear as a whole upon a personal situation, that it was all agent and in no way corrective environment. But there is one conspicuous exception—the action of conscience in a personality. An act performed in violation of a person's conscience encounters the sanction of remorse. Remorse here functions as a corrective, by the personality itself, of an action of the person just like the corrective sanctions of a cultural pattern in a social situation.

But notice this important corollary of the exception above. Conscience is the incorporation into the personality of the demands of the environing culture. So conscience is actually a social sanction rather than a personal sanction. We noticed that fact earlier when we showed that the irrational conscience is rooted in the repressed system, and so is outside the voluntary control of the personality. Conscience is one of the most powerful social sanctions. Mill calls it the internal sanction, and in his *Utilitarianism* gives more attention to it than to the more obvious external sanctions which are traditionally the civil, approbative, and religious. The civil sanctions are those of the police, the courts, and, in the last emergency, the army. The approbative sanctions are those of public approval and disapproval—more permeating in the long run than the civil, particularly since the approbative sanctions are usually instilled in a person's conscience by parents and other teachers. In fact, we might almost call the approbative sanction the externalized conscience. For there is nothing that arouses social disapproval so promptly as offended conscience. The religious sanction is the authority of the church and the control of conduct through beliefs in supernatural powers generally.

These four social sanctions are all cultural in origin. The civil has its source in institutions of political and legal authority; the approbative, in the customs and current beliefs of the community; the religious, in the institution of the church and traditional beliefs in the supernatural. And conscience, as we know, is the incorporation of the cultural pattern of a child's environment into his personality structure. Having been incorporated, it is then projected again into the environment in the form of the approbative sanction. This circular reciprocity between the internal sanction of conscience and the external sanction of community approval is the principal mechanism for the rigidity of custom and tradition and for the resistance to change of cultural patterns. It makes it possible for customs to persist long after their usefulness has ceased and they have become radically out of adjustment. But on the other side of the balance sheet is the fact that the stability of a cultural pattern is the docile animal's substitute for the firmness of the instinctive social organization of insect colonies. It guarantees to a society the almost blind loyalty and self-sacrificial behavior of its members in times of social emergency.

In terms of individualistic value theories, the function of the social sanctions is to make it prudent for individuals to act in the community interest. On the assumption that the resultant act of a social situation maximizes the purposive values for the total group of persons concerned, the sanctions are introduced to make it immediately to the advantage of each individual to perform what in the long run the reality of the situation would painfully force upon the group anyway. So we have fines for parking overtime or in socially dangerous places such as near fire hydrants. These penalties confront individuals with immediate artificial minor consequences; so they will find it prudent to avert serious social consequences that might occur from lack of consideration and foresight. On this principle the degree of punishment imposed by society for infringement should be just as much, and no more, as will induce individuals to have due consideration for others—as Gilbert and Sullivan summed it up, 'to make the punishment fit the crime.'

This theory for the social sanctions goes only part of the way, however. It covers type 1 and type 2 situations, but not type 3 situations. These last are the situations that individualistic theories of value systematically fail to take account of. For when it is a matter of the survival of a community, considerations of personal prudence are shoved entirely away. Then the social sanctions bite in with all their authority and with the biological aim of molding the individual to the social pattern in the interests of social solidarity and cultural survival. The authority of the cultural pattern assumes complete priority over the purposive values of the individual and exploits these as the dynamic instruments for its biological aim. Because of the legislative priority of a cultural pattern as a natural norm over the natural norm of purposive values in periods of emergency or extensive suffering, the cultural values are often referred to as the deeper values. And individualistic theories, in neglecting the solidifying force of survival values operating within cultural patterns in times of pressure, are often referred to as superficial.

In the end we must give each its full due—the aim of individual satisfaction and that of social survival. But at the moment we need to know much more about the latter. We proceed, then, to the study of the cultural pattern as a natural norm.[11]

# 19

## Cultural Pattern and Social Integration

### 1. A Descriptive Definition of Cultural Pattern

A cultural pattern is to a social situation what a personality structure is to a personal situation. And just as it was difficult to define a personality descriptively, so it will be for a cultural pattern. It was difficult to define a personality because it is a system of dispositions, and a disposition is notoriously puzzling to describe. However, having faced the problem and reached a hypothesis for its solution in the description of a personality, we now have only to carry over the same procedure into the description of a cultural pattern.

Earlier we found (chap. 17, §2) that a disposition could be regarded as a configuration of characters causally productive of certain other characters under specific conditions, and that the first set of characters constituted the *seat* or vehicle of the disposition, and the second set, causally related to the first, constituted the *character* of the disposition. In the description of a personality we indicated the physiological organism as the seat of the personality, and the types of response observed in the organism as its character.

Similarly, we must now ask what is the seat of a cultural pattern and what its character. For a cultural pattern, like a personality, must have a seat in order to be an object of description

571

and empirically verifiable. A cultural pattern is not a floating collection of traits. Swift's description of the Brobdingnag society presented a collection of cultural traits, but it was not a description of an existent culture open to verification. It was Swift's imaginative fiction. Ruth Benedict's description of the Kwakiutl culture is on a very different footing. The difference is that there was no seat for the Brobdingnag culture, but there was for the Kwakiutl. Or rather, the seat of Swift's fiction was that of an aesthetic vehicle (the printed pages of a book), whereas the seat of the Kwakiutl culture described by Ruth Benedict was a cultural vehicle. What constitutes a cultural vehicle?

The first thought is that the seat of a cultural pattern is the collection of organisms which are the seat of the personalities making up a given society. These are included in the seat, but they are not enough. The deficiency comes out as soon as we try to conceive what would be left of a cultural pattern if all its artifacts were removed. Imagine a selective bomb which destroyed all the cultural artifacts in America but left every organism intact. This collection of organisms would possess all the capacities they had before the bomb struck. But would the cultural pattern of American society remain unchanged? To control the imaginative experiment completely, let us suppose that the bomb set up an impenetrable screen between America and the rest of the world. Is it not clear that the pattern of American culture would have to be fundamentally reshaped to adjust to this catastrophe? Without means of extended communication or any tools to make tools, men would have to organize in small groups, and might well have to revert to the patterns of primitive culture.

A cultural pattern that is woven into its artifacts dies with the destruction of its artifacts, unless it retains the means of reconstructing the artifacts within the memory of the men then living who possess the skill to make and use them.

Artifacts are to a cultural pattern much what brain tracts are to a personality structure. If certain regions of the brain are injured, serious alterations take place in the personality. If the functions carried on by the injured region cannot be transferred to some other region of the brain, the personality is permanently affected. Just as certain personality dispositions have their seat in the brain, certain cultural dispositions have their seat in artifacts. If the artifacts are destroyed in a society, the capacities for functioning are likewise destroyed, and thereby alter the cultural pattern of the society unless they can be reconstituted.

But if this is so, why stop with artifacts? Do not changes in natural objects in the environment of a society also produce cultural changes? Should not these be included in the seat of a cultural pattern?

With man's increasing control of nature, the line between a natural object and an artifact is becoming more and more hazy. So far as man controls his environment by means of the knowledge he inherits from his culture, this environment takes on the form of an artifact. A farmer's fields are his artifacts as much as his plows, his reapers, and his barns. When forest lands are farmed, they likewise become artifacts. When water is channeled for irrigation and dammed for electric power, that becomes an artifact. When fish are planted in streams for the furtherance of the ritual of the sportsman, they are to that extent domesticated and institutionalized and become artifacts. When deer and elk and buffaloes are protected by law, and ducks and geese and doves, these take on the role of sacred animals. They become incorporated within the texture of the society, and as physical objects constitute part of the seat of the culture.

The seat of a cultural pattern evidently comprises both the physiological organisms that are in dynamic cultural relations with one another, and those other physical objects which are produced or controlled by these cultural relations. With a slight extension of the usual meaning of the term 'artifacts,' we can speak of culturally controlled natural objects along with tools as artifacts of a culture. Granted this clearly definable extension of the usual meaning of the term, we can say, on the basis of our analysis, that *the seat of a cultural pattern consists in the physical organisms of the persons interrelated by institutionalized behavior together with the artifacts embedded in these relations.*

The *character* of a cultural pattern will then be *the types of group activity that originate in the seat of the culture.* And a *cultural pattern* is the total set of dispositions having the above-defined seat and character.

The term 'cultural pattern' acquired prominence chiefly through being the title of a widely read book by Ruth Benedict. The term is so frequently identified with her use of it that I must point out how I may be slightly expanding her meaning of it. She does not make explicit the dispositional reference I do, or the distinction between 'seat' and 'character,' and she implies that a cultural pattern has a certain consistency or co-herence which I do not insist upon in my descriptive definition. For me, the cultural pattern of a society is whatever the dispositions discoverable for it turn out to be. To be sure, as we shall see, every cultural pattern tends to resolve its internal conflicts and become more integrated, just as with a personality structure. But just as we find that there are disintegrated personalities, so we shall wish to refer to poorly integrated cultural patterns. Sometimes Ruth Benedict writes as if a poorly integrated cultural pattern were, by her implicit definition, a contradiction in terms. This would seem to be an inconvenient stipulation because it blocks the inquirer's desire to follow out and describe cultural relations as he actually finds them.

The critical term remaining to be defined in the foregoing definitions is 'institutionalized behavior.' This will have to wait upon the analyses which follow. But as an initial approximation, it may be said this requires an interpersonal habit of response. Some individual's personal trick of sneezing or tapping with his fingers would not be institutionalized behavior; nor would an imaginative game invented by a group for an occasion and then abandoned. Institutionalized behavior is any acquired habit of response possessed by a number of persons who mutually anticipate its occurrence on suitable stimulation, generally for purposes of coöperation. The speaking of a language, the following of traffic rules, and the controlling of a machine in a factory are institutionalized responses.

## 2. A DEFINITION OF SOCIETY

Having thus described a cultural pattern, we can now ask what its relation is to a society. A society is a group of persons whose behavior is regulated by a common cultural pattern. This distributes the social functions of the persons concerned. These functions are regulated by the social sanctions characteristic of the cultural pattern. Sanctions do not necessarily involve punishments. The sanctions operating in a purely social club are mainly the rewards that a group of persons receive in carrying on the club functions—the opportunity to play bridge in a bridge club, or golf in a golf club.

A single person may belong to a number of societies. Moreover, lesser societies may be included in larger ones, or societies may overlap. Local labor unions in contemporary society are included in national organizations, local churches in a universal church. And today church organizations in their spatial spread may overlap political organizations. Also, there are degrees of dominance in the relation of societies to one another, depending upon the scope and power of the social sanctions which hold them together. Today political organizations are the most pervasively dominant, though there have been times when religious organizations were, or when the two shared the dominant power. Sometimes the two have been so fused in a cultural pattern as not to be discriminable. In many small primitive societies, social relationships are so interlocked that the concept of dominance becomes almost inapplicable. The social sanctions apply uniformly over the whole complex of customs.

Because we must place some limitation on the great amount of cultural material that has a bearing on values, we shall do well to confine our attention mainly to the groups controlled by the dominant sanctions. This restriction will hold wherever distinctions of dominance have relevance. For it is the dominant sanctions that give dynamic coherence to a group, and direct the conduct and policies of a society for better or worse in terms of the reality of the situation. So it is the sanctioned patterns—those that hold together a tribe in primitive society, or a nation or an empire in civilized society—which we shall emphasize. A Boy Scout organization, or an Olympic Games association, which draws members from many nations but is not very strongly sanctioned, does not require so much attention for our purposes as does a labor union or an industrial corporation, nor these so much as a political group like England, France, or India. What are the principal cultural sources of human attitudes and decisions? These we particularly want to know for our understanding of cultural values.

## 3. The Boundaries of Societies

From the foregoing conclusions the boundaries of a society can be described. The practical reason for determining the boundaries of a society is to know how far its sanctions carry in regulating the behavior of its members. Now the extent of jurisdiction of a cultural pattern is precisely the extent of its seat. And the seat of a cultural pattern comprises the organisms and the artifacts interrelated by institutionalized behavior. Accordingly, the boundaries of a society encompass the organisms and artifacts comprising the seat of a cultural pattern. The boundaries of a society thus extend beyond the number of persons included in it, and take in the artifacts of the cultural pattern. For these also are subject to selection by the cultural pattern operating as a selective system.

Although this definition of the boundaries of a society is clear enough, nevertheless in practice the boundaries are not always easily demarcated. Some of the most serious conflicts between societies have arisen over uncertainties regarding their cultural boundaries. One of the artifacts which many societies incorporate in their cultural patterns is land. When a society claims land as part of its seat, it literally lays off geographical areas as part of its cultural pattern. Contemporary maps of the world are indications of the cultural claims among the present nations of the world. So far as political sanctions are employed in maintaining these claims, land is part of the seat of the culture. This is essentially true even when a nation maintains jurisdiction over a people of different cultural tradition—as today the United

States does over Okinawa, or over the Navajo Reservation. The boundaries of American society include these lands. The cultural differences of the Japanese and the Navajos on these lands constitute a social problem for American society. They institute sub-cultures within the boundaries of our society.

But much more than land is included within the boundaries of a society. Conspicuously these boundaries must take in the human population that is governed by the institutionalized responses sanctioned by the cultural pattern. The boundaries include also tools, domesticated animals, wild animals so far as they are protected, and all that goes under the head of artifacts in the broad sense earlier defined. Among some societies the latter boundaries are the only effective ones, and no definite claims are made upon land any more than, until lately, claims have been made upon the seas or the air over the land and seas. In short, and in any case, the boundaries of a society extend only as far as its sanctions do.

Is this literally so? Do not the boundaries extend as far as the cultural pattern induces persons to claim or to believe that they extend? This question in value terms resolves into the following: Are the boundaries of a society determined by the anticipatory sets induced by a cultural pattern or by the reality of the situation which verifies these sets? The answer now is obvious. The believed boundaries are determined by the anticipatory sets, but the actual boundaries are determined by the reality of the situation, and the former may be in error with respect to the latter. If there is doubt, it can be tested by seeing whether in fact the social sanctions of the society's cultural pattern control the area or not. If you want to find out whether the deer in a forest are really wild or have become institutionalized and protected, one way to find out is to shoot them and see whether you are apprehended. If there is no ranger to catch you, and no questions are asked when you bring the deer into town, and no sanctions are applied anywhere along the line, then the deer are evidently wild. If someone calls your attention to an ancient ordinance for the protection of the deer, your answer must be that the cultural pattern has evidently ceased to incorporate it as one of its dispositional traits.

The spatial boundaries of a society are thus in theory easily determined from the effective sanctions of a functioning social institution. The temporal boundaries, however, do not at first blush seem to be so easily determined even in theory. The termination of a personality is clearly marked by the end of its functioning at the death of the physical organism. Only occasionally does anything so decisive happen to a society and its cultural pattern. Disaster and conquest can bring a primitive culture or a civilization to an end, but rarely by the total annihilation of the persons who are the dynamic seat of the cultural pattern. By conquest one people may be absorbed into another, and a new set of dominant sanctions may displace the old. A political revolution may have a similar effect. But ordinarily cultural change is gradual and is going on all the time. The rate of change in isolated primitive cultures seems generally to be very slow, and these remain relatively stable for many generations. In modern civilizations, cultural changes are relatively rapid; each generation finds itself in a pattern palpably different from its predecessor. Sons and fathers look out upon different social environments.

Cyclic theories of civilization like Spengler's and Toynbee's are apparently attempts to deal with the temporal boundaries of this genus of societies by indicating more or less predictable sequences of change in cultural patterns. These writers mark off such sequences in stages, which may be expected to repeat themselves. On the cyclic theory there are initial and terminal stages, and a civilization has a normal life somewhat analogous to the life of a physical organism. The evidence for something of the sort is rather impressive, especially in Toynbee's account. But the theory has not yet gained very wide acceptance. The analogy to the physiological life cycle is clearly inadequate. It seems more likely that the appearance of cycles in cultural change is due to the effects of social adjustments of large human groups— due, that is, to the prolongation of the evolutionary laws of natural selection into the area of human culturally organized societies.

Moreover, the dynamic groups which are the seat of social choices seem to be not primarily the broad homogeneous cultural areas which Toynbee describes—not the 'intelligible fields of historical study' which he denominates 'civilizations'—but rather the political communities which he refers to as 'simply articulations of the true social entities.' [1] For note, it is not Western society that determines the taxes and the economic and foreign policies of an Englishman, but the functional institutions of the British nation. Similarly with the Frenchman or American, who is also a member of Western society. A historian may be chiefly interested in following the spread of certain cultural traits and the number of societies exhibiting them, but a student of values is chiefly interested in the seat of a cultural pattern from which sanctioned social decisions emanate. For the latter the true social entity is the political community, or whatever the group may be that dynamically sanctions social acts.

This point is important, for it brings to a focus the object which a student of value needs to have described in the cultural field. What Toynbee is describing is perhaps not selective systems in dynamic operation but logical classes without intrinsic selective powers. It is not clear from his account whether he intends his twenty-one civilizations to be singular entities identified with proper names, or species with defined characters identified by class names. Is Western society—or Egyptian, Andean, Sinic, Minoan—a class like 'vertebrate' or an individual like Benjamin Franklin? Of course, only the latter has a personality. Only Franklin had a set of dispositions with its seat in a physical body that was alive over a certain period of time. Only Franklin made choices out of the dynamics of his personality. The class 'vertebrate' never made a choice, nor does it literally possess a personality, for it has no particular seat. It is a logical entity, not a particular existent.

Just as 'vertebrate,' being a logical class or species, has no personality, so 'Western society' regarded as a *species* of civilization could have no cultural pattern. It could not literally be a set of dispositions attached to a particular seat bounded by a particular group of organisms and their artifacts. Only if Toynbee conceived it as an individual would it literally have a cultural pattern—have a seat and a character in terms of a set of dispositions for social action.

If, then, by a civilization he means a species of society, his discussions have no particular bearing on the length of time a cultural pattern endures. But if by a civilization he intended to indicate an individual society, the areas covered by his names do not seem to bear out his intended result. For Western society, as he describes it, seems to be a name for a collection of individual societies rather than an individual functioning whole. The societies in the collection are similar by virtue of having similar cultural traits. But the dominant sanctioning agencies are the several political structures, not the area of spread of the similar cultural traits.

However, there is a sort of sanctioning of conduct that comes simply from mutuality of understanding among people from diverse political societies who have cultural traits in common. A common language, a common religion, common manners will bind persons together in a community of understanding even though the dominant sanctioning powers divide these people into different societies. This is something different from a class of similar societies. We shall call such instances of a community of cultural dispositions 'communal institutions' and contrast them with 'functional institutions' like a political society or an industrial corporation.[2]

So, in dealing with cultural subject matter, we must distinguish three things: (1) *species* or logical classes of cultures such as democracies, European societies, Christian societies, and the like; (2) *communal institutions* such as common languages; and (3) *functional institutions* such as tribes and nations. Toynbee does not clearly distinguish these. Only the latter two operate as selective systems instituting values. We shall have more to say about them presently. But only the last one institutes a society.

The search for the boundaries of a society, therefore, is a search for the extent of effective operation of a functional institution. The duration of a society is the length of time a functional institution continues to direct social policies and decisions and uphold customs and traditions by its dominant sanctions. If there is a sudden break because of conquest or revolution, this marks the end of one cultural pattern. It will mark the end of the society it bound together as an effective sanctioning unit, and perhaps the beginning of another. But if the transition from one dominant functional institution to another is gradual, we cannot say that there was a definite time span for these societies, a month or year in which one ended and the other began. In a human personality, such a complete gradual transformation from one character to another is very unlikely—as if Iago should be gradually transformed into Othello—but it is a common way with societies. For even a conquered society is tenacious of its traditions and surrenders them slowly and reluctantly. In the end the conquerors sometimes find themselves more transformed by the conquered than the reverse, and ironically in the final cultural reckoning it may be the conquerors who are conquered.

## 4. SOCIAL INSTITUTIONS

That which in a cultural pattern corresponds to a role, in a personality structure is a social institution. A social institution, like a role, is a cluster of dispositions acting as a selective system in its own right within the totality of the cultural pattern which determines the boundaries and the structure of a human society.

There are two sorts of social institutions in terms of their selective operations: *functional* institutions and *communal* institutions. A functional institution distributes the functions which members of a society are expected to fulfill. The function for each member generates a role for that member. Here we note the connection between a cultural institution in the structure of a cultural pattern and a role in the structure of a personality. The sanctioning of a role in a personality structure is ultimately derived from the social sanctions which support the functional institutions generating that role. A person may find it better to abandon some role he has taken up and to substitute another in the interest of personality integration. But so long as he remains in a role, the social sanctions bear down on him to fulfill it in accordance with the demands of the institution generating it. A man may change his profession, or a workman change jobs for something more congenial to him, but whatever profession or job he takes imposes its demands upon him and supports them with its sanctions. He does not get paid; he loses the respect of those who know his role; he may come into conflict with his conscience, of which more presently.

The functional institutions are the executive institutions in a society. As such they are constantly being tested for their satisfactoriness in working harmoniously within the society or in producing the expected or needed results in their adaptive operations in the environment. It is in respect to the functional institutions particularly that we come upon the concept of cultural lag. As we have seen (chap. 18, §5), this lag may occur in either of two directions. If the environmental conditions have changed so as to require more effort or a different mode of effort to fulfill the needs served by the institution, then a reorganization of the institution is in order to serve those needs. But if the change in the environmental conditions is such as to relax the call for these needs, then a reorganization of the institution is in order to render it more internally satisfying to the society.

All economic and political institutions are examples of functional institutions: a shop, a factory, a farm, a ship or harbor authority, a city government, a national government. Also a family, a school, a church. Included would be all functional arrangements which institute roles for persons to perform. Thereby ideals of attainment are set up which act as evaluative norms of great efficacy. These are the specific social ideals which groups of men aim for and often enforce rigorously. Such enforcement is what is meant by calling these norms selective systems in their own right.

Communal institutions may be distinguished from functional institutions in that they do not distribute specific functions among particular persons. They set up areas of mutual understanding. A common language is a ready example, or common customs, manners, faiths. A common area of understanding does not institute a society. Only functional institutions can do that. All the people who speak English do not make up a society of persons. They simply understand each other. Nevertheless, a communal institution has its sanctions, if these are nothing more than the frustration of being misunderstood. But often a communal institution becomes incorporated in a functional institution and acquires the full force of the latter's sanctions. Thus a language that is taught in a family or a school acquires the sanctions of the latter institutions.

Because a communal institution lacks the obvious social conditions of a functional institution, we might expect it to be dynamically much weaker and more fragile. This is by no means always true, and even the reverse may be suggested. Man's most deeply embedded habits and convictions are likely to lie in his communal rather than in his functional culture patterns. A political institution can often be changed more easily than a language, or a communal mode of thought or feeling, or a religious belief.

And in the mutual intercourse of persons in a society the distinction between a communal and a functional pattern becomes blurred, and can be sharpened only by an external analysis. A church as a functional institution embodies a faith which is apart from a church as a communal institution. For a member of a church in his religious activity, no line is felt or exhibited in behavior between his functioning as a member of the church and his communion with his fellow members as a participant in a common faith. It is only when he moves from one church to another of the same faith—from a Congregational church in one town to a Congregational church in another town—that the difference between his faith and his church can be felt. If there were no Congregational church in the town he moved to, the distinction would be still more pronounced, for then he would probably look for the church of a faith most nearly resembling the faith of the church he left. If the area of a faith corresponds exactly with that of a church, as supposedly it does for the Roman Catholic church or the Methodist church because of their hierarchical organization, then the distinction between church and faith is almost completely blurred.

Much of what we may call richness of culture comes from communal institutions. It is often said to be greatly lacking in our huge modern industrial civilizations. These have intricate functional institutions both economic and political. Men's functional relations may be intricately coördinated and their physical needs satisfied by a relatively high standard of living, yet their communal heritage may be thin. No deep tradition of myth or

ritual or literature or drama or art or celebration may permeate
the social fabric, as it does in many primitive societies and peas-
ant communities, and as apparently it once did in the medieval
cities of Renaissance Venice and Florence and in feudal China
and Japan. In such societies the emotionally charged communal
understanding gives a depth and a pervasive significance to life
which many people miss in modern industrial civilizations. Can
it be recovered in a new, more realistic way free from myth and
unwarranted supernatural authority? This is one of the great
value problems in modern society. But to recognize the problem
is likewise to recognize the enormous potential value embedded
in communal institutions.

## 5. The Values of Religious Faith

It is at this point that the religious values take off from our general study. These are the values derived from a certain type of
social institution. What is the nature of this institution? What is
religion?

This question is notoriously difficult to answer. Undoubtedly,
men give the name of religion to a great variety of things which
probably have no common attribute. But among them are
churches and the faiths which are functionally embodied in
them. Now a church is a functional institution and a faith is a
communal institution. It is possible that there could be a faith
without a church. At least in some periods and in some areas,
groups of persons may subscribe to a common faith without organizing into a church. And churches may continue to exist
which have lost their faith. Certainly, it is not uncommon to find
persons who continue to function as members of a church but
no longer subscribe to its creed. They sometimes justify their
continuance as churchgoers on the ground that the church is
necessary for the masses of the people and so needs to be supported. But as a church becomes separated from its creed, it
gradually loses its heart and requires a revival to become dynamic again; so it would appear that the dynamic element in a
church is its faith rather than its organization. The functional
institution appears to function only as long as it incorporates

with some conviction a communal institution of the sort we call a faith.

There is thus a difference between a church as a functional institution and an economic or a political institution. Shops or factories would not ordinarily be thought of as functional institutions organized to incorporate and perpetuate a faith.[3] They are organized to produce goods for the satisfactions of purposive demands. The manufacturers must believe that there is a demand for their goods, but they do not organize their institutions for the perpetuation of that belief. Nor do they, beyond the attractions of advertising and other devices of salesmanship, apply social sanctions to perpetuate among their customers or even employees belief in the values of their goods. In other words, the confidence attached to an economic institution is mainly an instrumental one depending on whether there truly is a demand for the goods and whether the goods truly satisfy the demands. It is a confidence depending on the reality of the situation; the confidence is more or less realistic and varies with the probabilities in terms of the evidence. Its credit value is proportioned to an ultimate cash value.

But for a church, faith seems to be its own justification, as if the function of the church were to maintain its own belief by its sanctions, and the belief were regarded as terminal and for its own sake. A church seems to enforce confidence in itself for confidence' sake. And the most powerful social sanctions are enlisted to enforce this confidence.

This is so extraordinary a situation that it seems incredible, the more so as the institution of religion both as a communal and a functional entity seems to be well-nigh universal in human societies. It would appear that it must be fulfilling some function consonant with the reality of the situation even if it is not one that can be justified by the correctness of the cognitive references of religious beliefs directed upon man's environment.

Let us delay our inquiry a moment, however, to assure ourselves that this last statement is probably true. Is it true that most religious beliefs are largely unverifiable, or, if verifiable, generally false or improbable? The animistic beliefs characteristic of primitive religions (with perhaps only such qualifications as may be necessary to do justice to some of the investigations of psychical research) would be so denominated. The elements of magic which make up another component of primitive religious beliefs do frequently have an empirically verifiable core, but the belief in a peculiar efficacy of magic which is supposed to distinguish it from common empirical causation has not stood up very well in the light of empirical observation and experiment.

When we turn from primitive religious beliefs to the creeds of civilized religions, we find a more articulate effort among theologians to give their creed a cognitive justification. The types of arguments suggested have been numerous. For the most part they reduce to four which have received well-worn traditional names: the cosmological, the teleological, the ontological, and the mystical. I shall not go into these. They have often been scrutinized—perhaps nowhere better than in Hume's *Dialogues Concerning Natural Religion*. The most appealing from the empirical standpoint was the teleological argument based on the evidences of order and adaptation in the world, inducing an inference from these evidences to a supernatural being with the intelligence and power to create them. But even apart from Hume's difficulties with the argument, it lost most of what was left of its appeal with the advent of Darwin and the evidences he produced for explaining adaptation as a type of natural causation in evolutionary terms.

The strongest of the traditional arguments is, in a certain sense, the mystical. But this is only because the mystical argument is not primarily a cognitive argument. It is primarily an emotional argument. It makes its appeal to the mystic experience of intense exhilaration and a sense of unity and illumination. It carries with it a feeling of essential reality, and it commonly attaches that feeling to whatever happens to be a person's supreme religious belief at the time he has the experience. Thus a religious belief appears to receive a seal of certainty from a mystic experience charging the belief. We are invited to credit the creed not on any specific evidence that tends to confirm it, but on the basis of the intensity of the emotional charge that fills the belief. The creed, it is felt, should be believed because the conviction of its truth is so intense. Here we have inverted inertial commitment (chap. 4, §9) at its peak.

A last and most common resort for the support of religious belief is to authority, preferably to revealed and infallible authority. Even Hume, after his brilliant critical analysis of the prevalent arguments in support of religious belief, seems to take this ultimate refuge. Practically his last words in the *Dialogues* are these:

> Some astonishment indeed will naturally arise from the greatness of the object: Some melancholy from its obscurity: Some contempt of human reason, that it can give no solution more satisfactory with regard to so extraordinary and magnificent a question. But believe me . . . the most natural sentiment, which a well-disposed mind will feel on this occasion, is a longing desire and expectation, that heaven would be pleased to dissipate, at least alleviate, this profound ignorance, by affording some more particular revelation to mankind, and making discoveries of the nature, attributes, and operations of the divine object of our faith. A person, seasoned with a just sense of the imperfections of natural reason, will fly to revealed truth with the greatest avidity.[4]

Even with Hume the drive of faith could apparently overpower his trust in 'natural reason.' He also seems to be saying, somewhat more reservedly, what Pascal said in distinguishing the reasons of the heart from the reasons of the head: "The heart has its reasons, which reason knows nothing about; we know it in a thousand things. I say that this heart loves the Universal Being naturally . . . It is this heart that feels God, and not the reason. This is faith: God sensible to the heart, not to reason."[5]

Now in view of our analysis of purposive behavior, and the modes of human association, and the place of impulse and cognition through all these relations of man to his environment, this attitude of man to his religion cannot but strike an observer as unusual. What is going on here, that the most docile of animals, whose success in the race of life he owes so conspicuously to his intelligence, should at this point be so eager to disavow his judgment and submit his beliefs to utter commitment? Arguments that in his practical life he would accept with the greatest skepticism he hastens to welcome and embrace for his religious belief and to seal with the signet of certainty, or else, like Hume, he maintains his skepticism concerning the worth of the arguments but hastens to disparage reason as a whole, pleading for an infallible authority.

When it comes to religion, man just does not seem to behave rationally. What does this mean? Suppose we first ask why man does not get himself into serious practical difficulties in his adjustment to his natural environment by filling it with all manner of fictitious entities. For this much is clear: his religious beliefs do not seem to have stood in the way of his survival. Then we notice that the magic and spirit world of primitive societies is rather carefully separated from the practical techniques so as not to get in their way physically. A guardian spirit of a New Guiana fisherman does not interfere with the accuracy and coördination of the man's techniques of fishing or handling his canoe. The spirit hovers above these executive techniques and does them no material harm. In the course of cultural evolution, religious operations have adapted themselves to the practical operations of society so as generally not to hamper them.

But, considering all the time spent on religious practices in primitive societies, we suspect that the prevalence of religion there must have had some positive benefit for cultural survival; otherwise it would gradually have been eliminated. It would look as if a set of religious beliefs has in some way proved to be an asset in the survival of human groups. Primitive societies which possessed the institution of religion would appear, at least sometimes, to have had an advantage in the competition for survival.

The reason for this comes to light when we observe the effect of a religion in producing group loyalty. It appears to be a principal cultural agent for social solidarity. Now social solidarity is essential for group survival. Among the insects this is attained by innate reflex systems built into the response mechanisms of the species. In man it must be attained by cultural means. Up to a point a man's prudence will recommend coöperation with other men. But for long-range consequences, and conditions which require, for the survival of the group, extreme exertion and personal self-sacrifice and the risk of death, individual prudence hardly suffices. It takes the compulsion of a social institution. And here the ordinary social sanctions (the civil and the approbative) will carry a group a long way, but if implicit loyalty is to be counted on, it appears ideal if the sanctions for social response are lifted out of the sphere of natural events and their consequences and placed in a supernatural realm. Then a social demand cannot be countered by reflection on its natural consequences. Questions of practical probability dissolve in confrontations with supernatural authority. What a cultural pattern demands when backed by the religious sanctions becomes an implicit and unquestioned obligation. Individual prudence and personal benefit then melt into insignificance, and a social group in its struggle for existence is able to meet opposition with a solid front. This seems to be what the institution of religion can do for a people.

In the course of producing this group solidarity for the preservation of a society, the institution of religion supplies many other values also. It presents the members of the society with an object on which they can depend—on the source, in fact, of man's basic strength and security against the pressures of his environment—namely, social solidarity. It presents men with a church and a priesthood which ministers to their mental health, often with the skill of a long-accumulated wisdom of tradition. It presents them also with rituals and visual and auditory accouterments of great depth of aesthetic worth. By these means a religion may permeate a cultural pattern and saturate with its emotional charge almost every detail of men's lives within the society.

If this analysis of the institution of religion is essentially correct, we can understand its powerful hold on society, and also why men cling to it so desperately and so blindly. It does possess a basic social value in providing a communal solidarity in which lies man's central strength as a docile social animal. Without such a communal solidarity men would have been scattered, isolated, and weak. Men instinctively shrink from the loss of such protection and security just as a child instinctively shrinks from the apprehension of losing his mother. And the attachment is essentially blind in most societies because its strength would have been weakened if men had been seriously tempted to adjust their beliefs in a religious creed to the empirical evidences that could be found to support it.

In short, in the communal institution of religion it is not so much what is believed that has great social value as that there should be a community of belief. Indeed, it apparently often makes for social solidarity if what is believed is not too closely scrutinized for its verifiability. This statement should not be taken to mean that the articles of religious belief make no difference in the social value of a religion. Some creeds can be greatly superior to others for their service to human social survival. What the statement does mean is that for many types of society the cognitive correctness of a religious belief may have little or nothing to do with its value as an article of faith conducive to the furtherance of social solidarity. For the sole importance of social solidarity apparently lies in its conduciveness to man's survival as a docile social animal.

Religious values have their roots in biological survival for man. If the full significance of this fact is taken in, it explains most of the paradoxes of religious faith as these emerge before the eyes of an empirical observer. It explains what can be meant by the reasons of the heart and their opposition to the reasons of the head, and yet that these reasons of the heart can be acknowledged as intelligent reasons of a sort, once the head has penetrated to the biological service these reasons perform; at the same time it explains the concern of religion to keep the head from penetrating through to the reasons of the heart, for then these reasons lose their immunity from rational criticism.

We suspected, when we were studying commitment to belief in a mediating judgment, that there might be some justification for inverted inertial commitment in the domain of religious values (chap. 4, §9). Then it seemed hard to believe that incorrect belief could ever be a source of value for a docile animal. From the point of view of a prudent individual, it never could be so. But now we see that from the point of view of society it is essential that men should not always be prudent. Under certain conditions for the preservation of the human species as a social animal, it is necessary that individual men should perform individually imprudent acts even to the sacrifice of their lives. Insects are motivated to sacrifice themselves for the continuance of their societies and their species by patterns of instinctive response embedded in their systems. The same result is obtained for man through derived drives incorporating social demands in the form of religious belief. Or, more precisely, religious faith through its sanctions has been one of the strongest supports in human society for self-sacrificing action whenever this has been called for in the interests of social solidarity. There are, of course, other sources of self-sacrificing action besides those of religious origin, but probably none which apply so forcefully to the whole area of human conduct.

## 6. Religion and Truth

Granted the values of a religious creed and likewise of a church as a social institution for the preservation of social solidarity, and granted also the essential irrelevance of the empirical truth of the creed in the performance of this biological function, would it not be better if the creed were true?

Much as it goes against the grain of the truth-seeking student, I think in all candidness we have to admit that, at least among primitive societies, the evidence does not indicate that the falsity of their religious beliefs, gauged by our cognitive standards, did any great harm. The same is possibly true of the religions of the earlier civilized societies. So far as this admission is justified, it arises from the fact of the relative stability and changelessness of these early civilizations and of the primitive societies that preceded and surrounded them. If the religious creed did not interfere with the economic and other practical operations essential to the life of the society, but maybe even charged them with additional motivation, the fictitiousness of the object of religious belief would not lessen the survival power of the society, would perhaps increase it by the use of well-chosen symbols for sublimating purposes. A set of religious beliefs cognitively unfounded but well selected for their emotional capacities to consolidate the attitudes of the people in a socially responsible way would have a high survival value under stable environmental conditions—better perhaps than a set of beliefs empirically more nearly true which men might find harder to believe. For men are inveterate personifiers and animists, and do not take easily to a creed of hypotheses and equations.

But it does not look as if the same can be said of a modern industrial civilization. Here every act is brought into contact with some tool or gadget which is a constant reminder of engineering and scientific principles. More important still, man has learned the art of invention and the efficacy of the method of hypothesis and experiment. In an industrial society a constant change is going on by means of a stream of startling inventions. That is not a condition suitable for static, supposedly infallible beliefs. No longer can social solidarity be safely founded on some 'higher truth' that can be guaranteed not to conflict with the empirical truths of science and their application in engineering, agriculture, and medicine, and also increasingly in education, economics, and politics. Formerly, a religious creed blindly accepted from tradition or ancient authority could permeate down and emotionally charge the techniques of fishing, boat-building, hunting, and warfare without apparent conflict with the effective operation of these techniques—rather the contrary. But today the beliefs generated by the empirical sciences, and belief in the scientific method itself, permeate the world and saturate our cosmology and our ideals. An authoritarian or mystical religion and its appeal to a 'higher truth' are crowded hard for a place of cosmic lodgment.

It is questionable if a religion based on faith alone, in disregard of empirical truth, is any longer a source of survival value. It is too necessary today for men to be adjusted to all the details of their environment, and quickly adaptable to social changes. If this observation is correct, it poses a serious problem for modern man. It means that religion as an institution in its own right sanctifying a species of truth apart from empirical truth is no longer the security that it used to be, but is becoming a hazard. Wherever in a modern industrial civilization it imposes its sanctions severely, it is likely to be acting as a cultural lag.

So religion as an inviolable institution for the preservation of a faith is, it would seem, to a cultural pattern what the irrational conscience is to a personality structure. The two are generated by very much the same forces, and are parallel in their dynamics. In fact, the content of a man's irrational conscience is very largely an embodiment of the religion prevailing in his culture; and reciprocally, having acquired his irrational conscience as a child, he later as a man, along with other men similarly brought up, projects his conscience into the cultural pattern as its traditional religion.

## 7. RELIGION AND CONSCIENCE

When we were discussing the nature of conscience (chap. 17, §§9, 10), we distinguished between an irrational and a rational conscience. The former had its roots in the repressed system of the personality, and its origin in parental authority. The latter, the rational conscience, was conceived of as free from the inhibitions and the cognitive blindness of the repressed system, and was identified with the integrative rationality of the voluntary system.

A similar contrast can be made between an irrational and a rational religion. The term 'religion' is ambiguous, and many persons will wish to confine its reference to the traditional creeds and their churches. Some, to be sure, would be content only if religions were confined to their own particular creed, all other believers being heathen! But there are two sides to the traditional creeds: on one side, the obscurantism and irrationalism which surround the biological survival function of group solidarity through the sublimation of group loyalty and individual self-sacrifice; on the other side, an integration, more or less deliberate, of the total value system of the society. Paul Radin, in his *Primitive Man as a Philosopher,* suggests that one of the principal functions of the medicine man in primitive society was to systematize the beliefs and attitudes of the culture to make them more harmonious. The harmony is not always sought, to be sure, in terms of cognitive consistency or of verifiability in reference to the reality of the situation. Various forms of emotional congruence may be satisfactory for the harmonizing of a creed if the beliefs are not too rigorously confronted with an insistent reality.

But even in a primitive society, an important function of religion is that of integrating the total value system of the society. And this is a serious and difficult matter because a docile organism learns to look after his personal needs and to preserve himself as an individual by prudence; but as a social animal and a member of an organized society, which is man's chief source of power and of his preservation as a biological species, he is compelled to perform acts of self-sacrifice which are often anything but personally prudent. A total human value system is thus inevitably loaded with internal conflict and constantly in need of adjustment. One of the great functions of religion, then, is to supply a society with a body of beliefs which are so adjusted to one another and to the environment that there will be a minimum of frustration for the individuals accepting the creed.

This function of the integration of the totality of human values, when separated from the irrational elements of religion, results in what may be called a *rational religion*. A rational religion, then, is a social integration of human values freed from dogma. Just as rational conscience is the natural integrative action of a personality freed from the inhibitions of the repressed system, so rational religion is the natural integrative action of social institutions once these are freed from the restrictions of dogma.

Now the question that arises from the preceding analysis is whether the modern civilized society is not in the process of substituting a rational religion for an irrational one. Has not human social organization reached a point at which an irrational religion no longer serves to preserve a society but rather to weaken it and expose it to destruction? Can a society any longer afford to institutionalize a creed which forbids a man to use his intelligence in solving the problems which are declared to trespass on the area of sacrilege? Can modern man afford to be forbidden to eat fish on certain days or pork on any day? Can he safely be forbidden to practice birth control? Can he safely be enjoined to believe in revelation and a truth above intellectual criticism and scholarly research and laboratory experiment? Can he safely accept a creed that conflicts with the reality of the present situation?

It looks as if the time has passed when religious beliefs and practical techniques can occupy separate compartments of a man's mind or be differently sanctioned. The integrative function of religion seems bound to bring man's beliefs and his techniques together in a systematic way. And it must be a way that does not embarrass a man's intelligence when the beliefs are opened to critical examination or are seen to conflict with reliable empirical techniques. The irrational elements of religion can hardly be expected to survive this integrative action except in the backwaters of modern society and among groups that do not greatly influence social policy.

Or put it this way: a society which in this industrial epoch fails to institutionalize science and the experimental method will lack the strength to resist a society which has done so, should any serious conflict develop between them. If an irrational religion stands in the way of the experimental method and its social contributions, the society so blocked is at a great disadvantage in competition with neighboring industrialized societies. If the social pattern is not gradually modified so as to reduce the irrational elements in its controlling religion, the society is likely to eliminate itself through internal revolution or through conquest from without. Just as primitive societies are being eliminated wherever they come into definite conflict with civilized societies, so we can anticipate that the irrational religions will be eliminated from civilized societies or else be so modified that their remaining dogmas become innocuous.

This trend toward a rational religion is already to be seen in the policy of religious tolerance which many of the great modern civilizations cultivate. For an institutionalized policy of religious tolerance stimulates criticism of religious dogmas. Each church is compelled to justify its creed in confrontation with the creeds of rival churches, and some of the irrational elements are forced up into the light of social consciousness. Brought out into this critical light and opened up for examination by the techniques of cognitive inquiry, church creeds and practices are confronted with the data of empirical knowledge. The church comes under pressure to conform to the reality of the situation or else to lose the confidence of its more intelligent believers.

The result is that in many of the religions a liberal church has emerged which is committed to the creed of a rational religion. A liberal Jewish church and a liberal Christian church are practically indistinguishable in creed, and the same seems to be true of the liberal movement within other religions of civilized society. In this respect a rational religion already exists and has its churches. And many persons not connected with any church are committed in their beliefs and manner of living to a rational religion.

What is the content of this religion? At the minimum it is committed to a deep respect for the truth as true belief unfolds in its contact with reality, and it is committed to a devotion to human fellowship and social solidarity. It looks toward an ideal of both cognitive and emotional integration. If a person wishes to give this ideal the name of God, he will not be taking that name in vain. For this ideal, unless our analysis of values is much mistaken, is the actual goal of the religious process from the beginning. It represents the achievement of a complete social integration, offering security because only in social solidarity and mutual trust does man find his security, and offering peace because only if this security is founded on true belief can it be expected to endure.

As a terminal ideal this total integration may well be unattainable. It may not even be the highest human ideal, since man thrives on a degree of conflict and struggle. But the process, of continual striving for integration and partial attainment of it over and over again, seems to be actual enough. Some may prefer to give this actual integrative process the name of God rather than the distant and perhaps unattainable terminal ideal of total integration. Then we have the conception of an active dynamic God moving in our midst always for closer and more harmonious social relationships, and always prepared to meet emergency or disaster in a realistic manner for social amelioration.

The process and its ideal terminus remain the same whichever one prefers to name God, or the name may be given to both together. In any case, the process of social integration is sufficiently well evidenced to be considered an actuality. As such it constitutes a natural norm operating as a selective system upon social institutions. Social integration is to a cultural pattern what personality integration is to a personality structure. But, as we shall soon see, social integration does not operate as simply as personality integration does.

Now we can profitably consider the natural norms which emerge among cultural patterns. These norms turn out to be social institutions operating as selective systems, and the processes of social integration.

## 8. PRIORITIES AMONG THE NORMS WITHIN A CULTURAL PATTERN

We have described a cultural pattern as a system of dispositions composed of the forms of group activity originating in the seat of the culture. The seat of a cultural pattern we identified with the physical organisms and artifacts interrelated by group responses of these organisms. We then noticed that a cultural pattern can be broken up into institutions, which behave in a culture as roles behave in a personality structure.

We considered two kinds of institution: the functional and the communal. The functional was so named because under the pressure of social sanctions it distributes the functions persons are expected to perform in a group relationship. These functions turned out to be the socially sanctioned roles in which individuals carry on their lives. It was then observed that a functional institution defines what we regard as a society. Among the numerous functional institutions, one attains a priority over the others in the application of its social sanctions. This becomes known as the political (or, in primitive society, the tribal) institution.

Communal institutions do not distribute functions, but consist in group responses affording attitudes of mutual emotional and intellectual understanding. Communal institutions often extend over many different societies as the latter are defined by a functional institution. They have some sanctioning power in their own right, but generally acquire their principal authority by being taken up by a functional institution which adds its own social sanctions to them. When we speak of a cultural pattern as a specific group of institutions controlling the behavior of a certain society, we are referring primarily to the cultural character of a political society or a tribe.

In the description of a single society's cultural pattern we take as our point of departure the dominant functional institution of the group of men under study. Then we observe what other institutions (functional or communal) these men are involved in. Thus we notice that the organization of a Hopi village is the dominant functional institution for the Hopi Indian. So we take the village as the point of departure for the description of the cultural pattern of the Hopi Indian. Then we observe that other Hopi villages have similar cultural patterns, and that accordingly they are all related by communal institutions.

Similarly we would take as our point of departure for the cultural patterns of contemporary civilizations such national units as England or the United States, because the dominant functional institution binding together the members of these groups is their national political institutions. Then we would observe that in their language, traditions, and political procedures England and the United States are closely related by their communal institutions. The principal dynamic entity, in other words, is the dominant functional institution.

This fact automatically reveals to us the line of priorities operating among the various institutions composing a cultural pattern. The institution with the dominant sanction has priority over other institutions in which members of this institution are involved. This does not mean that serious conflicts do not arise in practice. The conflicting demands of church and state, of state and family, of custom and moral principle, are notorious. Moreover, the conflict may be a constructive social conflict growing out of a cultural lag and in process of resolution, for which the ameliorating goal is still uncertain. But we can see what the answer to the integrative problem is theoretically, in terms of cultural pattern alone, apart from the emergence of a cultural lag (of which more presently). The answer is that the institution with the dominant sanctions has legislative priority as long as the sanctions can be maintained without succumbing to the pressure of cultural lag.

Then we noticed one institution that seemed to be different in its mode of functioning from the others. The institution of religion appeared to be organized not for some determinate end—political, economic, or aesthetic—but simply for the continuance of belief in itself. We noticed that these beliefs are well protected by the devices of dogmatism (cf. chap. 1, §2) as well as by the institutionalized sanctions of the church. It is furthermore characteristic of the institution of religion to claim an absolute priority for its sanctions whether these are enforceable over political and economic sanctions or not. We also noticed a linkage between the institution of religion within a cultural pattern and the operation of conscience within the personality structure. In both an unquestioning infallibility is ordinarily protected, and the beliefs and attitudes supported by the one are essentially those supported by the other for all the members of an orthodox church. We noticed that the irrationality of such an institution was an anomaly in the social life of a docile organism which survives mainly by the use of his intelligence. We had already noticed a similar anomaly in the operation of the irrational conscience in an intelligent man's personality structure.

When we were dealing with the evaluative priorities among natural norms of the personality, we found evidence for setting the voluntary system over the repressed system, but we deferred our decision in regard to the legislative priority of the voluntary system over the irrational conscience until we had more evidence on the relation of this conscience to man's wider social and biological relations (cf. chap. 17, §11). There was no question that within the sphere of a single personality the voluntary system legislates over the irrational conscience, since the repressions in which the irrational conscience is embedded limit the range of rational prudence open to a person's intelligent judgment. But the question remained whether this limitation on individual prudence might not be socially beneficial and whether, therefore, the irrational conscience was not the manifestation within the human personality of a natural social norm required for man's survival as a docile social animal. Speaking animistically, it looked as if nature trusted intelligence and docility only up to a certain point, and there blocked it off with irrational conscience within the personality structure, and with irrational religion within the social structure. If this inference is justified, it means that the institution of an irrational religion serves a biological function for the preservation of the human species by shutting off intelligence where this might weaken social solidarity, and that irrational conscience is the extension of this institution into the human personality structure. And if this conclusion is accepted, it follows that religion and conscience do have an evaluative priority among natural norms regulative of human decisions.

In a qualified manner, our analysis does seem to substantiate this conclusion. In a relatively stable social structure rendered appropriate by its location in a relatively stable environment, a rigid cultural pattern enforcing group loyalty and social solidarity would seem to have survival value. A society having efficient economic, political, and military organization to which is added an institution that sanctions the unquestioning loyalty and obedience of its members to the fulfillment of these social functions would appear to have an advantage over a society that lacks such an institution. Such an institution would be that of an irrational religion. The irrationality of the institution in its impact on individual prudence is advantageous, on this hypothesis, because the very function of religion is to inhibit a man's prudential behavior which might make him circumspect, self-concerned, and timid in the line of duty and in performing acts of self-sacrifice for the security of his society. Moreover, this irrationality of the institution must be carried down into the personality structure and protectively embedded there; otherwise man's natural prudence will perceive and puncture the irrationality of the social institution which compels him to acts of unquestioning self-sacrifice. Here we begin to understand the biological function of man's irrational conscience.

It does, then, appear that under stable social conditions a society that has an institutionalized irrational religion maintaining a set of beliefs well adjusted to the environment and firmly supporting group loyalty through coöperative behavior is better equipped for biological survival than a society lacking this institution. And the more thoroughly the beliefs of this social institution can be encapsulated protectively within each individual's personality structure in the form of irrational conscience, the more reliable the self-sacrificing behavior of the group.

Within the conditions for which a relatively changeless cultural pattern is appropriate for a society in its adjustment to its environment, it would appear that the institution of an irrational religion does have evaluative priority over the other institutions in the cultural pattern. And under the same conditions an irrational conscience reflecting this social institution within the personality structure would have priority over the voluntary system whenever a conflict arises between the two.

We must not, however, at this point leap to the conclusion that irrational religion and conscience in a stable society are lifted above all further evaluative selection. For these hold their priority in a stable society only through their survival value for that society. They are subject to the selective competition of any other stable societies in their environment. If a society is eliminated through war or cultural competition, and another social pattern is imposed upon the defeated group, the religion of the defeated group tends to be eliminated too. That is to say, a religion is subject to selection and modification for its adaptiveness in promoting group solidarity by the regular process of natural selection applied to cultural patterns. Natural selection as a selective system maintains a continuing evaluative priority, therefore, over religion and conscience, no matter how well adapted these may be for a given society in its particular environment. For the religion holds its high sanctioning powers only as a result of its biological adaptive properties for the human group, and that means subject to the natural norm of natural selection.

It is precisely for this reason, precisely because natural selection legislates continously over religion and conscience, that we have been led to surmise that within the sphere of a modern industrial civilization an irrational religion and an irrational conscience are no longer of adaptive value. Or, if they still have an adaptive value, only within limited domains where they do not influence social policy.

In modern industrial society men live under conditions which require a flexible and rapidly changing cultural pattern. Within any great political society of today will be found a diversity of customs in different strata of society and in the various regions over which it governs. A person moving from one place to another or from one social level to another has to be able to adjust rapidly. Moreover, constant internal cultural changes are occurring as a result of scientific inventions and discoveries. The reality of the contemporary situation thus seems to demand rapid adaptability and ready intelligence more than it does obedience and fixed loyalty. Today a self-effacing fanatic, even as an element in an army, is less serviceable to his society than a skillful mechanic.

So far as these conditions hold, it would appear that the adaptive function of irrational religion and of irrational conscience has ceased, and that these norms have lost their evaluative priority over other institutions and personality structures. A rational religion and a rational conscience become the appropriate norms to take the place of their irrational counterparts and are accordingly, we surmise, sanctioned above them by natural selection.

This outcome does not imply that men will not continue to seek comfort from their traditional religions. Men may crave the stability of a settled faith all the more because of the very instability of the social conditions under which they live. But this outcome does mean that where irrational religion conflicts with the rational integrative processes the latter now have the ultimate sanction of social survival value, which before they sometimes lacked. It means that a political institution so set up that it can develop social policy on the basis of expert scientific authority will obtain the ultimate sanction of social survival over an institutionalized irrational religion. The contribution of unquestioning faith to social survival is no longer sufficient to compensate for the contribution of institutionalized science to that end. Under rapidly changing conditions, a society guided by the experimental methods of science stands a better chance of survival than one guided by a rigid loyalty to an irrational religion.

Picking up again our earlier figure of speech personifying nature, we can say that nature now appears ready to put all her trust in human intelligence for the survival of the human species.

There is no longer any use in blocking off intelligence at a certain point to ensure social solidarity. Man today has to adapt his social policies so rapidly to changing conditions that he cannot wait for the slow adaptation of an irrational faith to the reality of a situation. Hence, at the risk of less human solidarity, nature now puts her complete confidence in human intelligence in the expectation that man will use his intelligence to develop a political institution capable of preserving his life and his species. If man fails, the penalty this time is probably not some other type of human society, but the end of man as a biological species and, of course, the end of human values also. It looks as if the human race were now engaged in a very interesting experiment!

At the same time, there is no reason to think that man is not intelligent enough to control the situation ultimately, and so provide for his own survival. But he must be vigilant, energetic, and patient, if he is to succeed.

Our conclusion regarding the evaluative priorities of cultural institutions one over another, then, is this: In general, the institution with the most effective social sanctions for holding men together as a group has priority. This institution is always a functional institution and is ordinarily a political institution. However, in a relatively stable society the institution of irrational religion may in certain spheres of action legislate over a political institution or so fuse with it that the two are not distinguishable. The legislative priority of irrational religion gives way, however, in a changing society, where rapid adjustability of behavior is socially more advantageous than implicit obedience to authority. The doctrine of the separation of church and state is a symptom of this change in evaluative priority, as is likewise a policy of religious tolerance. An institutionalized rational religion then becomes possible, and is actually to be observed in the liberal wings of a number of contemporary orthodox churches.

The strength of our conclusion lies in its thoroughgoing empirical verifiability. It asks the student simply to note the flow of social dynamics. It asks him to observe carefully what institutions apply the most effective correctives when someone in the community fails to conform. For a social institution as a selective system operates by demanding conformity. As such it is a natural norm to be observed and described. The legislative priority of a social institution functioning as a norm is in proportion to the strength of its sanctions to enforce conformity when violations occur.

## 9. SOCIAL INTEGRATION AS A NORM

The demand for conformity, however, is not the only natural norm operative among social patterns. We are aware also of what is frequently called 'cultural lag.' This concept calls attention to another dynamic factor active in this field—the integrative factor. Just as we observed an integrative action among roles within the personality structure, so we can observe an integrative action among institutions within a social pattern. In fact, the integrative action in the two spheres is often hard to differentiate. But they differ, as we have seen (chap. 16, §6), in their dynamics. The energy for the drives emerging in a personal situation all comes out of one energy source, that of a single physiological organism. But the energy for coöperative action emerging in a social situation comes from many separate sources—from the many separate organisms involved in a social situation having no channels of communication except those supplied by a superimposed cultural pattern. The dynamic action of social integration is consequently quite different in its details from that of personality integration.

In general form, however, the two are much the same. In personality structure the motive for integration is some frustration arising from a conflict of roles, or from a conflict between a role and an environing situation for which the role was unadapted or lacking. Similarly the dynamics impelling a process of social integration is either a conflict that proves chronic between institutions within a cultural pattern, or a lack of adaptation between an institution and its outer environment. Either an internal or an external adjustment is called for, or a combination of the two. These conflicts arise from changes occurring either within the institutions or in the environment. Portions of a cultural pattern, once adequately in adjustment, cease to be so. The result is a cultural lag.

It is easy to see that most instances of cultural lag involve a conflict of natural norms. The conservative habitual demand for conformity comes into opposition with the radical demand to change institutions so as to improve social integration and neutralize a cultural lag. It is easy to see that in the long run the norm of social integration will legislate over that of conformity to an institution. For if the inertia of a society for conformity goes on too long within a changing environment, the survival factor will take over, and the social pattern as a whole will be eliminated through some physical catastrophe inadequately provided for, or through conquest or even willing absorption by a superior neighboring group, or by revolution. This observation does not mean that the radical elements in a society are more often correct than the conservative in furthering social integration. The radical group may err in their judgment of the social change advisable or of the degree of change advisable. The reality of the situation is the steady, firm corrective determining what does or does not help to minimize social conflicts.

What is the reality of the situation? That depends on the situation. We were dealing with that problem when we distinguished the three types of social situation in chapter 18, §5. The type 1 situation requires no change of cultural pattern for the resolution of competing interests. In the type 2 situation the resolution of a social difficulty calls for a change in some institution so as to increase available individual satisfactions. In the type 3 situation the society is faced with an emergency that threatens its security; here the solution lies in changing an institution, not to maximize satisfactions but to maximize security.

The resolution in each type of situation is a mode of operation of the norm of social integration. In the type 1 situation, integration consists in minimizing interpersonal frustrations, where no need appears for institutional change. In the type 2 situation, integration again consists in minimizing interpersonal frustrations, but this time only by making the adjustments that appear necessary within the controlling social institution. In the type 3 situation, integration consists in preserving the integrity of the society, not only by strict enforcement of the existing institutions for social solidarity but also by changing existing institutions so as to increase the solidarity and security of the social structure. What integration signifies specifically depends, then, upon the type of situation. But in general, *social integration means the tendency of a society to preserve its integrity as a social group and to minimize frustration within the group.*

Social integration is thus a two-headed norm. In a type 1 or type 2 situation it is headed toward the maximizing of satisfactions for the individuals in a society. In a type 3 situation it is headed toward a maximizing of social solidarity for the preservation of a society. There are thus two ideals of social integration: first, the individualistic (leading to the ideal of an open, individualistic, democratic society), in which the dynamics comes from the purposive drives of the members of a society seeking as much satisfaction as possible for all concerned; second, the functionalistic (conveying the ideal of an authoritarian functional society), in which the dynamics comes from the mechanics of evolutionary survival. The one is clearly appropriate under conditions of social prosperity; the other, under conditions of great emergency. Some mixture of the two seems appropriate under the usual changing conditions of the contemporary social scene. One of the problems of social integration is to judge for any period the degree of individual freedom and of social compulsion appropriate to the social environment. The elevation of this sort of judgment to the role of a guiding principle yields the ideal of an *adjustable society:* a rationally organized political institution capable of fitting its social policies to the reality of the situation so as to permit the maximum freedom of satisfaction for its members that is consonant with the safety and preservation of society.

This is the terminus toward which the process of social integration actually tends, if our analysis of the dynamics of the situation is correct. For, on our evidence, this process is impelled by the two opposed forces which bear upon a social pattern from opposite sides. If either one is dominant beyond what the reality of the situation warrants, the other may be relied upon to come into action sooner or later. But ordinarily the process of social amelioration goes by fits and starts and overswings. The inertia of social institutions is great, and, besides, much irrational motivation is involved, with the result that social movements are often blind, or partly so. Nevertheless, through it all the social integrative process is at work, for if in any social group the development of an integrated structure is so retarded that the institutions of the society are entirely out of adjustment with the environmental situation, then that error proves fatal. That particular society goes out of existence, and its place is taken by a society with a better-integrated structure. The organisms composing the two societies may be practically the same. This is what happens in a social revolution. But the new society is controlled by a new political institution.

Our assumption has been that social integration works within the boundaries of a society. But may not the dynamics of integration lead to the amalgamation of a number of societies, thus extending the boundaries of societies? Might not either the individualistic or the survival factor or both indicate to one group of people the feasibility of uniting with another? Surely. This happens to a degree with all social federations. And then a federation may consolidate into a union. These expansions and consolidations seem generally to happen among political societies on the stimulus of fear. A society gives up its sovereignty to a wider social group with which it is friendly rather than risk the loss of sovereignty to a hostile society that is threatening. The motivation leading to expansion seems most often to be that of fear or aggrandizement rather than of brotherly love.

So here is a paradox: It is supposedly the survival factor that stimulates social solidarity, draws sharp boundaries around social groups, and stresses the in-group as opposed to the out-group. It is supposedly the individualistic factor that stimulates liberty and tolerance and a universal respect for men, and breaks down the line between in-group and out-group. Yet actually it is the survival factor that mainly induces self-effacement and group loyalty and drives societies to consolidate and so enlarges the boundaries of effective mutual concern. And actually the individualistic factor often appears inertial and inactive in spreading the effective boundaries of society, and may even encourage individualistic isolation.

For this reason it is unlikely that the individualistic factor alone would produce a universal integrated society of men unless this were sparked by its polar opposite, the survival factor. The norm of social integration thus appears to gain its dynamics chiefly from the survival factor driving for social integration, and this appears to get its primary purposive motivation from the injective drive of fear. This motive can be softened and ennobled by a sublimated love yielding the ideal of the brotherhood of man. Without this positive contribution of sympathetic concern for our fellow men a social integration is disciplinary, hard, and lacking in appeal. Once the circle of a group's concern for their fellow men is enlarged by fear, however, it can be stabilized and enriched by love and sympathy. But the motive of human sympathy alone would not appear to be sufficient to spread the range of effective social integration beyond the boundaries of an in-group so as to take in an out-group. It seems to be the survival factor and the threat of elimination that (apart from conquest) lead one political society to unite with another for mutual social integration.

If this observation is correct, an uncompelled universal integration of men into a world society is unlikely. Apparently men must be driven to any large-scale consolidation through fear. Since the only serious threat to an organized group of men in the present state of human culture is another competing organized group of men, what could induce two strong political societies competing for the earth's surface to enter into a single social integration? One could overwhelm the other by conquest. But after the conquest, with no competing society in view, we could anticipate a relaxation of social discipline and divisions springing up eventually, giving rise to a new period of competing societies. If there were some outer environmental pressure as a realistic ground of fear which only a universal human society could safely control, then, and apparently then only, could a fairly stable and continuous world society be reasonably predicted. It is possible that the hydrogen bomb constitutes such a realistic ground of fear.

Social integration as a natural norm operates initially only within the boundaries of a society. Its mode of operation, however, differs according to the reality of the social situation. If the demand for security is small, it operates with or without modification of the institutions so as to minimize frustrations within the group. But if the demand for security is great, it operates to insure this security by modifying the social pattern where necessary, and even by extending the boundaries of the dominant political institution through federation or amalgamation with other social groups.

Social integration seems, then, quite different in its operation from personality integration. The latter works in one continuous direction: that of organizing a system of dispositions which tends to maximize a person's purposive values. Social integration exhibits two opposite directions: that of maximizing the satisfactions of the individuals in the group, and that of maximizing the security of the group. Which of these directions social integration takes depends on the reality of the situation. What is correct for one type of situation would be an error for the other.

But, it may be asked, is this opposition final? Does not social integration move in one direction which includes due consideration of these poles of social concern? Has not this aim of social integration already been stated as the maximizing of individual satisfaction within the group so far as this is consonant with group security? And has not the form of the political institution to embody this aim been indicated—namely, that of an adjustable government? Here the political institution itself adjusts to the situation, centralizing functions for emergency, and decentralizing for individual liberty when the emergency ceases. Indeed, does not this polarity of values become reflected in personality integration, where a man must be equally prepared for achievement in periods of stress and for consummatory enjoyment in periods of relaxation?

Yes, this is all true, and yet a difference remains. And again the difference is due to the contrasting dynamics of the two processes. There is one energy source for a personality and this source is in a man's physical organism. A person is born and matures and lays down his dispositions in strata, and he acquires a character. His character is subject to adjustment and may be better or worse integrated, but it develops a degree of fixity, and adjustments have to be made according to the man's age and the stratification of his dispositions. At a more or less predictable time he dies. Personality integration goes on in the framework of this rather determinate life history of a physical organism. Because of the limits set for the normal life history of a physical organism, it is possible to be fairly specific in regard to what constitutes a healthy, well-integrated personality.

A society does not have the same unified dynamics, or the same maturing process, or a time of death. Theoretically, a society could be immortal and, never having had a revolution, still be quite different in its cultural pattern at one time from another two or three centuries earlier. It might have been socially well integrated all the while and it might never have set up an adjustable political institution.

A society is a much looser thing than a person. It is not tied to a physical organism with a specific anatomy and physiology. It has a much wider range of freedom for channeling dispositions. So there are many kinds of cultural patterns within which men can find satisfaction and security.

One other point: Before the advent of civilization it was irrelevant to speak of the superiority of a civilized society over a primitive tribal organization in terms of their survival values. Yet it is just this fact that has led to the displacement of primitive societies by civilized societies whenever serious competition occurred. For similar reasons, industrial societies can be expected to displace nonindustrial societies. A failure of a society to adjust to these changes is a failure in social integration. The ideal of an adjustable society is a form of civilized society with integrative capacities so much superior to those of other forms of civilization that we may reasonably predict its emergence if the social competition among civilizations continues.

The ideal of an adjustable society, however, is in a somewhat different status from that of the healthy personality. Both represent an ideal of integration for human values. But the healthy personality applies to any man at any time. There is always pressure to eliminate the mentally ill, and there is always a particularly favored position for the well-adjusted man. But there is no similar pressure for an adjustable cultural pattern. If a primitive cultural pattern is adjusted to its environment well enough to be stable, it will remain a long time without much need for change; and similarly with earlier civilizations like the Egyptian. The pressure for institutionalized adjustability is rather recent. In fact, there is probably an inverse relation between an irrational religion with a dominating role in a cultural pattern and a political institution with powers of rapid adjustment to the reality of the situation. The one that is strong in enforcing social conformity is weak in providing rapid adjustment, and vice versa. And since we hold that irrational religion has had a central function in maintaining social solidarity among men in primitive society and in the early civilizations, we cannot hold also that in those cultures an adjustable political institution would have served them better. In short, the ideal of an adjustable society is not the same for social integration as the ideal of the well-adjusted man is for personality integration. And yet both are terminal concepts, in their respective domains, for the integrative process.

So we have to conclude that social integration is bipolar. It is headed in either of two opposite directions, depending on the reality of the social situation. It heads for an individualistic political organization to maximize personal satisfaction if the situation is free from emergency; but it heads for a functional political organization to maximize security if the situation is threatening. However, the two opposite aims may be joined in one: that of an adjustable political institution which undertakes to reach the balance that will maximize satisfaction together with reasonable security. But the latter requires special conditions and an intelligently controlled society. This would be the ultimate ideal of social integration only when a society has reached the stage of an industrial civilization that must rapidly adapt to constantly changing conditions.

# 20

# Biological Evolution and Survival Value

## 1. Is SURVIVAL VALUE A VALUE?

Periodically, in the last few chapters, the material shaped up in such a manner as to induce references to an ultimate determining survival factor involved in human decisions. In an empirical treatment of values, the bearing of evolutionary principles cannot be ignored. Whether values or norms of value are to be found in the evolutionary process is a matter for questioning, but there is no question today that the evolutionary process is a condition underlying the particular repertory of needs and drives of any species of organism. So far as values are considered to have some roots in these dynamic sources of behavior, the evolutionary process is the selective agency explaining the origin of these sources. Moreover, since the evolutionary process is a selective process—and we have gradually come to see that the guiding concept in the dynamics of values is what we have called a selective system—it becomes not unlikely that the evolutionary process may itself be a selective system similar to that of a purposive structure, and so may properly be regarded as itself a source of values.

It is the aim of this chapter to explore this possibility. In the latter decades of the nineteenth century there was considerable interest in the bearing of evolutionary principles on values. This interest continues among many biologists and medical men and some anthropologists, but has lapsed among philosophers. Its persistence among the specialists who are most closely concerned with biological facts and with the application of these facts to man as a biological entity might, however, well give philosophers pause—particularly the philosophers who are looking toward an empirical treatment of values.

The ordinary textbook refutation of survival value, calling it a bare description of fact devoid of value significance, is much too smooth. The usual statement goes something like this: To speak of the survival of the fittest is to say nothing about the survival of the best; it is simply to note that those which survive are those which survive. The obvious answer to this argument is that 'fittest' does not denote *mere* survival. It denotes a *selective* survival in which those that survive are intrinsically connected through the process of selection with those that perish. Out of a single dynamically generated group, those that survive are selected pro as against those that perish, which are selected con. If there is any ground in this context for taking a pro selection as good and a con selection as bad, then the survival of the fittest can, in this specified sense of 'good,' properly mean the survival of the best out of the group subjected to such selection.

The survival of the fittest is thus not a concealed tautology or an empty phrase. It denotes the results of a complex selective process and in its significance denotes the mode of selection too.

The question of the value significance of the term then resolves itself into that of whether value can be equated with the results of such a selective process, or, further, whether the process itself might be regarded as a natural evaluative procedure. Is evolutionary natural selection a natural norm instituting values?

For an empirical theory of values this is an open question. We found good reason to equate purposive values (conative, achievement, and affective) with the selective processes of purposive structures. These selective processes conformed with many common uses of value terms. Once these processes were equated with the common value terms denoting them, and thereby descriptively defined, then with increasing degrees of refinement these processes were found to be dynamically closely interconnected through the selective action of needs and drives. The same dynamics extended with pertinent modifications into the fields of personality structures, into personal and social situations, and into culture patterns. In all these fields we found that human decisions are being made, and the relevancy of the term 'values' to the selective results of these various natural norms was clear enough once it was seen that the selective results of purposive structures were properly termed 'values.'

If natural evolutionary selection should prove to be an extension of the same dynamics, there would be no question of the consistency of regarding survival value as a value term as closely connected with achievement or affective values as are the values of personality integration and social conformity.

Even from an initial glance at the field of evolutionary selection, it is apparent, however, that the dynamic processes here are somewhat different in their action. Granted man's innate repertory of needs and drives, all the selective systems we have studied so far give man a wide range of voluntary control (in the particular sense of 'voluntary' developed in chap. 17, §10), but natural selection exhibits an inexorable character in relation to human wishes; this suggests that some other source of dynamics is operative besides innate and acquired drives.

Allowing this to be the case, would we still be justified in considering natural selection as a selective system generating values within human behavior? It is, of course, always possible to draw an arbitrary line, and stipulate by nominal definition that 'value' be limited to conation or affection or the results of purposive selection. This has frequently (indeed, customarily) been done by writers on value in the past. But we have steadily avoided such arbitrary definitions, being aware of the supreme legislative role of definitions as evaluative criteria in discourse (chap. 13, §2). We desire our definitions to follow descriptively the selective processes exhibited in human behavior and particularly in human decisions. Our practical test in this regard has been to ask ourselves whether a certain act or process had a dynamic bearing on an evaluative judgment determining a possible decision. On this basis, for instance, we ruled against Perry's insistence that the term 'value' necessarily includes a cognitive element. A simple riddance pattern or gratuitous satisfaction would thus have been excluded from the field of values by Perry's stipulation. These acts, however, would obviously figure in any evaluation of contemplated decision involving them as consequences. They are, in fact, among the ultimate rewards and punishments in the learning process, which, as we have seen, is a natural evaluative process.

The same sort of test is applicable to survival value. This can be excluded from the field of values by an arbitrary nominal definition stipulating that what we call 'values' shall be limited to selective acts performed on the dynamics of purposive drives. But then we shall find that we have excluded from evaluative judgment great areas of human concern which force themselves on human decisions in spite of our arbitrary definition. The restrictive definition becomes unrealistic. We find that men and societies do consider security and survival in making decisions and in developing their social patterns, and that unless the survival factor as it affects man is brought into the evaluative field the descriptive results are incomplete and erroneous. Or, to put it the other way round, as soon as natural selection is recognized as a natural norm of values to be considered in relation to the other selective systems we have been studying as natural norms, then the whole empirical field of values begins to become comprehensible and, within limits, rationally predictable.

When the question is approached in the foregoing manner, it becomes fairly obvious, from a superficial knowledge of how it works, that natural selection is a dynamic selective system. It becomes obvious, too, that this selective system has a selective relevancy to purposive structures, and to the dynamic elaborations of these in personal and social situations, in personality structures, and in cultural patterns. It would be arbitrary to deny the term 'value' to the selective action of the life processes in natural selection while allowing it for the selective action of purposive structures. Moreover, whether the term 'value' is denied or allowed, the selective interrelationships between the purposive and the evolutionary selective systems remain the same. It is, accordingly, more convenient and more consonant with the natural relationships between the two sets of selective systems to allow the term 'value' to spread over both, at least so far as they overlap in the area of human behavior.

The crucial evaluative consideration is this: Does the definition of survival value functioning as a criterion in discourse legislate as a matter of fact under certain conditions over the definition of purposive value functioning as a criterion? Does survival value (or, if you will, adaptation) sometimes take precedence over individualistic purposive values? For, if it does, it would be terminologically awkward to have to say that a nonvalue criterion under certain conditions legislates evaluatively (or in some way that demands a value synonym) over a value criterion. I may say at once that we shall, I believe, find natural selection functioning evaluatively in this manner. Accordingly, I propose to speak of survival value as a value. So, accepting this as a hypothesis, let us see whether it is not confirmed.

## 2. REJECTION OF THE TOOTH-AND-CLAW CONCEPT OF EVOLUTION

If we are to give serious consideration to survival value as a value generated by the selective action of the evolutionary process, how does this selective system operate? In the exposition which follows, I shall depend mainly on the writings of Darwin and G. G. Simpson. The ethical (and indeed the general value) implications of natural selection were never more clearly perceived than by Darwin himself, who had the insight to develop the evolutionary hypothesis essentially as it is now accepted, and to gather the data which substantiate in large degree the detailed operation of the selective evolutionary process. I am depending on Simpson, who also has a keen sense of the implications of this process for value theory, to bring the hypothesis up to date as a result of much added evidence and elaboration of detail.

There are two familiar conceptions of the bearing of the process on values, however, which do not appear to follow from the data, and these have to be cleared away to avoid misunderstanding. One is the tooth-and-claw conception of natural selection. The other is the continuous progress conception of evolution.

The first is particularly associated with Nietzsche; the other at present with Julian Huxley.

The tooth-and-claw conception errs from oversimplification and from a sort of melodramatic dramatization. It suggests that the evolutionary process is a succession of gladiatorial contests in the arena of life between competing individuals or groups. Such physical contests do occur, but the struggle for existence does not ordinarily go on in any such focalized dramatic scenes. Simpson writes:

A puma and a deer may struggle, one to kill and the other to avoid being killed. If the puma wins, it eats and presumably may thereby be helped to produce offspring, while the deer dies and will never reproduce again. Two stags may struggle in rivalry for does and the successful combatant may then reproduce while the loser does not. Even such actual struggles may have only slight effects on reproduction, although they will, on the average, tend to exercise some selective influence. The deer most likely to be killed by the puma is too old to reproduce; if the puma does not get the deer, it will eat something else; the losing stag finds other females, or a third enjoys the does while the combat rages between the two . . . Struggle is sometimes involved, but it usually is not . . . Advantage in differential reproduction is usually a peaceful process in which the concept of struggle is really irrelevant. It more often involves such things as better integration into the ecological situation, maintenance of a balance of nature, more efficient utilization of available food, better care of the young, elimination of intragroup discords (struggles) that might hamper reproduction, exploitation of environmental possibilities that are not objects of competition or are less effectively exploited by others . . . It is to be added that in intragroup selection . . . struggle is not necessarily or even usually of the essence. Precisely the opposite, selection in favor of harmonious or coöperative association is certainly common. It was a crude concept of natural selection to think of it as something imposed on the species from the outside. It is not, as in the metaphor often used with reference to Darwinian selection, a sieve through which organisms are sifted, some variations passing (surviving) and some being held back (dying). It is rather a process intricately woven into the whole life of the group, equally present in the life and death of individuals, in the associated relationships of the population, and in their extraspecific adaptations . . . Selection is not primarily a process of elimination. It is a process of differential reproduction and this involves complex and delicate interplay with those genetic factors in populations that are the substantial basis of evolutionary continuity and change.[1]

In short, natural selection is a selective system with a positive dynamic mode of operation involving a complex interplay of factors. It is not a sievelike process or a succession of elimination contests.

Darwin himself only partially gave grounds for the tooth-and-claw conception. Perhaps Simpson underplays the biological struggle, which in a definite though complex sense is necessarily involved in the concept of natural selection. He had the task of neutralizing the post-Darwinian exaggeration and dramatization of the struggle. But the sort of thing Darwin himself actually said does not sound much like tooth-and-claw contests:

> All that we can do, is to keep steadily in mind that each organic being is striving to increase in a geometrical ratio; that each at some period of his life, during some season of the year, during each generation or at intervals, has to struggle for life and to suffer great destruction. When we reflect on this struggle, we may console ourselves with the full belief, that the war of nature is not incessant, that no fear is felt, that death is generally prompt, and that the vigorous, the healthy, and the happy survive and multiply.[2]

Both of these men in the passages quoted are thinking primarily of organic evolution. But we shall presently see that this has a direct bearing on human social relationships.

### 3. REJECTION OF THE CONTINUOUS PROGRESS CONCEPT

The continuous progress concept of evolution, also, is the result of a hasty generalization and an oversimplification of the evolutionary process. It comes about through systematically neglecting certain rather obvious details, and not analyzing very carefully the meaning that is given to progress.

This concept in its bearing on evolution makes much of 'higher' and 'lower' forms of life, of the later development of the 'higher' from the 'lower,' and of man's place in the hierarchy of forms at the top, or at least near the top, as the 'highest' form yet realized. The tooth-and-claw concept can easily embrace the continuous progress concept, as in Nietzsche's 'superman.' But the two concepts do not necessarily go together. In Julian Huxley we have an exponent of the continuous progress concept without any admixture of the naïve tooth-and-claw concept. As with the tooth-and-claw concept, there is an element of truth in the evolutionary progress theory. There is a connection between the idea of progress and the operation of natural selection. To think of progress going on within the evolutionary process is not entirely false, but, as pictured in the continuous progress concept, it is falsifying.

Let us begin by asking what in the present discussion may be conveniently meant by 'progress.' It is a process of change; the change is directional; and, in the context here contemplated, the direction is positive. Moreover, in this context, the direction is evaluatively positive. Men often speak of the progress of a disease, but this is clearly not the sort of progress that an exponent of progress in evolution has in mind. The concept of progress here contemplated is an evaluatively positive one.

Such an evaluatively positive concept of progress clearly attaches to any successful act of purposive achievement. We should notice that achievement does not necessarily imply a goal. Appetitive achievement does, but the achievement of an act of aversion does not. Purposive progress may thus consist either in the successful approach to a goal or in the successful evasion of an object of apprehension. So progress, even in the restricted sense of 'continuous achievement,' does not necessarily entail a goal toward which the progress proceeds. A continuous decrease in negative values is an evaluative progress as much as a continuous increase in positive values. In both instances the opposite would be a retrogression.

It is now pretty clear that it is convenient and customary to speak of progress and retrogression wherever it is appropriate to speak of continuous changes in evaluation. In terms of our preceding analysis this means that evaluative progress would emerge wherever a selective system was in operation. There would be progress, then, not only in acts of achievement but also in the resolution of personal and social situations, in personality and cultural integration, and wherever selective systems were maximizing their values. The question whether there may be progress in the evolutionary process resolves itself, then, into our initial question of the present chapter: whether survival value is a value and natural selection a selective system. Since it did appear to us that natural selection probably is a selective system generating values in much the same sense that a purposive structure is a selective system, it would follow that we should probably be able to speak consistently of evolutionary progress in an evaluative sense.

Any difficulty that we should find with a concept of a continuous evolutionary progress would arise from a determination of the empirical locus of such progress. Just where does natural selection operate? What are the values it generates? And how may these values exhibit a progressive maximization? Answering these questions in a preliminary way sufficient for the present issue, we can say that natural selection operates to adapt living forms to their environment. It favors the more fully adapted forms and holds back in various ways or rejects the less well adapted forms. If, then, this selective process of adaptation is accepted as an evaluative process carried on by a natural norm, the gradual adaptation of a group of organisms or of a society of organisms to their environmental conditions would be a literal instance of an evaluative progress.

Progress in natural adaptation would not, however, be (this should be carefully noted) an instance of purposive goal-seeking progress. Natural selection is not a purposive appetitive act implying a drive and a goal. Certainly no intelligence or docility is implied in it. This was Darwin's great point. Human intelligence is not involved in natural selection. The reverse is the case, that human intelligence was evolved through natural selection.

But now our point is that, though natural selection does not generate purposive values, it is nevertheless a selective system in its own right and as such performs an evaluative operation (whether we are accustomed to call it evaluative or not) and institutes the values of adaptation and adaptability. These are not purposive values. But the adaptive purposive structures which generate purposive values do happen to be striking instances of adaptability, or (as more commonly called) survival values.

Well, then, if progress is properly to be ascribed, tentatively, to the process of natural selection, what is the error in the continuous progress conception of evolution? The error is that this conception ascribes progress not to the process of adaptation, where it is appropriate, but to the whole history of evolution, which is something quite different. It cannot be assumed that the later forms in the history of evolution are necessarily better adapted than the earlier. The later forms are better adapted only if they have been retained by the process of natural selection as against other forms that have been rejected. When earlier forms are not in biological competition with later forms, natural selection does not operate upon them, and there is no reason to consider the later forms better adapted than the earlier. Consequently, no progress from the earlier to the later is attributable to these forms as a result of natural selection. Man is a late evolutionary form with much to recommend him in his powers of adaptation. But some of the so-called lower forms which were generated much earlier in the history of evolution continue to live unchanged and in close adaptation to their particular environments.

On this theme Darwin writes with a sort of twinkle in his eye:

> On our theory the continued existence of lowly organisms offers no difficulty; for natural selection or the survival of the fittest, does not necessarily include progressive development— it only takes advantage of such variations as arise and are beneficial to each creature under its complex relations of life. And it may be asked what advantage, as far as we can see, would it be to an infusorian animalcule—to an intestinal worm—or even an earthworm, to be highly organized? If it were no advantage, these forms would be left, by natural selection, unimproved or but little improved, and might remain for indefinite ages in their present lowly condition. And geology tells us that some of the lowest forms, as the infusoria and rhisopods, have remained for an enormous period in nearly their present state.[3]

Darwin's point here is that a continuously surviving 'lower' form of life is just as well adapted to its living conditions as any contemporaneous surviving 'higher' form. If natural selection is properly to be regarded as a selective system, the normative action of this system is not that of selecting the 'higher' forms and rejecting the 'lower.' The selection goes on within determinate *zones of life,* and between different zones of life there may be no biological competition, or very little. The zone of life of the infusorian animalcule is entirely distinct from that of a vertebrate animal. And even many vertebrates have little biological relation to one another. Selective adaptation goes on only within a zone of life. Survival value thus signifies the adaptive capacity of a biological form within its zone of life, and there only. Consequently, there would be dynamic progress in adaptation only within a life zone, and there, definitely, progress would be observable in terms of the development of successively more and more fully adapted forms and the elimination of the less well adapted. The evolutionary evidence for progress of this sort is now incontestable.

But it is a very different matter to ascribe progress to the successive emergence of new and more complex living forms to fill successive zones of life as these open up in the course of life history on this globe. Yet this is the sort of progress that Julian Huxley apparently has in mind in his conception of evolutionary progress and ethical evaluation.

There is . . . one direction within the multifariousness of evolution which we may legitimately call progress. It consists in the capacity to attain a higher degree of organization without closing the door to further advance. In the organic phase of evolution, this depends on all-round improvement as opposed to limited improvement of one-sided specialization which, it can be demonstrated, automatically leads sooner or later to a dead end, after which no true advance is possible, but only minor variations. . . . [He then indicates that the insects reached a dead end thirty million years ago, birds a little later, and all the main lines of higher mammals except the primates at about the same time.] Most evolutionary lines or trends are specializations which either thus come to a stop or are extinguished; true progress or the unlimited capacity for advance is rare.[4]

The question that inevitably comes up is: By what natural norm is a surviving 'dead end' to be evaluated as inferior to a surviving form of later origin? Obviously not by the norm of survival operating through the process of natural selection. For both the dead end and the later supposedly more productive form are actively surviving. Gauged by length of survival and probability of continued survival, the dead end would appear to have even greater survival value than the more recent form. The infusorian animalcule would, in these terms, have more survival value than man.

But the preceding mode of argument is not actually to the point, anyway. For natural selection as a selective system does not operate over the whole domain of life. It operates over zones of life. There is effective competition for survival only within these zones, not with one zone against another. The infusoria are in one zone and man is in another. They do not compete. No selective system is selecting one as against the other. They cannot, therefore, be significantly compared for their survival value. The comparison suggested in the preceding paragraph in terms of actual past duration and probable future duration is not, as a matter of fact, a significant one for natural selection. For the basis of comparison was not instituted by natural selection as a natural norm. Length of life in the abstract is not a natural norm, but becomes so only as it is incorporated in the dynamic adaptive processes of a particular zone of life. If, for instance, the infusoria should enter into the human life zone in active competition for survival with the human species, and the recently originating human species should eliminate the ancient species of infusoria, the age of the perished species would not add a bit to its survival value. Survival value is not based on length of survival but on the capacity of a biological form to survive in the process of natural selection. However, length of survival is a fairly reliable secondary criterion of survival value within a life zone, for it indicates a high degree of adaptation.

The significant point is that natural selection as a dynamic selective system operates only within life zones. Consequently, there is no selective activity between life zones unless such zones should merge. It is possible, on the basis of our earlier analysis of the concept of evaluative progress, to speak of a progressive selection of life forms within any one life zone toward greater and greater adaptiveness to the environmental conditions within that zone. But it would not be possible to speak significantly of a progressive selection of life forms through a natural norm supervening over all the zones of life. For there is no evidence of a natural norm legislating over the whole course of evolutionary history.

When this fact is envisaged, it clears up many false issues that have littered the controversial field of survival value and evolutionary value theories. This point is so important that I should like to stress it by quoting a passage from G. G. Simpson which criticizes Julian Huxley to the same intent:

> In the search for, as nearly as may be, objective criteria of progress applicable to a particular case and yet widely valid, such considerations lead to the criterion of dominance, which has been stressed almost to the exclusion of any other by the leading student of the subject, Huxley. We have seen how throughout the history of life each group has tended to expand and to have one or more periods when it was particularly abundant and varied. We have seen, too, how at any given time certain groups tended to be much more varied and abundant than others, in other words to dominate the life scene, and that there has been a succession of these dominant groups. It is this succession that provides a criterion . . . of evolutionary progress. Thus among the aquatic vertebrates it is fully justified, as long as we keep in mind the particular *kind* of progress we mean, to say that successive dominance of Agnatha, Placodermi, and Osteichthyes represents progress and that Osteichthyes are the highest, Agnatha the lowest group among the three. . . . The same sort of sequence applies in the successive dominance of Amphibia, Reptilia, and Mammalia.
>
> We do not, however, find successive dominance between, say, Osteichthyes, Aves, and Mammalia. All three are dominant at the same time, during the Cenozoic and down to now. Taking the animal kingdom as a whole, it is clearly necessary to add insects, molluscs, and also the 'lowly' Protozoa as groups now dominant. If one group had to be picked as most dominant now, it would have to be the insects, but the fact is that all these groups are fully dominant, each in a different sphere.
>
> . . . The criterion of dominance is not invalidated by the fact that it does not yield a single sequence for progress in evolution. . . . The various different lines of progress that are involved in successive dominance are defined by adaptive types or corre-

sponding ways of life. Thus there is broadly one for aquatic vertebrates, and broadly another, quite distinct from this, for terrestrial vertebrates, with bony fishes at the top in the former and mammals simultaneously at the top in the latter. Within each of these groups there are other, more circumscribed ways of life and corresponding lines of dominance and of progress (in this sense) for each of these. Among the bony fishes, there are separate lines for marine and freshwater fishes, for shallow and deep sea fishes, and so on.[5]

All of this is simply an expansion of Darwin's original insight: "If it were no advantage, these [even 'lowly'] forms would be left, by natural selection, unimproved . . . for indefinite ages in their present lowly condition." Adaptation to the environment of a living group is what determines a line of progress for the group. When the adaptation is attained, there is no dynamic agency to induce or sanction further progress. Moreover, adaptive progress in one life zone is independent of that in another, and there is no dynamically sanctioned natural norm subordinating adaptation in one life zone to that in another. In short, there are as many dynamically sanctioned lines of biological progress as there are life zones within which adaptation is going on through natural selection. But there is no dynamically sanctioned line of progress across life zones, and consequently none for the course of evolutionary history as a whole.

Now man is a dominant species in his particular zone. Simpson describes the place of man in organic evolution as follows:

In relationship to man . . . adhering to strict dominance as objective criterion, we find that he is a member of a progressive group, and generally of the most progressive, in each of the various dominance sequences in which he can properly be placed. (His dominance cannot be compared with that of molluscs or insects, for instance, because the ways of life and corresponding dominance sequences are grossly different.) A major category might be that of self-propelled unattached organisms of medium to large size: vertebrates are dominant here; man is a vertebrate. Among these, terrestrial forms subdivide the major way of life: mammals dominant; man a mammal. Among land mammals as a whole, rodents are now clearly and strongly dominant, but within the Mammalia man belongs definitely to a dominant sequence quite different from that of the rodents and in this sequence he has recently and decisively risen to dominance. This criterion gives no justification for considering man the highest among all the forms of life, but it places him at least among the highest in his own general and particular sphere, and that is as far as the criterion can go.[6] . . . [Man's] general environment was among the last to be filled by life . . . It is really legitimate to go beyond this and to point out that man's particular adaptive type was the latest to be developed up to now in the history of life, one radically new, never before exemplified, and with extreme potentialities of expansion.[7]

Simpson is calling attention here to man's adaptability in terms of his docility, his tool-making capacities, and his social and linguistic powers—that is, in terms of his cultural capacities. Man's particular life zone is that of the cultural exploitation of his environment. Gradually man's environment has, through his cultural capacities, ceased to be something fixed that has to be rigidly conformed to, and has become something plastic that can be transformed to satisfy his needs and his desires. Man is the most adaptable of all animals, and there is evidence that natural selection generally, and perhaps in the long run always, favors adaptability over adaptation whenever the two come into competition. Probably this is one of the things Julian Huxley had in mind when he said, "There is one direction in the multifariousness of evolution," and disparaged the 'dead ends' as specialized adaptations liable to extinction. Perhaps he was thinking of man with his great capacities for adaptability as a form that could invade any other life zone successfully; or perhaps he was thinking of adaptability in the abstract as the life trait favored by natural selection and so giving direction to the whole history of evolution. But, as the facts stand, man has not supplanted or even domesticated all other living forms, nor does it appear likely that he ever will. And whereas adaptability will always, presumably, be favored over adaptation in man's particular life zone, since this is the distinctive trait by which man has attained his dominance in that zone, it does not follow that specialized adaptation in other life zones may not continue to provide other living groups with a dominance in their zones. There is no evidence that the highly specialized adaptations characteristic of insects are ceasing to be biologically advantageous to them in spite of the advent of man.

It is only in man's life zone that Julian Huxley's criteria of progress can have an application, and this would be sufficient unto man. But there is no adequate evidence for the continuous progress concept of evolution. Not through this concept shall we look for a natural norm of survival value. We shall find it operating in a much less grandiose manner, as the process of natural selection itself, operating wherever life is, in a multitude of rather separate zones of life, each zone instituting its own natural norm of adaptation or adaptability.

## 4. THE PROCESS OF NATURAL SELECTION

We are now prepared to consider the process of natural selection as a selective system instituting survival value. Because it is a selective system, we shall expect to find (1) a dynamic element comparable to the drive in a purposive structure, (2) a selective element comparable to the superordinate-subordinate act structure of a purpose, and (3) that peculiarity of a split dynamics which assures that the same dynamic element which puts in action the normatively correct result likewise charges the normatively corrected erroneous result.

The dynamic element for natural selection in organic evolution is the vital energy of an interbreeding population of individual organisms. The population constitutes a distinctive group by virtue of their reproductive association. Such a group is roughly what is known as a species. When two groups cannot reproduce by crossbreeding, they are generally referred to as different species. The converse, however, does not hold. Different species can sometimes crossbreed and produce hybrids. The determination of distinct species is consequently a difficult and controversial matter for technical biology. The basic principle which gathers a population of organisms into a species, however, is not controversial. It is the principle of heredity which maintains a constancy in the pattern of traits appearing in the offspring of an interbreeding group. It is the variations that occur within an interbreeding group which make it difficult to determine species. The factors producing these variations, however, are precisely the factors constituting the dynamic sources of selectivity for natural selection. For natural selection selects in favor of some of these variations and against others.

In the dynamics of natural selection there is a set of factors for change and a set of conservative factors. The conservative factors are those controlling heredity. A great deal has been learned about the latter in recent decades. Heredity is carried by genes, which are self-producing chemical units within the cells of organisms. Genes are gathered together into groups known as chromosomes, which reduplicate themselves whenever a cell divides. Ordinarily, chromosomes are passed on from one generation to the next by means of specialized germ cells. The individuals of the new generation develop from these germ cells, and the pattern of their development is controlled by the genes transmitted from the parents. By this process the pattern of traits characterizing the parents is reproduced in the offspring. And thus the dynamics of heredity maintains the constancy of a species throughout an interbreeding population.

But there are likewise factors for change in the dynamics of reproduction. The offspring are never exactly like their parents or even exactly like each other. Simpson enumerates three factors for change in the process of reproduction from one generation to the next.

There are, first, changes due to the environment and the development of organisms in their environment. For no two organisms are placed in exactly the same environmental conditions or develop in exactly the same way. This is particularly true of plants. Differences in soil, moisture, sunlight, exposure, prevalent winds, and so on produce differences in plants, even when they come from similar seeds. Animals, too, are affected by their environment, though the effects are often much more indirect. When docility is added to the physical effects of environment and growth, the variations of the offspring from their parents and from one another are augmented even more. Such variations, which are due to acquired characteristics, are not carried over from one generation to the next in organic evolution. There is no hereditary transmission of acquired characteristics. That theory, which was held even by Darwin, "has now been disproved beyond reasonable doubt," writes Simpson.[8] However, these acquired variations can be considerable and can become indirectly effective for selection pro or con, through the failure of individuals to propagate because they have been caught at a disadvantage by a chance environment.

A second and much more important factor for change in the dynamics of natural selection is sexual reproduction. It would be most unusual for two parents to have identical chromosome sets. In the mechanism of sexual reproduction, the offspring usually receives an equal number of genes from the chromosome sets of each parent in corresponding pairs.

> When the offspring, in turn, come to reproduce, each passes on to its progeny not simply the set of chromosomes it received from one parent or the other, but a random selection from both sets. Thus in continued sexual reproduction through the generations the genes and chromosomes are constantly reshuffled. Even in organisms with relatively simple gene sets and few chromosomes, the number of possible combinations of different genes and dissimilar chromosomes is astronomically large, far larger than the number of individual organisms in the line of successive interbreeding populations . . . Heredity is essentially conservative in its broad outlines, but this mechanism of shuffling in sexual reproduction makes it almost endlessly varied in detail.[9]

A third factor for change is mutation. There are both chromosome and gene mutations, but the latter are the more effective in evolving new species. A gene mutation may be large or small. It may affect the process of development early or only at a late stage. If the mutation is large it is generally lethal. If it has a late effect in the development of a trait, the change in the organism is slight. A small mutation of a gene which affects the early and cumulative development of a trait is the most effective. All genes seem to be open to mutation, but some are more susceptible than others. The frequency of mutations can be altered by heat, radiation, or chemicals, but the nature of the change is apparently not closely correlated with the nature of the cause. Such mutations when not lethal are inherited.

The last two factors for change are largely random. And the first factor, not being hereditary, is only indirectly effective in organic evolution. Consequently, the dynamic factors for change with respect to any interbreeding population are practically random. But this should not be taken to mean that the dynamic element in natural selection is entirely random. The random factors radiate from a rather firm dynamic core of inherited traits that maintains the characteristic pattern of the species. The random combinations of genes possible for a population of salmon, for instance, would be quite different in their range from those possible for a population of Jeffrey pines or even of jack rabbits. Presumably the ranges of probable mutations for these species would be similarly restricted. The characteristic inherited pattern of a species is in the nature of dynamic propulsion for its own preservation or survival, and the factors for variation are in the nature of insurance against destruction through environmental change. Random factors are to the conservative dynamic pattern of inheritance what in purposive behavior trial-and-error activity is to the impulse pattern of a drive. The chief difference is that the conservative pattern of inheritance has a long history of adaptive success and does not ordinarily have to depend on the random factors associated with it for its maintenance. But if the environment of an interbreeding population changes materially, then a gap opens between the inherited capacities of the species to cope with its environment and the demands for adaptation laid upon it. And then the random factors for organic change come in to function much like trial and error in purposive behavior when long-established habit no longer serves for the reduction of a drive.

Thus we do find in the dynamics of natural selection the characteristic form of a selective system comparable to that which we found in purposive structures. Nevertheless, natural selection is not a purposive structure. It does not institute, by its selective activity, purposive values, but a distinct type of value which has frequently and aptly been denominated *survival value*. Strictly speaking, natural selection is not teleological. For it does not operate through the medium of a purposive structure that has purposive drives and goals. But natural selection is, nonetheless, evaluative, since it operates through a selective system, which normatively evaluates variations as correct or incorrect by maintaining or eliminating them.

The dynamic element in the selective system of natural selection is the reproductive process of an interbreeding population operating through the mechanisms of inheritance and variation. The conservative core of the process is the mechanism of inheritance. It is the pattern of inherited traits that is, on the whole, being preserved by the reproductive process. But included in the dynamics of the process are the mechanisms of variation, which also serve to preserve the inherited traits of the interbreeding population. Thus one dynamic element in natural selection is split two ways. The dynamic element is the reproductive process. The dispositional reference of this process (call it 'aim' if you wish, so long as it is not confused with a purposive value reference) is to preserve the species. The aim of the process is to preserve, so far as possible, the pattern of traits characterizing an interbreeding population. This aim is served by a split in the dynamic element by which part of the dynamics goes toward the conserving of the pattern of traits through inheritance, and part toward the production of variations by mutation and sexual reproduction. The variations are then subject to selection pro and con in terms of their adaptation to the environment.

We must now turn to this latter phase of natural selection. But first let it be carefully noted once again that the selection pro and con of the variations generated by the reproductive process parallels in operation the selection pro and con of the subordinate acts generated by trial and error for a purposive drive. In both instances, moreover, it is the reality of the situation that determines the selection, subject to the dispositional reference of the dynamic pattern. The incorrect subordinate act of an appetitive drive is blocked and rejected by the reality of the environing situation in which that particular anticipated means for attaining the terminal reduction of the drive in fact did not causally obtain. A rat chooses a blind alley, or a man selects the wrong key to open his door. So, similarly (though with significant differences), an unadaptive variation is eliminated through natural selection by the reality of the environmental situation in which this particular living form is not in fact causally able to survive or to compete successfully with other variations which are more favorably equipped to survive.

It should be noticed also that the reproductive process of a biological species institutes a definite dispositional reference that is comparable to the conative reference of a purposive drive. This is implicit in the dynamic disposition of a species, in its propensity to propagate and to preserve its general character through inheritance. Just as the impulse pattern of a drive, through the very persistence of the drive to continue in action until it is finally reduced, institutes a conative reference toward the consummatory act of the drive as a goal, so the dynamics of the reproductive process of an interbreeding population sets up for any one generation a dispositional reference toward the reproduction, in the next generation, of the same general pattern of traits that characterized its own. Since we shall need a name for this reference, we may call it the *reproductive reference*. The mechanism of the reproductive process in a biological species is not for mere survival, or for mere survival of life, but quite specifically for the survival of that species. And, roughly, the intensity of that reproductive reference in a species is a function of the fertility of the interbreeding group, and indeed of those within the group which are most fertile.

We may now turn to a description, so far as it is known, of the selective process in natural selection. Darwin pictured it in relatively simple terms:

> A struggle for existence inevitably follows from the high rate at which all organic beings tend to increase . . . Although some species may be now increasing, more or less rapidly, in numbers, all cannot do so, for the world will not hold them . . . Owing to this struggle, variations, however slight and from whatever cause proceeding, if they be in any degree profitable to the individuals of a species, in their infinitely complex relations to other organic beings and to their physical conditions of life, will tend to the preservation of such individuals, and will generally be inherited by the offspring. The offspring, also, will have a better chance of surviving, for, of the many individuals of any species which are periodically born, but a small number can survive. I have called this principle, by which each slight variation, if useful, is preserved, by the term Natural Selection . . . Man by selection can certainly produce great results, and can adapt organic beings to his own uses, through the accumulation of slight but useful variations, given him by the hand of Nature. But Natural Selection . . . is a power incessantly ready for action, and is as im-

measurably superior to man's feeble efforts, as the works of Nature are to those of Art.[10]

Darwin knew nothing of the causes of variation, but assumed these as a postulate. He accounted for the development of a species in this way: when the reproduction of individuals of a species was in excess of what their environment could support, those best adapted to their environment were selected for survival. The principal selective agency for Darwin was adaptation, although he made some allowance for other factors such as sexual selection.

The principal selective agency is still adaptation. Though evolutionary theory has passed through numerous phases since Darwin wrote, the main features of his theory are standing up remarkably well. The principal differences arise from the greatly expanded knowledge of the causes of variation. These also have an effect on the grounds of selection. Here is Simpson's summary of the present-day views on natural selection:

> The history of life has not been strictly random or strictly oriented, but an odd mixture of the two, with one predominant here and the other there, but both generally present and almost inextricably combined in the evolution of any particular group. The orienting element was found rather surely to be adaptation.
>
> The mechanism of adaptation is natural selection. The idea of natural selection is very simple, even though its operation is highly complex and may be extremely subtle. Natural selection has this basis: in every population some individuals have more offspring than others. This obvious fact automatically accounts for the possibility of evolutionary change. It has been seen that individuals in any group differ in genetic make-up, hence pass on different heredity to their offspring, and also that mutations occur in a scattered way as such a group reproduces. It may happen, and is indeed the usual thing over small numbers of generations, that the new generation, in spite of its differences between individuals, has about the same average genetic constitution as the parent generation, and about the same incidence of mutations, so that no clearly evident change occurs from one generation to the next. It is, however, extremely unlikely that the new generation has exactly the same genetic make-up as the parental generation. Some individuals do have more offspring than others and their particular genetic characters, which differ to some degree from those of other individuals, will be more

frequent in the new generation . . . Even a very slight change
will produce evident, eventually large effects if it is cumulative
from one generation to the next . . . In nature the individuals
that tend to have more offspring are, as a rule and no matter
how slight the difference, either those best integrated with their
environment (including the association with their own species)
and most successful in it, or those best able to begin to exploit
an opportunity not available or less so to their neighbors. Thus
natural selection usually operates in favor either of increased
adaptation to a given way of life, organism-environment integration, or of such change as will bring about adaptation to another, accessible way of life. Natural selection thus orients evolutionary change in the direction of one or another of these two
sorts of adaptation.[11]

The second sort of adaptation to a new way of life would obviously be the beginning of a new species.

The chief difference between Darwin's theory of natural selection and the more recent one is in their emphasis. Simpson
stresses the selective factors operating in heredity because of the
greater fecundity of some individuals in a group in comparison
to others. They have a selective head start in the very dynamics
of natural selection. Darwin stresses the factor of adaptive selection by the environment. Yet in the end the latter is decisive
for Simpson, too, since he asserts that "the individuals that tend
to have more offspring are, as a rule . . . either those best integrated with their environment . . . or those best able to begin
to exploit . . . adaptation to another accessible way of life." In
both alternatives, the reality of the environmental situation is the
decisive orienting selective agency operating upon the range of
variations projected from the core of inherited traits that characterize an interbreeding group. Darwin's basic insight into the
mode of operation of natural selection has been corroborated
and amplified rather than corrected.

Now let me summarize these results in value terms, interpreting natural selection as a selective system instituting a natural norm of value. The dynamic element of this selective system is vital energy exhibiting itself as a pattern of inherited
traits characterizing an interbreeding population. One of the
traits of this dynamic pattern is a dispositional tendency to reproduce itself. This is exhibited in the mechanism of simple fis-

sion, or in the elaboration of this in the process of sexual reproduction. This dispositional tendency thus generates a reference
which may be called the *reproductive reference*. Within natural
selection as a selective system, it functions as a normative reference. That is to say, in the dynamics of this system a parent
generation has a disposition to reproduce itself in a succeeding
generation.

As part of the dynamics of this system, variations in the pattern of traits characterizing the interbreeding group are produced. These are subject to selection, partly by genetic factors
within the dynamics of reproduction, and partly, and in the end
decisively, by their degree of adaptation to the environment of
the group. An unadapted variation is immediately or slowly eliminated and is said to be lacking in survival value; an adapted
variation survives and propagates and is said to possess survival
value.

If a group is in a steady state, well adapted to its environment,
its character will change very little from generation to generation. But if through sexual reproduction and mutation, it is
capable of closer adaptation to its environment within its range
of variations, natural selection will gradually eliminate the less
fit and fill out the population with the more fit. If the environment changes radically, the norm of fitness obviously changes
accordingly. The dynamics of natural selection within the group
still operates as before to preserve the group by passing on to
the next generation as much as is adaptable of the pattern of
traits of the parent generation. This is what the survival of the
species means. If the resulting change is considerable, a new
species will be generated out of the old. The old species may or
may not continue to exist, depending on the continuance of
regions where some of the original group can continue to be sufficiently adapted. If an environmental change is so radical, and
the range of variations available to a species is so limited, that
no individuals of the species are capable of adapting to the new
conditions, then the species becomes extinct. The whole dynamics of an interbreeding group is directed to prevent extinction
and to further survival. So extinction is the nadir of survival
value. But it does occur in evolutionary history, just as animals

sometimes die of hunger and thirst, though the whole purposive dynamics of their systems is to satisfy these drives.

At this point the question of the relevancy of all this to human values is likely to arise. Suppose it is admitted that survival value is properly denominated a value in that it arises from a selective system comparable in its dynamics to systems motivated by purposive drives. What can a man or an animal do about survival value? Either he is fortunate enough to be an adapted variation and lives out his life and propagates, or he is unfit and, in spite of all his struggles, sooner or later is eliminated.

Man, at least, is in a position to do a great deal about it. Whether he survives or not as an individual has much to do with the purposive decisions he can and does make. The reason for this is that the pattern of traits for man as a biological species includes two traits which together place his capacities for survival within his powers of decision. These two traits are his extraordinary docility (the capacity to make decisions) and his social proclivities, which with the aid of language come out as cultural capacities. So far as man has control over his social relationships, he has control over his survival values.

For the course of biological evolution has in man taken a novel turn. As we have repeatedly had occasion to say in the earlier chapters, man is almost completely insulated as an organic being from competition with animals other than man. He has acquired so much power through his social organization and his inventions of tools that he has little to fear from his environment except other men. The competition of man with man has, to be sure, periodically become extremely severe. The competition here, however, shows up not mainly in terms of individual fitness of individual men for their physical environment, but as a competition of social group with social group, or as the differential adaptation of competing social groups to a particular environment. In man, biological evolution has turned from organic evolution into cultural evolution. It is no longer primarily the survival of an organic species but the survival of a society as a cultural group that is at stake. Man as a biological organism survives by reason of being incorporated in a social group. Consequently, the dynamics of survival for an interbreeding group characteristic of organic evolution is switched into the dynamics for the survival and preservation of a cultural group. It is definitely only a switching of these dynamics, for the organic survival of the human species is served by man's cultural organization. Man could not long survive outside his culture. Moreover, man interbreeds largely within his cultural group. Man has not escaped the demands of survival value by means of his cultural organizations. Survival value operates for man through his cultural organizations. And, as we shall see in our terminal chapter, under extreme conditions survival value legislates over all other values for man.

## 5. Adaptation versus Adaptability

But before we go into the operation of survival value in terms of human cultural evolution, attention must be given to a rivalry in the means for survival between adaptation and adaptability. Adaptation is the special fitness of a biological form for a specific environment. The closer the adaptation the more specialized the set of traits characterizing the species for living in its environment. The advantage of adaptation is the perfecting of the techniques of living for the species in its particular environment. This may be a decisive advantage for survival when the competition with other species or within a given species is severe. It often leads to extinction, however. The more highly specialized a species is in relation to its particular environment, the less its capacity to cope with environmental changes. The range of variation in sexual reproduction and nonlethal mutations, also, will be more limited. Specialized adaptation is thus a hazard for a species. Yet if at some stage this was the only means by which the species managed to survive, the selective direction was normatively correct. It provided survival value where otherwise the population would have perished.

Adaptability, if conditions permit it, is, however, less of a hazard. Adaptability is the capacity to adapt to a wide range of environments. Adaptability ordinarily entails a lesser degree of specialized conformity to a particular environment than adaptation does. The two concepts are evidently relative, but they point to divergent criteria for survival value.

According to adaptation, the closer the conformity of a species to its particular environment the better. This is the selection which the reality of the situation seems most obviously to enact. The greater the conformity of a group to its environment, the greater in that environment its likelihood for survival. But this formulation overlooks the possibility of conforming to another available environment, and the capacity of a group to do that depends not on its adaptation but on its adaptability.

Two ideals for survival are hereby projected by the mechanics of natural selection: that of the most efficient specialization of traits for the exploitation of a specific environment, and that of the most varied capacities for readiness to get along in a large variety of environments. Both ideals in the extreme are hazardous, and obviously the course of evolution keeps them both in action in various proportions depending on the conditions. But the two might be ingeniously combined if there were a life form which had a high degree of adaptability and at the same time a great capacity for adaptation which it could readily exercise or not as the environmental conditions demanded.

It was perhaps inevitable in the long course of evolutionary history that this particularly favorable type of adaptability (with a capacity for temporary specific adaptations included within it) should emerge. This is precisely the type of adaptability we obtain by means of docility. A docile organism is precisely one that has a general capacity to adapt to many environments and a specific capacity to learn to adapt in a highly specialized way to a particular environment. Man is the most docile of animals and probably also by this means the most adaptable. Through his docility man can direct his adaptability to a high degree of adaptation by learning just how best to utilize a particular environment. And then, through his social organization and language, he can transmit his learning from one generation to the next, thereby obtaining what organic evolution was never able to obtain otherwise than through culture—the transmission of acquired characteristics.

Docile animals, and particularly man, have that supremely flexible and effective combination of adaptability with adaptation which we may now technically call *adjustability*. Other modes of survival may be more suitable for other zones of life, but adjustability is the latest invention of the evolutionary process, and man is the species which through social organization has carried this mode farthest. Through the agency of cultural transmission, man is the most adjustable of animals. It is by means of his adjustability that man has been so successful in settling into his life zone and expanding its bounds wider and wider. This fact is something to be kept in mind. When man in any of his social relationships begins to set rigid bounds to his adjustability, he is acting directly counter to his fundamental mode of survival. This is the biological ground for the value ascribed to the all-round man, the rich personality. It is also safe to say that, for man in his cultural relationships, the greater the adjustability of the cultural organization through which he makes his living and survives, the greater his likelihood of survival. And since man's social organization is, in various complicated ways, under his purposive control (for this is just what is meant by man's exceptional adjustability), man actually does have control of his own evolutionary survival and so of his survival values in a manner that no other organism has. This does not mean that man has the power to do anything he wants. He must come into an adaptive relation with his environment. But he has greater powers of adaptability and so of maneuvering within his environment than any other species. He actually has the power to make new species (at least, new species of societies) by virtue of his power to develop new cultural patterns, for cultural patterns are the forms that life species take in the course of biological evolution in man's life zone.

## 6. CULTURAL EVOLUTION: ITS SIGNIFICANCE FOR HUMAN SURVIVAL

"The new sort of evolution so characteristic of man," writes Simpson, "is that of social structure and transmitted learning." [12] This is the sort of evolution that brought in "man's particular adaptive type," quoted earlier, "the latest to be developed up to now in the history of life, one radically new, never before exemplified, and with extreme potentialities for expansion." [13] It is because of this novelty, because evolution took a fresh direction when man emerged through natural selection, that the control of values and a concern as to how to control them emerged with him. Values are plentifully exhibited in other organic species, and evaluations through natural norms are constantly being carried out in their respective life zones. But man appears to be the only species that has a high degree of voluntary control over the course of his own evolution. This control is made possible by his exceptional adjustability as an organic species, which is projected with a comparable adjustability in the variety of his cultural patterns. For these are his basic instruments for adaptation, for the control of his environment, and for survival.

The significant point is that with man the course of evolution takes a new direction. With him—and so far, it would seem, with him alone—natural selection ceases to operate primarily on the hereditary constitution of the organism, and operates instead on the social constitution of a group organized within a dominant cultural pattern. The course of biological evolution turns from organic evolution to cultural evolution.

It is well to stress that this sort of turn does not take place in insect societies. These also survive chiefly through their social structures. But the structures for social specialization and coöperation are in these societies built into the organic structures of the organisms making up the societies. These social structures are built into the genes and chromosomes of the insects. Though there is evidence of some learning among ants and bees, relative to man their docility is greatly limited. Nothing in the nature of a cultural pattern is to be discerned among insects. Every hive of bees of the same organic species has the same social organization. This is equally true of ants and termites.

When, by means of natural selection, a new species of insect society comes into existence, this must occur by the process of organic evolution. It occurs by a selection of the more favored as against the less favored variations of individual insect organisms for their communal life zone. The insects themselves would not in any sense plan the change through the agency of purposive behavior. Some fine day an ancient species of ant would find in its environment another species of ant with a different type of social organization, and a different type of organic structure for the individuals composing the society. If the two groups compete for the same life zone and the latter is the better adapted, there is nothing the ancient group can do about it. They cannot change their social organization, for this is built into their individual organisms. As individuals they cannot be absorbed by and acculturated to the new group because their organic structure is not adapted to the new species of social organization. In short, there is no biological differentiation between a species of insect society and the organic species of insect carrying on that society. In a social insect, the social structure of its society is an organic trait of the insect carried in the genes like male and female in a species of plant or nonsocial animal.

The conditions are quite different in human societies. Man's social structures are not built into his organic structure. So man as a species is the same throughout all the many species of social organization within which he lives. The effectiveness of man's social organization has very largely insulated him from the effects of natural selection upon his organic structure. Instead, natural selection operates mainly upon his social structures directly, and when a certain type of social structure is eliminated by natural selection, the organic human species is often very little affected.

Thus survival value comes within the range of man's voluntary control because his capacities for voluntary control were the traits favorably selected for survival in his life zone. So to speak, natural selection with its norm of survival value gave him the capacity for purposive behavior and the capacity to transmit his learning through cultural tradition just so that he might survive in his life zone. Only by employing these modes of voluntary control over himself and his social organization has he successfully survived in his environment. Only if he continues to employ successfully these modes of voluntary control will he continue to survive. Survival value thus overarches the whole area of human values.

Survival value gave man his purposive values and his cultural values that these might favorably serve his survival values. It gave man the capacity purposefully to act for his own survival— apparently a unique gift in the history of life. Thus the very traits that were favorably selected by natural selection for human survival in man's life zone are traits by which man can purposefully create new life species within his life zone. The course of evolution in the production of new species of social organization with great survival value, and even perhaps of new varieties of men by social constraints upon breeding, is handed over to man for a large degree of voluntary control. In short, man holds his own survival in his own hands.

But, as with all voluntary control, he will succeed only if he respects the reality of the situation. Man can shape his future to his purposes so long as he has respect for the character of his total environmental situation, his life zone. But if this respect fails, if he fails to adapt to his environment or to control it by adapting it to his purposes according to predictable natural laws, the operation of natural selection inexorably takes over. Some type of society perishes, and perhaps many of the individuals in it who were specially identified with its unadapted ideals. And if man as a whole fails finally to respect the reality of his situation, he may well perish utterly as a species, and he will have done this by his own voluntary act through failure of social control. For man survives by his intelligence, and if he fails to survive as a group, be it a tribe or the whole human population, he perishes by a failure of intelligence.

There is a theological myth that God created man in His own image and thereby endowed him alone of all creatures in the world with a free will. By this act God made it possible for man to err. But He also made it possible for man to be creative like God. If man with his gift of freedom respected the will of God and voluntarily followed the divine decrees, he would prosper and be rewarded. But if he showed disrespect for the divine will, and sinned, God would punish him, and if he remained unrepentant, would visit eternal damnation upon him.

A religious myth can often exhibit an intuitive insight with a vividness and a presentiment beyond the powers of pedestrian intellectual concepts. God is to man in the myth as survival value to all the human values motivated by purposive drives and needs. The latter human values were created through natural selection, and eventually endowed man with the capacity to control his own survival and even to evolve biological species of his own making, but only so long as man also deeply respected the laws of natural selection and survival value. If any man or group of men failed in that respect, the error was fatal, and the whole race of man is subject to the final judgment of survival value.

## 7. CULTURAL EVOLUTION: DARWIN'S ACCOUNT

Despite many errors of detail which have been corrected by later research, Darwin probably had a clearer insight into the relation of human values to evolutionary theory than any other man. With a little screening and amplification, his statement of the relation of survival value to ethical evaluations can stand much as he gave it. This is perhaps not altogether astonishing, seeing that he is the man whose genius first saw and elaborated the relevant relations involved in the operation of biological evolution. Such a man would be the best equipped to mark the comparable relations determining cultural evolution and the relation of cultural to organic evolution.

The pertinent passages are to be found in *The Descent of Man.* His transition to the subject of man's social control is a passage on the weakness of man as an isolated organism. Referring to some of the critics of evolution, Darwin says:

It has often been objected to such views as the foregoing, that man is one of the most helpless and defenceless creatures in the world; and that during his early and less well-developed condition, he would have been still more helpless. The Duke of Argyll, for instance, insists that "the human frame has diverged from the structure of brutes, in the direction of greater physical helplessness and weakness. That is to say, it is a divergence which of all others is most impossible to ascribe to mere natural selection." [14]

Darwin thereupon turns the Duke of Argyll's evidence against him, precisely as there was a turn in the course of evolution to meet this condition. Darwin admits man's weakness as an isolated organism and even amplifies upon it, then turns the evidence to opposite effect.

In regard to bodily size or strength, we do not know whether man is descended from some small species, like the chimpanzee, or from one as powerful as the gorilla; and, therefore, we cannot say whether man was larger and stronger, or smaller and weaker than his ancestors. We should, however, bear in mind that an animal possessing great size, strength, and ferocity, and which, like the gorilla, could defend itself from all enemies, would not perhaps have become social; and this would most effectually have checked the acquirement of the higher mental qualities, such as sympathy and the love of his fellows. Hence it might have been an immense advantage to man to have sprung from some comparatively weak creature.

The small strength and speed of man, his want of natural weapons, etc., are more than counterbalanced, firstly, by his intellectual powers, through which he has formed for himself weapons, tools, etc., though still remaining in a barbarous state, and, secondly, by his social qualities which lead him to give and receive aid from his fellow men. . . . The ancestors of man were, no doubt, inferior in intellect, and probably in social disposition, to the lowest existing savages; but it is quite conceivable that they might have existed, or even flourished, if they had advanced in intellect, whilst gradually losing their brute-like powers, such as climbing trees, etc. . . . Natural selection arising from the competition of tribe with tribe, in some . . . large area . . . together with the inherited effects of habit, would under favorable conditions, have sufficed to raise man to his present high position in the organic scale.[15]

Just strike out the word 'inherited' in the last sentence (which implies the hypothesis of the inherited transmission of acquired characteristics), and the foregoing statement can stand not only as a brilliant initial insight but as still an essentially sound description of the place of man, his society, and his values within the evolutionary process.

For what Darwin is saying here is that out of man's very weakness as an organism was generated, through natural selection, his special strength as a social animal. Unless in his early ancestry man had been weak as an organism, the compensating traits could not have been selected by natural selection to give him a strength he otherwise lacked. These traits were intelligence (the capacity for purposive behavior) and his social instincts (gathered together under the term 'sympathy'). (Parenthetically, it is pertinent to notice that the trait of intelligence itself is founded on a potential weakness. For purposive behavior apparently is generated, as we observed (chap. 2, §2), from broken-down chain-reflex behavior, which produces the drive-gap-goal setup. The loss of the intermediate links of a chain reflex would seem at first to bode ill for the unfortunate organism. But when trial and error and the capacity for conditioning were added, then this organism became the fortunate possessor of the power of learning. And then he could fill in the gap between his drive and its goal in a variety of ways, not in the one way of a chain reflex, and thereby acquire a freedom of choice and a greatly expanded range of adaptability.) So, by the strengthening, through natural selection, of intelligence and certain social instincts, man acquired a prodigious strength and adaptability which emerged as a capacity for organization into culturally integrated social groups.

Darwin stresses, perhaps more than anthropologists would today, the improvement, through natural selection, of man as an organism in his capacities for social adaptation. But perhaps some contemporary anthropologists have been overstressing the influence of acculturation, as if in the course of cultural evolution no changes in the inherited structures of men had been produced by natural selection. Darwin refers approvingly to an article of Wallace's arguing that

> man after he had partially acquired those intellectual and moral faculties which distinguish him from the lower animals, would have been but little liable to bodily modifications through natural selection, or any other means. For man is enabled through

his mental faculties [i.e., purposive behavior] "to keep with an unchanged body in harmony with the changing universe." He has great capacity for changing his habits to new conditions of life. He invents weapons, tools, and various stratagems to procure food and to defend himself. When he migrates into a colder climate he uses clothes, builds sheds, and makes fires, etc.[16]

But this principle, Darwin adds, does not apply to man's intelligence and sympathy, on which he depends for his power of survival as a culturally social animal.

The case . . . is widely different in relation to the intellectual and moral faculties of man. These faculties are variable; and we have every reason to believe that the variations tend to be inherited. Therefore, if they were formerly of high importance to primeval man and to his apelike progenitors, they would have been perfected or advanced through natural selection. Of the high importance of the intellectual faculties there can be no doubt, for man mainly owes to them his predominant position in the world. We can see, that in the rudest state of society, the individuals who were the most sagacious, who invented and used the best weapons and traps, and who were best able to defend themselves, would rear the greatest number of offspring. [Notice how well this checks with the quotation from Simpson, above: "the individuals that tend to have more offspring are . . . those best integrated with their environment (including the association with their own species) . . ."] The tribes which included the largest number of men thus endowed, would increase in number and supplant other tribes. Numbers depend primarily on the means of subsistence, and this depends partly on the physical nature of the country, but in a much higher degree on the arts which are there practised. As a tribe increases and is victorious, it is often still further increased by the absorption of other tribes . . . From the remotest times successful tribes have supplanted other tribes . . . At the present day civilized nations are everywhere supplanting barbarous nations, excepting where the climate opposes a deadly barrier; and they succeed mainly, though not exclusively, through their arts, which are the products of intellect. It is, therefore, highly probable that with mankind the intellectual faculties have been mainly and gradually perfected through natural selection.[17]

And the same is true of the traits conducing to cultural social organization. Writes Darwin:

In order that primeval men, or the apelike progenitors of man, should become social, they must have acquired the same instinctive feelings, which impel animals to live in a body; and they no doubt exhibited the same general dispositions. They would have felt uneasy when separated from their comrades, for whom they would have felt some degree of love. They would have warned each other of danger, and have given mutual aid in attack or defence. All this implies some degree of sympathy, fidelity, and courage. Such social qualities, the paramount importance of which to the lower animals is disputed by no one, were no doubt acquired by the progenitors of man in a similar manner, namely, through natural selection . . . When two tribes of primeval man, living in the same country, came into competition, if (other circumstances being equal) the one tribe included a great number of courageous, sympathetic and faithful members, who were always willing to warn each other of danger, to aid and defend each other, this tribe would succeed better and conquer the other. Let it be borne in mind how all-important in the never-ceasing wars of savages fidelity and courage must be. The advantage which disciplined soldiers have over undisciplined hordes follows chiefly from the confidence which each man feels in his comrades. Obedience . . . is of the highest value, for any form of government is better than none. Selfish and contentious people will not cohere, and without coherence nothing can be effected. A tribe rich in the above qualities would spread and be victorious over other tribes; but in the course of time it would, judging from all past history, be in its turn overcome by some other tribe still more highly endowed. Thus the social and moral qualities would tend slowly to advance and be diffused throughout the world.[18]

I quote this passage at length, for, in admittedly oversimplified form, it describes the way in which man's repertory of drives and needs, out of which all his purposive and cultural values obtain their dynamics, have already been selected by the natural norm of natural selection. And this natural norm is surely still continuing its surveillance of the inherited basic repertory of human motivation, however far removed this may be through the intervention of cultural control. Darwin is saying here that we must not forget that man's cultural ideals and dynamics are all founded on a biological base (specifically on man's intelligence and his social instincts), and that this base has been subject to adaptation through organic evolution, and still is.

He does notice that "with highly civilized nations continued progress depends in a subordinate degree on natural selection." [19] He is concerned, as are some later biologists in even larger degree, with tendencies among civilized cultures toward deterioration of stock.

> We civilized men do our utmost to check the process of elimination; we build asylums for the imbecile, the maimed, the sick; we institute poor laws; and our medical men exert their utmost to save the life of every one to the last moment . . . Thus the weak members of civilized societies propagate their kind.[20] . . . [This] is mainly an incidental result of the instinct of sympathy. . . . Nor could we check our sympathy, even at the urging of hard reason, without deterioration in the noblest part of our nature.[21]

Darwin's dilemma shows his recognition both of the insulative effects of culture against organic selection and of the fact that a society of men cannot let its stock deteriorate too far without subjecting itself to risk of elimination through maladaptation. Darwin's conclusion is optimistic on the whole: even in a highly civilized society the more intelligent and sympathetic members will be the more successful and prolific. The commoner recommendation of later biologists is eugenics, cultural control of heredity in man. If effectively done, this would mean a deliberate acceleration of adaptability in the human stock by cultural planning—a supreme exemplification of adjustability.

So far, then, Darwin's analysis has brought out the following points: that man's power as a well-adapted species grew out of his physical weakness; that through natural selection his physical weakness was compensated for by a form of social organization generated from increased powers of intelligent behavior and certain social instincts; that his social organization in its evolutionary development increasingly insulated him from the direct effects of organic selection. The next question concerns the insulative dynamics of man's mode of social organization. What gives human society its coherence as an adaptive structure?

Here is where Darwin's theory of the 'moral sense' comes in.

> I fully subscribe to the judgment of those writers who maintain that of all the differences between man and the lower animals,

the moral sense or conscience is by far the most important . . .
It is summed up in that short but imperious word *ought*, so full
of high significance. It is the most noble of all the attributes of
man, leading him without a moment's hesitation to risk his life
for that of a fellow creature; or after due deliberation, impelled
simply by the deep feeling of right or duty, to sacrifice it in some
great cause.[22]

He then offers a rather detailed account of how he believes
conscience developed in man through the action of his social
instincts in concert with his intelligence.

[It seems] in a high degree probable . . . that any animal whatever, endowed with well-marked social instincts, the parental
and filial affections being here included, would inevitably acquire a moral sense or conscience, as soon as his intellectual
powers had become as well developed, or nearly as well developed, as in man. . . .[23] [At the same time, I do] not wish to
maintain that any strictly social animal, if its intellectual faculties
were to become as active and as highly developed as in man,
would acquire exactly the same moral sense as ours.[24]

For Darwin the dynamics of conscience comes from the social
instincts, guided with the aid of language by "the common
opinion how each member ought to act for the common good" [25]
and so consolidated by habit as to go into action automatically.
Thus conscience is properly recognized by Darwin as the carrier
of the demands of a cultural pattern within the personality of an
individual. He recognizes the influence of religion, also, in a
culture: "Another element is most important, although not necessary, the reverence or fear of the Gods, or Spirits believed in by
each man; and this applies especially in cases of remorse." [26]
Darwin could not elaborate the details of the dynamics of
conscience and its mode of incorporation of a cultural pattern in
the personality of an individual, as anthropological and psychological research has been doing for nearly a century since his day.
But he saw how it worked in main outline, and, by showing how
conscience is generated out of the operation of natural selection,
he made the connection between survival value in organic evolution and the cultural operation of purposive values in cultural
evolution.
Darwin does not make the distinction we did between irra-

tional and rational conscience. The two concepts are fused in his treatment. He had, of course, no knowledge of the mechanism of repression. But if he had known, he might well have observed, as we did, that though an irrational conscience is well adapted to a relatively stable primitive or civilized society in a relatively stable environment, it is not so well adapted to an intricate industrial civilization subject to constant internal changes and wide variations in physical environment. The same would hold for a dogmatic religion, which tends to be correlated with an irrational conscience.

Darwin, however, clearly perceived the link that connected man and his moral values with the essentially automatic operation of natural selection and survival value as the latter worked previous to the advent of man. The link is in the dynamics of man's social solidarity, which operates most effectively through conscience. Modern psychologists and anthropologists would wish to be able to distinguish between conscience and shame as dynamic agents and also between an irrational and a rational conscience. But the general concept is that of the dynamics of social solidarity in the human species. These dynamics have to be worked out on the basis of the two central features which characterize man's conduct: his intelligence and his social instincts. The particular development of man's intelligence (including his capacities for tool-making and articulated language) and the particular pattern of his social instincts (including his capacities for cultural transmission and conscience) are the results of natural selection. For their survival value they are continuously maintained today as inexorably as when man emerged. This was Darwin's great insight. And it seems to be as sound a view in its main outlines today as when Darwin announced it in *The Descent of Man*.

## 8. Cultural Evolution: Later Developments

Just as there has been development in the theory of organic evolution since Darwin's day, so there has in the theory of cultural evolution. The modifications have been in the same general direction—softening the emphasis on elimination through direct

competition and war. The selection is subtler and more dissem-
inated in its operation. Here I shall follow approximately the
view of G. G. Simpson in *The Meaning of Evolution*.

The title of Simpson's key chapter, in which he treats of the
relation of ethics to evolution, is "Knowledge and Responsibility."
Notice that these are synonyms for Darwin's two basic concepts
of intelligence and sympathy. Knowledge is the human result
of intelligence, and responsibility the outcome of social organization in a human society.

Adaptability, or rather adjustability, is in this area, for Simpson
as for Darwin, the guiding evolutionary concept. Human knowledge and responsibility are the products of evolution in man
that render him adaptable to his life zone, and may be expected
to render him still more adaptable. Future adaptation, however,
will not be guided by the threat of human extinction (unless
man perishes at his own hand), but toward a still greater adaptability of man to man and of man to his environment.

Yet Simpson does not anticipate an end of evolution in man or
in some future social equilibrium set up among men of the
present species:

> Some authorities do indeed maintain that evolution is through,
> that life has evolved as far as possible and all essential evolu-
> tionary change stops at this point . . . But evolution is not, in
> fact, finalistic and it seems to me quite impossible for it to come
> to a standstill so long as there are any living organisms left to
> evolve. Life and environment are in such a ceaseless flux that it
> is simply inconceivable that a permanent equilibrium will ever
> be reached.[27]
>
> It is, however, reasonably safe to assume that no animals able
> to compete with man in intelligence, socialization, and the other
> unique human characteristics will arise as long as man does in
> fact exist. *He has a firm grip on his adaptive zone and is fully
> able to defend it.*[28]

I italicize this sentence that its full implication may not be
missed, namely, that if man did not have a firm grip upon his
adaptive zone, his existence would be in great jeopardy until he
established it. It is only because man is so safe as an organic
species that he often forgets the supreme value of survival, without which all other human values would vanish utterly.

Unless man extinguishes himself (which Simpson observes is 'another of his unique capacities'!),

It is reasonably certain that he will evolve farther and will change more or less radically . . . Man has the power to modify and *within certain rather rigid limits* to determine the direction of his own evolution. [I italicize 'within certain rather rigid limits,' for these are the limits beyond which, if exceeded, natural selection takes its inexorable toll.] This power is increasing rapidly as knowledge of evolution increases. As regards biological evolution, this power has not as yet been exercised systematically and consciously to any effective extent. Control of social evolution has also been much less in the past than it can be and is likely to be in the future, and has likewise been highly unsystematic and often not really conscious.[29]

Yet this anticipated extension of human evolution through partial social control of man's own evolutionary future does not, Simpson is careful to state, lift man out of the operation of organic evolution. "Invention by man of the new evolution," he says, "based on the inheritance of learning and worked out in social structures, has not eliminated in him the old organic evolution. The new evolution continues to interact with and in considerable measure to depend on the old." [30]

The new cultural evolution operates by means of what Simpson calls 'interthinking groups,' somewhat comparable to the interbreeding groups of organic evolution.[31] The interthinking group transmits knowledge, as the interbreeding group transmits inheritance. As this knowledge becomes institutionalized in societies, these societies, differing in their institutionalized beliefs and modes of organizations, in short, in their cultural patterns, emerge as virtually different species of human societies.

The mode of transmission is by acculturation within an institutionalized society and by cultural diffusion from one such society to another. We have met the two concepts before (chap. 19). It is at this point that survival value intermingles with cultural value, and the norm of a cultural pattern becomes the vehicle for the norm of natural selection. There is a tolerance (and it may be a wide one) within which the normative action of a cultural pattern is unaffected by the normative action of natural selection. But when the demands of adaptation come to bear upon a society, either as a result of physical or social environmental changes, or as a result of inventions or other internal changes which often can indirectly increase the pressures upon a social group, then the normative action of natural selection makes itself felt.

The conservative element in cultural evolution corresponding to inheritance through the genes and chromosomes in organic evolution is tradition. The radical elements corresponding to the variations in organic evolution are inventions and other novel modes of thought, or belief, or social convention. They are subject to natural selection much as organic variations are. Such selection is made in terms of the reality of the situation. We have already dealt with these topics (chap. 19, §9; chap. 18, §5). We pointed out three types of problematic social situations, two of which involved changes in cultural pattern. Only these two would be involved in cultural evolution. In the type 2 situation the cultural change was in the direction of maximizing satisfactions within the society, or minimizing frustrations due to cultural lag. Many of these changes (like the many unadaptive 'accidental' traits in organic species) have little or no bearing on the adaptability of the society to its environment, and so have little or no effect upon survival value. They may, nevertheless, cumulatively bring about a whole new species of society, and so be very significant in cultural evolution. Not by natural selection alone, therefore, does cultural evolution operate any more than organic evolution does. But in the type 3 situation, where a cultural change is needed to increase the security of the society in the presence of a threat to its continuance, natural selection operates with decisiveness. And societies which fail to make the necessary cultural adjustments under such conditions, and so prove to be unadapted to their times and their environment, sooner or later by one means or another pass out of existence. For the type 3 situation the appropriate cultural changes have great survival value.

A notable difference between organic and cultural evolution hereby comes to light. Simpson has pointed out that the one and only directive factor in organic evolution is natural selection. But there are two decisive factors in cultural evolution. We have already called attention to them, and the observation is of supreme ethical significance. Natural selection for social adaptation is one of these; the other comes from the dynamics of purposive drives for the maximizing of satisfactions and the minimizing of frustrations. As we saw at the end of chapter 19, social integration is bipolar. We now see more clearly why. It is because the dynamics of purposive drives coming up from below meets, in a human culture, with the dynamics of biological evolution and natural selection as these come down from above upon the human species.

Man as a docile social animal capable of happiness through intelligent guidance of his purposive behavior is also, as a living creature, involved in the dynamics of biological evolution and concerned to live and not perish. These two evaluative forces, sometimes coöperative and sometimes opposed, are embedded in his make-up and in the dynamic make-up of his society. But if there is a genuine conflict between the two, natural selection overrules man's natural prejudice in favor of happiness. Usually it does this rather quietly by the demand for social conformity. The perverse, uncoöperative, solitary, or rambunctious man is shouldered away or neglected and has not the opportunity to propagate either his attitudes or his genes. And the greater the pressure upon a society, the greater the demand for social solidarity among its members.

In this rather quiet way, cultural evolution works its changes. Not so much by war and conquest as by communication, and trade, and example does one species of social pattern replace another. At present the industrial form of society is sweeping out the primitive forms and the less industrialized civilized forms. It is not a question whether some of the more primitive forms were not happier, on the whole, in their narrower environment, spiritually richer, or better in terms of numerous other ideals. Primitive societies are not adaptable to present conditions, and a decision on their part to delay or resist generally invites a good deal of unnecessary frustration and trouble. The natural norm of natural selection—biological evolution working here as cultural evolution —is evaluating these social structures and making a selection. The unadaptable forms of society by one means or another will simply evolve into other more adaptable forms. And, having an adaptable form of society, people can proceed to make it as happy and rich as possible. And there is no reason to think that a newly evolved industrial species of society has not even greater potentialities for human happiness and cultural richness than the species it is gradually displacing.

Another comment is pertinent at this point. Just as in organic evolution it was probably inevitable, given time enough, that an organic form should evolve which was not only adaptable but adjustable, so it is probably inevitable, given time enough, that a form of society will develop which is not only adapted to its situation but adjustable to a great variety of situations. There are evidences that such a development is now going on. Much waste of human comfort and life is involved in those cataclysmic modes of cultural evolution, by which every major change is a conquest or a revolution, and a better-adapted form replaces a less well adapted form by war and bloodshed. There is an advance both in human happiness and in survival value if a social form is evolved which is institutionally adjustable to great changes in social pressure and thus to great changes in environmental conditions. This would be, of course, the adjustable society envisaged in chapter 19 as an ideal for the minimization of frustrations and the maximization of security.

An adjustable society is nothing more or less than a docile society as contrasted with a rigid, unadaptable one. For, as experience has too clearly shown mankind, there is nothing inconsistent in a docile animal building up a social structure to live in which is rigid and incapable of learning anything. Then there is nothing to be done, when it is no longer adapted to its environment, but to destroy it. But it is even more consistent for a docile organism to learn eventually the advantages of a docile form of social organization within which to regulate his living in a constantly changing world. This means institutionalizing compensatory mechanisms within a cultural pattern to adjust to environmental changes. It means a form of social purposiveness comparable on the social level with purposive behavior on the organic level. It means the adjustable society.

Once a well-balanced adjustable form of society has evolved, it is a fair prediction that it will displace other social forms among mankind just because of its evaluative superiority both in its powers of purposive satisfaction and in its survival value.

## 9. THE LIMITS OF SOCIAL RESPONSIBILITY

One more very important point needs to be brought out before concluding these remarks on the bearing of the theory of evolution upon human values. The range of application of natural selection determines the limits of sanctioned social responsibility among ethical values. This is the empirical solution for an otherwise most puzzling problem for empirical ethics. Darwin also saw this point as few have since.

It is this: human social organization is sanctioned by the norm of natural selection as an instrument of adaptation for the survival of the human species. Consequently, the pattern of social relationships to which a man is required to conform in accordance with survival value is that of the community within which he lives. Just as a bee for its survival must coöperate with its own hive but not with any other hive, so a man for his survival has had to coöperate with his social group, but has had no such need to coöperate with members of any other social group. In fact, for his own survival and that of his group it was often necessary that he should not coöperate with members of other, and perhaps hostile, groups. The boundaries of a man's society thus became the boundaries of his sphere of obligation sanctioned by survival value and natural selection. To try to behave toward hostile animals (including other men) as if they were members of your society is often to risk destruction; and to fail to accept obligations within your own society is likewise to court destruction. So the ultimate sanction of survival sets the limits of human obligation quite definitely at the limits of social organization fitted for human adaptation.

Darwin makes the generalized statement as follows:

> With all animals, sympathy is directed solely towards the members of the same community, and therefore towards known, and more or less beloved members, but not to all the individuals of the same species. [This same principle applies to man.] The

virtues which must be practised, at least generally, by rude men so that they may associate in a body, are those which are still recognized as the most important. But they are practised almost exclusively in relation to men of the same tribe; and their opposites are not regarded as crimes in relation to men of other tribes.[32]

Darwin then runs over a number of the traditional virtues, bringing out some of the now familiar facts of cultural relativity, and concludes: "We have now seen that actions are regarded by savages, and were probably so regarded by primeval man, as good or bad, solely as they obviously affect the welfare of the tribe—not that of the species, nor that of an individual member of the tribe." [33] The last phase is the one for us particularly to notice: Darwin's observation that the approved cultural pattern determining obligatory behavior for a primitive tribe is sanctioned by natural selection for its bearing on the "welfare of the tribe—not that of the species, nor that of an individual member of the tribe."

Whether savages consciously regarded their obligations in that light is not relevant or, on present evidence, likely. Nor did Darwin probably mean to give that strict interpretation to these loose phases. But in the context he clearly does mean that there is a correlation between a cultural pattern with its repertory of 'oughts' and the welfare of the group in respect to the adaptation of the cultural pattern to the group's environment. If the cultural pattern were not adapted, it would be subject to alteration or elimination by natural selection. What is directly affected by natural selection is the culture of that group and nothing else. This is Darwin's crucial point. The locus of impact for natural selection on man is his cultural pattern. Any changes in the human species would result from the action of natural selection upon his social organization, and any effect upon an individual man would likewise come through his social organization. That, according to Darwin's insight, is why the ultimate sanction for human values is a social, not an individual, one. But it is a social one, because that is the way in which natural selection operates on the human species. So the ultimate sanction of all (if it comes to such an appeal) is that of natural selection, not that of cultural relativity, or that of maximizing an individual's satisfaction, or any of the other natural norms.

Suppose the social pressure is very strong. That would mean some maladaptation of the group to its environment, or a competition between groups and their presumably somewhat different social patterns. The survival of man as a species in either instance depends upon the survival of the group, and likewise the survival of any individual man depends largely on his doing his best for the adaptation of his group. It is group survival in either case, for this is the way in which natural selection operates on man. So, once more, it is survival value that ultimately determines the limits of the sphere of human obligation, and determines these limits as those of his cultural pattern subject to its adaptability.

Now this conclusion seems to head toward a cultural relativism subject to adaptability. Does this rule out the widespread but rather modern ideal among civilized peoples of a brotherhood of man? For the essence of this ideal is that the bounds of human obligation should be extended until they include all men.

An empirical value theory must insist that such ideals be empirically sanctioned. Assuredly Darwin is right in calling attention to the fact that no empirical sanction existed for such an ideal in the conduct of primitive societies, or in the evaluative action of natural selection. On the contrary, the immediate action of natural selection on man is to split the human population into many societies, and to limit the empirically justifiable range of human obligations to the boundaries of these several societies.

But this, observes Darwin, is only the beginning of the operation of natural selection on the human species. Eventually the boundaries of human obligation extend to the whole human race as civilization advances. Here is his argument:

> As man advances in civilisation, and small tribes are united into larger communities, the simplest reason would tell each individual that he ought to extend his social instincts and sympathies to all members of the same nation, though personally unknown to him. This point being once reached, there is only an artificial barrier to prevent his sympathies extending to all nations and races.[34]

This is a rather weak argument for an empirical evolutionist: no sanction is suggested but rational consistency, which is not a very strong empirical sanction in such a context of dynamic motivation. Why should a Frenchman have consideration for a German or even a Samoan any more than an ant has consideration for a anteater or even for an ant in another anthill?

Darwin senses a weakness in this argument and characteristically brings up a number of counter instances. "If men are separated . . . by great differences in appearance or habit, experience unfortunately shows us how long it is, before we look at them as our fellow-creatures . . . The very idea of humanity, as far as I could observe, was new to most of the Gauchos of the Pampas." [35] Darwin resorts to the spread of this humanitarian ideal "through instruction and example to the young" so that it "becomes eventually incorporated in public opinion." But this gives only *cultural* backing to the ideal, which is still a weak argument for its ultimate sanctioning by an empirical evolutionist who can call it a virtue, "one of the noblest with which man is endowed." Even his supporting of his suggested cultural conditioning with the doctrine of the inherited transmission of acquired habits, which Darwin proceeds to do in a paragraph or two, does not establish his conclusion, for as well might a provincial patriotism be so transmitted as the brotherhood of man.

Nevertheless, Darwin was probably voicing a correct intuitive induction from the evidence he had, though he stressed the wrong reasons. The reason for extending the limits of social obligation on evolutionary grounds is that the range of social organization for human survival has had to be extended under conditions of civilization, and must now or soon be extended world-wide under conditions of modern atomic civilization, else we lack the means of controlling the invention of our instruments of human destruction. We must extend our social organization in some effective manner to all men and extend our range of obligation similarly, or we risk our survival as a species. Survival value has at last embraced the brotherhood of man. Darwin stated the basic principle in his opening sentence on this topic: "As man advances in civilisation, and small tribes are united into larger communities . . . [a man] ought to extend his social instincts and sympathies to all members of the same nation." But he reversed the causal connection. The extension of the 'ought' follows the extension of men's sympathies by means of their becoming united in larger communities.

In our technical terms of this and the last chapter, since the boundaries of a society are determined by the effective functional institution which normatively binds men together into a coöperative community, the wider the range of the functional institution the wider the range of obligatory conduct sanctioned by that institution. And since the appropriate range for an effective functional institution is that sanctioned by its adaptation to the environmental conditions in which it functions, the ultimate empirically sanctioned norm for the range of a group's obligatory conduct is that determined by natural selection. Other norms—those, for instance, set by the ideals of a theosophical society, or by the gang laws of a band of bootleggers—may set different limits for their own obligatory conduct, and they can sanction them by such dynamic means as they can muster. But in a pinch, when the survival of the community is at stake, it is the sanctions of the functional institution controlling the effective political structure of the society that determine the limits. If these limits are over- or under-extended, in respect to the reality of the situation, the sanctioning effects of natural selection will come to bear on the group.

Darwin intuitively grasped the fact that the limits of ethical obligation were being steadily expanded by the norm of natural selection, as a result of human invention and social adjustability, to a point at which these limits would have to take in all men. For the very survival of mankind, not to mention their general comfort, this becomes even more predictively obvious today. If there were any other equally intelligent social animal competing for man's life zone, the same would hold, and the limits of obligation would need to be extended to include them too. But the same does not hold for other animals which do not compete on a par with man in his life zone. Natural selection does not require them to become incorporated into man's functional institutions, except in the subordinate role of domestication. And if they began to edge mankind out of his life zone, it is easy to see what man would do about it. Suppose cattle began to push men out of their towns and villages and take over their fields, even a religious taboo protecting the cattle would not save them from being put back into a place where men would be safe from their depredations. If a Hindu society could not do this, a neighboring Mohammedan society would be glad to take over their villages and do the cleaning-up job necessary.[36]

So, ultimately, it is adaptation through natural selection that determines the limits of human obligation. This is a very important point to notice. For it resolves a host of problems that have puzzled empirical moralists regarding the legislation of the various natural norms as these relate to one another. Now we are in a position to take up this final problem.

# 21

# The Lines of Legislation
among Selective Systems and
Final Demarcation of
the Value Field

## 1. SOME FINAL QUESTIONS

It turns out that the pivotal concept for an empirical theory of
value is that of *selective system*. The concept first came to light
in the description of the purposive act. We followed it through
many levels of human activity and discovered it again in the
operation of natural selection, which determines the course of
biological evolution. Here, so far as values are concerned, at least
in their bearing on human decisions, the application of the concept came to an end. No more selective systems affecting human
values exist beyond natural selection.

There remain, however, three or four important matters to
clear up in this final chapter in order to round out our study.
Having discerned a large number of types of selective systems,
we are now in a position to make a generalized inductive description of this particular sort of selective process. Heretofore we
have done this only tentatively. We are in a position also to
observe the lines of legislation which the series of selective systems follow in their operation upon one another. Since these

systems institute natural norms for the values that are generated from them, the lines of legislation by which some of these systems operate selectively over others are of cardinal importance for empirical evaluations. For these lines of legislation determine the ultimate empirical sanctions of evaluations.

Then we shall wish to consider the question raised at the beginning of this study whether a general definition of value is possible or convenient. Have we been dealing with a homogeneous type of activity or with a heterogeneous group of interconnected activities? The third possibility, that there is nothing which can be verifiably referred to as 'value,' as observably exhibiting characters appropriately called 'good' or 'bad' or 'better' or 'worse,' is, I take it, by now demonstrably excluded.

Finally, we shall want to look back at the original common sense test definition of our area of subject matter—of things commonly or traditionally called 'good' or 'bad'—to see if we have left anything out which we should wish to include after this extended study, or which we should be embarrassed for empirical reasons still to exclude.

## 2. Definition of Selective System

The principal selective systems we have examined are the following:

1. The structure of a purposive act
   A. Appetitive
   B. Aversive
2. The consummatory field
3. The personal situation
4. The personality structure
   A. Roles
   B. Irrational conscience
   C. Personality integration
5. The social situation
6. The cultural pattern
   A. Institutions
   B. Irrational religion
   C. Cultural integration
7. Natural selection

The distinctive feature of a selective system which marks it off from other natural modes of selection is its split dynamics. The same dynamic agency which charges the norm in terms of which the selection is made likewise charges the trials which are selected pro and con. This is very different from a sievelike selection. A sieve institutes no norm with respect to its selection. Larger particles are sifted one way, smaller ones the other. Neither selected group is correct or incorrect with respect to the other or to the structure of the sieve. Someone with a purpose may want the sand that passes through the sieve or, instead, the pebbles that are separated from the sand. But the sieve itself is not normative with respect to either side. Similarly, whether the rain from the clouds drains into the Atlantic or into the Pacific depends on which side of the Great Divide it falls. But the setup has no normative element to correct one drainage as against the other. In a selective system, however, the dynamics of the system institutes trials and corrects them, all by the same dynamics.

The dynamics charging the norm and that charging the trials selected pro and con by the norm is the same. This is what makes the trials relevant to the norm, and also the selection of them pro and con. So to speak, the trials are compelled to recognize the authority of the norm to correct them, because their energy, their very life, has all its source in the energy of the norm. If the norm ceases to energize the trials, the trials receive no more energy; their life goes out, they cease to exist, and no more selections are made among these trials by the norm.

Selective systems may differ from one another in respect to their dynamics, or in respect to the channeling through which the dynamics is structured, or in respect to both. Our inquiry has brought out that there are only two basic instigating dynamic sources for the selective systems listed above: one is the instinctive purposive drives; the other, the vital forces of evolutionary selection. The two dynamic sources overlap in many of the selective systems, and it is pertinent to remember that evolutionary selection underlies purposive selection even though the latter has acquired a sphere of independence among docile organisms. That is to say, purposive behavior with its repertory of drives is a product of natural selection, and will be maintained by natural selection as long as it remains adaptive, but it would surely be eliminated by natural selection if ever it should cease to be adaptive in its life zone.

The purposive drives thus operate as a dynamic agency, independent even in opposition to natural selection only on sufferance, only because they have proved so highly adaptable that they have been able to take over a large sphere of human activity and insulate it from the direct impact of natural selection.

In our study we did not, as a matter of fact, become aware of a dynamic source other than purposive drives for our selective systems till we encountered the operation of the irrational conscience. We suspected that its great power over human decisions might be an indication of some nonpurposive force outside the drive structures—a force that had a vital normative function different from that of rational prudence. This suspicion was confirmed in our study of the social situation and still more in our study of the selective operation of cultural pattern, and was finally explained by the relevancy of natural selection to human social behavior.

Roughly speaking, the dynamics of individual behavior—the operation of the first four selective systems—is carried on by the purposive drives. The dynamics of social behavior (that for the social situation or the cultural pattern) is a combination of drive dynamics and the dynamics of natural selection. Actually, however, as we shall see presently in following out the lines of legislation for the evaluations of the series of selective systems, the dynamics of natural selection makes itself felt far into the details of individual behavior as well as of social behavior.

Since there are only two basic instigating sources of dynamics for our selective systems, and we have distinguished seven principal types of selective system bearing on human decisions, it is clear that the differences among them are due especially to their mode of channeling this energy.

Let us, then, quickly review the types of norms and trials characteristic of the seven selective systems. This will amount to a brief reminder of their modes of channeling.

1. The norm for a purposive act is the reduction of the drive.

Specifically, this signifies escape from the field of a riddance pattern or object of aversion for aversive structures, and attainment of a consummatory goal or goal object for appetitive structures. The subordinate acts are the trials. The drive charging the norm likewise charges the subordinate acts, which are rejected if they fail to fulfill the norm.

2. The norm for the consummatory field is that of maximizing the gratuitous satisfactions available in the field. The trials are the acts of maneuvering to find the optimum conditions for satisfaction. The appetitive drive energizes the norm and also the trials with the characteristic split dynamics of a selective system.

3. The norm for the personal situation is that of the maximum of achievement and of gratuitous satisfaction available from the contributory drives in view of the reality of the situation. The trials are the resultant acts of the organism. The dynamics is that of all the contributory drives. A trial that increases rather than reduces the tensions, or a trial that lessens rather than increases or maintains the available consummatory satisfactions, is dropped and another is attempted when the situation permits.

4. The personality structure institutes two types of norms: the roles and conscience demanding conformity, and the maximum of integration for the dispositions of the personality. The trials for personality roles and conscience are acts of the person. If they fail to conform, they encounter the sanctions supporting the personality roles and conscience. The trials for personality integration are personality dispositions. If these are persistently frustrating, they tend to be eliminated or modified to harmonize with the main personality structure. The dynamics of the personality is complex, but the same dynamic personality which makes a trial applies the norm to correct it. The split dynamics characterizing selective systems is again exemplified here.

5. The norm for a social situation is that of the maximum reduction of tension or attainment of consummatory satisfactions for all the persons involved so far as the reality of the situation will permit. The dynamics of the social situation includes that of all the personalities involved, together with whatever may be the impact of the dynamics of natural selection. The trials, as with the personal situation, are the resultant acts performed. If

the tensions are increased, the dynamics of the situation demands another trial if it is still possible. Or perhaps a new and worse situation has been precipitated—which amounts to the same thing: a recognition by the group that the first trial was a mistake, and something else must be done. Still, the expected split dynamics holds of the charge for the norm that charges the trial also.

6. The cultural pattern, like the personality structure, institutes two types of norms: institutions, including religion, that demand conformity; and the maximum of cultural integration. The trials for the former are social acts occurring in a social situation involving a cultural institution. The trials for the latter are the institutions themselves, and cultural lag is the indication of inadequate integration. The dynamics here are the institutionalized social sanctions which are energized partly by the drives of the persons composing a society and partly by the forces of natural selection.

7. For natural selection, the norm is the continuance of an interbreeding population, which ordinarily signifies the continuance of the inherited characteristics of the species, but may signify the origin of a new species adapted to a new life zone. The trials are the individual offspring which are selected pro and con by natural selection. Among highly socialized species, however, the trials are the societies of coöperating organisms rather than the individual organisms themselves. For man (the only highly socialized docile species) the trials are chiefly his cultural patterns. Natural selection takes on the form of cultural selection. Again the same dynamic agency (here inheritance and adaptation instead of drives and drive reduction) that creates the trials (here the organisms or the societies) selects the fit and rejects the unfit, and persists as a tendency for the continuance of a life form.

Gathering together the results of this rapid survey, we are in a position to offer a more refined descriptive definition of a selective system than has been possible heretofore:

*A selective system is a structural process by which a unitary dynamic agency is channeled in such a way that it generates particular acts, dispositions, or objects (to be called 'trials'), and*

*also activates a specific selective agency (to be called 'the norm')
by which some of the trials are rejected and others are incorporated into the dynamic operation of the system.*

## 3. VALUES SELECTED BY SELECTIVE SYSTEMS

Having thus defined a selective system and described its operation, we have indicated a natural norm for values so far as this
norm bears on human decisions. But in describing the series of
selective systems in §2, we made no mention of values. Let us
now attach the values (as they are generally called) to these
selective systems viewed as natural norms.

A natural norm generates values in the sense that it evaluates
something by its selective action. It evaluates value facts, which
we shall call *selected values*. These can be truly described and
classified. A natural norm is also a fact—another sort of value fact,
a normative fact—in that it performs a normative function and also
can be described and classified. Such a description of value
norms is just what we were giving in describing selective systems
in §2. Now let us indicate the selected values generated by the
several selective systems.

There is a set of selected values that can be named for each
principal selective system listed in §2. From our study in the
preceding chapters we are familiar with them all. But they have
never been brought out in a row where we could look at them
side by side. Nor have we yet attached the selected values to
their respective selective systems, as it now appears we should
do, to establish their empirical status as specific value facts. Let
us, then, list the selected values generated by each of the principal selective systems.

1. The structure of a purposive act yields, by its selective activity, what we may call *conative-achievement values*. When
these were discussed in our detailed study of the structure of the
purposive act, we referred to them as two distinct sorts of purposive value. For it was clear that the interest school of value, including preëminently R. B. Perry, has, on the whole, regarded
conative value as value proper. Yet our analysis revealed another
evaluative criterion operative beside that for conation, namely,

achievement. At that time we did notice that conation and achievement are closely interrelated. Conation institutes a value, positive or negative, which achievement proceeds to realize. No achievement value would be possible unless it were instituted by a conative value (less technically: no achievement without a desire that seeks to be achieved). Nor would conative value ever be completed except through an achievement value. Each complements the other. Also we found that achievement value regularly legislates over conative value (chap. 14, §§5, 6, 8). But all those relationships were then worked over before we had fully taken in the significance of the concept of selective system for the understanding of the action of natural norms.

Now, looking back, we can see that neither conation nor achievement are attached to specific selective systems. The selective system which generates both together is a purposive structure. This structure, in its acceptance or rejection of subordinate acts, selects conative-achievement blocks of articulated acts. A subordinate act is initiated by conative references (anticipatory or apprehensive sets), which then, as quickly as possible, are followed out for their achievements; the realization of these conative references is accepted or rejected by superordinate conative references for further achievement. The values generated by a purposive structure as a natural norm are neither purely conative nor purely achievement, but the two wedded together. The separation of them is an empirical abstraction, and not falsifying unless we hypostatize for each a separate natural norm that cannot be empirically justified. The selected values generated by purposive structures are, then, conative-achievement values. Hereafter we shall refer to them more briefly as *achievement values*. An act of positive achievement is said to be successful; a failure, unsuccessful.

2. The values generated by the consummatory field are *affective values*. These are clearly separable from achievement values only in the consummatory field of an appetitive structure. The maximization of affective values in the consummatory field does not appear to be reducible to processes of achievement. Introspectively, pleasure is not obviously reducible to desire. Certain objective tests confirm this conclusion. Maneuvering for optimum

enjoyment in the consummatory field should not, therefore, be confused with the subordinate-superordinate act structure of an appetition. Consummatory pleasures, including gratuitous satisfactions, are distinct selected values.

In the riddance field of an aversion, however, which is structurally parallel to the consummatory field of an appetition, there seems to be no way of distinguishing the affective from the conative-achievement character of the act. Unpleasantness is indeed negative affection, but it is also automatically a stimulus for negative conation and immediate action for aversive achievement. There is, accordingly, no practical reason for speaking of the riddance field as a natural norm for negative affection. Maneuvering for optimum riddance is immediately telescoped into aversive achievement.

A positive affective value is commonly called pleasant; a negative one, unpleasant.

Since, in our analyses of purposive structures, we came upon the whole set of conative, achievement, and affective values, we lumped these together and called them *purposive values*. There is a practical use in this, for these are the values directly generated out of a docile organism's repertory of needs and drives. These are the values that come immediately out of such an organism's dynamic setup. Other values, from other selective systems, arise from a different mode of channeling and selection from these basic dynamic elements, or from a mingling of the internal dynamics of organisms with that of natural selection. Let us then nominally define purposive values as either conative-achievement values or affective values taken together.

3. The next of the principal selective systems listed was the personal situation. This yields what is commonly called *prudential values*. These are the acts resultant upon the mutual encounter of all the purposive values competing for achievement or satisfaction in an organism's or (if human) a person's life-space. The increased tension of the total situation induced by an imprudent act functions as a selective agency against imprudence and for prudence.

4. The personality as a selective system yields *character values*. In reference to the fulfillment of the demands of roles and of

conscience, these come out, in the terms G. G. Simpson employs (chap. 20), as instances of responsibility or irresponsibility. But these demands stress only one side of character values. The other side draws in the gratuitous satisfactions, and a richness of character that is consonant with wide adaptability rather than with strict adaptation. Since adaptability, rather than adaptation, is the predominantly human way of survival in man's life zone, an all-round man rather than a highly specialized duty-bound man would seem to have a biological sanction. At any rate, here in the human personality the biological rivalry between specialization and width of adaptability, including capacity for enjoyment, begins to be felt. The character values for the latter have lately come to be called 'personality integration.' A well-integrated personality is supposed to have the whole repertory of his purposive values available for use when a situation calls for any of them. This requires a firmly developed personality structure to maximize both achievement and enjoyment in terms of the reality of the situation. The selected values for a personality are not only acts, as with all the previous norms, but also dispositions for action.

5. The social situation yields *social values*. These are socially determined acts which are the resultants of the prudential values of all the persons involved in a social situation subject to modification by the dynamics of natural selection. Character values and cultural values are necessarily drawn into the resultant acts. The tensions in a social situation are the dynamic selective agency. An act which increases the tensions or fails to relieve them is rejected and another act is sought till the tensions are reduced. These acts—and there may be whole series of them to bring about the final solution of a problematic social situation— are often specifically called morally right or wrong. But economic values are included among the social values, and manners and propriety and some phases of aesthetic good taste, and a variety of other social acts which are not usually dignified with the name of moral values.

Moreover, some moralists tend to ascribe moral values primarily to human motives and character traits or to institutions and cultural patterns. Moral values are spread by different ethical systems over the whole gamut of selective systems, as will be explained more fully later (§8). There does not seem to be any term of common usage to denote specifically positive and negative social value as this is generated by the natural norm of the social situation. Nor have I any particularly felicitous term to suggest. So I shall just speak of social values as congenial or uncongenial social acts.

6. The cultural pattern as a selective system yields *cultural values*. These are of two sorts, parallel with the two sorts of character values generated by personality structure. There are the acts which are selected pro and con for their conformity to the dispositions making up the selective system; and there are the dispositions selected or modified pro and con in terms of their integrative capacities. For cultural pattern as a selective system, the first yield the values of acts (and here, it must be added, of personalities too who act) in respect to their conformity to the cultural institutions. The second yield the values of cultural institutions in respect to their harmoniousness with other institutions in a society, and also in respect to their adaptation or adaptability to the environment of the society. A person who fails to conform to an accepted institution is brought into line by the sanctions of the institution, *unless* the institution itself is exhibiting a cultural lag, and then the forces for integration will tend to support the nonconforming reformer and to modify or eliminate the institution. Here it is not only acts that are the selected values, as in the social situations, but persons as carriers of personality structures, and likewise institutions as cultural dispositions. Acts are corrected by cultural institutions if they fail to conform; persons are punished for nonconformity and rewarded for conformity; and institutions showing a cultural lag are changed. Thus acts, persons, and institutions get selectively evaluated through the dynamics of a cultural pattern as a natural norm.

7. Natural selection as a natural norm yields *survival values*. Here the evaluated objects of selection are organisms and social structures. In application to man, as we have seen, it is primarily the cultural pattern that is subject to selection for its survival value. We call such objects when positively selected, adapted or

adaptable; when negatively selected, unadapted or unadaptable.

The preceding list of selected values has been condensed in table 8. For a reason soon to be fully explained, I have this time placed affective values first. Conative-achievement values came first in our investigation, because we decided to consider purposive behavior first. But, as we have already seen, affective values have a legislative priority over conative-achievement values in an isolated purposive act. This is a very significant fact, and now that we are about to examine the lines of legislation followed by these selected values, this fact requires explicit acknowledgment in the manner of listing.

TABLE 8

| Selected values | Selective system | Positive and negative names for values |
|---|---|---|
| 1. Affective | Consummatory field and riddance field | Pleasant vs. unpleasant |
| 2. Conative-achievement | Structure of purposive act (appetitive or aversive) | Successful vs. unsuccessful |
| 3. Prudential | Personal situation | Prudent vs. imprudent |
| 4. Character | Personality structure | Personally responsible or integrated vs. personally irresponsible or unintegrated |
| 5. Social | Social situation | Socially congenial vs. socially uncongenial |
| 6. Cultural | Cultural pattern | Socially conforming or integrated vs. socially nonconforming or unintegrated |
| 7. Survival | Natural selection | Adapted or adaptable vs. unadapted or unadaptable |

## 4. LINES OF LEGISLATION AMONG SELECTED VALUES

If only one basic dynamic agency were operating upon selected values, there would be just one simple line of legislation. For instance, if affective values were the basic selected values, and the selective action of the consummatory and riddance fields was the basic selective system, then the line of legislation would run down from this selective system through the others. This would be the dominant selective system determining the mode of selection for all the other selective systems.

We have seen, however, that this is not the way in which the selective systems we have been describing work. Sometimes affective values are dominant, sometimes achievement values are dominant, and similarly with the selected values of the other selective systems. It is this inconstancy of legislative dominance that has made the value field so controversial. Different ethical writers pitch upon different selective systems as the systems to be dominantly legislative over all the others. On occasion each of the principal selective systems can be found to operate in this controlling manner. Then confusion arises from the fact that champions for each system can make about equally plausible claims. There are respectable schools of ethics pivoted on nearly every one of the principal selective systems.

Whenever we have been confronted with a serious difficulty in the course of this study, our consistent policy has been to observe carefully the empirical dynamics of the matter under consideration. What actually sanctions a choice or a decision? What precisely is the dynamics of the selection? So now let us ask what precisely are the dynamic agencies determining the legislative dominance of one selective system over another.

Approached in this way, the problem begins to clear up. There are, as we have seen, two main dynamic agencies operating among the seven principal selective systems. The one is the purposive drives of the individual organisms; the other is the reproductive process of an interbreeding population. The purposive drives are made up of riddance patterns and of impulse patterns with their correlative quiescence patterns or consummatory acts. The reproductive process is that of the transmission of genes and chromosomes through cell division. There are no other instigating dynamic agencies among the seven principal selective systems. What chiefly differentiates the various systems is the manner of channeling these two dynamic agencies for the selecting of their respective selected values. It turns out that each of the selective systems—except the first, yielding affective values, and the last, yielding survival values—is energized in some degree on some occasions by both dynamic agencies. This is what has caused the confusion in the value field.

Affective values are selected by pure drive dynamics. The repertory of drives with which an organism is endowed is given with the life of the organism. Natural selection has an overarching control over the survival of the organism, but, apart from gross organic maladaptation, the human socially oriented organism is thickly insulated from the direct impact of natural selection. It is a cultural pattern that is chiefly under trial for natural selection in the human species. A man's repertory of instinctive drives is thus essentially an independent dynamic agency in man. It spontaneously institutes the selective system of the consummatory and riddance fields to maximize affective values. In the consummatory field an impulse pattern maneuvers for the optimum of pleasant satisfaction. In the riddance field a riddance pattern acts for the speediest elimination of an unpleasant stimulus. This is all pure drive dynamics.

When we move up into the structure of a purposive act as a selective system, it does not seem at first that any new dynamic agency has come upon the scene. In terms of drive dynamics a purposive structure is instituted to guide the organism by means of subordinate acts to the attainment of consummatory satisfactions when these are not immediately offered by the environment at the emergence of an impulse pattern; or with aversions a purposive structure is instituted to guide the organism out of range of noxious objects when a riddance pattern is not automatically effective to this end. It would look as if the sole function of a purposive structure were to maximize affective values when this had to be done by means of subordinate instrumental acts.

The first inkling that this may not be the whole story comes when it is noticed that achievement value in man very often legislates over his affective values. This never happens, to be sure, with negative affective values because the minimizing of pain in the riddance field is automatically as speedy as possible and so automatically is a maximizing of achievement value. But speedy achievement of the reduction of an impulse pattern is not automatically the best way of maximizing enjoyment in the consummatory field. It is usually the worst way. Nevertheless, very often a man will act for maximum achievement at the sacrifice of considerable consummatory satisfaction, and this act seems to be fully sanctioned. This can only mean that the selective system for achievement value is legislating over that for affective value in the consummatory field.

However, perhaps this act was only conditional upon a maximizing of prudential values at the next level of selective systems. For prudence has reference to the total personal situation solely, it might be said, for the maximization of affective values. It is often prudent to sacrifice an immediate pleasure for a later one, to rush through a dinner at the station so as to catch the next train home. The legislative dominance of achievement value over an immediate consummatory value would then be dictated by the legislative dominance of prudential value, which, however, was still for maximizing affective values, but on a higher, more inclusive level.

It could also be indicated that the character values selected by a personality structure are such as to develop dispositions to maximize affective values for that person. According to this view, an integrated personality is one whose dispositions are so selected and organized as to give him the greatest amount of happiness in terms of pleasure and absence of unpleasantness.

In this sequence of evaluations we are obviously following the traditional movement of a hedonistic ethics. It goes along smoothly enough so far, except that it overlooks the dictates of a person's irrational conscience. This, however, may be set aside as something to be overcome by the substitution of a rational conscience, which will develop dispositions conducive to prudence in evaluating decisions.

The first really serious difficulty comes with the person's entrance into a social situation. Now prudence no longer works consistently as a dominant selective system. One person's prudence has to adjust itself to another's. In situations of simple trading, two experienced prudent traders can make a deal to their mutual advantage. But this sort of situation is exceptional. Usually, in a social situation, the maximizing of affective values for all the persons concerned demands sacrifices for some persons.

Sometimes these sacrifices would be imprudent acts for the person involved were he not acculturated to accept, or perhaps even conscientiously to welcome, the sacrifice for the general welfare. Now we begin to feel the force of the other dynamic agency in human evaluation. The pressure of a cultural pattern is now making itself felt as legislatively dominant over a social situation and the persons involved in it. Social conformity overrules the maximization of affective values at least some of the time, and in some societies most of the time. The best the hedonist can do now is to urge individuals to get as much happiness as they can within the restrictions of an unpropitious social system, and then as a reformer to do his best to change the social pattern so as to maximize as much as possible the affective values for the persons involved.

But it may be that the system is required for the survival of the group in its particular environment. Then we encounter without escape the legislative dominance of the dynamics of natural selection. And now, tracing this line of legislation back through the seven selective systems, we find it making its way into all of them but the first.

The survival values of natural selection as a natural norm are, of course, determined by the dynamics for the adaptation of the species to its life zone or for its adaptability for filling some other available life zone. The dynamics of affective values is not in any way legislative over natural selection. Like the wings of wasps, a repertory of purposive drives is an adaptive feature for a species in some particular life zone. But natural selection as a selective system does not make its selections to maximize happiness for its creatures, but to secure their adaptation for survival in a life zone. There is no element of purposive drive dynamics in the dynamics of natural selection. The selective system for survival values is energized solely by the dynamics of reproductive survival.

In the cultural pattern as a selective system, however, we find the dynamics of survival operating in conjunction with purposive drive dynamics. It is upon cultural patterns, as we saw in chapter 20, that natural selection chiefly operates in the human species. The selective action of survival dynamics will thence inevitably be reflected in pressures upon social acts in the social situation. If environmental conditions are such that these pressures are continuous, they will be reflected through acculturation in modifications of the personality structures of the individuals within the society.

The irrational conscience seems to have been biologically adaptive as a means of binding an individual into his social pattern. The presence of irrational conscience in the structure of a personality is thus mute evidence of the infiltration of the dynamics of survival into the interior motivation of the individual. Survival value thereby embeds a cultural pattern in the very body of an individual. In a less spectacular way a rational conscience would do the same thing. The pressure of conscience, whether rational or irrational, would then make itself felt in any personal situation which involved cultural factors. Survival value thus finds its way all the way down to the personal situation.

It finally has its effect on achievement values by means of cultural pressures coming to bear on the personal situation. One of the reasons why a person will let achievement values legislate over his consummatory satisfactions is the pressure of conscience, which gets much of its dynamics all the way back to its ultimate source in survival value.

Only affective values are in their selection free from the dynamics of natural selection. But the selective system for affective values is frequently subject to the selective dominance of natural selection operating through cultural conformity and conscience. For, while it is true that the selective system for affective values operates altogether independently of survival value or the pressures for survival transmitted through other selective systems, still it is possible for these survival pressures so to dominate a situation that the selective system for affective value is shut off and completely blocked from operating to maximize its selected values.

The principle revealed here is an important one for evaluation: when the survival of a group is at stake, the dynamics for survival values legislates over that for affective values. Affective values have an independence of operation only on sufferance.

Only as long as the pressures for group survival are held at a distance, so that they do not make themselves felt very strongly (or perhaps, under propitious conditions, not at all), are affective values free to maximize themselves without interference from the dynamics of survival.

## 5. Resulting Strategy for Maximizing Human Values

The strategy for man, who can to a considerable degree control situations, is hereby laid out with realistic clarity. Constituted as he is, a docile animal endowed through his inherited repertory of drives with a capacity for happiness (for maximizing pleasures as well as minimizing pains), he *naturally* (in the literal sense of the term) has a bias for maximizing affection and satisfying his own basic drives. But he can achieve much happiness for himself only if he can keep the pressures from survival values at a distance.

In the simplest terms, this dynamic interplay, or even opposition, between the demand of human drives for satisfaction and the demand of the evolutionary forces for survival is commonly referred to as the problem of impulse versus duty. This is surely an oversimplification, for there would still be duties on a purely prudential basis, even if the satisfaction of drives were all that had to be considered in human evaluations. The dynamics of the affective selective system would still make it a man's duty to act so as to maximize affection and not yield to the impulse of the moment. But the stern call of duty is not of this prudential sort. It comes from somewhere far outside a man's own drives (except as he finds this duty in his irrational conscience, but we now know where that comes from). The relegation of this stern duty to a supernatural source or to the sanction of some unempirical form of a priori intuition is not surprising. If a man does not know where this strong duty comes from, yet can feel and observe its inexorable power, what more likely than for him to invent an imaginary source for it?

But when he sees where it comes from and can understand why it is indeed inexorable wherever the pressure for human survival is severe, man can take measures to keep it mild and distant through his control of himself, his society, and his environment.

At the same time, man must not get the idea that he can entirely escape it, or that the survival values are not as much a part of him as the affective values. The dynamics of survival are just as deeply implanted in his body and behavior as the repertory of drives that give him his capacity for happiness. He is both a docile animal with drives and a social human animal conveying an inheritance to the next generation of his species.

Two ways for a man to increase his satisfactions and keep the pressures of survival at a distance have been discovered and tried out from antiquity. One is for a man to retire personally from the world's pressures as far as he can, and perhaps be willing to accommodate himself to few satisfactions provided he escape from the irritations of society and its frustrating duties. The extreme of this way of life is that of the hermit and the solitary mystic. In a qualified form it was recommended by the Epicurean school and similar schools of moral advice. This is the method of escape, and may work after a fashion. Under desperate social conditions, when a society is disintegrating and the individual is oppressed or ignored, it may even be the most realistic advice for individual men to follow. But human survival follows another more culture-bound course, a course which recognizes that cultural selection will inevitably operate in its own time.

This other course—and, for the docile and social animal that man is, the more realistic means of increasing his happiness and keeping the impact of survival pressures at a distance—is through social control. Since natural selection applied to man turns out to be mainly cultural selection, the obvious way for man to guarantee his survival and that of his group is to control his cultural pattern so that his society can be secure and then, on the base of this security, to obtain the maximum of satisfaction possible. If man does not control his social organization for his own security and happiness, he is simply letting his society meet the impact of adaptation to its environment the hard way. Cultural selection will inevitably force upon a cultural pattern changes which a society either accepts and so adapts to the environing conditions, or fails to accept and perishes as a society. That is the hard way. The more congenial way is to use intelligent foresight in social organization with a view to developing a social structure so well adapted to its conditions that the pressures for cultural survival will not disturb it and men can turn their attention to the attainment of the greatest happiness for the greatest number who will accept shelter within the social structure.

This is the social way of attaining happiness and keeping the survival pressures at a distance. This is the only way that will work for large groups of men, and with promise of a fairly enduring happiness. It is the intelligent employment of the methods of survival for man, to hold the pressures of survival at a distance so that a group of men can cultivate happiness behind their social fortifications of defense. It is just the opposite of the way of escape, which is the way of desperation, and cannot become very enduring or attain a socially solid assurance of widespread satisfaction.

The need for a socially intelligent mode of social organization is more than ever pressing today, when recently invented instruments of destruction, if left socially uncontrolled, could perhaps destroy the whole human population. Up till now, neglect of intelligent social control could lead to one society's perishing at the hands of another, or by the gentler means of being transformed through cultural diffusion. Through cultural selection, the less adapted societies perished and the more adapted survived. Thus formerly there was a certainty that some human group with a cultural pattern would survive, whether societies exhibited social intelligence or not. But today there is a practical certainty that unless the societies possessing the modern highly destructive instruments employ methods of social intelligence for the control of these instruments, there will be no human societies left for adaptation.

What, then, are the principal types of social organization open to intelligent human choice? For it appears that these are now the evaluative objects of greatest concern to mankind not only for the maximizing of human happiness but for man's very survival.

## 6. Types of Social Organization Controlling Human Values

Since man is probably the most adaptable of animals, we should plausibly expect him to develop the most adaptable forms of social organization. But this does not seem to be the general rule. Most human societies have been exceedingly rigid in their cultural pattern and have exemplified a specialized adaptation to a particular environment rather than adaptability to a wide range of changing conditions. Moreover, many customs that do not seem to have any obvious adaptive value get locked in a cultural pattern and persist with remarkable inertia. Rigidity rather than adaptability seems characteristic of most human cultural patterns. This has been often noted in primitive societies. It has not been much different in civilized societies.

Roughly speaking, most civilized societies can be divided into two types: the *authoritarian* (or functional) and the *individualistic*. Both of these exhibit adaptation rather than adaptability. The earlier forms of civilization seem to have been mainly, if not uniformly, authoritarian. The individualistic forms appear to be a later development. Absolute monarchies and totalitarian forms of government are authoritarian; nontotalitarian democracies are individualistic. The authoritarian (or functional) forms justify themselves in terms of survival values; the individualistic forms, in terms of affective values. Plato's *Republic* has frequently been regarded as the classical exposition of the ideals of a secure and duty-bound functional society. Locke's political writings and those of John Stuart Mill represent the ideals of an individualistic liberty-seeking society.

Thus, among civilized peoples, two opposite ideals of civilized society are common, and each has an empirical justification in the basic dynamics of human values. For the one is based on the dynamics of human drives yielding the affective values; the other, on the dynamics of human security in social organization, based on natural selection, yielding the survival values. The main traits of these two ideals for civilized society are listed side by side in table 9.

TABLE 9

| Functional authoritarian society | Individualistic democratic society |
| --- | --- |
| 1. Survival as dominant motive | 1. Happiness as dominant motive |
| 2. Basic right of society over individual | 2. Basic right of individuals and instrumental view of society |
| 3. Centralization in government | 3. Decentralization in government |
| 4. Efficiency as chief aim of social organization | 4. Opportunity for individual enterprise and satisfaction as aim of social organization |
| 5. Discipline or team-play as social attitudes sought | 5. Initiative or tolerance as social attitudes sought |
| 6. Duty or loyalty as personal attitudes sought | 6. Satisfaction or compromise as personal attitudes sought |

That the two systems are antithetical is obvious from a comparison of the two columns. The basic right of society over the individual runs contrary to the basic rights of individuals and the instrumental treatment of social organization, and so on down. That the concepts of each set are internally consistent and demand one another is also fairly clear.

For if survival is the underlying motive, men must organize for power. But organization for power calls for social efficiency, which calls for centralization of government, which demands the subordination of the individual to the social organization, and that means the basic right of the society. The subordination of the individual to the demands of efficient organization is achieved, if necessary, by discipline, but preferably without compulsion in the manner of team play. Discipline develops a sense of duty in the individual, but preferably he should act from a sense of loyalty, in the voluntary efficiency of team play. If loyalty cannot be counted on, discipline is invoked and duty demanded. All these concepts follow from the underlying demand for survival.

But if happiness is taken as the dominant motive, or the attainment of the greatest amount of satisfaction, then the rights of individuals become basic because satisfactions have their seat in the bodies of individual men. When impulses conflict, it follows that compromise will be instituted, so that the greatest amount of mutual satisfaction may ensue. It follows also that men will be tolerant of one another's satisfactions, and will be encouraged to use initiative in finding their own satisfactions, since no one knows better than the man himself what will please him most. From this it follows that opportunity will be given for men to find their satisfactions, and that there will be a minimum of interference. Lastly, it follows that a government will be instituted simply to guard against interference—that is, to guarantee opportunity, and tolerance, and compromise, and, if necessary, forcibly to protect the rights of individuals. Ideally there would be no government. But since experience shows that there must be some social organization to guarantee fair play, the less of it the better, and what there is should be well protected against itself to see that no man gets in a position of power to seize more than his share of satisfactions. The result is a decentralized form of government with checks and balances and the sovereignty carried back as directly as possible to the people.

The farther we get into the details of the two systems, the more closely their respective features knit together, and consequently the more distinct and opposed they become.

It can readily be seen that both ideals are relatively rigid and dogmatic and unadaptable. Each is dogmatic especially in regard to its basic dynamics. What is man if he is not a social animal strong only through the efficiency of his social relationships? On the dynamics of survival, the functional authoritarian ideal is unimpeachable. But likewise what is man if not a person with individual capacities for satisfaction giving him an inalienable right to liberty and happiness in the life at his disposal? And on the dynamics of his innate drives, this individualistic ideal is likewise unimpeachable.

What is not noticed by the exponent of each of these ideals is that each ideal is appropriate (I may even legitimately say adapted) to only a particular sort of situation. When there is great social pressure upon a society, the functional authoritarian ideal is appropriate, as in time of war. A functional authoritarian society has a great advantage over an individualistic society in speed of decision, control of the army, discipline of the people, efficiency of supply, and the like. An individualistic society can compete successfully only by taking on the features of a functional society under such conditions.

However, a functional authoritarian society is inappropriate and unadapted for long conditions of peace and prosperity. When men can see no reason for the imposition of authority, and the infringement on their freedom and on the potential satisfaction of their drives, they are frustrated, prepared to rebel, and threaten the stability of the authoritarian pattern. A clever and unprincipled ruler will even instigate trouble so as to create a social pressure to justify his authoritarian structure.

The obvious solution for the conflict of ideals is an adjustable social structure, one that can be centralized in authority during emergencies, and decentralized to make way for liberty and opportunity for individual satisfaction in times of peace and safety. We have seen the advisability of the adjustable type of society on two or three occasions already. Actually, the individualistic democracies of the Western world have been operating on that basis semideliberately for a century or more. Only so have they been able to survive against the onslaught of a most effective and resourceful totalitarian society in their environment. But these societies have not taken the full measure of their procedures, or institutionalized them effectively, or lifted them before their people as the features of a new social ideal that is as superior to dogmatic individualism (not to mention dogmatic authoritarianism) as adjustability is superior to rigid adaptation.

The adjustable society for a civilized culture is a social invention of a new era. It amounts to a new social species in the evolutionary history of man. It is the intelligent society, which bids fair to supplant all other forms of society from competition in its life zone, just as adjustable man through his purposive behavior has eliminated all effective competition from other organic forms in his life zone.

Just what features would distinguish the adjustable society? Its social aim would be to maximize happiness, subject to the legislation of human survival values over affective values. It would seek to keep issues of survival and the pressures for survival as far away as possible. It would, therefore, under present world conditions, seek to organize all men into one society (without, however, destroying subcultural differences) in order to eliminate cutthroat competition among human societies. It would probably soon have to consider means of limiting populations, to preserve man from the social effects of population pressures which are sure to invoke survival values and drive out affective values. It would do these things by regulatory social mechanisms administered by experts. Just what these would be or how they would operate to go on and off as needed is the experimental task of the generations ahead. But we have the tentative beginnings of such regulatory mechanisms in the numerous boards of state and federal regulation now in action, and in such institutions as the Federal Reserve Bank of the United States.

The inducement for men the world over to create such a society is strong. It is nothing less today than the survival of the human interbreeding population.

## 7. Demarcation of the Field of Values

With the preceding description of the lines of legislation among the selective systems, the task of making a survey of the field of values is completed. For the lines of legislation among the selective systems constitute the connective relations which bind the selective systems together and gather them into a single field of interconnected values.

At the beginning of this study we presented an ostensive common sense definition of the field of values. This was a list naming a great variety of things that are customarily included among values. It was a heterogeneous list. How could all those items be brought into order? The method of reduction has often been tried, the method of singling out some one element and seeking to reduce all other items to this one. This has never been worked out successfully in the value field. The method of generalization, too, has often been tried, the method of looking for some common quality in which all the items shared. And this too has never yet succeeded in drawing in all the items which competent students have thought should be included in the value field. The method of exclusion has often been resorted to in order to render the use of the previous two methods plausible. On occasion the exclusion of certain meanings of a term is legitimate, but an arbitrary verbal stipulation can never eliminate an actually observable connection between items in an empirical inquiry. We entertained the possibility that there was no field of values whatever, and that the term, together with its synonyms, was an ambiguous term enveloping heterogeneous items having no significant relations among them. This possibility seemed unlikely, and our inquiry has strengthened this belief. Another possibility was that many of the items were indeed heterogeneous but nevertheless interconnected in ways that did demarcate a determinate field of values. This possibility we believe our preceding inquiry has shown to be the correct one.

The connective agency that operates in the value field is what we have been calling a *selective system*. Each selective system binds together a considerable number of items from the common sense list, and sometimes reveals other items not clearly discriminated before. Each selective system institutes a norm for its selected values, together with the selected values themselves, and indicates numerous potential values (conditional objects and potential objects of value) which are also customarily and legitimately included within the value field. These various selective systems might have been found to operate quite independently of each other. Actually, however, we have found that they are intimately and dynamically interconnected. And this legislative dynamic interconnection among the various selective systems is what constitutes a single field of empirically related objects, appropriately called the *field of values*. Items within this field are appropriately described as good or bad according to the action of these selective systems operating as natural norms and dynamically selecting among them pro and con. There are as many different kinds of good and bad as there are kinds of selective systems selecting pro and con.

This point deserves to be stressed. For some may be led to the conclusion that our account institutes two basic values—affective and survival—to which all other values are reducible, or, indeed, to one basic value, since, under pressure, survival value legislates over affective value. The question could well be just one of words. For the facts are clear enough, if we observe and describe them in sufficient detail.

If we identify value with the instigating dynamics of selection, there are only two distinct dynamic sources of this kind, two instigating dynamic values, if you will. If, however, we identify value with the dynamic source which has ultimate legislative power over all other agencies in time of stress, then there will be only survival value. But affective value is not reduced to survival value through the foregoing observation. Affective value still makes its normative claims, but in emergency the normative claims of survival value are prepotent, and similarly with all the other selective systems. The normative action of a cultural pattern is subject to the legislative control of either survival value or affective value when it exhibits a cultural lag, but it makes its claims in its own selective manner just the same, and has an area of freedom of its own before a cultural lag is felt. Conformity to cultural pattern is not reducible without residue to either affective or survival values.

So I am holding, on the grounds of the evidence submitted, that each selective system constitutes a normative value in its own right. There are, accordingly, as many types of normative value as there are types of selective systems. And since every selective system generates selected values through its selective action, there are as many types of selected values as there are types of selective systems.

I return, then, to my original statement that there are as many different kinds of good and bad as there are kinds of selective system selecting pro and con. These are what we have been observing and describing.

Values are thus as much open to description as any other objects or events in the natural world. These descriptions are verifiable so far as relevant data are at hand, and the search for further data is of the same order as the search for further data in any other empirical inquiry. In spite of the length of this book, all that the present study has done or could expect to do is to direct attention to this empirical field of values, show where a quantity of relevant data are already to be found, suggest hypotheses for later confirmation, and solicit interest in seeking out more data and developing more refined hypotheses. From this empirical study of values reliable predictions can be anticipated, and accordingly the possibility of a rational and humane guidance of man's social relations and personality development can also be anticipated.

Another comment can now be made which may help to clarify a quantity of verbal problems that have gathered about the terms 'value,' 'good,' 'bad,' and their equivalents. These common terms could now be dispensed with and nothing of empirical consequence would be lost, though many rich literary connotations would vanish, as always happens when a word with a long literary history is abandoned. However, I am not recommending the abandonment of these terms. They are still, and probably always will be, the linguistically most convenient terms to use because they are the most familiar.

But what I am pointing out is that through our study we have acquired a number of fairly refined technical terms which can free us from being tied to the meanings of ordinary language. We can now use our language to conform to the facts instead of trying to find facts (sometimes hypostatizing them as G. E. Moore did his 'indefinable good') to conform to the language. Not but that linguistic studies may frequently bring to light empirical discriminations that have been overlooked. But too often the empirical approach to values has been blocked and side-tracked by disputes over linguistic references and connotations.

Let us look again at our list of the principal selective systems and their selected values (table 9). In place of 'good' and 'bad' we could, if we wished, now always use the more precise pair of terms in the extreme right-hand column. Some value paradoxes will then automatically disappear. Suppose the question is raised whether pleasure can be equated with 'good' or appropriately called positive value. Our answer is that pleasure is positive affection as selected by the selective system for affection. No mention of 'good' or 'value' is necesasry. To the argument that if anyone identifies good with pleasure he can mean only the empty tautology that pleasure is pleasure, our answer is that pleasure is positive affection, and this is often called 'good,' but so is successful achievement often called 'good,' which is a selection derived from a distinctly different selective system. Drop the term 'good' and the paradox and the tautology both disappear. For pleasure as positive affection is not likely to be confused with success as positive achievement. Positive achievement, as we know, does not always lead to pleasure—not ever in a simple aversive achievement. Drop the term 'good' and all ambiguities vanish and nothing of empirical import is lost.

Or suppose, with pleasure understood as good, somebody asks if pleasure is ever really better than success and whether pleasure is not sometimes *bad*. This sounds very paradoxical. But in our more refined terms this question turns out simply to be whether the natural norm for affection ever legislates over that for achievement, and whether pleasure is not sometimes negatively selected in a personal situation in terms of prudence. Again there is no need to use the terms 'good' and 'value,' and the confusions vanish as soon as these terms are eliminated. For without them we are referred directly to the facts—to the natural norms and their selected entities.

Then why not do without these terms? Because they are convenient. And because it is safer to keep them equated with the various selective systems than floating loose where ingenious men may note their freedom from attachment and proceed to hypostatize facts for them to refer to. However, we can obviate much ambiguity by always qualifying them with the selective system we have in mind when employing them. So we have consistently spoken of 'affective values,' 'achievement values,' 'prudential values,' and never of values *simpliciter* except as an enveloping term to cover the various types of selected entities. The same with 'good' and 'bad.' There is the 'pleasantly good,' the 'successfully good,' and so on to the 'adaptively good,' but there is no simple unqualified 'good.'

If we wished to define the application of the term 'good' as a result of this study, it would refer to a positive selection by a selective system relevant to human decisions, and 'bad' would refer similarly to a negative selection. The term 'value' would refer to all selections by a selective system that are relevant to human decisions and all such natural norms. By extension the terms 'value,' 'good,' and 'bad' could cover also any other selections pro or con by selective systems relevant to human decisions, even when these selections do not bear on human behavior. Thus all purposive selections would be values whether performed by men or by other docile animals. And all instances of natural selection would be survival values whether bearing on the human species or on other living species. If there are selective systems beyond the threshold of life, these systems and their selections are not, according to the present study, referred to as values.

## 8. Final Reference to Usage and Tradition Concerning Values

In §7 we referred to the common sense test definition of value given at the beginning of our study. Before this study is completed, we should consider whether all the items in the list have been taken care of; and, if any have been omitted, whether we are content to leave them so in the light of the final demarcation of the value field reached in §7.

If we now look back at the list in table 9, we notice that practically all the common sense value items are obviously lodged, and often much elaborated upon, in our descriptions of the various selective systems. Some of the less obvious items deserve a bit of comment, however.

Very little has been said about the term 'preference.' This will be the more noticeable since a number of writers on value appear to make it their pivotal value concept. From our study such a procedure would seem unfortunate, for it tends to fuse significant distinctions.

Preference is a selective act. On our view there would be as many sorts of preference as there are sorts of selection by different selective systems. Preference would also be exhibited in the legislation of one selective system over another.

Statistical summaries of human preferences are, for these reasons, often entirely valueless. They become significant only when the particular mechanism of selection has been identified, the selective system which determines that one and only one norm of selection is in operation. Preferences have thus by no means been neglected in our study. The term is absorbed in our uses of the terms 'selection' and 'legislation,' and the term 'preference' is less specific than the latter terms. 'Preference' is often a convenient term when we wish to refer loosely to some act of selection without specifying the mode of selection. The concept of preference is open to criticism only when it is assumed to be an ultimate value concept not open to, or requiring, more specific analysis.

The item 'reality' turns out to be an important factor in the value field by virtue of the concept of the reality of the situation, which comes in wherever mediating judgments are involved in instrumental acts. It is also one of the normative factors in personal and social situations, and in adaptation for survival values.

Speaking of reality, what about truth and falsity? Are these values? This is a debated question. On our view, they are definitely values. They are derived from the structure of a purposive drive—that part of the structure concerned with cognitive sets. All human judgments in action are cognitive sets. A true judgment is a cognitive set that serves for the attainment of its superordinate appetitive goal or (*when tested*) for the avoidance of a superordinate object of apprehension; a false judgment is one that fails to perform this services and thus delays achievement. This is the original source of the selective distinction between truth and falsity. The selection arises out of a selective system, an intrinsic feature of a purposive structure. As such, the distinction of true from false cognitive sets is definitely a value distinction.

But this distinction is so important in its bearing on human cultural relationships and human adaptation that it has been enormously elaborated. Conditional objects of truth value have been developed on a stupendous scale. For the various sciences are such conditional objects. They are symbolic systems of potentially serviceable cognitive sets. Then these systems are submitted to scrutiny to discover tests that can be relied upon to produce potentially serviceable cognitive sets. These tests come to be known as truth criteria. If there is a discrepancy of views regarding these criteria, the views become diverse theories of truth. Systems of interconnected true judgments develop also. These systems develop criteria of consistency and principles of valid reasoning. All these criteria are interrelated as various sorts of conditional objects of value or as potential objects of value. But they all find their source in the dynamic selection of the correct from the incorrect cognitive sets within purposive structures. Originating and functioning as they do within selective systems, they all fall within the value field.

Beauty and ugliness, the aesthetic values, are clearly included in the value field. But I am somewhat surprised, in looking back, to note that I have no section or chapter heading for them. Possibly because I have dealt with them so fully elsewhere,[1] I have turned my attention mainly to other sorts of values in this study. But all references to the maximizing of affective value in the consummatory field are references to aesthetic values, even if not so named. And there have been other references to aesthetic values (in the operation of the fatigue and habituation mutations, for instance). There is, moreover, an art of relief as well as an art of delight. The former figures prominently in religious art. Many of the cultural patterns of both primitive and civilized peoples are made up of institutionalized aesthetic behavior. Though these have been slighted in this study, let this paragraph act as at least a recognition of the fact, and as a tardy gesture of compensation.

Economic and religious values have received explicit attention, and their place in the field of value has been made clear. One aspect of the concept of God, however, has not been touched upon, and should be, to show we have not been unmindful of the exponents of a theological ethics. The concept of God is plainly interpreted as a derivative concept in the preceding study. In this study, anything in the nature of a transcendent personal being stationed outside nature as its creator and guide is taken to be unlikely. And the evidence of revelation frequently adduced to support such a belief is regarded as dogmatic in type and unreliable in the light of its employment in the past. But the following should also be pointed out in relation to our study. If such a Being does exist and His will and acts are relevant to human decisions, then He would clearly be a selective system in His acts of judgment relative to man. According to such theological doctrine, He would be the supreme selective system legislating over all others. In short, there is nothing in the conception of selective systems as the source of values that is inconsistent with a theological ethics which gives the will of God the supreme sanction over all human values. For the will of God, like the conscience of man, would be a selective system. It is merely that this study, out of respect for its standards for the testing of evidence, does not find the evidences for a transcendent supremely legislative selective system sufficient to warrant belief.

If, then, God is interpreted as an added selective system transcendent to those described in the present study, He is omitted from the value field not from any inconsistency between the concept of such a God and the concept of selective system but merely from a questioning of the evidence for His reality. But if He is interpreted as a derivative concept, central to religion treated as a cultural institution, which in the past has apparently contributed to human social survival, then God has been already included as a value concept in this study.

So, as far as the common sense test definition goes, our final demarcation of the value field seems to be sufficiently inclusive of the items listed. Our refined definition proves to be continuous with the common usage of value terms.

An even better test of a continuity of subject matter would be that of seeing how the traditional theories of ethics (as typical of value studies) tie into our analysis. The principal traditional theories of ethics are: (1) the hedonistic or pleasure theory, (2) the self-realizationist theory, (3) the pragmatic or problematic situation theory, (4) the cultural relativist theory, (5) the evolutionary ethical theory, and (6) various varieties of intuitionist and a priori duty theories.

The first five are definitely empirical in outlook and should find their places in our empirical account. Each of the five traditional empirical theories takes one of our principal selective systems as a value base, and attempts to make it legislate universally over all the others. Virtually every one of our principal selective systems has been treated in this way.

1. The typical hedonism takes affective and achievement values for its content, not distinguishing between them very clearly, and then takes the personal situation as its evaluative base. The theory recognizes that the prudential values legislate over the pleasures, the pains, and the desires which enter into the personal situation. It did not till lately notice that there is a distinction between pleasure (affective value) and desire (conative-achievement value), and that each of these has its distinctive selective system and evaluative operation. The issue within the interest theory of value (which is the most recent offspring of traditional hedonism), whether pleasure or desire is to be taken as the ultimate value element, amounted to a recognition of two natural norms for these elements. Meinong and Prall, for instance, took affection as legislating over conative-achievement. Ehrenfels and R. B. Perry took conative-achievement as legislating over affection.

On our view (§4) both groups are right, depending on the dynamics of the situation. If the social pressure is light, the lines of legislation originate in the drives and have their origin in the affective values. If the social pressure is strong, the lines of legislation originate in the survival values and give precedence to achievement over affective values. But thereafter, on either alternative, the resolution of conflicting interests is regarded as carried on by the selective operation of the personal situation. The pivotal system for both the older hedonistic theories and the later interest theories is the personal situation and the elaboration of the evaluative procedures of prudence.

For the prudential values these theories have been most illuminating. They have run into trouble whenever they attempted to extend the evaluative dynamics of the prudential values into the social situation. Immediately a dynamic gap opened up between egoistic and universalistic hedonism. The dynamic procedures which sanction prudence for the individual just did not factually carry over into the social situation to sanction the greatest happiness of the greatest number. In despair over the possibility of bridging this gap by empirical sanctions, Sidgwick, one of the most clearheaded of the traditional hedonists, gave up and resorted to an a priori appeal to self-evident principles to bridge the gap. The trouble arose from his trying to make individual drive dynamics and the personal situation as a selective system legislate over all other selective systems. There were other selective systems in the value field and there was another dynamic source in the survival values.

But for our present purpose we need only note that the hedonic and interest theories of value are fully taken care of in our account.

2. The traditional self-realization theory of ethics takes as its pivotal selective system the integrative action of the personality structure. This is something that traditional hedonism does not pay much attention to. From personality integration, the self-realizationist theory passes a little too easily into cultural integration, as if this were all one evaluative process, which it is not. When we go into the details, we find that both the mode of integration and the content are different in the two evaluative systems. But all these materials are well taken account of in our analysis.

3. Pragmatic ethics takes the social situation as the evaluative point of departure. We called attention to this fact when we were describing the social situation as a selective system (chap. 18, §5). We showed just how far we thought the Deweyan analysis was acceptable and where we thought it exceeded its evaluative capacities. Dewey's end-means continuum is the device by which he hoped to extend the sanctioning power of the social situation as a selective system over all other selective systems. Our criticism was that this device concealed the articulations of purposive dynamics in which drives really do get reduced and attain a terminal consummatory satisfaction. Dewey's concentration on the social situation thus distorted his treatment of the personal situation and of the selective systems associated with the conative-achievement and the affective values. It also kept him from distinguishing clearly between the evaluative operation of a cultural pattern and of a social situation, and, for all his emphasis on the biological aspect of human values, it restrained him from working out an evolutionary conception of values which would have revealed the survival values. But again

all we have to note is that the contribution of pragmatic ethics is fully taken account of by our analysis.

4. Cultural relativism as an ethical theory takes the cultural pattern as its central selective system, stressing particularly the demand for conformity to social institutions. This type of ethical theory tends to understress the integrative aspects of the cultural pattern as a selective system, and also the way in which this dynamic tendency leads into adaptation and adaptability. It is clear that this type of ethical theory has been fully incorporated in our analysis.

5. The evolutionary theory, of course, takes natural selection as its pivotal selective system. We have particularly insisted upon the relevancy of the contributions of this ethical theory to the value field. It affords one of the essential dynamic sources of value in our analysis.

6. This leaves only the intuitional and a priori theories. Their mode of cognitive appeal to the various suggested sanctions of certainty—self-evidence, indubitability, and the like—we reject as cognitively unreliable. We hold to the empirical methods only. And we willingly accept the conditions attached to these methods, that hypotheses and the evidence supporting them are all subject to critical scrutiny and in that sense are never more than highly probable or practically certain—never self-evident or indubitable.

However, the content of these theories is well covered by our analysis, and even the authoritarian and indefeasible appearance of this content is accounted for. For it is to conscience and the stern voice of duty that these theories chiefly make their appeal. The mysterious power of irrational conscience we traced to its roots in the repressed system of the personality structure. And we saw how conscience reflects and is reciprocally reflected in the culturally sanctioned institutions of a man's social environment, particularly his religion, and how the survival values dynamically sanction these cultural values without men being fully aware of the source of their sense of obligation. Nothing then was more natural than that men should believe that this voice of duty was supernaturally sanctioned or sanctioned by some inner intuition or a priori logical certainty. Man's sense of another dynamic agency beyond his drives is justified, we believe, but on our account this other dynamic agency is a natural one, as empirically cognizable as a man's drives and consummatory pleasures: nothing other than the reproductive dynamics of the life process manifesting itself in the survival mechanisms of the human species.

Thus all these ethical views of our philosophical tradition are taken up into our analysis, and their sources of justification shown, and their limitations, on our hypothesis, made evident.

It may be added for completeness that each of these ethical treatments of value has its corresponding aesthetic treatment. (1) There is a hedonistic aesthetic theory. (2) There is an integrative aesthetic theory stressing an organic interdetermination for the work of art, a creative imagination for the artist, and an imaginative re-creation for the spectator. (3) There is the vivid realization of the total fused quality of a given situation for pragmatic aesthetics. (4) There is a cultural relativism of styles of art as evaluative criteria of aesthetic expression. (5) There are aesthetic theories stressing criteria of health and normality which gain their sanction from the survival values. Even if we have not called attention to these, they are all implicitly taken account of within the field of values we have descriptively defined.

The continuity of our present analysis with the common sense and traditional field of value subject matter seems sufficiently well established. The field here demarcated does, however, extend farther than is usual for common sense and the philosophical tradition. For our analysis takes the evaluative dynamics of natural selection seriously, and this automatically draws into the value field all instances of evolutionary adaptation. However, according to a fairly wide usage, adaptation is recognized as good and maladaptation as bad. But more to the point, there is no question as to the facts of the matter, that natural selection is a selective system normatively selecting pro and con, and that in its operation as a natural norm it is one of the principal selective systems bearing upon human decisions.

The guiding maxim for any empirical approach to values is to seek out the natural sanctions for values. What specifically are the agencies that sanction evaluative criteria and institute values, positive or negative, through their action? These are the things to keep looking for. Whatever they are, they are what empirically verify evaluative judgments about values, and confirm an empirical theory of values. Follow the dynamics of values wherever they may lead. For it is only the dynamics of values that can guide a man to the natural norms and show him the lines of legislation running through them.

# Notes

# Notes

## Notes to Chapter 1

[1] For instance, S. C. Pepper, *World Hypotheses* (Berkeley and Los Angeles: University of California Press, 1942), chap. ii.

[2] This phase of the emotive judgment school, so far as it stipulates that the imperative is the verbal expression of a feeling such as pleasure or desire, virtually identifies value with pleasure or desire. The verbalizing of the emotion in the emotive expression is incidental. The value lies in what is verbalized. The view then becomes virtually a type of hedonism or motor-affective theory. And thus it borrows much of its plausibility by attaching itself to these well-known traditional theories. But these theories can, of course, be perfectly well presented (as usually they have been) as descriptive hypotheses open to confirmation by empirical evidence.

The main objection to the value judgment view thus interpreted as a type of hedonism or motor-affective theory would then be its particular use of the dogmatic device of definitional stipulation to remove its emotive theory of value from the sphere of criticism. For by defining ethical statements as imperatives (interpreted as emotive expressions) and pointing out that imperatives are not descriptive statements, the view by definition denies that ethical statements may be descriptive statements. It would be more direct and open for the writers to define value dogmatically at once as motor-affective feeling. Then the bias of the theory would be evident. But by passing the stipulation through the medium of a verbal imperative the bias is concealed from the unwary.

A further objection to treating ethical emotive expressions as verbal imperatives is that the verbal form merges into one form a great variety of dynamic elements, which need to be descriptively discriminated for their value significance. The dynamic emotive feeling that stimulates an imperative utterance may be a desire, a pleasure, a preference, a personality attitude, or other 'emotive' feelings. The imperative of the value judgment theory throws these all together in a single undiscriminated feeling, which the ethical student is discouraged from differentiating in descriptions. For imperatives are not descriptions, and descriptions of feelings are not ethical statements but merely psychological statements! What is descriptively many, thus becomes imperatively one.

[3] These warnings of the emotive judgment school have a deceptive clarity. They condense into neat maxims all the ambiguities we have been exhibiting

703

in the preceding pages. It should be pointed out that the expressions are not equivalent. The opposition of 'prescription' to 'description' is not parallel with that of 'ought' to 'is.' Both prescriptions and descriptions are verbal expressions. What the 'ought' is we do not yet know, but the 'is' refers to fact and is neither true nor false. Now, unless an 'ought' is spirited off into some nonfactual realm, it is difficult to see how it can be even referred to unless it is a fact of some kind—some sort of being, some sort of 'is.' The occurrence of an emotion is clearly a fact (an 'is') and so also is the occurrence of an emotional expression even when it is expressed in words. Likewise, any particular prescription or description is a fact, and in its occurrence an 'is.' So, in an ultimate sense, everything, including prescriptions and whatever an 'ought' may be, is an 'is.' If there are any occurrences of 'oughts' they would surely be some class or selection of 'is's.' Every 'is' is not an 'ought,' but every 'ought' is an 'is' or nothing.

The contrast, then, is not between an 'is' and an 'ought' that is not, but between the characteristics of a prescription and those of a description. These two verbal expressions have different references. The first has an obedience reference which may be satisfied or frustrated; the second has a reference to fact which may be true or false. These are different kinds of references. A prescription is thus clearly something that cannot be regarded as a kind of description or linguistically reduced to one. But prescriptions can be described like any other occurrences. And the relations of prescription to other facts can be described. And it may well appear, in the observation of these relationships, that prescriptions are controlled by factual structures which correct them and so legislate over them. These structures, being facts, are open to description. Such descriptions would show that the prescriptions are not final in fact, and that to regard them so is false. Such descriptions then have an authority over the prescriptions in this special sense that any writer who states that a prescription cannot be incorrect is making a false statement.

This is the crux of the issue between an empiricist in value theory and any linguist who takes a stand on the finality of imperatives and denies that they are subject to facts which may be truly described as regulative of them.

4 Most contemporary psychologists now use 'phenomenological' for what most other persons mean by 'introspective,' and reserve the latter term for a special technique of 'introspective' observation, such as the Titchenerian. But since the term 'introspective' in its older, broader sense will be more readily understood here, I am using it in this way throughout.

## NOTES TO CHAPTER 2

1 R. B. Perry, *General Theory of Value* (New York: Longmans, Green and Co., 1926), p. 159.

2 For the reasons why it seems inadvisable to follow Perry and many of his followers in this technical use of 'interest,' see chap. 6, §2.

3 Gontran de Poncins, in collaboration with Lewis Galantiere, *Kabloona* (New York: Reynal and Hitchcock, Inc., 1941), pp. 148–153.

## NOTES TO CHAPTER 3

1 Though this excellent term is taken directly from Perry, my use of it cannot be exactly equated with his. Perry never clearly differentiates between the drive and the anticipatory set; the cognitive references of an anticipatory set are always conceived by him to be present in an 'interest.' This definitely is

not true of all docile behavior, and gives a slightly intellectualistic bias to Perry's treatment of value. His analysis was remarkable enough at the time it was made. He could not be expected to make all the discriminations which came to light later, to a large extent as a result of his own searching earlier analysis.

2 E. C. Tolman, *Purposive Behavior in Animals and Men* (Berkeley and Los Angeles: University of California Press, 1949), pp. 32–33.

3 The arousal of consummatory satisfactions in the quiescence pattern of hunger, for instance, makes the difference between hunger proper, based on stomach contractions and whatever else contributes to the pattern of bodily tension for the hunger drive, and what is called 'appetite.' A gustatory appetite may go on after the hunger need is satisfied, and may be aroused without hunger need, as when we enjoy after-dinner condiments or eat nuts and fruit and candy between meals for the delight of their taste. 'Appetite' as distinguished from hunger need is based on the gratuitous satisfactions attendant on the quiescence pattern of hunger. These satisfactions can be gratified and even sought after without the motivation of a hunger drive. See chap. 14, §8, 4.

4 P. T. Young, "The Role of Hedonic Processes in the Organization of Behavior," *Psych. Rev.*, vol. 59, no. 4 (July, 1952).

5 I am heading off the assumption of psychological hedonism—the theory that human conduct (and possibly all animal activity) is motivated solely by pleasure and pain. These are strong motives in certain sorts of behavior. But actions do not seem to be always motivated by them. For examples to consider within the easy range of human introspection, watch any simple automatic reflex act, like the winking of the eye at a sudden flash of light, or the knee-jerk reflex. These acts occur with considerable intensity, but they do not seem to be either painful or pleasant. The whole chain of reflexes of the wasp may be like that. And, if you consider closely, so may be the incipience of hunger and thirst in ourselves. Is a little hunger painful or even uncomfortable? Is it not just an impulse to eat something if we can find it? Of course intense hunger becomes very painful. My point is simply that the impulse of a drive probably cannot be identified with the pain or pleasure attached to it, though these may reinforce it or eventually take it over.

## NOTES TO CHAPTER 4

1 Perry, *General Theory of Value*, p. 205.

2 With the exception of latent learning, perhaps, which, however, occurs only if *some* drive is in action, though not one served instrumentally by the acts latently learned. See also chap. 5, §2.

## NOTES TO CHAPTER 5

1 Tolman, *Purposive Behavior in Animals and Men*, pp. 320–321.

2 *Ibid.*, pp. 324–325.

3 This mutation will be further amplified in chap. 11, §6.

4 E. L. Thorndike, *Animal Intelligence: An Experimental Study of Associative Processes* (New York: The Macmillan Co., 1911), p. 35.

5 Wolfgang Köhler, *The Place of Value in the World of Facts* (New York: Liveright Publ. Corp., 1938). For the full treatment of this important link, which is the 'mediating judgment' of value, see chap. 4, §§4 ff.

6 See chap. 4, §6.

## Notes to Chapter 6

1 In the lingo of the experimental psychologist, this hierarchical set of responses is an example of 'secondary, tertiary, etc. reinforcement and higher-order conditioning.'

2 This reminds us of Aristotle's self-moved mover, the god at the apex of his cosmic hierarchy. We suspect that the appetitive hierarchy we are describing was the model somewhat vaguely in the background of his mind from which he drew much of the structure of his world hypothesis. The governing drive of an appetition is for that act a self-moved mover until it attains quiescence, and all other activities within its structure are moved only through its energy. A governing drive is the god of its appetitive hierarchy.

## Notes to Chapter 7

1 Some writers prefer to call these 'acquired' drives. These drives, of course, are acquired, not instinctive, and are derived from the subordinate acts of drives already active. Both terms are appropriate. I just happen to have fallen into the use of the latter.

2 William James, *The Principles of Psychology* (New York: Henry Holt and Co., 1918), vol. 2, pp. 522–523, 524–525.

3 Perry, *General Theory of Value*, p. 537.

4 *Ibid.*, p. 540.

## Notes to Chapter 8

1 See, for instance, E. B. Holt, *The Animal Drive and the Learning Process* (New York: Henry Holt and Co., 1931).

2 Something like this seems to be Gardner Murphy's conception in *Personality* (New York: Harper and Bros., 1947). There are signs of it in Dewey and many of his followers.

3 Tolman, *Drives toward War* (New York and London: D. Appleton-Century Co., 1942), p. 9.

4 I am referring to derived appetitions for consummatory satisfactions due to experience with these consummatory acts. When a person has gratuitously had the delights of sea bathing, the thought of these pleasures may stimulate him to act so as to have them again.

5 Self-love and benevolence were basic principles of motivation for many seventeenth- and eighteenth-century moralists such as Butler and Hutcheson, and survived even into the analyses of Sidgwick.

6 O. H. Mowrer, perhaps more than any other psychologist, has developed the theory of injectives in a manner comparable to the hypothesis suggested here. He calls them 'acquired drives,' however, which is likely to produce some confusion. For as drives in their own status, injectives are, in his treatment as in mine, original and innate. He observes (as I do also, chap. 11, §§1–5) that acquired drives derived by the independence (means-to-end) mutation get their dynamic motivation from the injectives fear and aggression. But the content (i.e., the goals and conative references) of the acquired drives come from the subordinate acts of the primary appetitive and aversive structures from which the acquired drives were derived. Only the dynamic motivation of these drives is injectives, and this dynamic motivation is the same for all acquired drives

with all their variety. It seems much clearer to me to identify the acquired drives with their content. For their content functions to make up their total impulse (or riddance—see chap. 10, §1) pattern. With this understood, it becomes clear that there are as many distinct acquired drives as there are varieties of content of subordinate acts that have acquired an independent status—as many as there are varieties of total acquired impulse (or riddance) patterns. Then we avoid the anomaly of an acquired drive having an apparently acquired motivation without any instinctive source. I prefer, therefore, to call the injectives 'instinctive drives,' and to name the acquired or derived drives by their content. Thus the love of mountain climbing for its own sake, and that of doing mathematics for its own sake, would be *two* acquired or derived drives, both energized by the *identical* injectives, fear or aggression, which are instinctive drives. The injectives, being originally instinctive, are always instinctive, but they may become the energizing agencies for acquired drives.

## NOTES TO CHAPTER 9

1 Tolman, *Purposive Behavior in Animals and Men*, pp. 27–28. From the context it is clear that Tolman's 'goal-object' is equivalent to our 'goal' and includes both our 'goal object' and 'quiescence pattern.

2 Perry, *General Theory of Value*, pp. 115–116.

3 *Ibid.*, pp. 173–174.

4 *Ibid.*, pp. 176–177

5 *Ibid.*, pp. 175–176.

6 *Ibid.*, p. 177.

7 *Ibid.*, p. 182.

8 *Ibid.*, p. 183.

9 *Ibid.*, p. 185.

10 *Ibid.*, pp. 185–186.

11 *Ibid.*, pp. 188–189.

12 *Ibid.*, pp. 204–208.

13 W. B. Cannon, *Bodily Changes in Pain, Hunger, Fear and Rage* (New York and London: D. Appleton and Co., 1916), pp. 233–235.

14 Perry, *op. cit.*, p. 272.

15 *Ibid.*

16 *Ibid.*, p. 273.

17 *Ibid.*, p. 318.

18 *Ibid.*

19 *Ibid.*, p. 358.

20 *Ibid.*, p. 346.

21 *Ibid.*, p. 316.

22 *Ibid.*, pp. 345–346.

23 *Ibid.*, pp. 183–195.

24 *Ibid.*, p. 185.

25 *Ibid.*, p. 227.

26 *Ibid.*, p. 230 (italics mine).

27 *Ibid.*, p. 116.

28 This motive in Perry's analysis shows the influence of Meinong, who made the subsistent 'objective' a central element in his analysis of value. It also fits in with Perry's espousal of subsistence as a tenet of the neorealistic school of which he was an exponent.

29 Perry, *op. cit.* Cf. p. 332: "Students of philosophy will perhaps be reluctant to recognize another member of the growing family of quasi-entities, such as 'intentional inexistence,' 'objective,' 'subsistent,' 'possibility,' etc.; but I prefer

the expression 'problematic object' for present purposes because I wish to be just as non-committal as possible regarding metaphysical questions, and this expression does not take one beyond the context of the cognitive situation."

30 *Ibid.*, p. 116 (italics mine).

31 *Ibid.*, p. 360.

32 See chap. 11, §6, chap. 14, §§7 and 8, and chap. 21, §4, for the full treatment of this problem.

## NOTES TO CHAPTER 10

1 Poncins, *Kabloona*, pp. 148–153.

2 Wallace Craig, *Biol. Bull.*, vol. 34 (1918), p. 91.

3 Perry, *General Theory of Value*, p. 235.

4 *Ibid.*, pp. 239–240.

5 *Ibid.*, pp. 237–238.

6 Tolman, *Purposive Behavior in Animals and Men*, p. 273.

7 Tolman, *The Wants of Men* (mimeographed by Associated Students Store, University of California, 1948), pp. 16–17.

8 The description offered earlier of the spontaneous injectives would be another illustration of a purely positive drive—positive high spirits in pursuit of consummatory triumph.

## NOTES TO CHAPTER 11

1 A miser's interest in money is, of course, something quite different. In the extreme case of a Père Goriot, money is a mania, a derived drive based on repression.

2 Sometimes called 'stimulus generalization' or 'response generalization.'

3 For an adequate account of this sort of mutation, a theory about the nature of affection (pleasantness and unpleasantness) is called for. This will be offered after all the typical structures of purposive behavior have been spread out to view. Then we can come to terms with the values to be found in these structures.

## NOTES TO CHAPTER 13

1 *The Arts*, vol. 13, no. 5 (May, 1928), p. 327. See also vol. 11, no. 3 (March, 1927), p. 113.

2 The principle of successive definition is clearly elaborated in V. Lenzen, *Physical Theory* (New York: John Wiley and Sons, 1931), pp. 47 ff. It presupposes a continuous close connection between definitions and the facts defined in the progress of empirical inquiry, and so assumes the concept of the descriptive definition implicitly if not explicitly. In our own inquiry into the nature of purposive behavior in the last twelve chapters, the principle of successive definition has been deliberately employed, as will be pointed out presently. If the actual steps of an extended empirical inquiry are recorded, they will always, I believe, exemplify the principle of successive definition.

3 It should not be necessary to point out that the foregoing analysis of the descriptive definition does not imply the Aristotelian notion of the 'real definition.' The Aristotelian 'real definition' involves the doctrine of essence and the formistic categories supporting that doctrine. If there were essences, clearly these could be described, and a descriptive definition of an essence would cor-

respond with the Aristotelian 'real definition.' But if the doctrine of essence is not accepted, then obviously the nature of any facts described by a descriptive definition would not be an Aristotelian 'real definition.' A metaphysical nominalist does not have to confine himself to nominal definitions. The doctrine of nominalism regarding the status of universals does not require a philosopher to define definitions as exclusively nominal. A metaphysical nominalist also acknowledges that there are fields of facts that can be truly described, and a definition of such a field intended as a true description of it would be a descriptive definition.

The possibility of confusing the descriptive definition with the Aristotelian 'real definition' is augmented by the fact that many of the older nominalistic logicians like Jevons distinguished the nominal from the real definition, ex‑hibiting the latter as the typical fruitful definition of the inductive sciences. His conception of the real definition would come very close to the conception of the descriptive definition given above. So it could be said that the descriptive definition as analyzed here is exactly what has sometimes been meant by the real definition. But that would be only because the real definition was sometimes formulated so as to involve no reference to Aristotelian essences. One of the reasons for my selection of the term 'descriptive definition' is to divest the conception of any involvement with the doctrine of essences.

4 It may be objected that the list of terms gathered together in chapter 1 to designate the field of our study in a rough common-sense way functions rather as an ostensive than as a descriptive definition. This may be true. But, if so, the objection merely strengthens the point alluded to in §3, that some ostensive definitions (and perhaps all) include implicit descriptions by which one particular set of facts rather than another is chosen for the ostensive reference.

That some sort of descriptive reference underlies this list of items is evident from the fact that a person may point out that another term should be added to the list and thereby make a true statement. If, for instance, pleasure had been omitted, it would be *true* that pleasure is a term referring to an experience customarily regarded as a value. The list is ostensive in appearance, but is selectively compiled by reference to a description stating that the terms chosen are those which by custom or tradition have roughly been considered constitutive instances of good or bad.

It may be pertinent to add that in the method of successive definition there is nothing methodologically wrong in starting with a pure ostensive definition (theoretically) containing no descriptive element and hence no attribute of truth or falsity; then from that ostensive indication making a first rough description; and proceeding thereafter by successive definition to more and more refined descriptive definitions.

5 The only exception (which is simply an apparent one) would be where the facts were themselves linguistic, such as evaluations of the correct use of words.

6 Perry, *General Theory of Value*, pp. 599–600.

7 Some concern has been voiced by a sympathetic critic that this test is not sufficient to guarantee that the subject matter of the present inquiry will end by encompassing that of the traditional fields of value such as ethics, aesthetics, and the like. In his words: "My point is—briefly—that 'to be responsible to the *relevant* field of value facts' one must be highly sensitive to common and traditional moral opinion (or common and traditional $\begin{cases} \text{meaning} \\ \text{usage} \end{cases}$ of value terms).

Otherwise one's 'test definition' may exclude something important (an area of *facts* indeed). In refining and refining the common sense definition one may consistently leave out this 'area of facts.' This is just the vice of so many naturalists, who seem prone to one set of facts, one selective system or group of them. It seems exceptionally important to me to go back and forth from one's theory to conventional and traditional opinion—to see whether or not something meaningful and relevant is being omitted entirely, or inadequately developed."

I had thought that a common sense test definition explicitly including tradition (as in chap. 1, §1) would guarantee both that the study lay within the traditional field and also encompassed it. But in case I have given too little attention to the contributions available from tradition, I quote this comment. So long as a factually responsible inquiry about values is not bound by tradition or held strictly to "the language of the ordinary man" (see chap. 1, §2), there is everything to be gained by listening, as the critic says, to the wisdom of the past through the "common and traditional $\left\{ \begin{array}{l} \text{meaning} \\ \text{usage} \end{array} \right.$ of value terms." Moreover, the terminal section of this study will consist in a check on our results not only with the initial common sense test definition but with the principal schools of thought in our long ethical tradition (chap. 21, §8).

## Notes to Chapter 14

[1] Perry, *General Theory of Value*, p. 600.

[2] For interpretation 1 see Perry; for interpretation 2 see C. I. Lewis, with his theory of 'inherent value'; for interpretation 3 see Pepper in the treatment following.

[3] It must not be assumed, however, that the efficiency of performance is proportional to the intensity of the drive. Up to a certain level it is, but beyond that level greater drive tension reduces efficiency. Referring to some experiments by H. G. Birch on the effects of different degrees of food deprivation on the problem-solving ability of six young chimpanzees, Krech and Crutchfield write: "The results of this experiment clearly indicated that with excessive tension . . . the perceptual processes of the animals were so interfered with as to reduce considerably their problem-solving efficiency." David Krech and R. S. Crutchfield, *Theory and Problems of Social Psychology* (New York: McGraw-Hill Book Co., 1948), p. 114.

[4] The detailed examination of the objects of conative value will be found in chap. 15.

[5] The line at this point between acts that are or are not incorporated in a purposive structure is not always easy to determine. Probably, wherever correct learning develops we should have to admit some degree of achievement, even in latent learning (see chap. 5, §2). Thus, if from sheer coincidence an object appeared that happened to satisfy a desire, and we saw its significance at once, and, as a result, *learned* the right answer through the accident of its being given to us, this would be a purposive achievement of a sort. If the thirsty geologist, for instance, happened to break open a species of cactus bud and noticed that it had a little water in it which could slake his thirst, that act and observation would have been an achievement. But if he happened upon a canteen full of water in the middle of the desert, that would certainly have been his good luck but hardly his achievement. For there was nothing to be learned from the latter occurrence. And if he jumped to the conclusion that canteens full of water are common in the desert, he would be giving himself a false anticipation and preparing for a painful awakening and a negative achievement value. So, though the line is sometimes hard to draw, provision needs to be made for the distinction between an earned achievement and a lucky accident.

[6] For the latest and probably most complete and systematic treatment of

the hedonic theory of value see A. L. Hilliard, *The Forms of Value* (New York: Columbia University Press, 1950).

7 The development of the personal situation as a natural norm with its value of prudence will be found in chap. 16. And other natural norms will be developed in subsequent chapters.

## NOTES TO CHAPTER 15

1 Those familiar with the history of the controversies over causality and natural law will recognize the extent of the issues involved in this section. It is clear that the position I have taken here is critical of Hume's position, which is widely accepted today. Hume's position and that of those who follow his mode of analyzing the subject of causality and natural law amounts, if I am not mistaken, to identifying these with what I am calling 'hypothetical potentiality.' They maintain that the relation of cause and effect is a human or behavior relation, and that there is no evidence and possibly no meaning for what I am calling 'inherent potentiality.' My position is that there is plenty of evidence for inherent potentiality, and that hypothetical potentiality loses most of its meaning and all its predictive justification unless it makes references to inherent potentiality.

Let me briefly review Hume's argument about causality and indicate the nature of my criticism of it. He showed, first, that there is no *logical* necessity in the relation of effect to cause. The denial of an effect to cause does not involve a self-contradiction. Second, he showed that there is no indubitably intuited connection between a cause and an effect. Observation seems to show only a sequence of occurrences. There is no intuitive way of distinguishing with certainty between a coincidence and a causal sequence. Third, he showed that our *belief* in causality is conditioned by past experiences which produce what we roughly call a habit. Fourth, he appears to suggest that the only basis we have for a judgment of causality is such a habit with its accompanying beliefs and anticipations. Fifth, he appears to deny that there is any evidence for, or meaning in, a causal relation other than the association of ideas controlled by habit.

On my view, outlined in §4, I should agree with the first three points. I should want to qualify the fourth and I should deny the fifth and assert its contrary. The qualification I should place on the fourth point is a distinction between uncritical beliefs and critically refined beliefs. The latter are controlled by methods for sifting evidence. Then I should assert that the difference between the two sets of beliefs is evidence that causal relations and natural laws are not determined by beliefs, but that the difference between the two sets of beliefs is determined by causal relations that hold apart from beliefs.

Hume is correct in suggesting that causal relations are known only through beliefs (hypotheses) about them. But it does not follow that causal relations are nothing but beliefs. The modern term 'correlation' contributes to this sort of confusion. For a correlation may mean a collection of observations systematically compared and so *brought* into relation by an observer. Or, again, it may mean a relation inferred in fact through a systematic comparison of data or through a hypothesis.

Furthermore, I am pointing out that if a causal relation or a natural law holds in fact, as I am asserting on the evidence of refined beliefs that it does, then we must face the fact squarely that such a relation holds lengthwise in time, and spreads in action from a present into a future. If, then, existence is identified with a present, the effect of a cause must be still nonexistent in the future, when the cause is in the present. I am pointing out that this sort of relation in fact needs to be distinguished clearly from a relation all of whose terms exist in some present. Therefore I distinguish an existential relation from a potentiality relation, and I further distinguish a hypothetical from an actual potentiality relation to indicate the difference between a judgment about an effect following a cause and the fact of a causal relation or natural law being actually in process.

Just how is an actual potentiality relation to be described? This clearly would be a hypothesis. There is a great preponderance of evidence, I maintain, on the basis of our present powers of prediction and control over natural events, that natural causal laws do hold in fact, but at the same time I maintain that we have conflicting evidence on the precise nature of these laws.

The variety of hypotheses about the nature of these laws, moreover, cannot be taken as evidence against inherent potentiality. The case is analogous to that of a city under attack. There would be overwhelming evidence that a force was attacking, but there might be very conflicting evidence about the nature of the attacking force, and much profit in considering a variety of hypotheses on the subject.

And so I hold in this issue over inherent potentiality. The evidence that there are objective grounds for predictions and consequently for inherent potentiality appears to be overwhelming, but the evidence is not sufficient to inform us of the precise nature of these grounds. Hypotheses in regard to the nature of these grounds can be found in world hypotheses. It could almost be said that this is the central aim of such hypotheses: to infer and describe the structures and inherent potentialities of the world. See Pepper, *World Hypotheses*.

[2] For a detailed study on the work of art as a conditional object, see Pepper, *The Work of Art* (University of Indiana Press, 1955).

## NOTES TO CHAPTER 16

[1] Kurt Lewin's chief works are: *A Dynamic Theory of Personality* (New York and London: McGraw-Hill Book Co., 1935), *Principles of Topological Psychology* (New York and London: McGraw-Hill Book Co., 1936), *Resolving Social Conflicts* (New York: Harper's, 1948), *Field Theory in Social Science* (New York: Harper's, 1951).

[2] Some of Lewin's statements will not entirely confirm this identification. We have already called attention to the confusions attendant upon the object of value (chap. 15). Lewin has not escaped these confusions. He was not interested primarily in the value problem, and never faced the distinctions between actual object of value, potential object of value, and object of potential value (the conditional object). Not having observed these distinctions, he did not distinguish between a personal situation and a social or interpersonal situation. I find his work particularly illuminating for the personal situation. So I wish to render his concept of life-space unambiguous for at least that sort of situation. This can easily be done by identifying his object of valence with the actual object of value in every instance, and then developing the concept of life-space consistently from there on. By this means it is possible to be clear about the distinction between a person's life-space and the reality situation to which it has reference. Similarly it is possible to show the interplay between the life-spaces of a number of individuals in a social situation, and the effect of a change of social situation on an individual life-space. If individual life-space is clearly distinguished from a social situation, both concepts are clarified, and the values connected with each stand out in firm outline.

For us, an individual life-space will be defined as the field of actual objects of value and their interrelationships for a given organism at a given time. A social situation, for us, is a field of interacting organisms, and constitutes one sort of reality situation to which an individual's life-space is under pressure to adapt. The concept of social situation is accordingly, for us, a totally different concept on a different level of values from that of individual life-space.

3 The typical pragmatic term 'situation' blurs three distinct selective systems: (1) purposive structures, (2) life-space, or the personal situation, and (3) the social situation. We shall come to the social situation in chap. 18. Since these three selective systems are all blurred, it is hard to say which is reduced to which. But the doctrine of relativity of means and ends definitely reduces away one prominent feature of purposive structures in terms of some sort of field structure. These remarks should not be taken as a disparagement of the great contribution of the pragmatists in calling attention to the 'situation' as a value criterion. Lewin's life-space concept might have been unborn but for the pioneering work of the pragmatists before him.

4 A friendly critic writes: "Section 6 seems to make freedom lie in (a feeling of?) spontaneity, which is quite mysterious. Any important response is socially conditioned in very high degree. Yet some are products of oppression, and others—even as a result of the learning which makes alternative paths possible and *which is a product of society*—are free. The freedom seems to depend *on the kind of social* influence. I suspect the root of the difference between the two kinds lies in whether or not the learning which is at the root of the choice is based on evidence, or other forms of conditioning such as punishment, threats, etc. Is this what you mean?"

'Freedom' is a term which has become heavily weighted with emotion and stretched into many meanings. I am here referring strictly to the traditional individualist's claim that individual liberty has a very high ethical priority. And I am pointing out that this claim is well justified in the dynamic structure of an individual organism's life-space, which is dynamically different in its structure from that of the social situation. From the viewpoint of any individual his personal situation has a dynamic priority which is well grounded in the individual's purposive drives. From the very nature of an individual organism's dynamic structure, these drives spontaneously correct themselves through the processes of learning, and integrate into acts of prudence. But there they stop at the boundaries of individual life-space.

Another mode of dynamics comes in to require an organism to conform to the demands of a social situation. The new dynamic agents are the drives of other organisms contributing to a social situation in which an individual organism is involved. When there is a conflict between an act, which is the spontaneous resultant of a man's individual drives in his life-space, and the dynamic pressures of other men's drives contributing to the (probably quite proper ethical) demands of a social situation, then the individual is restrained in his freedom of action. Here is an empirically well justified descriptive definition of individual freedom. It is a very important definition, for it defines a selective system. The selected values (in this instance, the acts of individual prudence) are dynamically sanctioned by a highly effective natural norm whose claims cannot be ignored. The claims may be overridden by the superior claims of some other selective system legislating over the norm of an individual's life-space. But the individual's prudential claims are dynamically steadily there even when they are overridden. A man's impulse for personal satisfaction and freedom of action is steadily there even when it is properly restrained by social demands.

The ethical individualist is a man who deeply respects these claims for freedom of individual satisfaction, and frames his social ideals on the principle that any one man's freedom is never to be restrained unless it can be shown to interfere with another man's freedom. And then some compromise is in order. This is the sense of freedom I am descriptively defining in §6.

The freedom I have defined there is not a *mere* 'feeling of spontaneity.' It is the action of a selective system descriptively defined, a dynamic structure, a natural norm, and one of fundamental significance for human decision-making. Individual freedom is action under this norm—the dynamic norm of the personal situation. When, however, a man acts in accordance with this norm without impediment of social restraints, then he does have a 'feeling of spontaneity.' This is the introspective quality accompanying untrammeled action in individual life-space. It is no *mere* feeling. It is the inner quality of a dynamic behavior structure in action. The feeling is a registering in consciousness of dynamically untrammeled action.

But there is another point in the penetrating criticism quoted—penetrating, for it raises all the pertinent issues. What if a man's personality at the time of action has already incorporated the social pressures in the form of deeply learned dispositions and habits of the individual? And are not most of an adult man's dispositions of this origin? Can he then be said to be free even if he behaves spontaneously in his life-space?

This is a complex question, and partly question-begging. An ethical individualist would at once retort that a man should not be compelled to live in a society which placed such restraints upon his capacities of satisfaction that he had no desires left except those for social conformity. The evaluative problem is that of why such restraint should be put upon a man, and of what it does to his values and to society's. A tentative answer is given in §7. More on the subject will come out in the discussion of conscience in chapter 17, §§7–11. But it cannot get a full answer until the final chapter (chap. 21) on the legislation of selective systems over one another. One of the important considerations, however, is that inhibited desires are not eliminated desires. Innate drives demand their consummation, and the diverted impulse theory does not work (see chap. 7, §2).

One last comment on this subject remains to be made. This follows a suggestion from another constructive critic. A distinction can well be made between freedom in the sense of (1) freedom from social compulsion and (2) freedom as a result of a large integration of dispositions for handling the environment. The first has to do with the freedom of an action; the second, with the development of a free man. The first is what I have been dealing with in §6. The second is undoubtedly in the long run the more important consideration, though still closely related to the first. The second, however, is essentially a problem in personality structure, which we shall consider at length in chapter 17 under the heading of personality integration. However, discussion of the reason for the general superiority and, in the wider sense, the greater freedom of the well-rounded man and rich personality over an efficient specialist or a man of rigid conscience must wait till our final chapter (chap. 21, §2, 4). But, by way of anticipation, let me say that the reason for the superiority of the rich, well-rounded personality is primarily his greater adaptability, from which follows secondarily his greater capacity for personal satisfaction.

[5] There is an illuminating exception to this statement: namely, if all the feasibility judgments (see chap. 4, §8) of all the component acts in a life-space are correct, then the reality judgment of the life-space as a whole will be correct also. But this is only because each feasibility judgment (by definition) takes account of the total situation. The final resultant reality judgment for the total life-space turns out to be precisely the feasibility judgment reached for each component act. That is, the same act is the best means, *in view of the total*

*situation,* for attaining the end sought by each component drive. This point is brought out later.

6 To which Santayana is really referring in his concept of 'shock.' This for him is the ultimate indication of existence—that is, of a reality beyond the qualities of immediacy (his 'essences'). Santayana is using these noncognitive conative references as a criterion of an ultimate reality. The suggestion should be taken very seriously. It is as strong evidence as we are likely to get.

7 A neurotic individual with repressions is blind to relationships in his environment much as the chick is. He is to a normal man like the chick to a human observer. When his repressions are released, his environment suddenly expands. He now has capacities for learning that were previously inhibited. His sense of reality, his insight, the scope and correctness of his reality judgments, are correspondingly increased.

8 Lewin, *A Dynamic Theory of Personality,* pp. 207 ff.

9 Lewin, *Resolving Social Conflicts,* p. 105.

10 Compare with the discussion of the scheme of conative references in chap. 14, §5, 1.

11 This is the sort of value act from which the emotive judgment school takes its point of departure. These noncognitive conative acts are indeed selective acts ('value judgments' in a Pickwickian sense of 'judgment'), and neither true nor false. But it does not follow that they are not themselves subject to selective action which may have a cognitive ingredient. And this, we seem to find, is the case. For riddance reactions and quiescence patterns occur in a man's life-space, and are, as we have seen, subject to adjustment and selection under a reality judgment. The terminal segments of aversive or appetitive structures are legislative over their own subordinate acts and the mediating judgments under them, but these whole structures are in turn subject to the legislation of life-space and the reality judgment mediating between life-space and the reality of the situation. A man may not like weak after-dinner coffee. But in view of the reality of the situation, in order not to hurt his hostess' feelings or risk her displeasure when her husband is his employer, he may drink it without a grimace. We should probably agree that his insight into the situation was correct. But that means that his reality judgment *truly* selected his *unpleasant* terminal reaction as a *good* thing to do. This was a choice *between ends,* and was nonetheless cognitively mediated.

We shall find later that there are circumstances in which a social situation legislates over a man's personal life-space. There is no empirical evaluative ultimacy in the terminating acts of individual purposive structures.

12 The attention given to the indeterminacy principle in physics shows how confidently scientists have believed in men's unlimited powers of discrimination. If, however, men can discriminate just where the limits of their discrimination are, this itself is a reference to ultimate reality. It is a verifiable fact of nature with a reality reference, not a mere blankness, as with the chick.

## NOTES TO CHAPTER 17

1 E. H. Erikson, "Growth and Crises of the 'Healthy Personality,'" in Clyde Kluckhohn, H. A. Murray, and D. M. Schneider, eds., *Personality in Nature, Society, and Culture,* 2d ed. (New York: Alfred A. Knopf Inc., 1953), p. 187.

2 *Ibid.,* p. 188.

3 *Ibid.,* p. 191.

4 See Frieda Goldman-Eisler, "Breastfeeding and Character Formation," in Kluckhohn *et al., op. cit.,* pp. 146–184.

[5] Erikson, in Kluckhohn *et al., op. cit.,* p. 193.

[6] *Ibid.,* p. 198.

[7] *Ibid.,* p. 199.

[8] *Ibid.*

[9] *Ibid.*

[10] *Ibid.,* p. 200.

[11] *Ibid.,* p. 205.

[12] *Ibid.,* p. 207.

[13] *Ibid.,* p. 208.

[14] "Adults generally report with conscious honesty that they only learned the facts of sex from high school comrades and never masturbated before puberty. At the same time as this *repression of infantile sexuality* sets in between the years of five and six—the coincidence cannot be accidental—the overt behavior of the child undergoes marked changes."

"Infantile sexuality is the only causal explanation ever given why normal human beings display complete forgetfulness of practically all events preceding a very definite period of their lives, usually a certain month in the fifth or sixth years. Yet we all recognize by watching children that the earliest years are most replete with vivid and intense emotional experiences." Ives Hendrick, *Facts and Theories of Psychoanalysis* (New York: Alfred A. Knopf, Inc., 1941), pp. 50, 62i.

[15] Erikson, in Kluckhohn *et al., op. cit.,* p. 209.

[16] Dorothy Eggan, "The General Problem of Hopi Adjustment," in Kluckhohn *et al., op. cit.,* p. 286.

[17] Erikson, in Kluckhohn *et al., op. cit.,* p. 222.

[18] *Ibid.,* p. 232.

[19] Perhaps it should be noted that all levels and constellations of dispositions constitute interests of the personality which are distributed (§1) in an individual's life-space.

[20] James's classical description of a conflict of roles as ego ideals, such as every young man must have had, cannot be omitted in this context: "I am often confronted by the necessity of standing by one of my empirical selves and relinquishing the rest. Not that I would not, if I could, be both handsome and fat and well dressed, and a great athlete, and make a million a year, be a wit, a *bon-vivant,* and a lady-killer, as well as a philosopher; a philanthropist, statesman, warrior, and African explorer, as well as a 'tone-poet' and saint. But the thing is simply impossible. The millionaire's work would run counter to the saint's; the *bon-vivant* and the philanthropist would trip each other up; the philosopher and the lady-killer could not well keep house in the same tenement of clay. Such different characters may conceivably at the outset of life be alike *possible* to a man. But to make any one of them actual, the rest must more or less be suppressed. So the seeker of his truest, strongest, deepest self must review the list carefully and pick out the one on which to stake his salvation. All other selves thereupon become unreal, but the fortunes of this self are real."

And then, apropos of levels of aspiration, about to be mentioned, James's next sentences make the point: "I, who for the time have staked my all on being a psychologist, am mortified if others know much more psychology than I. But I am contented to wallow in the grossest ignorance of Greek. My deficiencies there give me no sense of personal humiliation at all. . . . So we have the paradox of a man shamed to death because he is only the second pugilist or the second oarsman in the world. That he is able to beat the whole population of the globe minus one man is nothing . . . Yonder puny fellow, however, whom every one can beat, suffers no chagrin about it . . . So our self-feeling in this world depends entirely on what we *back* ourselves to be and do. It is determined by the ratio of our actualities to our supposed potentialities; a fraction of which our pretensions are the denominator and the numerator our success: thus, Self-esteem $= \dfrac{\text{Success}}{\text{Pretensions}}$. Such a fraction may be increased as well by diminishing the denominator as by increasing the numerator." James, *The Principles of Psychology*, vol. 1, pp. 309–311.

[21] Davies and Vaughan, eds., *Plato's Republic* (A. L. Burt Co., n.d.), Book IX, pp. 335–336.

[22] *Ibid.*, p. 336.

[23] *Ibid.*, p. 338.

[24] Spinoza, a self-realizationist too, but much later, saw this point and stated it in his *Ethics*, Part IV:

"Prop. XIV. A true knowledge of good and evil cannot check an emotion by virtue of being true, but only in so far as it is considered as an emotion.

"*Proof.*—An emotion is an idea, whereby the mind affirms of its body a greater or lesser force of existing than before; therefore it has no positive quality, which can be destroyed by the presences of what is true; consequently the knowledge of good and evil cannot, by virtue of being true, restrain any emotion. But in so far as such knowledge is an emotion if it have more strength for restraining emotion, it will to that extent be able to restrain the given emotion. Q.E.D." *Ethics*, trans. by R. H. M. Elwes (London: Geo. Bell and Sons, 1884).

[25] Hendrick, *Facts and Theories of Psychoanalysis*, pp. 6–7.

[26] Otto Fenichel, *The Psychoanalytic Theory of Neurosis* (New York: W. W. Norton and Co., 1945), pp. 102–103.

[27] *Ibid.*, pp. 103–104.

[28] *Ibid.*, p. 104.

[29] *Ibid.*, pp. 105–106.

[30] This account of Fenichel's indicates that Mill's description of conscience in his *Utilitarianism* was not far off as a first approximation. Only he failed to distinguish between the irrational and the rational conscience. The latter would ideally be entirely free from the feeling of guilt. Mill, of course, had no inkling of the repressed dispositions and their action upon the personality. His description is rather surprising for its insight, considering the data at his disposal:

"The internal sanction of duty whatever our standard of duty may be, is one and the same—a feeling in our own mind; a pain more or less intense, attendant on violation of duty, which in properly cultivated natures rises, in the more serious cases, into a shrinking from it as an impossibility. This feeling when disinterested, and connecting itself with the pure idea of duty, and not with some particular form of it, or with any of the merely accessory circumstances, is the essence of Conscience; though in that complex phenomenon as it actually exists, the simple fact is in general all encrusted over with collateral associations, derived from sympathy, from love, and still more from fear; from all the forms of religious feeling; from the recollections of childhood and of all our past life; from self-esteem, desire of the esteem of others, and occasionally even self-abasement. This extreme complication is, I apprehend, the origin of the sort of mystical character which, by a tendency of the human mind of which there are many other examples, is apt to be attributed to the idea of moral obligation, and which leads people to believe that the idea cannot possibly attach itself to any other objects than those which, by a supposed mysterious law, are found in our present experience to excite it. Its binding force, however, consists in the existence of a mass of feeling which must be broken through in order to do what violates our standard of right, and which, if we do nevertheless violate the standard, will probably have to be encountered afterwards in the form of remorse. Whatever theory we have of the nature and origin of conscience, this is what essentially constitutes it." J. S. Mill, *Utilitarianism, Liberty, and Representative Government* (Everyman Edition, New York: E. P. Dutton and Co., 1929), p. 26.

[31] The phrase 'really want' here signifies the legislation of a selective system over its own trials. And in this instance the legislating 'want' is not literally an appetition but the integrative action of the personality, which dynamically corrects appetitive dispositions that have continuously frustrating effects. If the term 'want' in any way confuses the issue here (for this is simply the colloquial way of expressing the observed fact), substitute 'value.' Then the sentence would read, "A neurotic does not really positively value his impulse to commit suicide." Expanded, this signifies that the suicidal impulse is a complex impulse of the person involving repressions which conceal certain relevant mediating judgments. If these judgments could be exhibited to the person so that he could recognize their relation to his voluntary system, he would see that they did not serve the goal of the drive charging them, and the suicidal impulse would cease. That is to say, this suicidal impulse was in error in regard to the integrative action of the personality. The error shows up as soon as the blockage is removed in the way of the dynamics of personality integration. In short, the integrative norm was functioning all the time, but was blocked off from its full selective action by the repressions.

But, someone may retort, the successful suicide (when it is successful) shows that the impulse was a real impulse of the victim, and can legislate over the integrative action of the voluntary system. In this one type of instance, of course, no correction of the error is possible. The victim is dead. However, in a broader sense, the error has in fact been decisively corrected in the death of the victim. He does not live to carry on his suicidal program. Those in whom the voluntary system and the integrative action of the personality legislate over the repressed system live on and carry on their integrative ideals and propagate their kind.

## NOTES TO CHAPTER 18

[1] D. O. Hebb and W. R. Thompson, "The Social Significance of Animal Studies" (unpublished MS).

[2] *Ibid.*

[3] *Ibid.*

[4] *Ibid.*

[5] *Ibid.*

[6] John Dewey, "Theory of Valuation," in *International Encyclopedia of Unified Science* (Chicago: University of Chicago Press, 1939), pp. 40–50.

[7] *Ibid.*, pp. 40–42.

[8] *Ibid.*, p. 43.

[9] *Ibid.*, p. 46.

[10] See Köhler, *The Place of Value in the World of Facts*, for an expansion of the concept of 'requiredness' which he sets up as the central notion for value.

[11] The discrimination, in this chapter and elsewhere, between Dewey's theory of the social situation and his theory of the end-means continuum, and their almost contrary implications for value theory, I owe to Dr. Raymond Jaffe's analysis of this subject in his doctoral dissertation, *The Pragmatic Conception of Justice* (in press).

## NOTES TO CHAPTER 19

[1] Arnold Toynbee, *A Study of History* (London: Oxford University Press, 1935–1954), vol. 1, p. 45.

2 I find that anthropologists customarily identify the term 'institution' with what I am calling a 'functional institution'; so a culture pattern includes 'institutions' in their sense and also noninstitutionalized configurations of culture traits. However, for evaluative purposes, our central concern in the present study, my use of 'institution' as signifying *any* cluster of cultural dispositions is much more convenient. Then the parallelism is plainly visible between the clusters of dispositions in a personality, which are known as 'roles,' and the clusters of dispositions in a culture pattern designated as 'institutions.'

For both functional and communal institutions operate as selective systems demanding conformity in a social situation, just as roles operate in a personal situation demanding conformity there. More than that, most personality roles are derived from the pressures of social institutions, and communal institutions as well as functional institutions determine roles for personalities. In fact, the line between functional and communal institutions is often difficult to draw, which adds another reason for not trying to separate them terminologically more widely than they are separated in action.

3 There are exceptions. Utopian groups that set up model farms incorporated a faith into their functional institutions. So, too, apparently, with the early Soviet farms and factories. So, too, with religiously inspired armies like those of the Mohammedans and the Crusaders—though these might be considered as wings of the church implementing church policies. Granted occasional exceptions, the statement in the text is, I think, essentially correct.

4 David Hume, *Dialogues Concerning Natural Religion* (Edinburgh and London: Wm. Blackwood and Sons, 1907), pp. 190–191.

5 Blaise Pascal, *The Thoughts, Letters, and Opuscules,* trans. by O. W. Wright (New York: Derby and Jackson, 1859).

## NOTES TO CHAPTER 20

1 G. G. Simpson, *The Meaning of Evolution* (New Haven, Conn.: Yale University Press, 1949), pp. 222–224.

2 Charles Darwin, *Origin of Species* (New York: Modern Library, n.d.), p. 62.

3 *Ibid.,* p. 95.

4 Julian Huxley, *Evolutionary Ethics* (London: Oxford University Press, 1943), pp. 36–37.

5 Simpson, *op. cit.,* pp. 245–247.

6 *Ibid.,* pp. 247–248.

7 *Ibid.,* p. 248.

8 *Ibid.,* p. 213.

9 *Ibid.,* p. 214.

10 Darwin, *op. cit.,* pp. 51–53.

11 Simpson, *op. cit.,* pp. 219–221.

12 *Ibid.,* p. 260.

13 *Ibid.,* p. 248.

14 Darwin, *op. cit.,* p. 443.

15 *Ibid.,* pp. 443–444.

16 *Ibid.,* p. 496.

17 *Ibid.,* pp. 496–497.

18 *Ibid.,* p. 498.

19 *Ibid.,* p. 509.

20 *Ibid.,* p. 501.

21 *Ibid.,* p. 502.

22 *Ibid.,* p. 471.

23 *Ibid.*, p. 472.

24 *Ibid.*, p. 473.

25 *Ibid.*, p. 472.

26 *Ibid.*, p. 485.

27 Simpson, *op. cit.*, pp. 325–326.

28 *Ibid.*, pp. 327–328.

29 *Ibid.*, pp. 328–329.

30 *Ibid.*, p. 329.

31 *Ibid.*, pp. 287 ff.

32 Darwin, *op. cit.*, p. 478.

33 *Ibid.*, p. 489.

34 *Ibid.*, p. 492.

35 *Ibid.*

36 Reported of a Kashmir Mohammedan: "How could we agree with the Hindus? They worship cattle; we eat them."

## NOTE TO CHAPTER 21

1 S. C. Pepper, *Principles of Art Appreciation* (New York: Harcourt, Brace and Co., 1949), details the main factors in the appreciative act of an individual spectator. In *The Work of Art* (Bloomington: Indiana University Press, 1955) will be found an analysis of the conditional object for aesthetic values. The norms of aesthetic criticism are studied in *The Basis of Criticism in the Arts* (Cambridge, Mass.: Harvard University Press, 1945). *Aesthetic Quality* (New York: Charles Scribner's Sons, 1937) brings out the importance of vividness in aesthetic experience.

# Index

# Index